Lecture Notes in Computer Science 9742

Commenced Publication in 1973
Founding and Former Series Editors:
Gerhard Goos, Juris Hartmanis, and Jan van Leeuwen

More information about this series at http://www.springer.com/series/7409

Gabriele Meiselwitz (Ed.)

Social Computing and Social Media

8th International Conference, SCSM 2016
Held as Part of HCI International 2016
Toronto, ON, Canada, July 17–22, 2016
Proceedings

 Springer

Editor
Gabriele Meiselwitz
Towson University
Towson, MD
USA

ISSN 0302-9743   ISSN 1611-3349   (electronic)
Lecture Notes in Computer Science
ISBN 978-3-319-39909-6   ISBN 978-3-319-39910-2   (eBook)
DOI 10.1007/978-3-319-39910-2

Library of Congress Control Number: 2016939997

LNCS Sublibrary: SL3 – Information Systems and Applications, incl. Internet/Web, and HCI

Printed on acid-free paper

This Springer imprint is published by Springer Nature
The registered company is Springer International Publishing AG Switzerland

Foreword

The 18th International Conference on Human-Computer Interaction, HCI International 2016, was held in Toronto, Canada, during July 17–22, 2016. The event incorporated the 15 conferences/thematic areas listed on the following page.

A total of 4,354 individuals from academia, research institutes, industry, and governmental agencies from 74 countries submitted contributions, and 1,287 papers and 186 posters have been included in the proceedings. These papers address the latest research and development efforts and highlight the human aspects of the design and use of computing systems. The papers thoroughly cover the entire field of human-computer interaction, addressing major advances in knowledge and effective use of computers in a variety of application areas. The volumes constituting the full 27-volume set of the conference proceedings are listed on pages IX and X.

I would like to thank the program board chairs and the members of the program boards of all thematic areas and affiliated conferences for their contribution to the highest scientific quality and the overall success of the HCI International 2016 conference.

This conference would not have been possible without the continuous and unwavering support and advice of the founder, Conference General Chair Emeritus and Conference Scientific Advisor Prof. Gavriel Salvendy. For his outstanding efforts, I would like to express my appreciation to the communications chair and editor of *HCI International News*, Dr. Abbas Moallem.

April 2016   Constantine Stephanidis

HCI International 2016 Thematic Areas
and Affiliated Conferences

Thematic areas:

- Human-Computer Interaction (HCI 2016)
- Human Interface and the Management of Information (HIMI 2016)

Affiliated conferences:

- 13th International Conference on Engineering Psychology and Cognitive Ergonomics (EPCE 2016)
- 10th International Conference on Universal Access in Human-Computer Interaction (UAHCI 2016)
- 8th International Conference on Virtual, Augmented and Mixed Reality (VAMR 2016)
- 8th International Conference on Cross-Cultural Design (CCD 2016)
- 8th International Conference on Social Computing and Social Media (SCSM 2016)
- 10th International Conference on Augmented Cognition (AC 2016)
- 7th International Conference on Digital Human Modeling and Applications in Health, Safety, Ergonomics and Risk Management (DHM 2016)
- 5th International Conference on Design, User Experience and Usability (DUXU 2016)
- 4th International Conference on Distributed, Ambient and Pervasive Interactions (DAPI 2016)
- 4th International Conference on Human Aspects of Information Security, Privacy and Trust (HAS 2016)
- Third International Conference on HCI in Business, Government, and Organizations (HCIBGO 2016)
- Third International Conference on Learning and Collaboration Technologies (LCT 2016)
- Second International Conference on Human Aspects of IT for the Aged Population (ITAP 2016)

Conference Proceedings Volumes Full List

1. LNCS 9731, Human-Computer Interaction: Theory, Design, Development and Practice (Part I), edited by Masaaki Kurosu
2. LNCS 9732, Human-Computer Interaction: Interaction Platforms and Techniques (Part II), edited by Masaaki Kurosu
3. LNCS 9733, Human-Computer Interaction: Novel User Experiences (Part III), edited by Masaaki Kurosu
4. LNCS 9734, Human Interface and the Management of Information: Information, Design and Interaction (Part I), edited by Sakae Yamamoto
5. LNCS 9735, Human Interface and the Management of Information: Applications and Services (Part II), edited by Sakae Yamamoto
6. LNAI 9736, Engineering Psychology and Cognitive Ergonomics, edited by Don Harris
7. LNCS 9737, Universal Access in Human-Computer Interaction: Methods, Techniques, and Best Practices (Part I), edited by Margherita Antona and Constantine Stephanidis
8. LNCS 9738, Universal Access in Human-Computer Interaction: Interaction Techniques and Environments (Part II), edited by Margherita Antona and Constantine Stephanidis
9. LNCS 9739, Universal Access in Human-Computer Interaction: Users and Context Diversity (Part III), edited by Margherita Antona and Constantine Stephanidis
10. LNCS 9740, Virtual, Augmented and Mixed Reality, edited by Stephanie Lackey and Randall Shumaker
11. LNCS 9741, Cross-Cultural Design, edited by Pei-Luen Patrick Rau
12. LNCS 9742, Social Computing and Social Media, edited by Gabriele Meiselwitz
13. LNAI 9743, Foundations of Augmented Cognition: Neuroergonomics and Operational Neuroscience (Part I), edited by Dylan D. Schmorrow and Cali M. Fidopiastis
14. LNAI 9744, Foundations of Augmented Cognition: Neuroergonomics and Operational Neuroscience (Part II), edited by Dylan D. Schmorrow and Cali M. Fidopiastis
15. LNCS 9745, Digital Human Modeling and Applications in Health, Safety, Ergonomics and Risk Management, edited by Vincent G. Duffy
16. LNCS 9746, Design, User Experience, and Usability: Design Thinking and Methods (Part I), edited by Aaron Marcus
17. LNCS 9747, Design, User Experience, and Usability: Novel User Experiences (Part II), edited by Aaron Marcus
18. LNCS 9748, Design, User Experience, and Usability: Technological Contexts (Part III), edited by Aaron Marcus
19. LNCS 9749, Distributed, Ambient and Pervasive Interactions, edited by Norbert Streitz and Panos Markopoulos
20. LNCS 9750, Human Aspects of Information Security, Privacy and Trust, edited by Theo Tryfonas

Social Computing and Social Media

Program Board Chair: **Gabriele Meiselwitz, USA**

- Areej Al-Wabil, Saudi Arabia
- James Braman, USA
- Ali Shariq Imran, Norway
- Tomas Kincl, Czech Republic
- Carsten Kleiner, Germany
- Soo Ling Lim, UK
- Fernando Loizides, Cyprus
- Anthony Norcio, USA

- Elaine Raybourn, USA
- Stefan Stieglitz, Germany
- Giovanni Vincenti, USA
- Evgenios Vlachos, Denmark
- Yuanqiong (Kathy) Wang, USA
- June Wei, USA
- Brian Wentz, USA

The full list with the program board chairs and the members of the program boards of all thematic areas and affiliated conferences is available online at:

http://www.hci.international/2016/

HCI International 2017

The 19th International Conference on Human-Computer Interaction, HCI International 2017, will be held jointly with the affiliated conferences in Vancouver, Canada, at the Vancouver Convention Centre, July 9–14, 2017. It will cover a broad spectrum of themes related to human-computer interaction, including theoretical issues, methods, tools, processes, and case studies in HCI design, as well as novel interaction techniques, interfaces, and applications. The proceedings will be published by Springer. More information will be available on the conference website: http://2017. hci.international/.

General Chair
Prof. Constantine Stephanidis
University of Crete and ICS-FORTH
Heraklion, Crete, Greece
E-mail: general_chair@hcii2017.org

http://2017.hci.international/

Contents

Enterprise Social Media

Designing and Developing Social Media

Interaction Design Patterns
from a Multicultural Perspective:
Case Studies Panama, Colombia and Spain

César A. Collazos[1(✉)], Jaime Muñoz Arteaga[2], Zayra Jaramillo[3],
Daniyal M. Alghazzawi[4], and Habib M. Fardoun[4]

[1] Universidad del Cauca, Popayan, Colombia
ccollazo@unicauca.edu.co
[2] Universidad Autónoma de Aguascalientes, Aguascalientes, Mexico
jmauaa@gmail.com
[3] Universidad Tecnológica de Panamá, Ciudad de Panamá, Panama
zayra.jaramillo@utp.ac.pa
[4] Ciudad Universitaria, Av. Universidad #904, C.P. 20131
Aguascalientes, Ags., Mexico
{dghazzawi,hfardoun}@kau.edu.sa

Abstract. By identifying interaction design patterns of an existing website with common language, it is possible to integrate cross-cultural features to the interaction design patterns. The purpose of this paper is the development of a set of interaction design patterns from a multicultural and emotional perspective. This research analyzes cultural behaviors of users from Spain, Panamá and Colombia, which is based on Geert Hofstede's theory of cultural dimensions, and Aaron Marcus's cross-cultural user experience design. In order to evaluate the impact of these patterns on users, the research proposes three prototypes using these patterns. Therefore, questionnaires were used as usability evaluation method, and the results showed acceptance by users. The PrEmo test was also used in order to recognize user's emotions. The results of the PrEmo test showed most people evoke positive emotions while interacting with the interface.

Keywords: Interaction design patterns · Emotions · Multicultural aspects · User interface · User experience · Usability

ACM Classification Keywords: H.5.2. [user interfaces]: User-centered design · H.5.3. [group and organization interfaces]: Web-based interaction

1 Introduction

In the developing of any kind of interactive and information applications, multicultural aspects, usually, have not been considered [1]. Therefore, people need to adapt to the interfaces instead the opposite, interfaces adapting themselves to the user characteristics. Designing products for international users all above the world is a non-solved challenge and will be one of the main goals for future marketing strategies. Differences in cultural mentalities and environments lead to different needs towards computing

G. Meiselwitz (Ed.): SCSM 2016, LNCS 9742, pp. 3–11, 2016.
DOI: 10.1007/978-3-319-39910-2_1

systems across different cultures, and this will often influence the interaction between computers and users [10]. Culture is a shared, learned, symbolic system of values, norms, beliefs and attitudes that shapes and influences perception and behavior. Multicultural aspect is one of the emerging research areas in HCI (Human Computer Interaction). The interface is one the main components of any interactive system, because it is the way of communication between the computer and the user, therefore, the design should be useful and usable. In that way, interaction design patterns [3] are used because they are widely accepted and they collect designers' prior experiences in creating users interfaces. So, those best practices are reused in development of inter-active systems. Interactive system interfaces have basic characteristics such as usability, usefulness and attractiveness that define the user experience [4]. The User eXperience (UX) is everything which stakeholders have contact, a product or a service [5]. Also, it takes into account the cultural context and emotions of users [6].

Patterns for HCI have recently been developed by a significant number of researchers [7]. This paper aims to present a set of interaction design patterns including multicultural attributes, in order to help to create usable interfaces and can increase the users' satisfaction degree. Usability techniques and an emotional evaluating tool were used with participants from Panama, Colombia and Spain.

The following section describes aspects related with cultural models, then some related works are presented, then the proposal is depicted. Finally, there is a section which presents some conclusions and further work.

2   Cultural Models

When talking about culture aspects, one quickly notices that many different under-standings and definitions have been derived from different methodological assumptions exist. Culture is hard to grasp in concepts, let alone to define in precise terms. Although many scholars in different disciplines have tried to come up with an all-inclusive and universal definition of what culture actually is, to this day is lacking a universally agreed-upon definition of culture. Culture could be defined as a way of life of a group of people [9]. Some scholars delved into finding what culture means and what the major components of culture itself are. Three of such studies are Hofstede's four cultural dimensions [2], Trompenaars' seven elements of culture [25] and Hall's high and low context cultures [26], which determine some cultural attributes studies.

3   Our Proposal

The proposal we design includes a set of steps allowing the integration of multicultural attributes into the interaction design patterns. The first part was to select the countries which will be analyzed: Panama, Colombia and Spain were the selected countries, they have a language like cultural element in common and there is a closer relationship between participants of these countries. These countries give a great opportunity for knowledge and value in the results.

Select a Website. Once the countries were selected, it is necessary to select a website of a company or organization which has been designed for the three countries. The interface of this website must have similar design in order to not create all the interface design for the prototype. Then a home page of any of the three countries is selected. For this work we selected the website of Toshiba (http://www.toshiba.co.jp/worldwide/ region/index.html); which has a version of the three countries selected. The interfaces for those three countries are very similar and have language as commonality.

Identification of Interaction Design Pattern. Interaction design patterns are a way to describe solutions to common usability or accessibility problems in a specific context [3]. They document interaction models that make it easier for users to understand an interface and accomplish their tasks. The interaction design patterns are identified taking into account the Home page of Spain. These interaction design patterns are taken from the repositories of Tidwell [7] and Van Welie [11]. These authors are selected because they have studied pattern designs and developed the most complete repositories. Moreover, these authors have established a structure to show the patterns, so stakeholders can reuse them and be guided by examples presented.

Select Multicultural Attributes. This research is based on dimensional Hofstede's model [2] to recognize cultural behaviors of users, UX implications [6] to know some relationship between culture and user interface design, and cultural markers [13] that define interface design elements influenced by culture. Multicultural attributes are studied in order to identify those markers that can be used in the design of web interfaces. Therefore, there is an analysis of the cultural characteristics and behaviors of the users that predominate in each country that are being studied. Table 1 shows the multicultural attributes that are extracted.

Table 1. Multicultural attributes

Marker	Interface design	Countries	References
Grouping	Symmetrical design	Panamá, Colombia and Spain	[6, 8, 15]
Language and verbal style	Spanish and style of text	Panamá, Colombia and Spain	
Color	Transmission of information and background contrast	Panamá, Colombia and Spain	[4, 10, 18, 19]
Design	Aesthetics and emotional design	Panamá and Spain	[2, 6, 16, 19]
Holidays themes	Memorable dates	Panamá	[17]
Local navigation	Memorable dates	Panamá, Colombia and Spain	
Collectivism	News titles or articles	Colombia	[10, 20, 21]
Individualism	News titles or articles	Spain	[2, 6, 10, 22]

Pattern with Multicultural Aspects. After identifying the multicultural attributes and interaction patterns, the next step is develop a list of interaction design patterns with multicultural aspects. For every pattern identified, the multicultural attribute is included that helps to achieve its function. The interaction design patterns with multicultural aspects are validated by designing prototypes for every country studied, see Fig. 1.

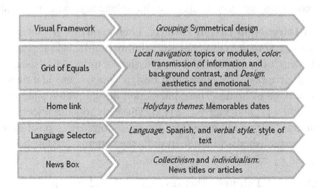

Fig. 1. Interaction design pattern with multicultural aspects

Prototyping. The interaction design patterns with multicultural aspects are applied on the home page for Toshiba's Spain website. This prototype is taken as a basis for the prototype for Panamá and Colombia. Additionally, the information in the home pages of the websites of Toshiba and Colombia are taking into account for the design. To design the prototypes is used the rapid prototyping tool Justinmind Prototyper [23]. The first prototype corresponds to Spain. The second prototype corresponds to the Republic of Panama, with an example for November month, to stands out the historical facts of the country in this month. So, in order to apply one of the multicultural patterns, it is taken this historical month for Panama. Finally, the third prototype corresponds to Colombia, which shares several cultural characteristics with Panamá, since both countries are part of Latin America. As a result, the interface design has some similarities.

The interaction design patterns used in each prototype are explained bellow in detail. In some cases, the interaction design pattern is repeated, because the pattern is represented in a different way for each prototype, see Fig. 2. The patterns are:

Visual Framework. (1): (a) The layout is symmetric, horizontal (top) for menus and images, and vertical (bottom) for categories, news and favorites section. (b) This prototype has symmetry both horizontal and vertical. At the top, the menus, banner and images gallery (horizontal symmetry) are shown. In the bottom, the section is divided in two columns (vertical symmetry), at one side the products categories are shown, and in the other side the news.

Grid of Equals. (2): (a) It is presented a set of grids that contains images. They are categories of information presented to the user by topics or modules. Soft colors were used for the background of the images. There are leaves shapes for larger images

Figure 2a. Home page prototype – Spain.

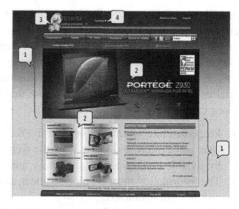

Figure 2b. Home page prototype – Panama.

Figure 2c. Home page prototype – Colombia.

Fig. 2. Websites prototypes

(aesthetic and emotional design). (b) It is represented a set of grids that contain images, that are categories of information presented to the user by topics or modules. The color tends to be strong, but also there are soft colors to contrast the interface.

Language Selector. (3): The option to select language is not shown, since the interface has been designed totally in Spanish. The reason is to show the information clearly and precisely.

News Box. (4): (a) In the Favorites section it is shown social responsibility topics (individualism) o offered by the company to its customers. (b) In the news section of Colombia, it is shown performance and humanistic titles. So, for this case Toshiba shows headlines about deals for father's date (humanism) as an important date for Colombians. Also, it shown headline about needs (performance) that requires the Colombian consumer from Toshiba products.

Testing. The prototypes were validated in order to know the impact of the interaction design patterns with multicultural aspects on users. A questionnaire was used as a usability measure tool of the interfaces, and PrEmo [24] as a tool to evaluate users' emotions about the prototypes. In the evaluations, five users from each country participated. Those users must have born and currently residing in their native country and also practice a profession related to computing system or Information Technologies (IT).

The questions presented in the questionnaire apply theory of heuristic principles of Nielsen and Molich [12]. Results show that users have commented about the prototypes or identified the following details:

- Properties like symmetry, uniformity, formality and order must be used in websites.
- User can explore and know what the website offers through information represented by modules or topic, and also show messages during the interaction.
- The information must be precise, clear, and aesthetically consistent so that the user will not get distracted.
- The colors are used for contrast in the background and text, order, attraction or changes. The Panamanian population rather uses soft colors because strong colors represent rudeness and sobriety.
- Panamanian population feels identified with the cultural elements shown with the company logo, even some of them have felt to see the "pintado" hat with the Holy Spirit flower which is a Panamanian unique cultural element. The people who did not like have said that the elements must be consistent to the festive season.
- Use native language. The users from Panama mentioned that when they display the menu Computers, they expected to find the word desktops not laptops. Generally, the word laptop is used to refer to laptop in Spanish, so it is recommended to use this word to avoid confusion.
- Users think some topics are relevant in some cultures. This is the reason why is taken into account the topics related to social responsibility and achievements.

Measure Emotions. PrEmo tool measures fourteen emotions, which are depict using a cartoon with universally known facial expression for each emotion. Seven feelings are positive (amusement, surprise, fascination, satisfaction, admiration, inspiration, and desire) and other seven are negative (boredom, disappointment, dissatisfaction, fear, sadness, disgusting, and shame). The purpose of this tool is to measure the level of emotional response of users without having a conversation to get the emotions [24].

The objective of the questions is to know what users feel toward the interface features. For each question, there are fourteen cartoons showing different emotions. The scale used is "−" to describe I do not feel, "+/-" to describe I feel some emotion, and "+" to describe I feel the emotion, and "+" to describe I feel the emotion [14]. The user must answer the question with each cartoon.

In order to show the results from the test, the emotions felt by users during the test are listed. Also, it is important to know the interest from users to identify cultural elements in the interface. Moreover, the results shown that users from Panama feel pleasantness when they identify Panamanian cultural elements, and also said that may be used to offer deals during the festivities. It is important to design the interface in a manner that shows clearly the information transmitted to user, so that the interface will not confuse the user. The users assessed the prototypes with positive emotions.

Also, users want to see an interface with good aesthetics that is why the aesthetics is a fundamental part of every design. The users from Panama and Spain perceived pleasantness from the appearance, however some users from Colombia expressed feeling somewhat displeased in the test.

About the contrast of background colors and text in the interface, the users from Spain felt high level of positive emotions. The users had no problem, while visualizing the information; therefore they rated the interface with positive emotions. However, the users from Colombia perceived positive and negative emotions about the contrast of the colors.

Users' reaction about the contrast of colors in the images is: the prototypes of Spain and Panama provoke few negative emotions in users, whereas the prototype of Colombia provokes positive emotions in users.

The results have shown that the design of the interface vary according to cultures, some results were expected while others no. In the next section it is discussed some ideas about the results from the usability test.

4 Conclusions and Further Work

HCI patterns research is still relatively new, and researchers have been debating the basic concepts of patterns. Many existing pattern collections do not include cultural aspects. Nowadays, there is no interaction design pattern with multicultural aspects for Spain, Panama, and Colombia users. This work presents five interaction design pattern with multicultural markers. It is proposed to use a methodological framework to increase the list of patterns with multicultural aspects, since the evaluations showed that these patterns were widely accepted by users. In fact, Panamá stood out by using cultural elements in the interface design during festive season, which provoked positive emotions. Each culture has words with different meaning in their language, so it is important to take into account the terms used in the interface. Hence, users will not reject the website or being confused by the words. Moreover, some topics of interest are more important than others for some cultures, so it is important to identify those topics and take into account in the design.

Furthermore, the aesthetics and colors have a significant role in every design. Some cultures feel pleasantness by the contrast of colors both in images and in the background of the interface. Due to this fact, it is recommend to know the colors will be used in the interface, whether strong or soft colors. The proper uses of colors evoke positive emotions in users, as well as attract users' attention, and show organization or changes. Additionally, the aesthetics of the design must be consistent for all the pages in the website.

In conclusion, the methodological framework proposed here may be considered as the beginning for studies to combine interaction design patterns and multicultural aspects. Therefore, their implementations can extent the list of patterns with multicultural aspects in order to identify characteristics in the design for other cultures. Also, those elements can be validated in real scenery by using websites' interfaces and evaluation methods, which involve the user.

References

1. Collazos, C.A., Granollers, T., Gil, R., Guerrero, L., Ochoa, S.: Multicultural aspects in HCI-curricula. Proc. Soc. Behav. Sci. **2**, 1584–1587 (2010). http://www.sciencedirect.com/science/article/pii/S1877042810002806
2. Hofstede, G., Hofstede, G.J., Minkov, M.: Cultures and Organizations: Software of the Mind. McGraw-Hill, New York (2010)
3. Borchers, J.O.: A pattern approach to interaction design. In: Gill, S. (ed.) Cognition, Communication and Interaction, pp. 114–131. Springer, Heidelberg (2008). https://guzdial.cc.gatech.edu/hci-seminar/uploads/1/BorchersInteractionPatterns.pdf
4. Jaramillo-Bernal, Z., Collazos, C.A., Arosemena, K., Muñoz, J.: Methodological framework for design and evaluation of interactive systems from a multicultural and emotional perspective. In: ChileCHI 2013, pp. 60–65 (2013). http://dl.acm.org/citation.cfm?id=2535605
5. Hassenzahl, M., Tractinsky, N.N.: User experience-a research agenda. Behav. Inf. Technol. **25**(2), 91–97 (2006). http://www.tandfonline.com/doi/abs/10.1080/01449290500330331
6. Marcus, A.: Cross-cultural user-experience design. In: Barker-Plummer, D., Cox, R., Swoboda, N. (eds.) Diagrams 2006. LNCS (LNAI), vol. 4045, pp. 16–24. Springer, Heidelberg (2006)
7. Tidwell, J.: Designing Interfaces. O'Reilly Media, Inc., Sebastopol (2010)
8. Barber, W., Badre, A.: Culturability: The merging of culture and usability, pp. 1–14 (1998). http://research.microsoft.com/en-us/um/people/marycz/hfweb98/barber/
9. Adler, N.J.: A typology of management studies involving culture. J. Int. Bus. Stud. **14**(2), 29–47 (1983)
10. Collazos, C.A., Gil, R.: Using Cross-cultural Features in Web Design Patterns, pp. 514–519 (2011). http://ieeexplore.ieee.org/Xplore/home.jsp
11. Van Welie, M.: Patterns in Interaction Design (2008). http://www.welie.com/
12. Molich, R., Nielsen, J.: Improving a human-computer dialogue. Commun. ACM **33**, 338–348 (1990). http://dl.acm.org/citation.cfm?id=77486
13. Russo, P., Boor, S.: How fluent is your interface?: designing for international users. In: Proceedings of the INTERACT 1993 and CHI 1993 Conference on Human Factors in Computing Systems, pp. 342–347 (1993). http://dl.acm.org/citation.cfm?id=169274
14. Magallanes, Y., Molina-Rueda, A., Sánchez, A., Mendez, Y.: Towards an emotional validation of heuristic approaches for usability evaluation. Acta Universitaria **22**, 119–125 (2012)
15. Mcmanus, C.: Symmetry and asymmetry in aesthetics and the arts. Eur. Rev.-Chichester **13**, 157 (2005)
16. Callahan, E.: Cultural similarities and differences in the design of university web sites. J. Comput.-Mediated Commun. **11**(1), 239–273 (2005)
17. Porras, A.E.: Cultura de la interoceanidad: Narrativas de la identidad nacional de Panamá (1990–2002), 2a. edn. Booksurge Llc, North Charleston (2009)
18. De Bortoli, M., Maroto, J.: Colours across cultures: Translating colours in interactive marketing communications (2009). http://www.globalpropaganda.fresa.net/articles/TranslatingColours.pdf
19. Marcus, A.: User-interface design, culture, and the future. In: Proceedings of the Working Conference on Advanced Visual Interfaces, pp. 15–27 (2002)
20. Ogliastri, E.: Culture and organizational leadership in Colombia. House, RJ & Chokkar, J. Cultures of the world, A GLOBE anthology of in-depth descriptions of the cultures of, vol. 14 (1998)

21. Marcus, A., Cultural dimensions and global web design: What? So what? Now What?: AM+ A (2001). http://www.amanda.com/cms/uploads/media/AMA_CulturalDimensionsGlobal WebDesign.pdf
22. Santos, S.S., Pérez Niño, C.A.: Responsabilidad social empresarial (2012). http://repository. unimilitar.edu.co/bitstream/10654/3721/2/SuarezSantosSandraYaneth2010.pdf
23. Justinmind: Justinmind Prototyper (2012). http://www.justinmind.com/
24. Desmet, P.: Measuring emotion: development and application of an instrument to measure emotional responses to products. In: Blythe, M.A., Overbeeke, K., Monk, A.F., Wright, P.C. (eds.) Funology, pp. 111–123. Springer, Heidelberg (2005). http://link.springer.com/chapter/ 10.1007/1-4020-2967-5_12
25. Trompenaars, F., Hampden-Turner, C.: Riding the Waves of Culture: Understanding Cultural Diversity in Business. Nicholas Brealey, London (1993)
26. Hall, E.: Beyond Culture. Anchor Press, New York (1976)

Towards Emotionally Intelligent Machines: Taking Social Contexts into Account

Han Lin[1,2]([⊠]), Han Yu[2], Chunyan Miao[2], and Lin Qiu[3]

[1] Institute of High Performance Computing, Agency for Science,
Technology and Research (A*Star), Singapore, Singapore
[2] Joint NTU-UBC Research Centre of Excellence in Active Living for the Elderly
(LILY), Nanyang Technological University (NTU), Singapore, Singapore
{linhan,han.yu,ascymiao}@ntu.edu.sg
[3] Division of Psychology, School of Humanities and Social Sciences,
NTU, Singapore, Singapore
linqiu@ntu.edu.sg

Abstract. Emotion is considered a critical component in human computer interaction and intelligent interfaces. However, the social context in which the emotion is manifested is rarely taken into account. In this paper, we present a set of two empirical studies, taking a social network perspective to examine the contextual effect on emotional expression. In study 1, we conducted a scenario-based experiment to examine people's intention to express in social networks with different structural properties. Study 2 investigated the actual expression on Facebook, and the roles of social network structure and personality traits play in the process. Altogether, it is found that an individual's tendency for expressing positive emotions and negative emotions is affected by the size and density of the social network he/she belongs to, and the effects vary with individual personality traits. Drawing on these findings, we propose to add the role of social context into existing emotion models, the context profile can be defined by each individual's social network structure. For different personality traits, the weightage of social context on the outcome expression will be adjusted accordingly. Implications on human-centered design are discussed.

Keywords: Emotion · Social network · Personality · Facebook

1 Introduction

Emotional intelligence enables people to have the capability to perceive, understand, and regulate emotions [32]. In the past decades, there is an increasing interest in humanizing machines by incorporating emotional intelligence to improve human-computer interaction. Specifically, emotion-related mechanisms have been considered and implemented in intelligent systems for enhanced functionalities, such as sensing and predicting users' affective states [47], generating human-like social behaviors among virtual characters [19,37], fostering lasting human-agent

© Springer International Publishing Switzerland 2016
G. Meiselwitz (Ed.): SCSM 2016, LNCS 9742, pp. 12–24, 2016.
DOI: 10.1007/978-3-319-39910-2_2

relationships [21,23], and facilitating negotiation and decision-making [1,2,22,33, 46]. In these works, a multitude of computational emotion models are developed to define the processes that activate emotional states and expressions in artificial agents [39,40,45]. However, most of them focus on the internal states of the agents and the direct external triggering factors (i.e., the particular incidents that cause the emotional responses). The social context in which the emotion is to be manifested has not yet received much attention.

The effect of social context on people's emotions has been an important research topic in the field of psychology. Ekman and Friesen [7] posited that certain emotions are constrained by the etiquettes that define proper behaviors in a given society. People tend to conform to such social rules so as to maintain a favorable image in front of others [9]. The presence of an audience may either facilitate or inhibit affective expressions, depending on the emotional content and the relationships between the emotion discloser and the audience [5]. For example, affective expression is more frequent and detailed between people who are intimately familiar than who mere acquaintances [28,31]. Overall, people are used to adjust their emotional expression according to audiences' different levels of significance and preferences.

However, social context has not yet been well incorporated into computational emotion modeling although some preliminary research started to addressed the importance of this issue. Endrass and colleagues [8] studied the agents' social and cultural signals in maintaining their believability and sustaining their relationships with people. The work demonstrates the role of social context in human-computer interaction. However, the context is defined at a macro level and the communication occurs in a simple human-agent setting. Ptaszynski [29] proposed a context-aware system to evaluate the appropriateness of user's emotions in a certain context. The system focuses on emotion recognition and the appropriateness of context that is defined by common associations between words. In general, what is lacking in existing computational emotion modeling literature is a way to quantify a particular social context and an implication beyond mere emotional perception.

Attention is needed on a complex interaction environment where multiple machines and/or multiple human users are involved, given the nature of complexity of human world and state-of-art systems. A better understanding of emotional expression in such a complex social context is meaningful for two reasons. First, social networks comprise important parts of individuals' societal life, hence it is necessary to understand not only the individuals but also their social relationships. Second, with better understanding about the contingency of affective expression, we can create a supportive context for beneficial disclosure of emotions.

To this end, the first step is to identify critical variables that can capture the important features of social context in influencing emotional expressions. Therefore, in this paper, we present two empirical studies, taking a social network perspective to demonstrate the contextual effect on emotional expression.

2   Related Work

Several psychological emotion models have been widely used in affective computing. The PAD emotional state model places emotions in a space with three continuous dimensions [20]. The dimensions represent the *pleasure* (P), *arousal* (A) and *dominance* (D) of each emotion. In parallel with the 3-dimensional approach, models classifying discrete emotions have been proposed. For example, the OCC model [25]–one of the most widely used models–proposes a hierarchy classifying 22 emotion elicitation conditions through appraising the emotion triggering event in terms of parameters such as desirability and likelihood. Based on the OCC model, a particular emotion can be triggered in an agent during an interaction and actions can then be taken accordingly. Models of this kind allow intelligent agents to identify elicitation conditions for a given emotion. In other words, whenever an incident occurs, it can be mapped onto a particular condition and trigger a corresponding emotion.

In addition to emotion appraisal highlighted in above-mentioned models, context is the other important source of information that accounts for the differences of emotional expressions in different scenarios [30]. Several studies have shown that by including contextual elements, systems can demonstrate better performance in various domains. For example, by considering the temporal dynamics of emotional states, virtual agents can not only better sense emotions in human-agent interactions [48], but also perform a variety of behaviors at different points in time in real-time interactive systems despite receiving the same stimuli [36]. In addition, a conversational agent with the detection of contextual appropriateness of emotions yields better emphatic capability and helps users to manage their emotions [29].

According to López and colleagues' [18] definition of context, these works mainly address the personal and environmental contexts, leaving another important context–social contexts–understudied. One study showed that culture, which is a representation of social context, can affect small talk behaviors in human-agent interactions [8]. It is an early attempt to bring social contexts into computational emotion modeling. An artificial agent attempting to integrate social contexts into the process of comprehending emotion and triggering appropriate emotion responses can benefit from a more in-depth understanding of how social contexts influence people's emotional behaviours. For this purpose, we conduct research reported in this paper to provide a premise for future work on social context-aware emotional intelligence for human-computer interaction.

3   Study 1

The social network perspective provides an approach to understand a social context [16,18]. It focuses on the relationships (also known as ties) that exist between individuals, as well as the interactions and outcomes of these relationships [38]. An ego-centered social network analysis examines a local network quantitatively from the viewpoint of a person at the center. Specific structural indices can be computed to indicate an ego's network structure, and contextual differences are thereby comparable among egos [14]. In other words, individuals who have structurally equivalent networks are supposed to exhibit similar responses by virtue of the similar facilitators and constraints in the context [3].

Past research has established several metrics to describe a personal social network, among which network size and density are two fundamental ones. The network size is defined as the number of nodes in a network, and the network density is defined as the ratio of existing relationships in the network over all possible relationships. The values of network density range from 0 to 1, ranking networks from completely sparse in which none of the members knows each other, to completely interconnected so that everybody is linked to everyone else. The two metrics capture distinct dimensions of a social network. Network size determines how many resources one can gain from the network, reflecting the quantity of connections [12]; while network density is usually interpreted as cohesiveness and closure of the network, reflecting the quality of interpersonal relations [13]. By investigating the effect of network size and density, we expect to gain insights into divergent dimensions of social context and their influence on people's tendency to express emotions.

3.1   Method

A between-subject design was applied with network size (10/50/200) and network density (sparse/dense) as two factors. Participants consisted of 296 (98 males and 198 females) undergraduate students. Their average age was 21.92. Each participant was randomly assigned to one of the six conditions.

During the experiment, participants were given a cover story stating that the purpose of this study was to evaluate a feature of Facebook, with which they would share their status updates to only a designated group of audience. Then, participants were presented with a description about the characteristic of the network:

> "This group has some characteristics: It involves *only 10 / 50 / 200* of your friends, *only a few / most* of them know each other."

We did not exactly define "a few" or "more" but left it to the participants to their own subjective interpretation. Next, following the scenario rating task paradigm [34], participants were asked to read the six scenarios (as shown in Table 1) that were adopted from [24,34]. Each scenario was 30–60 words long. Participants were instructed to imagine as if they were to encounter these situations. After each scenario, they were prompted to indicate how much they would be willing to share this emotional experience with the specific group on a 7-point Likert scale ranging from 1 (very unlikely) to 7 (very likely).

3.2   Results and Discussion

A repeated measure analysis was conducted with network size and density as two between-subject factors and the valence of emotion as the within-subject factor.

Table 1. Scenarios in study 1

Positive emotion	Negative emotion
I had some important job to do in my student organization. Last night, after having worked almost day and night for about a week, I finally finished my part	I had a paper due in one of my classes, and the night before my computer crashed.
My brother's birthday was coming up. So, I went to the store he likes, and found a gift that I think he would love	A friend of mine and I decided that we would go to a movie; But, my friend forgot about it, and didn't show up.
I found a summer job that would look really good on my resume. Getting a good summer job was really important to me because I am graduating this December, and I need good experiences to get a good full-time job	I am the president of the debate team this year. A freshman who joined our team this fall. After today's practice, I told him that his performance was very bad. Now I feel I shouldn't say that

Table 2. The main effect and interaction of network size and density on expression intention

Factor	F	df	p
Positive emotion			
Size	5.15	2, 290	0.006
Density	0.25	1, 290	> 0.05
Size × Density	0.17	2, 290	> 0.05
Negative emotion			
Size	33.26	2, 290	< 0.001
Density	0.31	1, 290	> 0.05
Size × Density	0.304	2, 290	0.049

In general, results showed that positive emotions on average were more likely to be expressed than negative emotions. More important, as shown in Table 2, network size has a main effect on expression of both positive emotions and negative emotions. Figure 1 shows that the intention to express positive emotion was significantly stronger in network size condition of 10 and 200, compared to that of 50. Regarding negative emotions, both network sizes of 10 and 50 afforded significantly higher intention to express than network size of 200.

Therefore, it suggests that social context which individuals interact with plays a key role in deciding emotional expression. In either a very small or a very large network, individuals are more likely to express positive emotions, compared to those in a network of medium size. In a very large network, broadcasting own emotions may raise a major concern about self-image. As the audience size grows, the need to be perceived as popular and competent (i.e., the impression concern) increases [17].

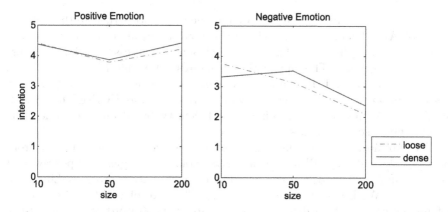

Fig. 1. Expression intensity as a function of network size and density.

To foster a desirable image, individuals are inclined to display positive emotions. Due to the same impression concern, people in a large social network would hesitate to express negative emotions. By contrast, individuals in a very small network may tend to exchange internal feelings as a means of bonding, because a small network is likely to offer more focused social attention and affirmation that are anticipated when sharing pleasure. Indeed, negative emotions are not always damaging. Expressing negative emotions when necessary, but not continuously, can be a demonstration of trust [26, 35, 43] and to improve intimacy [11]. This explains why negative emotions are acceptable in small networks where individuals' intimacy need is well supported and the impression concern is less intense.

In sum, the results presented a strong evidence for adding context variable in affective models. An expressed emotion is not only a reaction to the triggering event itself but also a decision made by taking the environment around into consideration.

4   Study 2

While Study 1 demonstrates how the social network around a person affects his/her intention to express emotions, how can the social context be added on to existing models that have incorporated personal attributes such as expression inclination in communication context [47]? This raises another empirical question about whether the contextual effect is homogeneous across individuals. In view of this issue, we conducted Study 2 with personality traits included as the individual attributes. Meanwhile, we analyzed the network structure and actual behaviors to provide convergent results to Study 1.

4.1   Method

One hundred and seventy-two undergraduate students (57 males, 115 females, mean age = 21.05) were included in this study. Upon their consent, we retrieved their most recent status updates as well as their network structure through the Facebook API. Then, they were asked to fill up a survey about their personality.

We used an application called "NameWebGen"[1] to access participants' information on Facebook. This application generates a text file listing all of one's Facebook contacts and the connections among these contacts. Then, these text files were imported into the social network analysis software UCINET 6 [4] which computes the egocentric network size and density based on the connections within a given social network.

The 100 most recent status updates of each participant were retrieved from Facebook through the API provided by Facebook. The frequency of positive and negative emotional words was computed by the test analysis program–Linguistic Inquiry and Work Count (LIWC2007) [27]. The core of LIWC is its internal default dictionary which defines a total of about 4,500 words and word stems falling into approximately 70 word categories. Given a writing sample, LIWC searches each word in the text and counts the frequencies of the words that are defined in the dictionary. The word frequency in each category is taken as a percentage of the total word count in the text sample. With regards to emotional disclosure in particular, LIWC contains two word categories that predominantly signify different expressions of emotions: positive emotions (e.g., love, nice, sweet) and negative emotions (e.g., hurt, ugly, nasty). These two categories of emotion words have been used to indicate temporal pattern of individual's happiness on Facebook and Twitter [6] and emotional fluctuations over time on Twitter [10]. In the current study, the ratio of negative emotion word frequency over positive emotion word frequency is taken to indicate the overall pattern of emotional expression.

Participants' personalities were measured by the Big Five Inventory [15] which is a widely used personality measure to classify people's personalities into the five dimensions: openness to Experience (e.g., being curious and imaginative), conscientiousness (e.g., being responsible and organized), extroversion (e.g., being outgoing and sociable), agreeableness (e.g., being cooperative and helpful), and neuroticism (e.g., being anxious and moody).

4.2   Results and Discussions

Linear regression analysis shows that there is no significant interaction between network size and personality traits (p's > 0.05), suggesting that the effect of network size did not differ between individuals. Interestingly, network density shows statistically significant interaction effects with four personality traits, namely, extroversion ($b = 1.44$, $SE = 0.22$, $p < 0.001$), agreeableness ($b = 1.55$, $SE = 0.32$, $p < 0.001$), conscientiousness ($b = -1.20$, $SE = 0.31$, $p = 0.002$), and neuroticism ($b = -1.10$, $SE = 0.26$, $p < 0.001$). In other words, the effect of network density on emotional expression pattern varies across people with different personality traits.

---

[1] http://namegen.oii.ox.ac.uk/fb/.

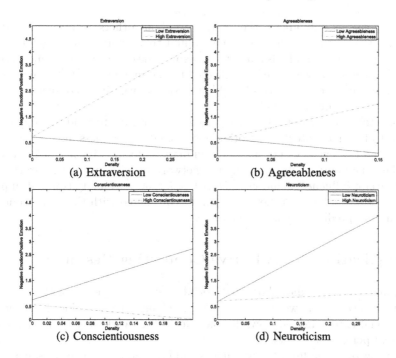

Fig. 2. The effect of network density on emotional expression varies with the personality. Lines are fitted by linear regression models. "Low" is defined as 1 standard deviation below the mean of the given trait, and high is defined as 1 standard deviation above the mean of that trait.

This can explain why network density has shown no contribution to emotional expression in Study 1. The effect of network density is high on some individuals yet low on others, resulting in null effect on average. As Fig. 2 shows, a person scoring high on extroversion is more likely to be affected by network density (i.e., the denser the network is, the more likely the person would like to express negative emotions over positive emotions). The effect is reversed for people who scored low on extroversion, though to only a mild extent. This patten is applicable to the trait of agreeableness, too.

Regarding individuals who scored high on conscientiousness, the network density showed a negative effect on expressing negative emotions. In contrast, for those scored low on conscientiousness, their tendency for expressing negative emotions increased as networks became denser. As for the neuroticism trait, network density increases the ratio of negative emotions over positive emotions for individuals who are less neurotic. For those who are highly neurotic, network density showed slight influence only.

It suggests that a closely connected network can support extroverted and agreeable individuals' tendency to share negative emotions, probably through fostering a safe environment to bear socially undesirable expressions. In contrast, a loosely connected social network may increase people's concern about self-image.

For conscientious individuals, they may care about others' feelings more in an interconnected network. Thus, they may inhibit their expression of negativity. In contrast, neurotic individuals may always express negative emotions due to their internal distress. They are the least affected by the social context. Those who are less neurotic may feel more comfortable to express negative emotions in a well-supported dense social network.

Taken together, this study provides convergent results to Study 1, supporting the effect of social context on emotion expression. Nonetheless, in some circumstances, the context does not affect individuals uniformly. Rather, it interplays with the personality traits. Particularly, network density, but not network size, makes variant influence on individuals with different personality traits. It implies that individual differences should be jointly considered with the social context, to accurately predict or generate emotions.

5   Implications for Affective Computing Research

In summary, both studies show that social contexts, in terms of the size and density of the social network which a person belongs to, determine the tendency of emotional expression. Meanwhile, the effect of network density differs across individual personality traits.

Drawing on these findings, we suggest adding the component of social contexts into existing emotion models. As illustrated in Fig. 3, previous emotion model directly links the stimuli to emotional expressions without considering social contexts. Based on our results, social contexts can be added between the emotion classification model and emotional expressions to provide another level of filtering. For a given emotion, social contexts will determine the extent to which it should be expressed. In particular, the context profile can be defined by each individual's social network structure. Following the computation of social contexts, an individual's personality profile can be included to determine the direction and magnitude of social context effects on the emotion expression.

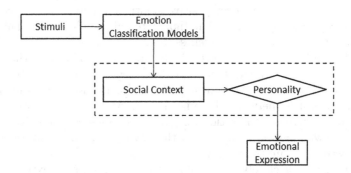

Fig. 3. A framework for integrating social contexts into emotion models. Components in the dashed box were overlooked in previous models.

Here, we use two instances of an intelligent agent to illustrate how the social context-aware framework can be applied in practice.

This framework can be used in intelligent agents. For a believable and empathetic agent, one of the core attributes is that the agent can understand and simulate how people feel. Based on our framework, agents should generate emotion in accordance with the social contexts. In a communicatively coordinated collaboration, multiple agents cooperate by using and responding to intentional acts [30]. Each agent may consider the impact of expressing positive or negative emotions as a function of the number of agents it needs to interact with over the long term. Meanwhile, each individual agent's personality trait can be predefined through specification of roles and abilities. If the communication takes place within a small network, the agent can safely express both negative and positive emotions in order to build trust with each other [41, 42, 44]. If the agent is designed as a conscientious one, it is expected to express less negative emotion in a sparse network.

The model can also be utilized for managing an online social network (e.g., discussion group, virtual game). Given that positive emotional expressions in a big social network are more expected than negative emotional expressions, there could be a mechanism that can remind the users, who are in a negative mood, to avoid strong negativity in their public expressions. An opposite strategy can be applied in a dense network, where users can be encouraged to disclose more negative emotions to seek social support. Alternatively, the system can intervene the social context formation to adapt to users' needs. For example, an online health community is expected to encourage people to share their distress or problems so as to receive attention and help. If it is detected that the community is too big such that negative emotional expression is very likely to be hindered, the system can generate new schemes to divide the community into smaller groups. According to the design objectives of different social networks, the system can take actions accordingly by releasing more connection resources for network expansion or putting constraints on it.

6 Conclusions and Future Work

This research is driven by concerns about the understudied variable–social contexts–in human computer interaction. As an empirical study, it always starts from a simple design, to eliminate confounding explanations and produce generic knowledge. Therefore, we only discuss the emotion valence in this paper. A finer categorization of emotions is expected in the future to integrate the concerns of discrete emotions into the examination of contextual effects. Also, by choosing two fundamental social network metrics (i.e., size and density), our studies demonstrate the initial step towards taking social contexts into account when modeling emotions. The proposed theoretical framework provides a promising starting point for integrating social contexts in computational emotion models. Future work will look into other social network metrics to develop a more comprehensive profile of social contexts. Meanwhile, the next step could include building up a computational model with the variables of social network size, density and personality for applications such as conversational agents. Eventually, this line of work is expected to establish an elaborative social context-aware affective model that can be applied to various infocomm applications.

Acknowledgements. This research is supported, in part, by the National Research Foundation Singapore under its Interactive Digital Media (IDM) Strategic Research Programme; and the Lee Kuan Yew Post-Doctoral Fellowship Grant.

References

1. Antos, D., De Melo, C., Gratch, J., Grosz, B.J.: The influence of emotion expression on perceptions of trustworthiness in negotiation. In: Proceedings of the 25th AAAI Conference on Artficial Intelligence (AAAI 2011), pp. 772–778 (2011)
2. Antos, D., Pfeffer, A.: Using emotions to enhance decision-making. In: Proceedings-International Joint Conference on Artificial Intelligence (IJCAI 2011), vol. 22, pp. 24–30 (2011)
3. Borgatti, S.P., Mehra, A., Brass, D.J., Labianca, G.: Network analysis in the social sciences. Science **323**(5916), 892–895 (2009)
4. Borgatti, S.P., Everett, M.G., Freeman, L.C.: Ucinet for windows: software for social network analysis (2002)
5. Buck, R., Losow, J.I., Murphy, M.M., Costanzo, P.: Social facilitation and inhibition of emotional expression and communication. J. Pers. Soc. Psychol. **63**(6), 962–968 (1992)
6. Dodds, P.S., Harris, K.D., Kloumann, I.M., Bliss, C.A., Danforth, C.M.: Temporal patterns of happiness and information in a global social network: hedonometrics and twitter. PloS ONE **6**(12), e26752 (2011)
7. Ekman, P., Friesen, W.: Unmasking the Face: A Guide to Recognizing Emotions from Facial Clues. Prentice-Hall, Oxford (1975)
8. Endrass, B., André, E., Rehm, M., Lipi, A.A., Nakano, Y.: Culture-related differences in aspects of behavior for virtual characters across Germany and Japan. In: Proceedings of the 10th International Conference on Autonomous Agents and Multiagent Systems (AAMAS 2011), pp. 441–448 (2011)
9. Goffman, E.: The Presentation of Self in Everyday Life. Anchor, New York (1959)
10. Golder, S.A., Macy, M.W.: Diurnal and seasonal mood vary with work, sleep, and daylength across diverse cultures. Science **333**(6051), 1878–1881 (2011)
11. Graham, S., Huang, J., Clark, M., Helgeson, V.: The positives of negative emotions: willingness to express negative emotions promotes relationships. Personal. Soc. Psychol. Bull. **34**(3), 394–406 (2008)
12. Hanneman, R.A., Riddle, M.: Introduction to Social Network Methods. University of California, Riverside (2005)
13. Hogan, B.J.: Networking in everyday life. Doctoral dissertation (2009)
14. Hogan, B.J.: A comparison of on and offline networks through the Facebook API (2008)
15. John, O.P., Donahue, E.M., Kentle, R.L.: The Big Five Inventory Versions 4a and 54. University of California, Institute of Personality and Social Research, Berkeley (1991)

16. Li, B., Yu, H., Shen, Z., Miao, C.: Evolutionary organizational search. In: Proceedings of the 8th International Conference on Autonomous Agents and Multiagent Systems (AAMAS 2009), pp. 1329–1330 (2009)
17. Lin, H., Tov, W., Qiu, L.: Emotional disclosure on social networking sites: the role of network structure and psychological needs. Comput. Human Behav. **41**, 342–350 (2014)
18. López, J.M., Gil, R., García, R., Cearreta, I., Garay, N.: Towards an ontology for describing emotions. In: Lytras, M.D., Damiani, E., Tennyson, R.D. (eds.) WSKS 2008. LNCS (LNAI), vol. 5288, pp. 96–104. Springer, Heidelberg (2008)
19. Mao, W., Gratch, J.: Modeling social causality and responsibility judgment in multi-agent interactions. In: Proceedings of the 23rd international Joint Conference on Artificial Intelligence (IJCAI 2013), pp. 3166–3170 (2013)
20. Mehrabian, A.: Basic Dimensions for a General Psychological Theory: Implications for Personality, Social, Environmental, and Developmental Studies. Oelgeschlager, Gunn & Hain, Cambridge (1980)
21. de Melo, C.M., Carnevale, P., Read, S., Antos, D., Gratch, J.: Bayesian model of the social effects of emotion in decision-making in multiagent systems. In: Proceedings of the 11th International Conference on Autonomous Agents and Multiagent Systems (AAMAS 2012), pp. 55–62 (2012)
22. Minsky, M.: The Emotion Machine: Commonsense Thinking, Artificial Intelligence, and the Future of the Human Mind. SIMON & SCHUSTER, New York (2007)
23. Murakami, Y., Sugimoto, Y., Ishida, T.: Modeling human behavior for virtual training systems. In: Proceedings of the 20th National Conference on Artificial Intelligence (AAAI 2005), vol. 20, pp. 127–134 (2005)
24. Oishi, S., Schimmack, U., Diener, E., Kim-Prieto, C., Scollon, C.N., Choi, D.W.: The value-congruence model of memory for emotional experiences: an explanation for cultural differences in emotional self-reports. J. Personal. Soc. Psychol. **93**(5), 897–905 (2007)
25. Ortony, A.: The Cognitive Structure of Emotions. Cambridge University Press, Cambridge (1990)
26. Pan, L., Yu, H., Miao, C., Meng, X.: A reputation pattern for service oriented computing. In: Proceedings of the 7th International Conference on Information, Communications and Signal Processing (ICICS 2009) (2009)
27. Pennebaker, J.W., Booth, R., Francis, M.: Linguistic inquiry and word count: Liwc [computer software]. Austin, TX: liwc. net (2007)
28. Pennebaker, J., Zech, E., Rimé, B.: Disclosing and Sharing Emotion: Psychological, Social, and Health Consequences, pp. 517–543. American Psychological Association, Washington DC (2001)
29. Ptaszynski, M., Dybala, P., Shi, W., Rzepka, R., Araki, K.: Towards context aware emotional intelligence in machines: computing contextual appropriateness of affective states. In: Proceedings of the 21st International Joint Conference on Artifical Intelligence. IJCAI 2009, pp. 1469–1474. Morgan Kaufmann Publishers Inc., San Francisco (2009)
30. Reich, W.: Toward a computational model of "context" (2011). http://www.aaai.org/ocs/index.php/SSS/SSS11/paper/view/2386
31. Rimé, B., Finkenauer, C., Luminet, O., Zech, E., Philippot, P.: Social sharing of emotion: new evidence and new questions. Eur. Rev. Soc. Psychol. **9**(1), 145–190 (1998)
32. Salovey, P., Mayer, J.D.: Emotional intelligence. Imagination Cogn. Personal. **9**(3), 185–211 (1989)

33. Scheutz, M.: Agents with or without emotions?. In: FLAIRS Conference, pp. 89–93 (2002)
34. Schimmack, U., Diener, E.: Affect intensity: separating intensity and frequency in repeatedly measured affect. J. Personal. Soc. Psychol. **73**(6), 1313–1329 (1997)
35. Shen, Z., Yu, H., Miao, C., Weng, J.: Trust-based web service selection in virtual communities. Web Intell. Agent Syst. **9**(3), 227–238 (2011)
36. Tanguy, E., Willis, P.J., Bryson, J.: Emotions as durative dynamic state for action selection. In: Proceedings of the 21st International Joint Conference on Artificial Intelligence (IJCAI 2007), vol. 7, pp. 1537–1542 (2007)
37. Tsai, J., Bowring, E., Marsella, S., Tambe, M.: Emotional contagion with virtual characters. In: Proceedings of the 11th International Conference on Autonomous Agents and Multiagent Systems (AAMAS 2012), pp. 1193–1194 (2012)
38. Wasserman, S., Faust, K.: Social Network Analysis: Methods and Applications, vol. 8. Cambridge University Press, Cambridge (1994)
39. Wu, Q., Han, X., Yu, H., Miao, C., Shen, Z.: The innovative applications of learning companions in virtual singapura. In: Proceedings of the 12th International Conference on Autonomous Agents and Multi-agent Systems (AAMAS 2013), pp. 1171–1172 (2013)
40. Yu, H., Cai, Y., Shen, Z., Tao, X., Miao, C.: Agents as intelligent user interfaces for the net generation. In: Proceedings of the 15th International Conference on Intelligent User Interfaces (IUI 2010), pp. 429–430 (2010)
41. Yu, H., Miao, C., An, B., Leung, C., Lesser, V.R.: A reputation management model for resource constrained trustee agents. In: Proceedings of the 23rd International Joint Conference on Artificial Intelligence (IJCAI 2013), pp. 418–424 (2013)
42. Yu, H., Miao, C., An, B., Shen, Z., Leung, C.: Reputation-aware task allocation for human trustees. In: Proceedings of the 13th International Conference on Autonomous Agents and Multiagent Systems (AAMAS 2014), pp. 357–364 (2014)
43. Yu, H., Shen, Z., Leung, C., Miao, C., Lesser, V.R.: A survey of multi-agent trust management systems. IEEE Access **1**(1), 35–50 (2013)
44. Yu, H., Shen, Z., Miao, C., An, B.: A reputation-aware decision-making approach for improving the efficiency of crowdsourcing systems. In: Proceedings of the 12th International Conference on Autonomous Agents and Multi-agent Systems (AAMAS 2013), pp. 1315–1316 (2013)
45. Yu, H., Shen, Z., Miao, C., Tan, A.H.: A simple curious agent to help people be curious. In: Proceedings of the 10th International Conference on Autonomous Agents and Multi-agent Systems (AAMAS 2011), pp. 1159–1160 (2013)
46. Yu, H., Yu, X., Lim, S.F., Lin, J., Shen, Z., Miao, C.: A multi-agent game for studying human decision-making. In: Proceedings of the 13th International Conference on Autonomous Agents and Multiagent Systems (AAMAS 2014), pp. 1661–1662 (2014)
47. Zhang, L.: Affect sensing in metaphorical phenomena and dramatic interaction context. In: Proceedings of the 22nd International Joint Conference on Artificial Intelligence (IJCAI 2011), vol. 22, pp. 1903–1909 (2011)
48. Zhang, L., Barnden, J.: Affect and metaphor sensing in virtual drama. Int. J. Comput. Games Technol. **2010**, 5:1–5:12 (2010)

Using Infographics to Represent Meaning on Social Media

Erick López-Ornelas[(✉)] and Saúl Hermilio Sánchez Hernández

Information Technology Department and Theory and Design Processes Department,
Universidad Autónoma Metropolitana, Cuajimalpa, Mexico
elopez@correo.cua.uam.mx, saulsan7@hotmail.com

Abstract. In this paper we focus on the automatic creation of infographics based on automatic extraction of tweets. To achieve this goal, we define a model where five types of information can be represented: spatial, chronological, quantitative, hierarchical, and contextual or, as is usually the case, a combination of all five. To demonstrate the suitability of this approach a prototype was generated in order to create automatic infographics without any user assistance.

Keywords: Twitter · Social Media · Infographics · Visualization

1 Introduction: Social Media and Infographics

Social Media has become an essential component in the navigation of everyday life [1]. Social Media influences some aspects of human behavior from the way in which organizations operate to the way people shop and spend their time. Using Social Media vast amounts of information can be disseminated to worldwide audiences in an instant, while the web simultaneously offers an arena for public and private social interaction.

Social network sites (SNS) can be defined as virtual collections of user profiles which can be shared with others. Despite the prominence of the internet and social networking in modern life, research concerning information representation and visualization has been limited. We focus on the use of Twitter and the large amount of information that is generated daily. Twitter is a popular social media service that allows people to share updates, news, and information (known at "tweets") with people in their Twitter network and beyond. In our approach we used tweets extracted from Twitter. A tweet is a little message of no more than 140 characters that users creates in order to communicate thoughts, feelings, or even participate in conversations.

In short, there is a large amount of information generated in social networks which is not properly explored or exploited by users. Even if the tweets have a lot of information, there exists much more information that can be extracted and analyzed automatically.

In the other hand, the human brain is more able to identify and understand relationships and patterns if data is encoded into visual forms [2]. One form that has being used frequently are infographics whose definition are: "The use of computer-supported, interactive visual representations of data to amplify cognition [3]"; infographic is graphic visual representation of information, data or knowledge intended to clarify and integrate difficult information quickly and clearly [4]. For education (definition) for

© Springer International Publishing Switzerland 2016
G. Meiselwitz (Ed.): SCSM 2016, LNCS 9742, pp. 25–33, 2016.
DOI: 10.1007/978-3-319-39910-2_3

infographic: a collection of graphic organizers integrates different media in simple diagrams: text, images, symbols and schemas [5]. In Human and Computer Interaction, infographics can improve user cognition by utilizing graphics to enhance the human visual system's ability to see patterns and trends. In other words, Infographic is a new way to visualize data. Another concept frequently used is information visualization (InfoVis) or data visualization [6]. Visualization is defined as [7] "mechanisms by which humans perceive, interpret, use and communicate visual information". The main aim of visualization is to communicate information more clearly and effectively by using graphical means [8].

Although infographics have been used for information visualization, they rarely have been used in Social Media and in any case created automatically. Usually it required user support for its coherent creation. In this article we explore the idea of using the large amount of information generated by Twitter and we propose the automatic construction of infographics coherently identifying the type of information we need to represent.

2   Types of Infographics

There are many graphic types for visualizing data, from bar graphics to pie charts, from tables to diagrams. Actually, most of the graphics used in visualization applications are a part of our lives since many years. Graphs allow us to explore data and observe patterns that no other approach can achieve.

Arabic numerals are preferable in infographics, the heading of table should put underlined and centered above them. Human mind can recognize visual information with more successful and lasting way when compared to with written or verbal information transfer [8]. Therefore, infographics design should be experienced to carry transmission of data visualization.

In informatics research [9], it is found that a rich interactive infographic capable of showing far more digestible information at a glance than conventional, tabular representations. The essential text content has been explained with well designed infographics. Just by reviewing the graphics, we can understand the whole idea of the reports. Moreover, with today's technology, infographics can also be transformed to animated images for the website version [9]. A graphical symbol or icon is defined as the smallest graphical unit that carries meaningful information.

Some major types of infographics base on its usability [10] are as follows:

- Statistical Based. This type of infographic includes diagrams, charts, graphs, tables, and lists. Among the most common devices are horizontal bar charts, vertical column charts, and round or oval pie charts, that can review statistical information. It can be made in interactive manner as well.
- TimeLine Based. Timeline show the sequence of events according to the time each event had happened. A timeline enables an audience to realize chronological relationships very quickly. Sometimes it shows in tabular, year-by-year paragraphs, etc.
- Process Based. These process based usually can be found in cooking magazines or explain about recipe using infographic. Also this type of infographic can be used to

clarify in workspaces of factory or offices. It can make readers to understand about its practices in limited space.

- Location or Geography Based. With widely use of GIS, maps can also consider as the best way to show geography based infographics. They include symbols, icons, diagrams, graphs, tables, arrows and bullets. There are many well known GIS notation that used in maps to identify highways, streets, subways, and facilities. Many familiar icons and symbols designed for places like tourist spots, hospitals, airports etc. Scale is the imperative consideration additionally because all places and landmarks are marked according to the exact scale or ratio.

3   Mining Twitter Data

Twitter has its own convention that renders it distinct from other textual data. Consider the following Twitter example message ("tweet"): RT @john has a cool #car. It shows that users may reply to other users by indicating user names using the character @, as in, for example, @john. Hashtags (#) are used to denote subjects or categories, as in, for example #car. RT is used at the beginning of the tweet to indicate that the message is a so-called "retweet", a repetition or reposting of a previous tweet.

The Twitter Application Programming Interface (API) [11] currently provides a Streaming API and. Through the Streaming API [12] users can obtain real-time access to tweets in sampled and filtered form. The API is HTTP based, and GET, POST, and DELETE requests can be used to access the data.

In Twitter terminology, individual messages describe the "status" of a user. Based on the Streaming API users can access subsets of public status descriptions in almost real time, including replies and mentions created by public accounts. Status descriptions created by protected accounts and all direct messages cannot be accessed. An interesting property of the streaming API is that it can filter status descriptions using quality metrics, which are influenced by frequent and repetitious status updates, etc.

Among all these elements extracted by the API, we are interested in analyze those listed in Fig. 1.

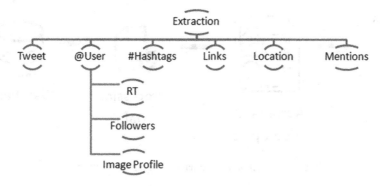

Fig. 1. Data extraction using the API of Twitter

The API uses basic HTTP authentication and requires a valid Twitter account. Data can be retrieved as XML or the more succinct JSON format. The format of the JSON data is very simple and it can be parsed very easily because every line, terminated by a carriage return, contains one object. Using this API, we can extract large amounts of data, however we need to find a better way to display and visualize this data.

4   Infographics: Modeling and Creating

Despite the difficulty in creating a design model, it would be useful to have one, in order to understand the overall picture of the infographic design process and especially the type of information that will be used.

The major challenge in order to design and create successful infographic is to understand what type of information it is trying to communicate. We have defined five different approaches – whether spatial, chronological, quantitative, hierarchical, contextual or, as is usually the case, a combination of all five.

The first three approaches are has been explored widely [13], but the hierarchical and contextual approaches are the most important contribution made in this work, together with the automatic creation process.

In the first step the user has to choose a topic of interest. This is defined using the #Hashtag that has to be entered to the system. The system has to extract, using the Twitter API, all relevant information related to this specific #Hashtag. Then the system asks what kind of representation has to be represented whether spatial, chronological, quantitative, hierarchical, and contextual. The system, process the data and define automatically the design of infographics and the most important the type of information that should be used. Then this infographic is presented to the user for validation.

In the Fig. 2 we shows the model used to create infographics focusing in the type of information that we need to visualize.

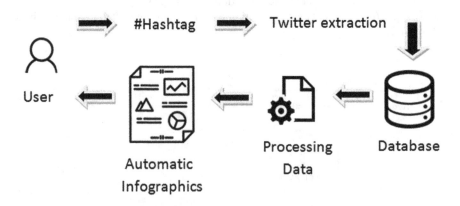

Fig. 2. Model of an automatic infographic creation

The different types of information that can be represented are described below.

4.1 Spatial

This information describes relative positions and the spatial relationships in a physical or conceptual location. Using this approach, it is possible to identify the spatial information and to determine where each Tweet has been written and published. The information is displayed using a map and we have the option to display the different geographical places. The essential elements for build this type of spatial infographics includes: the user profile, the user name, the tweet and the user location. In Fig. 3, we show an example of this approach.

Fig. 3. Spatial infographics using Twitter

4.2 Chronological

This information describes sequential positions and the causal relationships in a physical or conceptual timeline. In this type of infographics the result is displayed as a timeline, some chronological aspects can be discovered using this approach. In these representations we have to order all Twitter elements chronologically in order to be presented on the infographics, using this approach the date and time of tweet publication is determinant. In the Fig. 4, we show an example of automatic construction of a chronological infographic.

4.3 Quantitative

This Information describes scale, proportion, change, and organization of quantities in space, time or both. This infographic shows different data organized by different trends or details about the search in the form of numbers, graphics etc. So, the user can draw some conclusions and logic of their topics of interest.

Twitter elements required to build this type of infographics are the user names, the account names, the tweet, the platform where the tweet was published, the user profile

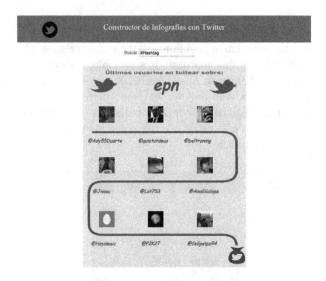

Fig. 4. Chronological infographics using the Hashtag #epn

(picture age, sex, etc.), and the numbers of times that the tweets is shared and marked as favorite.

With all this information we need to select and perform some operations in order to display the suitable infographics, using graphics or manipulating data. All this manipulation is performed based on style sheets and JavaScript. In the Fig. 5 we show the result of a quantitative infographics created automatically.

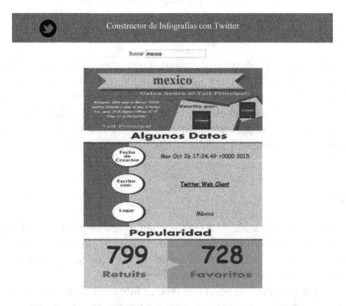

Fig. 5. Quantitative infographic using the Hashtag #Mexico

4.4   Hierarchical

Hierarchies are some structures based on a criterion of subordination, i.e., we can define different levels taking into account some factors such as scales, the influences degree, periods of time or importance of a subject. This category was a contribution in this article, which emerged thanks to the previous analysis to represent information.

Using this design we can simplify the infographic and obtain visually different trends, patterns, measuring the followers or shared publications. That is the main reason we include this type of representation in our design model.

For the automatic construction of this infographics, it was necessary to extract the following items from the tweet: the user names, the profile picture, the user account information, the number of times a tweet has been shared and bookmarked. Having this information we can identify the influential users, or some communities in social network. In Fig. 6, we show an infographic designed identifying the most popular tweets using the Hashtag #donaldtrump.

Fig. 6.   Hierarchical infographics using the Hashtag #donaldtrump

4.5   Contextual

Contextual information is also used to design infographics. Using this information, it is possible to represent symbolic data or graphics, and to explore a set of circumstances surrounding specific issues or facts for some behavior or pattern from the original topic.

We realized that extracting Twitter information, it could exist the interest of the user to know significant topics linked to an specific Hashtag, for example what are different Hashtag related to the original one or who is the most influential user that is not mention directly in the Hashtag but is related to the original keyword.

All these variables can also been extracted and represented with data in order to identify a context. To construct this infographics, we used Cloud Words in order to visualize all surrounding topics. Normally, the elements extracted: the tweet, the user profile, the original Hashtag and the related Hashtag. The visual design of the info-graphics can change according the context of each Hashtag search. In the Fig. 7 we show an example.

Fig. 7. Contextual infographic using the Hashtag #futbol

5   Conclusions

The Twitter messaging service is wildly popular, with millions of users posting more than 200 million tweets per day. This stream of messages from a variety of users contains information on an array of topics, including conventional news stories, events of local interest (e.g., social movements), opinions, real-time events (e.g., earthquakes or traffic jam), and many others. Unfortunately, all this information is not well exploited by users.

Automatic extraction using Twitter's APIs provide access to tweets from a particular time range, from a particular user, with a particular keyword, or from a particular geographic region. We think that this form of automatic extraction must be used regu-larly in order to have a better understanding of what happens on Twitter.

In other hand, infographics are traditionally viewed as visual elements such as charts, maps, or diagrams that aid comprehension of a given text-based content. We have shown in this paper how to represent Twitter data in order to get new meaning and discover new knowledge.

In this article, we have described an approach for efficient extraction of information from Twitter searching a particular subject (the use of Hashtag #). This information is properly reorganized and presented through infographics automatically. These infographics can be designed to represent Twitter information on qualitative, temporal, geographic, hierarchical or contextual. A prototype tool was created to determine the suitability of this kind of infographics.

In conclusion, we need to find new ways to represent all this large amount of data that is generated by Social Media. We argue that visualization and specifically Infographics has a great potential. Some aspects should be improved, like the visual design and the interactive interaction, but we think is a good beginning and research must continue in this direction.

References

1. Amichai-Hamburger, Y., Vinitzky, G.: Social network use and personality. Comput. Hum. Behav. **26**, 1289–1295 (2010)
2. Cleveland, W.S.: The Elements of Graphing Data, Revised edn. Hobart Press, New Jersey (1994)
3. Card, S., Mackinlay, J., Shneiderman, B.: Readings in Information Visualization: Using Vision to Think. Morgan Kaufmann Publishers, Los Altos (1999)
4. Smiciklas, M.: The Power of Infographics: Using Pictures to Communicate and Connect with Your Audience. Que Biz-Tech Series. Que Publishing, Indianapolis (2012)
5. Serenelli, F., Ruggeri, E., Mangiatordi, A., Ferri, P.: Applying the multimedia learning theory in the primary, school: an experimental study about learning settings, using digital science contents. In: Proceedings of the European Conference on e-Learning is the Property of Academic Conferences (2011)
6. Card, S.: Information visualization. In: Sears, A., Jacko, J.A. (eds.) Human-Computer Interaction: Design Issues, Solutions, and Applications, pp. 510–543. CRC Press, Boca Raton (2009)
7. Scaife, M., Rogers, Y.: External cognition: how do graphical representations work? Int. J. Hum. Comput. Stud. **45**, 185–213 (1996)
8. İnan, B., Dur, U.: Analysis of data visualizations in daily newspapers in terms of graphic design. Proc. Soc. Behav. Sci. **51**, 278–283 (2012)
9. Spry, K.C.: An infographical approach to designing the problem list. In: IHI 2012: Proceedings of the 2nd ACM SIGHIT International Health Informatics Symposium (2012)
10. Artacho-Ram, M.A., Diego-Mas, J.A., Alcaide-Marzal, J.: Influence of the mode of graphical representation on the perception of product aesthetic and emotional features: an exploratory study. Int. J. Ind. Ergon. **38**, 942–952 (2008)
11. Twitter API: (2010). http://apiwiki.twitter.com/
12. Kalucki, J.: Twitter streaming API (2010). http://apiwiki.twitter.com/Streaming-API-Documentation
13. Rajamanickam, V.: Infographics seminar handout (2005, 2011)

Automated Mobile Health: Designing a Social Reasoning Platform for Remote Health Management

Hoang D. Nguyen[✉] and Danny Chiang Choon Poo

Department of Information Systems, National University of Singapore,
Singapore, Singapore
{hoangnguyen, dpoo}@comp.nus.edu.sg

Abstract. With the drastic expansion of mobile technologies, mobile health has become ubiquitous and versatile to revolutionize healthcare for improved health outcomes. This study takes initiatives to investigate a new paradigm of automated mobile health as the process automation of mobile-enabled health interventions. Through the realisation of the paradigm, a novel social reasoning platform with a comprehensive set of design guidelines are proposed for efficient and effective remote health management. The study considerably contributes to the cumulative theoretical development of mobile health and health decision making. It also provides a number of implications for academic bodies, healthcare practitioners, and developers of mobile health.

Keywords: Automated · mhealth · Health management · Decision · Reasoning · Screening · Treatment · Social support

1 Introduction

Mobile health is going through a massive growth spurt that would promisingly extend the reach of healthcare to 1.7 billion patients, by 2018 [1]. Its technologies such as wireless sensing devices, and computation and memory resources have constantly been advanced to meet the worldwide escalating public expectations on healthcare [2]. By removing both spatial and time constraints, it is promisingly transforming healthcare services for improved health outcomes, higher quality of care, and reduced costs of healthcare delivery.

Today, mobile health has been evolved beyond classic data collection and reporting functions to provide better decision support capabilities [3, 4]. Therefore, this research takes an evolutionary approach in investigating the literature of mobile health and health decision making to propose a new paradigm of automated mobile health. It enables highly personalised health interventions for patients in managing their conditions by automating certain healthcare processes. Integration of reasoning processes on mobile devices unveils new capabilities of providing suitable and timely clinical alerts, action plans, and recommendations [5–8]. This study aims to address major boundaries of mobile computing resources [6], utilization of patient's information [9], and data

© Springer International Publishing Switzerland 2016
G. Meiselwitz (Ed.): SCSM 2016, LNCS 9742, pp. 34–46, 2016.
DOI: 10.1007/978-3-319-39910-2_4

privacy [10] by introducing a social mobile reasoning platform with a comprehensive set of design guidelines for remote health management.

Based on theoretical foundations, the study contributes to the cumulative theoretical development of mobile health and health decision making. It has drawn out many implications for academic theorists and healthcare practitioners.

The structure of the paper is as follows. Firstly, we review the literature background of our study in Sect. 2. Secondly, we introduce the paradigm of automated mobile health in Sect. 3. Section 4 presents our social reasoning platform with the design concepts of our mobile platform. Lastly, we conclude our paper with findings and contributions in the final section.

2 Literature Background

2.1 Mobile Health

The firm development of mobile technologies leading to a digital revolution in healthcare has started the path for a new health management model, "mobile health" or "mHealth" [11]. It is broadly defined as "healthcare to anyone, anytime, and anywhere by removing locational and temporal constraints while increasing both the coverage and the quality of healthcare" [12, 13]. With the prevalence of over 6 billion smartphone users [14], mobile health is moving away from typical hospital settings depending solely on clinicians to transform healthcare within existing resource constraints such as infrastructure, healthcare workforce, or financial limitations [15]. The applications of mobile health encompass a variety of activities such as disease management and prevention [4, 16, 17], care surveillance [18–20] and decision support [4, 21].

With the significant advantages of usability and mobility [22, 23], it is imperative to note that mobile health has been progressed beyond simple data collection and displaying functions [4] to link health observations with clinical knowledge to influence decisions for improved health outcome [3].

2.2 Health Decision Making

Making health decisions typically involves a number of parameters, factors and outcome possibilities; thus, it is always complex to both patients and healthcare professionals [24, 25]. The problem of decision conflict may arise when there are two or more clinically reasonable options in screening, treatments, or major life transitions for patients with preference-sensitive conditions (e.g., diabetes mellitus, back pain, early breast/prostate cancer...) [26]. Studies have shown that involvement of both patients and healthcare practitioners in considering various options, benefits, and risks of these health management processes reduces decision conflict, and improves adherence to treatment protocols and outcomes [27, 28].

Over the recent decades, the development of tools and interventions for improving health decisions has progressively innovated. On the one hand, computerized clinical decision support systems (CCDS) are designed to assist and improve clinical decision making [29] which have been found to reduce prescription errors, to increase adherence to guidelines, to improve healthcare professionals' performance and to enrich health interventions for patients [29–31]. On the other hand, patient decision aids (PtDAs) are developed as evidence-based tools to enhance patient's knowledge, to educate risk perceptions, and to increase participation in decision making [32–34]. Patients are engaged to make health choices based on their own preferences and values towards better decision quality and outcomes [35]. For instance, patients with schizophrenia, those who participated in decision aid interventions, acquired better knowledge about their health conditions and had higher perceived involvement in health decisions [36]. Therefore, the evolution of technology-based interventions for health management is moving towards shared decision making for reduced clinical workloads, and economical healthcare services [37, 38].

3   Automated Mobile Health

In recent research, automation of healthcare practices supported by mobile and wearable technologies has paved the way for new types of interventions that are capable of providing highly personalised health monitoring, timely alerts and suitable recommendations [6–8]. With the integration of reasoning processes in mobile apps, automated mobile health has become a viable paradigm for a wider reach of interventions, population-based patient engagement, and cost savings [39]. It is useful in remote health management as a collective process of screening, monitoring and following treatment in which many sub-processes can be selectively automated by linking health observations such as medications, vital signs, and environmental factors with health knowledge towards better clinical outcomes [21]. For instance, rectifying the issue of non-adherence to existing treatments through the process automation of context-aware reminders [40, 41] would lead to more health benefits worldwide than developing any new medical treatments [42].

Automated mobile health is closely related to health informatics and mobile health analytics. Health-related insights can be discovered and operated by mobile health analytics which can trigger automatic health decisions that are parts of health informatics-enabled workflows. Sophisticated interventions of automated mobile health, therefore, can be designed to improve medication adherence, avoid adverse drug events, as well as, connect patients with their social networks and healthcare practitioners in real-time.

3.1   Key Challenges of Automated Mobile Health

In the early development, automated mobile health meets several barriers such as data collection issues, reliability issues, and constraints on mobile computation and memory capabilities. In addition, there are some well-known problems of mobile health interventions such as human involvement, as well as security and privacy concerns. The key challenges of automated mobile health are described as the following.

Heterogeneous Data. Mobile sensing data such as vital signs, medical streams and environmental measures are being captured and processed continuously from a variety of sensing devices [43–49]. In many scenarios, such data are high-speed, high-density, high-volume, and multi-dimensional [50]; for example, Electrocardiogram (ECG) has a high sampling rate of 128 Kbps [51]. For the data to be useful, aggregating and combining the data from multiple sensors in conjunction with medical and related data stored in dispersed locations are a grand challenge for automated mobile health.

Reliability. The reliability of automated mobile health is susceptible to some validity issues of mobile sensing technologies [52]. These include the problems of excessive thermal effects, bad signal failures, short battery life, or conflicts in packet/data delivery [53]. In some cases, the quality of data is prone to errors in usage or placement of mobile sensing devices. For instance, wearable devices could be slipped away or detached to a wrong position due to the patient's movements; thus, the measurement data might be interrupted or distorted. The validity of mobile sensing data might be unexpectedly degraded which might lead to inaccurate health recommendations.

Security and Privacy. Privacy, security and confidentiality concerns exist as highly personal information are subjected to data transmission wirelessly [54]. A study has shown that sensitive location information and physical movements of patients can be revealed by sophisticated reverse-engineering algorithms [55]. Hence, sharing certain privacy-sensitive data outside the mobile devices is not recommended. It is also critical to conceal personal identifiable information over one or multiple wireless communications.

Energy and Resource Limitations. The power consumption of mobile sensing technologies has been known as a problem resulting in quick depletion of phone battery level. This issue leads to the usability and ecological issues of automated mobile health. D'Aquin and his team have reported that an elementary semantic data would take up to hundreds of KB in memory [56]; thus, direct processing over mobile sensing data would easily use up available memory resources on a mobile phone. The major challenge is to design a mobile companion of automated mobile health that is transparent to mobile users and other applications by consuming a low level of CPU and memory resources.

Complex Interventions. Many mobile health interventions require human involvement due to their nature and potential for harmful outcomes to the patient's health [24]. In these complex situations, the human interactions can be better utilized [12]; while some sub-processes with less chance of any risk to patients can be selectively supported by automated mobile health. It is intriguing to investigate the combination of automated and human-assisted care for highly personalized and improved remote health management.

3.2   Realisation of Automated Mobile Health

This study utilises Nguyen & Poo's framework for analysing automated mobile health interventions towards better remote health management [57]. Six core elements were assessed based on the Activity Theory [58], namely (1) subject, (2) objective, (3) tool, (4) control, (5) context, and (6) communication.

(1) **Subject.** Three key participants are identified in various scenarios of automated mobile health, namely: (i) patients, (ii) friends and family members, (iii) and healthcare practitioners. Patients are the centre and the most actionable subject of this paradigm; while their friends and family members, as well as their healthcare professionals, play a contributing role to support the patients in making health-related decisions.

(2) **Objective.** The primary objective is to automate certain healthcare processes in the direction of better decision efficiency and improved quality of outcomes. This can be achieved through mobile reasoning over sensing data and relevant knowledge to support decision automation of remote health management. It encompasses a number of scenarios such as providing suitable recommendations for improving adherence to treatment regimens, timely alerting for adverse events based on multiple sensors (e.g., accelerometers, ECG, pulse oximeter), and engaging patients and healthcare practitioners in shared decision making. The enabler of automated mobile health is a collection of patient's preferences and values which are integral parts of process automation and paths leading to proper health decisions [59].

(3) **Tool.** As a vital companion of remote health management [60, 61], mobile apps have excellent advantages of ubiquity, usability, and mobility [62, 63]. With the real-time connectivity between a mobile phone and multiple wireless-enabled medical devices, embedding a localized reasoning engine in mobile apps would unlock a full potential of automated mobile health without compromising the data security and privacy. As the result, a large number of healthcare workflows can be integrated and automated by reshaping the interactions amongst patients, their friends and family members, and healthcare practitioners.

(4) **Control.** There are boundaries in health practices such as regulations, policies, and cultural norms. It is critical to consider them as the guidelines for human-computer interaction design in which the user-friendly interface and the full control over information sharing are essential for automated mobile health interventions.

(5) **Context.** Both locational and temporal constraints have been removed in the environment of automated mobile health. Social connectivity amongst patients, their social networks, and their clinicians is strongly encouraged for shared understandings of healthcare processes including available options, benefits, risks, and outcomes. This provides opportunities for discovering and formulating decision rules in public communities over time.

(6) **Communication.** The use of mobile technologies empowers the participants with different forms of communication such as e-mail, short message service (SMS), and push notifications. One-to-one discussion and information sharing over a secured channel are essential for remote health management. Moreover, automated mobile health involves collaboration in automation of healthcare processes and automatic remote monitoring and alerts.

In summary, this section presents an analysis of the activity system of automated mobile health. It provides a ground for realising the process automation of mobile health as relevant interventions for improved health outcomes.

4 Designing a Social Reasoning Platform for Remote Health Management

Based on the realisation of automated mobile health interventions, this study takes an important step to propose a social mobile reasoning platform for remote health management. It utilizes a localized mobile reasoning engine where rules are implemented as the best choice and real-time sensing data collected become useful for health screening and management [10], even in the absence of network connectivity [64].

It aims to bring collaborative care to the next level where health knowledge is being exchanged, and social networks of patients are being involved in decision aid activities.

4.1 System Architecture

We architect the social reasoning platform for automating healthcare practices with two major components: (i) a cloud-based service platform, (ii) a mobile companion app. Figure 1 shows the overall architecture of the social reasoning platform.

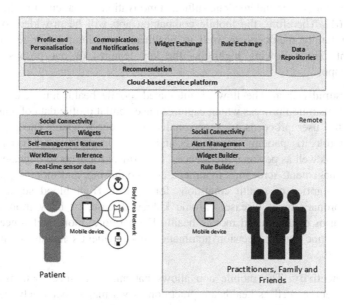

Fig. 1. Overall architecture

The cloud-based service platform employs an enterprise service architecture for modularity and extensibility [65]. It consists of five core services: profile and personalization, communication and notifications, monitoring widget exchange, rule exchange, and recommendation services. These services expose a RESTful interface for the mobile companion app to consume.

A minimal set of de-identified profile data, rules, widgets and alerts will be stored in the cloud-based data repositories. This practice ensures the data security and privacy in which privacy-sensitive data will not be transmitted outside mobile phones. In general, rules have no privacy issues, and rules exchange is introduced to empower patients with community standards. These data strategies minimize the network bandwidth between the server and the mobile companion app, thereby reducing the power consumption and computation resources on mobile phones.

The comprehensive feature set of the mobile companion app is described in the subsequent section for more details.

4.2   Design Concepts of the Mobile Companion App

In remote health management, while healthcare practitioners are expert about disease knowledge; patients are indeed experts about their own health observations [66]. Hence, constant cooperation between them plays a decisive role for effective health management [9]. Moreover, based on a strong theoretical foundation, the social support from those who are family members and friends involved in interventions helps to create persuasion power and generate sufficient motivation for patients to achieve better outcomes [61]. Therefore, the mobile companion app will be provided to patients, friends and family members, as well as healthcare practitioners for remote health management. The following highlights the key features of our proposed mobile companion app.

Profile Personalisation. The flow of automated mobile health interventions begins with a self-registration process which captures the essential profile data of a user. Once registered, the user proceeds to a personalisation process which encompasses the selection of role: (i) patients, (ii) friends and family members, and (iii) healthcare practitioners, as well as personal preferences. It is critical for users to indicate the types of health management: screening, treatment, and monitoring, and more importantly to select the categories of health conditions for control. High blood sugar (diabetes mellitus), coronary heart disease, chronic kidney disease, or baby monitoring are typical scenarios of automated mobile health. Furthermore, more preferences will be prompted for fine tuning decision automation once patient's health conditions are entered.

Social Connectivity. The mobile app allows patients to connect with friends and family members as well as healthcare practitioners via major social networking sites such as Facebook and Twitter (Fig. 2.). Once connected with appropriate permissions, the platform ensures the interactions and information exchange amongst the users in real-time. With the social support, the engagement between the users and the mobile app would strengthen the frequent usage leading to a healthier lifestyle.

Rule Management. This features the process of rule management where rules and action plans (e.g., alerts, reports) are being synchronized with the cloud-based service platform. Mobile users are allowed to create their rules with the antecedent (IF) clauses and the consequence (THEN) clauses from different data sensing sources. In Fig. 3 –

Fig. 2. Social connectivity

screen 1, the mobile is capable of establishing real-time connectivity with wearable devices such as a Bluetooth-enabled blood glucose meter or a temperature sensor to infer whether an adverse event of Hypoglycaemia is detected. Action plans such as alerting healthcare professionals are fully customisable and automated. Furthermore, the mobile app permits users to deposit their rules to the cloud-based repositories which can be flagged as private for personal use, shared for individual social networks, or public for the community. These rules can be exchanged and applied across users of the platform for remote health management as shown in Fig. 3 – screen 2.

Fig. 3. Rule management

Fig. 4. Monitoring widgets

Monitoring Widgets. The mobile app is capable of enriching the interactions between patients and their smartphone using widgets for real-time and continuous health surveillance. Figure 4 shows two monitoring widgets based on the user profile personalisation: (i) the heat rates being read (as a green dot) from a heart rate sensor in an intuitive meter, and (ii) the blood glucose readings are being reported in real-time for diabetes self-management. For more community widgets, users can search for relevant widgets from the cloud-based repositories.

Alerts and Notifications. This facilities effective interventions for health management over messaging, social networking sites, and SMS. Based on event triggers of decision rules, alert and notifications will be sent to families, friends, or healthcare practitioners timely.

5   Conclusion

Our study has several implications for theoretical literature and practice of mobile health. First, we propose a new paradigm of automated mobile health as the automation of healthcare processes supported by mobile technologies. Second, we elaborate this paradigm to propose a novel social reasoning platform to empower patients with more affordable medical information and less dependent on healthcare practitioners. Last but not least, we designed and prototyped a mobile platform which is capable of reshaping the current generation of mobile health interventions towards a more supportive and automatic direction. It unveils the capability of building knowledge repositories for effective health management using ubiquitous mobile and wearable devices.

This paper is not an end, but rather a beginning of future research. We are looking into ways of further refining our mobile platform through the process of knowledge discovery in mobile health analytics. Decision rules, therefore, can be dynamic and highly personalised towards more efficient and effective personal health management. Furthermore, we are in the process of evaluating automated mobile health interventions to figure out their effects on behavioural change and improvements in health outcomes.

References

1. Research2guidance: Global Mobile Health Trends and Figures Market Report 2013–2017. http://www.research2guidance.com/shop/index.php/mobile-health-trends-and-figures-2013-2017
2. Dobriansky, P.J., Suzman, R.M., Hodes, R.J.: Why population aging matters - a global perspective. US Department OFSS State, pp. 1–32 (2007)
3. Martínez-Pérez, B., de la Torre-Díez, I., López-Coronado, M., Sainz-de-Abajo, B., Robles, M., García-Gómez, J.M.: Mobile clinical decision support systems and applications: a literature and commercial review. J. Med. Syst. **38**, 4 (2014)
4. Van Woensel, W., Roy, P.C., Abidi, S.S.: A mobile and intelligent patient diary for chronic disease self-management. In: MEDINFO 2015 eHealth-enabled Health, pp. 118–122 (2015)
5. Ambroise, N., Boussonnie, S., Eckmann, A.: A smartphone application for chronic disease self-management. In: 2013 Mobile and Information Technologies in Medicine and Health Conference (MobileMED 2013), Vol. 1785 (2013)
6. Hommersom, A., Lucas, P., Velikova, M., Dal, G.: MoSHCA–my mobile and smart health care assistant. In: 2013 IEEE 15th International Conference on e-Health Networking, Applications and Services (Healthcom 2013), pp. 188–192 (2013)
7. van Woensel, W., Al Haider, N., Roy, P.C., Ahmad, A.M., Abidi, S.S.R.: A comparison of mobile rule engines for reasoning on semantic web based health data. In: 2014 IEEE/WIC/ACM International Joint Conference on Web Intelligence Agent Technology, vol. 1, pp. 126–133 (2014)
8. O' Connor, Y., O' Sullivan, T., Gallagher, J., Heavin, C., O' Donoghue, J: Developing eXtensible mHealth Solutions for Low Resource Settings. In: Prasath, R., O'Reilly, P., Kathirvalavakumar, T. (eds.) MIKE 2014. LNCS, vol. 8891, pp. 361–371. Springer, Heidelberg (2014)
9. Jung, H., Yang, J.G., Woo, J.-I., Lee, B.-M., Ouyang, J., Chung, K., Lee, Y.H.: Evolutionary rule decision using similarity based associative chronic disease patients. Cluster Comput. **18**, 279–291 (2015)
10. Nalepa, G., Bobek, S.: Rule-based solution for context-aware reasoning on mobile devices. Comput. Sci. Inf. Syst. **11**, 171–193 (2014)
11. Kumar, S., Nilsen, W., Pavel, M., Srivastava, M.: Mobile health: revolutionizing healthcare through trans- disciplinary research. Computer (Long. Beach. Calif). 28–35 (2013)
12. Varshney, U.: Mobile health: medication abuse and addiction. In: Proceedings of 4th ACM MobiHoc Work, pp. 37–42 (2014)
13. Varshney, U.: Pervasive computing and healthcare. Pervasive Healthcare Computing: EMR/EHR, Wireless and Health Monitoring, pp. 39–62. Springer, US (2009)
14. World Bank: Information and Communications for Development 2012: Maximizing Mobile. World Bank Publications (2012)
15. Steven, R., Steinhubl, M.: Can mobile health technologies transform health care? JAMA **92037**, 1–2 (2013)

16. Hervás, R., Fontecha, J., Ausín, D., Castanedo, F., Bravo, J., López-de-Ipiña, D.: Mobile monitoring and reasoning methods to prevent cardiovascular diseases. Sensors (Basel). **13**, 6524–6541 (2013)
17. Walton, R., DeRenzi, B.: Value-sensitive design and health care in Africa. IEEE Trans. Prof. Commun. **52**, 346–358 (2009)
18. Prociow, P.A., Crowe, J.A.: Towards personalised ambient monitoring of mental health via mobile technologies. Technol. Health Care **18**, 275–284 (2010)
19. Magill, E., Blum, J.M.: Personalised ambient monitoring: supporting mental health at home. In: Advances in Home Care Technologies: Results of the Match Project. pp. 67–85 (2012)
20. Paoli, R., Fernández-Luque, F.J., Doménech, G., Martínez, F., Zapata, J., Ruiz, R.: A system for ubiquitous fall monitoring at home via a wireless sensor network and a wearable mote. Expert Syst. Appl. **39**, 5566–5575 (2012)
21. Junglas, I., Abraham, C., Ives, B.: Mobile technology at the frontlines of patient care: understanding fit and human drives in utilization decisions and performance. Decis. Support Syst. **46**, 634–647 (2009)
22. Carroll, A.E., Marrero, D.G., Downs, S.M.: The healthpia glucopack diabetes phone: a usability study. Diabetes Technol. Ther. **9**, 158–164 (2007)
23. Istepanian, R.S.H., Zitouni, K., Harry, D., Moutosammy, N., Sungoor, A., Tang, B., Earle, K.: A: evaluation of a mobile phone telemonitoring system for glycaemic control in patients with diabetes. J. Telemed. Telecare. **15**, 125–128 (2009)
24. Varshney, U.: Mobile health: four emerging themes of research. Decis. Support Syst. **66**, 20–35 (2014)
25. Stacey, D., Murray, M.A., Légaré, F., Sandy, D., Menard, P., O'Connor, A.: Decision coaching to support shared decision making: a framework, evidence, and implications for nursing practice, education, and policy. Worldviews Evid. Based. Nurs. **5**, 25–35 (2008)
26. O'Connor, A.M., Tugwell, P., Wells, G.A., Elmslie, T., Jolly, E., Hollingworth, G., McPherson, R., Bunn, H., Graham, I., Drake, E.: A decision aid for women considering hormone therapy after menopause: decision support framework and evaluation. Patient Educ. Couns. **33**, 267–279 (1998)
27. Stewart, M., Brown, J.B., Boon, H., Galajda, J., Meredith, L., Sangster, M.: Evidence on patient-doctor communication. Cancer Prev. Control **3**, 25–30 (1999)
28. Stewart, M.A.: Effective physician-patient communication and health outcomes: a review. Can. Med. Assoc. J. **152**, 1423–1433 (1995)
29. Garg, A.X., Adhikari, N.K.J., McDonald, H., Rosas-Arellano, M.P., Devereaux, P.J., Beyene, J., Sam, J., Haynes, R.B.: Effects of computerized clinical decision support systems on practitioner performance and patient outcomes: a systematic review. JAMA **293**, 1223–1238 (2005)
30. Ammenwerth, E., Schnell-Inderst, P., Machan, C., Siebert, U.: The effect of electronic prescribing on medication errors and adverse drug events: a systematic review. J. Am. Med. Informatics Assoc. **15**, 585–600 (2008)
31. Chaudhry, B.: Systematic review: impact of health information technology on quality, efficiency, and costs of medical care. Ann. Intern. Med. **144**, 742 (2006)
32. Knops, A.M., Legemate, D.A., Goossens, A., Bossuyt, P.M.M., Ubbink, D.T.: Decision aids for patients facing a surgical treatment decision. Ann. Surg. **257**, 860–866 (2013)
33. Hoffman, A.S., Volk, R.J., Saarimaki, A., Stirling, C., Li, L.C., Härter, M., Kamath, G.R., Llewellyn-Thomas, H.: Delivering patient decision aids on the Internet: definitions, theories, current evidence, and emerging research areas. BMC Med. Inform. Decis. Mak. **13**(2), S13 (2013)
34. Trenaman, L., Bryan, S., Bansback, N.: The cost-effectiveness of patient decision aids: a systematic review. Healthcare **2**, 251–257 (2014)

35. Stacey, D., Légaré, F., Col, N.F., Bennett, C.L., Barry, M.J., Eden, K.B., Holmes-Rovner, M., Llewellyn-Thomas, H., Lyddiatt, A., Thomson, R., Trevena, L., Wu, J.H.: Decision aids for people facing health treatment or screening decisions. In: Stacey, D. (ed.) Cochrane Database of Systematic Reviews. Wiley, Chichester (2014)
36. Hamann, J., Langer, B., Winkler, V., Busch, R., Cohen, R., Leucht, S., Kissling, W.: Shared decision making for in-patients with schizophrenia. Acta Psychiatr. Scand. **114**, 265–273 (2006)
37. Wennberg, J.E., Fisher, E.S., Skinner, J.S.: Geography and the debate over Medicare reform. Health Aff. (Millwood). Suppl Web, W96–114 (2002)
38. Veroff, D., Marr, A., Wennberg, D.E.: Enhanced support for shared decision making reduced costs of care for patients with preference-sensitive conditions. Health Aff. **32**, 285–293 (2013)
39. Christofferson, D.E., Hamlett-Berry, K., Augustson, E.: Suicide prevention referrals in a mobile health smoking cessation intervention. Am. J. Public Health **105**, e1–e3 (2015)
40. Osterberg, L., Blaschke, T.: Adherence to medication. N. Engl. J. Med. **353**, 487–497 (2005)
41. Singh, N., Varshney, U.: An artifact for improving effective medication adherence. In: Tremblay, M.C., VanderMeer, D., Rothenberger, M., Gupta, A., Yoon, V. (eds.) DESRIST 2014. LNCS, vol. 8463, pp. 304–311. Springer, Heidelberg (2014)
42. De Geest, S.: Adherence to long-term therapies: evidence for action. Eur. J. Cardiovasc. Nurs. **2**, 323 (2003)
43. Abidoye, A.P.: Using wearable sensors for remote healthcare monitoring system. J. Sens. Technol. **01**, 22–28 (2011)
44. Bonato, P.: Wearable sensors and systems. IEEE Eng. Med. Biol. Mag. **29**, 25–36 (2010)
45. Allet, L., Knols, R.H., Shirato, K., de Bruin, E.D.: Wearable systems for monitoring mobility-related activities in chronic disease: a systematic review. Sensors (Switz.) **10**, 9026–9052 (2010)
46. Bonato, P.: Advances in wearable technology and its medical applications. In: 2010 Annual International Conference on IEEE Engineering in Medicine and Biology Society EMBC 2010, pp. 2021–2024 (2010)
47. Lane, N.D., Miluzzo, E., Lu, H., Peebles, D., Choudhury, T., Campbell, A.T.: A survey of mobile phone sensing. IEEE Commun. Mag. **48**, 140–150 (2010)
48. Chan, M., Estève, D., Fourniols, J.-Y., Escriba, C., Campo, E.: Smart wearable systems: current status and future challenges. Artif. Intell. Med. **56**, 137–156 (2012)
49. Mukherjee, A., Pal, A., Misra, P.: Data analytics in ubiquitous sensor-based health information systems. In: Proceedings of 6th International Conference on Next Generation Mobile Applications, Services and Technologies NGMAST 2012, pp. 193–198 (2012)
50. Catley, C., Smith, K., Mcgregor, C., Tracy, M.: Extending CRISP-DM to incorporate temporal data mining of multi- dimensional medical data streams: a neonatal intensive care unit case study. Comput. Med. Syst. **1**, 1–5 (2009)
51. Touati, F., Tabish, R.: U-healthcare system: state-of-the-art review and challenges. J. Med. Syst. **37**, 9949 (2013)
52. Kumar, S., Nilsen, W.J., Abernethy, A., Atienza, A., Patrick, K., Pavel, M., Riley, W.T., Shar, A., Spring, B., Spruijt-Metz, D., Hedeker, D., Honavar, V., Kravitz, R., Craig Lefebvre, R., Mohr, D.C., Murphy, S.A., Quinn, C., Shusterman, V., Swendeman, D.: Mobile health technology evaluation. Am. J. Prev. Med. **45**, 228–236 (2013)
53. Lee, H., Park, K., Lee, B., Choi, J., Elmasri, R.: Issues in data fusion for healthcare monitoring. In: Proceedings of 1st ACM International Conference on PErvasive Technologies Related to Assistive Environments - PETRA 2008, p. 1 (2008)

54. Raij, A., Ghosh, A., Kumar, S., Srivastava, M.: Privacy risks emerging from the adoption of innocuous wearable sensors in the mobile environment. In: Proceedings of 2011 Annual Conference on Human Factors in Computing Systems – CHI 2011, pp. 11–20 (2011)
55. Guha, S., Plarre, K., Lissner, D., Mitra, S.: Autowitness: locating and tracking stolen property while tolerating GPS and radio outages. In: ACM Transactions, pp. 29–42 (2012)
56. d'Aquin, M., Nikolov, A., Motta, E.: How much semantic data on small devices? In: Cimiano, P., Pinto, H. (eds.) EKAW 2010. LNCS, vol. 6317, pp. 565–575. Springer, Heidelberg (2010)
57. Nguyen, H.D., Poo, D.C.C.: Analysis and design of mobile health interventions towards informed shared decision making: an activity theory-driven perspective. In: IFIP WG8.3 International Conference on Decision Support Systems (DSS 2016) (2016)
58. Payam, S., Pavel, A., Morad, B., Kathryn, M., Craig E., K.: Activity theory driven system analysis of complex healthcare processes. In: Twenty Second European Conference on Information Systems, pp. 1–14 (2014)
59. Elwyn, G., Frosch, D., Thomson, R., Joseph-Williams, N., Lloyd, A., Kinnersley, P., Cording, E., Tomson, D., Dodd, C., Rollnick, S., Edwards, A., Barry, M.: Shared decision making: a model for clinical practice. J. Gen. Intern. Med. **27**, 1361–1367 (2012)
60. Saurer, J.: Pervasive and Mobile Sensing and Computing for Healthcare. Springer, Berlin Heidelberg (2013)
61. Nguyen, H.D., Jiang, X., Poo, D.C.C.: Designing a social mobile platform for diabetes self-management: a theory-driven perspective. In: Meiselwitz, G. (ed.) SCSM 2015. LNCS, vol. 9182, pp. 67–77. Springer, Heidelberg (2015)
62. Kollmann, A., Riedl, M., Kastner, P., Schreier, G., Ludvik, B.: Feasibility of a mobile phone-based data service for functional insulin treatment of type 1 diabetes mellitus patients. J. Med. Internet Res. **9**, e36 (2007)
63. Quinn, C.C., Shardell, M.D., Terrin, M.L., Barr, E.A., Ballew, S.H., Gruber-Baldini, A.L.: Cluster-randomized trial of a mobile phone personalized behavioral intervention for blood glucose control. Diabetes Care **34**, 1934–1942 (2011)
64. Kiran, M.P.R.S., Rajalakshmi, P., Bharadwaj, K., Acharyya, A.: Adaptive rule engine based IoT enabled remote health care data acquisition and smart transmission system. In: IEEE World Forum Internet Things, WF-IoT 2014, pp. 253–258 (2014)
65. OSGi Alliance: The OSGi Architecture. http://www.osgi.org/Technology/WhatIsOSGi
66. Bodenheimer, T.: Patient self-management of chronic disease in primary care. JAMA **288**, 2469 (2002)

Does Location Matter? The Efficiency of Request Propagation Based on Location in Online Social Networks

Salem Othman[✉], Javed I. Khan, and Fatema Nafa

Networking and Media Communication Research Laboratories,
Department of Computer Science, Kent State University, Kent, OH 44240, USA
{sothman,javed,fnafa}@kent.edu

Abstract. The centrality metrics such as Closeness and Betweenness in Online Social Network (OSN) determine how much end-to-end delay and queue-load of a node can have as a source or as a destination through Social Routing. Experimentally, we find that nodes with high Out-Closeness centrality in OSN suffer from high end-to-end delay as a target, but not as a source. We show that the cause of this end-to-end delay is that most nodes with high Out-Closeness centrality have low In-Closeness centrality. Moreover, we show that the increase in the local In-Degree centrality will increase the global In-Closeness centrality. We also find that the promised level to increase the In-Closeness centrality of a node is its Friends of Friends-Of-Friends (Level-3). An agent-based Model for Social Routing is proposed and a set of large-scale Google+ Graphs are used. A simulation study is also completed by propagating a set of requests in different societies with different routing schemes and diverse queue disciplines, in order to compare the average end-to-end delays from the source and target perspectives.

Keywords: Online social networks · Requests · Social routing and forwarding · Simulation of online social networks · Network centrality

1 Introduction

Social Routing [14] is an important component of Online Social Networks (OSNs) (e.g. Facebook, Twitter, and Google plus). The main goal of the social routing protocols such as our SOR protocol [14] is to help individuals to communicate with indirect neighbors by disseminating their requests in the OSNs. However, the location of individuals in OSNs can be a double-edged sword. Thus, it is imperative to study and understand how the node position in OSNs can affect the efficiency of message propagation and how nodes can cope with the increase in their queue loads and in their requests delays as a source or as a destination. Source individuals who request donations from others hope to be near them while those who are in the target position might try to be out of the way temporally or forever.

Identifying the location (centrally) of a node in OSNs has been introduced in social science to analyze the importance of nodes in social networks [7]. The three most popular individual centrality measures are Degree centrality, Betweenness centrality, and closeness centrality [7, 9]. Other definitions of closeness centrality are possible based on the

© Springer International Publishing Switzerland 2016
G. Meiselwitz (Ed.): SCSM 2016, LNCS 9742, pp. 47–58, 2016.
DOI: 10.1007/978-3-319-39910-2_5

direction of the edge such as In-Closeness centrality and Out-Closeness centrality which determine how close a particular node is to its incoming and outgoing neighbors respectively [4]. Recently, increased attention has been given to identifying the centralities in blogs, wikis, social annotation and tagging, media sharing, transportation, Brain and Online Social networks. These central nodes represent the most critical nodes that can have a major impact on the network operations.

In this paper, we therefore propose an agent-based Model for Social Routing which aims to mimic human interaction in OSNs. A set of Google+ social network large-scale Graphs with a set of human attributes are used for experimental studies. A simulation study using our protocol SOR [14] is conducted by propagating a set of requests in four different societies in order to compare the average end-to-end delays from the source and target perspectives. Experimentally, we find that (1) nodes with high Out-Closeness centrality in OSN suffer from high end-to-end delay as a target, but not as a source, (2) the cause of this end-to-end delay is that most nodes with high Out-Closeness centrality have low In-Closeness centrality, (3) the promised level to increase the In-Closeness centrality of a node is its Friends of Friends-Of-Friends (Level-3).

The reset of the paper is organized as follow: Sect. 2 presents the related work. Section 3 introduces the notation and formally defines the Closeness and Betweenness centrality metrics. Our agent-based model of Social Routing, SPPD Metric, and four societies are explained in detail in Sect. 4. The simulation and experimental results are given in Sect. 5 and the conclusion is in Sect. 6.

2 Related Work

Node position within the OSN has been studied in many domains in order to analyze important nodes. In Brain Networks, node position help to Identify and Classify Hubs [15]. In blogs, it is meant to identify influential bloggers in a blogging community [11]. In Transportation Networks, it is to determine critical nodes in order to improve the design of the network and devise plans for coping with network failures [6]. In computer networks (Internet), node position is studied in order to protect against threats of central nodes [5] and to analyze country-level routing which helps to answer questions about the influence of each country on the flow of international traffic [10]. In Online Social Networks, node position helps to evaluate the centrality of the node within the social network [3], to identify the social hubs which are nodes at the center of the influential neighborhoods [8], to examine the relationship between the type of flow and the differential importance of nodes with respect to the speed of traffic reception and the frequency of receiving it [2], and to evaluate ways of predicting a node's future importance under degree, closeness, and Betweenness centralities [12]. Our work is to investigate the efficiency of request propagation based on the node's location (In-Closeness, Out-Closeness, and Betweenness centralities) in the OSN.

3   Background

In this section, we formally define the Online Social Network, In-Closeness centrality, Out-Closeness centrality, and Betweenness centrality.

3.1   Online Social Network (OSN) Model

As shown in Fig. 1, Let $G = (V, E)$ be an OSN modeled as a directed graph where V is a set of n nodes and E is a set of m edges in the graph. Let $e_{u,v}$ denote a link (social relationships) of the graph connecting a pair of nodes (u, v) and let $P_{u,v}$ denote a path between the source node u and the destination node v; the path consisting of a series of intermediate nodes $(u, I_0, I_1, ..., v)$. Let $L_{anc}(v)$ be the set of predecessors (ancestors) which are connected to v in G, let $L_{neb}(v)$ be the set of incoming direct neighbors connected to v, let $L_{src}(v)$ be the set of source nodes sending their requests to v, let $L_{int}(v)$ be the set of intermediate nodes between node v and its sources, and let $L_p(v)$ be the set of paths which start from the source nodes and end at v as a target.

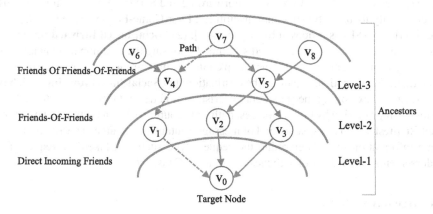

Fig. 1.   Target node v and its ancestors

3.2   Node Centrality in OSN

The three most widely used centrality measures are Degree, Closeness, and Betweenness.

Closeness centrality: is a measure of the mean geodesic distance between a node and all its reachable nodes. Therefore, it identifies node location. It also refers to how near a node is to all other nodes in the network. In a social network context, this means how fast this node can reach everyone in the network; which affects the rate at which the information is propagating throughout the network [2].

The used graph is directed, so we define two versions of closeness centrality which are In-Closeness centrality (In-CC) and Out-Closeness centrality (Out-CC) measures. The difference between them is that the node with high Out-Closeness centrality is close to its outgoing neighbors and the one with high In-Closeness centrality is close to its incoming neighbors.

Betweenness centrality: measures how important a node is by counting the number of the shortest paths that pass through a node. Therefore, it measures the load of a given node. In a social network context, it means how likely a node is to be the most direct path between two individuals in the network and how it can influence the flow of information between them [2].

4   Agent-Based Model for Social Routing

For the simulation of human interaction on the OSN, we propose an agent-based model with (1) **Social-based Human-Queue model** which is a way of governing how requests are buffered while waiting to be transmitted to the next hop or to get a service. We assume that each agent in OSN has two queues Forwarding and Servicing. Furthermore, in this paper we only focus on two queuing disciplines: First-Come-First-Service (FCFS) and Social Priority (SP) as proposed by Barabasi [1]; (2) **Social-based forwarding** which is simply a social characteristic-based scheme of choosing the next hop from neighbors to receive a particular request. The next hop could be either the destination of the request or an intermediate node in a path to the destination; (3) **Social-based Routing** which is the process of exploiting the social characteristics of nodes in OSN in order to make a better routing decision by finding the best path from source to destinations; (4) The agent used **Request** which is a special kind of message containing a source, a destination, and some information which determine the request type such as LinkedIn's request for endorsements, and Facebook's request to join in a Cause, etc.

4.1   Agent Architecture

As shown in Fig. 2, each agent is associated with (1) a queue named forwarding queue and denoted as Q_u^f which is a data structure for storing requests temporarily. (2) A queue manager which utilizes queue disciplines for inserting, dropping, popping, and ordering requests. The Forwarding queue has three parameters (a) request arrival rate, λ_u^f, which is the number of requests arriving at u's queue per unit time, (b) request forwarding rate, μ_u^f, which is the number of requests departing the u's queue per unit time, and (c) forwarding queue length, $L_u^f(t)$, which is the number of requests in the forwarding queue of node u at time t. (3) The forwarding manager which forwards the requests to the next neighbor based on forwarding strategies.

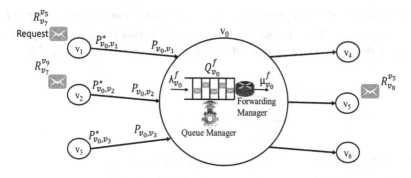

Fig. 2. Agent anatomy

4.2 Social Priority (SP)

The friendship edge, $e_{u,v}$, from node u to node v is associated with two values as shown in Fig. 2: an In-Social Priority (*iSP*) for forwarding and it represents a form of proportionate priority with which v will treat a request arriving from u and an Out-Social Priority (*oSP*) for determining the best path to forward. The value of *iSP* is known to v but, but we cannot expect v to reveal it candidly to u, thus, u continually learns *oSP* which is an estimate of *iSP*. If node u makes a correct estimation then $oSP = iSP$. In our model, we factor namely Gender, Degree, Betweenness, Closeness, Eigenvector centralities, etc. In order to generate social priorities for all potential senders (receivers), each node uses its own set of factors and uses singular value decomposition (SVD) [13] to generate a SP vector for the immediate in(out) circle made of adjacent neighbors.

4.3 Social Priority Based Path Delay (SPPD) Metric

In this subsection, we describe the SPPD metric and the information needed for it. The objective is to determine the end-to-end delay, $T_{\text{end-to-end}}$, experienced by a request R_s^d through simple and autonomous paths from a source node s to a destination node d. We assume (1) the node can use only one queue discipline (SP or FCFS) which is known to all nodes in the network, (2) the node u's queue parameters $\left(\lambda_u^f, \mu_u^f, L_u^f(t)\right)$ are also known. Table 1 summarizes the used parameters.

Table 1. Queue parameters

Parameter	Description
$L_u^f(t)$	The number of requests in forwarding the queue of node u at time t.
λ_u^f	The number of requests arriving at u's queue per unit time
μ_u^f	The number of requests departing the u's queue per unit time
$oSP_{u,v}$	Out-social priority
$\beta_u(t)$	The queue discipline of node u at time t. It is fixed all times?

Given a request $R_{v_1}^{v_k}$, a simple path $P_{v_1,v_k} = (v_1,...,v_k)$, and all parameters of intermediate nodes as depicted in Table 1, *find the end-to-end delay that the expected request will experience through a given simple path.* To find it, we introduce Eqs. 1 and 2:

$$T_{v_i}^f = \frac{L_{i+1}^f(t_0) + T_{v_{i-1}}^f * \lambda_{v_{i+1}}^f}{\dfrac{\mu_{v_{i+1}}^f}{oSP_{v_{i+1},v_i}} - \lambda_{v_{i+1}}^f} + \frac{oSP_{v_{i+1},v_i}}{\omega} \tag{1}$$

Where $T_{v_0}^f = 0$ and $i = 1, 2... v_{k-1}$, ω is a constant value.

Generally, the end-to-end delay for any number of intermediate nodes in the simple path is computed by Eq. 2:

$$T_{end-to-end}(v_1, v_k) = \sum_{i=1}^{k-1} T_{v_i}^f + c \tag{2}$$

The above equations can be modified to calculate FCFS queue discipline by putting $oSP_{v_{i+1},v_i} = 1$ which means the position of the request will be at the bottom of the queue regardless of how the out social priority is.

4.4 Societies in Online Social Networks

In this section we introduce a set of societies in OSN according to routing algorithms, the queuing discipline, and the forwarding schemes of nodes in OSN. We propose four societies. Two of them use the Social Priority-based routing algorithm and the others use the First-Come-First-Service based routing one. Moreover, the Social Priority-based queue and the First-Come-First-Service based queue disciplines are used to study the misalignment between routing algorithms and the queuing discipline. Let use discuss the differences and similarities between the four societies.

SP-SP society: In this social system, the source nodes use Social Priority-based routing algorithm to get the best paths to a particular target and the intermediate nodes use Social Priority-based queue discipline. This is an ideal society where there is no misalignment between the routing algorithms and queue disciplines, and where computing the best path to any target is possible and accurate.

SP-FCFS society: In this mock community, the source nodes use Social Priority-based routing algorithm in order to get the best paths to a particular target and the intermediate nodes use First-Come-First-Service based queue discipline. This is a factual society where there is a misalignment between the routing algorithms and queue disciplines and where computing the best path to a target is possible but not as expected because of the misalignment.

FCFS-SP society: In this group, the source nodes use First-Come-First-Service based routing algorithm in order to get the shortest paths to a particular target while the intermediate nodes use Social Priority-based queue discipline. The source nodes just know the number of hops between them and their destinations. They do not have access to critical information like the Social Priorities of nodes. However, the members of this society use Social Priority-based queue discipline which means there is a misalignment between the routing algorithms and queue disciplines.

FCFS-FCFS society: In this society, the source and intermediate nodes use First-Come First-Service based on routing and queue discipline. This is another example where the source nodes just know the number of hops between them and their destinations and hence there is no misalignment.

5 Experimental Results

In our previous work [14], we design and implement SOR using Omnet++ [16] to simulate human behavior and we also develop the Behavioral Data Analyzer (BDA) in Python and Apache Pig[1] to analyze and interpret the results. We perform a set of experiments to evaluate the efficiency of message propagation in the four societies: SP-SP, SP-FCFS, FCFS-SP, and FCFS-FCFS. We run all the experiments in amazon web services (AWS) using the instance of type t2.large[2]. For experiments, we use real social network datasets of different sizes of Google Plus platform. Table 2 lists the datasets (graphs) along with the vertex count, the edge count, the average degree, and the graph diameter. The graphs are directed and are available in the following web sites[3].

Table 2. Statistical information of Google + datasets

Dataset	#Nodes	#Edge	Avg. node degree	Graph diameter
DS-1	54	252	9.3	5
DS-2	120	1255	21.6	5
DS-3	498	13119	52.0	5
DS-4	1079	51953	96.0	6
DS-5	1648	166291	201.8	7
DS-6	2211	93509	84.5	8

We examine the impact of a node position (Closeness and Betweenness centrality) in OSN on the average end-to-end delay from the source and target perspectives. We use two performance metrics: *Target-based average end-to-end delay (T_AVG_EtoE_Delay)*, and *Source-based average end-to-end delay (S_AVG_EtoE_Delay)* to compare delays in the four societies. In general, the end-to-end delay of a request in a network is the time it takes the request to reach the destination from the time it leaves the source. Each source sends a set of requests to a different target and each target receives a set of requests from different sources. We compute the Target-based average end-to-end delay and Source-based average

---

[1] https://pig.apache.org/.
[2] https://aws.amazon.com/ec2/instance-types/.
[3] http://snap.stanford.edu/data/index.html.

end-to-end delay for each node separately by first getting all the node's received and sent requests and finding the end-to-end delays of these requests, then finding the average value of these delays. In our study delay comprises queuing and forwarding delays but not the service (processing) delay. Since we are focusing on routing and forwarding behaviors, we assign one millisecond to all service components. We use Closeness and Betweenness to measure the varying importance of the nodes in OSN.

Simulation setup: There are n forwarding queues in OSN, each with a single node. Requests generate in exponential distribution with a mean 15 min, forward in the exponential distribution with mean 5 min, and serve in 1 ms. We fix the number of requests for all of the experiments and we use the same sources and destinations. We notice that some scientists directly use distributions (e.g. Poisson or Exponential) in the simulator which may cause a different number of requests and/or different destinations. We use six datasets and for each dataset we have done four experiments (SP-SP, SP-FCFS, FCFS-SP, and FCFS-FCFS).

5.1   Source and Target Nodes Perspectives

We compare the Target-based and Source-based average end-to-end delays of SP-SP, SP-FCFS, FCFS-SP, and FCFS-FCFS societies using various datasets (graphs). Since the patterns of Target-based and Source-based average end-to-end delays of the four societies are similar in all datasets and because of the space limitation, we only show the Target-based and Source-based average end-to-end delays of the society SP-SP of the dataset DS-6 as shown in Figs. 3. The Figure shows that among the correlation between In-Closeness, Out-Closeness, and Betweenness Centralities and the Target-based and Source-based average end-to-end delays of SP-SP society, the patterns of In-Closeness centrality and Betweenness centrality are more similar to each other where nodes with high centrality get less delay than with Out-Closeness centrality. The nodes with high Out-Closeness centrality are close to their outgoing neighbors and this helps them as sources as shown in Fig. 3(c) while the same nodes with high Out-Closeness centrality suffer from very high Target-based average end-to-end delay as shown in Fig. 3(d). The following subsection introduces why nodes with high Out-Closeness centrality have this delay and how delay can be handled by nodes.

5.2   Closeness and Betweenness Centralities

We find, as shown in Fig. 4(a) where the x-axis is the position of nodes ordered by Out-CC and the y-axis is the difference between node's position in Out-CC and its position in In-CC (*Diff*), that most nodes with high Out-Closeness centrality have low In-Closeness centrality in OSN and this explains why these nodes suffer from delay as targets. We first order nodes by their Out-Closeness centrality, then we find the position of each node in the ordered In-Closeness centrality list and finally we calculate the difference between the two positions. For example, the highest Out-Closeness centrality node is node number 467 and its position is 1, however, its position in the ordered In-Closeness centrality list is 182, so, the difference is $1 - 182 = -181$. If we carefully observe Fig. 4(a)

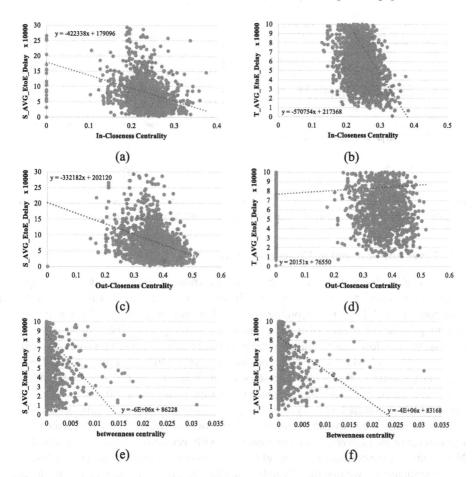

Fig. 3. Correlation between source-based average end-to-end delay and In-Closeness, Out-Closeness, and betweenness centralities in the left column and correlation between Target-based average end-to-end delay and In-Closeness, Out-Closeness, and betweenness centralities in the right column.

we can also see that some nodes with low Out-Closeness centrality have high In-Closeness centrality. Nodes can handle this problem by increasing their In-Closeness centrality and adding more edges. In Fig. 4 (b) we find the node with high local In-Degree centrality (which is a count of the number of links directed to the node) also has high global In-Closeness centrality. This pattern can be used to encourage nodes to increase their local In-Degree centrality to be globally important (High In-Closeness centrality) in the OSN which will help them to reduce the Target-based average end-to-end delay as shown in Fig. 3(b).

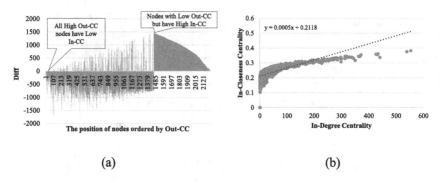

Fig. 4. (a) The difference between Out-Closeness centrality and In-Closeness centrality positions of nodes and (b) The correlation between In-Degree and In-Closeness Centralities

5.3   Level Ancestor and in-Closeness Centrality

We define a level as a distance (number of edges) from an ancestor node u to a target node v. Thus as depicted in Fig. 1, ancestors in level-1 are v's direct incoming neighbors, ancestors in level-2 are v's incoming friends-of-friends, ancestors in level-3 are v's incoming friends of friends-of-friends, and so on. Two types of edges can be added to increase the In-Closeness centrality of the target node v: *long-haul edges* from far away ancestors at level L where $L > 3$ edges or *short-haul edges* from ancestors at level $L = 2$ to the target node v. To find the ancestors and their levels, we first use an algorithm (traversing based on Breadth-First Search) to get the predecessors' list, $L_{anc}(v)$, of the target node v and their levels (How far they are from v). Then, we assume node v has some information (e.g. In-Closeness centrality) about its ancestors either from the plat-form owner or by analyzing the paths associated with received requests and their traffic. Node v ranks its ancestors in each level on the basis of their In-Closeness centrality.

Experimentally, we find that (1) adding an edge, $e_{u,v}$, from an ancestor u at any level to the target node v will only increase v's In-Closeness centrality (Other centrality measures might be effected, but this is not our goal in this study); (2) the most important nodes that dramatically increase the In-Closeness centrality when k is larger than 25, are friends of friends-of-friends at the level-3 of node v. As shown in Table 3, if we compare the increase in In-Closeness centrality after connecting a random number (150 edges in the shown experiment) of ancestors in each level to the target node v (nodes id: 764, 707, 19, 342, and 1535 of dataset DS-6) separately; (3), the maximum number of levels for most nodes is six. This is compatible with the six degrees of separation.

Each node in OSN has a different strategy and this strategy changes with time. Some Nodes sometimes need to increase their Out-Closeness centrality to be close to their targets and some other times they do not need to. Other nodes sometimes need to increase their In-Closeness centrality to be close to their sources and some other times they do not need to. It is the node's responsibility to make the trade-off between its desire to change centrality and the extra load/traffic which it might get. A node can use two tech-niques to increase its In-Closeness centrality: the *Adding* technique or the *Replacement* technique. The drawback of the Adding technique is that a target node after a period of

Table 3. The change of In-Closeness centrality of different nodes at different levels

Level/Node-ID	764	707	19	342	1535
Baseline	*0.287*	*0.274*	*0.298*	*0.245*	*0.192*
Level-2	0.322	0.314	0.329	0.308	0.274
Level-3	**0.344**	**0.335**	**0.351**	**0.310**	**0.293**
Level-4	0.316	0.312	0.328	0.287	0.299
Level-5	0.292	0.278	0.301	0.257	0.265
Level-6	0.289	0.275	0.298	0.247	0.200

time will be flooded with friends. The other option is to replace the edge (delete the existing edge before adding). A node is given k edges to add, but it must delete k (more or less based on equation) directly connected edges. Based on the finding number 2, a set of algorithms and techniques can be introduced to focus on friends of friends-of-friends at level-3 and ignore other levels.

6   Conclusion

In this paper, we experimentally find that (1) nodes with high Out-Closeness centrality in OSN suffer from high end-to-end delay as a target, but not as a source, (2) the cause of this end-to-end delay is that most nodes with high Out-Closeness centrality have low In-Closeness centrality, (3) the best level to increase the In-Closeness centrality of a node is its Friends of Friends-Of-Friends (Level-3). Moreover, we show that the increase in the local In-Degree centrality increases the global In-Closeness centrality. The Social Priority based Path Delay (SPPD) Metric is used for estimating the end-to-end social routing delay. An agent-based Model for Social Routing is proposed and a set of large-scale Google+ Graphs are used. We conducted a simulation study to compare the average end-to-end delays from the source and target perspectives by propagating a set of requests in four different societies with different routing schemes and diverse queue disciplines.

References

1. Barabasi, A.-L.: The origin of bursts and heavy tails in human dynamics. Nature **435**(7039), 207–211 (2005)
2. Borgatti, S.P.: Centrality and network flow. Soc. Netw. **27**(1), 55–71 (2005)
3. Brodka, P., Musial, K., Kazienko, P.: Efficiency of node position calculation in social networks. In: Velásquez, J.D., Ríos, S.A., Howlett, R.J., Jain, L.C. (eds.) KES 2009, Part II. LNCS, vol. 5712, pp. 455–463. Springer, Heidelberg (2009)
4. Carrington, P.J., Scott, J., Wasserman, S.: Models and methods in social network analysis, vol. 28. Cambridge University Press, Cambridge (2005)
5. Chapela, V., Criado, R., Moral, S., Romance, M.: Intentional Risk Management Through Complex Networks Analysis. Springer, Heidelberg (2015)

6. Cheng, Y.-Y., Lee, R.K.-W., Lim, E.-P., Zhu, F.: DelayFlow centrality for identifying critical nodes in transportation networks. In: 2013 IEEE/ACM International Conference on Advances in Social Networks Analysis and Mining (ASONAM). IEEE (2013)

7. Freeman, L.C.: Centrality in social networks conceptual clarification. Soc. Netw. **1**(3), 215–239 (1979)

8. Ilyas, M.U., Radha, H.: Identifying influential nodes in online social networks using principal component centrality. In: 2011 IEEE International Conference on Communications (ICC). IEEE (2011)

9. Kang, U., Papadimitriou, S., Sun, J., Tong, H.: Centralities in large networks: algorithms and observations. In: Proceedings of the SIAM International Conference on Data Mining, Society for Industrial and Applied Mathematics (2011)

10. Karlin, J., Forrest, S., Rexford, J.: Nation-state routing: censorship, wiretapping, and BGP (2009). arXiv preprint arXiv:0903.3218

11. Kayes, I., Qian, X., Skvoretz, J., Iamnitchi, A.: How influential are you: detecting influential bloggers in a blogging community. In: Aberer, K., Flache, A., Jager, W., Liu, L., Tang, J., Guéret, C. (eds.) SocInfo 2012. LNCS, vol. 7710, pp. 29–42. Springer, Heidelberg (2012)

12. Kim, H., Tang, J., Anderson, R., Mascolo, C.: Centrality prediction in dynamic human contact networks. Comput. Netw. **56**(3), 983–996 (2012)

13. Klema, V.C., Laub, A.J.: The singular value decomposition: Its computation and some applications. IEEE Trans. Autom. Control **25**(2), 164–176 (1980)

14. Othman, S., Khan, J.I.: SOR: a protocol for requests dissemination in online social networks. In: Agarwal, N., Xu, K., Osgood, N. (eds.) SocInfo 2012. LNCS, vol. 9021, pp. 394–399. Springer, Heidelberg (2015)

15. Sporns, O., Honey, C.J., Kötter, R.: Identification and classification of hubs in brain networks. PLoS ONE **2**(10), e1049–e1049 (2007)

16. Varga, A.: The OMNeT ++ discrete event simulation system. In: Proceedings of the European simulation Multi-conference (ESM 2001) (2001). SN

Usability Heuristics: Reinventing the Wheel?

Cristian Rusu[1], Virginica Rusu[2], Silvana Roncagliolo[1],
Daniela Quiñones[1(✉)], Virginia Zaraza Rusu[1], Habib M. Fardoun[3],
Daniyal M. Alghazzawi[3], and César A. Collazos[4]

[1] Pontificia Universidad Católica de Valparaíso, Valparaíso, Chile
{cristian.rusu,silvana}@ucv.cl, danielacqo@gmail.com,
rvzaraza90@hotmail.com
[2] Universidad de Playa Ancha de Ciencias de la Educación, Valparaíso, Chile
virginica.rusu@upla.cl
[3] King Abdulaziz University, Jeddah, Saudi Arabia
{hfardoun,dghazzawi}@kau.edu.sa
[4] Universidad del Cauca, Popayán, Colombia
ccollazo@unicauca.edu.co

Abstract. Heuristic evaluation is a well-known and widely accepted usability evaluation method. When performing a heuristic evaluation, generic or specific heuristics may be used. But forming heuristic evaluators may be a challenging task. The paper presents a study that evaluates the perception of (novice) evaluators on Nielsen's usability heuristics. A standard survey was applied in five experiments.

Keywords: Usability · User experience · Usability evaluation · Heuristic evaluation · Usability heuristics

1 Introduction

Usability is a well-known basic attribute in software quality. Over the last decades usability was defined and redefined by many authors. Formal usability definitions were also provided by ISO standards. However, there is still no clear and generally accepted usability definition. Usability's complex nature is hard to describe in a unique definition. User eXperience (UX) is usually considered as an extension of the usability concept. Usability evaluation methods may also be applied in order to assess UX.

Heuristic evaluation is one of the most common usability evaluation methods. Usability specialists (evaluators) examine an interactive software system based on a set of established usability design principles, called heuristics. Generic or specific heuristics may be used. We proposed sets of specific usability heuristics (and associated checklists) for several types of applications. We also proposed a methodology to develop usability heuristics.

We systematically conduct studies on the perception of (novice) evaluators over generic (Nielsen's) and specific usability heuristics. We developed a standard survey that assesses evaluators' perception on a set of usability heuristics, concerning four dimensions: D1 – *Utility*, D2 – *Clarity*, D3 – *Ease of use*, D4 – *Necessity of additional*

G. Meiselwitz (Ed.): SCSM 2016, LNCS 9742, pp. 59–70, 2016.
DOI: 10.1007/978-3-319-39910-2_6

checklist. All dimensions are evaluated using a 5 points Likert scale. The studies offer an important feedback for both teaching and research.

The paper presents a study based on five experiments. Section 2 briefly reviews the concepts of usability, UX, and usability heuristics. Section 3 presents the experimental results. Section 4 points out conclusions and future work.

2 Usability and User Experience Evaluation

A well-known usability definition was proposed by the ISO 9241 standard back in 1998 [1]. The ISO 9241 standard was updated in 2010 [2]. Yet a new revision started briefly after, in 2011 [3]. It proves once again the evolving nature of the usability concept. The current ISO 9241 definition of usability refers to "the extent to which a system, product or service can be used by specified users to achieve specified goals with effectiveness, efficiency and satisfaction in a specified context of use".

The UX concept gains popularity. To move from usability to UX is a tendency. ISO 9241-210 standard defines UX as a "person's perceptions and responses resulting from the use and/or anticipated use of a product, system or service" [2]. Most authors consider UX as an extension of the usability concept; others still use the terms usability and UX indistinctly.

Measuring effectiveness, efficiency and satisfaction does not represent the only way of evaluating usability. Two major conceptions on usability have been pointed out: (1) summative, focused on metrics, "measurement-based usability", and (2) formative, focused on usability problems detection and associated design solutions, "diagnostic usability" [4].

Usability evaluation methods are basically classified as: (1) empirical usability testing, based on users' participation [5], and (2) inspection methods, based on experts' judgment [6]. Usability evaluation methods may also be applied in order to assess UX. A broad collection of UX evaluation methods is provided by Allaboutux.org [7].

Heuristic evaluation is one of the most popular usability inspection methods. Usability specialists (evaluators) analyze every interactive element and dialog following a set of established usability design principles called heuristics [8]. Generic or specific heuristics may be used. Generic heuristics are familiar to evaluators and therefore (relatively) easy to apply, but they can miss specific usability issues. Specific heuristics can detect relevant usability issues related to the application area [9].

We proposed sets of specific usability heuristics (and associated checklists) for transactional web applications [10], touchscreen-based mobile applications [11], smartphones [12], grid computing applications [13], interactive digital television [14], virtual worlds [15], driving simulators, u-Learning applications, and virtual museums. We also developed a set of cultural – oriented usability heuristics [16]. The experience we had gained led to a methodology to develop usability heuristics [9]; the methodology is currently under review.

3   Heuristic Evaluators' Perception

SIGCHI acknowledges the importance of getting down Human-Computer Interaction (HCI) to the practical work [17]. But forming usability/UX evaluators is a challenging task. We believe that a strong relationship between HCI theory, research and practice is particularly important in countries were HCI communities are not yet well established.

Heuristic evaluations and usability tests are compulsory practice for all our students, at undergraduate and graduate level. As standard practice, at least one heuristic evaluation is performed based on Nielsen's set of 10 usability heuristics [8]. Sometimes a heuristic evaluation based on domain-specific usability heuristic is also performed. After each heuristic evaluation a survey is made, using a standard questionnaire. It gives us an interesting and useful feedback, for teaching and research. Some results have been previously published [18].

3.1   The Questionnaire

We systematically conduct studies on the perception of (novice) evaluators over generic and specific usability heuristics. All participants are asked to perform a heuristic evaluation of the same software product (case study). Then, all of them participate in a survey. We developed a standard questionnaire that assesses evaluators' perception over a set of usability heuristics, concerning 4 dimensions:

- D1 – *Utility*,
- D2 – *Clarity*,
- D3 – *Ease of use*,
- D4 – *Necessity of additional checklist*.

All dimensions are evaluated using a 5 points Likert scale. Five experiments are described below. All of them involved graduate/undergraduate Computer Science (CS) students from Pontificia Universidad Católica de Valparaíso, Chile. All heuristic evaluations were performed using Nielsen's usability heuristics. As observations' scale is ordinal, and no assumption of normality could be made, the survey results were analyzed using nonparametric statistics tests.

Mann-Whitney U tests were performed to check the hypothesis:

- H_0: there are no significant differences between evaluators with and without previous experience,
- H_1: there are significant differences between evaluators with and without previous experience.

Spearman ρ tests were performed to check the hypothesis:

- H_0: $\rho = 0$, the dimensions D_m and D_n are independent,
- H_1: $\rho \neq 0$, the dimensions D_m and D_n are dependent.

In all Mann-Whitney U and Spearman ρ tests, $p \leq 0.05$ was used as decision rule.

3.2   The Google Cultural Institute Experiment – Undergraduate Students

An experiment was made, involving 33 CS undergraduate students; 21 of them had previous experience in heuristic evaluations, and 12 others were novice evaluators. All participants were asked to perform a heuristic evaluation over the Google Cultural Institute website (www.google.com/culturalinstitute/). Google Cultural Institute is a web portal that provides access to a huge amount of information; it is in fact a "collection" of virtual museums. Later on a survey was conducted based on the standard questionnaire described in Sect. 3.1.

The Mann-Whitney U test results are shown in Table 1:

- There are no significant differences between the two groups of evaluators (with/without previous experience) in the case of dimension D1 – Utility and D4 – Necessity of additional checklist,
- There are significant differences between the two groups of evaluators in the case of dimension D2 – Clarity and D3 – Easy of use.

Table 1. Mann-Whitney U test for the perception of Nielsen's heuristics when evaluating Google Cultural Institute (CS undergraduate students)

	D1: Utility	D2: Clarity	D3: Ease of use	D4: Necessity of additional checklist
p-value	0.792	**0.018**	**0.006**	0.894

The Spearman ρ test results show that:

- In the case of evaluators with previous experience (Table 2), there are strong correlations between dimensions D1 – D2 and D2 – D3. If heuristics are perceived as clear (easy to understand), they are also perceived as useful and easy to use.
- In the case of novice evaluators (Table 3), there is moderate correlation between dimensions D2 – D3.
- When all evaluators are considered (Table 4), there is strong correlation between dimensions D2 – D3. There are moderate correlations between dimensions D1 – D2 and D1 – D4. If heuristics are perceived as useful, the necessity of additional evaluation elements (checklist) is also perceived.

Table 2. Spearman ρ test for evaluators with previous experience, CS undergraduate students (case study: Google Cultural Institute)

	D1: Utility	D2: Clarity	D3: Ease of use	D4: Necessity of additional checklist
D1	1	0.701	Independent	Independent
D2		1	0.672	Independent
D3			1	Independent
D4				1

Table 3. Spearman ρ test for novice evaluators, CS undergraduate students (case study: Google Cultural Institute)

	D1: Utility	D2: Clarity	D3: Ease of use	D4: Necessity of additional checklist
D1	1	Independent	Independent	Independent
D2		1	0.575	Independent
D3			1	Independent
D4				1

Table 4. Spearman ρ test for all evaluators, CS undergraduate students (case study: Google Cultural Institute)

	D1: Utility	D2: Clarity	D3: Ease of use	D4: Necessity of additional checklist
D1	1	0.592	Independent	0.500
D2		1	0.765	Independent
D3			1	Independent
D4				1

3.3 The Google Cultural Institute Experiment – Graduate Students

A similar experiment to the one described in Sect. 3.2 was made, involving 15 CS graduate students; 10 of them had previous experience, and 5 others were novice evaluators.

The Mann-Whitney U test results are shown in Table 5. There are no significant differences between the two groups of evaluators (with/without previous experience), excepting the dimension D4 – Necessity of additional checklist.

Table 5. Mann-Whitney U test for the perception of Nielsen's heuristics when evaluating Google Cultural Institute (CS graduate students)

	D1: Utility	D2: Clarity	D3: Ease of use	D4: Necessity of additional checklist
p-value	0.385	0.788	0.548	**0.022**

The Spearman ρ test results show that:

- In the case of evaluators with previous experience (Table 6), there is very strong correlation between dimensions D1 – D2.
- In the case of novice evaluators (Table 7), there is very strong correlation between dimensions D2 – D3.
- When all evaluators are considered (Table 8), there are strong correlations between dimensions D1 – D2, D2 – D3, and very strong correlation between dimensions D1 – D3. If heuristics are perceived as easy to use, they are also perceived as useful.

Table 6. Spearman ρ test for evaluators with previous experience, CS graduate students (case study: Google Cultural Institute)

	D1: Utility	D2: Clarity	D3: Ease of use	D4: Necessity of additional checklist
D1	1	0.898	Independent	Independent
D2		1	Independent	Independent
D3			1	Independent
D4				1

Table 7. Spearman ρ test for novice evaluators, CS graduate students (case study: Google Cultural Institute)

	D1: Utility	D2: Clarity	D3: Ease of use	D4: Necessity of additional checklist
D1	1	Independent	Independent	Independent
D2		1	0.917	Independent
D3			1	Independent
D4				1

Table 8. Spearman ρ test for all evaluators, CS graduate students (case study: Google Cultural Institute)

	D1: Utility	D2: Clarity	D3: Ease of use	D4: Necessity of additional checklist
D1	1	0.738	0.816	Independent
D2		1	0.753	Independent
D3			1	Independent
D4				1

3.4 The www.tripadvisor.com Experiment

An experiment was made using Tripadvisor as case study. 31 CS undergraduate students participated; 8 of them had previous experience, and 23 others were novice evaluators. All participants performed a heuristic evaluation of www.tripadvisor.com, a popular platform that shares reviews, compares prices, and offers links to several virtual travel agencies. The standard questionnaire was then applied.

The Mann-Whitney U test results are shown in Table 9. For all dimensions, there are no significant differences between the two groups of evaluators (with/without previous experience).

Table 9. Mann-Whitney U test for the perception of Nielsen's heuristics when evaluating www.tripadvisor.com

	D1: Utility	D2: Clarity	D3: Ease of use	D4: Necessity of additional checklist
p-value	0.101	0.803	0.085	0.138

The Spearman ρ test results show that:

- In the case of evaluators with previous experience (Table 10), there are strong correlations between dimensions D2 – D3, D2 – D4, and very strong correlation between dimensions D3 – D4. Even if heuristics are perceived as easy to use, the necessity of additional evaluation elements (checklist) is also perceived.
- In the case of novice evaluators (Table 11), all dimensions are independent.
- When all evaluators are considered (Table 12), there is weak correlation between dimensions D3 – D4.

Table 10. Spearman ρ test for evaluators with previous experience (case study: www.tripadvisor.com)

	D1: Utility	D2: Clarity	D3: Ease of use	D4: Necessity of additional checklist
D1	1	Independent	Independent	Independent
D2		1	0.743	0.798
D3			1	0.858
D4				1

Table 11. Spearman ρ test for novice evaluators (case study: www.tripadvisor.com)

	D1: Utility	D2: Clarity	D3: Ease of use	D4: Necessity of additional checklist
D1	1	Independent	Independent	Independent
D2		1	Independent	Independent
D3			1	Independent
D4				1

Table 12. Spearman ρ test for all evaluators (case study: www.tripadvisor.com)

	D1: Utility	D2: Clarity	D3: Ease of use	D4: Necessity of additional checklist
D1	1	Independent	Independent	Independent
D2		1	Independent	Independent
D3			1	0.380
D4				1

3.5 The www.expedia.com Experiment – Undergraduate Students

An experiment was made, involving 21 CS undergraduate students; 13 of them had previous experience, and 8 others were novice evaluators. All participants performed a heuristic evaluation of the www.expedia.com website. The standard questionnaire was then applied. Expedia is a popular virtual travel agency.

The Mann-Whitney U test results are shown in Table 13. There are no significant differences between the two groups of evaluators (with/without previous experience), excepting the dimension D3 – Ease of use.

Table 13. Mann-Whitney U test for the perception of Nielsen's heuristics when evaluating www.expedia.com (CS undergraduate students)

	D1: Utility	D2: Clarity	D3: Ease of use	D4: Necessity of additional checklist
p-value	0.466	0.743	**0.045**	0.913

The Spearman ρ test results show that:

- In the case of evaluators with previous experience (Table 14), there is strong correlation between dimensions D2 – D3, and moderate correlation between D3 – D4.
- In the case of novice evaluators (Table 15), there is a very strong negative correlation between dimensions D3 – D4. When heuristics are perceived as easy to use, there is no perceived need for additional evaluation elements (checklist).
- When all evaluators are considered (Table 16), all dimensions are independent.

Table 14. Spearman ρ test for evaluators with previous experience, CS undergraduate students (case study: www.expedia.com)

	D1: Utility	D2: Clarity	D3: Ease of use	D4: Necessity of additional checklist
D1	1	Independent	Independent	Independent
D2		1	0.614	Independent
D3			1	0.582
D4				1

Table 15. Spearman ρ test for novice evaluators, CS undergraduate students (case study: www.expedia.com)

	D1: Utility	D2: Clarity	D3: Ease of use	D4: Necessity of additional checklist
D1	1	Independent	Independent	Independent
D2		1	Independent	Independent
D3			1	−0.976
D4				1

3.6 The www.expedia.com Experiment – Graduate Students

A similar experiment to the one described in Sect. 3.5 was made, involving 15 CS graduate students; 10 of them had previous experience, and 5 others were novice evaluators.

Table 16. Spearman ρ test for all evaluators, CS undergraduate students (case study: www.expedia.com)

	D1: Utility	D2: Clarity	D3: Ease of use	D4: Necessity of additional checklist
D1	1	Independent	Independent	Independent
D2		1	Independent	Independent
D3			1	Independent
D4				1

The Mann-Whitney U test results are shown in Table 17. There are no significant differences between the two groups of evaluators (with/without previous experience).

Table 17. Mann-Whitney U test for the perception of Nielsen's heuristics when evaluating www.expedia.com (CS graduate students)

	D1: Utility	D2: Clarity	D3: Ease of use	D4: Necessity of additional checklist
p-value	0.461	0.157	0.356	0.711

The Spearman ρ test results show that:

- In the case of evaluators with previous experience (Table 18), all dimensions are independent.
- In the case of novice evaluators (Table 19), there is a perfect correlation between dimensions D1 – D4.
- When all evaluators are considered (Table 20), there are strong correlations between dimensions D2 – D3, and D1 – D4.

Table 18. Spearman ρ test for evaluators with previous experience, CS graduate students (case study: www.expedia.com)

	D1: Utility	D2: Clarity	D3: Ease of use	D4: Necessity of additional checklist
D1	1	Independent	Independent	Independent
D2		1	Independent	Independent
D3			1	Independent
D4				1

Table 19. Spearman ρ test for novice evaluators, CS graduate students (case study: www.expedia.com)

	D1: Utility	D2: Clarity	D3: Ease of use	D4: Necessity of additional checklist
D1	1	Independent	Independent	1.000
D2		1	Independent	Independent
D3			1	Independent
D4				1

Table 20. Spearman ρ test for all evaluators, CS graduate students (case study: www.expedia. com)

	D1: Utility	D2: Clarity	D3: Ease of use	D4: Necessity of additional checklist
D1	1	Independent	Independent	0.651
D2		1	0.696	Independent
D3			1	Independent
D4				1

3.7 Discussion

The results of The Mann-Whitney U tests indicate that, in general, evaluators' perception (with or without previous experience) over the Nielsen's usability heuristics is quite similar. In two experiments there are no significant differences in none of the four dimensions: D1 – *Utility*, D2 – *Clarity*, D3 – *Ease of use*, and D4 – *Necessity of additional checklist*. In two experiments there are significant differences regarding only one dimension (D3 and D4, respectively). In one experiment there are significant differences regarding two of the four dimensions (D2 and D3). When occur, differences were related to three of the four dimensions: D2, D3, and D4. Differences related to dimension D1 never occurred.

The results of Spearman ρ tests show that most correlations between dimensions occur in the case of evaluators with previous experience (8); only 4 correlations occur in the case of novice evaluators. When all evaluators are considered, 9 correlations occur. When occur, correlations are usually strong or very strong. All correlations are positive, excepting one.

The most recurrent correlation is between dimensions D2 – D3. It occurs in three experiments when considering all evaluators, in three experiments when considering evaluators with previous experience, and in two experiments when considering novice evaluators. When heuristics are perceived as clear, they are also perceived as easy to use.

Correlation between dimensions D1 – D2 occurs twice in the case of evaluators with previous experience, twice when all evaluators are considered, but never occurs for novice evaluators. In some experiments, when heuristics are perceived as clear, they are also perceived as useful.

Correlation between dimensions D1 – D4 occurs twice when considering all evaluators, and once when considering novice evaluators. But in this particular case the correlation is perfect. So, in some experiments, when heuristics are perceived as useful, there is also a perceived necessity for additional evaluation elements (checklist).

Correlation between dimensions D3 – D4 occurs twice in the case of evaluators with previous experience, once when all evaluators are considered, and once for novice evaluators. But in the last case the correlation is negative (and very strong). So when heuristics are perceived as easy to use, the necessity for additional evaluation elements (checklist) is perceived very differently.

4 Conclusions

Heuristic evaluation is a well-known and frequently applied usability evaluation method. Nielsen's generic heuristics are employed for more than two decades. They are familiar to evaluators and therefore (relatively) easy to apply, but they can miss specific usability issues. Many alternative heuristics were proposed, usually specific for a certain type of applications. Specific heuristics may (potentially) detect relevant usability issues related to the application area.

Forming usability/UX evaluators is a challenging task. A study on the perception of (novice) evaluators over Nielsen's usability heuristics was conducted; five experiments were performed. In general, evaluators' perception (with or without previous experience) is quite similar.

When occur, dependencies between the four surveyed dimensions are somehow expected. The most recurrent correlation is between dimensions D2 (*Clarity*) – D3 (*Ease of use*). When heuristics are perceived as clear, they are also perceived as easy to use. The only unexpected correlation is between dimensions D3 (*Ease of use*) – D4 (*Necessity of additional checklist*). Twice the correlation is positive for evaluators with previous experience, but once is negative and very strong for novice evaluators.

The study offered an important feedback for both teaching and research. The number of correlations within the four surveyed dimensions is relatively low for evaluators with previous experience, and very low for novice evaluators. Nielsen's heuristics are not perceived as one would expect, even when evaluators have previous experience in their use. The study offered relevant information particularly for the refinement of the set of usability heuristics for transactional web applications, and for the development of a new set of heuristics for virtual museums.

We examined the results only at dimension level. A more detailed study will be done at heuristic level. Quantitative analyze will be also complemented with qualitative data, collected through surveys and interviews.

References

1. ISO 9241-11: Ergonomic requirements for office work with visual display terminals (VDTs) – Part 11: guidance on usability. International Organization for Standardization, Geneva (1998)
2. ISO 9241-210: Ergonomics of human-system interaction – Part 210: human-centred design for interactive systems. International Organization for Standardization, Geneva (2010)
3. Bevan, N., Carter, J., Harker, S.: ISO 9241-11 revised: what have we learnt about usability since 1998? In: Kurosu, M. (ed.) Human-Computer Interaction. LNCS, vol. 9169, pp. 143–151. Springer, Heidelberg (2015)
4. Lewis, J.: Usability: lessons learned... and yet to be learned. Int. J. Hum.-Comput. Interact. 30(9), 663–684 (2014)
5. Dumas, J., Fox, J.: Usability testing: current practice and future directions. In: Sears, A., Jacko, J. (eds.) The Human – Computer Interaction Handbook: Fundamentals. Evolving Technologies and Emerging Applications, pp. 1129–1149. Taylor & Francis, New York (2008)

6. Cockton, G., Woolrych, A., Lavery, D.: Inspection – based evaluations. In: Sears, A., Jacko, J. (eds.) The Human – Computer Interaction Handbook: Fundamentals, Evolving Technologies and Emerging Applications, pp. 1171–1189. Taylor & Francis, New York (2008)
7. Allaboutux.org: All About UX. http://www.allaboutux.org/. Accessed 7 Jan 2016
8. Nielsen, J., Mack, R.L.: Usability Inspection Methods. Wiley, New York (1994)
9. Rusu, C., Roncagliolo, S., Rusu, V., Collazos C.: A methodology to establish usability heuristics. In: The Fourth International Conference on Advances in Computer-Human Interactions (ACHI2011), pp. 59–62, IARIA (2011)
10. Quiñones, D., Rusu, C., Roncagliolo, S.: Redefining usability heuristics for transactional web applications. In: 11th International Conference on Information Technology: New Generations (ITNG2014), pp. 260–265. IEEE Computer Society Press (2014)
11. Inostroza, R., Rusu, C., Roncagliolo, S., Rusu, V.: Usability heuristics for touchscreen-based mobile devices: update. In: First Chilean Conference on Human - Computer Interaction (ChileCHI2013), pp. 24–29. ACM International Conference Proceeding Series (2013)
12. Inostroza, R., Rusu, C., Roncagliolo, S., Rusu, V., Collazos, C.: Developing SMASH: a set of SMArtphone's uSability heuristics. Comput. Stan. Interfaces **43**, 40–52 (2016)
13. Roncagliolo, S., Rusu, V., Rusu, C., Tapia, G., Hayvar, D., Gorgan, D.: Grid computing usability heuristics in practice. In: 8th International Conference on Information Technology: New Generations (ITNG2011), pp. 145–150. IEEE Computer Society Press (2011)
14. Solano, A., Rusu, C., Collazos, C., Arciniegas, J.: Evaluating interactive digital television applications through usability heuristics. Ingeniare **21**(1), 16–29 (2013)
15. Rusu, C., Muñoz, R., Roncagliolo, S., Rudloff, S., Rusu, V., Figueroa, A.: Usability heuristics for virtual worlds. In: The Third International Conference on Advances in Future Internet (AFIN2011), pp. 16–19. IARIA (2011)
16. Diaz, J., Rusu, C., Pow-Sang, J., Roncagliolo, S.: A cultural - oriented usability heuristics proposal. In: First Chilean Conference on Human - Computer Interaction (ChileCHI2013), pp. 82–87. ACM International Conference Proceeding Series (2013)
17. ACM SIGCHI: ACM SIGCHI Curricula for Human-Computer Interaction. http://old.sigchi.org/cdg/cdg2.html#2_1. Accessed 7 Jan 2016
18. Rusu, C., Rusu, V., Roncagliolo, S., Apablaza, J., Rusu, V.Z.: User experience evaluations: challenges for newcomers. In: Marcus, A. (ed.) DUXU 2015. LNCS, vol. 9186, pp. 237–246. Springer, Heidelberg (2015)

Circles: Enhancing Effective Interactions by Quantitative and Qualitative Visualization in User-Centered Design

Diana Sepúlveda Barrera, Erick Monroy Cuevas, and Rocío Abascal Mena[✉]

Master in Design, Information and Communication (MADIC),
Universidad Autónoma Metropolitana, Cuajimalpa, Mexico
dcg.disb@gmail.com, ermoncu@gmail.com,
mabascal@correo.cua.uam.mx

Abstract. In this paper we analyze how effective the interactions between Mexican individuals that share a relationship, like family or friends, can be measured with a proposed social network tool. This tool is called *Circles* and its main function is to apply visualization methods to show graphically parameters like quality and quantity of time, where quality becomes more important due to the relation within interests or hobbies sharing. The process was based on User-Centered Design methods in order to find the main user's needs, build prototypes according to final users, test the prototypes and get knowledge about the tool's relevance in improving life quality.

Keywords: Media-based social interaction · Social media · Online involvement · User-Centered design · Social circles · Information visualization · Usability

1 Introduction

Lifestyle in big, urban cities is chaotic, but not only lifestyle, also the ways we develop our daily activities; traffic jams, crowds, long journeys between places, are some of the main problems for urban people which also suffer from tight schedules and poor organization of their daily routines.

While living fast, people do not have an efficient tool to know how they invest their time and how they organize their activities. They also ignore how much time they invest in their relationships, within different social circles, or if those relationships are really significant in their lives according to the quality of time, hobbies, interests and life plans in common.

One of the solutions for time measurement in order to strength relationships are social networks. We can use Valerio Arnaboldis and Marco Conti's definition of social network as an *"ensemble of ties denoting the existence of a social connection between two individuals"* [1]. This definition describes, in a good way, the social process of bonding and the importance of having a connection or a link where individuals interact and exchange information about interests, hobbies and lifestyles with their different social circles. However, until now, one of the biggest problems lays on information saturation, that leads to wrong and imprecise guidance to achieve effective relationships with family, friends and co-workers. Some researches show that some users, which are exposed to

© Springer International Publishing Switzerland 2016
G. Meiselwitz (Ed.): SCSM 2016, LNCS 9742, pp. 71–80, 2016.
DOI: 10.1007/978-3-319-39910-2_7

larger amounts of time using social networks, can suffer depression and isolation because of the misleading perception of information joined to an excessive saturation of data. Also, they believe that social networks improve relationships based on the amount of contact over the quality of it [3].

In Sect. 2, we analyze the state of art in social networks and Internet usage. As we present some mobile apps that were designed as tools for improving relationships among social circles and activities organization.

The Section is concern to the contextual study. This section explains the process and methodology followed for developing our prototypes and evaluating them with final users as we demonstrate usability and relevance.

In the Sect. 4, we present a description of our prototype's functions and how the app works. Finally, conclusions are given as future work.

2 Background and Related Work

According to AMIPCI (Mexican Internet Association, 2015) nine of every ten Mexicans web surfers are frequent social networks users. This is the main reason why they use Internet, and we can translate this behavior in an importance of reaching social interactions. 85 % of regular Internet users adopt social networks to keep in touch with family and friends and to inform about what happens around the world [2].

The main device for social networks access is the laptop, however, the sum of mobile devices such as tablets and smart phones, lead the access to social networks. People aged between 18 and 44 years old, are the ones that use social networks in their daily basis; this segment represents 87 % of total Internet users. Here, we can highlight a special group between 25 and 34 years old that represent 45 % of total Internet users [3].

In Mexico, some of the most used social networks are: Facebook, Twitter and Instagram. Although, there are others that are gaining ground between Mexican users, like: Snapchat, Vine, Periscope, Tinder and Foursquare. We will focus on the last one in this paper.

Some of the essential reasons for using social networks in Mexico are mainly associated with relationships maintenance and news consumption. Young adults, between 18 and 34 years old, who develop full-time professional activities, have a lack of time to grow effective relationships. In this way, social networks become a crucial key to maintain, develop or strengthen links between individuals. Until now, social networks research has analyzed these phenomena in diverse ways and from different backgrounds: sociology, psychology, marketing, administration, economy and computer sciences.

In literature, we find many works that analyze Facebook and Twitter and their impact in relationships [4–6]. In spite of being social networks used to keep in touch with friends and family, these apps have other main purposes that lay on information exchanging more than activities and interests' organization. Most of these studies were interested in finding common structures to measure human interactions between them by using Graphic Users Interfaces (GUI). Another field of study involves similar interests' communities and their possibilities to strengthen social networks as tools for communal living [7, 8].

As we described above in this section, some social networks that used to be less popular are gaining ground (Snapchat, Vine, Periscope, Tinder and Foursquare), which essentially allow multimedia exchange about interests and personal preferences. These include dating, suggesting places, and each one of these apps has particular and diverse main objectives, but they have something in common: lifestyle sharing among social circles.

We'll focus in analyzing Foursquare and it is crowd-sourcing scheme. This social network is based on geo-localization and user-experience evaluation of places. Since it's developing, in 2009, it has grown its database thanks to the community collaboration, where anyone can grade places to let the world know how great -or how bad- is a mall or a restaurant. Also, users can leave tips for the community, where they share their wisdom of the experience they had and they can add new places to the database. Gamification is another of the reasons that made this app popular among users: the possibility to get the best rank in the leader board where users compete with their contacts. Also achieving masteries, a progressive system that acknowledges users as "masters" in certain category, like some region or food style. Suggestions of places pop out when the user is near to a popular place or if it matches with his/her list of interests. Places that are liked can be saved in a wish list in order to be visited later. Foursquare is great for sharing places, but its main objective is not to enhance interactions between individuals that have an important relationship. It is possible to see graphically how many times the user has been in a place, but not how many times he or she has been with someone, and more important, how many times he or she spent with someone. Even more, it is not possible to measure quality of time based on the user's interests.

Arnaboldis *et al.*, analyze the processes in online social relationships, where they found a gradual decay between most users' relationships as time passes due to a high percentage of weak ties [3].

In the next section, we present our contextual study in order to find user's needs and propose a prototype according to them.

3 Contextual Study

Methodologically, we used a contextual study, which is a User-Centered Design (UCD) method, to discover urban inhabitant needs by using direct observation and interviews in the environment of the users.

We chose UCD method because even though we were the ones that pointed out what the problem was, and we could propose a list of features the app "should" have, it is important to consider final users. In this way, they were those whom showed us how functional these features were, based on their experience and not in our assumptions.

We observed people from different group ages, economic income and academic backgrounds in 3 regions of Mexico: Mexico City, Toluca (Estado de México) and Acapulco (Guerrero). They showed us the importance they give to relationships development; their need to visualize how they invest time, not only while doing activities, also with their loved ones. Finally, their need to get information in an easy way. In order to gather relevant information about people's social habits, we designed an interview composed by eleven questions. We chose two principles of design: (1) time and (2) change; every question had a specific objective according to the principles above mentioned. Table 1 shows each question and its objective. With the findings obtained during the observation phase, a brainstorm was generated to detect the best ideas in order to solve user's needs and to choose a couple of them for focusing on our possible solutions (Fig. 1).

Table 1. User's social habits interview

No.	Question	Objective
1	How many social circles do you think you have?	Change
2	How often do you contact your dearest ones?	Time
3	Which situations make difficult, for you, to contact your dearest ones?	Change
4	How do you contact important people you care for?	Change
5	Which kind of activities do you consider relevant to spend quality time with people you care?	Time
6	How many hobbies do you think you know from your dearest ones?	Change
7	Do you think there's a way to measure how much time you spend with important people for you?	Time
8	If a tool existed to keep record about the time you spend with your important people, would you use it?	Time
9	Which things in your life could be improved if you have more quality time with your dearest ones?	Change
10	Have you lost any important relationship due to a lack of time or contact?	Change
11	Why haven't you used an existent tool, like an agenda or an app, to organize your time so you could keep in touch with important people for you?	Time

Fig. 1. Through contextual study we could analyze the way users interact with people they care using social networks and messaging apps.

3.1 Contextual Study

Strategy becomes scope when you translate user needs and product objectives into specific requirements for what content and functionality the product will offer to users [9]. Table 2 shows 15 needs detected or deduced from the answers we got in the Contextual Study phase.

Table 2. User's needs

	Organization	Accessing information in a simple way
	Time administration	Redefining social media's concept and it's value for communal living, beyond idleness
User's Needs	Relationships bonding	To find new uses for existing tools
	Improvement of life quality	To visualize and control time
	Reaffirming self-assurance	To identify different social circles people are involved into
	Priority hierarchy	To use hobbies and likes for effective interactions building
	Communication efficiency	To diversify activities and hobbies
	To open to new horizons for social inclusion	

3.2 Rapid Prototyping

We made two storyboards, two paper and two digital prototypes that were given to ten end users to get usability feedback about the proposal.

To develop both storyboards we have been inspired in products, places and programs that were relevant for us, such as Swarm [10] and Foursquare [11] apps, because of their user's interaction based on places of interest and tips given by the community (Fig. 2).

Fig. 2. Storyboards were an important step in building a bridge between user's needs and our tool.

Interviewed users had different academic backgrounds, level of tech experience and they used diverse mobile operating systems (Android, iOS and Windows Phone). Their ages ranged between 21 and 45 years old.

With the feedback we got for each paper prototype, we made graphic and usability changes to make our digital prototypes; most of the changes involved suggestions to improve interaction and usage of existent apps to take advantage of the information gathered there to enrich our apps.

In Figs. 3 and 4 we can see some screens of the paper prototypes. The first one shows the step to import contacts from a list of existent apps to ours to get that linking feature that was important for interviewed users. Figure 4 shows the qualitative and quantitative charts screen that results from evaluations made to a certain contact for each encounter.

Fig. 3. Paper prototypes were tested to get features feedback from final users.

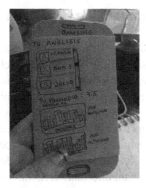

Fig. 4. Paper prototypes were tested to get features feedback from final users.

Users need to link their existing social network apps to make quicker and easier their profile filling process. The users also pointed the importance of visualization patterns of time administration as a preview step before planning activities to improve effective interactions among them.

In Fig. 5 we can see the contacts screen of one digital prototype that organizes people in social groups for detecting easily all the circles the user is involved into and how many members share that group in common.

Fig. 5. Digital prototype based on social circles.

3.3 Usability Testing

We had two really significant findings while testing prototypes: the first one, was that users identify healthy relationships based in the quality and not in the quantity of time spent. The second one was about interests and hobbies as symbols of having quality time.

Most of the mid-level-tech-experienced users interacted in a very natural way with both prototypes, pointing some doubts about icons design and sharing options (for example, if it was possible to hide the location or if contact grading -for qualitative experiences visualization- had private access).

4   Creating a Tool for Enhancing Effective Interactions: *Circles*

Our proposal is to develop a digital tool to visualize how people invest time between their social circles and to use significant information, such as interests and hobbies to suggest activities that could strengthen effective relationships. Our hypothesis is: if people had a social network capable of showing graphically how time is invested between their activities and social groups, they could be able to measure quantitatively and qualitatively their encounters to enhance effective interactions between individuals.

This tool is called *Circles*, which we conceive as a social network for community, activities and time visualization. Its main goal is to provide tools for constructing effective relationships by using significant information exchange about specific communities, such as family, friends, co-workers, or any group that share a particular interest (Fig. 6).

Fig. 6. Digital prototype based on evaluating social encounters to show qualitative and quantitative visualization between contacts with a relationship.

The prototype uses existing social networks and messaging apps (Facebook, Twitter, LinkedIn, Instagram, Google+, Swarm, Foursquare, Skype, Spotify and WhatsApp) to link information that enriches our user database and to create more helpful interest's profiles, routines and social circles. With all this information, users can organize their most relevant contacts or social circles to register activities done with them, also to produce more accurate activities suggestions (based in coincidences between users and geo-localization) in real time or to make future plans. After each meeting, *Circles* allows users to grade the experience as it registers all the meetings by makings graphics, so the user can visualize the quality of these experiences. Users are able to analyze this information and decide if they need to make new habits or if it is healthy for them to keep some relationships. To make introspection about how they keep in touch with people and how they affect their lives.

A strengthen of social circles is the result of arranging information about likes, hobbies, appointments and contacts (friends, family, etc.) according to the principles we chose at the beginning of the project, both, time and organization; also, information design's principle: to organize an amount of information in different ways to visualize and analyze new patterns and relations [12].

5 Conclusion

We conclude that time and organization are two linked factors that usually are hard to measure because of their intangibility. However, they can be represented in a graphic way to make easier to know, by using visualization, our activities and the amount of time we spend daily in each one. In this way, activities can be organized effectively and this can be also applied in the developing of social relationships where quality is more important than quantity. This could be translated in the raise of productivity and self-esteem as a lowering of stress levels.

Sharing hobbies and interests is an important key to improve effective interactions in relationships. The suggestions feature based on contact coincidences was widely appreciated with interviewed users, allowing them to have a deeper knowledge of the ones they care about and to discover new places and activities to enjoy together.

User-Centered Design was an effective method to know final users in a holistic way: their habits, their needs, their desires and how they interact with technology to do everyday tasks. We believe this is an essential step in app and websites development.

In future work we intend to improve the social media linking and to add a quiz tool to gather more particular information in an entertaining and fun way. This could provide us more valuable and consistent data to create more significant and accurate profiles and suggestions for final users in *Circles*.

References

1. Arnaboldi, V., Conti, M., Passarella, A., Dunbar, R.: Dynamics of personal social relationships in online social networks: a study on Twitter. In: Proceedings of the First ACM Conference on Online Social Networks, pp. 15–26. ACM, New York (2013)
2. Asociación Mexicana de Internet (2015). https://www.amipci.org.mx
3. Echeburúa, E., de Corral, P.: Adicción a las nuevas tecnologías y a las redes sociales en jóvenes: un nuevo reto. Rev. Adicciones **22**, 91–95 (2010)
4. Tran, T.B., Joormann, J.: The role of Facebook use in mediating the relation between rumination and adjustment after a relationship breakup. Comput. Hum. Behav. **49**, 56–61 (2015)
5. Jin, C.H.: The role of Facebook users' self-systems in generating social relationships and social capital effects. New Media Soc. **17**(4), 501–519 (2015)
6. Goodman-Deane, J., Mieczakowski, A., Johnson, D., Goldhaber, T., Clarkson, P.J.: The impact of communication technologies on life and relationship satisfaction. Comput. Hum. Behav. **57**, 219–229 (2016)

7. El-diraby, T.E.: Communities of interest-interest of communities: social and semantic analysis of communities in infrastructure discussion networks. Comput. Aided Civil Infrastruct. Eng. **31**(1), 34–49 (2016)
8. Yang, J., Leskovec, J.: Defining and evaluating network communities based on ground-truth. Knowl. Inf. Syst. **42**(1), 181–213 (2015)
9. Garrett, J.: Elements of User Experience, the: User-Centered Design for the Web and Beyond. Pearson Education, Berkeley (2010)
10. Swarm (2015). https://www.swarmapp.com/
11. Foursquare (2015). https://foursquare.com/
12. Wurman, R.: Hats. Des. Q. **145**, 1–32 (1989)

A Recommender System Research Based on Location-Based Social Networks

Jianmin Wang[1], Ruhuo Tan[2(✉)], Ri-Peng Zhang[2], and Fang You[1]

[1] School of Arts and Media, Tongji University, Shanghai, China
{wangjianmin,youfang}@tongji.edu.cn
[2] School of Information Science and Technology, Sun Yat-Sen University, Guangzhou, China
{891567977,pk_mati}@qq.com

Abstract. Nowadays, with the rapid development of Location-Based Social Networks, information presents a trend of explosive growth. In order to locate the valuable information in tremendous amounts of location-based service data and prosperi O2O business through LBS, recommender system based on location-based service was presented. This paper takes Sina Microblog LBS data as research object. By analyzing the features of the crawled data and the existing problems of current LBS recommender systems, we present Region-density-based Clustering (RC) recommendation algorithm. For optimization, this paper also presents another algorithm called Distance-and-Category-based Clustering (DCC). This algorithm is mainly about clustering spots base on their distance similarity and category similarity. If two spots are nearby and both category attributes are similar, they will be more likely to gathered into a cluster. Finally, this paper also proposed the visualization method of the LBSNs recommender system.

Keywords: Location-based service · Sina microblog · Cluster · Location recommendation · Visualization

1 Introduction

With the rapid development of mobile Internet and mobile terminal location technology in recent years, location-based service (LBS), which has been applied to various applications, is becoming the standard configuration of mobile Internet applications. All kinds of LBS applications, which can be mainly categorized as entertainment, social networking, life service, and business service, are merged into social networking services (SNS), thereby changing the way people socialize. For instance, the traditional relationship of sociality is based on friends or some kind of stable social relation constructed by interests. However, through the LBS, we can find a user who is engaged in the same activity, in the same place, and at the same time. As a result, we build a new social relation based on location. Moreover, as a dimension of information filter, location can be used to improve the validity and accuracy of a user's fetching and sharing of information. Furthermore, relying on their significant relationship and interest spectra, location-based social networks (LBSNs) construct an online to offline (O2O) pattern [1]

© Springer International Publishing Switzerland 2016
G. Meiselwitz (Ed.): SCSM 2016, LNCS 9742, pp. 81–90, 2016.
DOI: 10.1007/978-3-319-39910-2_8

through releasing text, images, videos, and audios that possess location information. The O2O pattern improves the propagandist strength of a businessman as well as makes finding valuable locations easy for a user.

2 Background

As LBSNs develop, information overload appears inevitable because of the promotion of user-based and location information. To solve such a problem, a recommender system based on location service is proposed and is gradually becoming a popular subject of current studies. In current mainstream LBSNs, a user's location preferences are mainly measured by the number of check-ins. For example, Berjani and Strufe [2] established a user-site score matrix by crawling Gowalla's data, after which they gain results by using orthogonal matrix decomposition. Ying et al. [3] established UPOI-Mine, a recommender system driven by a prediction model based on a regression tree. Ye et al. [4] combined the geographic feature of social relation and location, and proposed the geo-measured friend-based collaborative filtering algorithm. While the above methods are only concerned with check-in records and ignore the semantic information between locations, which may easily lead to a problem of identifying similar locations, Lee and Chung [5] used semantic information of sites to compute the similarity of users for the first time. However, they neglected the effect of distance. Currently, research on LBSNs is mainly based on collaborative filtering [6], but the large data in LBSNs will result in sparsity of check-in matrix. Thus, Leung et al. [7] used community location model (CLM) to show the relations among users, activities, and locations. They used community-based agglomerative-divisive clustering to cluster CLM and reduce the sparsity. In addition, for a better universal method of reducing the dimension of user check-in matrix, Zhou et al. [8] proposed the use of PLSA topic model to determine the implicit subject between users and locations.

In LBSNs, each user's check-in information of location becomes easy to obtain because of the openness of such information. By analyzing different users' check-in behaviors, we can recommend users with similar location preferences and possible interesting locations, which makes finding valuable user and information in massive data effective for users as well as increases O2O business through location recommendation. SNS data are characterized by a large order of magnitude, authenticity, and instantaneity. Therefore, we believe it can reflect users' behavior effectively.

3 RC Algorithm

In this paper, clustering all the sites is an important part of the location recommendation algorithm because it can reduce the dimension and improve the recommendation accuracy. Clustering, which is mainly based on the similarity of data objects, involves dividing data objects with similar characteristics based on certain rules into different subsets, which are usually called clusters or groups. The goals of clustering are to make object similarity in a cluster as high as possible and make the object similarity among clusters as low as possible [9]. The common clustering algorithm can be divided into partitioning methods [10], hierarchical methods [11], density-based methods [12], grid-based methods [13] and model-based methods.

The RC algorithm clusters sites based on the domain density according to the aggregation effect of geography so that it can reduce the dimension and avoid user similarity reduction because of check-in error. Subsequently, it calculates the signed location for each cluster from the clustering result and transfers a cluster that contains multiple locations into an abstract signed location with the geographic coordinate and hierarchical category. Then, it transfers the check-in vector of a user relative to the location into the check-in vector of the signed location of the location cluster and calculates the similarity among users. Finally, it selects users with Top-K similarity as a user recommendation, after which we use the recommended users for collaborative filtering calculation based on location preferences. We obtain the Top-N score locations as the location recommendation when we have finished adding the preference of the target user relative to this class of location to the calculation of unvisited sites.

Here i would like to introduce user similarity calculation based on hierarchical category tree. As shown in Fig. 1 we can construct a hierarchical tree based on the location cluster by transferring the category property to the location cluster. The bottom of the tree is the location cluster layer, while CategorySmall, CategoryMedium, and CategoryLarge are the small, middle, and large categories, respectively, to which the location cluster belongs. A high hierarchy corresponds to a large grain size and more location clusters. Constructing the hierarchical category tree improves the calculation of the similarity among users. For instance, user u_a always checked in location cluster c_1, whose signed location is Commercial Street of Beijinglu, while user u_b always checked in the

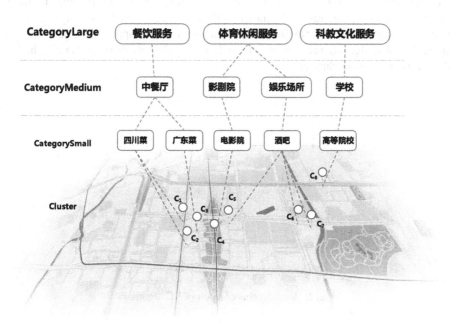

Fig. 1. Hierarchical categories tree based on location cluster

location cluster c_2, whose signed location is Commercial Street of Shangxiajiu; the abovementioned two users will have no similarity because they have not checked in the same location cluster if we consider the cluster layer only. However, if we consider the small category property of c_1 and c_2, then we will find that both c_1 and c_2 belong to the characteristic commercial walking street. Thus, users u_a and u_b possess a similarity in the CategorySmall layer. For the other hierarchy, if users do not possess a common check-in category in a hierarchy, then we could consider a higher hierarchy. If users have a similarity in the lower hierarchy, then their similarity is higher. For example, users u_a and u_b have common check-in location clusters in the cluster layer, while users u_a and u_c do not possess a similarity in the same layer. But if users u_a and u_c have a common check-in category in the CategorySmall layer, then the similarity between users u_a and u_b is higher than the similarity between users u_a and u_c. Therefore, to reduce the weight of hierarchy in the user similarity calculation, the hierarchy with a higher grain size should be multiplied by the corresponding coefficient.

4   DCC Algorithm

The RC algorithm contains different kinds of locations after clustering, and the category property of the signed location would cover the category property of other locations when using the signed location conversion algorithm. Therefore, the final check-in vector of the user to the location cluster cannot represent the true preference of the user in each category. To maintain the user's original location category preference when clustering the location, we propose the DCC algorithm. DCC algorithm clusters the locations that are near each other or have similar categories to improve the similarity among locations in the cluster. As shown in Figs. 2 and 3, while the RC algorithm can find only conglomerated location clusters, which are not overlapped in the geographical space, the DCC algorithm can find the crossed location clusters, thereby obtaining higher flexibility in location clustering.

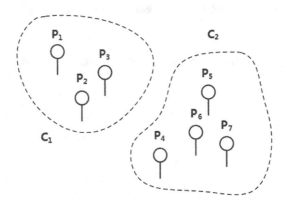

Fig. 2. location cluster result of RC algorithm

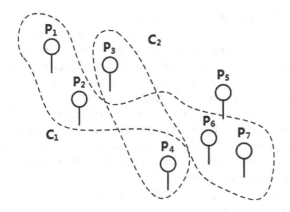

Fig. 3. Location cluster result of DCC algorithm

4.1 Similarity Based on Distance and Category

(1) Similarity in location distance

Locations have geographical position attributes, and they are represented by two points in a two-dimensional orthogonal coordinate system. In the two-dimensional space, we can use the Euclidean distance to measure the distance between two locations. However, we should use spherical distance formula to calculate the actual distance of two locations because Earth is a sphere. If location p_i's geographic coordinate is (log_i, lat_i), location p_j's geographic coordinate is (log_j, lat_j), and $R = 6370856$ (meters) is the rough radius of Earth, then the distance formula of the two locations can be shown as:

$$Dis(p_i, p_j) = R \cdot \cos^{-1}(\sin(lat_i) \cdot \sin(lat_j) + \cos(lat_i) \cdot \cos(lat_j) \cdot \cos(lon_i - lon_j)) \quad (1)$$

According to the geographical agglomeration effect, the locations with closer distances will have higher similarities. Thus, location distance similarity is inversely related to their distance.

$$Sim_{distance}(p_i, p_j) = \frac{1}{1 + Dis(p_i, p_j)} \quad (2)$$

(2) Similarity in location category

Aside from the similarity in distance, locations have similarity in category. According to Fig. 1, for independent trees "catering service" and "sports and leisure service," calculating the similarity between the c_3 in "catering service" and c_4 in "sports and leisure service" is possible. However, it is not different from the common classification recommendation if we cannot calculate the similarity among different large categories. As a solution, we defined that it has similarities with different degrees with each location in the location model based on distance and category. Therefore, we add a root layer upon the CategoryLarge layer so that all the nodes in the hierarchical category tree possess a common ancestor node, that is, the root category. As a result, the hierarchical category tree becomes a connected graph.

Intuitively, the category similarity of the two locations can be transferred into the distance between the two leaf nodes in the hierarchical category tree, and a higher distance, which is indicated by the number of edges between the two leaf nodes, corresponds to lower similarity. However, we cannot obtain a satisfactory accuracy if we use only the edge number between the two leaf nodes as the measurement standard of the similarity. For instance, the two leaf nodes, (cinema) and (Cantonese restaurant) have an edge number of eight. The nodes (cinema) and (colleges and universities) also have an edge number of eight, but obviously, we are more likely to have dinner in a nearby Cantonese restaurant after watching a movie. Therefore, to show this kind of similarity, we set different weights for each edge.

(1) Division of the category of edges

First, we divide the edges from the cluster layer to the CategoryLarge layer into two categories: one is the $e_{cluster}$, the edges from the cluster layer to the CategorySmall layer, which is a known value; the others are the $e_{categorysmall}$, $e_{categorymedium}$, and $e_{categorylarge}$, which correspond to each hierarchy in CategorySmall, and this kind of edges should be constructed from low to high.

(2) Construction of the weights of $e_{categorysmall}$

In this paper, we use the dataset crawled from Sina microblog to construct $e_{categorysmall}$. We count the total number of check-ins of every category in the CategorySmall layer, and we label it $CheckinNum_j$

$$e_{categorysmall} = \frac{1}{1 + \log_{10} CheckinNum_j} \tag{3}$$

We use the log function to reduce the effect on the calculation of similarity because of significant data diversity. We add one to avoid a zero denominator. The $e_{categorysmall}$ is inversely related to the check-in number, that is, a higher check-in number corresponds to lower weights of its edges. Therefore, clustering is simplified because of the close distance to other categories.

(3) Construction of the weights of $e_{categorymedium}$ and $e_{categorylarge}$

We take the average of the edge weights of the lower class that is connected directly to the edge as the weights of $e_{categorymedium}$ and $e_{categorylarge}$.

$$w_{categorymedium} = \frac{\sum w_{categorysmall}}{n_{categorysmall}} \tag{4}$$

$$w_{categorylarge} = \frac{\sum w_{categorymedium}}{n_{categorymedium}} \tag{5}$$

(4) Construction of the weights of $e_{cluster}$

We define the weights of $e_{cluster}$ as half of the minimum value in $w_{categorysmall}$.

$$w_{cluster} = 0.5 \times \min(w_{categorysmall}) \tag{6}$$

(5) Category similarity calculation among the locations

After finishing the construction of the weights of each hierarchy's edge, we calculate the category similarity among the locations in the dataset. We define the category similarity by the following formula because it is inversely related to distance.

$$Sim_{category}(p_i, p_j) = \frac{1}{\sum w_{cluster} + \sum w_{category}} \tag{7}$$

(3) Total similarity of locations

Location similarity based on distance and category essentially involves clustering related locations through the balance of distance and category. If two locations p_a and p_b have a close range but they belong to two large categories with significant difference, then they cannot be clustered. By contrast, if the above locations have a far range but they belong to the same small category, then they are likely to be clustered.

$$Sim(p_i, p_j) = \alpha \cdot Sim_{category}(p_i, p_j) \cdot Sim_{distance}(p_i, p_j) \tag{8}$$

4.2 Location Clustering Based on Affinity Propagation (AP) Algorithm

We will obtain a location similarity matrix S after calculating the similarity of N locations. This section will cluster the location similarity matrix through the AP algorithm and select the clustering center automatically through the information delivered by the locations. Compared with the DBSCAN algorithm, the AP algorithm effectively confirms the parameters of the clustering algorithm, and we could obtain a satisfactory result if we use only the default value. In addition, selecting a signed location after clustering to ensure a practical clustering effect is unnecessary. Furthermore, the AP algorithm can handle a massive dataset in a short time and obtain an ideal result.

We add the similarity of distance and category into the definition of similarity among locations, after which we use the AP algorithm to select the most representative location as the typical point of clustering. Therefore, the nodes in the result set may have a close range or similar category. In conclusion, the RC algorithm has a better effect on location clustering than the algorithm based on space density.

4.3 Calculation of User Similarity and Recommendation Result

After clustering the location, we transfer the user check-in vector, calculate the location preference of each user, and calculate the Top-K similar users of each user. Finally, we calculate the prediction score of the unvisited location according to the location preference of the target recommendatory user and show the locations with Top-N prediction scores to the target user as the final recommendation.

5   Experimental Results and visualization

5.1   Evaluation criteria

We use an offline experiment method to evaluate the effect of the algorithm in this paper. The data for the experiment is crawled through the Sina microblog API. For each target user, we use 80 % of their check-in record as the training set and the remaining 20 % for the test set, which is used to verify the effect of the recommendation. In addition, we select precision and recall, which are the most common index in the evaluation of the recommender system performance.

$$Precision = \frac{\sum_{u \in U} |R(u) \cap T(u)|}{\sum_{u \in U} |R(u)|} \tag{9}$$

$$Recall = \frac{\sum_{u \in U} |R(u) \cap T(u)|}{\sum_{u \in U} |T(u)|} \tag{10}$$

Here, $R(u)$ is the location recommendation based on the user's check-in record in the training set, and $T(u)$ is the user's check-in record in the test set.

5.2   Visualization

To strengthen the ability to display the multidimensional information of this recommender system and improve the intuition of the recommendation, we created a visualization model for the user recommendation that is based on force-directed algorithm, and a visualization for location recommendation is implemented.

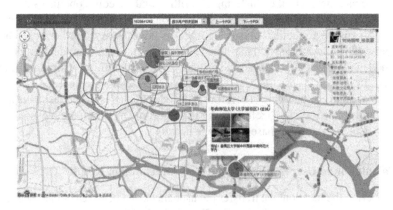

Fig. 4. Visualization of historic check-in record

We concentrated on elaborating the design of the recommendatory algorithm. Thus, we display only the interfaces of historic check-in record (Fig. 4), DCC user recommendation (Fig. 5), and DCC location recommendation (Fig. 6).

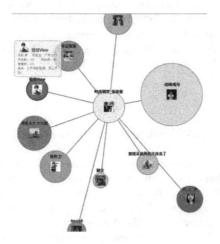

Fig. 5. Visualization of DCC user recommendation

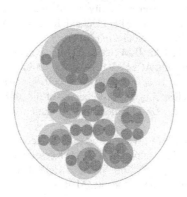

Fig. 6. Visualization of DCC location recommendation

6   Conclusion and Future Work

Social networking based on location service is a network platform with multidimensional information. It reflects extensive information about an individual in society to facilitate a thorough understanding of problems and laws in our daily life through the study of LBSNs.

Except for distance and category, we did not include additional feature information in the business of location into location clustering, such as the law of check-in time, location tag, and user comments. We expect to enhance the effect of location clustering by including additional feature information in future research.

Acknowledgements. This work was supported by the National Natural Science Foundation of China under Grant Nos. 61073132 and 60776796; the Fundamental Research Funds for the Central Universities (101gpy33); Special Project on the Integration of Industry, Education and Research of Guangdong Province (No. 2012B091000062); Project 985 of Innovation Base for Journalism & Communication in the All-media Era, Sun Yat-sen University.

References

1. Chen, Y.: Analysis in SoloMo application pattern of mobile internet. Telecommun. Sci. **03**, 18–22 (2012)
2. Berjani, B., Strufe, T.: A recommendation system for spots in location-based online social networks. In: Proceedings of the 4th Workshop on Social Network Systems, p. 4. ACM (2011)
3. Ying, J.J.-C., Lu, E.H.-C., Kuo, W.-N., et al.: Urban point-of-interest recommendation by mining user check-in behaviors. In: Proceedings of the ACM SIGKDD International Workshop on Urban Computing, pp. 63–70. ACM (2012)
4. Ye, M., Yin, P., Lee, W.-C., et al.: Exploiting geographical influence for collaborative point-of-interest recommendation. In: Proceedings of the 34th International ACM SIGIR Conference on Research and Development in Information Retrieval, pp. 325–334. ACM (2011)
5. Lee, M.-J., Chung, C.-W.: A user similarity calculation based on the location for social network services. In: Yu, J.X., Kim, M.H., Unland, R. (eds.) DASFAA 2011, Part I. LNCS, vol. 6587, pp. 38–52. Springer, Heidelberg (2011)
6. Goldberg, D., Nichols, D., Oki, B.M., et al.: Using collaborative filtering to weave an information tapestry. Commun. ACM **35**(12), 61–70 (1992)
7. Leung, K.W.T., Lee, D.L., Lee, W.C.: CLR: a collaborative location recommendation framework based on co-clustering. In: Proceedings of the 34th International ACM SIGIR Conference on Research and Development in Information Retrieval, pp. 305–314. ACM (2011)
8. Zhou, D., Wang, B., Rahimi, S.M., Wang, X.: A study of recommending locations on location-based social network by collaborative filtering. In: Kosseim, L., Inkpen, D. (eds.) Canadian AI 2012. LNCS, vol. 7310, pp. 255–266. Springer, Heidelberg (2012)
9. De Sa, J.M.: Pattern Recognition: Concepts, Methods, and Applications. Springer, Berlin (2001)
10. Cheu, E.Y., Keongg, C.,Zhou, Z.: On the two-level hybrid clustering algorithm. In: International Conference on Artificial Intelligence in Science and Technology, pp. 138–142 (2004)
11. Fred, A., Leitao, J.M.: Partitional vs hierarchical clustering using a minimum grammar complexity approach. In: Amin, A., Pudil, P., Ferri, F., Iñesta, J.M. (eds.) SPR 2000 and SSPR 2000. LNCS, vol. 1876, pp. 193–202. Springer, Heidelberg (2000)
12. Nanni, M., Pedreschi, D.: Time-focused clustering of trajectories of moving objects. J. Intell. Inf. Syst. **27**(3), 267–289 (2006)
13. Yanchang, Z., Junde, S.: GDILC: a grid-based density-isoline clustering algorithm. In: 2001 International Conferences on Info-tech and Info-net, 2001 Proceedings ICII 2001-Beijing, pp. 140–145. IEEE (2001)

Users Behaviour in Social Media

User's Understanding of Reputation Issues in a Community Based Mobile App

Orlando P. Afonso[✉], Luciana C. de C. Salgado, and José Viterbo

Department of Computer Science, Fluminense Federal University (UFF), Niterói, Brazil
{oafonso,luciana,viterbo}@ic.uff.br

Abstract. With the emergence of the Web 2.0, (digital) services are coverging and moving into the digital and mobile world, producing lots of information in real-time, such as traffic conditions, points of interests and so on. With the big amount of collected data from community-based applications, it becomes necessary to know wheather such content is trustworhty. When using applications such as Waze, we are supposed to trust in the information provided by unknown users, which act as digital content producers. However, it needs to be transparently clear where this information comes from and how trustable are its providers/endorsers. This paper presents the results of a two-step study to investigate how users recognize (or not) the signs and the reputation model of digital content producers in Waze app. We analysed and found out how the reputation is communicated to the users and the potential impacts on human computer interaction.

Keywords: Reputation · Community based app · Trust · Semiotic engineering · Communicability

1 Introduction

Community based applications, in general, aim at bringing users interested in work together toward a common goal, such as, finding a best route in a city or the best toilet in a town. With these interactive systems, users may collaborate and interact with instant messaging, profiles, forums and other social networking features. Furthermore, each participant may include, edit, exchange, share and evaluate interactive systems' content that may influence community members in decision-making process. Each participant may act as a consumer and/or a producer of digital content.

This work focus on investigating user's understanding of reputation issues in a Community based Mobile App and the potential implications to Human-computer Interaction (HCI). Reputation can be defined as what is said or believed about a person or thing as said by Josang et al. [6]. Josang and co-authors [6] consider reputation as the collective measure of trustworthiness or reliability based on the referrals or ratings from members in a community too. On the Web, the concepts of trust and reputation are applicable in virtual interaction environments through the Reputation systems [6, 8, 10]. These systems collect, distribute and aggregate information based on the behavior of the participants through their interactions. Thus, they help users to decide in whom to trust, to motivate good behavior among them, and to control the participation of those who are considered

© Springer International Publishing Switzerland 2016
G. Meiselwitz (Ed.): SCSM 2016, LNCS 9742, pp. 93–103, 2016.
DOI: 10.1007/978-3-319-39910-2_9

dishonest. The concepts of Reputation are considered a long time in our society and now, it extends to the web. Strahilevitz [18] presents that one of the most significant developments during the last decade has been the growing availability of information about individuals, making possible analyze with whom make deals, sells etc.

Donavan and Smith [12] investigated trust models in recommendation systems where trust is estimated by monitoring the accuracy of a profile at making predictions over an extended period. As seen in [19], in many community-based web applications, trust is a very important issue to make users' experience comfortable.

The reputation of a digital content producer, i.e. a user that provides digital content on the Web, involves characteristics like credibility, reliability and so on. If these aspects are not communicated properly or cause breakdowns at interaction time, they can cause misunderstandings and problems for users to complete their tasks successfully. In this research, we focus on understanding the potential breakdowns (in interaction) related to how interactive applications treat the reputation of digital content producers (by whom it is provided and/or endorsed) and communicate it to the end-users.

In this paper, we present and discuss the main results of a two-step study carried out to characterize the reputation model of a mobile application. To understand how the reputation questions affect the human-computer interaction, the first study (Study One) was proposed to investigate how the reputation of the content producers is communicated to users. We chose a mobile application, Waze©[1], whose purpose is to promote a smart traffic, where users interact and inform traffic conditions in real-time, aiming at collaborating and helping other users. Applying the Semiotics Inspection Method (SIM) [17], by two researchers, it was possible to: (a) analyze how Waze deal with reputation issues; (b) identify the Waze strategies to classify an information as reliable or not; (c) identify the potential breakdowns in the communication of reputation issues.

In Study Two we conducted an empirical experiment to observe (in practice) how users recognize (or not) the signs and the reputation model of information sources in Waze app. The results show that many users are not aware about reputation of digital content producers in community-based apps. It was also possible to confirm (and find out new ones) some breakdowns in communication strategies of Waze, identified in Study One.

This paper is divided as follows. In Sect. 2, we present an overview of some related work. In Sect. 3 we detail de methodology and findings of our study. Finally, in the Sect. 4, we conclude and discuss the results that we have found.

2   Reputation in HCI

People often base their relationships with others in values like trust, reliability and reputation. When we heard some news (in digital medias or not), for example, it would be appropriate to consider the content producer to decide if that information is reliable or not. In other words, the reputation of a content producer is an important issue to evaluate something as reliable or not.

---

[1] Waze, https://www.waze.com/.

As the amount of information produced by community-based apps increases, it is necessary to recognize the importance of reputation issues in this kind of places. Over the last 15 years the HCI research community has been researching this topic [13, 14, 21]. Dwyer and co-authors [4], for instance, studied social networks, where privacy and reliability are barely perceived by the end-users. The authors investigated and compared if the confidence in people in two social networking (Facebook[2] and MySpace[3]) affect the desire of sharing information and establishing new relationships. Facebook is supposed to guarantee the authenticity of its members due the associations with physical entities (e.g. university). MySpace, in turn, has a bad reputation in terms of reliability. Despite the study limitation (the veracity of profiles was not considered), the main findings include: subjects from Facebook and MySpace expressed similar levels of concern regarding internet privacy, but the members of Facebook were more trusting of the site and other members. Although the members of MySpace are more active in developing new relationships. These results show that the interaction of trust and privacy concern in social networking sites do not show enough to create a model of behavior and activity in an accurate way.

Ganesh and Sethi [5] presented a work about trust and reputation in Social Networks, showing empirical results from Facebook Reputation System where a score is associated to a person's profile, reflecting their extreme negativity or positivity. In this study, the users are divide into two groups: personal and professional. In the personal group, profile features like predictability, care, expertise, altruism and honesty. In the professional group: leadership, organization, punctuality, reliability and expertise. As limitation, the authors relate that the reputation can change over time and the proposed model does not cover that. Another limitation refers to engagement of the users.

Kittur and co-authors [7] discuss some risks related to trust in online environments such as Wikipedia. In this collaborative based environment any user can include, edit e consume the information available in the articles there. Among the risks, stands out: precision (not knowing if the subject is accurate, frequently perceived for lack of references); reasons (not knowing the reasons' editors, which can deflected for many reasons); expertise (it is not possible to know the level of editors' knowledge; stability (it is not possible to know the number of changes in the paper). The work presents a list of best practices to improve reliability, such as including history of record changes involving subject and their authors. One of the metrics founded in the study is to use percentage of words included by anonymous users. These users are supposed to offer more chances to commit vandalism and spam. Zeng and co-authors [22] use Dynamic Bayesian Networks to calculate the evolution of trust using as input status of editors' writing and inserted texts.

Luca and Zerva [9] relate that most researches about trust present as study case e-commerce situations and is focused on credibility, not trust. To understand how users consider a site as trustable, some aspects were analyzed such as: design look, information structure, information focus, underlying motive, usefulness of information, accuracy of information, name recognition and reputation, advertising, information bias, tone of the

---

[2] www.facebook.com.
[3] www.myspace.com.

writing, identity of the site operator, functionality of the site, customer service, past experience with the site, information clarity, performance on a test, readability of text and site affiliations. In e-commerce sites, for instance, the most relevant features are name recognition and reputation; in new sites, information bias; in nonprofit organizations sites, less information structure is considered important. In Opinion/Review sites, information sites and information accuracy; in Travel sites, customer service. In web search sites, information design, functionality, advertising.

Massa and Avesani [11] analyze the potential contribution of trust metrics to get better performance in Recommendation Systems, presenting a filtering process that can be informed between users reputation, being propagated by other users through evaluations and the trust model, creating a trust network.

Some studies also were focused on crowdsourcing environments. Alperovich and co-authors [1] propose a system and a method to calculate the reputation of mobile apps. It is done by collecting some attributes of mobile apps and its behavior. It is compared with crowdsourcing data in real-time, changing the reputation score of the application. Accordingly to a score, an application is classified in a level that represents its reputation and a probability to be malicious, identifying some risks.

Varshney and co-authors [20], in turn, suggest through coding, to promote the trust in crowdsourcing environments using control of errors and mathematic models. This work differs from ours because mathematic models are used to indicate when an information can be considered as trust or to identify attacks by malicious crowd workers. Our work uses a different methodology to comprehend these questions: our focus is on the communicability of reputation issues and how it affects interaction.

In HCI research area, we found the work from Shneiderman [15], that claims that the publication of users' past performance patterns and a rich feedback about subjects and authors/users are the best practices to increase the trust in this kind of environments. It presents guidelines to designers involving trust in online experiences. The main ones are disseminate past performance history, indicate references to create reputation systems, obtain certification of third parties as stamps of approval.

Our work presents an exploratory research to understand better the communication of the reputation questions of digital producers.

3 Investigating Reputation Issues in Waze App

The purpose of this study was to investigate user's understanding of reputation issues in a Community based Mobile App and the potential implications to HCI. The general research question we were asking was: How users recognize (or not) the signs and the reputation model of information sources in community-based apps?

This study is part of a broader research to investigate reputation issues in crowdsourcing apps. In our study, we chose the app Waze (shown in Fig. 1), which is about a smart traffic through information in real-time posted by users. In Study One, we conducted a semiotic [16] inspection and found out that Waze has some strategies to classify whether an information posted by a user can be considered trustworthy or not.

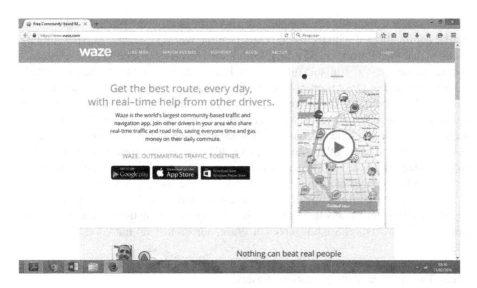

Fig. 1. Waze website (https://www.waze.com/)

Other findings from Step One show that there are potential breakdowns in the communication of reputation issues. Waze has some strategies to classify an information as trustworthy or reliable as said before, but these forms to help the users are now well communicated to the users, causing some problems to understand these questions. In summary, with the application of the Semiotics Inspection Method (SIM) [11], it was possible to: (a) analyze how Waze deal with reputation issues; (b) identify the Waze strategies to classify an information as reliable or not; (c) identify the potential break-downs in the communication of reputation issues. With respect to category (b), Waze offers verification mechanisms to try to ensure the integrity and accuracy of information that are: alerts and number of thanks and comments; threshold alerts per day; option "does not exist". To prevent cheating and abuse of function "alert", Waze put a limit on the number of alerts that each person can make in one day or even in one hour. If a user informs something that is incorrect or wrong, he may lose points of his classification level or be prohibited to post information in the app for a period. However, it happens only if the user report that the warning does not exist to the app. If a person decides to block the street for personal proposals, for instance, and a group of friends confirms that information, it can cause incorrect decisions to other drivers. Some users could assign that this message was incorrect, but what could happen to other drivers while the information was still visible? The number of comments associated to a post may influence the Waze reputation model, because it keeps the information available in the app for more time than usual. Our study also revealed that the number of "thanks" in the app suggests that the information is reliable. But, sometimes the sign of "thanks" does not represent that the users agree with that information. The users usually use that sign only to thank to the information posted.

As to the category (c), Waze is not clear about how the user is informed of the reliability of information. The communication lies with the interpretation of each user, and is therefore a point where the application should be improved. The track interdictions can be communicated with the hazard classification, works or events. Another limiting factor is that the information be available until the other user to enter its non-existence, leaving in the interval available information. It is not clear to the user when a source is reliable or not. For those users who know the application documentation, information that has a higher number of required become more reliable. Each user has an avatar that can change its level before some tasks such as driving a specific distance. Some problems were identified in this kind of situation. This resource (the avatar) is to promote engagement of the users, but in other situations, it could be the unique form that the user likes to customize his profile. At the map, when a user click on an avatar, some information is shown like: number of points, a classification of the user, how long the user is on Waze, etc. However, it is difficult to get these information on the fly, when the user is driving. Furthermore, many taxi drivers drive all the time during the week and get many points only for driving. So, big scores in Waze, sometimes, do not correspond to the idea of trust.

To a better comprehension about how and whether it affects the users' interaction, Study Two focused on the reception of users.

3.1 Methodology

We used a qualitative approach because it is especially appropriate for studies like ours [2, 3], which explores intensively and at greater depth a specific research question. Our primary data was produced by six participants (P1, P2, P3, P4, P5 and P6). The main empirical evidences were collected in post-evaluation interviews: the participants' discourse about the experiment and answer some questions about the test and reputation issues in Waze. Secondary empirical data was collected from the questionnaire sent before the tests including question about profile of participants and questions about reputation. The participants' interviews were analyzed separately, using discourse analysis techniques. This analysis consisted of a systematic exploration to find out major meaning categories in discourse relating intra-participant analysis and inter-participant analysis. In order to run the empirical study, a real route was selected. To conduct the tests, a scenario of use was elaborated, to motivate the participants and guide them about the tasks they should achieve during the study. This scenario presented a situation where a worker used the Waze to get the best route to a specific destiny, considering trust and the information reliability. The researcher also included a fake warning (in the Wazes' route) to observe the participants reaction. In order to avoid distractions we elaborate a questionnaire that prepared our participants to comprehend a little about the question of reputation. Beyond this, we introduced Waze and explain the objectives around the tests and characteristics about the route selected. It was possible, at any time of the test, that the participant interact with the interface of the app.

Participants and Procedures. The 6 (six) participants had little experience with Waze app in real experiences sucha as using the app while driving a car. The entire experiment had a duration of about 30 min.

Firstly, a pilot test was conducted to verify the viability of the test and making some adjusts. The participants were invited to answer a questionnaire and after that, inside the car, some aspects of Waze were presented and the scenario of use. Each participant should act like the character of the scenario. Then, after this, an interview was conducted to comprehend better some situations during the test and to understand how the participants lead with the reputation questions.

4 Experimental Results

The empirical data collected in the tests was examined using discourse analysis technique. It generated categories which are part of the broader results of the research. We arrived on evidences provided by six specific subcategories of meanings: (i) the participants are not worried about reputation issues in this kind of app; (ii) the participants do not recognize a reputation model in Waze; (iii) the participants believe that to trust in the information posted in the app is necessary another kind of knowledge; (iv) the participants credit to the app the provided information reliability; (v) the participant trust in information provided by friend and family.

As evidence for (i), we see the following excerpts:

P1: "If it was easy to post, I posted". The criterion that I used to select a route was the short time".
P2: "To help the Waze working well, I put the information, but I don't have this habit". "I used as criterion to select the route, the smaller traffic".
P3: "The selected criterion to choice a route is the smaller distance (if it shows)". "I posted the information, because it is an app which depends on that to help other users".
P4: "If I know how to post the information, I posted. Nevertheless, if I was driving, I do not. I don't have the habit to do this".

During the interview, a question was included: If you are driving and heard about an accident in the road, would you post this information? The point here is identify if the participants are worried about their own reputation and if they look for more information before post something. It demonstrate that participants do not matter about the information sources.

As evidence for (ii), we see in the following excerpts some breakdowns in communication of Waze and the reception of users:

P1: "I didn't see any element in the interface different from the others to give best routes. It presented the same icons etc.".
P2: "When we pass around the mall, it show me the traffic. It is important to help the drivers".
P3: "The app show the traffic condition (heavy or low)".
P4: "I think that trust in an information posted is responsibility of each user because it is not possible to verify by the app".
P5: "I guess if the app show the number of evaluations about an information, it would be a better model to trust in that information".

Many elements present in the interface of Waze are not well communicated to the users. The participants did not see aspects like information sources, accidents and other conditions of traffic during the tests. Therefore, we identify some ruptures in communicating these elements.

As evidence for (iii), we see in the following excerpts that the participants think that is necessary to have some knowledge to compare with what is showed by Waze.

P2: "In an unknown city I trusted based on following example: if in the cities that I know it works well, it will work well there too".
P3: "I trusted only if I can compare it with other app similar".
P4: "If the app suggest a different place from I know, I don't select the suggested route".
P5: Places that we know by magazines, tv programs are shown with intense traffic and I pass there and the traffic is that way, I can trust".

Waze presents as one of its strategies to identify an information the number of likes. However, the participants associated this to the Facebook, not associating to the idea of confirmation of trust.

As evidence for (iv), we see in the following excerpts that sometimes users credit to the app the function of analyze if an information is reliable.

P3: "The app show the traffic condition (heavy or low)".
P5: "This information posted on Waze means that someone inform that? Or not? Because only one or two can post something and it will be considered reliable"?

The choice of a direct observation was due to the difficulties in reproducing traffic situations on the laboratory. Participants were recruited after answering a questionnaire about their technological profile and experience about social media, especially mobile community based apps. During the study, their task was to use the Waze app to find a route to a specific address in the city, in a typical scenario. In this route, each participant analyzed the traffic conditions and the content confident. We then interviewed participants, individually, to find out what meanings and use they associated with reputation while using Waze app.

As evidence for (v), we see in following excerpt that a known information by the participants is easier to trust in.

P5: "One of criterion adopted by me to consider an information as trust is its origin. If the information source is my friends or my family, I can trust".

The following evidences was identified: the participants have not provided no care about their own reputation, posting information listened by third parties without confirming its veracity and validity, attributing ease of use as criteria as task. The participants did not perceive elements of interface used by Waze to communicate features reputation and trust. In this point, the users did not demonstrate preoccupation in knowing information sources to analyze and make their decisions. So, the reputation is not considered when selecting a route. Waze bring many information about information sources like avatars, time of use, etc. However, the users recognized none of them during the tests. Another aspect that was identified is: many times the participants consider localization or previous knowledge to classify an information as trust forgetting the role of the participants that are subject producers. This way, the responsibility and veracity of information was attributed to the app. Aspects like reliability and credibility only are considered when the participant compare the results demonstrated by the app with other one on same function The doubt of information and reputation only appear when errors are detected (wrong routes etc.). Some participants attribute totally to the app the information that are posted and others understand the role of users (producing and consuming information in real time).

The participants presented a profile that use the app many times only to know a route in an offline way, not demonstrating so much interesting in real time traffic. As seen in Study One, some breaks in communicating strategies of confirm the information and its authors happen. The Reputation Model adopted by Waze is not comprehended so well by the users.

5   Conclusions

This research intended to understand how users deals with reputation issues, i.e., given some content, how they recognize (or not) aspects related with the credibility and reliability of the content producers. Another aspect of reputation analyzed in this study is how the users see their self-reputation and if they are worried about this. We conducted 2 studies: one focused on how the message is communicated to the users, other has focused on reception of this message, by the users.

Our findings show that reputation is something that the apps needs to work better. The reputation models of apps are weak and communicate not so well about it. It should exist more resources to help the users to make decisions based on information posted by other users.

During the test was possible to see how difficult is to drive and use the app to get more information. Many decisions are made in a question of seconds and how better it is communicated to the users, more important it becomes.

It is important to develop in an easy way to communicate this kind of information, because it is not possible to stop the car in any part of a road to verify what is happen. The fake warning created to see the reaction of the participants was not communicated by Waze and the participants didn't see it.

The evidences collected in the Study One have improved our understanding of the interactive strategies to communicate reputation issues in crowdsourcing apps. The empirical evidences from Study Two showed to us that novice users are not aware about the app mechanisms to deal or classify the reputation of a content and they believe that content reliability is provided by the app. With a characterization of the reputation model of a community based mobile application we aim at give a contributing to HCI design process.

In the results we can also understand see that at many times the users are not aware of their own reputation beyond to attribute to the app itself the function of communication traffic conditions, ignoring the collaborative aspects os the app. The model reputation of Waze is not perceived correctly by the users as the study demonstrates.

To help the users to decide better the best route and other situations of traffic, the designers should making easier to understand the reputation model of their apps. In a technology age, many users do not think about their digital attitudes and consequences yet.

This works is our first attempt in trying to characterize the reputation model of a community based mobile application. As next steps, we intend to compare the reputation model of another community-based app to confirm (or not) what was discovered in this study. This experiment was made on Sunday, at the city Campos dos Goytacazes, Rio de Janeiro. In this day of week, the traffic is less than days like Monday, Tuesday etc. Maybe it be interesting to apply the test in these days and verify if the users recognize the same signs or have the same behavior.

References

1. Alperovitch, D., Krasser, S., Brinkley, M.: U.S. Patent Application No. 13/426, 363 (2012)
2. Creswell, J.W.: Research Design: Qualitative, Quantitative, and Mixed Methods Approaches. Sage Publications, Beverley Hills (2013)
3. Dezin, N.K., Lincoln, Y.S. (eds.): The Landscape of Qualitative Research. Sage Publications, Thousand Oaks (2008)
4. Dwyer, C., Hiltz, S., Passerini, K.: Trust and privacy concern within social networking sites: a comparison of Facebook and myspace. In: AMCIS 2007 Proceedings, p. 339 (2007)
5. Ganesh, J., Sethi, P.: Reputation and trust in Social networks: empirical results from a Facebook reputation system. In: 19th Americas Conference on Information Systems, AMCIS 2013 Chicago, Illinois, USA, 15–17 August 2013, Association for Information Systems (2013)
6. Josang, A., Ismail, R., Boyd, C.: A survey of trust and reputation systems for online service provision. Decis. Support Syst. **43**(2), 618–644 (2007)
7. Kittur, A., Suh, B., Chi, E.H.: Can you ever trust a wiki? Impacting perceived trustworthiness in wikipedia. In: Proceedings of the 2008 ACM Conference on Computer Supported Cooperative Work, pp. 477–480. ACM (2008)
8. Kraut, R.E., Resnick, P.: Building Successful Online Communities: Evidence-Based Social Design. MIT Press, Cambridge (2012)
9. Luca, M., Zervas, G.: Fake It Till You Make It: Reputation, Competition, and Yelp Review Fraud. Harvard Business School NOM Unit Working Paper No. 14-006 (2013)
10. Malaga, R.A.: Web-based reputation management systems: problems and suggested solutions. Electron. Commer. Res. **1**(4), 403–417 (2001)
11. Massa, P., Avesani, P.: Trust-aware collaborative filtering for recommender systems. In on the move to meaningful internet systems. In: Meersman, R., Tari, Z. (eds.) CoopIS, DOA, and ODBASE, pp. 492–508. Springer, Berlin (2004)
12. O'Donovan, J., Smyth, B.: Trust in recommender systems. In: Proceedings of the 10th International Conference on Intelligent User Interfaces, pp. 167–174. ACM (2005)
13. Resnick, P., Kuwabara, K., Zeckhauser, R., Friedman, E.: Reputation systems. Commun. ACM **43**(12), 45–48 (2000)

14. Rowley, J., Johnson, F.: Understanding trust formation in digital information sources: the case of Wikipedia. J. Inf. Sci. (2013). 0165551513477820
15. Shneiderman, B.: Designing trust into online experiences. Commun. ACM **43**(12), 57–59 (2000)
16. De Souza, C.S.: The Semiotic Engineering of Human-Computer Interaction. The MIT Press, Cambridge (2005)
17. De Souza, C.S., De Leitão, C.F.: Semiotic engineering methods for scientific research in HCI. Synthesis Lectures on Human-Centered Informatics, vol. 2(1), pp. 1–122. Morgan & Claypool, Princeton (2009)
18. Strahilevitz, L.J.: Reputation nation: law in an era of ubiquitous personal information. Nw. UL Rev. **102**, 1667 (2008)
19. Teruel, M.A., Navarro, E., López-Jaquero, V., Simarro, F.M., González, P.: A comparative of goal-oriented approaches to modelling requirements for collaborative systems. In: ENASE, pp. 131–142 (2011)
20. Varshney, L.R., Vempaty, A., Varshney, P.K.: Assuring privacy and reliability in crowdsourcing with coding. In: Information Theory and Applications Workshop (ITA) 2014, pp. 1–6. IEEE (2014)
21. Woodruff, A.: Necessary, unpleasant, and disempowering: reputation management in the internet age. In: Proceedings of the SIGCHI Conference on Human Factors in Computing Systems, pp. 149–158. ACM (2014)
22. Zeng, H., Alhossaini, M.A., Ding, L., Fikes, R., McGuinness, D.L.: Computing trust from revision history. Stanford Univ Ca Knowledge Systems LAB (2006)

Modeling of User's Tweet Behavior to Enhance Profile's Influence

Esraa Almajhad, Abdullatif M. AlAbdullatif, Esam Alwagait,
and Basit Shahzad(✉)

College of Computer and Information Science,
King Saud University, Riyadh, Saudi Arabia
bent.majhad@hotmail.com,
{amalabdullatif,alwagait}@ksu.edu.sa,
basit.shahzad@gmail.com

Abstract. The communication among the individuals having commonality in interests has been empowered by the emergence of the social media. Twitter is one of the social media platform used by individuals, activist, politicians, academicians and celebrities and is used for diversified purposes. Despite being a brilliant medium in facilitating the process of communication, Twitter still has a gap in targeting specific people, attracting attention, and increasing the opportunity to get more interaction with the user's followers. This is due to the nature of the timeline that presents the recent tweets every time the user logins his account. In this situation the many significant tweeters may go un-noticed. In this paper we have addressed this problem by proposing a system that uses a novel method dedicated to discover the appropriate times to tweet based on the analysis of the active followers' usage behavior. Then, a tool that utilizes this method launches tweets during the time these followers are expected to be active. The tool helps the tweeters to receive the highest percentage of engagement and the proliferation of tweets among their targeted followers by finding the best times to tweet. The results of the experiments show the effectiveness of this system in raising the level of activity and interaction with the user's tweets.

Keywords: Tweeter's behavior · Active followers · Predictive behavior · Online following behavior

1 Introduction

Online social networks have become a social phenomenon that is growing day by day. Along with many other social networks available, Twitter is one of the media that helps in the rapid spread of short messages (so-called Tweets) if properly used; this means reaching thousands of people in a short period of time and at a lower price. The difficulty the tweeter sometimes faces is the dynamics of the followers' timelines [1–3]. With the ability to follow a large number of tweeters, the timelines of the followers are becoming much longer, which will decrease the possibility of interaction and paying attention to all tweeters' tweets. This may occur because the followers focus their attention on the tweets that appear in the visible region and display the last events in

© Springer International Publishing Switzerland 2016
G. Meiselwitz (Ed.): SCSM 2016, LNCS 9742, pp. 104–113, 2016.
DOI: 10.1007/978-3-319-39910-2_10

their timelines without paying attention to reading other tweets in the middle. This interview asked people about the tweets they are interested to read and interact with when they login to their accounts on Twitter. The result was that 86 % of the answers are limited to the latest news that appear in the visible region. What we need is a study to pinpoint the "best" time window to tweet. This time window will have most of the active followers connected to a tweeter. This time window will be classified by the followers' activities.

The focus of this paper is to develop a system that finds out the best times to launch tweets at a particular user level, instead of guessing times. This is achieved through design and implementation of an algorithm that will analyze and mine the user's tweets. We fetch the user's tweets from Twitter API to extract the useful metadata that will help us specify the active followers. Then, we analyze and mine the user's active followers' timelines to identify time windows of their presence. This will helps calculate the best times for a particular user with respect to the times when most active followers are online. Finally, when the user types certain tweets, the tool built in our system stores and launches tweets in the best times in order to obtain the maximum rate of interaction from the followers. We demonstrate the efficiency of our system by choosing random samples taking into account they contain activities to identify the peak times. Then, we calculate the rate of communication and activities before and after using the proposed system. Several measures are used to demonstrate the increase that occurs by identifying the peak times to post tweets for a particular user.

2 Related Work

Online social networks are useful for studying collaboration relationships, the structure of groups, learning opinions/or sentiments [4] and have an ability to produce a huge amount of data through review, text, discussion, blogs, news and reactions that will help to understand the people, communities and organizations. Social media therefore assist to establish relational data such as information about a user's friends, people who live in the same area and people who enjoy the same things. These data help to increase the chances of understanding the social world around the users [5, 6] has been identified that Six Degrees.com is the first social media network launched in 1997. Then a series of social media networks emerged such as MySpace, Facebook, YouTube, Skyblog and more [7]. Through these media, the consumer is able to learn from the experiences of others and find more information about a specific product before he/she makes a purchase decision [8]. This research is based on Twitter, a brief introduction and composition of twitter is presented here [8–10].

In 2006, Dorsey launched an online social networking service called Twitter. Since its launch, Twitter gained a great popularity to become the most visited site on the Internet. The number of users in Twitter service reached more than 500 million people in 2012 [8]. Twitter is a real-time and highly social micro-blogging service that allows twitter users to communicate with text messages consisting of maximum 140 characters called (tweets) which appear on a timeline. Despite this limitation of characters, users can broadcast information including daily activities, give opinions on a particular topic, status, current events and more by tweets [8, 11]. The best time to launch tweets is from 1 pm to 3 pm, while the worst time is between 8 pm to 9 am. In addition, the organization identifies that Friday after 3 pm is the time that must be avoided to post tweets. The results of this study did not target users based on specific time zones similar to what was done in [12]. Alwagait and Shahzad [1] performed a statistical study that aimed to determine the peak times in the Twitter social network. This study targeted fixed time zone (Saudi Arabia). This study was conducted to identify the best time of the maximum number of online followers for a specific sample of Twitter users.

Holmes et al. [13] proposed a tool called HootSuite that works to manage and organize multiple social media networks. This tool was used to launch advertising campaigns and marketing on a number of social media like Facebook, LinkedIn and Twitter from one secure place. This tool allows monitoring more than 100 profiles during one dashboard. Furthermore, it allows adding more than one member for the management and assigns tasks to them. It provides reports and gives an overview of users' accounts showing the extent of the growth of followers and their engagement rate. In addition, it allows the scheduling of 100 messages and posts at specific times. For Twitter, in particular, it has facilitated the work for businessmen to monitor their brands and follow up statistics [14].

Su.pr [15] is a tool that provides URL shortening service to allow deployment on a number of social media networks due to limitations in the number of characters in messages such as those on Twitter. Tweet Reports takes a different approach from the other tools in the collection of information to provide statistics of the ideal time to post tweets. This approach relies on two methods: one method depends on the analysis of the optimal 25 influential user's followers last week. Then, it submits an hourly report including statistics for tweets and retweets [1, 2, 16–21]. The other method relies on the analysis of the tweets containing certain keywords to know the best times. Hence, the user can look for a specific word or name for a brand to discover the best times of circulation per day in the past week. As a result, it offers a report showing the times of most active users who post tweets or retweets related to a keyword. It is a very useful tool, but it can become better if it can also collect statistics about the most influential followers online and when users are active for a certain keyword [22]. Widrich [16] proposed a tool that shows the peak times for Twitter users. It depends on an algorithm to analyze 1000 past tweets and the response to them. This simple tool lacks other criteria, as it does not take into account the user's followers.

From the above discussion it is evident that there are some recent studies focused on identifying the best time to tweet and to identify the times when more followers of a given user are online. However, it is also evident that these studies have been undertaken in different contexts and parameters. This study will describe the best time to tweet considering the local data and hence addressing the social, cultural, and technological habits as well. The study will conclude by suggesting an algorithm, designing and implementing a tool and assuring that the suggestions made in this research are worthwhile for the individuals by validating the tool.

3   Proposed Algorithm

As we mentioned earlier, the Twitter's timeline consists of a set of tweets. This set is constantly increasing with a high number of tweeters and passage of time, which causes problems. Consequently, the probability that a follower interacts with Tweeter's tweets decreases. This is because the follower often focuses on the visible area, which is the first page of the timeline. Meanwhile, the follower does not give attention to the old tweets that do not appear in the visible timeline even when they are of great importance. This problem occurs because of the dynamic nature of the timeline that scrolls down tweets to other pages that become invisible to the follower when the number of tweets increases. To address this phenomenon, we propose an algorithm that works to launch tweets in the visible area of the followers in order to increase the rate of activity and response. This can be done by searching the best times when the user's followers are more active to post their tweets. Unfortunately, in the Twitter world, there may be users who have followers but do not communicate with them. This fact made our algorithm focus its attention only on the followers who interact with the user's tweets by replying or retweeting. These are called *active followers*. Therefore, the method starts with finding the active followers of the user. Then, it divides the timeline for each active follower into Hit/Miss Windows. Hit Windows means the time windows when the followers are active, while Miss Windows means the time windows when the followers are absent (i.e., not active). Consequently, our algorithm finds the common Hit Times of active followers to ensure the posting of tweets in the Hit Windows of the user's followers. Figure 1 displays the timeline of follower (n).

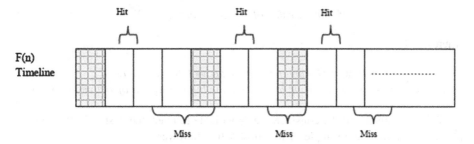

Fig. 1. Follower (n) timeline

Therefore, our algorithm consists of three stages:

(a) Finding active followers.
(b) Finding the Hit/Miss rate of time windows for each active follower.
(c) Finding Global Hit Time of active followers.

3.1   Finding Active Followers

In order to find active followers, we analyze the user's tweets. Every tweet has some metadata associated with it. These metadata contain the creation time of tweets, the user who posts tweets, the number of retweets, the number of replies, the identifier of the followers who retweet or reply and more. Thus, in order to determine active followers, we rely on two parameters, namely the number of replies and the number of retweets. Socially, each response to the user's tweet has a certain weight. Thus, the user's followers who reply to the user's tweet are more active than those who retweet. As a result, we assume (α) as a weight for each reply and (β) as a weight for each retweet, and then we find the best value for each variable after experiments. Then, we calculate the weight of each active follower through the following formula:

$$W(fn) = (\# \text{ of replies } (fn) * \alpha) + (\# \text{ of retweets } (fn) * \beta) \tag{1}$$

Where

$W(fn)$: *The weight of follower n*
$\#$ *of replies*(fn) : *Number of replies for follower n.*
$\#$ *of retweets* (fn) : *Number of retweets for follower n.*
α : *Weight for a reply,* β : *Weight for a retweet.*

Sometimes we face a problem when the weight of the active follower is too small. This occurs because some followers do not interact with the user significantly. In order to exclude such followers, we need to determine the *most active followers* with a high weight. Therefore, we take a certain percentage from the top weight of the active followers to calculate the smallest weight value that can be regarded as an active follower by the following formula:

$$Minimum \; value \; of \; weight = max\,(w) * X \tag{2}$$

where

$max(w)$: *Maximum value of active followers weight.*
X : *The percentage that will be taken from the highest weight of active followers*

This percentage will be considered as a variable to reach the best ratio that can be found to determine the sample of the most active followers.

3.2 Finding the Hit/Miss Rate of Time Windows for Each Active Follower

From the first stage, we have a group of the most active followers. For each of them we identify the Hit/Miss rate of time periods for his/her timeline. Figure 2 represents the timeline for a single active follower. It can be observed that in some of the time slots, the follower is more active, while his/her participation in other slots is non-existent.

Therefore, we can determine that whether the follower is interactive or not based on the total practiced activities in each slot of time such as posting tweets, retweets or

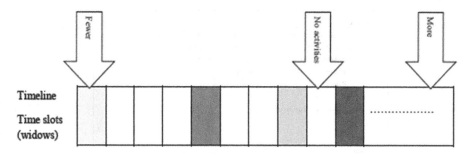

Fig. 2. A single active follower timeline

responding to them. All these activities are considered equal as far as the weight is concerned. Consequently, we can classify the time periods of active followers into: high interaction, called *Hit* period and low or non-existent interaction, called *Miss* period. We assume that dividing the timeline into equal periods takes (t) seconds. Then, we normalize the value of the total activities in each time period to a scale from zero to one. Figure 3 displays the scale to normalize total activities in each time slot.

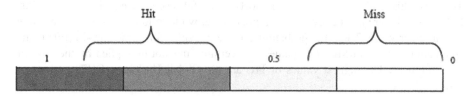

Fig. 3. Normalization scale for total activities in each time slot

All values from 0 to 0.5 are considered Miss time periods, while all values greater than 0.5 to 1 are considered Hit time periods, but this boundary may be altered after experiments as this is based on the initial assumption. The flow chart for Hit/Miss rate of time window for each active follower is shown in Fig. 4. This normalization applies to the total activities in each time slot according to the following equation:

$$Tx\,(Vfn) = \frac{Vfn - \min(fn)}{\max(fn) - \min(fn)} \tag{3}$$

Where

$Tx(Vfn)$: *The value from 0 to 1 represents the total activities of follower(n) in time slot(x)*

Vfn : *Total activities of follower (n) in time slot(x)*

$\min(fn)$: *Minimum number of total activities of follower(n) over the timeline.*

$\max(fn)$: *Maximum number of total activities of follower(n) over the timeline.*

```
Start
        Request active follower' s timeline from Twitter
        Download activities (tweet, retweet, reply)
        Calculate activities for each user in intervals
        If activities count >0.5 and <=1
            Place in Hit area
        Else
            Place in Miss area
End
```

Fig. 4. Finding the Hit/Miss rate of time windows for each active follower

3.3 Finding Global Hit Time of Active Followers

Global Hit Time is a time when most active followers are Hit. From the previous stage, we have the timeline for each active follower segmented into Hit/Miss periods of time. At this stage, we should look for common Hit time periods for all active followers in order to post the tweets in them. However, finding a common Hit time period for all active followers is difficult, especially if the user has a large number of active followers. To solve this problem we rank the most active followers based on their weights. Followers who are most active take a higher value, while followers who are less active take a lower value. Then, the probability of the activities for each time slot P(t) is the summation of the Hit/Miss rate value for a certain time slot multiplied by the rank of each follower. The highest values of P(t) are the Global Hit Time (GHT) periods of active followers.

4 System Design and Implementation

The objective of this proposed system is to develop a tool that can be used in a Twitter platform. This system provides a new way to find the best times to tweet along with posting tweets in these times. The basic functional requirements consist of allowing any Twitter user to register in our system, retrieve the best times that will be calculated by a proposed algorithm. In addition, the proposed algorithm enables the system to send requests to Twitter API to download a particular user's and his/her followers' timelines using an information retrieval component, store the information in the system database, extract statistical data from the queried data, compute the best times and allow a weekly update of this data. Therefore, we need an application that handles the computation of the best times and the creation of tweets in a user-friendly way with good efficiency.

Apache is a most popular Web Server on Linux systems environments that was used in our project. It is used in a combination with the MySQL database engine and (PHP) scripting language. This configuration is called LAMP (Linux, Apache, MySQL and PHP), and forms a powerful and robust platform for the development of web applications [23]. In addition, Twitter API is a rich source that allows third party applications to retrieve data from Twitter. Therefore, in this application, we used a ready-made

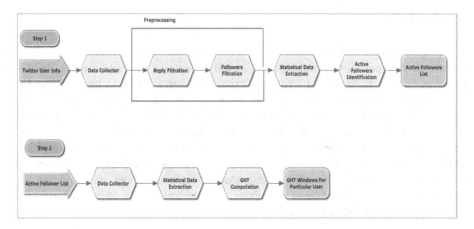

Fig. 5. System implementation flow chart

developed component to connect to Twitter API and retrieve useful information to compute GHT for a particular user. This environment is programmed in Java, and uses RSET API calls to get the required data. Figure 5 displays the sequence of the implementation of the system. This phase is focused to implement the basic objectives as mentioned in Sect. 3.1, 3.2 3.3.

- Data Collector: Twitter API allows third party applications to fetch data that aids developers in their applications. The data collector is responsible for requesting data that helps our application to compute GHT. It works to collect user information such as user tweets (user timeline), mention timeline, retweet to each tweet and followers ID. It can also obtain followers' timelines.
- Reply Filtration: Focusing on the timeline of a particular user we can determine that it contains tweets that are considered @replay or @mention. The main difference between them is their purpose and their delivery. Typically, @reply is directed to the particular user, but in @mention the username of the particular user may appear but it is not directed to him. Therefore, at this stage the system filters timeline based on the user replied to.
- Followers Filtration: It is common to observe that sometimes people do not follow back the twitter user. Yet, they reply and retweet his tweets. Thereby, by this stage the system filters persons who reply or retweet based on user followers ID. Such situations have not been addressed in this study and are considered out of scope.
- Statistical Data Extraction: In this stage, the system counts the reply tweets and retweets for each follower to determine active followers. In addition, it counts the activities for each active follower to maintain all possible statistical data that can be generated based on the available information.
- Active Followers Identification & GHT Computation: Based on proposed algorithm discussed in Sect. 3, the system calculates active followers for each Twitter user. The status of a follower is determined as proposed in Sect. 3. Also, the system computes the GHT windows for particular users depending on algorithm proposed in Sect. 3.

5 Validation

Our project aims to find the best time for the Twitter user to post his/her tweets with respect to the most active followers to identify the most interactive times. In the previous section, we proposed a solution to this problem in order to help the Twitter user release tweets in the visible region of the active followers to gain the highest level of communication with them. The proposed solution depends on selecting the Global Hit Times (GHT) for active followers of a particular user to launch tweets. Thus, the percentage of activity increases because of the increased response and the retweet rate. In this section, we investigate the effectiveness of the proposed algorithm developed as a tool in our system. This will ensure that we have achieved our objective of demonstrating an increased level of activity and interaction with active followers by targeting the time windows when active followers are online.

6 Conclusion

The results that emerged after using the proposed system gave a good indication of the success of the tool. By considering the more active followers the activity of the tweet viewership increased as the active follower's tweet got more visibility. For that, it cannot rely on the peak times or days for the majority of people because there are special times of the individual achieves high probability of activities, thus guaranteeing greater interaction and engagement with posted tweets. From the results of the experiments it can be deduced that there is a direct relationship between the number of followers and number of active followers. It was also noted that the for some accounts the number of followers increased while the experiments were completed. This may be due to an increase in the activity level of active followers by retweet, which contributed to the spread of tweets significantly and the gaining of new followers. This assumption provides an area of research which can be addressed in the future.

References

1. Alwagait, E., Shahzad, B.: Maximization of tweet's viewership with respect to time. In: 2014 World Symposium on Computer Applications and Research (WSCAR), pp. 1–5 (2014)
2. Alwagait, E., Shahzad, B.: When are tweets better valued? An empirical study. J. Univers. Comput. Sci. **20**, 1511–1521 (2014)
3. Shahzad, B., Alwagait, E.: Best and the worst times to tweet: an experimental study. In: 15th International Conference on Mathematics and Computers in Business and Economics (MCBE 2014), pp. 122–126 (2014)
4. Barbier, G., Liu, H.: Data mining in social media. In: Aggarwal, C.C. (ed.) Social Network Data Analytics, pp. 327–352. Springer, Heidelberg (2011)
5. Hansen, D., Shneiderman, B., Smith, M.A.: Analyzing Social Media Networks with NodeXL: Insights from a Connected World. Morgan Kaufmann, San Francisco (2010)

6. Adedoyin-Olowe, M., Gaber, M.M., Stahl, F.: A survey of data mining techniques for social media analysis (2013). arXiv preprint arXiv:1312.4617
7. Chen, G.M.: Tweet this: a uses and gratifications perspective on how active Twitter use gratifies a need to connect with others. Comput. Hum. Behav. **27**, 755–762 (2011)
8. Gomathi, C., Gowtham, P.: Social media networking state of social media. In: Proceedings of National Conference on New Horizons in IT-NCNHIT, p. 205
9. DNA Kingston Training: Social Media Policy and Procedure. Kingston Training and Employment Pty Ltd, vol. 1 0113 SM SL, January 2013
10. Kaplan, A.M., Haenlein, M.: Users of the world, unite! The challenges and opportunities of social media. Bus. Horiz. **53**, 59–68 (2010)
11. Java, A., Song, X., Finin, T., Tseng, B.: Why we Twitter: understanding microblogging usage and communities. In: Proceedings of 9th WebKDD and 1st SNA-KDD 2007 Workshop on Web Mining and Social Network Analysis, pp. 56–65
12. Fisher, J.D.: Maximizing your Tweets—Twitter Infographic, May 2014. http://www.fuseworkstudios.com/maximizing-your-tweets-infographic/
13. HootSuite: About HootSuit, May 2014. https://hootsuite.com/company
14. Comm, J.: Twitter Power 2.0: How to Dominate Your Market One Tweet at a Time. Wiley, Hoboken (2010)
15. StumbleUpon: What features does Su.pr have? May 2014 http://www.stumbleupon.com/help/business-tools/supr/
16. Widrich, L.: Top 5 Tools to Better Time Your Tweets, May 2014. http://mashable.com/2011/10/28/best-time-to-tweet/
17. Al-Mudimigh, A.S., Ullah, Z., Shahzad, B.: A model for the efficient implementation of portals. In: 2010 2nd International Conference on Computer Engineering and Technology (ICCET), pp. V7-552–V7-554 (2010)
18. Al-Ohali, Y., Al-Oraij, A.A., Shahzad, B.: KSU news portal: a case study. In: International Conference on Internet Computing (ICOMP 2011) (2011)
19. Alwagait, E., Shahzad, B., Alim, S.: Impact of social media usage on students academic performance in Saudi Arabia. J. Comput. Hum. Behav. **51**, 1092–1097 (2014)
20. Shahzad, B., Alwagait, A.: Does a change in weekend days have an impact on social networking activity? J. Univers. Comput. Sci. **20**, 2068–2079 (2015)
21. Shahzad, B., Alwagait, E.: Utilizing technology in education environment: a case study. In: 2013 Tenth International Conference on Information Technology: New Generations (ITNG), pp. 299–302 (2013)
22. Aronica, J.: 4 Tools To Better Time Your Twitter Updates, May 2014. http://socialfresh.com/how-to-target-your-twitter-audience-at-the-right-time/
23. Pitt, L.F., Watson, R.T., Kavan, C.B.: Service quality: a measure of information systems effectiveness. MIS Q. **19**, 173–187 (1995)

The Impact of Social Context and Personality Toward the Usage of Stickers in LINE

Ya-Chiao Chang$^{(\boxtimes)}$ and Jiunde Lee

National Chiao Tung University, Hsinchu, Taiwan
ycc6625@gmail.com, jiulee@mail.nctu.edu.tw

Abstract. Instant Messenger is a social media which is focused on communication. The aim of system is to enhance relationships of acquaintances. Stickers of Instant Messenger are popular with persons, so there is a big business opportunity in the design market of the stickers. The main findings are as follows: the impact of social context and personality toward the usage of stickers in Instant Messenger are significant. Persons use the most of stickers in chat contexts, and persons use the fewest of stickers in business contexts. Furthermore, high extraversion persons use more stickers than low extraversion persons. In business contexts, high extraversion and low neuroticism persons use more stickers than low extraversion and high neuroticism persons. The most usage of sticker is emotion type, the second are atmosphere and personality type, appearance and story type are used the least.

Keywords: Extraversion · Instant · Messenger · Neuroticism · Personality · Sticker · Social context

1 Introduction

Except for only text, people can use text with emoticons in Instant Messenger. Furthermore, people can also use stickers. In this study, the stickers in Instant Messenger LINE is to be examined. How can people use stickers in their conversation? How the stickers are impacted by individual difference and social context? Present studies rarely talked about stickers, which are new nonverbal cues for people. This study tried to realize the stickers. In order to provide designer to design more and more stickers, which are useful for person when they communicate with others.

1.1 Social Interaction

Social interaction refers to the way people interact. Blumer interprets fashion's origin as an example for social interaction. Fashion is from people's tastes. Tastes is an experience for the product, and the process of taste is from ambiguous to explicit. The shaping of taste is under the context of social interaction by others' responses [1]. In this framework, people will have a similar taste experience, and to develop common taste feeling. Based on social interaction, people could shape their communication through information exchange. Of course, emoticons and stickers are included on the online communication.

© Springer International Publishing Switzerland 2016
G. Meiselwitz (Ed.): SCSM 2016, LNCS 9742, pp. 114–122, 2016.
DOI: 10.1007/978-3-319-39910-2_11

1.2   Online Relationship

In the social information processing theory, Walther proposed two points. One point is that people will adapt communication environment, although they use only text in the online communication environment. The other is that people have similar communication effect between real life and virtual environment when they have sufficient time to communicate online [2]. As more and more pictures, like photos or image icons, appear on the virtual environment, these information bring positive communication effect in the past literatures. Related study indicate visual presentation makes a significant influence for people. In the results of study, persons post more pictures, images which are their favorites, and they will receive more amount of "likes" and amount of comments [3].

Social information processing theory based on the basic theories of the interpersonal relationship. People reduce uncertainty for themselves and relationships. Furthermore, they do more self-disclosure to develop relationship with others. Empirical studies about online communication indicate three emphases. The first is that people do more self-disclosure to reduce their uncertainty [4]. The second is that people do more self-disclosure to improve interpersonal intimacy [5–9]. The final is that people, who do more self-disclosure, have more truthfulness and respect from others. Moreover, people disclose honesty, the relationship with acquaintances could be maintained [10, 11].

1.3   Nonverbal Communication

Nonverbal communication refers to three dimension: communication environment, communicators' appearance and communicators' behavior [12]. In the virtual environment, nonverbal cues are complex, because nonverbal cues are integrated reality, social context and virtual environment [13]. There are variety of forms for the nonverbal cues in the online environment, including symbols, images, pictures, time information etc. In this study, Stickers of Instant Messenger is a type of image, and they are used in the conversation with the corresponding text. So stickers are considered as nonverbal cues.

In the past studies, online nonverbal cues, like punctuation, are viewed as one type of emotion expression, attitude utterance, disagree mitigation, the topic of conversation extended and the maintenance of friendship [7]. Emoticons, compared to languages, can be regarded as a form of dialogue, its placement is systematic, and it may be at the beginning of a dialogue, end of a dialogue, dialogue halfway or appearing alone. The usage of the rules doesn't fixed, and it may be regarded as pause, the invitation of responses, punctuation, but most of them are used to be an utterance interrupted [14]. Related literatures about emoticons refer to emoticon have a few functions: to enhance effect of communication [15–18], to make communication more harmonious environment and promote interpersonal intimacy [19, 20], to enhance a sense of confidence between the communicators [21].

1.4 Social Context and Individual Difference

Communication environment impacts individual's emotion, discourse selection and behavior. People evaluate environment no matter which place. People affect the environment, and also be affected by the environment. There are six perceptions of environment, like perception of formality, warmth, privacy, familiar, constraint and distance [12]. Some literatures refer to the relationship between social context and emoticons. The first is that people in the social emotional context uses more emoticons than in the context of social tasks. People, who in the negative, task-oriented situations, uses the least emoticons. Secondly, people who in the workplace, tries to use more positive emoticons.

Besides the factor of social context, some literatures indicates that individual difference is another factor which affect human's behavior. Some literatures are examined by McCrae and Costa s' five factor model which includes neuroticism which means that someone is anxious, insecure, and nervous frequently; extraversion which means that someone is social, humor and friendly. According to the literatures, extraverts tend to use social media frequently, because of their social personality, and neurotic persons tend to use social media frequently as well, because of their belonging sense. Therefore, this study uses extraversion and neuroticism to be the factors of individual difference.

1.5 Research Question and Research Hypothesis

- Q1: How the differences of social contexts impact the usage of stickers?
  - H0 1-1: The differences of social contexts have a significant influence on the amount of stickers.
  - H0 1-2: The differences of social contexts have a significant influence on the personality stickers.
  - H0 1-3: The difference of social contexts have a significant influence on the appearance stickers.
  - H0 1-4: The differences of social contexts have a significant influence on the story stickers.
  - H0 1-5: The differences of social contexts have a significant influence on the atmosphere stickers.
  - H0 1-6: The differences of social contexts have a significant influences on the emotion stickers.
  - H0 1-7: In the social contexts of casual conversation, the usages of each types of stickers have a significant difference.
  - H0 1-8: In the social context of private conversation, the usages of each types of stickers have a significant difference
  - H0 1-9: In the social context of business conversation, the usages of each types of stickers have a significant difference.

– Q2: How the personality impact the usage of stickers?
  • H0 2-1: Extravert people have a significant influence on the usage of stickers.
  • H0 2-2: Neurotic people have a significant influence on the usage of stickers.
– Q3: Social contexts and personality can impact the usage of stickers together.

2   Research Method

The aim of this study is to examine the usage of stickers in Instant Messenger LINE. Moreover, social context and personality are two factors which evaluate the effect of behavior. The main research methods are focus group, affinity diagram and online survey. In the first stage, focus group and affinity diagram are used to realize which types of stickers could be used by persons and to realize which types of social contexts could be happened in LINE. In the second stage, online survey are used to collect the usage of stickers.

2.1   Focus Group and Affinity Diagram

Researcher invite 15 respondents to execute focus group and affinity diagram. These respondents were between 20 to 30 years old. All respondents were recruited in Taiwan and used LINE frequently. The results of this stage are as follows, three social contexts: chat, privacy and business, five types of stickers: personality, appearance, story, atmosphere and emotion. The definitions for each types of social contexts and stickers are listed in the table [Table 1]. In the focus group, we focus on asking respondents the aim of sticker usage when they communicate with others in LINE. Related questions are as follows: Why do you like to use these kind of stickers? What kind of reasons are important for you to choose the stickers? When do you use stickers?

2.2   Questionnaire

This survey was released on Facebook from July 24, 2015 to August 8, 2015. All respondents should use LINE 1 h a day in order to collect regular persons' data. The number of valid survey is 452. There are three parts in the questionnaire, the first part is to record stickers, and each social context has five options which are the types of sticker. The second part is the scale of personality extraversion and neuroticism from McCrae and Costa s' five factor model. The third part is personal information. The process of stickers' record which can be divided into six main steps. At the beginning, respondents should open LINE application in the mobile phone. In the second step, looking through the dialogue list and selecting two friends' dialogue. In the third step, finding stickers in the conversation to categorize social contexts and stickers' types which are according to the definition for the social contexts and stickers' types [Table 2, Fig. 1]. In the fourth step, recording the types of social context and stickers in the survey. In the final step, repeating the above steps until two friends' stickers are recorded during three day's conversations.

Table 1. The definition of social contexts

Social context	The definition of social context
Chat	To share daily life
Privacy	Express secret things about yourself or your friends, and you don't want other people know these things
Business	Inform or handling important matters

Table 2. The definition of stickers

Sticker	The definition of sticker
Personality	To show individual personality, interests, preference and so on
Appearance	To show favorite style of stickers
Story	The sticker is retrieved from the characters of fictional story or the characters in the real world, such as cartoons, animation
Atmosphere	The sticker make a sense of atmosphere or scene
Emotion	To express emotion fully, such as happy, anger, sadness and so on

Fig. 1. The sample of the screenshot of LINE from the respondent (Source of sticker: LINE store https://store.line.me/home/zh-Hant).

3 Results

This study used Two-way ANOVA to examine the impact of social context and personality toward the usage of stickers in LINE. In the first research question: social contexts affect the usage of stickers. The hypothesis 1-1 is valid, people use the most of stickers in chat context, and following is in privacy context and the least is in business context. The hypothesis 1-2 is valid, people use the most of personality stickers in chat context, and following is in privacy context and the least is in business context. The hypothesis 1-3 is valid, people use the most of appearance stickers in chat context, and following is in privacy context and the least is in business context. The hypothesis 1-4 is valid partially, people use more story stickers in chat context than in business context; people use story stickers in chat context as much as in privacy context; people use story stickers in privacy context as much as in business context. The hypothesis 1-5 is valid partially, people use more atmosphere stickers in chat context than in business context; people use more atmosphere stickers in privacy context stickers than in business context; people use atmosphere stickers in chat context than in privacy context. The hypothesis 1-6 is valid partially, people use more emotion stickers in chat context than in business context; people use more emotion stickers in privacy context than in business context; people use emotion stickers in chat context as much as in privacy context. The hypothesis 1-7 is valid, the stickers types people used sequentially in chat context as emotion, personality, atmosphere, appearance and story. The hypothesis 1-8 is valid partially, the stickers types people used sequentially in privacy context as emotion, personality, appearance and story; the personality stickers people used as much as atmosphere stickers. The hypothesis 1-9 is valid partially, the stickers types people used in business context is as follows, emotion stickers more than personality and atmosphere; personality and atmosphere stickers more than appearance and story; personality stickers as much as atmosphere stickers; appearance stickers as much as story stickers.

In the second research question: personality affect the usage of stickers. The hypothesis 2-1 is valid partially, high extraversion person use more stickers than low extraversion person; high extraversion person use more personality stickers than low extraversion person; high extraversion person use more appearance stickers than low extraversion person; high extraversion person use more story stickers than low extraversion person; high extraversion person use atmosphere stickers as much as low extraversion person; high extraversion person use emotion stickers as much as low extraversion person; high extraversion person use more personality, appearance, story, atmosphere, emotion stickers than low extraversion person in business context; high extraversion person use stickers as much as low extraversion person in chat and privacy context. The hypothesis 2-2 is valid partially, low neuroticism person use more personality, appearance, story, atmosphere and emotion stickers than high neuroticism person in business context; high neuroticism person use stickers as much as low neuroticism person in chat, privacy context. In the third research question: Social contexts and personality cannot impact the usage of stickers together.

4   Discussion

According to the result from statistic analysis, high extraversion person tend to do more self-disclosure than low extraversion person, and more personality, appearance and story stickers are presented in LINE.

In business contexts, high extraversion and low neuroticism persons use more stickers than low extraversion and high neuroticism persons. People use stickers no difference no matter whom they are in chat and privacy context.

Generally speaking, the most usage of sticker is emotion type, the second are atmosphere and personality type, appearance and story type are used the least. Furthermore, persons use the most of stickers in chat contexts, and persons use the fewest of stickers in business contexts.

5 Conclusion

People exchanges information every day, one of the most important factors which impact human communication is nonverbal communication. People disclosure themselves in order to reduce uncertainty and increase intimacy. Personality and social contexts not only impact human behavior in real life, but also impact the stickers of online exchange.

Nowadays, stickers becomes a new nonverbal clues in Instant Messengers, especially in LINE. In this study, stickers not only can be an emotional expression in LINE, but also can be other clues which include personality, appearance, story, atmosphere and emotion as the results from this study. Personality is to show individual personality, interests, preference and so on; appearance is to show favorite style of stickers; story is the sticker which retrieved from the characters of fictional story or the characters in the real world, such as cartoons, animation; atmosphere is the sticker make a sense of atmosphere or scene; emotion is to express emotion fully, such as happy, anger, sadness and so on. In addition, there are three types of social contexts in LINE which are the result of interview in this study, such as chat, privacy and business.

Based on Walther's information processing theory, people would be able to adapt text-based computer-mediated environment. Extend to this theory, image becomes more and more popular in Instant Messenger environment. Stickers is the image-based form, differ from the original Instant Messenger based on texts and emoticons, exchange over and over among people who talk In LINE. This study uses two factors in the McCrae and Costa s' five factor model in order to explore the individual difference for the exchange of stickers, which are extraversion and neuroticism. One is Extraversion means someone is social, humor and friendly. The other is Neuroticism means someone is anxious, insecure, and nervous frequently. This study also uses social contexts to examine the difference of the usage of stickers. People would be able to adapt the text-based online environment by using lots of stickers.

Emotion type is one of the most usage of stickers, the second are personality and atmosphere type. It indicates that people prefer to express their emotion in LINE and it is necessary that people take emotion, personality and atmosphere for granted in the conversation. The stickers of story and appearance are used the least. However story and appearance type of stickers might not be ignore by stickers' designers, because these types of stickers play an important role in helping people to start a new topic in conversation and find out the common interests between people.

In the year of 2015, LINE announced the global survey for the frequently usage of stickers and emoticons. In the top of 100, 48 percent of stickers and emoticons in joy and happy, 10 percent of stickers and emoticons in sad emotion, 6 percent of stickers of stickers and emoticons in angry emotion, 5 percent of stickers and emoticons in surprise emotion, 14 percent of stickers and emoticons in gesture and daily term and 16 percent of stickers and emoticons in other types [22]. It explains that the usage rate of emotional stickers is highest, especially for the positive emotion. This is similar to the result about this study.

In the study, high extraversion persons use more stickers and use more personality, story and appearance stickers than low extraversion persons. It indicates that high extraversion persons expose themselves to perform individuality more than low extraversion persons. However, there are no difference in atmosphere and emotion type of stickers' usage between high extraverts and low extraverts. It indicates that atmosphere and emotion are two important elements in the daily conversation.

In addition, high extroversion persons use more stickers than low extroversion persons in business contexts. It is not similar to the past studies about social media which indicate high extraversion persons and high neuroticism persons prefer to use social media frequently, however high neuroticism persons doesn't use more stickers than low neuroticism persons in this study. The reason is that people behave differently in the different social context. In business contexts, which makes people feel formal and serious, high neuroticism persons would be more sensitive than low neuroticism persons so that high neuroticism persons use fewer stickers than low neuroticism persons in business contexts. Comparing to face to face conversation, the usage of LINE makes grey area bigger which could impact the effect of execution of business. Moreover, the stickers are not suitable for communicating with superior in the official workplace, because of the funny appearance. It explains the least usage of stickers for high neuroticism persons in business contexts.

Apart from the individual difference, the social context also be a factor in this study to examine the usage of stickers. People use the most of stickers in chat, next is in privacy context, the least usage of stickers is business context. Similarly, people use five types of stickers in business context and other two types of social context, however the most difference between business and other two types: chat and privacy is that people use the least of stickers in business context. This result reflects on the individual difference in the usage of stickers. According to the result, high extroversion persons and low neuroticism persons use fewer stickers than low extroversion persons and high neuroticism persons.

To sum up, people make relationships with others through exposing themselves. In the computer-mediated environment, people communicate with other people with text, emoticon and stickers. Personality and social context are two main factors to examine the usage of stickers in LINE.

References

1. Blumer, H.: Fashion: from class differentiation to collective selection. Sociol. Q. **10**(3), 275–291 (1969)
2. Knapp, M.L., Daly, J.A. (eds.): The Sage Handbook of Interpersonal Communication, 4th edn. SAGE, Thousand Oaks (2011)
3. Howley, I., Newman, T.: Factors impacting community response in an interest-sharing network. In: CHI 2013 Proceedings of the SIGCHI Conference on Human Factors in Computing Systems, pp. 2283–2286 (2013)
4. Palmieri, C., Prestano, K., Gandley, R., Overton, E., Zhang, Q.: The Facebook phenomenon: online self-disclosure and uncertainty reduction. China Media Res. **8**(1), 48–53 (2012)
5. Ma, M.L., Leung, L.: Unwillingness-to-communicate, perceptions of the internet and self-disclosure in ICQ. Telematics Inform. **23**, 22–37 (2006)

6. Park, N., Jin, B., Jin, S.: A. Effects of self-disclosure on relational intimacy in Facebook. Comput. Hum. Behav. **27**, 1974–1983 (2011)
7. Utz, S.: The function of self-disclosure on social network sites: not only intimate, but also positive and entertaining self-disclosures increase the feeling of connection. Comput. Hum. Behav. **45**, 1–10 (2015)
8. Seidman, G.: Expressing the "true self" on Facebook. Comput. Hum. Behav. **31**, 367–372 (2014)
9. Vetere, F., Gibbs, M.R., Kjeldskov, J., Howard, S., Mueller, F.F., … Bunyan, M.: Mediating intimacy: designing technologies to support strong-tie relationships. In: CHI 2005 Proceedings of the SIGCHI Conference on Human Factors in Computing Systems, pp. 471–480 (2005)
10. Ku, L.: Self-disclosure in online intimate relationship. J. Cyber Cult. Inf. Soc. **24**, 1–26 (2013)
11. Yu, J., Qiu, H., Tseng, H.: Self-disclosure in social media: the case of Facebook. Chin. Commun. Soc. (2012)
12. Knapp, M.L., Hall, J.A.: Nonverbal Communication in Human Interaction, 7th edn. Wadsworth Cengage Learning, Boston (2010)
13. Teigland, R., Power, D. (eds.): The Immersive Internet (2013). http://www.palgraveconnect. com/pc/doifinder/10.1057/9781137283023.0001
14. Garrison, A., Remley, D., Thomas, P., Wierszewski, E.: Conventional faces: emoticons in instant messaging discourse. Comput. Compos. **28**, 112–125 (2011)
15. Luor, T.T., Wu, L., Lu, H., Tao, Y.: The effect of emoticons in simplex and complex task-oriented communication: an empirical study of instant messaging. Comput. Hum. Behav. **26**, 889–895 (2010)
16. Walther, J.B., D'Addario, K.P.: The impacts of emoticons on message interpretation in computer-mediated communication. Soc. Sci. Comput. Rev. **19**(3), 324–347 (2001)
17. Leung, L.: Impacts of net-generation attributes, seductive properties of the internet, and gratifications-obtained on internet use. Telematics Inform. **20**, 107–129 (2003)
18. Tung, F., Deng, Y.: Increasing social presence of social actors in e-learning environments: effects of dynamic and static emoticons on children. Displays **28**, 174–180 (2007)
19. Huang, A.H., Yen, D.C., Zhang, X.: Exploring the potential effects of emoticons. Inf. Manag. **45**, 466–473 (2008)
20. Janssen, J.H., IJsselsteijn, W.A., Westerink, J.H.D.M.: How affective technologies can influence intimate interactions and improve social connectedness. Int. J. Hum.-Comput. Stud. **72**, 33–43 (2014)
21. Scissors, L.E., Gill, A.J., Geraghty, K., Gergle, D.: In CMC we trust: the role of similarity. In: CHI 2009 Proceedings of the SIGCHI Conference on Human Factors in Computing Systems, pp. 527–536 (2009)
22. LINE: Thanks for 4 Great Years! (2015). http://official-blog.line.me/tw/archives/34902589. html

Factors Leading to Viral Intention on Exercise Posts

Wonkyung Kim[1] and Taiwoo Park[2(✉)]

[1] Department of Advertising and Public Relations,
Michigan State University, Michigan, USA
kimwonkl@msu.edu
[2] Department of Media and Information,
Michigan State University, Michigan, USA
twp@msu.edu

Abstract. Exercise report posts generated by mobile exercise apps (i.e., Nike Plus and Endomondo) have shown potential to encourage exercisers (e.g., runners) by providing them a sense of social support from others. From the perspective of support-givers, the motivational factors for engaging in such exercise-related posts are largely underexplored. Under the framework of Self-Determination Theory, this study investigates associations among need satisfaction for relatedness, autonomy, tie-strength, exercise intention and viewers' viral behaviors for exercise posts in social media. Study findings highlight the importance of increasing viewers' relatedness through engaging exercise posts.

Keywords: Self-Determination theory · Tie-strength · Exercise · Social media · Viral intention

1 Introduction

Exercise-related studies have shown that social support from others motivates and encourages exercisers [19]. With the advances of Internet and mobile computing technology, it is even possible for exercisers to solicit support from others from long distance. Mobile exercise apps, which track and summarize activities of runners, have gained momentum by enabling sharing functions on social media. For example, Nike Plus offers app-generated posts in social media, along with real-time message delivery for readers to send a cheering message to the app owner immediately. A recent study revealed that such a peer-feedback system, which connects runners and friends through social media, enhanced runners' experiences along with their completion rates [23].

Despite the advances in remote exercise supports, made available by new technologies, the motivational factors of viewer's participation in exercise posts (e.g., like, comment and share) are largely underexplored. Under the framework of Self-Determination Theory, this study aims to explore the motivation to support others' exercise activity by participating in exercise posts in social media, in terms of perceived autonomy and relatedness.

© Springer International Publishing Switzerland 2016
G. Meiselwitz (Ed.): SCSM 2016, LNCS 9742, pp. 123–129, 2016.
DOI: 10.1007/978-3-319-39910-2_12

2   Determinants of Viral Intention on Exercise Posts

2.1   Need Satisfaction for Perceived Autonomy and Perceived Relatedness

One of the most common approaches to shed light on motivational factors is the Self-Determination theory (SDT) [3]. It distinguishes motivation as intrinsic and extrinsic motivation, which bring different outcomes. The SDT argues that intrinsic motivation leads to greater enjoyment [15] and greater persistence at activities [7, 20]. There are three essential needs to be fulfilled as to facilitate intrinsic motivation: autonomy, relatedness, and competence [16]. Autonomy, the extent to which individuals feel their own control over tasks, was a significant predictor that creates persistent behaviors [19]. Relatedness, which drives intrinsic motivation by maintaining psychological relatedness with others, was found to be a critical factor for user's engagement in social media [12]. Competence refers to the extent to which individuals feel they can successfully complete tasks [16].

Fulfilling the three needs is important for both original posters and people who view the exercise posts on social media. An experimental study showed that an exercise intervention using social networking sites improved participants' perceived competence and enjoyment [22]. From the exerciser's point of view, posting their exercise achievement on social media would increase their autonomy and relatedness. We expect the same applies to those who view the exercise posts in social media. For instance, a study investigating motivational factors for Facebook use revealed that the need for relatedness is an important factor, rather than an outcome of interacting with people on Facebook [18]. We assume that viral behavior such as commenting, sharing, liking the post would follow as a consequence of self-determination. Post viewers' need satisfaction for autonomy and relatedness should be fulfilled in order to facilitate viewers' viral behavioral intention.

H1: Need satisfaction for autonomy of the exercise post on Facebook positively influences viral behavioral intention.

H2: Need satisfaction for relatedness of the exercise post on Facebook positively influences viral behavioral intention.

2.2   Tie-Strength

The strength of tie is a crucial variable for users' engagement of viral behaviors in social media [5, 13]. As Granovetter states, "the strength of a tie is a (probably linear) combination of the amount of time, the emotional intensity, the intimacy (mutual confiding), and the reciprocal services which characterize the tie" [6]. Chu and Kim [2] found tie-strength as an influential predictor that positively predicts the engagement of viral behavior on social media. Kim [8] 's study on official Facebook brand pages showed that users are more likely to engage into liking, commenting, and sharing brand-related contents when their need satisfaction of relatedness was high. Applying these findings into exercise posts in social media, we expect that as the relationship between an original poster and a viewer is closer, the viewer would be more willing to show increased viral behavioral intention for the post.

H3: Tie-strength between the original poster and viewers of the exercise post on Facebook positively influences viral behavioral intention.

2.3 Exercise Intention

We expect that viewers of exercise posts would be willing to perform viral behaviors out of their intrinsic motivation, since viral behaviors for someone's exercise posts usually do not offer any monetary incentives or rewards. Building on previous studies as well as our insights on viral behaviors, we expect that people will be more likely to engage in exercise posts when they are willing to engage in their own exercise activities.

H4: Exercise intention of viewers of the exercise post on Facebook positively influences viral behavioral intention.

2.4 Mediating Role of Perceived Relatedness

There have been volumes of SDT research, which found the mediating role of need satisfaction for autonomy, competence and relatedness on desirable outcomes in many different contexts [14]. Relatedness, one's psychological connection with people, is an important factor to look at since our study deals with engagement in social media [12]. We expect that need satisfaction for relatedness via exercise post will mediate the relationship between participants' attitude toward the exercise and viral behavioral intention. Similarly, relatedness will mediate the relationship between tie-strength and viral intention.

H5: Need satisfaction for relatedness mediates the relationship between tie-strength and viral behavioral intention.

H6: Need satisfaction for relatedness mediates the relationship between exercise intention and viral behavioral intention.

3 Method

3.1 Participants and Procedures

A total of 163 participants (81 male, 82 female, M age = 34.6 years; SD = 10.35) were recruited through Amazon Mechanical Turk online survey system. Only people who have seen exercise posts from social media were included in this study. At first, examples of exercise posts using mobile apps were shown. Participants were asked to recall the most recent experience of reading their Facebook friends' exercise posts. Regarding that particular experience, they were asked to answer a questionnaire, which included measures for the need satisfaction for autonomy, relatedness, tie-strength, exercise intention and viral behavioral intention for the exercise posts. Upon finishing the survey, each of the participants was compensated with 50 cents for their participation.

3.2   Measurements

Viral Behavioral Intention. Viral Behavioral Intention was measured on a 5-point scale, which was adopted and revised from Alhabash et al. [1]. Participants were asked whether they would like, share and comment on the post. *(Cronbach's α = .82).*

Perceived Autonomy. To measure the perceived autonomy, 3 items on a 7-point scale were adopted from Mathwick and Ridgon [11]. An example of item would be "I have flexibility in my interaction while reading this exercise post". *(Cronbach's α = .76).*

Perceived Relatedness. The measure for perceived relatedness was adopted from La Guardia et al. [9] and Sheldon et al. [18] and was adjusted using a 7-point scale. Participants were asked to indicate their feelings while engaging in exercise post on social media: "I felt connected when reading this exercise post." *(Cronbach's α = .70).*

Tie-Strength. Three items for tie-strength on a 7-point scale were adopted from Frezen and Nakamoto [4] as well as Ryu and Feick [17]. Participants were to answer the questions regarding closeness and intimacy with a person such as "How likely would you be to share personal confidences with this person?"

Exercise Intention. To measure participants' exercise intention, a 7-point scale from Lowe, Eves and Carroll [10] was used *(Cronbach's α = .70)* (Table 1).

Table 1. Detailed items, means and standard deviations for each construct

Constructs	Items	α	M	SD
Viral behavioral intention (5-point scale)	I will "like" this message on Facebook. I will "share" this message on Facebook. I will "comment" on this message on Facebook.	.82	3.22	1.12
Need satisfaction for autonomy (7-point scale)	While reading this exercise post, I felt (1) I could make a lot of decision on my own (2) I had a choice to voice my opinion (3) I had a flexibility in my interaction	.76	5.50	1.21
Need satisfaction for relatedness (7-point scale)	While reading this exercise post, I felt (1) appreciated (2) a lot of closeness and intimacy (3) disconnected (R)	.70	4.27	1.51
Tie-strength (7-point scale)	How likely would you be (1) to share personal confidences with this person? (2) to spend free time socializing with this person? (3) to perform a large favor (e.g. lending the person your car, typing a paper for this person because he/she is too ill, etc.) to this person?	.76	5.21	1.37

(Continued)

Table 1. (*Continued*)

Constructs	Items	α	M	SD
Exercise Intention (7-point scale)	Exercising in my leisure time over the next 6 months would be (1) extremely boring/interesting (2) extremely unenjoyable/enjoyable (3) extremely harmful/beneficial (4) extremely unhealthy/healthy	.70	5.56	1.05

4 Results

Structural Equation Modeling using AMOS 22.0 was performed to test the hypotheses on need satisfaction for autonomy, relatedness, tie-strength, exercise intention on viral behavioral intention. The results of maximum likelihood analysis using the bootstrapping method revealed that the proposed model demonstrated to be a poor fit for the data, $\chi^2 = 314.12$, $df = 94$, $p = .00$, CFI = .80; TLI = .75; RMSEA = .12. Modification indices indicated that misfit was associated with correlation between two items on exercise intention, which made theoretical sense. The addition of this correlation had a significant effect on fit, $\chi^2 = 189.04$, $df = 93$, $p = .00$, CFI = .91; TLI = .89; RMSEA = .08. In support of H1 and H2, the model showed that participants' perceived autonomy and relatedness positively predicted their intention to like, share, comment on others' exercise posts. Analysis showed that viral behavioral intention is positively influenced by 'relatedness' ($\beta = .58$, $p < .05$) and 'autonomy' ($\beta = .12$, $p = .058$). However, 'tie-strength' ($\beta = .30$, $p > .05$) and 'exercise intention' ($\beta = .02$, $p > .05$) did not show significant relationships on viral behavioral intention, disconfirming H3 and H4.

Next, indirect effects were tested. The indirect effect of tie-strength on viral behavioral intention through perceived relatedness was not significant, $\beta = .18$, 95 % CI = [−.01, .41]. Thus, H5 was not supported. However, the indirect effect of exercise intention on viral behavioral intention through perceived relatedness was significant and positive, $\beta = .36$, 95 % CI = [.206, .589]. 9.4 % of variances in viral behavioral intention were accounted for exercise intention through perceived relatedness. Therefore, H6 was supported. The findings are discussed with regard to enhancing viral intentions for the exercise posts.

5 Discussion and Implications

Though advancement of technologies has enabled real-time interaction between original posters of the exercise post and viewers, there has been only some attention given to this new invention. In this study, we aimed to find a way to motivate people on social media to give real-time social support to original posters of exercise posts, by exploring the relationship between motivational factors and viral behavioral intention.

Building our study on the constructs of SDT, we found significant path between the need satisfaction for relatedness and autonomy on intention to like, comment and share. Findings highlight the importance of elements of exercise posts, which in turn satisfy viewers' need for relatedness and autonomy. For instance, by explicitly stating that one's liking or commenting would be influential on posters' exercise activity would help by increasing the sense of autonomy of the viewers.

It was interesting that we did not find a direct effect between exercise intention and viral behavioral intention, but only the indirect effect through relatedness. This result indicates that exercise intention would increase the viewers' need satisfaction for relatedness, which in turn leads to viral behavioral intention. In this regard, practitioners could think of designing the exercise activity post that highlights the viewer's role, which heightens their feeling of being appreciated and connected. For instance, adding function to exercise posts such as explicit request for feedbacks from the original poster of the exercise posts would increase the feeling of connection for viewers.

Our disconfirmed hypotheses for the relationship between tie-strength and viral behavioral intention explain that viewers' engagement cannot be achieved by relying on existing relationship between the original posters and viewers. This result highlights the importance of satisfaction for relatedness through exercise posts once again.

This study also provides some further implications. While contributing on theory building by applying SDT in the context of exercise posts, this study has practical implications for exercise application designers. In this study, we could not incorporate the need satisfaction for competence; however, future research will investigate the effect of competence as well.

References

1. Alhabash, S., McAlister, A.R., Hagerstrom, A., Quilliam, E.T., Rifon, N.J., Richards, J.I.: Between likes and shares: effects of emotional appeal and virality on the persuasiveness of anticyberbullying messages on Facebook. Cyberpsychol. Behav. Soc. Netw. 16(3), 175–182 (2013)
2. Chu, S.C., Kim, Y.: Determinants of consumer engagement in electronic Word-Of Mouth (eWOM) in social networking sites. Int. J. Adverts. 30(1), 47–75 (2011)
3. Deci, E.L., Ryan, R.M.: Intrinsic Motivation And Self-Determination in Human Behavior. Plenum, New York (1985)
4. Frenzen, J., Nakamoto, K.: Structure, cooperation, and the flow of market information. J. Cons. Res. 20, 360–375 (1993)
5. Gilbert, E., Karahalios, K.: Predicting tie strength with social media. In: Proceedings of the SIGCHI Conference on Human Factors in Computing Systems, pp. 211–220 (2009)
6. Granovetter, M.S.: The strength of weak ties. Am. J. Socio. 78(6), 1360–1380 (1973)
7. Grouzet, F.M.E., Vallerand, R.J., Thill, E.E., Provencher, P.J.: From environmental factors to outcomes: a test of an integrated motivational sequence. Motiv. Emot. 28(4), 331–346 (2004)
8. Kim, E.E.S.: Consumer engagement and relationship building in social media: the effects of consumer self-determination and social relatedness (Doctoral dissertation) (2014)

9. La Guardia, J.G., Ryan, R.M., Couchman, C.E., Deci, E.L.: Within-person variation in security of attachment: a self-determination theory perspective on attachment, need fulfillment, and well-being. J. Pers. Soc. Psychol. **79**(3), 367 (2000)
10. Lowe, R., Eves, F., Carroll, D.: The influence of affective and instrumental beliefs on exercise intentions and behavior: a longitudinal analysis. J. Appl. Soc. Psychol. **32**(6), 1241–1252 (2002)
11. Mathwick, C., Rigdon, E.: Play, flow, and the online search experience. J. Consum. Res. **31**(2), 324–332 (2004)
12. Miller, L.M., Prior, D.D.: Online social networks and friending behaviour: a self-determination theory perspective. In: Proceedings of Australian and New Zealand Marketing Academy Conference, Christchurch, New Zealand (2010)
13. Okazaki, S., Rubio, N., Campo, S.: Do online Gossipers promote brands? Cyberpsychol. Behav. Soc. Netw. **16**(2), 1–8 (2012)
14. Roeser, R.W., Midgley, C., Urdan, T.C.: Perceptions of the school psychological environment and early adolescents' psychological and behavioral functioning in school: the mediating role of goals and belonging. J. Educ. Psychol. **88**(3), 408–422 (1996)
15. Ryan, R.M., Connell, J.P.: Perceived locus of causality and internalization: examining reasons for acting in two domains. J. Pers. Soc. **57**(5), 749–761 (1989)
16. Ryan, R.M., Deci, E.L.: Intrinsic and extrinsic motivations: classic definitions and new directions. Contemp. Educ. Psychol. **25**(1), 54–67 (2000)
17. Ryu, G., Feick, L.: A penny for your thoughts: referral reward programs and referral likelihood. J. Mark. **71**, 84–94 (2007)
18. Sheldon, K.M., Abad, N., Hinsch, C.: A two-process view of Facebook use and relatedness need-satisfaction: disconnection drives use, and connection rewards it. J. Pers. Soc. Psychol. **100**(4), 766–775 (2011)
19. Teixeira, P.J., Carraça, E.V., Markland, D., Silva, M.N., Ryan, R.M.: Exercise, physical activity, and self-determination theory: a systematic review. Med. Sci. Sports Exerc. **43**(4), 728–737 (2011)
20. Treiber, F.A., Baranowski, T., Braden, D.S., Strong, W.B., Levy, M., Knox, W.: Social support for exercise: relationship to physical activity in young adults. Prev. Med. **20**(6), 737–750 (1991)
21. Vallerand, R.J., Blssonnette, R.: Intrinsic, extrinsic, and amotivational styles as predictors of behavior: a prospective study. J. Educ. Psychol. **60**(3), 599–620 (1992)
22. Wang, C.J., Leng, H., Kee, Y.: Use of Facebook in physical activity intervention programme. Int. J. Sport. Psychol. **45**(6), 1–15 (2014)
23. Woźniak, P., Knaving, K., Björk, S., Fjeld, M.: RUFUS: remote supporter feedback for long-distance runners. In: Proceedings of the 17th International Conference on Human-Computer Interaction with Mobile Devices and Services, pp. 115–124 (2015)

Do Users Express Values During Use of Social Systems? A Classification of Their Postings in Personal, Social and Technical Values

Denilson C. Oliveira[1(✉)], Elizabeth Furtado[1], and Marilia S. Mendes[2]

[1] University of Fortaleza (Unifor), Fortaleza, CE, Brazil
denilsoncursinol@gmail.com, elizabethsfur@gmail.com
[2] Federal University of Ceará (UFC), Russas, CE, Brazil
mariliamendes@gmail.com

Abstract. Nowadays Social Systems (SS) are widely used by users who want to interact expressing their thoughts and values in their posts. In this study, we present a research over the values expressed in user posts to investigate the following questions: what are the relationships between personal and social values in the users posts; which social or personal values can express (positively or negatively) the technical values and; how the expression of personal and social values in SS posts can assist in SS evaluation. The results showed that the analysis of values can be used as filters for an empirical assessment of the quality and technical problems of SS as well as a source of knowledge for the construction of new SS requirements.

Keywords: Human computer interaction · Usability · User experience · Personal and social values

1 Introduction

Concerning on Human Computer Interaction (HCI) field, studies related to User Experience (UX) of SS to get a holistic view of the users participation are always needed. The SS (e.g. twitter, Facebook, LinkedIn, WhatsApp, etc.) are used by a wide range of user profiles and each with different objectives: simple interactions with other individuals, marketing of products and services, knowledge, among others. The users' motivations in interaction are always accompanied by values, expressed in their posts: personal values; social values, mainly formed by the interaction of their personal values and the socio-cultural context, which they are inserted. That thought about the social value is corroborated by [20] when he says: each individual, when born, is inserted in a social system established through generations and is assimilated through social inter-relationships. [13] defines value as something that a person or group of people, considers important in life.

In [18], a SS honeycomb was created by aiming to provide a basis for understanding the functioning of a SS and, consequently, determining the elements (or values) that should be considered when designing it. The concept of SS and the analysis of the SS honeycomb are examined by [14] which presents a framework to help in understanding

© Springer International Publishing Switzerland 2016
G. Meiselwitz (Ed.): SCSM 2016, LNCS 9742, pp. 130–140, 2016.
DOI: 10.1007/978-3-319-39910-2_13

this kind of system and to describe new elements to such honeycomb, such as: object, collaboration, emotion and affection, adaptability, usability, accessibility. In [10], a discussion is presented about the evaluation on the context of human and technical values. The meaning of each value is displayed, along with its classification regarding a semiotic onion.

Previous research acknowledged that posts of users, created during user interaction in the SS, may have different implications in the SS development and evaluation processes. The research carried out in [11] aimed to study the Posts with content Related to the Use of system (called PRU) for the evaluation process.

However, how useful is the study of user values (personal, social and technical, etc.) expressed in PRU for such processes?

We propose to explore the relationships among personal and social values through the lens of PRU classification in order to meet later standards to help at two different contexts: the development of systems with the concept of VSD (Value Sensitive Design) and evaluation of quality user interaction in ready-made systems.

During this research it was possible to confirm and establish a correlation of personal and social values in SS posts, consequently, building a framework to be used as a tool to assess the UX in SS. The posts of the database used in this study were obtained from public posts of Twitter users with careful to get different contexts [11]. 1,452 PRU (N = 1,2 %) from the total of 68,888 posts were identified. The studies presented in this article randomly separated in 1,000 posts to be analyzed.

This paper is organized as follows: in Sect. 2, we present a background with some concepts about SS, posts in SS and new concepts about value related to use of system. In Sect. 3, we present some related works. In Sect. 4, we present our research of posts in SS. In Sect. 5, we present the considerations and future work.

2 Background

2.1 Social Systems

The first definition of the term was described by [16] where SS are described as software that provides group interaction. [9] went further stating that SS not only have the possibility of interaction, feedback and conversations among users but also have the ability to recombine everything and establish new tools. In [24], the SS were taken to the field of educational technologies and defined SS as a tool that provides activities in online social networks.

[10] took the SS concepts to another level, analyzing them from the precepts presented by [18]: honeycombs elements. [10] used some values (e.g. autonomy, collaboration, trust, etc.) to analyze the quality of use of a SS called rich village.

2.2 Posts in Social Systems

Posts are characterized as a representative element of the interaction of SS users: their views, small reports, public or private messages, and so on. In [12] is investigated how users express their emotions regarding the system through their postings in order to support the UX evaluation in SS. The same authors in [13] have Investigated usability and UX from the user postings in SS from the PRUs. PRU is a Post Related to the Use of the system, for example, the following post is a PRU: "*My twitter has some problem. It's giving an error when I want to give an answer*", but the following post is not related to the use of the system: "*I want to study, but the problem is I'm too lazy.*" [11].

The posts are the main objects of study of this research. [4] analyzed how deep the sentiments are manifested into the posts and the specific vocabulary used by the authors when they want to express a strong sense of danger about events that occurred or will occur. The goal is to find security patterns in words in order to develop search algorithms. In [21] was carried out an analysis of the influence of the users feelings of posts as a major factor of attention of other users to interact. The authors compared this fact in many SS. A study about the possibility of malicious links in posts on Facebook was carried out in by [1].

2.3   VRU and N-VRU Concepts

As a step belonging to methodology to be followed in this research, the PRUs are classified as Value Related to Use of system (VRU) and Value Non Related to Use of system (N-VRU) as a previous step of classification in social and personal values.

Posts classified as VRU show a positive or negative content related with the system in use. Table 1 shows same examples of VRU.

Table 1. Examples of VRU posts

N^0	VRU (posts)
1	"My twitter is presenting problem"
2	"I need to change my icon but twitter had a problem right now"
3	"Looks, twitter to Windows 8 Pro is bad like all others"

Posts classified as N-VRU are related to any other matters which aren't related to use of the system. Table 2 shows same examples of VRU.

Table 2. Examples of N-VRU posts

N^0	N-VRU (posts)
1	"Almost reaching 1000 tweets ... but it's still very little"
2	"We must tweet because, according to the new promotion, how much more tweets more followers"
3	"Good morning, who now came to Twitter"

3   Related Works

[18] bought altogether social elements that should be considered when developing social interaction tools. In [14] a review of the concepts related to SS and SS HoneyComb was performed. The social values initially pointed out by Smith were classified in social,

personal and technical values. In [14], a social tool called "Vila na Rede" was used as a reference to know how much the values are important in evaluation processes. The same author, in [15], presented some activities, during a system development process, to consider cultural requirements of target audience. He called this artifact as V4FSS (Valuation Frame For Social Software).

A study of the construction and/or acquisition of knowledge was approached by [23]. Here the construction of knowledge was attributed to interaction between participants and the authors suggested two ways: Inflow, where the sense of knowledge comes from another person; outflow, which knowledge is produced by the individual to others.

A study regarding how the social networks influence the dissemination of knowledge is argued in [17]. In [24] a social network with P2P architecture is built to facilitate the interconnection of those users who need the knowledge with who owns it.

[3] proposed a conservation model at social networks based on the principles of Hippocrates. These principles were mentioned by [2], namely: specific motivation, consent, minimum set, limited use, limited disclosure, limited retention, accuracy, access and compliance. To [7, 19], privacy preserving of SS user information must be provided and be one of the main goals of the developers.

[22] asserted the importance to know how people feel about certain topics that they find in SS. It proposed a classification of these feelings using of rating Naïve Bayer algorithm. The author emphasized the complexity because the feelings could be represented in various ways within users posts.

[8] researched about user behavior and content of social community in terms of reciprocity. The authors claim that when a user is faced with some content that considers important, made available by another user, beget a sense of reciprocity with whom released. The authors observed other points: who provides the knowledge want to take advantage of reciprocity from other users; what can be the impact of these contents to the SS and what types of content more cause reciprocity.

[5] asserted that the identity notion plays a key role in virtual communities: to know the identity of those with whom the user communicate is essential to understand and assess an interaction. The authors described about the ambiguous side of identity in virtual communities stating that the basic tips on personality and social roles used in the real world are missing into the virtual one.

Analyzing these related works regarding the study of human values, we noted the studies correlate the maximum number of three values: [6] worked with the informed consent of values, privacy and autonomy. The personal value of emotion and affection is one of personal values developed in our research and considering the various feelings represented by this value, is the most studied [4, 11, 12, 21, 22]; evaluation of SS [9, 11, 24]; sharing (social value) and Safety (technical) by [1, 17, 23, 24] study the personal value of knowledge; the personal value of privacy is studied by [7, 19], reciprocity [8] and the personal value of identity by [5].

The current state-of-art have a lot of work directed to the study of values in the IHC area, nevertheless, none discusses the relationship of various values, merely limited to some. We propose a study on the relationship between human values as a source of information for assessing the SS and to the development of the SS considering VSD.

4 Research of Posts in SS

The classification of posts was conducted in two steps: The first step was to classify 1,000 (one thousand) posts as a VRU post or a N-VRU post. The selection process of such posts was the following [4]: 295,797 postings of users with public profiles on Twitter were collected focusing only the Portuguese language. Retweeted messages and noisy post, such as misspellings, absence of space between words and HTML tags were also discarded. We also considered the PRU as valid for analysis [5]. The second step was to associate each classified post to one or more personal and social values. This second step required the classification of each value so that we had established the interconnections among them. The result is a table (See Fig. 4 to VRU and Fig. 5 to N-VRU), showing the relationship among values.

4.1 VRU Classification

4.1.1 The Process

During the classification process, the concepts relatives to each value were used to connect the posts and values. The classification was initially held by the author of this research and, given the manual nature of the classification process, it was put in proof: a sample of 100 VRU posts was released to a HCI specialist and other 100 N-VRU posts to another one. A meeting was held with the specialists to present: the classification reasons to be performed by each one; the meaning of each value [4] and the difference between VRU and N-VRU.

After receiving the classification made by each specialist, another meeting was held to conduct a comparison between these and performed by the author of this research until have a final result (described below).

On the VRU, percentage of correct answers between the two classifications was always above 88 % (knowledge): 91 % for emotion and affection, 100 % confidence. During the meeting, some cases were discussed and one of them concerned the classification of the Autonomy value: the sample possessed 3 posts classified with the value of autonomy by the author and the specialist only 2 of them generating an assertiveness rate of only 67 %. During the meeting, they both agreed with the classified posts. The Table 3 shows some examples of VRU classification.

Table 3. Classification of VRU posts in personal and social values

Posts	Personal Value	Social Value
"Twitter already changed the way of tweeting, soon takes the 140 character limit"	Emotion and Affection	(Standards, Rules and Policies) and object
"Wanted twitter I read all the rules and not committed any error, not punish me for nothing again please	(Emotion and Affection) and trust	(Standards, Rules and Policies) and object
"Twitter launches official app for Windows 8 and Windows RT: It took a while, but Twitter finally released her to... http://t.co/GJKvnQuXKU"	(Emotion and Affection), autonomy	Object, sharing

4.1.2   Analysis and Results

As previously described the first action of the research was the classification of posts in VRU and N-VRU and the subsequent expression of personal and social values in each of the messages of the two posts banks (See Fig. 1).

		Social							
		Standards, Rules and Policies	Collaboration	Sharing	Conversation	Groups	Object	Relationship	Property
Personal	Autonomy	•		•			•		
	Trust	•		•	•		•	•	
	Informed consent								
	Emotion and Affection	•					•	•	
	Identity								
	Presence	•					•		
	Privacy								
	Reciprocity								
	Reputation								
	Visibility								
	Knowledge	•		•			•		
	Prestige								
	Social responsability								

Fig. 1. Classification of VRU posts in personal and social values

In Fig. 1 social values are interconnected with person's values, characterizing a result of this research. It can be used as a source for different analysis of a system in study. Considering a database of 1000 VRU posts, Fig. 2 shows the amount of personal values expressed in VRU posts. Some values (as informed consent, identity, privacy, reciprocity, reputation, visibility, prestige and social responsibility) weren't expressed in the VRU posts.

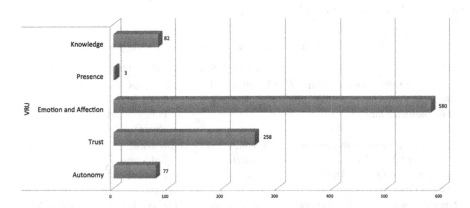

Fig. 2. Amount of each value in VRU posts

The Pareto chart (See Fig. 3) shows the three more expressed values in sentences (emotion/affection, trust and knowledge) and they represent 92 % of all posts. We emphasize the presence emotion/affection representing 76 %. We can infer, across the high expression of this value in posts, a deep user involvement with the system when he praises or complains about something related to the use of that system. The content of the posts, which expressing these values cited, we find compliments and complaints concerning the system that lead us to possible technical problems (technical values).

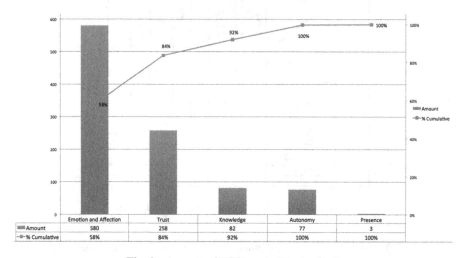

Fig. 3. Amount of VRU posts (Pareto chart)

The second question of this research was: which social or personal values can express (positively or negatively) the technical values and how this expression can be useful in evaluation systems. To answer this question the contents of each message was analyzed to identify the technical values represented in each post (as seen in Table 4). The Fig. 4 depicts the results of this study.

Table 4. Examples of technical classification of VRU posts

Posts	Personal Value	Social Value	Technical
"*RT{user}_: twitter already changed the way of tweeting, soon takes the 140 character limit*"	Emotion and Affection	(Standards, Rules and Policies) and object	Usability
" Do not Like More Of this For now I'll Be Thank Sticky Tweets quotient Who Occupy The Full Screen From My Phone"	(Emotion and Affection) and trust	(Standards, Rules and Policies) and object	Appearance
"Enter the twitter by phone is very bad, photo does not appear"	(Emotion and Affection), autonomy, trust	Object, sharing	Availability

		Social								Technical								
		Standards, Rules and Policies	Collaboration	Sharing	Conversation	Groups	Object	Relationship	Property	Accessibility	Adaptability	Appearance	Awareness	Availability	Scalability	Portability	Safety	Usability
Personal	Autonomy	•		•			•					•				•	•	•
	Trust	•		•	•		•	•			•	•	•	•	•	•	•	•
	Informed consent																	
	Emotion and Affection	•					•	•		•	•	•	•	•				•
	Identity																	
	Presence	•					•							•				
	Privacy																	
	Reciprocity																	
	Reputation																	
	Visibility																	
	Knowledge	•		•			•					•				•		•
	Prestige																	
	Social responsability																	

Fig. 4. Interconnection between human values and technical of VRU posts

A possible scenario to illustrate the utility of interconnection between human values and technical is the following: a company wants to find out what technical issues are related to portability, but the content of the client messages did not phrase this problem explicitly. A filter could be executed with sentences that only express the personal values of autonomy, confidence and learning.

4.2   Classification, Analysis and Results of N-VRU Posts

All the procedure described for VRU is also valid for N-VRU posts. The result of the classification of N-VRU posts with interconnection between personal and social values (shown in Fig. 5).

		Social							
		Standards, Rules and Policies	Collaboration	Sharing	Conversation	Groups	Object	Relationship	Property
Personal	Autonomy								
	Trust								
	Informed consent								
	Emotion and Affection		•	•	•		•	•	
	Identity								
	Presence			•			•	•	
	Privacy								
	Reciprocity			•	•		•	•	
	Reputation								
	Visibility								
	Knowledge			•	•		•		
	Prestige				•		•	•	
	Social responsability			•	•		•	•	

Fig. 5. Interconnection between human values and technical of N-VRU posts

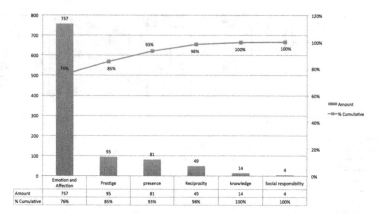

Fig. 6. Personal values expressed in N-VRU posts (Pareto Chart)

A number of posts about emotion and affection values is expressed by users (See Fig. 6). Three values (emotion/affection, prestige and presence) represent 93 % of the six values found in N-VRU posts.

A point to note is the widespread expression of prestige value by users. Considering this value, as an example, we believe in the use this information (be a very value expressed by users) as a reason for the development of new SS requirements which encourages the use from this value, considering the perception its importance to users. We would use the information learned from analysis of N-VRU posts as differential is compared with other tools and to improving usability by the user. Like this example, many others analysis could be done in N-VRU posts to improve the UX of SS. As seen in Fig. 7, the occurrence of personal values in VRU and N-VRU posts It has some peculiarities, with values present in only one of them.

		VRU	N-VRU
	Autonomy		
	Trust	•	
	Informed Consent		
	Emotion and Affection	•	•
	Identity		
Personal Values	Presence	•	•
	Privacy		
	Reciprocity		•
	Reputation		
	Visibility		
	knowledge	•	•
	prestige		•
	Social responsability		•

Fig. 7. The occurrence of personal values found in VRU and N-VRU

We argue for the use of VRU posts as an information source for a system in use evaluation or even to help in its development phase. In general, the state-of-art of human values don't use posts that aren't related to use of the system, as a source of information. The comparison between VRU and N-VRU is unique in this work related to other tools and it is interesting to: (i) provide developers with a vision about what values are expressed in both and which appear in only one of them; (ii) set patterns of users' behavior and; (iii) use the feelings of users as a source of information in order to raise new requirements for the system being evaluated.

5 Considerations and Future Work

This research aims at studying the relationship between personal values, social and technical requirements to assist in evaluation systems in use or in development. During the research we have established an interconnection between the values, both to VRU as for N-VRU.

As for VRU posts, was shown that is possible deal with potential technical problems studying the posts that express personal values that, in turn, portray about these problems. With respect to N-VRU posts, they can be useful as source information for creating new SS requirements to positively exploit the values expressed by the users. As future work we intend to follow three lines of study:

- To apply the studies in other types of SS and to make comparisons;
- To establish patterns for identify each value to permit the development of algorithms to do automatic classification;
- To study the possibility of further analysis considering the interconnections presented to help in a VSD development.

References

1. Abu-Nimeh, S., Chen, T., Alzubi, O.: Malicious and spam posts in online social networks. IEEE Comput. Soc. **44**, 23–28 (2011)
2. Agrawal R., Kierman J., Srikant R., Xu Y.: Hippocratic databases. In: Em 280 VLDB Conference, Hong Kong, China (2002)
3. Bedi, R., Gove, N.R.: Application of Hippocratic principles for privacy preservation in social network. In: Information and Communication Technologies (WICT), pp. 95–101 (2012)
4. Bolea, S.C.: Vocabulary, synonyms and sentiments of hazard-related posts on social networks. In: 2015 International Conference on Speech Technology and Human-Computer Dialogue (SpeD), pp. 14–17 (2015)
5. Donath, J.S.: Identity and deception in the virtual community. In: Kollock, P., Marc, S. (eds.) Communities in Cyberspace. Routledge, New York (1999)
6. Friedman B., Kahn Jr., P.H., Boring, A.: Value sensitive design and information systems. In: Human-Computer Interaction in Management Information Systems: Foundations, pp. 348–372 (2006)
7. Kleinberg J.: Challenges in mining social network data: processes, privacy and paradoxes. In: KDD, EUA, pp. 4–5 (2007)
8. Lee J. G., Antoniadis, P., Salamatian, K.: Faving reciprocity in content sharing communities: a comparative analysis of Flickr and Twitter. In: ASONAM, pp. 136–143 (2010)

9. McLoughlin, C., Lee, M.: Social software and participatory learning: pedagogical choices with technology affordances in the Web 2.0. In: Ascilite Singapore, pp. 664–675 (2007)
10. Pereira, M., Baranauskas, C.: Softwares sociais: uma visão orientada a valores. In: IHC, pp. 149–158 (2010)
11. Mendes, M.S., Furtado, E., Castro, M.F.: Do users write about the system in use? An investigation from messages in Natural Language on Twitter. In: 7th Euro American Association on Telematics and Information Systems, Valparaiso, Chile (2014)
12. Mendes, M.S., Furtado, E., Furtado, V., Castro, M.F.: How do users express their emotions regarding the social system in use? A classification of their postings by using the emotional analysis of Norman. In: 6th International Conference, SCSM, pp. 229–241 (2014)
13. Mendes, M.S., Furtado, E. S., Furtado, V., Castro, M.F.: Investigating usability and user experience from the user postings in social systems. In: 17th International Conference on Human-Computer Interaction (HCII 2015), Los Angeles, CA, USA (2015)
14. Pereira, R., Baranauskas, M.C.C., Silva, S.R.P.: A discussion on social software: concept, building blocks and challenges. Int. J. Infonomics (IJI) 3(4), 533–542 (2010). ISSN: 17424712
15. Pereira, R., de Miranda, L.C., Baranauskas, M.C.C., Piccolo, L.S.G., Almeida, L.D.A., Dos Reis, J.C.: Interaction design of social software: clarifying requirements through a culturally aware artifact. In: Information Society (i-Society), pp. 293–298 (2011)
16. Shirky, C.: A group is its own worst enemy: social structure in social software. In: O'Reilly Emerging Technology Conference, CA (2005). http://www.shirky.com/writings/group_enemy.html. Accessed on Dec 2015
17. Sorenson, O., Rivkin, J.W., Lee, F.: Complexity, networks and knowledge flow. Res. Policy 35, 994–1017 (2006)
18. Smith, G.: Tagging: People-Powered Metadata for the Social Web. New Riders, Berkley (2008)
19. Srivastava J., Ahmad, M.A., Pathak, N., Hsu, D.K.W.: Data mining based social network analysis from online behavior. In: 80 SIAM International Conference on Data mining (SDM) (2008)
20. Strey, M.N.: Psicologia Social Contemporânea, 7th edn. Vozes, Rio de Janeiro (2002)
21. Sun B.: Analyzing sentimental influence of posts on social networks. In: IEEE International Conference on Computer Supported Work in Design, pp. 546–551, Hong Kong Polytechnic University, Hong Kong, China (2014)
22. Troussas, C., Virvou, M., Espinosa, K.J., Llaguno, K., Caro, J.: Sentiment analysis of Facebook statuses using naive Bayes classifier for language learning. In: Information, Intelligence, Systems and Applications (IISA), pp. 1–6 (2013)
23. Wang, B., Yang, J., Liu, H.: Understanding the mechanism of social network in the knowledge transfer process. In: PICMET, pp. 1–6 (2010)
24. Ying, Y., Ziran, Z.: Contemporary social design principles in HCI design. In: Control, Automation and Systems Engineering (CASE), pp. 1–4 (2011)

Judgment Making with Conflicting Information in Social Media: The Second-Order Judgment Problems

Mina Park[1(✉)] and Poong Oh[2]

[1] Annenberg School for Communication and Journalism, University of Southern California, 3502 Watt Way, Los Angeles, CA, USA
minapark@usc.edu
[2] Annenberg School for Communication, University of Pennsylvania, 3620 Walnut Street, Philadelphia, PA, USA
poongoh@asc.upenn.edu

Abstract. In online settings, people often face inconsistent or conflicting information about a target of judgment. To make an accurate judgment, they need to determine which information is most relevant, reliable, and trustworthy and how to incorporate it into their judgment making processes. In this paper, we call this the *second-order judgment problem*—evaluating the value of the information on the target of judgment before making judgments. Extending previous research on online impression formation [1], this study examined the impact of perceived social closeness between the target person whose personality is to be judged and those who provide the information about that person (e.g., comments), which is, in particular, in conflict with the information generated by the target person (e.g., online profiles) on impression formation. To this end, a web-administered experiment was performed, where participants were asked to judge the personality of a target person after reviewing the person's Facebook page, which had conflicting information. The results showed that the information generated by distant others was more influential on judgment making than that generated by close others, confirming that perceived social closeness functioned as a critical cue for judging the value of the available information. The current findings provide an important implication for the design of the interface of social media: the method of presenting the information about the available information can alter the allocation of judgment makers' attention, and thereby, final judgments.

Keywords: Second-order judgment problems · Information incompatibility · Judgment formation · Perceived social relationship · Social media

1 Introduction

The information provided by others, who presumably better know about the target of judgment, is useful in judgment making, in particular, in online settings [2–4]. For example, online shoppers look at the reviews submitted by others who have already used the products before they make purchases. However, information about the target of judgment is often inconsistent, or even conflicting, because it is created by multiple sources with different interests, tastes, and perspectives. Online sellers always advertise

© Springer International Publishing Switzerland 2016
G. Meiselwitz (Ed.): SCSM 2016, LNCS 9742, pp. 141–150, 2016.
DOI: 10.1007/978-3-319-39910-2_14

their products by demonstrating their benefits, but product reviews may not be as positive as advertised. Even for the best-rated products, some people may still complain and leave negative reviews. If inconsistent or conflicting information is the only available information about the target of judgment, judgment makers have to determine which information (or its sources) is more relevant, reliable, and trustworthy, and therefore, to be incorporated into their judgment-making processes. Put simply, judgment makers need to judge the informational value of the information on the target of judgment, which we shall call the *second-order judgment problem* in this paper.

Given that online environments are characterized by open-participation, diversity, and decentrality [5], it is reasonable to expect that there would be diverse opinions and views on the same objects. Therefore, inconsistent and conflicting information is very common, and online users frequently face second-order judgment problems. From this perspective, the current study explores the strategies people adopt to cope with information incompatibility in making judgments online. In particular, this study extends previous research on online impression formation, where the task is to judge the personality of a target person based on his/her conflicting online profile information [1]. Whereas previous research focused on the authorship of the information as a critical factor for judging the informational value, this study emphasizes the perceived relationship between the target and the creator of the information, as well as the authorship of the information. To this end, we conducted a web-administrated experiment in which participants were to judge the personality of target people based on their online profile information.

This paper is organized as follow: The next section briefly reviews previous literature on online impression formation and establishes research hypotheses. The following two sections—Methods and Results—describe the participants, the experiment design, the study procedure, and reports the results of statistical analysis. The final section discusses the theoretical and practical implications of the current findings and also suggests the directions of future research.

2 The Second-Order Judgment Problems in Social Media

2.1 The Impacts of the Authorship on Information Trustworthiness

Judgment formation based only on available information, as opposed to complete and perfect information, has long been studied, even before the advent of the internet. Perhaps, the first theoretical approach would be Spence's job-market signaling model published in 1973 [6]. The model assumes that employers need to make a correct judgment about job applicants (e.g., their skills and expertise) based on the information provided by the applicants themselves and little else. In that case, job applicants are incentivized to provide false information about themselves to get hired or for higher wages. For this reason, employers need to carefully review all the provided information, and further, determine which information should be weighted more instead of considering all the information equally. Spence's cost-benefit analysis of informational values suggests that the information that costs less to create (i.e. easy to manipulate) should be excluded from consideration.

Spence's signaling model has been further elaborated and successfully applied to impression management and formation in online contexts [2]. On one hand, early research on online impression management has found that people tend to construct and selectively present their positive images, as job applicants would do in job markets. For example, users in online dating sites manage their online profile to appear more likable or competent than they are [7]. Furthermore, they often engage in deceptive communication to compare favorably with others [8]. On the other hand, the literature on online impression formation suggests that people want to know others' authentic identities, as employers would do in job interviews. In the case of online dating sites, users have to decide whether to pursue the relationship by looking at any information available on the sites. To make a correct judgment of others, the users pay attention to information that reduces uncertainty about others' offline authentic identities and personalities [8, 9]. Given the tension between impression management and impression formation, judging a target's authentic identity requires the correct evaluation of the informational values of information about the target before making a judgment. Spence's signaling model would suggest that the information that costs less to create in the online environment should be carefully examined and excluded, if necessary, in judgment making processes [2].

Previous research on impression formation in social media has found that the value of the information about the target of judgment is perceived differently depending on the authorship of the information [1]. Specifically, the information generated by the target him or herself (i.e., self-generated information) is unlikely to be perceived as reliable because such information tends to be biased in favor of the target [8, 10]. For instance, a target can easily self-present a heavy community service-oriented image after a few clicks of the mouse on his/her online profile. The target would not display any information about him or herself drinking at a party or procrastinating at work to maintain the self-image in a positive light. On the other hand, the information generated by others than the target (i.e. other-generated information) is perceived as more objective and trustworthy. This is because other-generated information is not easily controlled or manipulated by the target, and thus, more "costly" in Spence's [6] term. The example includes a personalized message such as the following: "Jane, thank you so much for your consistent commitment to providing a service at our retirement home." Such an other-generated comment would have clearly required significantly greater offline time and effort than can be assumed from self-generated information. Therefore, people tend to rely on other-generated information more than self-generated information, when the two kinds of information are incompatible [11].

From this perspective, the authorship of information is expected to play as a critical role in the second-order judgment problems. More specifically,

H1: Other-generated information will have greater influences on judgment making than self-generated information in the presence of information incompatibility.

2.2   The Impacts of Social Closeness on Information Trustworthiness

As its name itself implies, a major function of social media is to build and maintain social relations among users, leading to the emergence of unprecedentedly large-scale social networks [12]. In social networks, individuals are connected in pairs by social ties. Some pairs are connected by "strong" ties, whereas others are loosely connected [13, 14]. Strong ties imply frequent interactions, long-lasting relationships, sharing mutual friends, common affiliations, and social *closeness* above all [15]. These social ties among users are recognizable in social media because the networked communication platform allows individuals to communicate with all of their social pairs in one place (e.g. individuals' profiles). For example, both the comments generated by the target's best friends and those generated by someone who just met the target are available on the target's profile page.

Previous research on interpersonal relationships implies that people would perceive the same information about a target differently depending on the information providers' relationship with the target. Studies have found that close others are motivated to deepen and intensify the experience of closeness while distant others concern the formation and stability of long-term relationship [16, 17]. Thus, close others tend to share thoughts, information, and feelings favorable to their communication partners. On the other hand, distant others involve boundary settings and developments of a sense of self and autonomy [16]. Having experienced this communication behavior with their close and distant others, people may perceive a target's close others' comments about the target as more subjective and emotional, whereas distant others' comments as more objective and informational.

Given the role of social closeness in message perception and the feature of social media platform, the dichotomy between selves and others appears to be too simple to fully capture judgment making with conflicting information in social media. The present study suggests that *social closeness* may play a critical role in the second-order judgment problems (Fig. 1). Based on the literature, judgment makers would think that the information generated by distant others reflects more objective and accurate offline identity about the target than that generate by close others. Thus, judgment makers would be

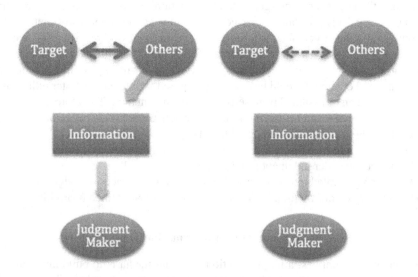

Fig. 1. The information generated by close others (left) and distant others (right)

more influenced by information generated by others who have relationships that are relatively independent of the target person than that generated by close others in the judgment-making process.

More specifically, the present study hypothesized that.

H2: The information generated by *distant* others will have a greater influence on judgment making than that generated by *close* others in the presence of information incompatibility.

3   Methods

3.1   Participants

Participants (N = 88; 20 male and 68 female) were undergraduate students from a university in California who volunteered to participate in the study in exchange for extra course credit or in partial fulfillment of a class research requirement. The sample identified their ethnic background to be 58.0 % Caucasian and 42.0 % others. Facebook use was assessed by the item "How often do you use Facebook." The present study only included participants who use Facebook everyday in order to control their familiarity of Facebook. Thus, 11 participants (14.1 %) who did not use Facebook everyday were excluded.

3.2   Procedure

Main Study. An experiment was carried out to test these hypotheses. The experiment started with an informed consent form where the participants were briefly introduced to the study. After participants understood that their responses were anonymous, they viewed the mock profile of the target person, Chris Kim. After viewing the profile, they rated their impressions of Chris Kim. A total of 2 stimuli were created with mock-up Facebook profiles.

Stimuli and Design. This study focused specifically on measurement of extraversion in social media setting in testing for impression formation [1]. Extraversion is among the Big Five personality dimensions along with experience, conscientiousness, agreeableness, and neuroticism [18, 19]. In addition to its wide empirical support as a personality dimension, extraversion is also often extracted and assessed from social media profiles [20]. Prior studies have found that online presentations of extraversion in social media profiles differ from online presentations of introversion in the amount of information displayed and the nature of content displayed [21, 22].

The experiment randomly assigned participants each to two conditions. Both conditions included conflicting information of a target person between self-(e.g., the target claimed to be an introvert) and other-(e.g., the other suggested the target was extrovert) generated comments in a mock-up Facebook profile (H1). The difference between the two conditions was in the social relationships between the target person and others: close others for one condition and distant others for the other condition (H2). Participants were then asked to make judgments of the target person. In essence, this design allowed for the testing of two hypotheses at the same time.

Manipulation Check. To determine that the stimulus statements induced intended social relationships, a pretest was administered to undergraduate students ($N = 25$) from a university in California, who were independent from the main study participants. Participants were asked to evaluate the degree of closeness in a relationship between the target and the target's Facebook friends after reading a set of descriptive statements about the target. They each rated two conditions, close others and distant others. The sample items for the close others' statements included "hey, call me when you hear where the partyz at… you will hear before I do lol" The statements in the distant others condition included "hey it was great meeting you last night! I think you drank twice as much as me, but still managed to be the life of the party!!" Participants responded to items such as "This person and others who comment on her Facebook are close to each other."

A paired-sample t test showed that the statements produced differences in the degree of closeness of social relationships. The close others' statements had significantly greater scores on closeness in relationship, $M = 3.56$, $SD = 0.77$, than did the distant others' statements, $M = 2.08$, $SD = 0.86$, $t(24) = 6.59$, $p < .001$.

Measures. The dependent variable of extraversion was assessed via an online questionnaire. The experiment used a subscale of the NEO-Five Factor Inventory (NEO-FFI) [19] that was adapted for judgment makers [23]. Scales included items such as "This person likes to have a lot of people around," and "This person really enjoys talking to people." Participants responded to these items on five-interval Likert-type scales, ranging from strongly disagree to strongly agree. Reliability among items was acceptable, Cronbach's $\alpha = .81$.

Time to complete the survey was also measured in order to exclude insincere response. Manipulation checks provided the mean time for judgment makers in reading Chris's Facebook profile and perceiving the relationship between Chris and her friends ($M = 57.79$ (seconds per one stimulus)). Considering that participants were asked to respond to 24 items (taking two to three seconds per item) after viewing the Facebook profile, those who spent less than two minutes were excluded. Thus, a total of 64 participants (72.73 %) were included in the analysis.

Data Analysis. In order to compare the mean of conditions, one-sample t test and an independent sample t test were performed for the experiment. The one-sample t test was used to test whether participants perceived the target as an extravert. Since self-generated information indicated that the target is introvert and other-generated information indicated the target is extrovert, greater than neutral (value $= 3$) assessments of extroversion can be considered as judgment makers' perception of target extraversion. An independent sample t test allowed the comparison of the target's mean extraversion between intimate relationship and less intimate relationship conditions.

4   Results

Hypothesis 1 predicted that judgment makers attribute other-generated information with greater weight than self-generated information. It was supported by one sample t test showing that judgment makers perception of extraversion of the target ($M = 3.40$, $SD = 0.47$) was significantly higher than 3, $t(63) = 6.80$, $p < .001$. The results suggest that although the target described themselves as introvert, judgment makers tended to judge the target as extravert in accordance to others' description of the target as an extravert. The reason for this is because judgment makers attributed other-generated information with greater weight than self-generated information.

The second hypothesis was that information about a target generated by distant others will have more influence on judgment of the target's impression than information about the target generated by close others. The result also supported the Hypothesis 2, showing that the perception of extraversion of the target in the distant other condition ($M = 3.52$, $SD = 0.46$) was significantly higher than that of the target in close other condition ($M = 3.29$, $SD = 0.47$), $t(62) = 2.02$, $p < .05$. This indicates that judgment makers attributed distant others' comments about the target with greater weight than close others' comments about the target.

Effect size was also measured in order to look at the amount of variance explained. Although the mean difference of two conditions seemed small, the results showed that different relationships had medium effects on judgment makers' perception of extraversion of the target, $\eta^2 = .061$ [24]. This indicates that social relationships between the target and others effectively explain judgment makers' impression formation of the target.

5   Discussion

This study found that judgment makers attributed other-generated information about a target person with greater weight than self-descriptions. In addition to the authorship of information about the target, participants valued distant others' comments more than close others' comments. The findings suggested that participants used the perceived social closeness between the target person and the authors of information as meta-information to judge the trustworthiness of the information in social media.

The current study extends previous research by incorporating the perceived social closeness between the authors of information and the target person to whom the information refers as an important moderator into the model. Although previous research explained well the impact of the authorship of information in social media, it did not consider the major feature of social media, social tie-based platforms, and thus did not adequately capture judgment making with conflicting information in social media. By applying social network features to the existing model, the present study confirmed that perceived social closeness functioned as a critical cue for judging the trustworthiness of the available information and that final judgments varied depending on whether and in what way the social closeness was perceived.

One potential concern with this study is the small mean difference of close and distant others' influence on extraversion judgment. Although the different relationships had medium effects on judgment maker's perception, the small mean difference cannot be considered as trivial. However, recent research suggested that extraversion is cued from observable dynamic behavior, such as frequency of posting messages and quick responses than static sources [1, 25]. Thus, the small difference of extraversion judgment could be considered as less sensitive to variation in Facebook pages. On the other hand, one can consider the case of diluting of influence of distant others' comments. When judgment makers think close others barely need to exaggerate or lie about a target, such as the extraversion in this study, some judgment makers can rely more heavily on the close others' comments because the information could be more accurate. Thus, if judgment makers have to make attractiveness judgments of a target, which can be more favorably generated by close others, the effects of distant others' comments can be increased.

6   Conclusions

The abundance of information does not immediately result in the accurate judgment or evaluation. Instead, it may require additional efforts to judge the informational value of the available information. If it is the case, as the volume of available information increases, the amount of effort required will increase accordingly. This, in turn, implies that information systems that merely contain huge amounts of information may not be useful at all, no matter how much information they have. Rather, information systems should be designed to solve *the second-order judgment problems.* In an online market, such system designs are well established to help consumers' judgment-making processes. For example, Netflix recommends videos that might be relevant to a specific customer's interest rather than displays all the videos that are available. In the case of Amazon, if a user values customer ratings, the search result page shows the list in order of highly reviewed products. The recommendation systems in Netflix and Amazon not only save customers' time and effort but encourage informed decisions by providing valuable information specific to each customer.

In the era of the deluge of social media, with the availability of too much information, it is getting more difficult to accurately judge people. As social media is used more and more in everyday life ranging from personal (e.g. online dating) to professional (e.g. the job market), there is increasing friction between impression management and impression formation. In this sense, social media interface designs (e.g., whether or not the information about the available information are provided) can help users effectively seek and process information which will be enable them to eventually make informed judgments and decisions.

References

1. Walther, J.B., Van Der Heide, B., Hamel, L.M., Shulman, H.C.: Self-generated versus other-generated statements and impressions in computer-mediated communication a test of warranting theory using Facebook. Commun. Res. **36**, 229–253 (2009)
2. Donath, J.: Signals in social supernets. J. Comput. Mediat. Commun. **13**, 231–251 (2007)
3. Walther, J.B., Liang, Y.J., Ganster, T., Wohn, D.Y., Emington, J.: Online reviews, helpfulness ratings, and consumer attitudes: an extension of congruity theory to multiple sources in web 2.0. J. Comput. Mediat. Commun. **18**, 97–112 (2012)
4. DeAndrea, D.C., Van Der Heide, B., Easley, N.: How modifying third-party information affects interpersonal impressions and the evaluation of collaborative online media: influence of third-party content on impressions. J. Commun. **65**, 62–78 (2015)
5. Dahlberg, L.: The internet and democratic discourse: exploring the prospects of online deliberative forums extending the public sphere. Inf. Commun. Soc. **4**, 615–633 (2001)
6. Spence, M.: Job market signaling. Q. J. Econ. **87**, 355–374 (1973)
7. Ellison, N., Heino, R., Gibbs, J.: Managing impressions online: self-presentation processes in the online dating environment. J. Comput. Mediat. Commun. **11**, 415–441 (2006)
8. Toma, C.L., Hancock, J.T., Ellison, N.B.: Separating fact from fiction: an examination of deceptive self-presentation in online dating profiles. Pers. Soc. Psychol. Bull. **34**, 1023–1036 (2008)
9. Gibbs, J.L.: Self-presentation in online personals: the role of anticipated future interaction, self-disclosure, and perceived success in internet dating. Commun. Res. **33**, 152–177 (2006)
10. Walther, J.B.: Computer-mediated communication impersonal, interpersonal, and hyperpersonal interaction. Commun. Res. **23**, 3–43 (1996)
11. Walther, J.B., Parks, M.R.: Cues filtered out, cues filtered in: computer-mediated communication and relationships. In: Knapp, M., Daly, J. (eds.) Handbook of Interpersonal Communication, pp. 529–563. Sage Publications, Thousand Oaks (2002)
12. Kwak, H., Lee, C., Park, H., Moon, S.: What is Twitter, a social network or a news media? In: Proceedings of the 19th International Conference on World Wide Web, pp. 591–600. ACM, New York (2010)
13. Wasserman, S., Faust, K.: Social Network Analysis: Methods and Applications. Cambridge University Press, Cambridge (1994)
14. Granovetter, M.S.: The strength of weak ties. Am. J. Sociol. **78**, 1360–1380 (1973)
15. Burt, R.S.: Neighbor Networks: Competitive Advantage Local and Personal. Oxford University Press, Oxford (2011)
16. Ben-Ari, A.: Rethinking closeness and distance in intimate relationships: are they really two opposites? J. Fam. Issues **33**, 391–412 (2012)
17. Birtchnell, J., Voortman, S., DeJong, C., Gordon, D.: Measuring interrelating within couples: The Couple's Relating to Each Other Questionnaires (CREOQ). Psychol. Psychother. Theory Res. Pract. **79**, 339–364 (2006)
18. John, O.P., Srivastava, S.: The big five trait taxonomy: history, measurement, and theoretical perspectives. In: Pervin, L.A., John, O.P., Pervin, L.A. (eds.) Handbook of Personality: Theory and Research, pp. 102–138. Guilford Press, New York (1999)
19. McCrae, R.R., Costa, P.T.: The five-factor theory personality. In: John, O.P., Robins, R.W., Pervin, L.A. (eds.) Handbook of Personality, Third Edition: Theory and Research, pp. 139–153. Guilford Press, New York (2008)
20. Utz, S.: Show me your friends and i will tell you what type of person you are: how one's profile, number of friends, and type of friends influence impression formation on social network sites. J. Comput. Mediat. Commun. **15**, 314–335 (2010)

21. Marcus, B., Machilek, F., Schütz, A.: Personality in cyberspace: personal web sites as media for personality expressions and impressions. J. Pers. Soc. Psychol. **90**, 1014–1031 (2006)
22. Krämer, N.C., Winter, S.: Impression management 2.0: the relationship of self-esteem, extraversion, self-efficacy, and self-presentation within social networking sites. J Media Psychol. **20**, 106–116 (2008)
23. Hancock, J.T., Dunham, P.J.: Impression formation in computer-mediated communication revisited an analysis of the breadth and intensity of impressions. Commun. Res. **28**, 325–347 (2001)
24. Cohen, J.: Statistical Power Analysis for the Behavioral Sciences. L. Erlbaum Associates, Hillsdale (1988)
25. Tong, S.T., Van Der Heide, B., Langwell, L., Walther, J.B.: Too much of a good thing? the relationship between number of friends and interpersonal impressions on Facebook. J. Comput. Mediat. Commun. **13**, 531–549 (2008)

Checking Information Reliability in Social Networks Regarding User Behavior and Developers' Effort to Avoid Misinformation

Alexandre Pinheiro[1]([⊠]), Claudia Cappelli[1], and Cristiano Maciel[2]

[1] Universidade Federal do Estado do Rio de Janeiro - UNIRIO,
Rio de Janeiro, Brazil
{alexandre.pinheiro,claudia.cappelli}@uniriotec.br
[2] Universidade Federal de Mato Grosso - UFMT, Mato Grosso, Brazil
cmaciel@ufmt.br

Abstract. The increasing number of users and data generated is leading the Social Networks to a scenario where the information cannot be verified. Social networks developers have faced problems about unreliable information sharing and availability of content intentionally prepared to confuse or mislead users. This paper presents a solution to add audit capacity in social networks. It is based on a catalog that organizes characteristics and operationalizations which support auditability of information in social networks and a guide that can help developers to build software that allow evaluation of information reliability.

Keywords: Social networks · Information · Developer · Auditability

1 Introduction

Due to the evolution of Online Social Networks (OSNs), a new feature emerges to increase the information exchange in this kind of system. Nowadays OSNs users can publish texts, photos and videos on their profiles, create links, chat by direct messages, manage their relationships, find content and other users who share common interests. Concerning that activities happen in a space with abundant information and where people are responsible for their own publications, it is possible to imagine scenarios where problems may occur due to misunderstandings.

Users frequently believe that all information published on social networks is reliable [1]. This harmful behavior contributes to misinformation spreading, lack of concernment with content evaluation and, in extreme circumstances, users distorting stories believing that opinions without alignment with their point of view are wrong or inaccurate. In most cases, users do not care about evaluating information before reading or discussing about it. Sometimes they think checking information is not important, but most of times they do not do it because OSNs do not have elements to help users with information analysis. An example of fake information listed among the most frequent ones in the social network Facebook [2] is that it owns the copyrights of content published by users. In this hoax, users are encouraged to post on their walls a text

© Springer International Publishing Switzerland 2016
G. Meiselwitz (Ed.): SCSM 2016, LNCS 9742, pp. 151–161, 2016.
DOI: 10.1007/978-3-319-39910-2_15

explaining that they do not allow Facebook[1] to use their publication contents. Information regarding copyrights in social networks that easily clarify this subject can be found at the privacy policy section, but users do not check this section believing the hoax and ending up reinforcing the misinformation chain.

This paper is based on an explanatory research and is presented as follows: the concept of auditability used as reference in this article, the relationship between this concept and other works that apply HCI practices are showed in Sect. 2. A catalog that organizes characteristics and operationalizations for OSNs in order to enable the auditability of information in these systems using influences of the HCI topics is presented in Sect. 3. A guide that can help developers to implement the catalog operationalizations and characteristics described in Sect. 3, followed by some examples of these implementations is available in Sect. 4. In Sect. 5 we present the conclusion of this article and suggestions of future works that can explore the discussed issues.

2   Auditability and HCI Related Issues

An auditable system allows better management of content when information can be discovered and evaluated by a monitoring process [3]. With this idea there are many efforts to evaluate information in all kinds of system, but on dynamic systems such OSNs, information auditability is a task that may consider variables related to the environment, development and the system users. Unlike traditional system audit actions that are performed after the identification of disruptions in data integrity, the definition of auditability enhances the claim of a social network with the capacity of constant audit of information by users and the easy implementation of features that support audits.

The definition of auditability that guides this paper is the capacity of OSNs systems to promote the audit aspects of information exchanged and disseminated on their core, especially the aspects derived and aligned with the definition of auditability described in the catalog of information transparency [4]. Once the concept of auditability of information is considered a quality requirement of software it's necessary to analyze the use of HCI foundations in this topic, especially those related with usability and which encourage users satisfaction, improving their experience of use and information understanding.

2.1   Working on Improvements of OSNs Elements

Some researchers studied the design of elements presented in OSNs and the user behavior during the use of these tools. It's possible to observe that misunderstanding or mistakes committed by users during the use of an element may result in the spread of unreliable information. In some cases, the system element can be manipulated to confuse the user. Given these possibilities, the developer should be prepared to build features that minimize or do not allow the incorrect system usage and dissemination of information created under this circumstances.

---

[1] http://www.facebook.com.

According to Lipford et al. [5], the difficulty that users face to set up their data and privacy settings within social ends up compromising the information exchanges. The research report shows mechanisms made to allow information sharing are purpose fully formulated to explore the users anxiety with the content flow. Those kinds of mechanisms and features do not follow HCI best practices. In these studies, the concern is that elements designed to raise security and privacy for users of social networks do not interact with other parts of the system. Some examples related to the user behavior using dubious elements and settings in Facebook are posts with information having public access when the user wanted to publish only for a group of friends and wrong system language and time zone setup compromising the understanding of displayed information. Despite the focus on improving the implementation of elements responsible for user settings, the research [5] do not worry about other elements in the social network that deal with content spread by users.

The research of Medeiros and Cybis [6] sets users satisfaction assessment activity regarding interfaces built from the use of various International Organization for Standardization (ISO) guidelines regarding user experience. This activity consists of a questionnaire designed to be applied, identify the users satisfaction with usability factors of a given system and associate it with international standards like ISO 9241 [7]. Although the questionnaire was not made for evaluation of user experience on social networks, it served as guidance during the elicitation of characteristics that combines usability and information auditability in the work presented on this paper. The HCI literature is rich of works related to usability of systems and user experience, but it has a lack of associations between the false or unreliable information generation and the difficulty that some users have to deal with the interfaces used to generate the information.

Brown et al. [8] analyzed the content manipulation in OSNs relying on social aspects of information presentation mixed with negligence of users during the system usage. The characteristics of OSNs are widely exploited by individuals interested in all kinds of information distortion. Users can be tricked by a friend request from a suspicious profile, without basic information details or click on a malicious link in a message sent internally by the system messaging service. The approach of this work classifies the types of attacks that may occur and the interface elements that allow information manipulation. An example of this subject is the spreading of users status updates with URLs containing headlines that use sensationalist content or manipulated metadata tags of web pages to attract the user access also known as clickbaits. The HCI concepts cited by the works above and their relation with OSNs elements allowed the choice of characteristics of the catalog of auditability that counts on the importance of user experience and also the implementation of features by system developer.

3 Projecting a Catalog of Information Auditability in Social Networks

To implement auditability characteristics in a social network interface, a catalog of information auditability in social networks was first created [9] and after improved, according to the settings and notations of the NFR Framework [10] and it is composed of features that contribute to achieve information audit capacity for OSNs. This catalog is based on the foundations of an information transparency catalog. A bundle of knowledge represented as a catalog supports the developer with topics constantly highlighted when the influence and contribution of HCI to the process of development of systems is discussed and the mechanisms and operationalization of the catalog considers it, since all user interaction in OSNs is made through their interface elements. The Table 1 shows the catalog with characteristics that must be implemented in a social network to support auditability of information.

Table 1. Catalog characteristics and definitions

Characteristic	Definition
Accountability	Capacity to explain the information
Adaptability	Capacity to show information and elements according user needs
Clarity	Capacity to show information in a clear and comprehensible way
Completeness	Capacity to provide complete information
Composability	Capacity to create elements using information of other elements
Correctness	Capacity to provide information free of errors
Extensibility	Capacity to provide details about the information
Traceability	Capacity to trace information
Uniformity	Capacity to show elements following patterns
Validity	Capacity to make information evaluation
Verifiability	Capacity to certify that the system works properly

3.1 Operationalizations and Mechanisms to Support Auditability

The main actions for the project of a catalog to provide information auditability in social networks were identifying the characteristics that could be applied to improve auditability in OSNs and the next step is to define and explain operationalizations and implementation mechanisms of each characteristic. Although the Table 1 contains 11 characteristics, in this work are addressed the mechanisms and operationalizations those related to spread of misinformation caused by lack of usability in the system or those require the attention of developers about unexpected user behavior. The characteristics chosen as example are: clarity, uniformity and verifiability.

Clarity is one of the key features to ensure a good experience to the user during the use of a system. An approach related to this feature is the capacity of reading graphics elements on a website [11]. The clarity in the system design allows the user to be guided during the system usage, navigation and interaction with the elements in an objective way. On repetitive tasks involving some activity, the clarity characteristic should be applied, indicating the users actions and where they are on the system [7]. Prioritize clarity, simplicity and assessing which elements should be considered in the interface over those one that may disrupt or incorrectly display information to the user [12]. Clarity enables "understanding without training". The human being has a visual system suitable for recognition of elements. When a design element is displayed with clarity the users perception is easier and helps in understanding the whole system [13].

This feature is aligned with clear and objective presentation of images and texts for a variety of purposes like better navigation on pages and menus. The use of a communication language without technical details on the system is also aligned with characteristic of clarity.

Uniformity contributes with the understanding of the meaning of a system by the user, keeping it focused on tasks and preventing distractions to the ambiguities of the application. Uniformity is based on ensure that users do not allocate all their cognitive ability in other marginal aspects of the content of the system. Elements such as visual hierarchy, proportion, alignment and typography appear as important parts of uniformity in a project of a system based in web pages [14]. The formation of a mental model for navigation enables the extraction of information quickly and concisely by the users [15]. The uniformity in design enhances the feeling of efficiency in the use of a system and impacts in sense of control of the people over information [16]. A uniform system has a consistent distribution of elements following layout schemes and enables the user to find similar information in the same position on different sections. The mechanisms of uniformity implementation are aligned with the provision of icons used to navigate in the system, elements with important information and standardization of names.

Verifiability provides details about the system elements that promote the information audit. Interface elements with auditable purpose should be properly identified to the users [17]. The verified users are an example of feature that reinforces auditability concepts. A verified user is recognized by the system authority due his qualities like reputation or because this user is a public personality. Some elements related to navigation security are also indicators of verifiability. For example, a post that contains a secure URL using HTTPS protocol can display the lock icon next to the link, using the same meaning of this icon in web browsers and showing to the users that it is safe to access the published link. This kind of element is important to help the users to judge the legitimacy of the URL and consequently the reliability of information that comes together with this link [18]. The mechanisms of implementation of verifiability will highlight and explain the elements that help with audit of information.

4 A Guide to Implement the Catalog of Information Auditability in Social Networks

After the catalog presented in the Sect. 3, the second tool that composes the solution is a Developer Guide. The guide provides options of system features that once implemented can promote credibility and avoid misinformation in OSNs. The features are based in the catalog of information auditability for social networks and described along with their operationalizations and implementation suggestions, duly adjusted to the context of social networks. It's important to remember that the examples of implementation mechanisms are suggested based in the Facebook, emulating a social network with the same characteristics, but as the system that needs elements with capacity of auditability of information enabled. Examples of implementation of suggested operationalizations mentioned on item 3.1 are presented next, with one or more description of problems that affect OSNs and the orientation for developers to use the guide.

The use of the guide begins at the start of development or in the maintenance phase of a social network. On this moment one or more developers should analyze the system elements looking forward to improve the information auditability. With the guidance, the developers must exercise their capacity of abstraction, analyzing problems related to the auditability information on their systems that already exists or may exist in certain time.

The next step predicts that the developer made a review of the operationalizations proposals listed in the guide. If the developer verifies the absence of an operationalization on his system but the operationalization is present in the guide, the suggested implementations should be evaluated. Stated the unapplied operationalizations, the developer will need to check the suggestions of mechanisms of implementation for it in the guide and if these implementations can be applied to solve some problem or lack of information auditability. If this flow is positively followed, the developer will ensure the auditability capabilities for his social network. If the developer identifies an operationalization or implementation not listed in the guide further research should be made to verify the need to include these items.

4.1   Examples of Characteristics and Operationalizations with Respective Implementations Mechanisms

The guide contains, for each characteristic, an operationalization, an example of a problem to be solved and the suggested implementations to solve or minimize the problem. This information is represented in Tables 2, 3 and 4 for clarity, uniformity and verifiability respectively. The guide also contains one or more images for each possible implementation (Figs. 1, 2 and 3), using the social network Facebook as example.

Table 2.   An example of Clarity characteristic in the guide

Characteristic: clarity
Operationalization
Highlighting identification of the users and their activities.
Problem to be solved
A user shared a post that had been shared a lot of times by other users and the original publication was very old. It is not clear who was the user that originally published the information, the subject is old and may lead to new sharing with content out of the context.
How-to (Implementation mechanisms)
Showing the name of the owner of the original publication and even after several shares of this publication the username should remain highlighted. The system should also highlight the postdate even if it were made a long time ago, preventing reactivations of topics with out-of-time content.

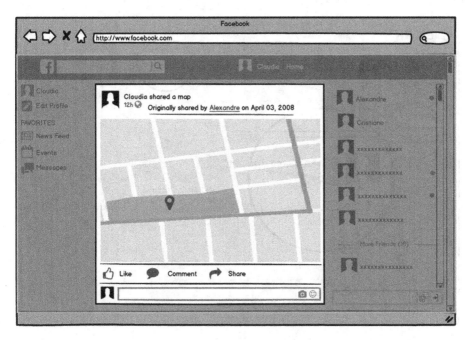

Fig. 1. An image as example for Clarity characteristic implementation

Table 3. An example of Uniformity characteristic in the guide

Characteristic: uniformity

Operationalization
Standardizing elements next to the piece of information. In this approach, standardization portray the use of icons and textual links without ambiguity of meaning across the whole system interface.

Problem to be solved
The system presents the same icons for different functions in the interface, sometimes at the same page. In Fig. 2, the same icon used for notifications is also used to show that a status update can be viewed by any user. Descriptions of links with the same name but different destination pages can be found too.

How-to (Implementation mechanisms)
Designing and using corresponding icons for each function without duplicity. The meanings of the icons should also be appropriate. The links with text description must follow the same orientation.

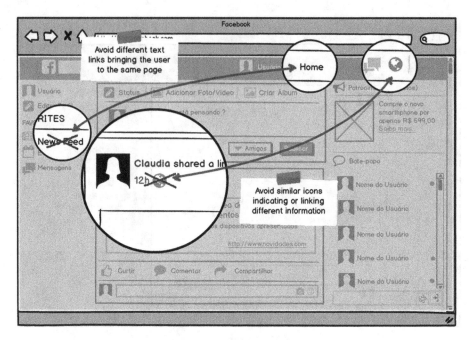

Fig. 2. An image as example for Uniformity characteristic implementation

Table 4. An example of Verifiability characteristic in the guide

Characteristic: verifiability
Operationalization Providing knowledge about the mechanisms of credibility assessment used in OSNs.
Problem to be solved Posts published by a user masquerading his or her real identity, with malicious links referring to sensitive content sites (e.g.: fake URLs of banks or government websites) in order to mislead other users.
How-to (Implementation mechanisms) Displaying an icon with padlock symbol next to the URL that directs to a website with safety certificate (e.g.: HTTPS). The absence of the icon of verified user in the profile of a person that shares content related to sensible information means that this user may have malicious intention and that other users should analyze the publication before any action regarding it.

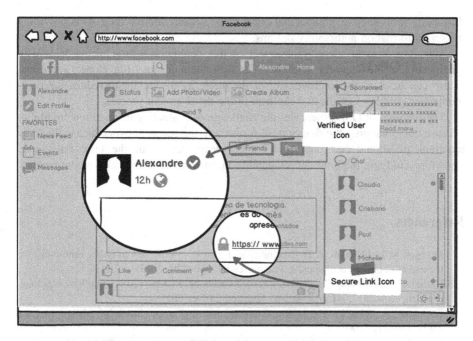

Fig. 3. An image as example for Verifiability characteristic implementation

5 Conclusion

The solutions presented on this paper can contribute to the refinement and quality of the information spread in social networks through the adoption of mechanisms targeting the evaluation of content. Since OSNs have become a source of information, the users should evaluate the content they access before share it or take it as trustful. Another goal is reinforcing the idea that the developer should be concerned about the development of systems with usability and auditability of information for users enabled. The actions that promote the development of tools focused in auditability are aligned with issues of critical design in HCI [19], since the developer needs to analyze the impacts that his software may cause in various aspects (like cultural or ethical) due to the emerging possibilities of design. During the system development, the developer should be prepared to estimate the behavior of users and their understanding of computerized communication technologies with critical skills of seeking, choosing and evaluating information in different contexts [20].

The adoption of the catalog of Information Auditability in Social Networks and the guide, suggests implementations in new OSNs in or for review systems already exist. The challenge in OSNs development, even after the use of guide suggestions presented in this paper is the users cognitive ability, their informational literacy and ability to interpret the spread content and adherence to auditability features.

The future works about the theme addressed in this paper include guide evaluation for refinement and creation of new operationalizations and mechanisms of implementation for auditability. In social networks like Facebook, it's possible to create third-party tools such as plugins that connect the system through their APIs providing missing information auditability options.

Some concepts of semiotics engineering like communicability, which deals with qualification of the communication between the system designer (developer) and users, it also can be used for improvement of the guide in an attempt to reduce the communication problems of the stakeholders in the development process.

The ubiquity of OSNs increases the challenge of evaluating information credibility because only changing the device used for browse the social network means that new requirements should be considered by the developer about the user experience. Therefore, studying the limits of auditability in different devices is also recommended.

References

1. Metzger, M.J., Flanagin, A.J.: Credibility and trust of information in online environments: the use of cognitive heuristics. J. Pragmatics **59**, 210–220 (2013)
2. Dashevsky, E.: 10 Huge Hoaxes that Fooled Facebook. PCMag (2015). http://www.pcmag.com/article2/0,2817,2475514,00.asp. Accessed 28 Dez 2015
3. Buchanan, S., Gibb, F.: The information audit: role and scope. Int. J. Inf. Manag. Elsevier **27**(3), 159–172 (2007)
4. Cappelli, C.: An approach for business processes transparency using aspects. Dissertation, Pontifícia Universidade Católica do Rio de Janeiro (2009)
5. Lipford, H.R, Besmer A, Watson, J.: Understanding Privacy Settings in Facebook with an Audience View. vol. 8, pp. 1–8. UPSEC (2008)
6. Medeiros, M, Cybis, W.: Método de Avaliação de Usabilidade de Software a partir da Satisfação de Usuários e da Aplicação de Quesitos da Norma ISO 9241. In: Proceedings of IHC'2000-III Workshop sobre Fatores Humanos em Sistemas de Computação. pp. 93–101 (2000)
7. Ergonomics of Human-system Interaction, Part 151: Guidance on World Wide Web User Interfaces. ISO 9241–151:2008(E), Switzerland
8. Brown, G, Howe, T, Ihbe, M, Prakash, A, Borders, K.: Social networks and context-aware spam. In: Proceedings of the 2008 ACM Conference on Computer Supported Cooperative Work, pp. 403–412 (2008)
9. Pinheiro, A., Cappelli, C., Maciel, C.: Increasing information auditability for social network users. In: Yamamoto, S. (ed.) HCI 2014, Part I. LNCS, vol. 8521, pp. 536–547. Springer, Heidelberg (2014)
10. Chung, L., Nixon, B.A., Yu, E., Mylopoulos, J.: Non-functional Requirements in Software Engineering. Springer Science & Business Media, New York (2002)
11. Misanchuk, E.R, Schwier, R.A, Boling, E.: Visual design for instructional multimedia. In: World Conference on Educational Multimedia, Hypermedia and Telecommunications. n.1, p. 1621 (1999)
12. WCAG2 (2016) Web Content Accessibility Guidelines 2.0. World Wide Web Consortium (W3C). https://www.w3.org/TR/WCAG20/. Accessed 05 Jan 2016
13. Ware, C.: Information Visualization: Perception for Design. Elsevier, Amsterdam (2012)
14. Faraday, P.: Visually critiquing web pages. In: Correia, N., Chambel, T., Davenport, G. (eds.) Multimedia'99. Eurographics, pp. 155–166. Springer, Vienna (2000)
15. Hervás, R., Bravo, J.: Towards the ubiquitous visualization: adaptive user-interfaces based on the semantic web. Interact. Comput. **23**(1), 40–56 (2011). Oxford University Press

16. Song, J, Zahedi, F.: Web design in E-commerce: a theory and empirical analysis. In: ICIS 2001 Proceedings, p. 24 (2001)
17. Engenharia de software– Qualidade de produto - Modelo de qualidade, Parte 1. NBR ISO/IEC 9126-1: 2003, Brazil
18. Alsharnouby, M., Alaca, F., Chiasson, S.: Why phishing still works: user strategies for combating phishing attacks. Int. J. Human Comput. Stud. **82**, 69–82 (2015)
19. Pierce, J, Sengers, P, Hirsch, T, Jenkins, T, Gaver, W, DiSalvo, C.: Expanding and refining design and criticality in HCI. In: Proceedings of the 33rd Annual ACM Conference on Human Factors in Computing Systems, pp. 2083–2092 (2015)
20. Silva, A.M.: Inclusão Digital e Literacia Informacional em Ciência da Informação. Revista PRISMA.COM ed. 7 (2010)

The Influence of Technology on Romantic Relationships: Understanding Online Dating

Stephanie Tom Tong[1(✉)], Jeffrey T. Hancock[2], and Richard B. Slatcher[3]

[1] Department of Communication, Wayne State University, Detroit, MI, USA
`stephanie.tong@wayne.edu`
[2] Department of Communication, Stanford University, Palo Alto, CA, USA
`jeff.hancock@stanford.edu`
[3] Department of Psychology, Wayne State University, Detroit, MI, USA
`slatcher@wayne.edu`

Abstract. A culture's social fabric is deeply dependent on how its members establish romantic bonds. What happens when the way those bonds are formed is radically changed over the course of a single generation? This is the case with the rise of online dating, which is now the second most common way for people to meet a romantic partner. Despite existing research exploring issues such as mate selection, self-presentation, and impressions, we still do not know how online dating systems affect people's perceptions—about technology, relationships, romantic partners, and themselves—and how these perceptions affect behavior. In this paper, we introduce and explicate the *Source Multiplicity, Attribution, Recognition, and Transformation (SMART) Model of Online Dating*. The SMART model is a comprehensive theoretical framework that has interdisciplinary roots in human-computer interaction (HCI), computer-mediated communication (CMC), psychology, and decision science.

Keywords: Online dating · Decision-making · Choice · Algorithms · System design · Affordances

1 Introduction

Technology often plays an invisible role in our lives by quietly influencing our perceptions, communication, and behavior. Since "good design" is often seamless, the inner-workings of many systems are hidden from users' view. Particularly influential are the algorithms that silently lurk in background of many computing systems. Through the organization and presentation of information, algorithms are capable of shaping human behavior by recommending what products to buy or which friends to include in our social networks. Yet despite their ubiquity, we still don't know how most people perceive the algorithms that are embedded in the systems that they use every day and how such perceptions affect behavior. How much trust do users place in technology when making decisions? Are people aware of technology's influence, or do they simply take these systems for granted?

© Springer International Publishing Switzerland 2016
G. Meiselwitz (Ed.): SCSM 2016, LNCS 9742, pp. 162–173, 2016.
DOI: 10.1007/978-3-319-39910-2_16

Researchers have recently called for more investigation into the impact of algorithms on human decision making—and no decisions are more important than the ones people make about their personal relationships. With over 30 million people using online dating, the algorithms embedded in dating websites have an enormous influence over the formation of relational bonds. A review of the existing online dating research shows that social scientists have examined factors such as self-presentation, ethnicity/race, and physical attractiveness in mate selection, but few have investigated how sociotechnical features like algorithms influence people's behaviors and decisions. In contrast, work in decision science, human-computer interaction (HCI), and information science (IS) has examined algorithmic influence in contexts like product selection and online shopping. But online dating provides a unique, theoretically rich context that demands research attention given the important role it now plays in human bonding. What happens when systems make recommendations about people instead of products? Is the popular use of online dating websites changing the landscape of romantic relationship formation in American society? To answer these questions, we propose the SMART model to explain how technology influences the perceptions, attributions, and decisions people make in online dating. This paper begins by outlining important theoretical frameworks that provide the foundation for the SMART model. We then proceed by defining each component of the model in detail.

2   The Algorithmic Curation of Choice

Online dating companies often advertise that they provide users with access to a large dating pool filled with potential partners. But is this too much of a good thing? Theories in decision science and psychology state that when people are faced with an enormous amount of selection they are often unable to evaluate all of their available options. As a result, most people will screen options and then filter down to a smaller choice set that contains a smaller number of promising alternatives [1]. Work in HCI has found that computer-curated choice sets are capable of influencing people's decisions by directing attention toward specific options [2]. Oftentimes, computer-curated choice is a simple default rather than calculated strategy: research suggests that most people are unaware of the presence of algorithms in the systems they use [3, 4]. But because most existing studies have examined algorithmic influence in contexts like online shopping, movie selection, and news aggregators [5–7], the impact of algorithms on choice sets featuring potential wives, husbands, and lovers is unknown. Do daters naively assume that the computer-curated alternatives are the best or only alternatives from which to choose? And, to the extent that they are conscious of the algorithmic involvement, do they view it as an advantage to finding love? As current research is silent on these issues, SMART examines how the algorithms in dating websites affect people's attention to alternatives during romantic mate selection.

3   Online Self-Presentation and Impression Formation

A central framework embedded in the foundation of SMART is the hyperpersonal model of CMC [8] which has been used by many scholars in communication to explain people's self-presentation and impression formation behaviors in online environments. In the model, senders are predicted to use the sociotechnical features of CMC channels (e.g., editing, asynchronicity) for selective-self presentation, allowing them to display especially desirable characteristics to others. As receivers get to know senders based on their selectively self-presented attributes, they often form overly idealized impressions. Lastly, mediated interaction between senders and receivers is predicted to form a reciprocal feedback loop that simultaneously reinforces the other three components as interaction unfolds between partners creating "hyper"-personal effects.

Applications of the hyperpersonal model to online dating have found robust evidence of selective self-presentation: In an investigation of self-authored dating profiles, Hancock et al. [9] found that on average, heavier daters tended to strategically represent themselves as weighing less than they actually did. Similarly, with respect to height, shorter daters presented themselves as being taller than they were in reality. Hitsch et al. [10] found that that the body-mass index reported by their sample of online daters was distinctly lower than the national average. And several respondents in Ellison et al.'s [11] study reported strategically exploiting CMC features for self-presentational gain. Furthermore, literature suggests that most online daters are aware that others engage in selective self-presentation: The more daters tend to misrepresent themselves in their profiles, the more they believe others do the same [11–13].

Yet a central issue that is overlooked by many of these existing online dating studies is how daters' knowledge of others' (and their own) self-presentation behaviors may affect how they judge the credibility of others' information as they make mate selection decisions. Online daters' sharpened recognition of information manipulation in CMC may influence the ways in which they process information, form attributions, and make decisions.

4   Information, Feedback and Self-Perception

The hyperpersonal model has also been used to examine the intrapersonal (i.e., individual-level) effects of online self-presentation. Integrating the hyperpersonal model with theory from psychology, Gonzales and Hancock [14] examined *identity shift*, which refers to the changes in self-perception that result from observations of one's own self-presentation behaviors in public online settings. In their study, participants (Ps) were asked to display either introversion or extraversion in written responses to interview questions. Identity shift occurred when Ps came to view themselves as being more like the trait they were asked to portray by the end of the interview. Notably, identity shift was stronger when Ps believed their responses were being collected and posted to an online weblog versus a private text file. The public nature of blogs made Ps more likely to incorporate their openly displayed behaviors into their self-concepts in an effort to balance their external performance with internal identity.

Walther et al. [15] extended Gonzales and Hancock's findings by examining the additive effects selective self-presentation and feedback. In their experiment, Ps performed the same interview task in public blog and private text document settings. Afterwards, half of the Ps were given (bogus) feedback on their responses, while the other half received no feedback. Those in saw feedback were led to believe that it came from either a person (i.e., a college student who supposedly read blog responses looking for introversion/extraversion) or the computer system (i.e., results of a software program that supposedly analyzed responses for linguistic markers of introversion/extraversion). Results indicated that Ps who received feedback confirming their self-presented introversion or extraversion experienced greater identity shift in the direction of enacted personality characteristics compared to those who saw no feedback. This was true for Ps who saw human-generated and system-generated feedback.

As self-presentation is both highly selective and very public in online dating contexts, Gonzales and Hancock's study provides good evidence to predict the occurrence of transformative identity shift effects on daters' self-concepts. And while Walther et al. provide a solid basis for predicting feedback effects, their work also raises questions about how variations in the valence of that feedback would affect self-perception. Ps receiving feedback in this study only saw information that was consistent with their self-presentation of introversion or extraversion. Within online dating contexts, it is likely that daters will sometimes receive inconsistent feedback from others who reject or refuse them. Thus daters' reactions to inconsistent feedback remain unknown.

5   The SMART Model

The SMART model is grounded in the hyperpersonal model of CMC, but we also rely heavily on models of decision making, psychological theories of self-perception, and design research from HCI. In the SMART model, source multiplicity reflects the two classifications of information sources present in online dating: human information sources and technological information sources. Both are predicted to influence daters' attributions regarding partners, decisions during mate selection, and expectations for relational development. Secondly, a sub-process predicted to affect daters' information processing is their level of conscious recognition of technology during online relationship formation. Lastly, a second set of arrows running from attribution to information sources in a cyclic fashion indicates transformative feedback effects: As daters process information to make attributions, it is predicted that they will experience reciprocal effects on identity, thereby transforming self-perception (Fig. 1).

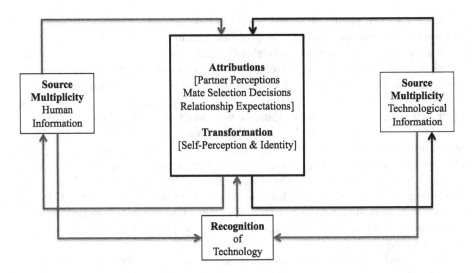

Fig. 1. The Source Multiplicity, Attribution, Recognition, and Transformation (SMART) Model of Online Dating.

6   Source Multiplicity

6.1   Human-Sourced Information

Previous CMC research indicates that people evaluate others' self-authored profile information when forming impressions and making attributions in contexts like Facebook [16]. In line with this research, we assert that such "human-sourced" profile content is important information used in mate selection. However, because most profile content is self-authored, daters must also assess the credibility of the others' self-presented information when making attributions. Daters do this by evaluating the *warranting value* of information. *Warranting value* refers to the extent to which people believe a piece of information is immune to manipulation by the source it describes [17]. For example, Abby's self-authored declaration of "I'm a fantastic rock climber" would have comparatively less warranting value than if she were to post a link from her profile to *Rock & Ice Magazine* that announces her victory at a recent competition. Because the competition results are being communicated by a third-party source, this information is presumably more difficult for Abby to manipulate, thus giving it greater warranting value. SMART asserts that the judgments daters' make regarding the warranting value of others' information affects the way they process and evaluate information during initial stages of profile review.

6.2   Technology-Sourced Information

As noted above, online dating systems have the potential to influence daters' mate selection decisions by algorithmically aggregating alternatives into computer-curated choice sets. Consistent with this reasoning, SMART predicts that the extent to which algorithms are featured in the design of dating systems may also affect people's subsequent interpersonal attributions. Of the many dating websites currently available, most follow one of two primary designs that reflect different levels of algorithmic involvement: Algorithmically-driven websites, such as eHarmony.com, begin by asking daters to supply information about their personalities, interests, and mate preferences through lengthy questionnaires. Responses are then fed into the company's algorithm, which matches partners based on the similarity or complementarity of those dimensions [18]. Contrastingly, "see-and-screen" websites like Match.com allow user to browse through a database of profiles. These websites provide search tools that help daters narrow down the list of potential mates.

One critical way these two design formats differ is the amount of perceived control daters experience when making mate selection decisions. Research from psychology [19] has documented the *illusion of control* effect, defined as people's unrealistically high level of confidence in their ability to exert influence over the outcomes of chance-based events. Romance can feel to many people like a chance-based or random event. Following this logic, it would appear that most people would prefer to maintain control over mate selection decisions. In fact, work in cognitive science [20] suggests that since choice allows humans to feel capable of regulating our environment we have adapted to seek it out as a way to boost our self-efficacy.

Thus compared to the one-on-one matching process of algorithmic websites, see-and-screen websites give daters more control over mate selection by allowing them to view the entire dating pool to make decisions. However, the increased control may also produce an increased likelihood of choice overload, which often occurs when people are overwhelmed with too many options. Iyengar and Lepper [21] demonstrated how the feelings of choice overload created during product selection resulted in diminished decision making satisfaction, greater difficulty, and more frustration. Additionally, they suggest that choice overload may be "further exacerbated" in contexts where "(a) the costs associated with making the 'wrong' choice, or even beliefs that there are truly 'wrong' choices, are much more prominent, and/or (b) substantial time and effort would be required for choices to make truly informed comparisons among alternatives" (p. 1004). Both conditions apply to the decision context of partner selection in online dating where the costs of choosing the "wrong" partner are high, and the time and effort needed to evaluate each person in the dating pool are extensive. When online daters feel overwhelmed by too much choice, they may rely on algorithms to ease choice overload and simplify mate selection.

As daters process information in the source multiplicity stage, SMART asserts that they use that information to make attributions about (a) potential partners' attractiveness and (b) a relationship's potential for future romantic development. Regarding human information sources, previous research has shown that people assign information with a higher warranting value more "attributional weight" during the impression formation process. Effects have been demonstrated in venues such as Yelp.com [22] and Facebook [23], but the effects of judgments of warranting value on attributions in online dating environments have not yet been tested.

Regarding *technological information sources*, we noted in the source multiplicity section how differences in system design features, such as algorithms, could affect the amount of control daters experience during mate selection. SMART predicts that the amount of control afforded by different dating systems will affect daters' attributions about the decision making process itself, prospective romantic partners, and a relationship's future potential.

Our preliminary experiment investigating how the differences in the design of *algorithm-based* and *see-and-screen* dating websites influence daters' attributions regarding: (a) psychological feelings of personal control over mate selection, (b) satisfaction with the mate selection decision making process, and (c) expectations regarding the relationship's potential for future development. Using an adaptation of the "bogus stranger" paradigm, 43 participants (Ps) were recruited and told that they were helping to test a new dating website aimed at college-aged singles. Ps developed profiles and filled out questionnaires about their mate preferences. A group of 24 Ps randomly assigned to the algorithm condition received a single profile (ostensibly) chosen by the dating system's algorithm as their most "optimal" partner match. This condition was designed to mirror websites like eHarmony that match daters on a one-on-one basis. Another 19 Ps randomly assigned to the see-and-screen condition were given four (bogus) profiles and asked to select the one person they found most attractive. This condition reflected websites like Match.com, which allow daters to maintain more control over mate selection. In actuality, all profiles that Ps saw were created by the researchers using content gathered from publicly available dating profiles. Profiles were pretested to ensure that there were no systematic differences in attractiveness prior to being used in the main study. Ps then completed measures of the dependent attribution variables detailed above. The results indicated:

- Website design affected daters' feelings of *personal control* over mate selection decisions, such that daters felt more control in see-and-screen formats than algorithmic formats
- Differences in personal control affected the overall amount of *satisfaction* daters' experienced during the decision making process, such that less control resulted in less satisfaction
- Decision making satisfaction mediated the relationship between control and daters' overall feelings of enthusiasm regarding *future relationship pursuit*

Taken together, findings from our preliminary test of SMART's source multiplicity and attribution components suggest that the ways in which dating systems present information can impact daters' attributions, decision making, and expectations regarding romantic relationships. Consistent with theory from psychology and cognitive science we found computer-supported decision making reduced feelings of personal choice and perceived control over mate selection, which ultimately reduced people's optimism about the relationship's developmental potential.

While promising, our initial findings suggest necessary extensions: First, daters saw different amounts of profiles across see-and-screen and algorithm conditions (e.g., four vs. one). The choice to operationalize the algorithm condition as a single, optimal profile was a deliberate decision to maximize ecological validity of algorithmically-based dating systems. According to the frequently asked questions portion of their website, eHarmony states that it may be a while before daters receive any matches, with some people being "not suitable" for matching due to various reasons. On average, eHarmony states most daters receive only 10 to 25 matches per year. Therefore, the choice to mirror the "one-on-one" matching procedures of algorithmic websites motivated our experimental manipulation of the algorithm condition. However, we realize that our effort to reproduce user experience of dating websites like eHarmony may be perceived as a naturally-occurring confound between the see-and-screen and algorithm conditions. Relatedly, our decision to create choice sets in the see-and-screen condition that contained only four profiles was guided by previous research [24]. But it remains to be seen if the designs of dating websites function the same way when the amount of choice varies. Amount of choice (e.g., low, moderate, high) becomes a critical process variable, because as amount of choice increases, the likelihood of overload also increases [22].

7   Recognition of Algorithmic Involvement

The next component of the SMART model addresses the issue of technological recognition. Research in HCI and IS suggests that most people remain unaware of the algorithms embedded in many popular platforms. This is especially true in online dating where companies often highlight the power of their algorithms while simultaneously obscuring their operation. For example, eHarmony members pay a monthly fee of $19.65 to get matched with others based on eHarmony's algorithm that features "29 dimensions of compatibility." Given that eHarmony surpassed the $1 billion revenue mark in 2010, people are clearly willing to pay for the privilege of algorithmic selection in their search for love. Even though eHarmony does not provide its members with an explanation of how the algorithm actually works, they have successfully created the semblance of algorithmic effectiveness as an advantage in romantic relationship formation—whether or not they empirically produce better romantic matches may not affect their bottom line [18]. Importantly, we are not interested in uncovering the actual technical processes of different dating website algorithms. Instead, SMART predicts that it is people's perceptions of what algorithms do that affect the subsequent stages of relationship formation: If people's perceptions shape their reality, then we must have a better understanding of perceptions to understand how they influence behavior [4].

7.1   Subconscious Attention During Decision Making

In addition to people's conscious recognition of technological influence, research from many fields has measured people's subconscious attention to information by tracking their eye movement behaviors (e.g., pupil dilation, gaze duration, scanpath). To obtain a complete understanding of people's recognition of technology in online dating, SMART explores three issues regarding daters' attention.

First, SMART examines subconscious attention and information utility. Previous large-scale studies of mate selection from psychology, sociology, and IS have suggested that human characteristics such as physical attractiveness, race, or age [25], are the most influential. However, such assertions have not been empirically verified; daters' attention to system-generated content (i.e., match scores, rankings, etc.) may also influence attributions and decisions.

Secondly, SMART examines how a website's visual layout affects daters' attention to information. Work in decision science and HCI has found evidence of stimulus-driven attention: Factors like size, saliency, and viewing position have all been shown to influence attention to and processing of information [see for review, 26].

Lastly, SMART examines the nature of attention processes over time. Consumer behavior research has demonstrated learning effects in which people who engaged in repeated decision making tasks learned to focus their gaze on more important attributes, and reduced gaze fixations on less salient information [27]. It is possible that learning effects also occur as daters become more familiar with the system and selection task.

8   Transformation of Self-Perception Through Feedback

SMART predicts that daters' recognition and interpretation of information from multiple sources will not only produce attributional effects at the interpersonal level, but also at the individual level by transforming daters' self-concept. Identity shift refers to changes in self-perception that arise from daters' observations of their own self-presentation behaviors in public settings. The environment of online dating is ripe for triggering identity shift given that: (a) daters consistently strive to present themselves as attractively as possible, (b) the online dating arena is by nature very public, and (c) daters often seek confirmation of their self-presented attractiveness in the form of attention, communications, and flirtations from other daters.

While Walther et al. [15] indicated that confirmatory feedback increases the likelihood of online identity shift, the SMART model extends previous CMC research to consider the role of negative, or disconfirmatory, feedback. Research from psychology suggests that when faced with negative feedback like rejection, daters may engage in protective tactics such as self-serving bias, which would allow them to maintain their own positive self-perception by derogating the source of the negative feedback [28]. Thus when daters are rejected, they might actually "double down" on their self-perception, creating a stronger belief in their own attractiveness, and displaying a greater propensity to attack the source of the rejection.

But with regard to romantic rejection in online dating, a novel issue that arises is the concept of feedback absence. Since daters may be inundated with request messages, their ability to respond to each and every person is limited [13]. As a result, daters may ignore messages from people that they do not find attractive by simply being unresponsive. *Online Dating for Dummies* advises that "Internet-appropriate ways to say no" include: "Don't reply at all, ever. Just delete the message. In Internet-speak, this tactic is completely understood to mean 'Not interested at all, ever'" [29]. However, as there is little existing psychological or communication theory to predict daters' response to lack of feedback, the transformation component of the SMART model advances an important question about feedback absence.

8.1   Interaction of Source Multiplicity and Transformation

As feedback can be communicated by human and system sources in dating websites, SMART predicts that the source multiplicity component will interact with feedback to produce transformative effects on self-perception. Though dating systems vary in the type of feedback they provide to their users, some examples include: "winks," or "smiles," automated indications that a dater has viewed a specific profile, and a dater's last active login into the system. Some platforms also provide notifications indicating when a message has been seen or read, as well as timestamps noting time/date of delivery. Match.com provides a "No Thanks" button that, when clicked, sends a pre-scripted, automated romantic refusal message [29]. Previous research indicates that these system-generated cues are used in online impression formation [11], but their role as a form of feedback affecting self-perception is unknown.

To illustrate the transformative effect of system-generated feedback on self-perception, imagine Abby sends a message to Bill using Match.com's messaging system that reads: "Hi, Bill, loved your profile. We have so much in common, we should chat!" A week later, Abby still has not received a reply from Bill, but when she checks her Match.com account, she finds a system-generated cue telling her that Bill viewed her profile five days ago. She also receives the system notification: "message read 5 days ago". Abby now knows that Bill viewed her profile and read her message, but never responded. Interestingly, Abby is only made aware of Bill's lack of response because of the system's responsiveness.

So how does this system feedback affect Abby's self-perception? The existing theories from psychology, communication, and HCI point in three different directions: Self-serving bias research from psychology would predict that Abby would be most likely to derogate Bill in this scenario ("Bill never responded, he must be a jerk"). Alternatively, the hyperpersonal model of CMC and identity shift research suggest Abby would internalize Bill's lack of feedback as part of her own self-concept ("Bill never responded; I must not be as attractive as I thought"). Work from HCI might suggest Abby would use the system as an attributional "scapegoat" ("Bill never responded; Match.com is not giving me access to the right kind of guys"). Because the SMART model considers theory from all three disciplines, it offers novel, but competing, predictions about how these dynamics of feedback might affect daters' self concept. Therefore, a central focus within the transformation component of SMART is to uncover daters' attributional responses to system- and human-generated feedback as they attempt to protect their self-perception.

9   Conclusions

It is clear that the process of relationship formation is being shaped mediated technology. Drawing from communication science, social psychology, and HCI, the SMART model offers a unique interdisciplinary conceptualization of this process. Although only one preliminary test of the model's first component has been conducted, more is underway. Researchers should continue to look across disciplines to provide more powerful and parsimonious explanations for human behavior. Future research will tell us if the components of SMART offer such an explanation regarding online dating and mate selection.

References

1. Howard, J.A., Sheth, J.N.: The Theory of Buyer Behavior. John Wiley, New York (1969)
2. Haubl, G., Trifts, V.: Consumer decision making in online shopping environments: the effects of interactive decision aids. Mark. Sci. **19**, 4–21 (2014)
3. Gillespie, T.: The relevance of algorithms. In: Gillespie, T., Boczkowski, P., Foot, K. (eds.) Media Technologies. MIT Press, Cambridge (2014)
4. Sandvig, C., Karahalios, K., Langbort, C.: Uncovering Algorithms. http://cyber.law.harvard.edu/events/luncheon/2014/07/sandvigkarahalios
5. Castagnos, S., Jones, N., Pu, P.: Eye-tracking product recommenders' usage. In: Proceedings of the Fourth ACM Conference on Recommender Systems, RecSys 2010, pp. 29–36. ACM Press, New York (2010)
6. Hallinan, B., Striphas, T.: Recommended for you: The Netflix prize and the production of algorithmic culture. New Media Soc. **18**, 117–137 (2016)
7. Sundar, S.S., Nass, C.: Conceptualizing sources in online news. J. Comm. **51**, 57–72 (2001)
8. Walther, J.B.: Computer-mediated communication: Impersonal, interpersonal, and hyperpersonal interaction. Comm. Res. **23**, 3–43 (1996)
9. Hancock, J. T., Toma, C., Ellison, N.: The truth about lying in online dating profiles. In: Proceedings of SIGCHI Conference on Human factors in Computing Systems, CHI 2007, pp. 449–452. ACM Press, New York (2007)
10. Hitsch, G.J., Hortacsu, A., Ariely, D.: Matching and sorting in online dating. Am. Econ. Rev. **100**, 130–163 (2010)
11. Ellison, N., Heino, R., Gibbs, J.: Managing impressions online: Self-Presentation processes in the online dating environment. J. Comp.-Med. Comm. **11**, 415–441 (2010)
12. DeAndrea, D.C., Tong, S.T., Liang, Y., Levine, T.R., Walther, J.B.: When do people misrepresent themselves to others? The effects of social desirability, accountability, and ground truth on deceptive self-presentations. J. Comm. **62**, 400–417 (2012)
13. Fiore, A.T., Donath, J.S.: Online personals: an overview. In: Extended Abstracts on Human Factors in Computing Systems, CHI 2004, pp. 1395–1398. ACM Press, New York (2004)
14. Gonzales, A.L., Hancock, J.T.: Identity shift in computer-mediated environments. Med. Psych. **11**, 167–185 (2008)
15. Walther, J.B., Liang, Y.J., DeAndrea, D.C., Tong, S.T., Carr, C.T., Spottswood, E.L., Amichai-Hamburger, Y.: The effect of feedback on identity shift in computer-mediated communication. Media Psych. **14**, 1–26 (2011)
16. Tong, S.T., Van Der Heide, B., Langwell, L., Walther, J.B.: Too much of a good thing? The relationship between number of friends and interpersonal impressions on Facebook. J. Comp.-Med. Comm. **13**, 531–549 (2008)
17. DeAndrea, D.C.: Advancing warranting theory. Comm. Theory **24**, 186–204 (2014)
18. Finkel, E.J., Eastwick, P.W., Karney, B.R., Reis, H.T., Sprecher, S.: Online dating: a critical analysis from the perspective of psychological science. Psych. Sci. Pub. Int. **13**, 3–66 (2012)
19. Langer, E.: The illusion of control. J. Pers. Soc. Psych. **32**, 311–328 (1975)
20. Leotti, L.A., Iyengar, S.S., Ochsner, K.N.: Born to choose: the origins and value of the need for control. Trends Cog. Sci. **14**, 457–463 (2010)
21. Iyengar, S.S., Lepper, M.R.: When choice is demotivating: Can one desire too much of a good thing? Pers. Pro. Indiv. Diff. **79**, 995–1006 (2000)
22. Lim, Y.-S., Van Der Heide, B.: Evaluating the wisdom of strangers: the perceived credibility of online consumer reviews on Yelp. J. Comp.-Med. Comm. **20**, 67–82 (2015)

23. Walther, J.B., Van Der Heide, B., Hamel, L.M., Shulman, H.C.: Self-generated versus other-generated statements and impressions in computer-mediated communication: A test of warranting theory using Facebook. Comm. Res. **36**, 229–253 (2009)
24. Lenton, A.P., Fasolo, B., Todd, P.M.: The relationship between number of potential mates and mating skew in humans. Ani. Beh. **77**, 55–60 (2008)
25. Rudder, C.: Dataclysm: Who We Are (When We Think No One's Looking). Crown Publishing, New York (2014)
26. Orquin, J.L.: Mueller Loose, S. Attention and choice: a review on eye movements in decision making. Acta Psychol. **144**, 190–206 (2013)
27. Jovancevic-Misc, J., Hayhoe, M.: Adaptive gaze control in natural environments. J. Neuro. **29**, 6234–6238 (2009)
28. Campbell, W.K., Sedikides, C.: Self-threat magnifies the self-serving bias: a meta-analytic integration. Rev. Gen. Psych. **3**, 23–43 (1995)
29. Tong, S.T., Walther, J.B.: Just say "No thanks": The effects of romantic rejection across computer-mediated communication. J. Soc. Per. Rel. **28**, 488–506 (2011)

Social Media, Policy, Politics and Engagement

Social Communities in Urban Mobility Systems

Tarfah Alrashed[1(✉)], Jumana Almahmoud[1], Mohamad Alrished[1],
Sattam Alsubaiee[1], Mansour Alsaleh[1],
and Carlos Sandoval Olascoaga[2]

[1] Center for Complex Engineering Systems CCES, King Abdulaziz City
for Science and Technology, Riyadh, Saudi Arabia
{t.alrashed, j.almahmoud, m.alrishe,
s.alsubaiee, m.alsaleh}@cces-kacst-mit.org
[2] Massachusetts Institute of Technology MIT, Cambridge, MA, USA
csandova@mit.edu

Abstract. Social and traffic dynamics of mobility in urban areas can be derived
from people's behavior on social networks. In this research study, we take steps
towards a conceptual framework for visualizing the social and traffic dynamics
of urban mobility. We present an overview of transportation modes and services
that have a digital presence, and illustrate these with a number of examples,
along with the information available from public and private modes of transportation. Further, we derive insights gained from investigating social media
communities that are active in the scope of mobility, using Saudi Arabia as a
case study. By conducting an exploratory survey of related social media communities, we describe the socio-cultural factors that were considered in the
design of mobility-oriented services. We also provide insights for investigating
social communities in urban mobility.

Keywords: Mobility · Transportation · Social Computing · Location Sensing ·
Social Network Analysis

1 Introduction

The widespread use of online social media and the ubiquity of low cost computing
have increased the possibilities for understanding socio-cultural behaviors in urban
mobility and the attitudes of people in transit. At the same time, these aspects have
facilitated opportunities to make shared-interest social communities accessible,
detectable, and comprehensible [28]. Gadgets such as smartphones, tablets, personal
computers, and other GPS-enabled devices leave digital footprints of the user's
activities. These proliferating digital footprints that people leave as they crisscross
cities offer a treasure trove of mobility patterns and socio-cultural information [29].
This information is valuable for understating the social and traffic dynamics in an urban
area and can consequently aid in city planning, policymaking, and traffic management.
The individual, community, city, and regional dynamics can be extracted from the
interconnected information that is readily available on social media. Despite the rapid
growth in the social media presence of mobility services and communities in Saudi
Arabia, the understanding of the landscape of services in the geographic region is

© Springer International Publishing Switzerland 2016
G. Meiselwitz (Ed.): SCSM 2016, LNCS 9742, pp. 177–187, 2016.
DOI: 10.1007/978-3-319-39910-2_17

inadequate and the literature on the topic is scattered across multiple disciplines [1]. This paper aims to address this issue by providing a descriptive overview of the Web landscape of mobility services and social communities.

While researchers have sought insights from communal behavior in contexts of mobility in countries across the world [2, 3], the literature is scarce on the Arab region in general and Saudi Arabia specifically. However, recent studies have shown that social media activity is rapidly growing in Saudi Arabia [4, 5]. In fact, Saudi Arabia has one of the highest penetration rates in the world when it comes to social media interactions [24]. However, it is surprising that the understanding of both the use of social media by Saudi residents and the impact of such are mostly derived from anecdotal sources (e.g. news reports and a scarce body of scholarly research on social analytics). What remains to be examined are the self-organizing urban mobility systems that have emerged in Saudi Arabia in recent years.

This research goal is to understand the transportation modes and services that have a digital presence in social media as well as the diffusion of technology in the context of urban mobility systems. More specifically, the following research questions have been formulated: What are the entities that have a digital presence, and how are they utilizing existing social media platforms? To answer these questions, an exploratory study of social communities have been conducted—contrasting privately owned and government public services—in order to understand the landscape and modes of communication of entities that are operating in the context of urban mobility in Saudi Arabia.

2   Related Work

In urban contexts, mobility is a multidisciplinary field. This research intersects social analytics, urban studies, transportation, civil engineering, planning, and policy. Prior research has often focused on each of the above separately and from a specific point of view [25–27]. This paper provides an overview of social communities of mobility from those different perspectives. The following subsection outlines Saudi Arabia as a unique context of study for social and traffic dynamics and the mobility research for examining social and traffic dynamics.

2.1   Saudi Arabia as a Unique Context of Study for Social and Traffic Dynamics

The investment in taxi service app companies has rapidly grown globally to more than $1 billion in venture capital [6]. Saudi Arabia has a population of about 30 million and has a markedly high mobile phone penetration rate reaching roughly 74 % of the country's inhabitants according to a recent report by PayFort [6, 7]. Moreover, none of Saudi Arabia's cities have a reliable metro or bus system; most importantly, almost half of the population (i.e., the female population) is not allowed to drive. Recent studies on the social traffic dynamics in Riyadh, Saudi Arabia's capital and main financial hub have provided insight into the patterns of mobility on the roads [1], an analysis conducted by the Center for Complex Engineering Systems in their City Dynamics Project[1] on the observed movements of Riyadh's urban population provided a better understanding of the city's demographics, the distribution of amenities and services, the flow of the existing transportation networks, and the temporal and spatial dynamics of traffic in Riyadh, which was visualized in an interactive web-based platform as it shown in Fig. 1. Such platform was develop to facilitate access to these complex datasets for policy-makers and the general public.

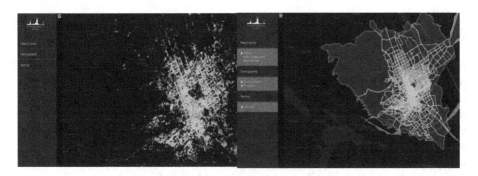

Fig. 1. City Dynamics visualization platform

In Riyadh, privately owned vehicle is the main transportation system for the urban and suburban population [8]. The Institute for Mobility Research (IFMO) study in 2015, which involved a cluster analysis from a mobility perspective of 45 cities around the world, classified Riyadh as an "auto-city" (encouraging the movement of people via private transportation) along with Houston, Texas and Phoenix, Arizona in the US [9]. Private taxi services are ground transportation technology companies that offer mobile location-based apps. These companies have rapidly scaled the transportation market in Saudi Arabia due to the perceived reliability, safety, convenience, and affordability of their chauffeur-driven vehicles. Customers track their rides in real-time, pay with credit cards, cash, or telecom-based credit systems, and access receipts online. The persis-tence and sense of safety associated with private modes of transportation clearly contrast with the perceived lack of reliability associated with the public transportation alternatives. Recent initiatives have sought to engage with the public by offering ser-vices to aid inhabitants in their travels within the city of Riyadh.

2.2 Mobility Research for Examining Social and Traffic Dynamics

Social analytics research has investigated the mobility patterns of populations. Early work examined individual human mobility patterns and modeled the dynamics between social media and mobility behavior [12–14]. Other work focused on investigating urban population activity and mobility patterns through social networks data [15, 20] or

---

[1] http://www.cces-kacst-mit.org/project/city-dynamics.

from cell phone data [21]. More recent work has focused on leveraging the ubiquity of sensors in mobile phones for monitoring road and traffic conditions [22]. In the space where people get from point A to point B, the transportation network is a rich, varied composition of mobility patterns of people and objects (vehicles). Social dynamics aim to understand people's mobility patterns, and traffic dynamics investigate the population's flow through transportation networks. This type of research and analysis is often conducted with the objective of predicting traffic conditions and providing real-time traffic and mobility indicators [12].

3   Social Media Landscape

Inspired by research methodologies developed for analyzing urban dynamic systems, this paper explored computational methods that measure various static and dynamic aspects of social networks and their relation to an underlying mobility pattern of specific demographics in a given urban area. It mainly investigated social media communities that are active and have a digital presence in the scope of mobility in Saudi Arabia. This section presents the main private mobility systems taxi services in Saudi Arabia (Riyadh in particular), some of the government-based and community-based traffic notifications systems, and some of the trends that have emerged in social media conversations about urban mobility in Saudi Arabia. Figure 2 shows a conceptual framework for classifying the social and traffic dynamics of mobility in an urban area, where systems can be classified under offline and online communities. Offline communities are government public and private mobility systems, and online communities are traffic notification systems and social networks. These communities are aligned and insights that can be gained from drilling deeper into social/traffic dynamics with analytics and visualizations.

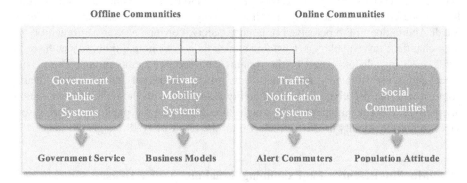

Fig. 2. Framework for visualizing the social and traffic dynamics of mobility

3.1   Privately Owned Transit Systems

The movement paths of people, which can be captured using trajectories of journeys, can represent human mobility or a sequence of events produced from the same person within a time window (e.g., geo-tagged tweets, photos, or check-ins in social apps [10]). For example, Riyadh is the home of more than 6 million people and has witnessed a significant increase in its population [23]. Moreover, for a long time, low gasoline prices offered an incentive for people to use their own vehicles to move around. Nevertheless, the increase in gasoline prices and traffic congestion, along with the absence of a public transit system, people (especially female) has started using taxi services and self-organizing ride-sharing communities more frequently. Therefore, mobility through taxi routes as a means for sampling and gaining insight into mobility patterns in Saudi Arabia have been captured. Table 1 shows basic information about some of the most popular taxi services in Saudi Arabia.

Table 1. Taxi services' apps in Saudi Arabia

Service	Launched	Based in	Cities	Payment Method
Uber	2012	United States	Riyadh, Jeddah, Dammam	Credit Cards, Cash (Riyadh/Jeddah)
Careem	2012	United Arab Emirates	Riyadh, Jeddah, Dammam, Makkah, Madina, Al Hasa, Jubail, Qassim	Credit Cards, Cash, Saudi Telecom Company (STC) Qitaf[a]
Easy Taxi	2014	Brazil	Riyadh, Jeddah	ET pay, Credit Cards, Cash
Taxi "Aujrh"	2015	Saudi Arabia	All Cities	Cash
MyTaxi Saudia	2009	Saudi Arabia	Riyadh, Jeddah, Dammam, Makkah, Medina	Cash
Mishwar	2014	Saudi Arabia	Jeddah	Credit Cards
Mondo	2014	Saudi Arabia	Riyadh, Jeddah	Cash
Taxi Pixi	2013	India	Riyadh, Jeddah, Makkah, Abha	Cash

[a]http://www.stc.com.sa/wps/wcm/connect/english/loyaltyPrograms/tamayouz/briefOnTamayouz

Several taxi services have started to take advantage of the lack of public transit systems. One of the factors that affect the popularity of a taxi service is the method of payment. Therefore, the more popular taxi service apps in the region allow their customers to pay in cash to accommodate their preferred method of payment [12].

By looking at the mobile app market in Saudi Arabia, insight can be gain from the presence taxi services have within the transportation ecosystem. According to AppAnnie[2], a platform that provides app market analytics and data, the most popular apps in transportation are Careem, Uber, and Easy Taxi in both iOS and Android

---

[2] https://www.appannie.com.

platforms. To further understand the market of taxi service apps in Riyadh, a survey has been conducted and collected answers from 280 participants in the city. The goal was to validate the findings shown in Table 2 and get specific answers. The participants were recruited from social media and messaging apps. Figure 3 shows the demographics of the participants.

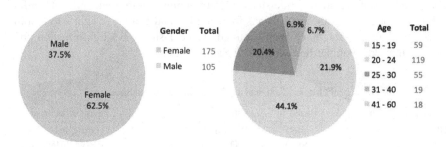

Fig. 3. The demographics of the survey participants (gender and age group)

The survey asked the participants a set of questions to understand the current transportation services and their presence in the online market. First, the participants were asked about their familiarity with a set of the most popular apps according to Table 2. The results indicate closeness in the degree of familiarity that participants had with the apps. The second questions asked the users about their usage of the same set of mobility apps shown in Fig. 4. The results indicate the popularity of some apps relative to others. For instance, when comparing Uber to Careem, it is clear how Careem is more popular in terms of usage. Also, the number of females using Uber, Careem, and Taxi London surpasses the number of males, which is opposite to the larger usage by males of the local taxi service (Aujrh) and Easy Taxi.

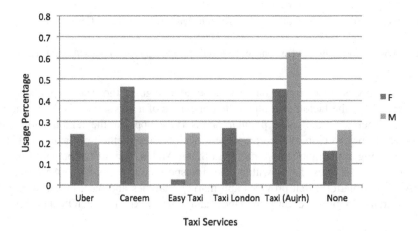

Fig. 4. Percentages of positive answers to the question: Have you used the following service?

Looking at the Twitter accounts of the most used, on-demand taxi services in Saudi Arabia, it was noticeable that the accounts are actively engaging with their customers in information dissemination, marketing, and in conversations with their followers. The data on the Twitter accounts listed in Table 2 were collected on 30/10/2015 and show the number of followers, the number following, the number of Tweets, the language used for communication, and whether or not promotions are shared. The language used most is Arabic given that the targeted audience of those Twitter accounts is in Saudi Arabia.

Table 2. Snapshot of Twitter accounts of key players in Saudi Arabia's mobility services

Account	Followers	Following	Tweets	Language
@Uber_KSA[a]	9179	712	2361	Arabic & English
@CareemKSA[b]	15400	7	4230	Arabic
@EasyTaxiSA[c]	6981	1163	2210	Arabic

3.2 Traffic Notification Systems

This section introduces some of the traffic notification systems that have been launched by government entities and self-organizing services that emerged by the community. These systems have been established to help notify commuters in Saudi Arabia in general and Riyadh in particular. The Arriyadh Development Authority (ADA)[3], the urban planning entity of the capital city, recently launched the Delilat Arriyadh app in 2014, which provides full coverage of Riyadh's road network with over 50,000 POIs, live traffic info that is updated in near real-time, and traffic flow visualizations on the map in four different colors indicating different levels of congestion (green, orange, red, and dark red indicate normal, moderate, slow, and heavy traffic). The app also displays road closures and other related road incidents. Another initiative is Hather "حاذر", an app that has been developed by AlRiyadh Municipality[4], a governmental entity, which notifies and warns Riyadh's residents from critical roads during floods and enables them to avoid these critical sites. In addition, several Twitter accounts for awareness have been introduced by some of the government entities in Saudi Arabia as shown in Table 3.

Ubiquitous technology has been playing a noticeable role in social communications in urban environments and city-wide awareness of urban issues (e.g., mobility and health outbreaks), which have been examined extensively in the design literature [18, 19]. In the context of Saudi Arabsia, several examples of urban mobility technology solutions have emerged that are aligned with citizen-science, allowing members of the community to share and help others. In terms of navigating the city and avoiding congested or blocked parts of the road network, apps have recently been introduced from community-based initiatives that provide ways for frequent users of Web apps to better understand which parts of the city road network are congested, unsafe, or

---

[3] http://www.ada.gov.sa/ada_e.

[4] https://www.alriyadh.gov.sa/en/news/Pages/hazer.aspx.

blocked. Table 3 shows some of the apps and Twitter accounts that have been developed by the community. Some of these accounts are to notify commuters of critical traffic issues in general (e.g., @ArRiyadh_ADA, @Amanatalriyadh, @RiyadhTraffic, and @jed_rd1 Twitter handles), and some accounts have been initiated to inform commuters to avoid blocked roads due to current metro construction (e.g., @Riyadh_Metro and @RiyadhTransport Twitter handles). Other apps and Twitter accounts are to notify border crossers between Saudi Arabia and Bahrain of the traffic status at the borders (e.g., Zahma O La and Eljisr apps, and the @Eljisir Twitter handle).

Table 3. Some of the apps and Twitter accounts initiated by the community

Apps	Twitter accounts
Government	
Delilat Arriyadh	@ArRiyadh_ADA
Hather	@Amanatalriyadh
	@RiyadhTransport
	@Riyadh_Metro
Community	
Zahma O La	@RiyadhTraffic
Eljisir	@Eljisir

[a]https://twitter.com/Uber_KSA
[b]https://twitter.com/CareemKSA
[c]https://twitter.com/EasyTaxiSA

3.3   Tapping into Social Conversations About Urban Mobility in Saudi Arabia

To acknowledge the efforts of the governments in engaging with the public in traffic issues, tapping into social networks is needed. Conversations around mobility and transportation trends continue to happen through multiple channels, including social media. This section focuses on those conversations happen on Twitter. Looking at Table 3, it can be seen that government entities responsible for planning or mobility (e.g., the ADA and Alriyadh Municipality) have a presence on Twitter and engage in conversation with their followers by sharing news and updates on new or existing projects. Figure 5 illustrates an example of the type of conversation shared by the @ArRiyadh_ADA Twitter account. In this Tweet, the ADA is sharing the Investment Climate report for Arriyadh.

Other conversations that occur on Twitter are through hashtags in which users Tweet notifications regarding traffic or other mobility issues targeted to both the public and the authorities in order to get their voices and concerns heard. The following are some Twitter hashtags in which traffic, roads, metro, construction, and other mobility issues are often discussed: #قطار_الرياض، #أين_المرور، #طرق_الرياض، #مترو_الرياض and #Riyadh_Metro.

Fig. 5. An example of the Tweets sent by government entities

The collected hashtags are all related to the mobility dynamics in Riyadh and were selected to show how citizens engage in social conversations. For example, Fig. 6 depict the network of related hashtags for the hashtag #أين_المرور though hashtagify.me.

Fig. 6. Network of hashtags related to the hashtag # أين_المرور

The network of the hashtag of # أين_المرور (translates to 'where is the traffic police' and shown in the red node) displays hashtags that are relevant to car accidents and traffic, such as speed cameras and emergency hashtag the nodes shown in grey. The other hashtag is about Riyadh roads and is showing related hashtags about traffic. The edges of the network indicate the correlation of the node connected from the hashtag of interest. The size of the node indicates the popularity of the hashtag.

4   Conclusion

Given that capturing the mobility patterns of people on transportation networks presents clear challenges; the results of this work suggest numerous avenues of possible exploration. Anecdotal evidence indicated an increasing use of social media in the Saudi population and suggested potential for tapping into social media conversations for insight into understanding urban dynamics. Using Twitter and the other social media accounts of the three popular taxi services (Careem, Uber, and Easy Taxi) as examples, a descriptive statistics is presented to characterize and measure the potential influence of social media on the mobility dynamics in Saudi Arabia in general and in the city of Riyadh in particular. One area where this research work of establishing an in-depth understanding of social communities of urban mobility has the greatest potential is in understanding the relationship between online and offline communities in an urban context. These insights provide a step towards understanding and visualizing mobility patterns of citizens in an urban context.

Based on this exploratory study of social media communities and the Web presence of the mobility services in Saudi Arabia, our findings suggest that mobility service apps that have a strong presence in social networks (such as Careem, Uber, and Easy Taxi) are used more than other mobility services. Also, active mobility services on the Web that interact with their customers through social media seem to attract much more people. Transportation services' presence in social networks enables researchers to analyze mobility patterns and model the dynamics between social networks and mobility behavior. In contrast, few studies have been conducted on how conversations about taxi services and road issues (congestion, weather-related blockages, construction rerouting, traffic accidents, drifting, etc.) on social networks could impact the ways those services are used [16, 17].

References

1. City Dynamics 2016. Technical report, Center for Complex Engineering Systems, King Abdulaziz City for Science and Technology and Massachusetts Institute of Technology
2. López-Ornelas, E., Zaragoza, N.M.: Social media participation: a narrative way to help urban planners. In: Meiselwitz, G. (ed.) SCSM 2015. LNCS, vol. 9182, pp. 48–54. Springer, Heidelberg (2015)
3. Sui, D., Goodchild, M.: The convergence of GIS and social media: challenges for GIScience. Int. J. Geogr. Inf. Sci. **25**(11), 1737–1748 (2011)
4. Abokhodair, N.: Transmigrant Saudi Arabian youth and social media: privacy, intimacy and freedom of expression. In: Proceedings of the 33rd Annual ACM Conference Extended Abstracts on Human Factors in Computing Systems, pp. 187–190. ACM, April 2015
5. Al-Khalifa, H.S., Al-Razgan, M.S., Al-Rajebah, N.I., Almasoud, A.M.: Exploring social media usage in Saudi e-government websites. In: Proceedings of the 6th International Conference on Theory and Practice of Electronic Governance, pp. 243–247. ACM, October 2012
6. Jones, R., Alomran, A.: Ban on Women Drivers in Saudi Arabia Gives Taxi Apps a Boos. The Wall Street J., 17 October 2014. http://www.wsj.com/articles/ban-on-women-drivers-in-saudi-arabia-gives-taxi-apps-a-boost-1413456923
7. PayFort Report 2014. http://www.payfort.com/press/payfort-to-enable-the-regions-travel-and-hospitality-industry-to-harness-the-benefits-of-online-payment/
8. Ansari, S., Akhdar, F., Mandoorah, M., Moutaery, K.: Causes and effects of road traffic accidents in Saudi Arabia. Public Health **114**(1), 37–39 (2000)
9. Mobility in Large Cities: Transport Typologies and Their Meanings, Being prepared for an influenza pandemic: a kit for small businesses, Government of Australia (2006). http://future-megacities.org/fileadmin/documents/El-Gauna_Symposium/13-JeffreyKenworthy.pdf

10. Yuan, J., Zheng, Y., Xie, X.: Discovering regions of different functions in a city using human mobility and POIs. In: Proceedings of the 18th ACM SIGKDD International Conference on Knowledge Discovery and Data Mining, pp. 186–194. ACM, August 2012
11. Demographics 2014, State of Payment, Payfort (2014). http://www.stateofpayments.com/#demographics
12. Gonzalez, M.C., Hidalgo, C.A., Barabasi, A.L.: Understanding individual human mobility patterns. Nature **453**(7196), 779–782 (2008)
13. Urry, J.: Social networks, travel and talk1. Br. J. Sociol. **54**(2), 155–175 (2003)
14. Sharmeen, F., Arentze, T., Timmermans, H.: Modelling the dynamics between social networks and activity-travel behavior: literature review and research agenda. In: 12th World Conference on Transport Research, Lisbon, July 2010
15. Hasan, S., Zhan, X., Ukkusuri, S.V.: Understanding urban human activity and mobility patterns using large-scale location-based data from online social media. In: Proceedings of the 2nd ACM SIGKDD International Workshop on Urban Computing, p. 6. ACM, August 2013
16. Howard, P.N., Hussain, M.M.: The role of digital media. J. Democracy **22**(3), 35–48 (2011)
17. Ghannam, J.: Social media in the arab world: leading up to the uprisings of 2011. Cent. Int. Media Assistance **3**, 1–44 (2011)
18. Chang, M., Jungnickel, K., Orloff, C., Shklovski, I.: Engaging the city: public interfaces as civic intermediary. In: CHI 2005 Extended Abstracts on Human Factors in Computing Systems, pp. 2109–2110. ACM, April 2005
19. Cuff, D., Hansen, M., Kang, J.: Urban sensing: out of the woods. Commun. ACM **51**(3), 24–33 (2008)
20. Le, A., Pelechrinis, K., Krishnamurthy, P.: Country-level spatial dynamics of user activity: a case study in location-based social networks. In: Proceedings of the 2014 ACM Conference on Web Science, pp. 71–80. ACM, June 2014
21. Isaacman, S., Becker, R., Cáceres, R., Kobourov, S., Rowland, J., Varshavsky, A.: A tale of two cities. In: Proceedings of the Eleventh Workshop on Mobile Computing Systems & Applications, pp. 19–24. ACM, February 2010
22. Mohan, P., Padmanabhan, V.N., Ramjee, R.: Nericell: rich monitoring of road and traffic conditions using mobile smartphones. In: Proceedings of the 6th ACM Conference on Embedded Network Sensor Systems, pp. 323–336. ACM, November 2008
23. General Authority for Statistics, Kingdom of Saudi Arabia (2016). http://www.cdsi.gov.sa/english/
24. Newton, A.: 4 ways how Twitter can keep growing. 07 November 2015. Peerreach Blog (2007). http://blog.peerreach.com/2013/11/4-ways-how-twitter-can-keep-growing/
25. Evans-Cowley, J., Griffin, G.: Microparticipation with social media for community engagement in transportation planning. Transp. Res. Rec. J. Transp. Res. Board **2307**, 90–98 (2012)
26. Kitamura, R., Fujii, S., Pas, E.I.: Time-use data, analysis and modeling: toward the next generation of transportation planning methodologies. Transp. Policy **4**(4), 225–235 (1997)
27. Haghshenas, H., Vaziri, M., Gholamialam, A.: Evaluation of sustainable policy in urban transportation using system dynamics and world cities data: a case study in Isfahan. Cities **45**, 104–115 (2015)
28. Bregman, S., Watkins, K.E. (eds.): Best Practices for Transportation Agency Use of Social Media. CRC Press, Boca Raton (2013)
29. Noulas, A., Scellato, S., Lambiotte, R., Pontil, M., Mascolo, C.: A tale of many cities: universal patterns in human urban mobility. PLoS ONE **7**(5), e37027 (2012)

Feasibility and Framing of Interventions Based on Public Support: Leveraging Text Analytics for Policymakers

Philippe J. Giabbanelli[1,2(✉)], Jean Adams[2], and Venkata Sai Pillutla[1]

[1] Department of Computer Science, Northern Illinois University, Dekalb, IL, USA
giabba@cs.niu.edu, z1780791@students.niu.edu
[2] UKCRC Centre for Diet and Activity Research (CEDAR),
MRC Epidemiology Unit, University of Cambridge School of Clinical Medicine,
Institute of Metabolic Science, Cambridge CB2 0QQ, UK
jma79@medschl.cam.ac.uk

Abstract. Public opinions play an important role in planning policies. A beneficial population intervention may not be publicly acceptable, or policymakers may be over-cautious and believe their constituents do not sufficiently support it. Understanding the feasibility and framing of interventions based on public support is thus an important endeavor for public health. While surveys or qualitative analyses are a typical approach, they can require significant time or manpower. In contrast, algorithms for text analytics are now available that could be readily used by policymakers. As a case study, this paper used the debate that surrounded taxes on sugar sweetened beverages (SSB) in California. Our main contribution lies in detailing the process of automatizing the analysis of public health opinions, particularly using off-the-shelf software that policymakers can use, and exemplify the types of policy questions that can be investigated.

1 Introduction

Close to two thirds of US adults are currently overweight or obese [1]. This has major consequences on quality of life as well as on healthcare costs, which are projected to reach 860 to 960 billion US dollars by 2030 [2] in the absence of long-term solutions. Several policies have been proposed to tackle the obesity epidemic [3–5]. These include economic measure, such as taxes on healthy food items [6–8] or subsidies for healthier ones [9]. There is growing evidence from both modelling and pragmatic studies [10,11], that taxes on less healthy foods can reduce sales and consumption of those foods. However, many of these more structural, population interventions may not be publicly acceptable, meaning that policymakers choose not to implement them and their potential is not realized [12]. Furthermore, policymakers may be over-cautious, thinking that some measures may not

Research funded by the Department of Computer Science and the College of Liberal Arts and Sciences at Northern Illinois University, and the Centre for Diet and Activity Research (CEDAR), a UKCRC Public Health Research Centre of Excellence.

© Springer International Publishing Switzerland 2016
G. Meiselwitz (Ed.): SCSM 2016, LNCS 9742, pp. 188–200, 2016.
DOI: 10.1007/978-3-319-39910-2_18

be acceptable to their constituents without having strong evidence of this. Consequently, there is a need to better understand public opinions regarding these sorts of public health policies. This can help not only decide which policies to pursue, but also how to frame them in a more publicly acceptable way.

Surveys have long been used to assess public opinions about public health policies [13]. However, they need time to be deployed and analyzed, and may only provide limited insight into policy debates. Qualitative analyses of documents that are readily available (e.g., news stories, blogs, editorials) provide an alternative source of information on public opinions concerning public health policies. Information includes the topics or sentiments expressed by constituents. For example, Nixon et al. performed an ethnographic qualitative analysis (i.e. a type of qualitative analysis) of news reports on soda tax initiatives in 3 US cities [14]. However, content analyses typically require a significant amount of time and/or manpower as each article is read and coded by humans for sentiment, topic, or other variables of interest [15]. Some of these tasks can actually be performed by computers using text analytic algorithms, many of which are now part of off-the-shelf software. As recently highlighted by Hamad et al. [16], the automated analysis of news media in obesity is still in its infancy. Given the importance of addressing obesity, and the complexity of the public policy debates surrounding it, understanding how to use mature techniques from text analytics in this domain could offer important insights for public health researchers and policymakers.

The use of text analytics in public health research is part of the growing area of 'infodemiology', which studies the distribution and determinants of information in an electronic medium in order to inform public health and public policy [17]. Twitter has been the electronic medium of choice for many studies, as it provides publicly available data together with a social network and sometimes geo-coding [18–21]. However, Twitter messages ('Tweets') can be at most 140 characters long, which limits the information that they contain regarding a public health debate. In contrast, news articles allow arguments to be more fully developed. Newspapers are also one of the most trusted information sources, encountered by 65 % of US adults each week [22] with most readers being registered voters [23]. In addition, some US newspapers are still considered to clearly impact policy agenda [24]. While written news provides depth in arguments, it can be narrow in the breadth of opinions represented. For example, analyses of public debates regarding soda taxes have found that they mostly received positive news coverage even though the public ultimately voted against these taxes [14,25]. One way to capture both the breadth of opinion included in social media such as Twitter, and the depth of opinion included in written news media, is to include both news reports and on-line reader responses to these. Consequently, we perform text analytics of news articles supplemented by readers' comments. As a case study, we used the debate that surrounded taxes on sugar sweetened beverages (SSB) in California in 2014-15. While the results are thus most informative to that specific debate, the main contribution of this paper resides in detailing the process of automatizing the analysis of public opinions and exemplifying the types of public health questions that it supports.

This paper is organized as follows. In Sect. 2, we provide a brief background on policies regarding SSB taxes in California. Section 3 describes how we performed data collection and cleaning. After preparing the corpus, we analyze it in Sect. 4 using a variety of algorithms from text analytics, and we explain how these analyses provide different types of information in order to understand the public debate. Finally, we address technical limitations in Sect. 5 and provide a brief discussion on future work.

2   Public Policy Background

Despite evidence from modelling studies for a beneficial health effect of SSB taxes [10,11], concerns over public acceptability of such policies are one reason why policy-makers and politicians appear reluctant to publicly consider them. The two SSB taxes in our case study were put to the vote in 2014 in Berkeley and San Francisco, California. An earlier 2011 survey in nearby Santa Clara county found that 67 % would support a SSB tax and 37 % would oppose it [26].

In Berkeley, CA, the tax was $0.01 per fluid ounce on the distributors of sugar sweetened beverages (SSB), and syrups operating within the city. The proposal was for a tax that would apply to sugary soda, energy drinks, juice with added sugar, and syrups that go into sugary drinks. 100 % juice and drinks with milk as the first (primary) ingredient were exempt because of their nutritional value. Diet soda and alcoholic drinks were also exempt. The tax revenue was designed to go into the city's general fund, and a Sugar-Sweetened Beverage Product Panel of Experts had to publish an annual report forming recommendations on how to allocate the funds to "reduce the consumption of sugar sweetened beverages in Berkeley and to address the results of such consumption" [27]. During the run-up to the November 2014 ballot, there was significant campaigning from those both opposed to, and in favour of, the SSB tax. Support for the tax focused around the campaign group *Berkeley vs Big Soda* funded primarily by contributions from local residents, public health organisations, and former New York City Mayor Michael R. Bloomberg. Opposition to the tax was driven by *Californians for Food &Beverage Choice* in association with the American Beverage Association, who reportedly spent around $2.4 m on campaigning [28]. This intense level of local campaigning generated substantial media coverage. Ultimately, the tax was put to the vote and received support from 76.16 % of voters. A simple majority was required. By adopting this tax, Berkeley became the first city in the USA to introduce an SSB tax and one of the first jurisdictions to do so world-wide.

The same day and less than a 30 mins drive away, citizens of San Francisco, CA voted on a proposition for a tax of $0.02 per fluid ounce payable, as in Berkeley, by SSB distributors. This was an 'hypothecated' tax with generated funds (estimated at $31 million per annum) earmarked for health, nutrition and physical activity programmes in public schools and parks, at the direction of a Healthy Nutrition and Physical Activity Access Fund Committee. The proposition was sponsored by six local Supervisors. The official opponents were the Libertarian Party of San Francisco. However, the American Beverage Association also funded opposition through both the Coalition for an Affordable City, a local pressure group formed specifically to oppose the ballot, and, as in Berkeley, *Californians for Food & Beverage Choice*. The proposition received 55.59 % support from voters. However, because the proceeds from the tax were dedicated to specific purposes, approval of this measure required a 2/3 super-majority. Thus, the tax passed in Berkeley while it did not pass in San Francisco.

3 Creating a Corpus: Data Collection and Cleaning

3.1 Data Collection

The time period of interest and the main events are summarized in Fig. 1. We included news reports published between 1 January 2014 and 31 January 2015. On 11 February and 4 February, the decisions to vote on SSB tax through a formal ballot were made in Berkeley and San Francisco respectively. This represents the first formal step towards a decision to hold a ballot. By extending the data collection period back to 1 January 2014 we captured any coverage related to the run-up to this decision. The Berkeley tax was implemented on 1st January 2015. Extending the inclusion period to 31 January 2015 gave the opportunity to capture short, but not long, term reflections on the process of implementation.

In order to explore any changes in reporting over the time-periods before the ballot, after the ballot but before implementation, and after implementation, reports were considered in three groups. Reports published between 1 January 2014 and 4 November 2014 were *pre-ballot*; reports published between 5 November 2014 and 31 December 2014 were *post-ballot* but *pre-implementation*; and reports published between 1 January 2014 and 31 January 2015 were *post-implementation*.

We performed text analytics on all types of newspaper text articles (including news, features, editorials and other comment) as well as readers' comments. Infographics, videos or raw poll results were not considered as text articles. This

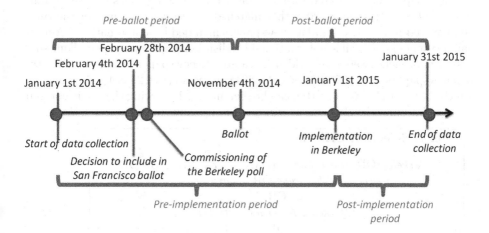

Fig. 1. Timescale for the data collection and main periods used in the analysis.

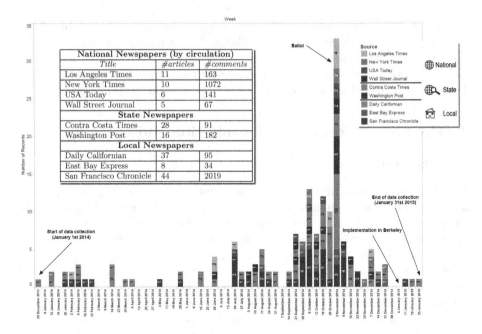

Fig. 2. Collected news articles by source and time. The inset summarizes selected newspapers with the number of articles (as found per selection criteria in Box 1) and corresponding comments.

strategy was chosen to capture comment articles written by leading members of the pro- and anti- lobbies, which go beyond news articles written by journalists. In addition, reader responses to these articles provide an insight into public perception and can potentially show a divide between the arguments used in newspapers and those held by the readers.

Newspapers were selected if they published at least 4 articles between 1 January 2014 and 31 January 2015 that matched our target content, per the rules summarized in Box 1. Candidate newspapers included local and national American newspapers, as well as international English-language newspapers. Four successive approaches were used to identify candidate newspapers, resulting in a total of 9 newspapers with 165 articles and 3,864 comments (Fig. 2 inset). The times at which these articles were written can be seen in Fig. 2, showing that articles often appeared around the elections as witnessed in previous policy research [14].

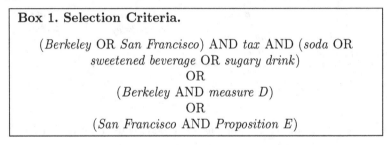

First, we applied the search criteria via the LexisNexis database, which has a wide reach, particularly of American content. Using this database as the first step is a common approach [14]. This resulted in including the *Contra Costa Times*, *Los Angeles Times*, *New York Times*, and the *Washington Post*.

Second, we repeated the search criteria on each of the 5 largest daily newspapers in the USA (measured by the 2013 combined circulation and on-line viewing data compiled by the Alliance for Audited Media) via their own search facility. This resulted in adding *USA Today* and the *Wall Street Journal*. Third, we repeated the search criteria for newspapers that had a significant readership in either Berkeley or San Francisco. This resulted in inclusion of the *Daily Californian* (local Berkeley newspaper), the *East Bay Express*[1], and the *San Francisco Chronicle*[2].

Finally, we also applied the search criteria to the top 5 English-language newspapers outside the USA, by circulation figures. None were retained for analysis since our search criteria did not find enough documents in these newspapers.

3.2   Data Cleaning and Wrangling

Each document was separated into the news article and the readers' comments. For each article, we removed all parts that were not part of the article itself (e.g., advertisements, links to other articles). Meta-data about the article was kept in a separate database and contained the article's title, author(s), publication date, newspaper, type of newspaper (i.e., local/state/national), number of readers' comments, and search terms that led to finding the article. As there were only 165 articles following 9 different formats, cleaning of the article and preparation of the database was done manually, rather than investing in developing cleaning scripts tailored to each newspapers' format.

In contrast to the articles, having 3,864 comments made it necessary to process them using scripts. Our scripts can be accessed online at https://osf. io/3x6av/. Writing such cleaning scripts can be time consuming, partly because of the wide differences in functionality and formats across newspapers (Table 1). For example, most allowed users to 'like'/'recommend' a comment but only two allowed users to 'dislike' a comment. Comments sometimes include conversations, but tracking who a user was answering heavily depended on how it was managed by a newspaper's website. Most had a straightforward structure (e.g., indenting answers using spaces, or embedding an answer within the HTML block of a comment) but some had no structure and it was up to the users to correctly write @*name* at the beginning of their comment (thus leaving room for errors).

---

[1] The *Daily Californian* reports a press run of 10,000, while the *East Bay Express* reports a press run in Berkeley of 13,442. The average number of persons who read a copy (i.e., the pass-along rate) is estimated at 2.3 by the National Newspaper Association. As Berkeley had an estimated 116,768 inhabitants in 2013 according to the US Census Bureau, these two newspapers may be read by approximately 20 % and 26 % of the population.

[2] The combined circulation and on-line viewing data reported 20 % of the market in Alameda county (where Berkeley is located) as well as 12 % in San Francisco.

Table 1. Differences in comments across newspapers

Newspaper	Comment functionality				Comment structure	Encoding
	Likes	Dislikes	Reply	Full date		
Contra Costa Times	No	No	Yes	No	Set spaces	Text
Daily Californian	Yes	No	Yes	No	Set spaces	Text
East Bay Express	Yes	Yes	No	Yes	N/A	Text
Los Angeles Times	Yes	Yes	Yes	No	Depends on people's use of @	Text
New York Times	Yes	No	Yes	Yes	HTML Structure	HTML
San Francisco C.	Yes	No	Yes	No	Depends on people's use of @	Text
USA Today	Yes	No	Yes	Yes	Set spaces	Text
Wall Street Journal	No	No	Yes	Yes	HTML Structure	HTML
Washington Post	Yes	No	Yes	Yes	HTML Structure	HTML

Newspapers' formats were sufficiently different that we recommend taking this into account when writing data collection scripts (e.g., by driving Selenium from Python): some formats can best be cleaned when copy/pasted from the user display, while for others the HTML page is best.

4   Applying Text Analytics to the Corpus

4.1   Solutions Most Readily Available to Policymakers

This section shows what policymakers *could* typically have access to in order to analyze news articles and associated reader comments. Thus, we focus on well-established text analytics software such as `Jigsaw` or `IN-SPIRE`; more functionalities could be obtained using newer, more specialized, or research software (e.g., Luminoso from the MIT Media Lab [29] or TopicNets [30] from the University of California). Additional examples can be found in [31].

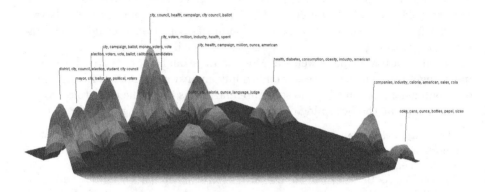

Fig. 3. Using the Galaxy view from `IN-SPIRE` [32] on the articles.

Documents are typically coded for themes. Both `Jigsaw` or `IN-SPIRE` allow themes to emerge (through clustering), as illustrated in Fig. 3. The height of each theme indicates the number of documents in it, while the words above the theme show the main keywords used by the algorithm to define that theme. The distance between themes indicates how they relate. In this example, it is immediately apparent that there were three broad categories: elections and ballots (left), health (center), company regulations (right). The specific themes within the last category include company sales (which may get impacted by the tax) and changes in can sizes (to compensate for the tax). The software allows correlations between themes or how they change over time (available as supplemental material at https://osf. io/3x6av/), which are other typical tasks for qualitative analysis.

When trying to assess public opinion, one may seek to examine the context in which specific words are used. An example of a motivating question would be: 'what do people say about *tax*?' One way to do this is to build a word tree using `Jigsaw`. Figure 4 shows such a word tree using readers' comments, and several of the main arguments already appear: some consumers see it as an attack against their freedom to eat a wide range of foods (e.g., a 'regressive sin tax' along the lines of taxing cookies or 'everything that can kill you'), have doubts about the use of proceeds (e.g., 'revenue to fund other projects or even their own generous pay raises'), fear a disproportional impact on the poor, or even on jobs ('corporations absorb the hit and reduce jobs'). A similar word tree built on the news articles (provided at https://osf.io/3x6av/), rather than the readers' comments, depicts a different picture with benefits on childhood obesity and funding health programs more prominently featured.

Finally, a policymaker may be interested in knowing who is behind certain arguments, or how organizations are associated. This can be achieved by entity

Fig. 4. Finding readers' arguments that followed the word 'tax' using `Jigsaw`. The full-sized figure is available at https://osf.io/3x6av/ together with the wordtree based on the articles.

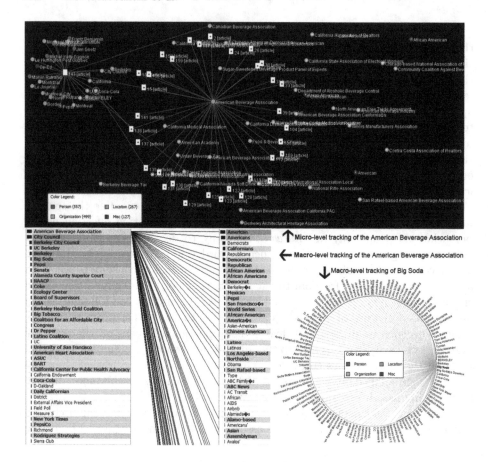

Fig. 5. Using entity tracking in `Jigsaw` on the articles.

tracking. `Jigsaw` automatically processes the documents to identify organizations, persons, locations, and other types of entities. Entity tracking can be done at the micro-level by following links (displayed as lines in Fig. 5 top): for example, one can start with the American Beverage Association, pick a document in which it is mentioned, and see what else is being mentioned. Alternatively, it can be done at the macro-level by finding the entities that co-appear the most with the American Beverage Association (e.g., showing that African-Americans are particularly co-mentioned), across all documents (Fig. 5 bottom left).

4.2   Advanced Solutions

The previous section emphasized techniques that policymakers could access using off-the-shelf software. There is still a variety of analyses that can be useful but may be less accessible to policymakers through current software. We provide additional examples of quantitative analyses on readers' comments at https://osf.io/3x6av/. Text summarization is of particular interest when policy-makers are faced with a large corpus that they need to quickly condense.

There are two broad ways of summarizing a text: extraction (also known as the shallow technique) and abstraction (also known as the deep technique). Extraction uses the words and phrases of the actual text and applies smoothing techniques to address any incoherence. Abstraction may not contain the explicit words of the text. As an example of extraction, we implemented the (graph-based ranking) LexRank algorithm [33]. One issue with this algorithm is that policy-makers cannot simply pass it the text and get a summary: they need to choose the value of a parameter, which has a large impact on results. For example, one value can produce an irrelevant summary ("the issue with Fructose is way it is metabolized only by the liver") while another value produces a very relevant one ("the proposed law benefits San Francisco bureaucrats like Scott Wiener who would like to get their hands on that expected $30 million a year by taxing"). By carefully choosing the right value, it is possible to generate summaries and compare how they change depending on the source (news vs readers' comments) or time (pre-ballot, post-ballot, etc.). The temporal difference is clear. For example, the readers' comments post-implementation are summarized as "While some local businesses have felt the effects of the citywide ordinance, sales of sugary drinks sold on campus have not and will not be affected because the UC system is not bound by city laws." In contrast, their comments pre-implementation were (perhaps sarcastically) summarized as "If this passes, please continue on and tax red meats, ice cream, donuts, fast food [etc.]". The difference between the article summary and the readers' comments summary echoes observations from word trees (Fig. 4).

5   Discussion

In this paper, we exemplified how current methods and software in text analytics could answer questions of interest to policymakers. We used SSB taxes as a guiding example to detail the process of collecting, cleaning, and analyzing data. We emphasized software that policymakers could directly use, while highlighting that there are other relevant analyses such as text summarization.

As we noted in the creation of the corpus, preparing the data is time consuming. Thus, one should not simplify text analytics as being immediate while qualitative analyses takes time: *both* approaches need time and manpower (particularly in the set-up phase) but they do not scale the same way. In text analytics, time is spent in writing scripts (e.g., to collect or clean data), and the time it takes is proportional to the number of different data sources (e.g., one has to decode the format specific to each newspaper). Passed this set-up cost, the cost of analyzing one additional article is negligible. In qualitative analyses, substantial time would be spent in developing the coding framework but analyzing each additional article will also require a small amount of additional time. As an example, in the supervised approach used by Hamad and colleagues, three people were involved in manually coding 354 articles to set-up the system, but it was then able to process 14,302 articles within a few days [16].

The off-the-shelf solutions that we presented have in common that they see all documents as being equally relevant. However, this is not the case in reality. For example, the *San Francisco Chronicle* (which had the most articles per our search criteria) also had articles of which the SSB tax was not the subject; instead, the tax may have been briefly mentioned as part of a subject's past records of political endorsements. This could lead to finding irrelevant themes or entities that are not truly connected. Consequently, a more accurate analysis would have to ensure that only relevant parts of the article (if any) are used. Similarly, when assessing public opinions via readers' comments, we need to ensure that the article they comment on strongly relates to the SSB tax. As the software capabilities evolve over time [34], such issues of relevance should gradually be addressed.

While the emphasis of this paper was on the generic process needed to perform text analytics, and on the type of questions that can be addressed, we note several limitations affecting the results specific to the guiding example. First, our search procedure cannot claim to have found all articles relevant to the SSB tax debate in California. While it is common to use only one database for text analytics (e.g., [16]), we searched within the LexisNexis database as well as daily newspapers with a large readership either locally or nationally, and the top 5 English-language newspapers outside the USA. This procedure is skewed towards large newspapers, and could be complemented by other online databases such as Access World News (http://infoweb.newsbank.com). In addition, using the largest newspapers does not guarantee that their articles have been at the core of the debates. The Topsy database can be used to find such 'hot' articles, by identifying the ones that are linked to retweets on Twitter. Using this procedure to identify articles has recently been shown to lead to different results in terms of sentiment or themes [15], although further research is needed to identify the procedure that selects the articles most representative of public opinions.

References

1. Flegal, K., Carroll, M., Ogden, C., Curtin, L.: Prevalence and trends in obesity among us adults, 1999–2008. JAMA **303**, 235–241 (2010)
2. Wang, Y., Beydoun, M., Liang, L., Caballero, B., Kumanyika, S.: Will all americans become overweight or obese? estimating the progression and cost of the us obesity epidemic. Obesity **16**, 2323–2330 (2008)
3. Zhang, D., Giabbanelli, P.J., et al.: Impact of different policies on unhealthy dietary behaviors in an urban adult population: An agent-based simulation model. Am. J. Public Health **104**(7), 1217–1222 (2014)
4. Giabbanelli, P.J., Jackson, P.J., Finegood, D.T.: Modelling the joint effect of social determinants and peers on obesity among canadian adults. In: Theories and Simulations of Complex Social Systems, pp. 145–160 (2014)
5. Verigin, T., Giabbanelli, P.J., Davidsen, P.: Supporting a systems approach to healthy weight interventions in british columbia by modeling weight and well-being. In: Proceedings of the 2016 Annual Simulation Symposium (ANSS) (2016)
6. Mytton, O., Clarke, D., Rayner, M.: Taxing unhealthy food and drinks to improve health. BMJ **344**, e2931 (2012)

7. Powell, L., Chaloupka, F.: Food prices and obesity: evidence and policy implications for taxes and subsidies. Milbank Q **87**(1), 229–257 (2009)
8. Brownell, K., Farley, T., et al.: The public health and economic benefits of taxing sugar-sweetened beverages. NEJM **361**, 1599–1605 (2009)
9. An, R.: Effectiveness of subsidies in promoting healthy food purchases and consumption: a review of field experiments. Public Health Nutr. **16**(7), 1215–1228 (2013)
10. Eyles, H., Mhurchu, C.N., Nghiem, N., Blakely, T.: Food pricing strategies, population diets, and non-communicable disease: A systematic review of simulation studies. PLoS Med **9**(12), e1001353 (2012)
11. Briggs, A., Mytton, O., Kehlbacher, A., Tiffin, R., Rayner, M., Scarborough, P.: Overall and income specific effect on prevalence of overweight and obesity of 20% sugar sweetened drink tax in uk: econometric and comparative risk assessment modelling study. BMJ **347**, f6189 (2013)
12. Pope, T.M.: Limiting liberty to prevent obesity: Justifiability of strong hard paternalism in public health regulation. Conn. Law Rev. **46**, 1859–1876 (2013)
13. Rivard, C., Smith, D., McCann, S.E., Hyland, A.: Taxing sugar-sweetened beverages: a survey of knowledge, attitudes and behaviours. Publ. Health Nutr. **15**(8), 1355–1361 (2012)
14. Nixon, L., Mejia, P., Cheyne, A., Dorfman, L.: Big soda's long shadow: news coverage of local proposals to tax sugar-sweetened beverages in richmond, el monte and telluride. Crit. Publ. Health **25**(3), 333–347 (2015)
15. Mahoney, L., Tang, T., et al.: The digital distribution of public health news surrounding the human papillomavirus vaccination: a longitudinal infodemiology study. JMIR Publ. Health Surveill. **1**(1), e2 (2015)
16. Hamad, R., Pomeranz, J., Siddiqi, A., Basu, S.: Large-scale automated analysis of news media: a novel computational method for obesity policy research. Obesity **23**, 296–300 (2015)
17. Eysenbach, G.: Infodemiology and infoveillance: framework for an emerging set of public health informatics methods to analyze search, communication and publication behavior on the internet. J. Med. Internet Res. **11**(1), e11 (2009)
18. Salathe, M., Khandelwal, S.: Assessing vaccination sentiments with online social media: implications for infectious disease dynamics and control. PLoS Comput. Biol. **7**(10), e1002199 (2011)
19. Bodnar, T., Salathe, M.: Validating models for disease detection using twitter. In: Proceedings of the 22nd International Conference on World Wide Web Companion, pp. 699–702 (2013)
20. Ji, X., Chun, S.A., Geller, J.: Monitoring public health concerns using twitter sentiment classifications. In: IEEE International Conference on Healthcare Informatics (ICHI) 2013, pp. 335–344 (2013)
21. Dredze, M., Cheng, R., Paul, M., Broniatowski, D.: Healthtweets.org: A platform for public health surveillance using twitter. In: AAAI Workshop on the World Wide Web and Public Health Intelligence (2014)
22. The Media Insight Project: The personal news cycle (2013)
23. Sasseen, J., Olmstead, K., Mitchell, A.: Digital: as mobile grows rapidly, the pressures of news intensify. Pew Center Project for Excellence in Journalism (2013)
24. Dolsak, N., Houston, K.: Newspaper coverage and climate change legislative activity across us states. Global Policy **5**(3), 286–297 (2014)
25. Niederdeppe, J., Gollust, S., Jarlenski, M., Nathanson, A., Barry, C.: News coverage of sugar-sweetened beverage taxes: pro- and antitax arguments in public discourse. Am. J. Publ. Health **103**, e92–e98 (2013)

26. Stoddard, P., van Erp, B., Induni, M., Reedy, A., Broderick, B.: Sugar-sweetened beverage tax acceptability in the u.s. versus foreign-born population: Results from a large northern california county. In: 142nd Annual Meeting & Expo of the American Public Health Association (APHA), p. 303809 (2014)

27. The People of the City of Berkeley: Imposing a general tax on the distribution of sugar-sweetened beverage products. Ordinance (2014)

28. Dinkelspiel, F.: A record $3.6 million spent in berkeley campaigns, November 2014

29. Speer, R., Havasi, C., Treadway, N., Lieberman, H.: Visualizing common sense connections with luminoso. In: Proceedings of the First International Workshop on Intelligent Visual Interfaces for Text Analysis, pp. 9–12 (2010)

30. Gretarsson, B., O'Donovan, J., et al.: Topicnets: Visual analysis of large text corpora with topic modeling. ACM Trans. Intell. Syst. Technol. **3**(2), 23 (2014)

31. Giabbanelli, P.J., Jackson, P.J.: Using visual analytics to support the integration of expert knowledge in the design of medical models and simulations. In: Proceedings of the 8th Workshop on Biomedical and Bioinformatics Challenges for Computer Science (2015)

32. Wong, P., Hetzler, B., et al.: In-spire infovis 2004 contest entry. In: IEEE Symposium on Information Visualization (2004)

33. Otterbacher, J., Gunes, E., et al.: Biased lexrank: passage retrieval using random walks with question-based priors. Inf. Process. Manage. **1**, 42–54 (2009)

34. Gorg, C., Liu, Z., Stasko, J.: Reflections of the evolution of the jigsaw visual analytics system. Inf. Vis. **13**(4), 336–345 (2014)

Chrono-Spatial Intelligence in Global Systems Science and Social Media: Predictions for Proactive Political Decision Making

Niki Lambropoulos[1(✉)], Habib M. Fardoun[2], and Daniyal M. Alghazzawi[2]

[1] University of Patras, Panepistimioupoli Patron, 265 04 Rion, Greece
nikilambropoulos@gmail.com
[2] King Abdulaziz University of Saudi Arabia,
Jeddah 21589, Kingdom of Saudi Arabia
{hfardoun,dghazzawi}@kau.edu.sa

Abstract. This paper discusses the advantage of social media in providing continuous non-liner, non-redundant information, taking advantage Global Systems Science (GSS) research tools and techniques. GSS matrix can indicate series of fortunate and unfortunate events that are not isolated but rather connected in time and space, sometimes appearing as events rising from serendipity. This proposition suggests that such hidden connections can be a new form of multiple intelligence named Chrono-Spatial Intelligence This is occurring by apparent or hidden connections between human or machine generated data and the time these occur so to investigate their connecting nodes, also linked to political decision making and learning. Although major prediction frameworks and systems exist as part of the GSS, it seems they cannot not successfully indicate or predict major or massive activities with global impact following the latest global events. Social media, semantic associations, local security camera data and other information have not been connected and analysed enough to predict undesirable events. Therefore, the main aim of this proposition is the identification, analysis and understanding connections between real-time political events for time-space investigation as Chrono-Spatial Intelligence. A second aim is to identify tools, methodologies and evaluation techniques to facilitate shedding light in Chrono-Spatial Intelligence understanding, analysis and impact related to political decision making, as for example quality in education. Future research suggests the proposition implementation.

Keywords: HCI · Chrono-Spatial Intelligence · Global Systems Science

1 Global Systems Science (GSS) and Serendipity

According to the EU, Global Systems Science (GSS) is to provide scientific evidence to support policy-making, public action and civic society to collectively engage in societal action (https://ec.europa.eu/digital-agenda/en/global-systems-science).

Crisis was a window to reality regarding the inability of the world states to deal with the global challenges such as wars, climate change, financial crises or energy sufficiency

© Springer International Publishing Switzerland 2016
G. Meiselwitz (Ed.): SCSM 2016, LNCS 9742, pp. 201–208, 2016.
DOI: 10.1007/978-3-319-39910-2_19

to name a few without apparent and promising solutions depicted in the horizon. As the impact and effects of such problems are indeed global, and following the expansion of the locus of research the recent years, it is obvious that only global actions connected to local solutions may provide hope for change. In this proposition, the Internet as the global connecting network and an interdisciplinary ecosystem is the place to identify expanded areas for specific locus of research. It is also the exact paradigm of the ways citizens create their own space of communication and collaboration acting locally with potential for global impact. Identifying communication and interoperability between systems, connections and orchestrating actions with global impact may be the ultimate vision for GSS; in fact, any citizen can 'go viral' at any moment using the social media.

In this proposition, we utilise GSS systems thinking in connection to social media by integrating and linking data from different social media resources across diverse sectors and global actors. The challenges addressed here are related to policy design and political decision making on specific challenges, as for example, quality in education in order to incorporate and address the exact and future students' needs and responses connected to the global job market.

Politicians nowadays need to make decisions under uncertainty or conflicting evidence; also, as human beings and representors of specific political systems, they cannot follow disruption and uncertainty as expressed today. For this problem, the serendipity identification and advantage is proposed in this paper to fill in, according to Roland Burt University of Chicago sociologist, the structural holes and therefore, aid in proactive decision making. This is possible via mathematics and Big Data analysis, integration and visualisation, cascading and escalating effects in social networks and media, also taking advantage of indicator-based and event-based surveillance from cities and police cameras.

Other than following the events, social media are events creators and social reactors for even more ideas, social interactions and events to be created. Hence, informal learning creates great leaps of behavioural change. As such, causal collisions indicators in social media can build upon appearing randomness of events for predictions. Coming across ideas and event son social media can create the canvas for new ideas to appear and advance creativity to its most. This exact nature and characteristic of social media infuse more ideas and events flow as actions indicate ideas priorities in reality, producing events. Eventually, harnessing creativity and taking advantage of digital serendipity in social media costs mush less as the cost of having barriers for collaboration and the cost of not knowing is rather higher.

2   Chrono-Spatial (Time-Space) Intelligence: An Introduction

Series of fortunate and unfortunate events are not isolated but rather connected in time and space and may be occurring by apparent or hidden connections. Although major prediction frameworks and systems exist as part of the Global Systems Science (GSS), it seems they cannot not indicate or predict major or massive activities with global impact. Social media such as Twitter, Facebook, sematic associations as with annotation homogeneity or other in correlations and associations with local security camera data and other information such as local police data can provide hints or possible undesirable movements that have not taken advantage so far. Moreover, it appears that there is a need for optimization methods for training forecast algorithms, distributed forecast and knowledge management in the cloud as well as streaming media visualisation such as special purpose accelerators (H/W) for streaming media processing for knowledge extraction. As the World Wide Web and the Internet of Things offer the widest range of data in the human history, it is possible to identify the ways and impact that these are connected for predictions, aid or prevention for effective and efficient proactive actions long before events visibility occurs. The main aim of the project is the identification, analysis and understanding connections between real-time political events for time-space investigation as Chrono-Spatial Intelligence on individual level regarding leadership and European level. A second aim is to identify tools, methodologies and evaluation techniques to facilitate shedding light in Chrono-Spatial Intelligence Analytics understanding, analysis and impact.

Rapid capture of information of events and real time analysis and visualisation is a challenge we are attempting to address. The same GSS tools can create and group recommendations based on data analysis according to specific hierarchical categories. Discovering lines of actions behind appearance of events and unexpected actions processes can create specific motives and patterns to be identified, studied, analysed and understand under GSS analytics, so to transfer these patterns and structures in different fields and disciplines.

3   Chrono-Spatial Intelligence Research

Rapid technological changes influence communication, collaboration, information and knowledge management. Within the context of these new challenges, research design needs to explore human-human and human-computer interactions as lack of an agreed GSS research strategies at the moment leaves researchers planning without coherent frameworks. Also, the ethical principles for conducting research with human participants include general principles that may differ in e-research.

Chrono Spatial Intelligence Research contexts under investigation are based on global events, people, time and locations can generate visible pathways and connections via Chrono-Spatial Intelligence Analytics. These are: Chrono-Spatial Intelligence Analytics Design Methodologies as with Time series design; Chrono-Spatial Intelligence Analytics Methodologies, as with Quantitative and Qualitative mainstream methods, Specific Focus Groups and Interviews; data analysis via Sequential Analysis, Natural Language Processing and Social Network Analysis. Therefore, the proposition refers to the design and development of a new Chrono-Spatial Intelligence Platform for data visualisation, semantic annotations, analytics predictions Interface via forecasting algorithms.

The identified factors would be related to: (a) the context under investigation related to forecasting intentions identified in linear and non-linear actions; (b) timelines on past, present and future actions and activities as well as associations and links towards forecasting; (c) spatial intelligence referring to locations and links between time and space events; (d) individuals and lists of individuals and groups as information and events hubs identified via social network analysis, natural language processing, focus groups and interviews; (e) contexts as with news channels, social networks with care on personal data and blogs feeds; and (f) identification of context conditions and dei-ex-machine. As such, the proposed research design is the time-series with time series real time streaming data visualisations (time) for predefined patterns and peak points identifications, abnormalities identification, and decision making identification points. The research methods are proposed to be the following: (a) Spatial Analysis (space – locations); Sequential Data Analysis (events - contexts); Social Network Analysis; and Natural Language Processing. The Data Analysis Outcomes are suggested to be identified based upon: Converged peaks from comparisons, Convergences, Divergences, People flow movement, Individuals identification, Valid Predictions and Forecast, Mistakes, Deus Ex Machina: non-apparent evens / individuals working at the background and appearing the last crucial moment, as well as Insights from past to future; Insights from future to past and Forces and Initial Conditions identifications.

The practical implications are related to advanced types of machine learning for computer vision and text analysis by deep learning algorithms for certain tasks. Such deep learning models and systems for Global Systems Science can create learning nets provide the mathematical framework for an estimation problem analysis anchored in previous 8 case studies analysed backwards. This means start by major events and tracking them backwards to their initial conditions and origins appeared on the internet and social media in particular.

Chrono-Spatial Intelligence platform proposition can provide insights for diverse utilisation. Here, the advanced and proactive political decision making is targeted, based on the recent crisis event around the globe. Therefore, relationships between information, events, people, time, locations can be identified by Chrono-Spatial Intelligence Analytics.

Indicated Chrono-Spatial Intelligence Analytics Design Methodologies is real-Time series design with streaming data real-time visualisation.

Time-based coordination was used to capture the development and to triangulate sides of space and time of the unit of analysis. The use of quasi experimental time-short-series design was found a suitable approach to set a timeframe [7]. Time settings refer to two main sets, defining the baseline(s), and time series. Baseline refers to the observation of behaviour prior to any treatment designed to alter behaviour. As such, the treatment effect is demonstrated by a discontinuity in the pattern of pre-treatment and post-treatment responses. The groups which are going to be used in this study are inactive. The latter suggests a solid baseline for treatments and effects related to causal inference, not affected by threats like history, natural development and maturity for studies mostly observed in children's research. In time-short-series design aggregation and causal inference are not necessarily affected if a detailed amount of data could be collected. There are three dimensions to be investigated in order to examine the nature of intervention: (a) the form of the effect (the level, slop, variance and cyclicity); (b) its permanence (continuous or discontinuous) and (c) its immediacy (immediate or delayed).

Social Network Analysis (SNA) has been used to visualize communication and relationships between people and/or groups through diagrams by depicting social relationships between a set of actors [2]. The most widely used SNA attributes are nodes (the actors of study), relations (the strands between actors), and centrality (central or isolated person). SNA focuses on complete (or group) and ego networks; however, only group analysis on cohesion and centrality was found suitable for this study. In addition, several tools were considered for SNA as well as their integration in discussion forums as to support co-presence.

Cohesion: Network density for group thickness, reciprocity, cliques, and structural equivalence were used to measure the level of cohesion. Network density is the proportion of possible links in network that actually exist; it was evaluated by the adjacency connection reports. Sent-Received (S-R) number of messages is related to participants' reciprocity. More specifically, reciprocity is the number of ties that are involved in reciprocal relations relative to the total number of actual ties. A clique is a set of actors with each being connected to each other in smaller groups. Structural equivalence and in particular the CONCOR technique (CONvergence of iterated CORrelations [1]), describes the actors that have similar relations to others in the network with dendrogrammes. So the degree to which two nodes are structurally equivalent can be evaluated by measuring the degree to which their columns are identical:

Centrality: Group centrality [3] refers to the distribution of power between the community members and is measured by centrality, closeness and betweenness. In this study it referred to the total number of Sent-Received Messages (direct links), out-degree (replies made) and in-degree (received messages) centrality. Group closeness is defined by the normalised inverse sum of distances from the group to a node outside the group and related to reciprocal distances. Betweeness is the number of indirect links in which the actor is required as an intermediary; this characterise the mediator as the controller of the information flow in a network.

Knowledge of the ways and weight of ties between actors and events can indicate ways to strengthen collaboration and thus, engineering digital serendipity.

Social Network Analysis is a research methodology suggested for analysing interactions between humans. In GSS and in this paper, such connections need to also be related to Spatial Analysis of interactions between users and locations triangulated with other Big Data collection as for example police cameras and reports.

Time Series Design and Sequential Data Design and Analysis can shed light on the processes so to engineer serendipity in data not fixed in advance but incoming in a nonlinear and agile format. The data is not stopped but continuous to be collected in time series and analytics, including usability analytics can be adjusted and also edited depending on the next incoming data. Comparisons and visualisations at earlier and later stages can provide insights for proactive decision making. Sequential Data Analysis (SDA) include transition matrix analysis, lag sequential analysis, frequency of cycles, graphical summarization techniques, and most importantly, pattern analysis techniques. Semantic Analysis such as Latent Semantic Analysis, optimization methods for training forecast algorithms and Natural Language Processing are also suggested as appropriate methodologies for quantitative and qualitative data analysis, however, not discussed in this paper.

Early identification for futile actions or beneficial ones can shed light for adjustment, enhancement or re-adjustment on proactive decision making. In some cases specific cycles and routines can be identified and utilised. Analysis and understanding of multiple matrices data provide the ecology for Chrono-Spatial Intelligence to arise.

4 Serendipity Engineering Economy with CSI

Serendipity Engineering builds upon randomness, interaction, chaos and complexity for innovative aspects and directions to be identified and taken advantage in favour of the user. In this way, serendipity and unintended outcomes can be manipulated to orchestrate pleasant surprises. According to [5]: "*Serendipity is the process through which we discover unknown unknowns. Understanding it as an emergent property of social networks, instead of sheer luck, enables us to treat it as a viable strategy for organizing people and sharing ideas, rather than writing it off as magic. And that, in turn, has potentially huge ramifications for everything from how we work to how we learn to where we live by leading to a shift away from efficiency—doing the same thing over and over, only a little bit better—toward novelty and discovery.*"

Accidental intentions can be engineered by directions and flow identification and moreover, enhance what is already there and moving [6]. Social media provide the mixed reality matrix with people, concepts, ideas and their relationships. Serendipity Economy is related to hidden value and potential in constantly shifting ecosystems that operate in rather apparent chaotic environments. Therefore, Serendipity Engineering Economy is related to return-on-investment on proactive decision making when taking advantage the social media for specific purposes, based on potential and anticipated outcomes from open, cross-organizational networking.

Social media research and CSI can built upon the structural holes for organisations, companies of even countries based on the following aspects:

- Predefined patterns and peak points identifications for both benefits and problems, so to apply restrictive or enhancing actions
- Abnormalities identification and study both the nature and characteristics as well as the impact on the context and the time series effects
- Decision making identification points and triangulation of chrono-spacial and human events earlier or later
- Converged peaks from comparisons and routines identifications
- Convergences and divergences on data visualisation as well as
- People flow movement can indicate both intentions and repeated activities in specific locations
- Individuals identification depending on specific criteria can also be more effective
- Deus Ex Machina for serendipity engineering reveals non-apparent evens / individuals working at the background, lastly
- Forces and initial conditions identifications to identify, restrict or enhance and recreate.

The financial benefits for providing such information towards proactive decision making can bring major advantages for the economy as the cost of resources would be minimised and directed to most effective situations and people support.

5   Concluding Remarks and Future Work

This paper described the advantage of utilising the power of social media utilising Global Systems Science (GSS) research tools and techniques. Fortunate and unfortunate series of events can reveal the matrix of creation for reality by revealing hidden connections in a new form of intelligence named digital Chrono-Spatial Intelligence (CSI). Digital CSI depends on the effectiveness for recognising apparent or hidden, serendipitous connections between human or machine generated data and the time. Such information can be the torch for proactive political decision making and learning bringing major benefits for the organisation that can adopt CSI in strategic thinking. Social media data in correlations with other data formats can provide information for real-time political impact related to political decision making, as for example quality in education.

Such GSS and machine learning also indicates scalable learning for us as humans and operators behind the machines. New tools can provide new lenses and extensions of our thinking processes; we are building the tools and then the tools impact us back in our perspectives. Social media is an emergent field and property for all to re-organise our strategies for collaboration and proactive decision making in an era of complexity and huge ramifications. In such chaotic environments, GSS can provide methods and tools for efficient actions with major impact for all in the direction we choose. Instead of repeating the same patterns and mistakes we can drive a different route towards serendipity for creativity and innovation with much lower financial and human cost and resources.

Among the 21st Century Skills [4] we consider to be the Chrono-Spacial Intelligence, also dynamic competence for a successful leader; bringing the right people to the right place at the right time for creating something new is indeed a combination of time, space and people intelligence. Nowadays, technology and social media in particular provide us with the methods, approaches and tools to discover the connected links between people and events and be responsive about the consequences. Future research suggests optimization methods for training forecast algorithms and streaming media visualisation as well as our proposal implementation.

Chance favours the connected mind.

References

1. Breiger, R.L., Boorman, S.A., Arabie, P.: An algorithm for clustering relational data with applications to social network analysis and comparison with multidimensional scaling. J. Math. Psychol. **12**, 328–382 (1975)
2. Baroudi, J.J., Olson, M.H., Ives, B.: An empirical study of the impact of user involvement on system usage and information satisfaction. Commun. ACM **29**(3), 232–238 (1986)

3. Everett, M.: Extending centrality. In: Carrington, P.J., Scott, J., Wasserman, S. (eds.) Models and Methods in Social Network Analysis, pp. 57–76. Cambridge University Press, New York (2005)
4. Lambropoulos, N., Romero, M.: 21st Century Lifelong Creative Learning: A Matrix of Innovative Methods and New Technologies for Individual, Team and Community Skills and Competencies. Nova Publishers, New York (2015)
5. Lindsey, G.: Engineering Serendipity (2014). https://medium.com/aspen-ideas/engineering-serendipity-941e601a9b65#.d5hjz08d6
6. Maurer, T.: Serendipity and the 'Aha' Moment – Unexpected Insights in the Innovation Process (2014). https://www.uschamberfoundation.org/blog/post/serendipity-and-aha-moment-unexpected-insights-innovation-process/34418
7. Shadish, W., Cook, T., Campbell, D.: Experimental & Quasi-Experimental Designs for Generalized Causal Inference. Houghton Mifflin, Boston (2002)

Designing for Neighbourhoods and Citizen Engagement

The Case of MyNeighbourhood

Sobah Abbas Petersen[1(✉)], Manuel Oliveira[1], and Grazia Concilio[2]

[1] SINTEF Technology and Society, S.P. Andersensv. 5, 7465 Trondheim, Norway
{sobah.petersen,manuel.oliveira}@sintef.no
[2] Department of Architecture and Urban Studies, Politecnico di Milano, Milan, Italy
grazia.concilio@polimi.it

Abstract. Citizen engagement, human infrastructure and engaging citizens to facilitate bottom up social innovation through technology is an important part of Human Smart Cities, which was the main focus of the EU MyNeighbourhood project. The main research question addressed in this paper is how to design social software to support neighbourhoods and encourage the social cohesiveness through social-spatial spaces in the real and virtual world where neighbours could come together and act towards improving the neighbourhood. The paper describes the co-design process in the project to design services and a technological platform for citizen engagement. The co-design process provided a rich set of requirements for a diversity of users. The challenges in designing the technology and the user engagement activities that were experienced and addressed during the project are discussed.

Keywords: Co-design · Citizen engagement · Design challenges · Human Smart Cities

1 Introduction

Most social networking software has been designed to bring together people through technology, often to connect people who are geographically distributed. Social networking applications such as Facebook, Flickr, Instagram, Twitter and LinkedIn, have brought people together for social and professional purposes; long lost friends and relatives are now connected and sharing photos and various aspects of their lives, and discussion groups agree and debate over issues that are of interest to them. Communities of Interests form groups to address specific things. Social networks have no doubt changed our lives in ways that were not anticipated and people are connected through technology more than ever before. While we are connected with our long distance contacts, colleagues, friends, relatives, it is unclear if we know our neighbours any better or if we can utilise the resources and the human infrastructure around us in our neighbourhoods and cities better through the social networking technologies available today [1]. The EU MyNeighbourhood project focused on the human infrastructure and engaging citizens to facilitate bottom up social innovation through technology [2]. The main research question addressed in this paper is how to design social software to support

© Springer International Publishing Switzerland 2016
G. Meiselwitz (Ed.): SCSM 2016, LNCS 9742, pp. 209–220, 2016.
DOI: 10.1007/978-3-319-39910-2_20

neighbourhoods and encourage the social cohesiveness through social-spatial spaces in the real and virtual world where neighbours could come together and act towards improving the neighbourhood.

Cities are moving from their traditional modes of engaging citizens to leveraging on ICT for reaching their citizens [3]. Engaging citizens in the co-design of services and solutions has become popular [4]. Similarly, the MyNeighbourhood project aimed at using 'smart' ICT services and citizen/neighbourhood generated data to help recreate the social mechanisms which, in the past, ensured that urban neighbourhoods coincided with a social system of connected and trusted communities, where people felt safe and happy with a true sense of belonging. The project had four pilot cities; Birmingham in UK, Milan, in Italy, Lisbon in Portugal and Aalborg in Denmark. The city councils were partners in the project. Specific neighbourhoods from each city were identified as the pilots and citizens and all the stakeholders were engaged from the onset to foster a sense of ownership as well as to ensure that the design of services and technologies met the needs of the end users. Co-design and Co-creation and Urban Living Labs were central to the work of the project. The aim was to co-design a set of services for each pilot and to create a common platform to engage the citizens and to facilitate dialogue among the citizens and between the citizens and the city councils.

A social networking platform for engaging citizens in neighbourhoods, the MyN Platform [5], was co-designed and developed in the project. Several co-design workshops were conducted to identify the needs of the citizens. The approach that was taken was to gather individual needs, select the ones that were most popular and use these to create scenarios of how people in a neighbourhood would do things if there were a common social platform available to them.

The neighbourhoods were selected by the Municipalities of each pilot city. The main criterion for selection was the municipalities' interest in improving the neighbourhoods and the activities that were already taking place in those neighbourhoods. Milan, Birmingham and Lisbon had neighbourhoods with ethnic diversity and challenges in integration, high unemployment and school dropout rates. Milan, in particular, had a geographical challenge where one neighbourhood was separated by a bridge, which increased the challenges. Aalborg, a relatively smaller city than the others, focused on a neighbourhood where the municipality was working closely with other organisations to engage volunteer citizens in the care of handicapped citizens.

This paper describes the co-design process and citizen engagement activities in the MyNeighbourhood project. The co-design process provided a rich set of needs and requirements for MyN Platform. One of the challenges during the project was meeting the expectations of the numerous stakeholders and the diverse user groups of the MyN platform. The paper provides an overview of the challenges in designing the platform and the citizen engagement activities. The rest of the paper is structured as follows: Sect. 2 describes the co-design process; Sect. 3 describes the citizen engagement process; Sect. 4 describes the challenges in the design and Sect. 5 summarises the paper.

2   Co-design Process

2.1   The MyN Handbook

Several methods and tools to support service design are available; e.g. [6]. In the MyNeighbourhood project, the co-design process in each MyN pilot was guided step by step and supported by a co-design handbook developed for the project [7], which contained a collection of methods and tools. The handbook also included methods and tools that could be used by operators in the public administration or by groups of citizens to promote innovative ideas in their neighbourhoods. It was clarified from the beginning that these tools and methods could be modified, adapted or even distorted, in order to achieve a practical result. For this reason, it was complemented with an online repository of cases, examples and templates: cases included illustrations on how the various methods could be used; templates included outlines, schemas, forms and checklists that the pilot could use to support the co-creation process with users; examples included pictures and schemes illustrating how the tools had been used in other co-design activities.

The MyN co-design handbook was organized around three main work phases: context analysis, design (concept generation and detailing), and application/test (see Fig. 1).

Overall design phase	Context Analysis		Design		Application/test
			Concept generation	Detailing	
Mode	Exploring	Making Sense	Proposing		Iteration

Fig. 1. MyN co-design work phases

The Context Analysis generally started with *explorative activities* aimed at entering the context, trying to keep interaction with people as small as possible and to identify possible situations as possible context entry points. This explorative work was "expansive", i.e. it was a process in which all the factors that could influence a social context were considered. The exploration was transformed slowly into a *sense making* work where the rich amount of information collected in the exploration phase was analysed and interpreted, in order to work out facts that could be usable in the design phase. This was also the work during which a first hierarchy of priorities was outlined, issues to address and change were clarified and consensus was developed among the actors, on what problem to work on.

The Service Design phase generally started with the *concept generation* activity as generative work. It was about working up and sharing provisional ideas – new activities, processes, systems or touch-points, which address the issue that have been identified during the context analysis phase. This stage usually led to open definitions of possible solutions, without investing too much in one idea, but rather collecting pros and cons about different hypotheses. This generative phase was followed by a *concept specification* work, a process of exploring what the concepts proposed would really be like in practice, to refine or rework an idea. This also implied a revision of concepts and iteration of concept-detailing phases. This phase also included methods to scale up co-design initiatives, to engage stakeholders into a continuous improvement and learning process.

2.2 Co-design in the MyN Pilots

The co-design work was divided into two main phases: the Context Analysis phase and Service Design phase. The contexts of the pilots influenced their interpretation of the phases and the activities that were conducted varied accordingly. An example of the activities is shown in Fig. 2. Nevertheless, all the pilots had used a good selection of tools from the Handbook coherently and conducted several activities in both the phases.

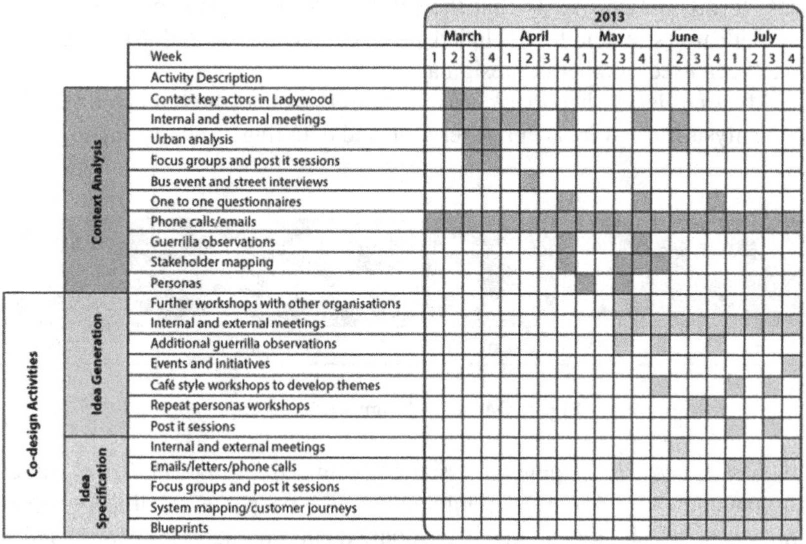

			2013																					
			March				April				May				June				July					
		Week	1	2	3	4	1	2	3	4	1	2	3	4	1	2	3	4	1	2	3	4		
Co-design Activities	Context Analysis	Activity Description																						
		Contact key actors in Ladywood																						
		Internal and external meetings																						
		Urban analysis																						
		Focus groups and post it sessions																						
		Bus event and street interviews																						
		One to one questionnaires																						
		Phone calls/emails																						
		Guerrilla observations																						
		Stakeholder mapping																						
		Personas																						
	Idea Generation	Further workshops with other organisations																						
		Internal and external meetings																						
		Additional guerrilla observations																						
		Events and initiatives																						
		Café style workshops to develop themes																						
		Repeat personas workshops																						
		Post it sessions																						
	Idea Specification	Internal and external meetings																						
		Emails/letters/phone calls																						
		Focus groups and post it sessions																						
		System mapping/customer journeys																						
		Blueprints																						

Fig. 2. Co-design activities in Birmingham

The context analysis mainly enabled pilots to identify problems in the neighbourhoods, the actors involved and the related stakeholder maps; (an example is shown in Fig. 3). In addition, personas were developed to describe the typical actors involved or considered as key actors in the context; see an example in Fig. 4.

In the concept generation phase, all the pilots produced different service ideas and they were described with a goal, how it would work and the actors involved. Some of the service ideas that were developed were safer transport routes (in Birmingham), Volunteers for handicapped citizens (in Aalborg) and a food service for the elderly provided by a catering school (in Milan).

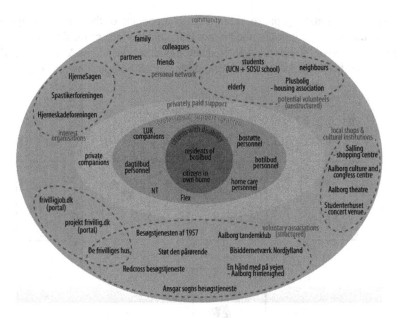

Fig. 3. Stakeholders map of the Aalborg Pilot

LONELY OLD LADY

1- Name: Luciana   Aged: 79   KW: widow, housewife

Typical day: I live alone in a rented flat in Quarto Oggiaro neighbourhood.
I wake up early in the morning, I turn on the radio that is my morning friend, than I prepare my breakfast and take my morning medicines, I can't go out of my flat very easily, infact my legs don't work anymore very well, you know, I feel tired very soon when I try to walk... .
I often would like to talk to someone, even for a little while, so I pick up the phone and call some old friend or my daughter that lives in another city, with his 3 kids. But sometimes our times for conversation don't match, and I feel very lonely at times.
When I turn off the radio, I turn on television. When the program "The chef competition" starts, I know it's time to cook my lunch and to take my "noon medicines". In the afternoon I often fell asleep because I am tired to do nothing. In the evening, after dinner and my evening medicines, I watch a bit of television, and also have a look at the televideo for the results of the lottery, then I go to bed. And that's it.

Lifestyle: I stay into my home mostly, sometimes I go to my doctor's when I need new medicines. Unfortunately he is quite far for me, every time is a journey. On Tuesday and Friday I go to the bar just under my home to buy a lottery ticket. Once or twice a month my son and his family came to visit me, and when it happens I feel very glad but also tired, because I like to prepare a cake for my grandson who is five years old and has a sweet tooth.

Opportunities: I'd like very much to see or talk with persons, or at least to have the opportunity to use someone's computer or that kind of telephone that makes you able to see the person who you are talking with...you know, I'd like to talk and see my grandsons more often, but it's only a dream, because those kind of things are very expensive and in addition they are very difficult to manage. But if I won the lottery...

Fig. 4. One of the personas of the Milan Pilot

In the concept detailing phase, three main components of the service design were developed: the customer journey, the system map, and the blue print. This was done for each pilot, for each of the services selected among the service ideas. An example of one of these, the system map for the volunteer service in Aalborg is shown in Fig. 5.

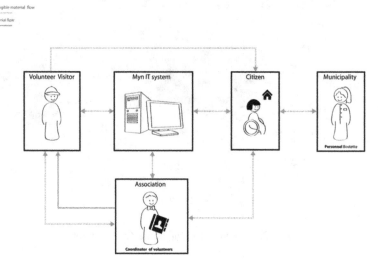

Fig. 5. System map of the volunteer service in Aalborg

The system maps and the blueprints helped identify the different components of the services and the support that was necessary. In particular, the blueprints identified the technological components that were required and the functionalities that needed to be designed. The material from the context analysis phase provided a good understanding and a rich set of requirements for the design of the technological components.

3   Citizen Engagement

As one of the main focus in the MyNeighbourhood project, the MyN Platform was designed to support citizen engagement. However, it did not take very long to see that the technology alone was insufficient to engage citizens on a new platform and a critical mass of users were crucial for the success of the technology. Thus, user engagement activities were planned as a part of an iterative development process which was composed of six distinct phases as illustrated in Fig. 6.

- **Platform Development.** The development of the MyN Platform was done using an agile approach where the product owner, represented by the key stakeholders of each pilot neighbourhood, prioritised the backlog of features and functionality resulting from the co-design activities;
- **Platform Release.** Throughout the development process, the MyN Platform was released periodically;

- **Citizen Engagement Activities.** With the release of the platform, planned user engagement activities were carried out in the field, involving the citizens in the neighbourhood;
- **Monitoring and Analysis.** The user engagement activities were closely monitored on the platform supported by evaluation work carried out in the field. The monitoring was based on assessment indicators, which were complemented by Google Analytics and analysis of platform logs. The analysis also considered cumulative effects of the user engagement with MyN Platform;
- **Correlation and Understanding of Context.** The resulting data gathered from the monitoring was analysed and correlated to determine the effectiveness of the activities and the performance of the MyN Platform. This was more than capturing error and functional mishaps, but included determining the shortcomings on the platform supporting user engagement;
- **Insights and Lessons Learnt.** The correlated data yielded important insights and lessons learnt that shaped the planning of user engagement activities and improvements to the MyN Platform.

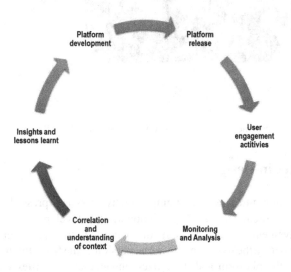

Fig. 6. MyNeighbourhood deployment process

These citizen engagement activities were carefully designed to promote the use of the MyN Platform and where the platform played a central role. The engagement activities included field work, activities on the MyN Platform and most importantly creating synergy between the two. One successful example of citizen engagement that resulted in increased activity and interactions among the neighbours through the MyN Platform was a photo competition, where citizens took pictures from their neighbourhoods and shared them through the platform. They then encouraged their friends to vote for the pictures, on the platform, to find the best or the most popular photo. This was a competition among neighbours within one neighbourhood as well as across the four pilot neighbourhoods where the winners were the most popular picture in each neighbourhood and the most active neighbourhood among the four pilot neighbourhoods. At the end of the competition, the photos were exhibited in a public place, such as the local library in Aalborg, and the competition results were announced in a small ceremony; see photo in Fig. 7.

Fig. 7. Prize ceremony of the photo competition in the Marvila pilot in Portugal

4   Challenges in Design

Designing for communities are challenging in many ways as expressed by other authors too [8]. A key challenge in the MyNeighbourhood development process was the continued involvement of the champions that were identified and engaged during the co-design phase before the release of the initial version of the MyN Platform. Challenges to the design of the platform and the citizen engagement activities were from many perspectives and these are described in the following subsections.

4.1   Diversity

In the MyNeighbourhood project, the pilot neighbourhoods were from four different countries with different cultures and languages. While the cultural diversities enriched the design, it also introduced challenges in supporting a multicultural, multilingual interface. The pilot neighbourhoods themselves were multicultural with a variety of people; immigrants with limited knowledge of the local language (e.g. in the Birmingham pilot), elderly citizens with little or no digital literacy (e.g. in the Milan pilot) and mentally or physically handicapped citizens (e.g. in the Aalborg pilot). Consequently, a major challenge to the design of the MyN Platform was the drive to support multiple dimensions of diversity such as elderly vs. digital natives (e.g. [9]), designing the right user interface and interaction design for different user groups and achieving the right balance of privacy. In the four pilot neighbourhoods, there was a clear digital divide, with the elderly suffering from poor digital literacy and the generation designated as digital natives being more digital savvy. The design of the interface posed challenges to meet the needs of a wide range of users with different requirements, such as in the case of handicapped users in Aalborg, and the use of symbols to support users who were not confident with the languages supported by the Platform or with poor literacy skills.

Achieving the right balance of privacy to safeguard the online information shared by the citizens within a neighbourhood was an important design issue. There was a need to provide functionality that would protect special user groups that required a closed and private community. Additionally, the need for fostering community trust amongst the non-citizen stakeholders, such as non-government organisations and the municipalities, was equally important.

4.2   Synergy Between Field Activity and the Digital Platform

Citizen engagement activities were aimed to foster community engagement through the use of the MyN Platform where the synergy between the work done in the field and the activity on the MyN Platform would contribute to enhance the feeling of a community, build trust and a sense of belonging among the neighbours and between the citizens and the public authorities. Thus, the design of the relevant and appropriate activities posed requirements on the platform too as illustrated in some examples listed in Table 1.

Table 1. Design challenges for citizen engagement activities

Citizen engagement activity	Field work	MyN Platform support
Photo competition (all pilot neighbourhoods)	-Taking photos -Talk to neighbours, inform and encourage them to vote for the photos	-Support user contributions (uploading of photos) -Access to photos for all users -possibility to vote online -display results of voting polls at any time
Hooking to local community activities.	Be present where it happens; e.g. at funfairs (Birmingham) or other community events (Lisbon)	-Mobile access to the platform from anywhere -Easy and fast registration process
Cibo Vicino (near food service in Milan)	Engaging neighbours and bringing relevant actors together	Interaction with existing or other ICT solutions
Flash mob (Lisbon)	Engaging neighbours to join a community event; e.g. a group of dancers on a train.	-Possibility to upload and share information by users

4.3   Iterative Releases

The iterative deployment shown in Fig. 6 required continuous analyses of data and understanding the synergy between the field work and the activities on the MyN Platform. Traditional evaluation approaches proved inadequate as the data was analysed in a working and development setting [10, 11]. This required a work process that supported it, a clear idea of the indicators for community engagement as well as appropriate and timely data from the platform that reflected the engagement. A task force was established with at least one representative of the development team, evaluation and user engagement activities. The role of the task force was to extract data logs from the platform and analyse them with data mining and sense making tools and methodologies; correlate the processed data with the evolving contexts in the pilots and to determine recommendations based on the distilled insights.

The graph of Fig. 8 illustrates a sample of the data gathered for the task force to assess and carry out the analysis. The graph represents the delta values over time of key indicators, such as the total number of registered users, total number of contributions, total number of supports on ideas, etc. Taking a closer look at the pattern of activity on the platform, the sudden changes such as a peak or a drop were considered and the activities of the pilots corresponding to those times were reviewed.

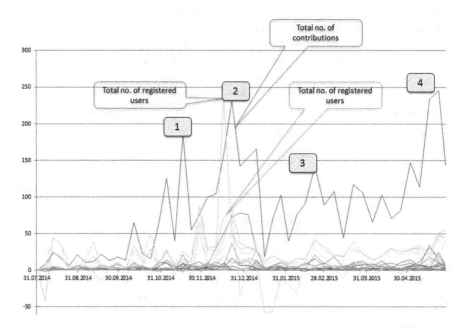

Fig. 8. Illustrative example of the analysis of the data collated from the MyN platform

The peak that is marked "1" on the figure corresponds to the time of the Magusto festival in Lisbon and the MyN team worked actively promoting the project and the MyN Platform. The peak that is marked "2" corresponds to the time when the photo competition took place, which generated a lot of activity on the platform. The exhibitions of the photos from the competition raised the level of activity two months after the photo competition, labelled "3". A few smaller peaks followed during the following months when all the pilots worked intensely presenting the MyN Platform to various associations and stakeholders in their own neighbourhoods and other neighbourhoods and munici- palities. This effort by the pilot teams resulted in increasing the level of activities in the initial neighbourhoods as well the emergence of new neighbourhoods and communities. The final peak of activities, labelled "4", is explained by the increased level of activity in general, some new activities by the Lisbon pilot such as the flash mob and activities from the new neighbourhoods. By the end of the project (June 2015), the no. of neigh- bourhoods had increased from the initial 4 to 23, spanning different cities in both Italy and Denmark.

5   Summary and Future Work

In this paper, we have described the co-design process in the MyNeighbourhood project to design services and a technological platform for citizen engagement and addressed the challenges in designing social software for engaging citizens at the neighbourhood level. The variety of methods and tools were used to co-design services where an exten- sive context analysis was done followed by systematic design of the services and even- tually the technical functionality of the MyN Platform. An iterative development process was followed, where releases of the platform were followed by user engagement activ- ities in the field, careful analysis of the data, experience sharing and reflection, followed by recommendations for new releases of the platform.

The rich set of requirements and contexts posed a no. of challenges, both for the user engagement activities as well as the design of the technology. The challenges could be categorised as ones related to the diversity of the stakeholders and user groups, creating synergy between the platform and the field activities and identifying and evaluating relevant data that reflected citizen engagement.

Further analyses of the data and contents on the platform will contribute to under- standing citizen engagement and the role of technology. Several improvements to the platform have been identified which will be considered in future projects. An example of this would be to develop a mobile platform to enhance accessibility.

Acknowledgments.   The authors would like to thanks the partners in the EU MyNeighbourhood project.

References

1. Gaudin, S.: Social networks make us feel more connected, survey says, in Computer World (2010)
2. MyNeighbourhood. The MyNeighbourhood project (2015). http://my-neighbourhood.eu/. Accessed 6 December 2015
3. Forlano, L., Mathew, A.: Codesigning Urban Technology for Citizen Engagement: From Citizen-Centered to Collaborative Cities. Institute of Design, Illinois Institute of Technology

4. Rizzo, F., Deserti, A.: Small scale collaborative services: the role of design in the development of the human smart city paradigm. In: Streitz, N., Markopoulos, P. (eds.) DAPI 2014. LNCS, vol. 8530, pp. 583–592. Springer, Heidelberg (2014)
5. MyNeighbourhood. MyN Platform (2014). http://www.my-n.eu/. Accessed 1 December 2015
6. Tassi, R.: Service Design Tools - Communication Methods Supporting Design Processes (2009). http://www.servicedesigntools.org/. Accessed 29 2016 February
7. Morelli, N., Würtz, P.: MyNeighbourhood Deliverable 2.2 - Handbook of co-design activities for co-designing services. Department of AD:MT, Aalborg University, Aalborg, Denmark (2013)
8. Morelli, N.: Challenges in designing and scaling-up community services. In: Fourth Service Design and Innovation Conference ServDes. (2014)
9. Blat, J., et al.: Cross-cultural aspects of ICT use by older people: preliminary results of a four-country ethnographical study. In: Irish Human Computer Interaction Conference Integrated Practice Inclusive Design, Cork, Ireland (2011)
10. Patton, M.Q.: Evaluation for the way we work. Nonprofit Q. 13(1), 28–33 (2006)
11. Patton, M.Q.: Developmental evaluation applying complexity concepts to enhance innovation and use. Guilford Press, New York (2010)

Social Media - New Face of Collaborative Policing?

A Survey Exploring Perceptions, Behavior, Challenges for Police Field Officers and Residents

Niharika Sachdeva$^{(\boxtimes)}$ and Ponnurangam Kumaraguru

Indraprastha Institute of Information Technology, Delhi, India
{niharikas,pk}@iiitd.ac.in

Abstract. Online social media (OSM) has become a preferred choice of police to communicate and collaborate with citizens for improved safety. Various studies investigate perceptions and opinion of high ranked police officers on use of OSM in policing, however, understanding and perceptions of field level police personnel is largely unexplored. We collected survey responses of 445 police personnel and 204 citizens' survey in India to understand perceptions on OSN use for policing. Further, we analyzed posts from Facebook pages of Indian police organizations to study the behavior of police and citizens as they pursue social and safety goals on OSN. We find that success of OSN for policing demands effective communication between the stakeholders (citizens and police). Our results show preliminary evidences that OSN use for policing can help (1) increase participation in problem solving process, (2) increase community engagement by providing unique channel for both Feedback and Anonymity. However, such a system will need appropriate acknowledgment and trustworthiness channels to be successful. We also identify challenges in adopting OSN and outline design opportunities for HCI researchers and practitioners to design tools supporting social interactions for policing.

1 Introduction

Crime and safety issues disquietude most urban communities. Collaboration between police and residents often play a significant role in addressing crime and safety issues in varied context including Hurricane and fires [5,13]. In such collaborations, Online Social Media (OSM) is a preferred technology (see Fig. 1) as it provides massive civic engagement and social support [3,4,19,22,28]. OSM role becomes even more significant for developing region with limited police staff. UN guideline suggests 270–280 police-personnel per 1,00,000 residents whereas developing countries like India have 130 personnel per 1,00,000 residents [7]. Realizing the potential of OSM, Indian police have started exploring its use for day-to-day policing.

Literature extensively studies human behavior, perception and OSM adoption for policing in crisis and post-crisis situation [3,5,13,19,22,28]. However, OSM

© Springer International Publishing Switzerland 2016
G. Meiselwitz (Ed.): SCSM 2016, LNCS 9742, pp. 221–233, 2016.
DOI: 10.1007/978-3-319-39910-2_21

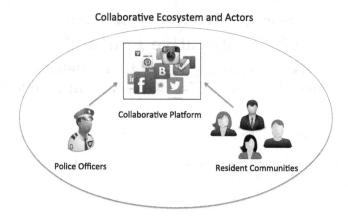

Fig. 1. Actors (Police and Residents) collaborating through various platform (Facebook, Twitter) for safety issues (EarthQuake, Hurricane).

use for day-to-day policing is largely unexplored. Few HCI studies that explored OSM in day-to-day policing investigated the opinion of command ranked officers (involved in the decision-making) but lack the understanding of field officers (who execute the decision) [1, 26]. Criminology research shows that field officers are the first point of contact and have maximum interaction with residents [23]. Therefore, understanding perceptions of field officers are necessary to improve collaborative policing. To understand OSM use for policing, we use a multi-stakeholder approach involving surveys of 445 police officers and 204 residents (Demographic details in Table 1). We analyze perceptions, behavior, and challenges experienced by police-personnel and residents while interacting on OSM. This includes investigating that why police and resident use OSM, what are their concerns, hindrances, and expectation as they interact on OSM.

Our work makes following contributions:

- We found that OSM can improve *transparency in problem solving process* by offering an open platform to engage communities for discussing safety issues/activities. However, we found residents and police differ on activities to be discussed on OSM. Top three activities for residents were – notifying about crime, emergency or disaster related issues, and crime prevention activities. Contrastingly, police-personnel preferred crime investigation, intelligence, and reputation management.
- We showed that the preferred OSM were *Facebook and WhatsApp*. Even though the preferred platforms for both were the same, we observed significant difference between officers and residents for choice of other OSM (χ^2 test, p-value < 0.001).
- We identified two distinct opportunities – *Feedback mechanism* and *Anonymity* to increase community engagement. Our results show that anonymity offered by OSM could help obtain more information from residents.

- We identified two deterrents to community engagement – lack of acknowledgement and trust. Residents (32 %) said that police should provide acknowledgement with an hour of residents posting the message. With limited resources, this can overload the police but to sustain collaboration, acknowledgement may be an effective tool.
- We suggest technological and design opportunities for effective community engagement and to innovate policing through OSM.

2 Related Work

Recent studies show increase in need of OSM as a plausible resource for police forces [6]. Police in developed nations have realized effectiveness of OSM in various activities such as investigation, identifying crime, intelligence development, and community policing [6,15,18]. However, interactivity and pace at which information diffuses on OSM results in additional pressure on police departments [6]. We found that police departments in developed countries have made reasonable efforts and progress to adopt OSM, whereas developing countries are still evolving skills to use OSM for policing [24]. Developing nations like India are not untouched from the influence of OSM. India has 92 million Facebook users (7.73 % of total Facebook user base) who are spread across both major (34 % of user base) and small cities (24 % of user base) of the country [21]. Various studies in Indian context showed that OSM was used to spread misinformation and public agitation during crisis events such as Mumbai terror attacks (2011), Muzzafarnagar riots and Assam disturbance(2012) [8,17,30]. In both the events (Assam, and Muzzafarnagar riots), panic was spread through fake images, messages, and videos on OSM [30].

Existing studies have shown effectiveness of OSM for crises like Boston bombings, Sichuan earthquake (2008), Haiti earthquake (2009), Oklahoma grassfires (2009), and Chile earthquake (2010) [9,10,20,25,29,31]. These studies demonstrate that OSM could provide critical real time information and reduce misinformation during crisis events. Researchers found that citizens used OSM for public coordination during crises. They categorized public response received during crisis on OSM and showed different communities which developed during crises [11,14]. We found few studies which analyzed police – public use of OSM [5,12,27]. Studies showed that police organizations need effective communication strategy to provide timely information to various groups [2]. These studies provide insights on different strategies and activities police perform on OSM. However, these provide little insight about police rationale and expectations behind these actions and citizen acceptance of these actions. Surveys showed that OSM introduced challenges for police officers such as fake/impostor accounts which target law enforcement agencies, security and privacy concerns, civil liabilities and resource constraints like time, and staff [15,18]. Another challenge was easy accessibility of OSM to malicious people, which could make sharing information with citizens a complex task [5]. Very few studies analyze citizen and police perceptions/concerns which lead to these challenges. However, these studies analyse the behaviour of higher ranked police officers and not of the ground staff who interact with the citizens more often. To best of our knowledge, this is the first study, which analyzed police personnel (ground staff) and citizen behavior/expectation regarding OSM use for policing. We present expectations gaps between police and citizens on OSM use for policing. We believe the insights from our study would provide opportunities to develop better communication strategy for police and motivate technologist to build secure system designs for effective policing using OSM.

3   Background

In this section, we give a qualitative review of different kind of posts made by different police departments in India. We found that police activities mainly include maintenance of law and public order, crime prevention and detection, traffic management, and enforcing laws of the land. To perform these activities police departments require active and dynamic interaction/participation from citizens. We found that police in India used OSM tasks such as traffic management, posting personal achievements and appreciation received by citizens. These pages also highlighted security conditions in disturbed/riots affected areas, educate citizens about current beat (patrols), and safety programs undertaken by city police. Figure 2 shows tag-cloud of most frequent words of posts and comments on these pages. Bangalore City Police (BCP) page provided one such platform to report issues related to policing. Figure 2(a) shows popular discussions on Bangalore City police page were regarding phone/mobile, finance problems, issues on roads, traffic, drivers, buses, lost objects, and First Information Reports (FIR). The comments below show complaints filed on OSM police pages.

Respected Commissioner, I wish to inform FIR No.07XX/20XX is registered in H.A.L. PS.GSC No. is PXXXX61301XXXXX. Registration No.: KXX5HXXX, Chassis No.: ME11CK0XXX, Engine No.:1XX2011XXX, Bike Model: Yamaha R15 white color, Phone: 8XX886XXXX & 80XX39XXXX.

People addressed various authorities like inspectors and commissioner to file complains and inquired about time constraints in which problem could be solved/addressed. To further understand citizens' view, we analyzed comments on BCP page. Mostly people reported issues in polite words – request, please and addressed officers as "Sir" (see Fig. 2(c)) but some people made rude statements about police. We found people thanked police, appreciated their work and inquired about action taken, and nearest station. Some examples below:

Great !! absolutely great !! Reading all the complaints and statuses. I am so very happy that police is doing great job in helping people via FB as well

People posted sensitive information and crime tips on Bangalore City Police page such as drug dealers active in the city, people in serious distress, and money laundering issues.

Drug dealer X. Phone number is 9XX02XXXXX. Please track him down. Selling ganja/pot/weed/marijuana.

(a)   (b)   (c)

Fig. 2. (a) shows popular discussions on Bangalore City Police (BCP) page, (b) shows Chennai police page, a relatively new page, was dedicated to city issues (c) shows comments posted on BCP page

Chennai police page, a relatively new page, was dedicated to city issues. Posts included questions regarding police action taken, complaints about phone, money, shops, traffic issues on roads, and few posts were regarding blackmailers. Figure 2(b) shows frequent words in these discussions. On analyzing comments on this page, we found popular topics were about blackmailers, money, police and station. We found some violent reactions on this page, people used words like Kill, torching, techniques etc. Outstation people in Chennai also posted their issues like:

We the people of INDIA from West Bengal want to say that some very dangerous groups want to kill many poor Indians for MONEY.

Delhi police did not have city police page but maintained a traffic police page. We analyzed this page and found that popular issues were traffic, vehicles, people, and car. Delhi police appreciated citizen participation for informing them about routine problems and also provided assistance if needed.

Thanks, matter will be looked into and you may also contact to TI/XXX at 87XXX7XXXX.

Similar to Bangalore City Police page, people gave their feedback to Delhi Traffic Police on these pages. Some people regarded these pages as eye wash whereas some people asked for status of their complaints and actions taken. For instance a citizen wrote

You are right XX, but DTP can never improve. FB page is also an eye wash.

People looked disappointed for not getting a reply/action taken against their complains in a given time frame. However, Delhi Traffic Police tried to keep citizens informed about actions taken and also posted other advisories as required. Some examples below:

The following vehicles/owners have been prosecuted by issuing notice on the basis of photographs on dated 08/02/2014 Vehicle no. - Notice no [XXXX]

Citizens also posted a variety of personal information on these pages such as phone numbers, IMEI numbers, and identity cards to report complains on these pages. Sometimes, police departments posted contact details as a reply to these post. People also posted irrelevant content on these pages such as publicity of a political party or general complaints against politicians. So far we analyzed messages on Facebook and Twitter to understand the policing landscape on OSM. This introduced many questions like how much information was useful for police departments, and were there some posts which could create problems for citizens. It was not clear, how OSM could help police departments to achieve their goals and what were the security/privacy/legal implications of sensitive information shared on OSM? Success of police pages could not be measured without understanding citizen's expectations and satisfaction. We conducted surveys with both the stakeholders to gain insights about experiences with, and expectations from OSM.

4   Methodology

The survey questionnaire was created to understand general activities on OSM for policing, concerns, scope of use, hindrances, and need for policies. To understand why OSM is needed, we asked police personnel questions such as *"for which of the policing activities can you use OSN e.g. Facebook?"* and options given included choices such as *crime investigations, listening/monitoring, notifying the public of crime*, and *donot use social media tools*. We also included *Others* as an option for police personnel to write their own choice. This list was constructed based on interviews and similar surveys conducted in the developed nations [6].

Next, we surveyed citizens on the use of OSM for policing, concerns regarding police presence on OSM, and activities that police can perform using OSM. For instance, we asked citizens *for which of the following activities should police use OSM e.g. Facebook?* and showed them same options as shown to police personnel. To understand the challenges and expectation on how citizens will like to communicate with police on OSM, we asked *how would you like to communicate information (e.g. complaints and feedbacks) to police using Online Social Media?* Participants could choose to *post anonymous information, post on police page with minimal personal information e.g. email id, send direct messages, create a fake account to inform police*, or *would use police pages to get information only*.

In total, we collected responses from 445 police personnel and 204 citizens. Table 1 shows the demographics of the survey participants. Our questionnaire included demographics questions such as age, gender and profession of the participants. We administered surveys via services such as Google forms and Survey Monkey. The number of male police personnel in our survey is dominant, however male and female ratio in our survey, is representative ratio of the genders in Indian police services [16]. Almost equal number of male and female citizens participated in the survey. To compare citizen and police perception, we used the same questions in the two surveys with minimal modification to suit the concerned group. In some questions, we used a 5-point Likert scale ranging from *Strongly agree* to *Strongly disagree* to capture participant's response. Further, we applied statistical tests such as Mann-Whitney U Test to analyze the difference in opinion for survey questions using likert scales.

Table 1. Demographics of the participants in the interviews and surveys. Values in the table are in percentage. Almost equal number of male and female residents participated in the survey.

	Resident Survey N = 204	Police Survey N = 445
Gender		
Female	40.66	8.98
Male	56.59	85.85
Not shared	2.75	5.17
Age		
18–24	80.22	3.05
25–34	16.48	37.79
35–44	0.55	21.36
45–55	0.55	27.93
55- 65+	–	9.87
Not shared	2.20	–
Education		
Computer IT	54.40	Field Officers
Teaching/Research	10.99	
Fashion Designing	10.99	
MBA	3.30	
CA	0.55	
Others	19.77	

5 Survey Results

We conducted surveys in the quest for empirical understanding of citizens and police expectation from OSM. These helped clearly quantify the similarities and differences between police personnel and citizens. Community policing requires citizen and police collaboration to prioritize the tasks.

5.1 Transparency in Problem Solving Process

Participants believed that OSM can improve *transparency in problem solving process* by offering an open platform to discuss crime and safety related issues/activities. We found that citizens were interested in reporting different issues to police through OSM, such as eveteasing (73 %), child labour (71.4 %), traffic issues (59.9 %), domestic violence (57.7 %), neighborhood issues (56.6 %). This shows OSM can increase the number of community volunteers to identify crime. Citizens agreed that they will like to give feedback (67 %) to police through OSM (Fig. 3).

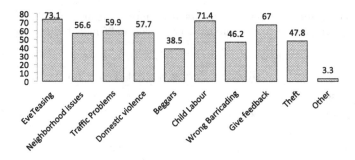

Fig. 3. Citizen (N = 204) issues which they will like to report using OSM.

We found different expectation between police and citizen with respect to policing activities can be performed using OSM. Top three activities for which citizens thought police can use OSM were – notifying the public about crime, emergency situation or disaster related issues, and crime prevention activities. In contrast to this, top three activities which police personnel preferred were crime investigation, intelligence, and public relation/reputation management (see Fig. 2). We found statistical difference between the citizens and police for preferred policing activities (χ^2 test, p-value < 0.001).

Survey analysis confirms that OSM offers opportunities for citizens and police identify and improve law and order situation in the society. Police develop better understanding about citizens' need using the feedback and information available on OSM. For improved citizen satisfaction, police can consider using OSM for notifying the public about crime, emergency situation or disaster related issues, and crime prevention in addition to the activities they will like to perform.

5.2 Community Engagement Through Feedback and Anonymity

OSM was a preferred platform to give Feedback which provides an opportunity to increase community engagement between residents and police. We asked citizens what will they like to do with a tweet/post with a positive feedback about police organization of your area/Estate, e.g. *We thank the police for reducing crime in our city.* Citizens could choose to share/retweet, like/favorite, comment/reply, delete, report–abuse/spam or Ignore the message. Almost 65 % citizens said that they will like or favorite the post with positive feedback and 30.77 % said that they will repost/share. Thus showing the effectiveness of OSM generated feedback in building police - citizen community. We also found that 52.20 % citizens said that they will share/retweet the post with negative comments about police and 39.01 % said they will comment or reply to such posts. This shows potential of OSM to understand the disagreement expressed by the citizen's community to strategize better and communicate police opinion (Fig. 4).

Citizens responded that they will like to leverage the anonymity offered by OSM to communicate with police. We asked citizens, – *"How will you like to communicate information (e.g. complaints and feedbacks) to police using Online*

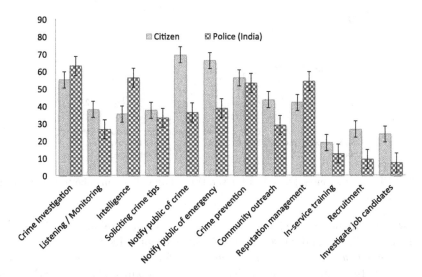

Fig. 4. Choices of Indian citizens (N = 204) and police personnel (N = 445) for policing activities on OSM.

Social Media?" We found that 36.26 % of citizens will like to post anonymous information on police page, whereas, 29.67 % will like to reveal minimal personal information e.g. email id. Only 2.75 % might create a fake account. This shows that anonymity offered by OSM can help in providing more information to police from citizens. We contemplate that anonymity offered increased the chances of citizens interacting with police as they would now share their thoughts without being fearful that police could harass them or people against whom they are complaining can identify and attack them [26].

Challenges to community engagement via OSM: We identified following challenges for the adoption of OSM – acknowledgment from police, lack of policies, and lack of trust on information available. Survey shows that absence acknowledgement can be a challenge for successful use of OSM. We found that 31.87 % said that police should take less than an hour to acknowledge that they had seen the post/message (See Fig. 5). With crunch of police personnel, this can slightly overload the police but police departments will need to setup a concrete acknowledgement process for community sustain over a long period.

Lack of policies is a concern for both police and citizens. We asked both citizens and police that *how much would they agree that Police should make an Online social media usage policy (rules and regulation) for using and benefitting from Online Social Media effectively.* Almost 94 % police strongly agreed or agreed with this statement and 75 % citizens strongly agreed or agreed that policy is needed. Police seemed to be significantly more concerned than citizens. We found this difference to be statistical significant (Wilcoxon rank-sum test, $z = -7.54$, $p < 0.001$) between citizens (M = 2.03, SD = 0.84, N = 204) and police (M = 1.79, SD = 0.58, N = 399).

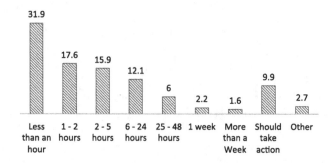

Fig. 5. Citizens' responses (N = 204) for the time that police can take to acknowledge the citizens' post.

Few participants trusted the information that was available on OSM. We asked both citizens and police to mark on a 5-point likert scale, *how much will they agree with the statement that the information obtained via OSM is trustworthy*. In comparison to 49.63 % police personnel (M = 2.4, SD = 0.84, N = 391), only 17.03 % (M = 3.15, SD = 0.9, N = 204) citizen agreed with statement (Wilcoxon rank-sum test, z = −1.19, p>0.05).

5.3   Preferred OSM Platform:

We asked police officers which OSM they will use for day to day activities. Similar to interviews, our survey results showed that Facebook and WhatsApp were the preferred networks; 72.17 % officers preferred Facebook and almost 60 % preferred WhatsApp. We asked citizens which OSM they will like to use to communicate with police. Almost 80 % citizens preferred to use Facebook, followed by WhatsApp (44.54 %) whereas 42.02 % citizens prefer Twitter in comparison to 15.80 % police personnel, see Fig. 6. We found statistically significant difference between police personnel and citizens choice of OSM (χ^2 test, p-value < 0.001). However, preferred platform for both was the same.

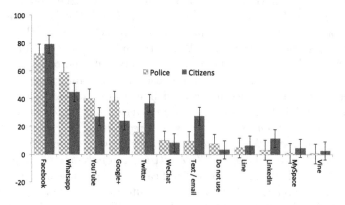

Fig. 6. Comparison of citizens (N = 204) and police (N = 445) choice for OSM as policing tool.

Design Implication and Conclusion: In this work, we provide insights for HCI researchers and technologists building social media technologies for policing (See Fig. 7). Our research is necessary to formulate appropriate communication strategies and collaboration methods.

We found that legitimacy of information is concern for residents, and they feel it is challenging to verify information posted on OSN. The implication of this on technology suggests that verification and validation applications should be an essential part of technology design.

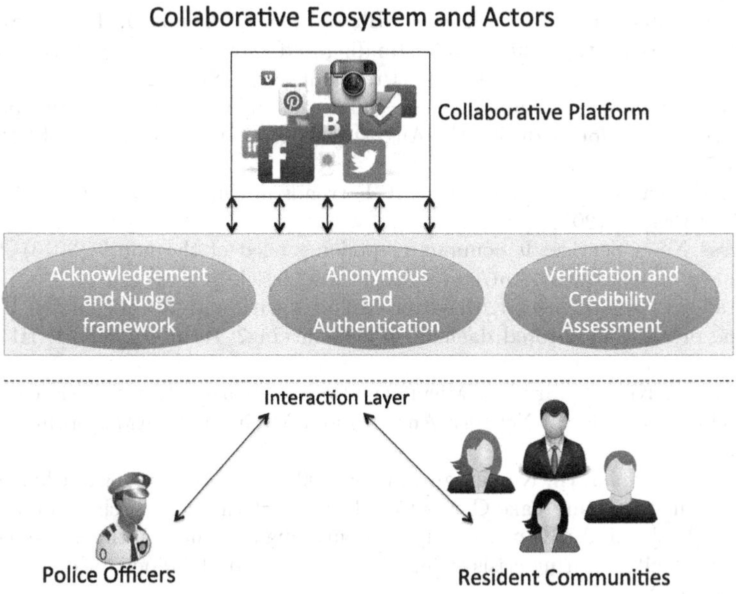

Fig. 7. Design and technological opportunities for collaborative innovation in policing on OSM

We find that residents may not trust community-policing technology that does not keep their submission anonymous. However, anonymous posts involve legitimacy issues that make it difficult for police to take actions. We believe that security and the HCI community should design mechanisms that provide anonymity and also keep minimal checks to authenticate information, if needed.

Our results show that residents post defamatory content inhibiting meaningful information exchange. To develop accountability among residents, HCI researchers can design appropriate nudges [32] that educate residents about the legal and social implications of abusive content on OSN.

References

1. Abdalla, A., Yayilgan, S.Y.: A review of using online social networks for investigative activities. In: Meiselwitz, G. (ed.) SCSM 2014. LNCS, vol. 8531, pp. 3–12. Springer, Heidelberg (2014)
2. Chermak, S., Weiss, A.: An analysis of police-media relations. J. Crim. Justice **33**, 501–512 (2005)
3. De Choudhury, M., Monroy-Hernandez, A., Mark, G.: "Narco" emotions: affect and desensitization in social media during the mexican drug war. In: Proceedings of CHI 2014. ACM (2014). http://research.microsoft.com/apps/pubs/default.aspx?id=208580
4. Cobb, C., McCarthy, T., Perkins, A., Bharadwaj, A., Comis, J., Do, B., Starbird, K.: Designing for the deluge: understanding and supporting the disturbed, collaborative work of crisis volunteers. In: Proceedings of CSCW 2014 (2014)
5. Denef, S., Bayerl, P.S., Kaptein, N.: Social media and the police - tweeting practices of British police forces during the August 2011 riots. In: Proceedings of CHI 2013, pp. 3471–3480. ACM (2013)
6. Denef, S., Kaptein, N., Bayerl, P.S.: ICT Trends in European Policing: The COMPOSITEProject (2011)
7. Express News Service: Is community policing need of the hour? (2013). http://www.newindianexpress.com/states/karnataka/article1430481.ece
8. Gupta, A., Kumaraguru, P.: Twitter explodes with activity in mumbai blasts! a lifeline or an unmonitored daemon in the Lurking? Technical report, IIIT-Delhi (2011)
9. Gupta, A., Kumaraguru, P.: Misinformation on twitter during crisis events. In: Encyclopedia of Social Network Analysis and Mining (ESNAM), Springer Publications (2012)
10. Gupta, A., Lamba, H., Kumaraguru, P.: $ 1.00 per RT #BostonMarathon #PrayForBoston: Analyzing Fake Content on Twitter. eCrime Research Summit (2013)
11. Gupta, A., Joshi, A., Kumaraguru, P.: Identifying and characterizing user communities on Twitter during crisis events. In: Workshop on UMSocial, Co-located with CIKM (2012)
12. Heverin, T., Zach, L.: Twitter for city police department information sharing. In: Proceedings of ASIST 2010 (2010)
13. Hughes, A.L., St. Denis, L.A.A., Palen, L., Anderson, K.A.: Online public communications by police & fire services during the 2012 Hurricane Sandy. In: Proceedings of CHI 2014 (2014)
14. Hughes, A., Palen, L., Sutton, J., Liu, S., Vieweg, S.: "Site- Seeing" in disaster: an examination of on-line social convergence. In: Proceedings of ISCRAM 2008 (2008)
15. 2013 IACP Social Media Survey (2013). http://www.iacpsocialmedia.org/Portals/1/documents/2013SurveyResults.pdf
16. Joshi, S.: Only 442 women police stations across India: Police research data (2012). http://www.thehindu.com/todays-paper/tp-national/tp-newdelhi/only-442-women-police-stations-across-india-police-research-data/article4236877.ece
17. Kumaraguru, P.: Riots in Muzaffarnagar (Uttar Pradesh), India. Technical report, IIIT-Delhi, September 2013
18. Lexis Nexis Risk Solutions: Survey of Law Enforcement Personnel and Their Use of Social Media in Investigations (2012). www.lexisnexis.com/investigations
19. López, C.A., Butler, B.S.: Consequences of content diversity for online public spaces for local communities. In: Proceedings of CSCW 2013, pp. 673–682. ACM (2013)

20. Mendoza, M., Poblete, B., Castillo, C.: Twitter under crisis: can we trust what we RT? In: Proceedings of Social Media Analytics, SOMA 2010 (2010)
21. Nayak, V.: 92 Million Facebook Users Makes India The Second Largest Country[STUDY] (2014). http://www.dazeinfo.com/2014/01/07/facebook-inc-fb-india-demographic-users-2014
22. Palen, L., Vieweg, S.: The emergence of online widescale interaction: assiatance, alliance and retreat. In: Proceedings of CSCW 2008 (2008)
23. Peak, K.J., Glensor, R.W.: Community Policing and Problem Solving: Strategies and Practices. Prentice Hall, Upper Saddle River (2002)
24. Plane, B.: [Infographic] How Police Departments Use Twitter (2013). http://connectedcops.net/2013/04/23/infographic-how-police-departments-use-twitter/
25. Qu, Y., Wu, P., Wang, X.: A case study of Tianya forum in the 2008 China earthquake. In: Proceedings of 42nd Hawaii International Conference on System Sciences (2009)
26. Sachdeva, N., Kumaraguru, P.: Online social networks and police in India - understanding the perceptions, behavior, challenges. In: Proceedings of ECSCW 2015, pp. 183–203 (2015a). http://dx.doi.org/10.1007/978-3-319-20499-4_10
27. Sachdeva, N., Kumaraguru, P.: Social networks for police and residents in India: exploring online communication for crime prevention. In: Proceedings of dg.o 2015, pp. 256–265. ACM (2015b)
28. Semaan, B., Mark, G.: 'Facebooking' towards crisis recovery and beyond: disruption as an opportunity. In: Proceedings of CSCW 2012, pp. 27–36 (2012)
29. Starbird, K., Palen, L.: "Voluntweeters": self-organizing by digital volunteers in times of crisis. In: Proceedings of CHI 2011, pp. 1071–1080 (2011)
30. The Times of India: Fearing attacks, 5000 people from northeast flee Bangalore (2012). http://timesofindia.indiatimes.com/city/bangalore/Fearing-attacks-5000-people-from-northeast-flee-Bangalore/articleshow/15512723.cms
31. Vieweg, S., Hughes, A., Starbird, K., Palen, L.: Micro-blogging during two natural hazards events: what twitter may contribute to situational awareness. In: Proceedings of CHI 2010, pp. 1079–1088 (2010)
32. Wang, Y., Leon, P.G., Acquisti, A., Cranor, L.F., Forget, A., Sadeh, N.: A field trial of privacy nudges for Facebook. In: Proceedings of the 32nd annual ACM Conference on Human Factors in Computing Systems, pp. 2367–2376. ACM (2014)

The Influence of Social Media on the Design of the National Image in the Globalization Context

Minggang Yang and Hongling Wan[✉]

School of Art, Design and Media, East China University of Science and Technology,
NO. 130, Meilong Road, M.Box 286, Shanghai, 200237 Xuhui, China
yangminggang@163.com, 2498007448@qq.com

Abstract. With the constant improvement of the science & technology and the rapidly spread mobile internet, the information dissemination method is also appeared a variety around the world. And the position of the social media being the main force of information dissemination is also much more prominent. In contrast, the speed of information dissemination is also becoming faster and faster, the rapid and convenient information dissemination has accelerated the globalization process, making the relations between the countries all over the world much closer. Today, while the exchange of information among different countries in both the economic, political and cultural fields etc. Becoming more frequent, the quality of the national image shall influence the speaking right and competitiveness of one country among the international society directly. Therefore, being the important part of the national "soft power", the design of national image is becoming crucial. In this paper, it took the Weibo of China Sina - such an important social media as the study platform, by selecting the Weibo accounts that certified by Sina and having the important influence on the design of American national image as the object of study, including the Weibo account of American Embassy in China that representing American political affairs, the TNC (The Nature Conservancy) Weibo account that representing the non-governmental organizations, and the personal Weibo account of Rupert Murdoch - the famous pressman, the executive chairman of US-based News Corp, by using the study methods of statistical analysis and text analysis, it focused on the analysis of the popular micro-blogging inside the three Weibo accounts, to analyze the important influencing effects that the Sina Weibo made on the design of the American national image, summarize the strategy and inspiration that using the social media to make the framework for national image, in order to provide some practical proposals for each country using the social media to improve their national image under the new media environment.

Keywords: Globalization context · Social media · The design of the national image

1 Introduction

With the coming internet era especially the rapidly popularized mobile internet, it makes the information dissemination more convenient and free, the interpersonal relationship

© Springer International Publishing Switzerland 2016
G. Meiselwitz (Ed.): SCSM 2016, LNCS 9742, pp. 234–246, 2016.
DOI: 10.1007/978-3-319-39910-2_22

is becoming quite closer, and the exchange of information among different countries is also more frequent. The internet crossing the barrier of time and space has made the information dissemination becoming more instant and interactive. Along with the development of internet technology, online social media has been grown so rapidly. Undoubtedly, at present the online social media was becoming the backbone force to guide the public opinion and one of the effective carriers for international propaganda.

2   The Social Media Under Globalization Context

2.1   The Social Media Is Creating the New Model of Information Dissemination

The social interactivity and expressing superiority of the social media enables the receivers getting the rights of information dissemination in a wider range, largely enhancing the subjective initiative of the receivers in dissemination. In the social media, people can access the mass information conveniently and rapidly and give comments freely based on the received information, it integrates the interpersonal communication, organizational communication and the mass communication together. At the same time, such an unprecedented interactivity enables people making the barrier-free communication across the boundary, and makes the world more and more liking a "global village".

2.2   The Social Media Enables Communication Subject Becoming Towards Diversification

Essentially, the social media shall be the effective carrier for information sharing and knowledge sharing, the platform for the public declaring their opinions and views. In such a internet era, every one could express their own voice through all kinds of social media openly. The internet has popularized the communication object from those special groups such as the reporter to each ordinary people who having certain expression and dissemination foundation. Everybody shall have the speech right on the social media, and the communication object of the information dissemination is also becoming more diversified accordingly.

2.3   The Social Media Accelerated the Speed of Information Dissemination

The social media that taking the Weibo as the representative shall have the biggest difference apart from the traditional media, that is its fission propagation mode in "One to N to N" style, such propagation mode promoted the freedom of information dissemination and accelerated the speed of information dissemination, enabled the social media presenting the academic and instant network structure for information sharing dissemination. At the same time the accelerated speed of the information dissemination also accelerated the globalization process. Currently, every country is coming to realize that under such new media environment, to positively and proactively utilize the internet for effective national communication and better design of national image shall play the important role on the improvement of the nation's international prestige, maintenance of national security and social stability.

3 The Design of National Image Through the Social Media

Till now there's still no unified definition on the "national image" in the academic circles. Chinese Scholar Liu Xiaoyan did think that the national image is the "overall evaluation that the international community and the public made on a certain country in the relative stable level", it's the "projection that the national objective state did make on the public opinions i.e. the overall reflection that the social public did think about the national influence, views, attitudes and evaluation - the summation of the emotion and will that the public did take to the country". In a word, the national image is one of the indispensable parts of the national soft power, it does not influence the external diplomatic policies and styles of the country, but also play the important role for the country getting the speech right and improving its own international position among the international community. Currently we're just at the active age to utilize the social media for diplomacy. From the International Monetary Fund in 2011, to the Prime Minister of UK - Cameron in 2014, then the executive chairman of the US-based News Corp - Rupert Murdoch in 2015, more and more international organizations and foreign dignitaries celebrities have opened their own account in the Weibo of China Sina. The social media shall have the incomparable advantages on the design of national image with its better characteristics in openness, interactivity and communitization.

3.1 The Manifestation Modes to Utilize the Social Media for Design of National Image

One of the difference between the social media that taking Weibo as the representative and the traditional media, is the diversification of the communication subject. Thus the communication subject of the national image in Weibo shall include not only the government and its subsidiary media, but also the organizations and ordinary people outside the government. From the perspective of communication subject, the themes for national image propaganda in Weibo can be mainly classified into the Weibo account of government body, such as the Weibo account of US Embassy in China; the personal Weibo account of state leaders, such as the personal Weibo account of the Prime Minister of UK Cameron; the Weibo account of non-governmental organization, such as the Weibo account of American's National Geographic and the personal Weibo account, such as account of the executive chairman of US-based News Corp Rupert Murdoch.

3.1.1 The Weibo Account of Government Body

The Weibo account of government body refers to the official Weibo account that the government and relevant agencies opened in the Weibo of Sina, such as Weibo account of US Embassy in China - it mainly introduce their national conditions and culture & arts, provide social service information accordingly. According to the search engine of Sina's Weibo, it shows that there are already 193 Weibo accounts related to the Embassy and got certified by the Weibo of Sina, among them there are not only the official Weibo account of the various countries' embassy in China, but also the official Weibo account of their culture office related to their embassy in China.

3.1.2   The Personal Weibo Account of the State Leaders

Currently so many state leaders has opened their social media account, for example, there are already the Twitter accounts for US President Obama, the Russian Prime Minister Dmitry Medvedev and German Prime Minister Merkel et al. In Weibo of Sina, there are also accounts of the former Australian Prime Minister Rudd Kevin and Prime Minister of US- Cameron et al. Those foreign dignitaries often declared some political, cultural and diplomatic topics related to their home country in Weibo and communicated with the people of the host countries. For example, while paying the visit to China in 2013, the Prime Minister of UK - Cameron has published the new of "thanks for your attention. And I'm glad to visit China again as the Prime Minister of UK. I want to get the knowledge of your ideas, please leave your questions here and I may arrange some answers according before I finished my visit in China." such micro-blog has been forwarded more than 39000 times and with 21000 comments until now. This micro-blog did not only express Cameron's willing to get knowledge of Chinese people, but even more important thing is that it gets the closer distance between Cameron and Chinese ordinary people effectively, and brings such a good feeling of kindness and friendship.

3.1.3   Weibo Account of Non-governmental Organization

The non-governmental organizations shall play the important role on diplomacy, whatever for government's decision making or the public opinions, it shall have the far-reaching influence accordingly; it is not limited within the activities of information dissemination and initiatives, but what is more to establish the relationship between them and the behavioral agent of citizen society of other countries and promote the network connection among the non-governmental organizations and groups at home and abroad. During the Weibo diplomacy, the non-governmental organizations usually play the essential role accordingly, many diplomatic actions that the state government is not convenient to do directly can be spread out through the non-governmental organizations. Such as The Nature Conservancy of American in Weibo name of "The Nature Conservancy TNC" has got more than 60000 fans in Weibo, and their micro-blog contents are taking nature environment protection as the theme, to convey the advanced concept of environmental protection, designing the American's national image from one side.

3.1.4   Personal Weibo Account

The figures who enjoyed the higher reputation among the world usually act the role of opinion leader while designing the national image in Weibo, being with higher awareness and wider range of social communication with national characters, while becoming the subject of Weibo they can also make the very direct influence on the Weibo fans with attention on them. For example the executive chairman of US-based News Corp - Rupert Murdoch has opened his own Weibo account in Sept. 2015 and now his fans are already more than 380000 person. Even though his Weibo update quantity and speed is quite slow, but each micro-blog did get thousands of comments, forwarding and likes in average. Thus it can be seen that the personal Weibo account shall also have the power on design of national image that cannot be ignored accordingly.

3.2 The Characters to Utilize Social Media for Design of National Image

In recent years, along with the continuous progress of media technology, the platform for design of national image gradually shifted to the network media and new media accordingly, thereinto the use of social media, especially the use of Weibo has been drawn the attentions from more and more countries and presented the situation with more and more popularity. By combining the character of social media and making a general survey of diplomatic activities by each country, it summarizes the features that the design of national image on social media may have.

3.2.1 The Design of National Image on Social Media Is More Open and Transparent

The features of good openness and interactivity that the social media may have enables the designing activities of national image on social media becoming more open and transparent, it provides the wider public with such a channel to understand the national images of each country more conveniently and rapidly. Foe example, through the Weibo account of US embassy in China, Chinese people could learn more about American's local customs & practices and social culture directly and participated in corresponding discussion, that makes the design of American national image more transparent and direct & stereo.

3.2.2 The Design of National Image on Social Media Is More Direct and People-Oriented

In comparison with the output model by using traditional culture, the design of national image on social media can touch the people in the country more directly and widely. For example, through the platform of Weibo of Sina, the state institution could connect and communicate with billions of netizen and people directly, thus can save many intermediate links among the design of national image. While saving the cost of dissemination, it shall also achieve the better propagation effects.

3.2.3 The Design of National Image on Social Media Has the Participants in Diversity

Everyone shall have speech rights on social media and everybody can be the communication subject also. Therefore. The participants for the design of national image on social media are diversified, they are no longer the task performed by only one department or institution, but with the participation by more and more organizations, individuals - including the non-governmental organizations and individuals. With the further development of the social media like the Weibo etc., the design of national image may have more obvious trend towards the diversified main body, any organization and individual could participate in the design of national image through Weibo of Sina.

3.3 The Important Significance to Utilize Social Media for the Design of National Image

Under the new media ecological environment, the better social interactivity, topic timeliness and expression superiority presented by social media has provided a brand new method for the countries all over the world to make the design of national image, it made the national image of each country more stereo and diversified, and made the diplomatic system that being ever in closer state becoming more free and open, endowing the diplomacy of each country with more personal characteristics. With the continuously accelerated pace of globalization, the demand of each country community to design the positive and active national image is becoming stronger increasingly, the good and bad national image on the international stage shall directly influence the international competitiveness and influence of one country.

3.3.1 The National Image Shall Be the Important Part of the Soft Power of the Country

The overall national strength of a country does not only include the hard power, such as the state economic strength, army force and technology power, but also contain the soft power - such as the culture & arts, values and national image of the country. The soft power of the country is such an intangible power, it presents the attraction of the values and the ability of political orientation of one country. Under the globalization context, both the countries of the world is positively designing their better national image, transmitting the culture and values and life concept of their own country, so as to guide foreign people being melt with the state interests of their native country, further to form the stronger national soft power, to realize the maximization of state interests. In recent years, from the mutual Cultural Year hosted among the European countries such as UK, France, Russia and China, to the opened Weibo account of several foreign dignitaries, these do not only present the changes of current art & culture output and values concept propagation mode, but also highlight the emphasize that each country made to the design of national image.

3.3.2 Better National Image Shall Be the Important Guarantee for National Interests

With the rapid growth of internet technology, the boundary between the countries is becoming blurring gradually, the economic trade flow and art & cultural exchange are also becoming closer increasingly. Under current international environment, to design the good national image shall be the important path for one country achieving international speech rights, improving its international position and securing state interests. The negative national image shall be not only isolated and resisted by other countries, the more important is to obstruct the external political, economic and cultural exchange, then bring severe damage to state interests. The good and bad national image shall be the key factor of whether this country could stand firmly among the nations of the world, it shall have the great impact on it to accomplish the maximization of state interests, play the national power and promote the overall national strength.

3.3.3   The Design of National Image Shall Be Important Means for Improving International Influence of the Country

Under the great environment with increasingly fierce competition, many countries has incorporated the design of better national image as their state strategy. The cultural values of their own country, the media organization and dissemination ability the country may have in the international community and the state discourse construction ability should be the foundation for the design of national image. Obtaining the strong media dissemination ability may help the country gaining the speech rights in the international community, and enable the country protecting the national rights in international stage and improving the international influence of the country. In contrast, for those countries with the weak media dissemination ability and relatively deprivation of material culture at present, because they did not construct the positive and true national image, they are always in the aphasic situation among the dissemination of national image, thus also damaged both the national interests and international influences accordingly.

4   The Survey and Analysis on American's National Image Based on Weibo of Sina

The China-US relations should be one of the most important relations in the 21st century, in this paper, the reason for the US being selected as the behavioral agent is that, on one hand is based on the leading position of that the US has utilized the social media for their diplomacy, on the other hand it is because of that to explore the diplomatic behavior of US made on the social media shall have certain realistic and reference significance, through the survey and analysis on the American's national image in Weibo of Sina, it shall provide certain guide suggestions for other country to carry out the public diplomacy accordingly. Usually there are four forms to express the design of national image in Weibo of Sina, they are: the government organization's Weibo account, personal Weibo account of the state leaders, the Weibo account of non-governmental organizations and personal Weibo account. Thus, for the study on American's national image in Weibo of Sina, in this paper it selected the Weibo account of US embassy in China, the Weibo Account of The Nature Conservancy TNC and the personal Weibo account of the executive chairman of US-based News Corp - Rupert Murdoch as the object of study, to focus on the study of these hot micro-blog contents in the three Weibo accounts, through the text analysis method to explore the American's national image formed by these Weibo accounts in three different categories. For it still haven't found the quality personal Weibo account certified by Weibo of Sina that related to US leaders, this time the expression form for the personal Weibo account of the state leaders is not included in the analysis range accordingly.

4.1   Its Political Image Is Spread Out Around the "Democracy System", "Legal Human Rights" and "Public Supervision"

For the design of American's political national image, this paper mainly focused on the text analysis of the Weibo account of US embassy in China, it selected 45 hot micro blogs in this Weibo account during Jan of 2016 that been widely noted by the fans for classification. Through study it was found that among these 45 micro blogs, 20 of them are about American politics/society categories, 10 for bilateral diplomacy, 5 for culture/ exchange, and 7 for environment/energy sources/technology, 2 for education/visa, and 1 for others. For 2016 is just the US election year, besides creating the topic of # the Primary Election in US # in its Weibo account of Sina, the US embassy in China did also interact with Chinese netizen positively, to popularize the relative knowledge of American Votes. Among them, the reading quantity of # the Primary Election in US # is as high as 8.131 million people and with discussion in 1283 times. The US embassy in China did not only discuss the issue of "American Votes" with Chinese people in Weibo of Sina, but also discussed the problems related to the U.S. fiscal spending with the people, making the efforts to form the American's national image with transparent & in-corrupt government, maintaining the Constitution and securing citizen's rights.

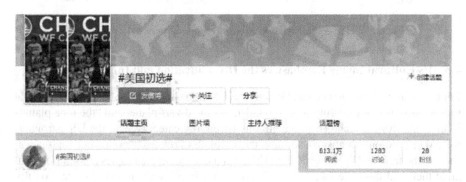

Fig. 1. #The US primary elections# Weibo Topic

4.2   It Social Image Is Mainly Presented Through Rendering the Welfare Benefits of the National Life

The study on American's social image is taken from the text data in both the official Weibo accounts of both the US embassy in China and The Nature Conservancy TNC. For example, upon the request of netizen, the Weibo account of US embassy in China has discussed the fiscal spending of American government made for people;s livelihood and education. Another example is that, for the environmental protection, the official Weibo account of The Nature Conservancy TNC has released the micro blog in name of Leonardo donated One Million US Dollars again to TNC and got the unanimous praise from the netizen of Weibo. Meanwhile, the Weibo account of US embassy in China did also set the dissemination and discussion on those topics such as "wild animals protection" and "global warming" etc. At the same time they've also given the clear attitude for some inherent social problems, such as the reporter's personal safety. And the dissemination of such a micro blog has been got the highest record in the history, gaining forwarding in 5262 times and 3179 comments, also induced the resonance of Chinese people. Through the dissemination of such series micro blogs, it outlined the great-nation image with high welfare, responsibility and high gross national happiness accordingly.

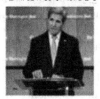

"对于那些试图恐吓或监禁记者的人，我们需要站出来大声、清晰地说从事新闻业、报道真相不是犯罪。它是荣誉的象征。它是一种公共服务。" — 克里国务卿在华盛顿邮报总部强调美国致力于保护新闻业。

1月29日 14:45 来自 微博 weibo.com

收藏   转发 5262   评论 3179   👍 1469

Fig. 2. Weibo communication effect of reporters' personal safety issue

4.3   Its Cultural Image Emphasizes the Diversification and Innovation

For the design of national cultural image, the US embassy in China has spread multiple topics, such as that the Pluto was "degraded" as the dwarf planet and "the nine planets in the solar system changed into eight" in astronomy category, and the US astronaut-related in aviation category, in addition the travel news related to American landscapes-such as the famous US Route 66 etc. Although the disseminated topics are multiple, but all of them did show the core values of American's bravery and innovation etc. To fully

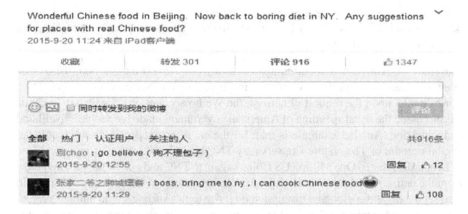

Fig. 3. Communication effect of the personal Weibo account of Rupert Murdoch

propaganda American's culture, the US embassy in China did also create the Weibo topic of #2016 wandering to the US#. For the aspect of cultural image propagation, the executive chairman of the US based News Corp - Rupert Murdoch did also show some in his few micro blogs released before, one of them is the micro blog asking for help to seek the real Chinese food in N.Y., gained the forwarding in 301 times and 916 comments. Rupert Murdoch has conveyed such a kind and friendly image to Chinese people through his personal Weibo account, and made the good impression in the netizen.

5 The Strategy for Design of National Image in Sina's Weibo

5.1 The Propagation Mode Based on the Opinion Leader

"The Weibo information & content should be spread through the network layers with the attention or being concerned." Among the Weibo propagation, the opinion leader with even higher credibility shall have more influence on the design of national image. By taking the personal Weibo account of Rupert Murdoch at his age of more than 80 as the example, there have the micro blog of meeting with the general secretary Xi Jinping of CCCP, the micro blog of visiting the Xiaomi Company and also the micro blog of asking for help from the netizen to seek for the real Chinese food in N.Y. etc., all the three micro blogs has got the good communication effect. For individual, it outlines such a personal image of down-to-earth, up to the design of national image, it shows the national image with the diversified country, innovation and hating to lose. Through the communication with hot nodes of the opinion leader on social media, to create the better communication and designing effects with quite small even the cost without expense, this should be incomparable for the traditional media.

5.2 To Make the "Built-in" Real Time Dissemination on the Hot Topic

By taking the Weibo as the representative, the social media shall have so many terminal sharing platform. At the same time it has the flexible method of information publish and with the strong interactivity, can realize the real time dissemination on the hot topics. For example the American Votes in 2016, it did not only create the topic of #the American Votes#, but also release the micro blogs such as "what is the political congress of party representatives", "who has the right to run for the president?" and "how did a midterm election influence the Votes?" etc., to carry out the warp-up of the hot topic on American Votes. Meanwhile, it also follow up the 2015 World Climate Conference in Paris, North Korea nuclear problem and the news of American government leader visiting China through Weibo. Through the publication of those micro blogs, it did not only improve the timeliness of the news, but also form the good interaction with Chinese people. In comparison with the traditional media, the social media such as Weibo can accelerate the communication speed of information on one hand, on the other hand can also more directly face to the audience widely for designing the national image.

5.3 To Integrate Online/Offline Sources Effectively

Whatever it is the US embassy in China or The Nature Conservancy TNC, on one hand, it did effectively integrate the network resources like the official website, blog and other related websites through the open interface of Weibo, on the other hand it shall also positively integrate the online and offline resources while there's hot topic. For example the hot topic of American Votes, it may ask the offline audience and give the answer for their concerned problems, enable the audience participating in this process and forming the good interaction accordingly. It shall perform the live broadcast on the high-level visit to China through Weibo, meanwhile invite audience to participate in their offline activities in the form of giveaway program. The social media that taking Weibo as representative has the good cross-platform characteristics, it can effectively integrate all kinds of communication resources.

5.4 The Propagation Mode by Utilizing the Agenda-Setting

By taking the agenda-setting method to accomplish the guiding effects on the public opinion, guide the thinking direction of the audience, it manifests in two ways: the one is focusing on the setting of Weibo content agenda, the other one is to make the continuous report by using Weibo. For example the Weibo account of US embassy in China, in order to draw attention of the audience, it always releases the relative hot topic or comments related to China in time, such as the North Korea nuclear problem. Through the attention paid on these hot events, it shall gradually bring out the values their native country have hold, further to expand the communication effects and seize the market opportunity in time. Through the continuous follow-up and creating the topic on 2016 American Votes through Weibo, the US embassy in China has fulfilled the attitude of the audience on the hot events, meanwhile effectively popularized the knowledge of the democratic system in their own country.

6 The Inspiration from the Improvement of National Image by Utilizing Social Media

6.1 To Emphasize the Localized Operation, Positively Cultivating the Opinion Leader

The design of national image by using so-called localized operation of social media shall contain two aspects: the one is the localization of content selection, the other one is the localization of operating staff in social media. For the content, it may meed the demand of the audience, which is related to the audience and loved by the audience. The operating stuff in social media shall be local people, for they may write, select and propaganda the content for design of other national image in more true and comprehensive way, and can be easily fit the demand of the audience. By designing the national image through the opinion leader, it not only enables the information content more feasible, but also improves the depth and width of the information dissemination during the designing process.

6.2   To Master the Hot Topic, Building the Communication Subject in Diversity

While performing the design of national image, the country shall positively grab the hot topic, chase the speech right among the international community, guide the direction of public opinion among the audience. In such an era with economy of attention, the country should learn to grab the attention of audience, because that grabbing the attention may equal to having the influence, but while grabbing the hot public opinion it shall fully understand the audience psychology. With the good cross-platform attribution of social media, each behavioral agent shall focus on playing more interaction between the subjects of public opinion, break the barriers among the information dissemination platform to fully develop their own characteristics, to mutually play the role by combining the multiplex subjects of public opinion.

7   Conclusion

In the gradually accelerated globalization process of today, the design of national image shall have the unprecedented significance than ever before, because the national image may impact the speech rights and influence of one country among the international community. Along with the continuous development of network technology and the increasingly changed ecological environment of media communication, the social media shall gradually become the important means for the design of national image. In this paper, it took the design of American national image on Weibo for study, as a case study this paper may have the limitation accordingly. But in light of the leading position that the US may have in the fields of designing national image and national relation practice, the research findings it has made may also have certain reference meanings then.

References

1. Zhong, X.: Public diplomacy version 2.0 - the study on micro blog and blogs of the US embassy in China. J. Int. Commun. 47–55 (2011)
2. Feng, Y.: The study on the influence that the Weibo may have on propagation of national image - the empirical study based on the intentions of college student users. University of electronic science and technology of China (2014)
3. Zhihong, D., Yue, H.: The weibo diplomacy: the study on the situation that the US embassy in China using the weibo modern. Media (3):150–151 (2013)
4. Guo, J.: The importance and urgency for media diplomacy and design of national image. Young Reporters **02**, 76–77 (2012)
5. Chen, J.: The study on social media dissemination strategy that foreign government agencies made in China. Shanghai International Studies University (2014)
6. Huang, S.:The study on the Weibo diplomacy used by the UK/US embassy in China. Hunan University (2014)
7. Zhang, L.: A study on the design of national image in Weibo - by taking the official Chinese Weibo account of foreign media as the example. Heilongjiang University (2015)

8. You, K.: The analysis on usage and communication strategy of Weibo of Sina by the US embassy in China. Shandong University (2014)
9. Yang, Y.: A study on how to improve Chinese internet international propagation power under the globalization context. Chine Youth University for Political Sciences (2012)
10. Liu, Y.: The discussion on the cultural communication and the design of Chinese national image under the globalization context. J. Yangtze Norm. Univ. (2):98–100

Social Network Analysis

Urban Analytics in Crowd Management in the Context of Hajj

Lamia Alabdulkarim$^{(\boxtimes)}$, Wafa Alrajhi, and Ebtesam Aloboud

College of Computer and Information Sciences,
Al-Imam Muhammad Ibn Saud Islamic University, Riyadh, Saudi Arabia
{lamia,walrajhi,ebtesam}@ccis.imamu.edu.sa

Abstract. The efficient management of crowded events remains a challenge, mainly due to several factors involving infrastructures, crowd dynamics, and service provision. In spite of recurrence of disasters such as stampedes, fires, and riots resulting in many situations which pose serious threats to the personal safety and security in crowds, there are no universal criteria and standards for controlling and managing crowds. The Hajj pilgrimage is the fifth pillar of Islam. Every year, muslims around the world gather in Mecca, Saudi Arabia to perform a series of rituals and prayers. In this paper, we describe crowd analytics in the study of masses of pilgrims taking part in the annual Muslim ritual of the Hajj. Technology solutions have been proposed for crowd analytics in the Hajj. Those solutions from Unmanned Aerial Vehicles (UAVs) to Mobile Crowd Sensing and Computing (MCSC). We describe trends and challenges in urban analytics for crowd monitoring and management in the Hajj.

Keywords: Hajj · Crowd analytics · Computer vision · Crowd management system · Location-based techniques in the Hajj · Pilgrims · Big data

1 Introduction

An urban area is a densely populated city with visible and invisible infrastructures such as water supply, energy networks and Information and Communication Technology (ICT) [1, 2]. Population in urban areas has spiked as never before, which introduces numerous challenges that span across several domains, such as transportation, health, and environment [1, 2]. Urbanization and the wide spread of ICT transform urban cities into big data pools. There has been a proliferation of research in urban analytics that analyze data to tackle the aforementioned challenges and help to make decisions [1].

One of the integral tasks of city management is planning, monitoring and managing crowds [3]. Crowd management is evolving as a field of interest to a variety of specialists such as computing, health and police force. Mecca confronts crowds regularly. Mecca is located in Saudi Arabia, and is one of the holiest cities in the world due to the existence of the holy mosque, which, Muslims visit for prayers and practice throughout the year (Fig. 1). The Hajj is an annual ritual where Muslims go to Mecca to perform acts of worship in several sacred rituals. Muslims are committed to perform the Hajj at least once

© Springer International Publishing Switzerland 2016
G. Meiselwitz (Ed.): SCSM 2016, LNCS 9742, pp. 249–257, 2016.
DOI: 10.1007/978-3-319-39910-2_23

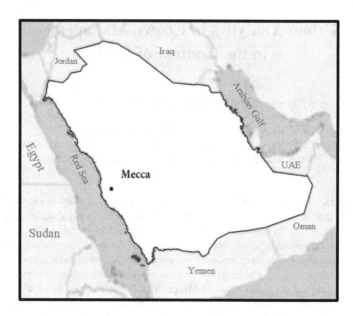

Fig. 1. The geographical location of Mecca, the site for the annual Hajj

in their lives and many of them are keen to repeat the Hajj experience more than once, leading to a recurring mass gathering that is often beyond the estimated crowd [4–7].

Recent statistics provided by the General Authority for Statistics in Kingdom of Saudi Arabia (GASTAT) showed that the number of pilgrims reach 3 million Muslims in 2012 and by 2019, this number is expected to increase to reach 3.75 million [8, 10]. To perform Hajj, all pilgrims need to congregate in several holy places over several days where the movement of pilgrims at the same time makes managing the hajj crowd a very critical operation. Other complicating factors include heterogeneous population, varying velocity of pilgrims, and different motion flows [4, 12]. Thus, avoidance of safety hazards, calls for real-time information about the facilities, density and behavior of the crowd.

In this paper we review a number of urban data collection and analysis studies. Moreover, we illustrate how new trends can be effective to manage crowded areas. Subsequently, we provide a number of suggestions to customize these works based on Hajj characteristics.

This paper is structured as follows: Sect. 2 provides an overview of background research on crowd analytics in the broad scope of events and the scope of cultural and religious events such as Hajj. Section 3 describes the trends and challenges in urban analytics for Hajj. We conclude in Sect. 4 with key insights and future directions for research.

2 Background

Nowadays, the world is witnessing the largest wave of urbanization in world history. In 2050, as per the United Nation's (UN)'s forecast, around 66 % of the world's population will be intensified in urban centers, as compared with 54 % in 2014 and 30 % in 1950 [13].

Understanding and managing crowd behavior is a critical mission in several application domains such as religious events, sports and festivals. Kumbh Mela, an Indian event, takes place every 12 years and gathered tens of millions Hindus in the same timeframe [9]. Incidents can occur when crowds of massive scale are not managed properly, such as the New Year celebrations on the Bund, a waterfront promenade in Shanghai, China, overcrowding on a staircase to an observation platform left 36 people dead and 49 more injured. In the city of Duisburg in Germany, a parade music festival, around 1 million festival goers crowded into a venue that could only hold 250,000. As a result, 21 died from suffocation and more than 510 were injured [14].

Crowd management is a practice that is used to control crowd events before, during, and after events, which include dealing with all elements of an event such as people, sites, facilities, data and technology. The key requirements in mass gathering and successful crowd management are ensuring the safety and security of people in the crowd and the facilities, and avoiding stampedes and loss of public life [3].

2.1   Crowd Management in the Hajj

According to the Pew Research Center [15], as in 2010 23 % of world population is Muslims, which is approximately 1,599,700,000 people, live in more than 100 countries. Annually, Mecca draws millions of Muslims to perform the Hajj ritual. In 2015, the number of pilgrims reached 1,952,817 [16] and as mentioned in the introduction, this number is expected to increase in the following years. Therefore, authorities in Saudi Arabia need to address and manage not just the growing numbers of pilgrims', but also challenges relating to safety, security, and culture differences. The Saudi authorities has provided wide infrastructure to support Hajj but significant problems of crowding still result in catastrophe such as stampedes, fires and spread of diseases [17].

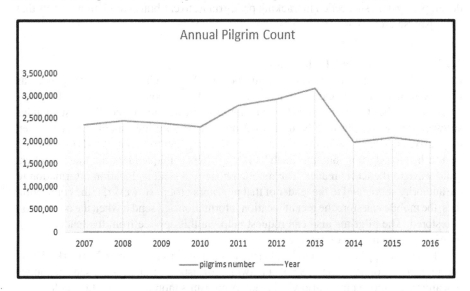

Fig. 2. The Annual pilgrim number [16]

2.2   The Hajj and Social Computing

Many researchers from different fields have contributed to the management of the pilgrimage. Among them are computer scientists, whose contributions comprise computer vision and location-based techniques (Fig. 2).

2.2.1   Computer Vision-Based Technique

As the name indicates, these techniques depend on detecting and counting the individuals [3]. According to Saudi Press Agency (SPA) in the last Hajj season, Saudi Authorities increase the number of surveillance cameras used by television surveillance department, to exceed 7,000 digital cameras from the 4200 cameras that were used in the past two years to monitor pilgrims, throughout Mecca in the Hajj time-frame, focusing on the holy sites [18].

In [19], the Forward-Looking Infrared (FLIR) technique determined the crowd density by using the output of thermal cameras and producing an estimation of the crowd. The FLIR images are affected by the time of capturing the image (day or night), ground temperature and the crowed density. Moreover, in [20], several thermal cameras are deployed as sensors at points of some roads, especially those considered access roads that suffer from congestion. The developed system acquires and processes data via thermal cameras linked to an analysis module. The module measures crowd flow and density in real time and thus determines the priority of roads with respect to widths and lengths. The roads priority is based on the road width, length, and the crowd density on the road. The system then sends its recommendations to authorities.

Extracting some useful parameters from videos (such as speed of the pilgrims) was the main purpose in [8]. To understand very high dense crowd phenomena, cameras focused on a gate of the holy mosque. Using image processing and computer vision, the developed system succeeded in tracking pedestrians, to calibrate simulation models that will disperse crowds.

2.2.2   Location-Based Techniques

Location-based applications leverage the power of smartphones technology such as GPS, AGPS, Wi-Fi, and cameras. The authors of [11] proposed two different location-based approaches to monitor the Hajj and minimize crowd turbulence. The first includes software that would need to be downloaded to all the pilgrims' mobile phones when they arrive in Mecca. In addition, a Radio Frequency Identification (RFID) tag should be attached to pilgrims' phones. Each RFID tag offers a unique identifier that is sent via radio wave to the RFID reader. The mobile phone will send its location information to the authority server and to the leader of that pilgrim's group. However, if the connection dies, the mobile can store the recent location information and send it when the connection is restored. The pilgrims also can request help via this service from the leader of that pilgrim's group in case of emergency.

The second approach offered by [11] is a system of Wireless Sensor Network (WSN) and pilgrims' mobiles. The WSN is a network consisting of distributed sensors, nodes that aim to monitor a physical environment. A pilgrim's mobile transmit his/her location to nearby fixed sensors. Data collected from the sensors is then transmitted to a WSN server ready for authorities to use for crowd detection.

3 Urban Analytics Trends and Challenges

As we race towards fully connected living environments, urban stakeholders and author-ities are exacting analytic solutions that provide actionable insights about citizens and their interactions with these environments. Information gathering and data collection play an important role in the crowd management. Following are trends of crowd moni-toring and detection of potential hazards from different dimensions such as human, data and resources, their applicability, and challenges.

3.1 Data Collection and Information-Gathering

Different methods play key roles in crowds', data collection and information gathering. Classical methods, such as surveillance cameras, helicopters, and government entities responsible for the security, compliance with safety regulations and emergency response eco-systems (e.g. Municipalities, Red Crescent, and Ministry of the Interior) face chal-lenges in scalability, the need for human intervention, and robustness [21]. Following is different methods that employ machine intelligence for scalable, robust, and effective crowd management.

3.1.1 Unmanned Aerial Vehicles

Unmanned Aerial Vehicles (UAVs) are increasingly used as tools to different systems, such as transportation, military, and reconnaissance, because of its low manufacturing cost and its ability to go far into remote and hazardous locations [22, 23]. UAVs have different degrees of autonomy, from Remote-Piloted Vehicles (RPVs) to intelligent, autonomous UAVs which control the flight, collect data, and make decisions [23]. UAVs operated by humans might be prone to errors because of human distractibility and is often associated with an increase in the operating cost. However, autonomous UAVs might require multiple hardware and software components and machine intelligence in many fields, such as computer vision, machine learning, and natural processing language [22]. Table 1 compares UAVs to surveillance cameras. Surveillance cameras requires human intervention for periodic maintenance and installation, since they are distributed in different places, while, as we know, UAVs, like any hardware, need periodic main-tenance but no installation. Surveillance cameras are fixed and cannot move; UAVs can, and can thus cover more ground. Surveillance cameras are connected to electrical power whereas UAVs lives on battery. Many research studies use wireless power transfer for UAVs. The study in [24] proposes an application to recharge UAV, using Wireless Energy Transfer (WET). Moreover, there have been multiple research studies to auto-mate UAVs such as [20]. It proposes a planning and control framework based on Dynamic-Data-Driven, Adaptive Multi-scale Simulation (DDDAMS). The simulation system is fed by dynamic data to use alternative control policies. It also claims that the higher the number of crowds, the better the result. The authors in [25] propose an agent-based hardware-in-the-loop simulation framework to model the UAV surveillance and crowd control system. It contains sensors to collect dynamic data, in order to track and detect crowds. It finds out that finer grid scale and larger vehicle detection range generate a better crowd coverage percentage.

Table 1. Comparison between surveillance camera and UAVs

Attribues	Surveillance Camera	UAVs
Power Source	Electricity (infinite)	Battery (Limited)
Picture stability	Stable	Unstable
Location	Fixed	Mobile
Installation Cost	Yes	No

3.1.2 Mobile Crowd Sensing and Computing

Mobile Crowd Sensing and Computing (MCSC) is a new sensing paradigm based on collecting real-time data from two participatory sources: sensing and social media. Therefore, it allows ordinary users to contribute with data sensed or generated from their mobile devices, aggregates and processes heterogeneous crowdsourced data in the cloud for intelligent service provision to control and monitor the crowd [21, 26]. MCSC collects data from devices to analyze them and identify spatiotemporal patterns [21, 30, 31].

Smartphones, tablets, and wearable devices are equipped with many sensors such as GPS, microphones and cameras, along with data information trail (such as social media posts) generated by users explicitly and implicitly, to integrate Human and Machine Intelligence (HMI) into sensing and computing process [27].

The advantage of MCSC is that the data collection is usually very short and less expensive than traditional methods such as surveillance cameras, which need humans, expensive utilities and sensors installations. In this model, collecting data manually will consume crowds' time, which might reduce its effectivity. The study in [6] suggests a centralized platform that has a comprehensive database that holds information related to pilgrims, medical, health care, emergency centers, educational contents about the hajj in different languages, and guidance model. However, in disaster situation, [29] claims that decentralized data from crowdsourcing applications might be more useful for gathering information about the disaster than the centralized platform, even though the data might not be accurate. It suggested an approach that enables collaborations amongst organizations to provide disaster relief using crowdsourcing applications.

Ushahidi [28] is a Web 2.0 site that uses crowdsourcing in crisis management works. It is based on allowing users to report a specific story using various methods such as SMS, email, web-form, and social media and accompanied by GPS location when it is possible. It shows each report on a map. Another example is the Large Emergency Event Digital Information Repository (LEEDIR) [26] launched recently by the US law enforcement agencies which was designed to collect video and images from crowds about an incident. The application receives the image/video and the metadata related to it such as GPS.

4   Conclusion and Future Directions for Research

Recently, interest has grown in urban analytics researches for the Hajj. Furthermore, researchers in [8, 11, 19, 20] have developed methodologies and techniques for controlling crowds in the context of the annual pilgrimage to Mecca. In this paper we reviewed different techniques that have been used in the Hajj. Computer vision-based techniques were used in the Hajj such as CCTV surveillance cameras that transmit the videos and audios. Moreover, many researchers used FLIR techniques to detect crowd density and then take the corresponding action accordingly. In addition to the former, different location-based techniques were proposed, such as attaching RFID tags in pilgrims' phones which will allow to follow-up the pilgrims.

In recent years, different techniques were developed to help avoid accidents that may result from the sense of urgency causing a rush toward an entry or exit point in the holy sites at the same time. However, there are precise crowd management trends in data and information gathering that are applicable for the Hajj context. Due to the location of Mecca, where it is located in a valley surrounded by mountains, such as Arafat Mountain that pilgrims need to visit to complete their Hajj, recent developments in UAV technologies suggest that they can be considered remote monitoring of mountainous contexts. Although the pictures provided by UAVs might not be stable but the UAVs will be able to move to new places without the need for installation. Moreover, with the raise of wireless networking, and mobile social techniques, MCSC based applications were developed in [6, 28]. MSCS web such as [28] might help pilgrims and authorities to avoid a crisis.

Acknowledgement. This research was supported in part by the Software and Knowledge Engineering Research Group (SKERG) at King Saud University through grant (RGP-VPP-157) provided by the deanship of Scientific Research. We are thankful to them.

References

1. Zheng, Y., Capra, L., Wolfson, O., Yang, H.: Urban computing: concepts, methodologies, and applications. ACM Trans. Intell. Syst. Technol. (TIST) 5(3), 38 (2014)
2. Psyllidis, A., Bozzon, A., Bocconi, S., Titos Bolivar, C.: A platform for urban analytics and semantic data integration in city planning. In: Celani, G., Sperling, D.M., Franco, J.M.S. (eds.) CAAD Futures 2015. CCIS, vol. 527, pp. 21–36. Springer, Heidelberg (2015)
3. Franke, T., Lukowicz, P., Blanke, U.: Smart crowds in smart cities: real life, city scale deployments of a smartphone based participatory crowd management platform. J. Internet Serv. Appl. 6(1), 1–19 (2015)
4. Al-Salhie, L., Al-Zuhair, M., Al-Wabil, A.: Multimedia surveillance in event detection: crowd analytics in Hajj. In: Marcus, A. (ed.) DUXU 2014, Part II. LNCS, vol. 8518, pp. 383–392. Springer, Heidelberg (2014)
5. Fardoun, H.M., Mashat, A.S., Ciprés, A.P.: Mecca access and security control system. In: Proceedings of the 13th International Conference on Interacción Persona-Ordenador, p. 30. ACM, October 2012

6. Jain, R.S., Kumar, N., Kumar, B.: Design and simulation of security sub-layer of WMAN IEEE 802.16 standard (Wi-Max Compliant). In: Das, V.V., Vijaykumar, R. (eds.) ICT 2010. CCIS, vol. 101, pp. 1–7. Springer, Heidelberg (2010)
7. Ahmad, A., Rahman, M.A., Rehman, F.U., Lbath, A., Afyouni, I., Khelil, A., Hussain, S.O., Sadiq, B., Wahiddin, M.R.: A framework for crowd-sourced data collection and context-aware services in Hajj and Umrah. In: 2014 IEEE/ACS 11th International Conference on Computer Systems and Applications (AICCSA), pp. 405–412. IEEE, November 2014
8. Al-Khaffaf, H.S., Haron, F., Sarmady, S., Talib, A.Z., Abu-Sulyman, I.M.: Crowd parameter extraction from video at the main gates of Masjid al-Haram. In: Sambath, S., Zhu, E. (eds.) Frontiers in Computer Education. AISC, vol. 133, pp. 727–736. Springer, Heidelberg (2012)
9. Bisht, A., Singh, S.: Environmental management in mass gatherings: a case study of Maha Kumbh Mela 2013 at Prayag, India. Int. J. Innovative Res. Sci. Technol. **1**(7), 107–115 (2015)
10. Ben-Mahmoud C., AbouChalbak, M., Plumb, C., Moore, K.: Holy Cities: Saudi's Unique Real Estate Markets. On point Jones Lang LaSalle IP, Inc. (2010). Retrieved from http://www.joneslanglasalle-mena.com/MENA/EN-GB/Pages/Home.aspx
11. Mohandes, M., Haleem, M., Deriche, M., Balakrishnan, K.: Wireless sensor networks for pilgrims tracking. IEEE Embed. Syst. Lett. **4**(4), 106–109 (2012)
12. Fruin J.: The causes and prevention of crowd disasters. In: Engineering for Crowd Safety, pp. 1–10. Elsevier, New York (1993)
13. United Nations, Department of Economic and Social Affairs, Population Division (2014). World Urbanization Prospects: The 2014 Revision, Highlights (ST/ESA/SER.A/352)
14. Höglund, F.: The Use of Resilience Strategies in Crowd Management at a Music Festival: and the safety organization's role in avoiding crowd conflict (2013)
15. The Future of World Religions: Population Growth Projections, 2010-2050. http://www.pewresearch.org
16. General Authority for statistics. http://www.stats.gov.sa
17. Yamin, M., Albugami, M.A.: An architecture for improving Hajj management. In: Liu, K., Gulliver, S.R., Li, W., Yu, C. (eds.) ICISO 2014. IFIP AICT, vol. 426, pp. 187–196. Springer, Heidelberg (2014)
18. Saudi Press Agencey. http://www.spa.gov.sa/viewstory.php?lang=en&newsid=1401176
19. Abuarafah, A.G., Khozium, M.O., AbdRabou, E.: Real-time crowd monitoring using infrared thermal video sequences. J. Am. Sci. **8**(3), 133–140 (2012)
20. Khozium, M.: A hybrid intelligent information system for the administration of massive mass of Hajjis. Life Sci. J. **9**(4), 171–180 (2012)
21. Guo, B., Wang, Z., Yu, Z., Wang, Y., Yen, N.Y., Huang, R., Zhou, X.: Mobile crowd sensing and computing: the review of an emerging human-powered sensing paradigm. ACM Comput. Surv. (CSUR) **48**(1), 7 (2015)
22. Wang, Z., Li, M., Khaleghi, A.M., Xu, D., Lobos, A., Vo, C., Lien, J.M., Liu, J., Son, Y.J.: DDDAMS-based crowd control via UAVs and UGVs. Proc. Comput. Sci. **18**, 2028–2035 (2013)
23. Eisenbeiss, H.: A mini unmanned aerial vehicle (UAV): system overview and image acquisition. In: International Archives of Photogrammetry. Remote Sensing and Spatial Information Sciences, vol. 36(5/W1) (2004)
24. Simic, M., Bil, C., Vojisavljevic, V.: Investigation in wireless power transmission for UAV charging. Proc. Comput. Sci. **60**, 1846–1855 (2015)
25. Khaleghi, A.M., Xu, D., Lobos, A., Minaeian, S., Son, Y.J., Liu, J.: Agent-based hardware-in-the-loop simulation for UAV/UGV surveillance and crowd control system. In: Proceedings of the 2013 Winter Simulation Conference: Simulation: Making Decisions in a Complex World, pp. 1455–1466. IEEE Press, December 2013

26. Guo, B., Chen, C., Zhang, D., Yu, Z., Chin, A.: Mobile crowd sensing and computing: when participatory sensing meets participatory social media. IEEE Commun. Mag. **54**(2), 131–137 (2016)
27. Guo, B., Yu, Z., Zhou, X., Zhang, D.: From participatory sensing to mobile crowd sensing. In: 2014 IEEE International Conference on Pervasive Computing and Communications Workshops (PERCOM Workshops), pp. 593–598. IEEE, March 2014
28. Okolloh, O.: Ushahidi, or 'testimony': Web 2.0 tools for crowdsourcing crisis information. Participatory Learn. Action **59**(1), 65–70 (2009)
29. Gao, H., Wang, X., Barbier, G., Liu, H.: Promoting coordination for disaster relief – from crowdsourcing to coordination. In: Salerno, J., Yang, S.J., Nau, D., Chai, S.-K. (eds.) SBP 2011. LNCS, vol. 6589, pp. 197–204. Springer, Heidelberg (2011)
30. Ganti, R.K., Ye, F., Lei, H.: Mobile crowdsensing: current state and future challenges. IEEE Commun. Mag. **49**(11), 32–39 (2011)
31. Ma, H., Zhao, D., Yuan, P.: Opportunities in mobile crowd sensing. IEEE Commun. Mag. **52**(8), 29–35 (2014)

Towards Urban Tribes in Saudi Arabia: Social Subcultures Emerging from Urban Analytics of Social Media

Tariq Alhindi[1(✉)], Salma Aldawood[1], Jumana Almahmoud[1],
Carlos Sandoval[2], Areej Al-Wabil[1], Mansour Alsaleh[1],
and Sarah Williams[1]

[1] Center for Complex Engineering Systems, King Abdulaziz City for Science
and Technology, Riyadh, Saudi Arabia
{talhindi,saaldawood,jalmahmoud,aalwabil,
maalsaleh}@kacst.edu.sa, sew@mit.edu
[2] Civic Data Design Lab, Massachusetts Institute of Technology's (MIT),
Cambridge, MA, USA
csandova@mit.edu

Abstract. Analyzing and accessing information related to coupled urban socio-technical systems can provide insights into social subcultures, mobility patterns and behavior that are critical to decision making systems at an urban scale. In this paper, we examine the question of how can urban analytics provide a classification of subcultures or urban tribes for the context of Saudi Arabia. Data analytics and classification methodology of urban tribes will be used to guide the discussion, and computational challenges and directions for future research will be discussed.

Keywords: Urban analytics · Social media analytics · Urban tribes

1 Introduction

French sociologist Michel Maffesoli coined the term "urban tribes" more than 30 years ago in 1985 [1]. In recent studies of social computing, the concept of urban tribes has evolved from simple classifications of subcultures to inform policy and decision making, to complex metrics for automating the extraction and analysis of urban subcultures [2, 3].

The goal of this work is to describe social subcultures in Saudi Arabia from urban analytics of check-ins and social media sharing of locations. A remarkable amount of social media in the context of Saudi Arabia takes the form of geo-tagged check-ins, images or videos, and is a largely untapped resource for understanding emergent phenomena in social behavior. Insights into mobility, consumer behavior, communication activity can be acquired from analyzing these vast amounts of information.

The applied context of this research is examining the urban tribes' classification in the scope of decision making and informing policy for urban planning. Situated in a socio-technical context, urban analytics, for the purpose of city planning requires a close

© Springer International Publishing Switzerland 2016
G. Meiselwitz (Ed.): SCSM 2016, LNCS 9742, pp. 258–266, 2016.
DOI: 10.1007/978-3-319-39910-2_24

dialogue between social, engineering and design-oriented fields of research as well as their methods. We are particularly interested to look closely at the ways in which points of interest in the urban fabric of the city are visited. Different 'urban tribes' may occupy space (i.e. places in Riyadh) in different ways, unbeknownst to each other. Indicators of social subcultures include the density of activity in the location, topics discussed around points of interests, and demographics of frequent visitors to points of interest.

Problem Definition. This work is focused on the analysis of geo-tagged tweets, a common type of activity in the social media. We focus on the problem of how to extract behavior patterns that facilitate meaningful comparison, i.e., a metric that captures tribal characteristics. To this end, we make use of recent advances in social network analytics SNA, and we show that it is possible to extract social semantic meaning from geo-tagged content. Our urban analytics approach is rooted in synthetic information and data analytics in urban contexts.

Contributions. Recent advances in social computing have created new opportunities for collecting, integrating, analyzing and accessing information related to coupled urban socio-technical systems. Innovative systems designed for urban analytics that leverage this new capability have recently been recognized as useful. The first contribution is a framework to learn and recognize types of social categories in an urban context from social media. The second contribution is an insight into the spatial distribution of urban tribes which can consequently be a source for recommendations for introducing integrated transit systems, resources allocation and development of infrastructure. Although the applied context is a city in Saudi Arabia, we foresee the contribution to be generalized to some extent to the global scope in similar urban mobility contexts.

This paper is structured as follows. Section 2 provides an overview of background research on urban analytics and the emergent research on urban tribes. Section 3 describes the different approaches we used to conduct the analysis. An experiment is presented and discussed in Sect. 4. We conclude in Sect. 5 with key insights and future directions for research.

2 Background

While cities are spatially structured, they are considered intricate socio-economic entities that depend for their existence on their links with the natural environment. Several disciplines are attempting to tackle the problem of understanding the complex systems of cities and the underlying socio-economic ecosystem theories of their constituent elements (people, places, and environment). These disciplines range from economics, physics, and social sciences to applied domains of engineering, computing and urban studies. Notably, the dynamic and complex systems approach to studying urban spatial data (location-based data) has only been possible with computer-based modeling.

Geo-social media data is essentially heterogeneous. It is a mixture of geographical information (location), mobility footprints (check-in data), visual snapshots (images or videos), and social interactions (social conversation around the post or activity). Research on urban analytics for the purpose of identifying subcultures and addressing the intricacies and coupling of socio and technical systems have provided an insight into the key metrics for urban tribe classification [4].

Observing mobility data bring up important insights regarding people's behavior and trends. These insights could be used by planners and business owners to study the area and to help them make an informed decision regarding the location of their businesses and offices. Location data provides useful insights in an aggregate level without being constrained to an individual level, which can be aligned with maintaining the privacy of the users of mobile devices. One example, to illustrate the use of location data to elicit urban insights, is Sense Network; an analytical platform by a company based in New York. The software analyzes location data and presents recommendations to shop owners and business stakeholders on several topics like for example the location of new branches of a shop [5].

Our project is part of a collaborative effort to understand how open data and social media can be used to provide a fine-grained and more holistic understanding of urban groups by using social media and locality information. In the following sections, we provide an overview of projects that have provided methods for an augmented analysis of urban tribes by using algorithmic approaches and social media data. Our methodology not only differs in the data computation, but also in the clustering through a spatial network of spaces.

2.1 Hoodsquare

The Hoodsquare project developed an algorithm for extracting neighborhood boundaries in cities, including New York City based on social media data [6]. The algorithm works by using data related to foursquare venue types, spatial distribution of local and tourists in the city, and the timestamps of check-ins in venues. Hoodsquare built a tool that can be used to "recommend geographic areas that are small in size and that maintain a balanced trade-off between prediction accuracy and geographic precision" [6]. The ranking attempts to go beyond the neighborhoods as administrative or politically defined units in order to unearth neighborhood geographies that are much more in accord to the actual behavior of people in the streets, and with the way they occupy the city. Their exercise provides a predefined spatial clustering within neighborhoods [6].

2.2 City Sense

CitySense is a discovery tool for temporal and spatial hot-spots of activity in the city that has been implemented as a mobile application [7]. It allows people and businesses to detect how the city is inhabited in real time, and take decisions on whether to go out, where to go, and where to locate franchises. Moreover, CitySense also allows for the exploration of how people is on the move in the city, by evaluating where they come from and where they go. The CitySense algorithm, is focused on discovering the circadian rhythms of the city [7].

2.3 Livehoods

The Livehoods project is based on the development of an algorithm that uses four-square data in order to produce neighborhoods classifications based on spatial and social proximity of venues in New York City [3]. Livelihood addresses the need to provide a more automatized and data-based approach to the characterization and understanding of neighborhoods to aid both urban computing and city planning projects. The Livehoods project has developed a compelling method to unearth a classification of New York City neighborhoods by taking advantage of massive data sets and unsupervised learning approaches. A significant result of this approach is the Livehood's definition of a neighborhood as "an urban area is defined not just by the type of places found there, but also by the people that choose to make that area part of their daily life" [3].

3 Methods

This section describes the collection and setup of the dataset used in our study. We focused on analyzing Twitter and Point of Interests (POI) datasets. At the time of conducting the fieldwork, there was no public dataset to provide insights into social subcultures in Saudi Arabia. Therefore, we created a dataset by scraping data from Twitter search APIs. The data collected was geo-tagged activity in Riyadh city for the months of October, November and December, 2015 with a total of 125 thousand geo-tagged tweets. The POI dataset was provided by Arriyadh Development Authority that has a comprehensive list of amenities in the city of Riyadh.

Social media applications facilitate spatially marking the activities of Riyadh residents, creating rich databases that hold digital imprints of their interactions. Although these datasets only represent the portion of the population who are active on social media, insights obtained from trends in interactions are often reflections of behavior patterns in the urban community. In our analysis, we observe the density of activity, the variation across space, and the cultural cues with regard to the interactions, the perceived narrative, and the place.

We follow a pipeline of three steps where in the first step we detect the type of activity based on the main topic discussed in each tweet. In the second step, we breakdown the city into clusters based on Traffic Analysis Zones (TAZ) which capture the mobility dynamics, based on the origin and destination of trips throughout the day. In the third step, we look at patterns of these clusters with respect to their spatial distribution and correlation with surrounding POIs.

3.1 Detecting Activity Type

We start by creating a list of eight categories of tweets derived from previous studies and inspired from anticipated popular categories in the Saudi context [8]. For each category, we define a set of four to ten keywords that are relevant to the topic of the category and are expected to occur frequently in Twitter. The keywords were selected based on our knowledge of the Arabic language and the local context in the social media. We chose keywords with direct-mapping in terms of their association with a certain category. An example of some of the categories and keywords used is show in Table 1.

We then assign multiple scores to each tweet in the dataset where each score resembles the number of keywords for a certain category in a single tweet. The category of the tweet will be the one with the highest score. The tweets are then aggregated on the urban level to generate clusters of human activity in the city. Figure 1 shows the architecture of the framework guiding our analysis in this approach.

Table 1. Sample list of Arabic keywords used with their translation in English

Category	Keywords	Translation to English
Weather	مطر, الجو، شمس، حر	Rain, weather, sun, hot,
Sport	دوري - هلال, نصر...	League, Hilal, Nasser (local clubs in Saudi)

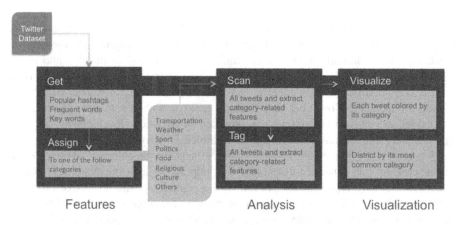

Fig. 1. Pipeline of steps to detect categories; showing complete list of categories

3.2   Clustering

To visualize urban tribes from tweets and correlate it to Points of Interests (POI) types, we used the Arriyadh development Authority (ADA) POI data and Riyadh Traffic Analysis Zones (TAZ) data derived from the ADA origin destination dataset as source of input. A TAZ is a geographical unit that is used in transportation modeling. The ADA data highlights all landmarks and amenities which are around 12000 points around the city. The POIs are categorized into six types including: restaurants, hotels and apartments, shops and services, Community services, health and education, and Tourism. Figure 2 shows the Riyadh TAZ map and POI distribution across the city.

By joining TAZ data and POI data we identified the different types of amenities that resides within each TAZ. We then split TAZs into six clusters, each of which highlights TAZ areas that contain a specific amenity type. It should be noted that a particular TAZ area can exist in more than one cluster based on whether a POI of a specific type exists or not.

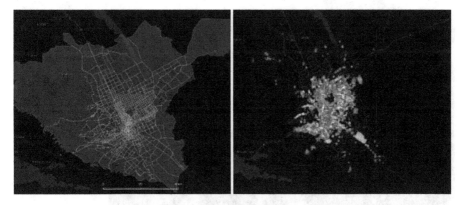

Fig. 2. (Left) Riyadh TAZ areas, (Right) Riyadh POI points.

3.3 Analysis

In our analysis, we examined patterns that emerge when correlating the most dominant tweet category in each TAZ with two main dimensions. First, we look at the spatial distribution of different categories in the city with regards to the location and the size of each TAZ. Second, we look at correlation of the category of tweets in each TAZ with the type of POIs in that TAZ. The overall goal of this analysis is to study the influence of urban features on the social dynamics of people in the city [9].

4 Exploratory Study

We applied our tweet categorization method explained earlier on the geo-tagged tweets collected in Riyadh to sense spaces as done in earlier studies [10–14]. Figure 3 shows the different subcultures within the city of Riyadh when overlaying tweets categories, extracted spatially over the TAZ areas, where clusters are color-coded by the category of tweets. The complete list of tweet-categories was described in the framework depicted in Fig. 1.

We look closely at Food, one of the tweet-categories, to examine relationships with related venues in the city (i.e. restaurants). Figure 4 shows the distribution of Food tweets around the city in contrast with TAZs that have restaurants. The levels of the pink color represent tweets about food with varying density (i.e. number of tweets) and the grey color represent all other tweets. We can see that dense food tweets (i.e. dark red) are found in locations that have restaurants, which are circled with red in Fig. 4.

Overlaying tweet-categories, extracted spatially over the clusters identified, and visualizing them on a map help in understanding the correlation between both POI and tweets-categories as we saw earlier. Also, we look at the number of tweets in each category in the six types of clusters we have. Table 2 shows the summary of these counts. It should be noted that each count is normalized by the total number of tweets in that category to address the issue of favoring categories that have more tweets.

Fig. 3. TAZs in Riyadh colored by most dominant tweet category (Color figure online)

Fig. 4. (Left) Food Tweets (Pink-scale) and all other tweets (Grey-scale) in the city. (Right) Food Tweets (Pink-scale) and all other tweets (Grey-scale) in Restaurant areas (Color figure online).

Table 2. Percentage of tweet categories in each TAZ cluster normalized by total number of tweets in each category.

TAZ	Food	Transportation	Politics	Religious	Weather	Culture	Sport	Other
Restaurants	0.21	0.18	0.20	0.21	0.18	0.28	0.18	0.19
Hotels and Apt	0.26	0.25	0.17	0.25	0.21	0.36	0.27	0.27
Shops	0.23	0.24	0.16	0.24	0.19	0.34	0.21	0.24
Tourism	0.21	0.21	0.28	0.23	0.19	0.22	0.22	0.22
Commercial	0.25	0.32	0.26	0.46	0.35	0.28	0.37	0.35
Health and Education	0.25	0.33	0.33	0.53	0.38	0.45	0.35	0.34

The findings show categories of tweets are distributed among the TAZ clusters of the six types of POIs with no clear patterns. Notably, the numbers are influenced by the selection of keywords, the corresponding categories defined, and the types of POIs. Also, the analysis was based on the assumption that the list of categories that were defined in the framework are aligned with the list of types of POIs in the dataset. Further investigation of the mapping in the POI dataset is planned. A larger dataset along with a more comprehensive list of keywords is sought to address the sensitivity and specificity of the tweet categorization conducted in this round of analysis.

5 Conclusion

In this paper we examined the question of what can be determined about the social categorization of people from their social media activity. The model we propose captured social dynamics within mobility patterns from activities extracted from social media. A number of limitations were noted in the study. First, a relatively smaller subset of Saudis share their location when they post in twitter, when compared to global trends in posting on twitter. This was evident in our dataset where the most popular hashtags were not in Arabic, an indicator that they were posted by expatriates rather than natives of the urban context of analysis, which limits the activity that can be collected about the city's local inhabitants. Second, the keywords and categories that were selected impact the effectiveness of categorization and clustering of twitter activity. Nevertheless, the potential in this methodology in gaining insights into the relationships between activity in social media and urban features in the city is evident. Tweet-categories with direct relationships to venues in the city, such as: food tweets with restaurants, sport tweets with stadiums and other sport venues, were used to validate the findings. The detection of less obvious relationships, such as the places that attract social, political or religious conversations remains a challenge. Identifying these relationships can be used to evaluate the influence of newly introduced venues to the social conversation in a given location.

Tweet categorization will be further improved in future work by redefining the list of keywords and categories selected. Also, other spatial clustering techniques will be examined to find unrevealed patterns in the data with respect to spatial elements in the city. In addition, a temporal dimension will be added to see differences in activity throughout the day and during different times of the week.

Acknowledgment. This work was sponsored by King Abdulaziz City for Science and Technology in Riyadh, Saudi Arabia.

References

1. Maffesoli, M.: The Time of the Tribes: The Decline of Individualism in Mass Society, vol. 41. Sage, Beverley Hills (1995)
2. Hsieh, H.P., Yan, R., Li, C.T.: Dissecting urban noises from heterogeneous geo-social media and sensor data. In: Proceedings of the 23rd Annual ACM Conference on Multimedia Conference, pp. 1103–1106. ACM, October 2015

3. Cranshaw, J., Schwartz, R., Hong, J.I., Sadeh, N.: The livehoods project: utilizing social media to understand the dynamics of a city. In: International AAAI Conference on Weblogs and Social Media, p. 58, June 2012

4. Marathe, M.: Resilient cities and urban analytics: the role of big data and high performance pervasive computing. In: Proceedings of the 2nd IKDD Conference on Data Sciences, p. 4. ACM, March 2015

5. Fitzgerald, M.: Predicting Where You'll Go and What You'll Like (2008). On the Web at http://www.nytimes.com/2008/06/22/technology/22proto.html

6. Zhang, A.X., Noulas, A., Scellato, S., Mascolo, C.: Hoodsquare: modeling and recommending neighborhoods in location-based social networks. In: 2013 International Conference on Social Computing (SocialCom), pp. 69–74. IEEE, September 2013

7. Loecher, M., Jebara, T.: CitySense: multiscale space time clustering of GPS points and trajectories. In: Proceedings of the Joint Statistical Meeting, August 2009

8. Refaee, E., Rieser, V.: Can we read emotions from a smiley face? Emoticon-based distant supervision for subjectivity and sentiment analysis of Arabic twitter feeds. In: 5th International Workshop on Emotion, Social Signals, Sentiment and Linked Open Data, LREC (2014)

9. Foth, M.: Networking serendipitous social encounters in urban neighbourhoods. In: Social Implications of Data Mining and Information Privacy: Interdisciplinary Frameworks and Solutions: Interdisciplinary Frameworks and Solutions, p. 71 (2009)

10. Al-Husain, L., Kanjo, E., Chamberlain, A.: Sense of space: mapping physiological emotion response in urban space. In: Proceedings of the 2013 ACM Conference on Pervasive and Ubiquitous Computing Adjunct Publication, pp. 1321–1324. ACM, October 2013

11. Al-Barrak, L., Kanjo, E.: NeuroPlace: making sense of a place. In: Proceedings of the 4th Augmented Human International Conference, pp. 186–189. ACM, March 2013

12. Mody, R.N., Willis, K.S., Kerstein, R.: WiMo: location-based emotion tagging. In: Proceedings of the 8th international Conference on Mobile and Ubiquitous Multimedia, p. 14. ACM, November 2009

13. Almaatouq, A., Alhasoun, F., Campari, R., Alfaris, A.: The influence of social norms on synchronous versus asynchronous communication technologies. In: Proceedings of the 1st ACM International Workshop on Personal Data Meets Distributed Multimedia, pp. 39–42. ACM, October 2013

14. Alhasoun, F., Almaatouq, A., Greco, K., Campari, R., Alfaris, A., Ratti, C.: The city browser: utilizing massive call data to infer city mobility dynamics. In: 3rd International Workshop on Urban Computing (UrbComp 2014). UrbComp, New York, NY (2014)

Arabic Sentiment Analysis Resources:
A Survey

Areeb alOwisheq[1(✉)], Sarah alHumoud[1], Nora alTwairesh[2],
and Tarfa alBuhairi[1]

[1] Computer Science Department,
Al-Imam Muhammad ibn Saud Islamic University, Riyadh, Saudi Arabia
{a.alowisheq,s.alhumoud}@ccis.imamu.edu.sa,
tmalbuhairi@imamu.edu.sa
[2] Information Technology Department, King Saud University,
Riyadh, Saudi Arabia
twairesh@ksu.edu.sa

Abstract. Research interest in Arabic sentiment analysis (ASA) is rapidly increasing, therefore it is important to compile, document and analyze efforts in this area to facilitate further development. These ASA efforts aim to create tools that can sift through and gain meaningful knowledge from the unending data explosion. ASA approaches have continued to evolve despite lack in Arabic linguistic resources. In this paper we conduct a comprehensive and up-to-date review of recent resources for ASA.

Keywords: Social networks · Sentiment analysis · Arabic · Lexicon · Corpus

1 Introduction

Large-scale data stream analysis has lately become one of the important business and research priorities. Social networks like Twitter and other micro-blogging platforms hold an enormous amount of data. Extracting valuable information and trends out of these data would aid in a better understanding and decision-making. Multiple analysis techniques are deployed for English content, and although the Arabic language is one of the languages that has a large amount of content over social networks, yet it is least analyzed.

As of March 2014, there are over 5.7 million Arab Twitter users, 2.4 million of those are from Saudi Arabia[1], together producing an average of over 17 million tweets per day. This huge volume of data provides the opportunity of *Sentiment Analysis* (SA), enabling organizations to observe feelings and opinions of twitter users towards products, policies or people. Existing solutions to Arabic SA are limited compared to English SA approaches, the unique nature and complexity of the Arabic language requires researching appropriate solutions. Arabic is a morphologically rich language

---

[1] Twitter in the Arab Region, Arab Social Media Report
http://www.arabsocialmediareport.com/Twitter/LineChart.aspx?&PriMenuID=18&CatID=25&mnu=Cat.

© Springer International Publishing Switzerland 2016
G. Meiselwitz (Ed.): SCSM 2016, LNCS 9742, pp. 267–278, 2016.
DOI: 10.1007/978-3-319-39910-2_25

where important grammatical information is expressed at word level. Moreover, Arabic language is a collection of multiple variants, where the everyday spoken language Dialectal Arabic (DA) is different from the formal language Modern Standard Arabic (MSA). In social media, Arab users have started using their own dialect in expressing themselves. This has complicated the task of SA since most Arabic NLP tools have been developed for MSA.

Although Research in Arabic SA is still in its early stages, it is rapidly increasing. As shown in Fig. 1, which is adapted from work done by [1], the number of scientific publications (conference papers and journal articles), have rapidly risen in the last couple of years.

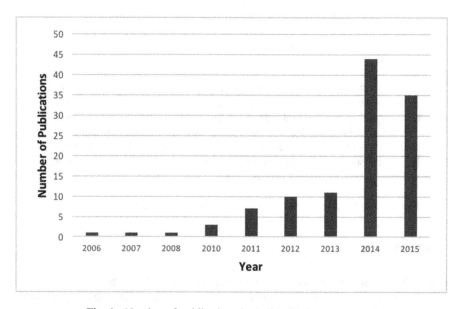

Fig. 1. Number of publications in Arabic SA in recent years

This increase in interest demands formal and systematic reviews of the area. It is highly important for the scientific community to recognize the state of the art, realize existing methodologies and tools; and address challenges and open issues.

One of the main obstacles in Arabic SA is the scarcity of high quality resources, such as datasets, corpora, and lexicons. This paper reviews main methods used to create them, their targeted dialects, and their size, in addition to their utilization by the reviewed SA approaches. The paper is organized as follows, Sect. 2 presents the survey methodology. Section 3 provides an overview of lexica resources which were used by the ASA approaches and Sect. 4 concludes the paper.

2 Survey Methodology

We followed the process from [1] in collecting the articles. The search process was conducted using keywords: 'Arabic subjectivity and sentiment analysis', 'Arabic opinion mining', 'Comparative opinions Arabic', and 'Opinion spam Arabic' in these databases: Google Scholar, Springer, IEEE explorer, ACM digital library, and Science Direct. Reviewed papers covers papers written until 2015. A total of 28 articles were selected from the retrieved publications: these included ones that introduced a new ASA resource, and that was not covered in [1]. The articles were then categorized into either an ASA approach or a resource depending on their contributions. For the ASA resources, we included ones that were used by the surveyed approaches in addition to any resources that have not been covered by previous surveys. The following sections review resources, which are divided into lexicons and corpora/datasets. In each section, the articles are presented in a tabulated form to ease readability. The aim is to provide a valuable resource for researchers when considering ASA.

3 Resources

In this section we cover linguistic resources essential to ASA approaches; these are sentiment lexicons, and corpora.

3.1 Sentiment Lexicons

Here we review papers that reported the construction of a lexicon without presenting any new methods in SA. Papers that constructed a new lexicon and developed a new approach that uses the lexicon are mentioned in the summary table (Table 1) for referencing. Where the proposed lexicons are mentioned if they were available publicly otherwise NA is written denoting that lexicon is not available or AOR if lexicon was available on request.

In an attempt to produce an Arabic SentiWordNet (SWN) Al-Hazmi et al. [2] proposed a methodology for mapping SWN 3.0 to Arabic. However, this resource has limited coverage (10 K) and was not tested in a sentiment analysis setting and is not publicly available. Badaro et al. [3] however, present pioneering work in the same direction by constructing ArSenL a large scale Arabic sentiment lexicon. They relied on four resources to create ArSenL: English WordNet (EWN), Arabic WordNet (AWN), English SentiWordNet (ESWN), and SAMA (Standard Arabic Morphological Analyzer). Two approaches were followed producing two different lexicons, each validated separately. Then the union of the two lexicons was validated and produced the best performance. The first approach used AWN, by mapping AWN entries into ESWN using existing offsets thus producing ArSenL-AWN. The second approach utilizes SAMA's English glosses by finding the highest overlapping synsets between these glosses and ESWN thus producing ArSenL-Eng. Hence ArSenL is the union of these two lexicons. They evaluated the lexicon by comparing it to SIFAAT lexicon [4], and it gave the highest coverage and best performance in subjectivity and sentiment

Table 1. Lexica used in ASA techniques

Article	Lexicon	Method of construction	Size	Sentiment Score	Arabic varia	Evaluated
[2]	NA	Mapping of English SWN 3.0	10000 lemmas	as in ESWN	MSA	No
[12]	NA	Extracted from a dataset of 22550 tweets. Jordanian dialect words manually translated to MSA.	16420 words	No	MSA / Jordanian	Yes
[13]	NA	Arabic translation of MPQA lexicon, and mappings of synonyms from AWN, manual annotations, entries from multi-lingual sentiment lexicons.	8133 words	-ve strong -ve weak +ve strong +ve weak	MSA	Yes
[3]	ArSenL[a]	Used EWN/AWN/ESWN and SAMA (Standard Arabic Morphological Analyzer) to construct the lexicon.	157969 Synsets 28760 Lemmas	As in ESWN 3 scores: +ve -ve neutral	MSA	Yes
[14]	NA	Extracted stems from a publicly available corpus [15]. Then crawled Arabic news websites to collect texts to expand the lexicon. The resulting stems were translated to English using Google Translate. The polarity of the terms was taken from an English sentiment lexicon.	120,000 terms	-Positive: (60%–100%), -Neutral: (40%–60%) -Negative: (0%–40%),	MSA	Yes
[16, 17]	AOR	Three methods for creating the lexicon **1. Manual Approach** 300 seed words were taken from SentiStrength[b] then translated into Arabic using English-Arabic dictionary. Synonyms of each word were added and assigned the same polarity. Then the lexicon was extended with Arabic dialects such as Egyptian, Khaliji, Levantine, etc. **2. Direct-translation Approach** Translated the SentiStrength lexicon using Google translate. Human experts normalized the lexicon, removed duplicates, and corrected the errors.	**1st lexicon** 4,815 words 1,942 +ve 2,873 −ve **2nd lexicon** 9,100 words 2,670 +ve 6,430 −ve **3rd lexicon** 8,618 2,075 +ve 6,543 -ve	No	MSA/ Dialect	Yes

(Continued)

Table 1. (*Continued*)

Article	Lexicon	Method of construction	Size	Sentiment Score	Arabic varia	Evaluated
		3. Corpus-based Approach Applied to a labeled and balanced corpus of +ve and -ve comments. Removed stop words, TF weighting scheme applied on classes to generate 2 lists of +ve and -ve words.				
[6][e]	BiSaL	Words were extracted form Dark web forums and annotated manually by linguistic experts.	1019 words	Yes	Not determined	No
[18][d]	NA	Unigrams and bigrams were extracted from the dataset which was a collection of hotel, restaurant, movies, product reviews. Then utilize a 1-norm SVM to select the most significant features. Then the resulting lexicon was manually reviewed and corrected by two Arabic speakers.	2000 words	No	MSA/ Dialect	Yes
[9, 19]	NA	**ArSeLex:** Started with a 400 adjective list as seed then manually expanded it by adding synonyms and antonyms for each word. Also propose an automatic way to expand the lexicon utilizing the synonym/antonym relations found in Arabic online dictionaries. **AIPSeLEX:** Also constructed a lexicon for common phrases and idioms for the Egyptian Dialect and manually annotated it.	5244 words 2003 +ve 2829 −ve 412 neutral. 3296 phrases and idioms	No	MSA/ Egyptian	Yes
[20]	NA	An Arabic lexicon was constructed by merging two MSA lexicons: MPQA [21] and ArabSenti [22] with two Egyptian Arabic lexicons: the lexicon constructed in [23] and a manually created lexicon by the authors.	Not available	No	MSA/ Egyptian	Yes
[24, 25]	AOR	1000 MSA sentimental words From the Arabic MPQA subjective lexicon and 2690 Saudi dialect sentimental words were extracted manually from a set of tweets.	3690	No	MSA/Saudi	Yes

(*Continued*)

Table 1.　(*Continued*)

Article	Lexicon	Method of construction	Size	Sentiment Score	Arabic varia	Evaluated
[5][e]	SLSA	The lexicon was constructed using AraMorph and SentiWordNet by relating the glosses of AraMorph to the synset terms in SentiWordNet. POS was taken into consideration since the glosses and synset terms might not be enough to disambiguate an entry.	35000	Yes	MSA	Yes
[7]	NA	Starting from a small seed list of positive and negative words, used semi-supervised learning to propagate the scores in the Arabic WordNet by exploiting the synset relations.	7576 885 +ve 616-ve 6075 neutral	Yes	MSA	Yes
[26]	NA	Used SentiwordNet to extract some sentiment words, then added words manually.	1500 words 1000 -ve 500 +ve	No	MSA/Saudi	Yes
[27]	NA	A seed of 300 words were taken from SentiStrength and translated to Arabic. Then synonyms were added from an Arabic dictionary. Words were stemmed using Khoja stemmer, and the stems added to the previous list. Some words with opposite polarity had the same stem, such words were removed from the lexicon.	2376 words: 1777 +ve 600 -ve	No	MSA	Yes
[28]	NA	This work is concerned with Aspect-Based SA. For every word in the dataset of book reviews LABR, its frequency in each of the classified reviews of the 4 polarities (+ve, -ve, neutral, conflicting) is depicted as its weight. Then to expand the lexicon, if a word is not found it is translated to English and its polarity value is looked up in Sentiwordnet. In a further attempt to expand the lexicon, a PMI method was also applied using a set of seed words from the lexicon.	Not available	Yes	MSA	Yes

(*Continued*)

Table 1. (*Continued*)

Article	Lexicon	Method of construction	Size	Sentiment Score	Arabic varia	Evaluated
[29]	NA	Has 13 parts constructed manually, by extracting the terms from a dataset of 1500 tweets. 6 parts are for Arabic text in 3 domains sports, news, economics, each divided into +ve and -ve. 2 parts are for audio files. And 3 parts for emoticons (+ve, -ve, and neutral). The last 2 parts (+ve and -ve) for the special symbols used in textual chat.	**452 words:** 171 +ve, 281 –ve, **Emoticons:** 61 +ve 65 -ve 68 neutral **Special symbols:** 99 +ve, 80 -ve.	No	MSA/Dialect	Yes
[11]	SentiRDI	Exploits relations of synonymy antonymy, hyponymy & causality in an Arabic Semantic Database.	3156 +ve 4169 -ve 10,839 neutral	No	MSA	Yes

[a]http://Oma-project.com
[b]http://sentistrength.wlv.ac.uk/
[c]http://www.abulaish.com/bisal
[d]http://bit.ly/1wXue3C
[e]http://volta.ldeo.columbia.edu/~rambow/slsa.html

classification. Although this lexicon can be considered as the largest Arabic sentiment lexicon developed to date, it is unfortunate that it only has MSA entries and no dialect words and is not developed from a social media context which could affect the accuracy when applied to social media text. Following the example of ArSenL, the lexicon SLSA (Sentiment Lexicon for Standard Arabic) [5] is constructed by linking the lexicon of an Arabic morphological analyzer Aramorph with SentiWordNet. Although the approach is very similar to ArSenL since both use SentiWordNet to obtain the scores of words, the authors argue that SLSA uses Aramorp which is a free resource while ArSenL use SAMA which is not free and thus makes ArSenL not publicly available. Also the linking algorithm used to link the glosses in Aramorph with those in SentiWordNet is different. SLSA starts by linking every entry in Aramorph with SentiWordNet if the one-gloss word and POS match. Then to accommodate the unlinked entries the POS match is relaxed further as to include the cases where the same lemma has POS noun and adjective, the next step ignores the POS completely. In case of multi-word glosses, the stop words are removed and the relaxed condition is tested on each word separately. This covers 98.2 % of the entries in Aramorph. Intrinsic and extrinsic evaluations were performed by comparing SLSA and ArSenL which demonstrated the superiority of SLSA. Nevertheless, SLSA like ArSenL does not include dialect words and cannot accurately analyze social media text.

In [6] a bilingual sentiment lexicon was developed especially for mining Dark Web forums. Two lexicons were developed SentiLEn for English and SentiLAr for Arabic. The Arabic lexicon was constructed by extracting sentiment words related to cyber threats, radicalism, and conflicts from 2000 message posts of Alokab Web forum. Three Arabic language experts annotated the extracted terms' polarity by giving each term a positive score [0, 1] and a negative score [0, 1]. If a word is always positive its positive score is 1 and the negative score is 0. Similarly, if a word is always negative its negative score is 1 and positive score is 0. For words that are used in both positive as well as negative contexts, positive and negative polarity scores are assigned in the range of 0 and 1 in such a way that their sum is 1. Also two different scores are given for each term for strong and hostile valences. Then the scores given by the three experts are aggregated and normalized to be between [-1,1]. The paper only reported the construction of the lexicon but nothing was reported about validating the lexicon in a real application.

Starting from a small seed list of positive and negative words, Mahyoub et al. [7] used semi-supervised learning to propagate the scores on the Arabic WordNet by exploiting the synset relations. They used the same relations that were used by [8] in developing WordNet-Affect to expand the seed list. These relations include eight semantic/lexical relations {near_synonym, verb_group, see_also_wn15, has_derived, related_to, has_-subevent, causes and near_antonym}. The lexicon was evaluated on two corpora's of movie and book reviews. Although reaching a high accuracy when evaluated, the lexicon still has a low coverage (7576 words) and does not include dialect words.

One of the challenges in sentiment analysis is handling phrases and idioms that convey sentiment. While sentiment words are significant clues to detect sentiment in text, users tend to use common phrases and idioms to express their opinions. These phrases are made up of a different number of words that are usually not sentiment bearing words, and when treated separately by any sentiment analysis algorithm would not be detected as a sentiment clue. Consequently, some efforts have been initiated to deal with this challenge. Authors in [9] constructed an idioms/proverbs lexicon for the Egyptian dialect. They collected 32785 idioms/proverbs from Arabic websites that present directories and encyclopedias of common Egyptian idioms and proverbs. Then they selected 3632 common phrases and manually annotated them for polarity (positive, negative). To check the coverage of this lexicon they developed a technique to detect and extract phrases in text using similarity measures (cosine similarity and Levenshtein distance) combining these measures with n-gram, they reached a 98 % accuracy when applied on tweets and reviews.

The Arabic lexical semantics database (RDI-ArabSemanticDB) [10] was exploited in [11] to construct an Arabic Sentiment Lexicon. The RDI-ArabSemanticDB contains approximately 150,000 Arabic words, 18,413 semantic fields, and 20 semantic relations, including synonyms, antonym, hyponymy and causality. These relations were used to expand a seed list of positive, negative, and neutral words. The lexicon was tested by first comparing it to a translated version of the MPQA lexicon and a manually annotated subset of the lexicon. The results showed that the translation of an English lexicon does not give accurate results. Also the lexicon was tested using different machine learning classifiers of Arabic sentiment using a translated version of the MPQA corpus.

Table 2. Corpora used in ASA techniques

Corpora	Size	Type/Domain	Resource	Dialect	Collection approach	Based On
Not named [31]	400 documents include 2855 sentences (+ve, -ve, neutral)	Document/Newswire	Al Jazeera Arabic news network bilingual website	MSA	**Collection** Manual **Annotation** Manual	**Penn Arabic Treebank: Part 1 v 3** [32]
OCA [33]	500 reviews: 250 +ve 250 −ve	Review/Movie & book reviews	Websites and blogs	MSA	**Collection** Manual **Annotation** Manual	-
HAAD [35]	2,389 reviews	Review/Book reviews	Websites	MSA	**Collection** Manual **Annotation** Manual	**LABR** [36]
LABR [36]	Over 63,000 reviews	Reviews/Book review	Website: (www.goodreads.com)	General	**Collection** Independent **Annotation** Independent	-
Not named [40]	2300 tweets (neutral, +ve, −ve, both, or sarcastic).	Tweets/Independent	Twitter	MSA and dialect	Collection Twitter4j API Annotation Manual	-
ATSD [41]	10000 tweets	Tweets/Independent	Twitter	Egyptian	**Collection** Independent **Annotation** Manual (Amazon Mechanical Turk (AMT))	-
MIKA [42]	4000: 2154 +ve 1648 −ve 198 Neutral	Tweets Mircoblogs/Product, hotel, TV reviews and comments comments	Twitter and Arabic microblogs: (social media, blogs, forums, e-commerce web sites?)	MSA and Egyptian dialect	**Collection** Tweets: Twitter API. Microblogs: manually **Annotation** Manually	

3.2 Corpora and Datasets

Applying sentiment analysis requires a corpus to train a classifier or to evaluate it. This section covers Arabic sentiment analysis researches, and reviews that used corpora. Mostly used corpora were collected from social media; because the content is provided freely, easily, and instantaneously. Users can express, reach, and share opinions in public. Table 2 shows the most available corpora in MSA or dialect which is used in sentiment analysis.

Authors in [5] and [30] used the corpus of [31] which was based on [32]. While the OCA corpus [33] was used by [13] and [34]. The authors in [28] used the HAAD corpus which was produced by [35]. The HAAD [35] minimized and utilized LABR corpus [36]. The authors [37] used the corpus of [38]. [39] utilize the corpus created in [40].

References

1. Al-Twairesh, N., Al-Khalifa, H., Al-Salman, A.-M.: Subjectivity and sentiment analysis of Arabic: trends and challenges. In: 11th International Conference on Computer Systems and Applications (AICCSA), IEEE/ACS, 2014, pp. 148–155 (2014)
2. Alhazmi, S., Black, W., McNaught, J.: Arabic SentiWordNet in relation to SentiWordNet 3.0. 2180 **1266**(4), 1 (2013)
3. Badaro, G., Baly, R., Hajj, H., Habash, N., El-Hajj, W.: A large scale Arabic sentiment lexicon for Arabic opinion mining. In: ANLP 2014, p. 165 (2014)
4. Abdul-Mageed, M., Diab, M.: Toward building a large-scale Arabic sentiment lexicon. In: Proceedings of the 6th International Global WordNet Conference, pp. 18–22 (2012)
5. Eskander, R., Rambow, O.: SLSA: A sentiment lexicon for standard Arabic presented at the empirical methods in natural language processing, Lisbon, Portugal (2015)
6. Al-Rowaily, K., Abulaish, M., Haldar, N.A.-H., Al-Rubaian, M.: BiSAL–a bilingual sentiment analysis lexicon to analyze dark web forums for cyber security. Digit. Investig. **14**, 53–62 (2015)
7. Mahyoub, F.H., Siddiqui, M.A., Dahab, M.Y.: Building an Arabic sentiment lexicon using semi-supervised learning. J. King Saud Univ.-Comput. Inf. Sci. **26**(4), 417–424 (2014)
8. Valitutti, A., Strapparava, C., Stock, O.: Developing affective lexical resources. PsychNology J. **2**(1), 61–83 (2004)
9. Ibrahim, H.S., Abdou, S.M., Gheith, M.: Idioms-proverbs lexicon for modern standard Arabic and colloquial sentiment analysis. Int. J. Comput. Appl. **118**(11), 26–31 (2015)
10. Attia, M., Rashwan, M., Ragheb, A., Al-Badrashiny, M., Al-Basoumy, H., Abdou, S.: A compact Arabic lexical semantics language resource based on the theory of semantic fields. In: Nordström, B., Ranta, A. (eds.) GoTAL 2008. LNCS (LNAI), vol. 5221, pp. 65–76. Springer, Heidelberg (2008)
11. Mobarz, H., Rashown, M., Farag, I.: Using automated lexical resources in Arabic sentence subjectivity. Int. J. Artif. Intell. Appl. **5**(6), 1 (2014)
12. Duwairi, R.M.: Sentiment analysis for dialectical Arabic. In: 2015 6th International Conference on Information and Communication Systems (ICICS), pp. 166–170 (2015)
13. Bayoudhi, A., Belguith, L.H., Ghorbel, H.: Sentiment classification of Arabic documents: experiments with multi-type features and ensemble algorithms (2015)

14. Al-Ayyoub, M., Essa, S.B., Alsmadi, I.: Lexicon-based sentiment analysis of Arabic tweets. Int. J. Soc. Netw. Min. **2**(2), 101–114 (2015)
15. Abuaiadh, D.: Dataset for Arabic Document Classification (2011). http://diab.edublogs.org/dataset-for-arabic-document-classification/
16. Abdulla, N., Majdalawi, R., Mohammed, S., Al-Ayyoub, M., Al-Kabi, M.: Automatic lexicon construction for Arabic sentiment analysis. In: 2014 International Conference on Future Internet of Things and Cloud (FiCloud), pp. 547–552 (2014)
17. Abdulla, N.A., Ahmed, N.A., Shehab, M.A., Al-Ayyoub, M., Al-Kabi, M.N., Al-rifai, S.: Towards improving the lexicon-based approach for Arabic sentiment analysis. Int. J. Inf. Technol. Web Eng. IJITWE **9**(3), 55–71 (2014)
18. ElSahar, H., El-Beltagy, S.R.: Building large Arabic multi-domain resources for sentiment analysis. In: Gelbukh, A. (ed.) Computational Linguistics and Intelligent Text Processing. LNCS, vol. 9042, pp. 23–34. Springer, Heidelberg (2015)
19. Ibrahim, H.S., Abdou, S.M., Gheith, M.: Sentiment analysis for modern standard Arabic and colloquial. Int. J. Nat. Lang. Comput. **4**(2) (2015)
20. El-Makky, N., Nagi, K., El-Ebshihy, A., Apady, E., Hafez, O., Mostafa, S., Ibrahim, S.: Sentiment Analysis of Colloquial Arabic Tweets (2015)
21. ALTEC, Arabic MPQA Subjective Lexicon and Arabic Opinion Holder Corpus, Arabic Langauge Technology Center (2011). http://www.altec-center.org/Repository_61.html
22. Abdul-Mageed, M., Diab, M.T.: Subjectivity and sentiment annotation of modern standard Arabic newswire. In: Proceedings of the 5th Linguistic Annotation Workshop, pp. 110–118 (2011)
23. El-Beltagy, S.R., Ali, A.: Open issues in the sentiment analysis of Arabic social media: a case study. In: 2013 9th International Conference on Innovations in Information Technology (IIT), pp. 215–220 (2013)
24. Alhumoud, S., Albuhairi, T., Alohaideb, W.: Hybrid sentiment analyser for Arabic tweets using R. In: Proceedings of the 7th International Joint Conference on Knowledge Discovery, Knowledge Engineering and Knowledge Management (IC3 K 2015), vol. 1, Lisbon, Purtogal (2015)
25. Alhumoud, S., Albuhairi, T., Altuwaijri, M.: Arabic sentiment analysis using WEKA a hybrid learning approach. In: Proceedings of the 7th International Joint Conference on Knowledge Discovery, Knowledge Engineering and Knowledge Management (IC3K 2015), vol. 1, Lisbon, Purtogal (2015)
26. Aldayel, H.K., Azmi, A.M.: Arabic tweets sentiment analysis–a hybrid scheme. J. Inf. Sci. (2015)
27. Duwairi, R., Ahmed, N.A., Al-Rifai, S.Y.: Detecting sentiment embedded in Arabic social media–a lexicon-based approach. J. Intell. Fuzzy Syst. **29**(1), 107–117 (2015)
28. Obaidat, I., Mohawesh, R., Al-Ayyoub, M., AL-Smadi, M., Jararweh, Y.: Enhancing the determination of aspect categories and their polarities in Arabic reviews using lexicon-based approaches. In: 2015 IEEE Jordan Conference on Applied Electrical Engineering and Computing Technologies (AEECT), pp. 1–6 (2015)
29. Khasawneh, R.T., Wahsheh, H.A., Alsmadi, I.M., AI-Kabi, M.N.: Arabic sentiment polarity identification using a hybrid approach. In: 2015 6th International Conference on Information and Communication Systems (ICICS), pp. 148–153 (2015)
30. Al Sallab, A.A., Baly, R., Badaro, G., Hajj, H., El Hajj, W., Shaban, K.B.: Deep learning models for sentiment analysis in Arabic. In: ANLP Workshop 2015, p. 9 (2015)
31. Abdul-Mageed, M., Diab, M., Korayem, M.: Subjectivity and sentiment analysis of modern standard Arabic. In: 49th Annual Meeting of the Association for Computational Linguistics: Human Language Technologies: Short Papers, vol. 2 (2011)

32. Maamouri, M., Bies, A., Buckwalter, T., Mekki, W.: The Penn Arabic treebank: building a large-scale annotated Arabic corpus. In: NEMLAR Conference on Arabic Language Resources and Tools, vol. 27, pp. 466–467 (2004)

33. Rushdi-Saleh, M., Martín-Valdivia, M.T., Ureña-López, L.A., Perea-Ortega, J.M.: OCA: opinion corpus for Arabic. J. Am. Soc. Inf. Sci. Technol. **62**(10), 2045–2054 (2011)

34. Ahmed, W.A., El-Halees, A.: Arabic Opinion Mining Using Parallel Decision Trees

35. Al-Smadi, M., Qawasmeh, O., Talafha, B., Quwaider, M.: Human annotated Arabic dataset of book reviews for aspect based sentiment analysis. In: 2015 3rd International Conference on Future Internet of Things and Cloud (FiCloud), pp. 726–730 (2015)

36. Aly, M.A., Atiya, A.F.: LABR: A large scale Arabic book reviews dataset. In: ACL, vol. 2, pp. 494–498 (2013)

37. Khalil, T., Halaby, A., Hammad, M., El-Beltagy, S.R.: Which configuration works best? An experimental study on supervised Arabic twitter sentiment analysis (2015)

38. Refaee, E., Rieser, V.: Subjectivity and sentiment analysis of Arabic twitter feeds with limited resources. In: Workshop on Free/Open-Source Arabic Corpora and Corpora Processing Tools Workshop Programme, p. 16 (2014)

39. Badaro, G., Baly, R., Akel, R., Fayad, L., Khairallah, J., Hajj, H., El-Hajj, W., Shaban, K.B.: A light lexicon-based mobile application for sentiment mining of Arabic tweets. In: ANLP Workshop 2015, p. 18 (2015)

40. Mourad, A., Darwish, K.: Subjectivity and sentiment analysis of modern standard Arabic and Arabic microblogs. In: Proceedings of the 4th Workshop on Computational Approaches to Subjectivity, Sentiment and Social Media Analysis, pp. 55–64 (2013)

41. Nabil, M., Aly, M., Atiya, A.F.: ASTD: Arabic sentiment tweets dataset. In: Proceedings of the 2015 Conference on Empirical Methods in Natural Language Processing, pp. 2515–2519 (2015)

42. Ibrahim, H.S., Abdou, S.M., Gheith, M.: MIKA: a tagged corpus for modern standard Arabic and colloquial sentiment analysis. In: 2015 IEEE 2nd International Conference on Recent Trends in Information Systems (ReTIS), vol. 2, pp. 353–358 (2015)

Surfing the Social Networks

Cristóbal Fernández Robin[1]([⊠]), Scott McCoy[2], and Diego Yáñez[1]

[1] Universidad Técnica Federico Santa María, Valparaíso, Chile
{cristobal.fernandez,diego.yanez}@usm.cl
[2] Mason School of Business, Williamsburg, VA, USA
scott.mccoy@mason.wm.edu

Abstract. This research aims to determine why people use Social Networks using an adaptation of the UTAUT2 model. The proposed model considers Subjective Norm, Perceived Playfulness, Perceived Ease of Use, and Perceived Usefulness as predictors of the Intention to Use. Five social networks were chosen in order to carry out this research: Facebook, Twitter, Instagram, WhatsApp, and LinkedIn. Findings shows that social networks are more useful to serve his or her purposes when more people close to the individual are using them. Perceived Playfulness proves to be a strong predictor of Intention to Use Facebook, Instagram, and WhatsApp, all these social networks are used for leisure purposes. Perceived Usefulness proves to be the most powerful predictor for Intention to Use in LinkedIn, this social network is mainly used for work purposes. Finally, both Perceived Playfulness and Perceived Usefulness are good predictors of Intention to Use Twitter. Implications are discussed.

Keywords: Social Network · Internet · Intention to Use

1 Introduction

It is usual to find people walking the streets while they interact with their smartphones as there are millions of applications that can be used at all times. According to Smith (2015), 45 billion messages are sent daily on Facebook, more than 30 billion Whatsapp messages are sent daily, and more than 80 million photos per day are shared on Instagram. However, what determines why a user utilizes a social network? Is it simply an application design that capture a large number of people or is there something else? Does it only depend on the users to decide which social networks will be used and which will not? This article seeks to answer these questions using an adaptation of the UTAUT2 (Venkatesh et al. 2012) model.

2 Literature Review

Created as an extension to the technological world of Theories of Reasoned Action, the Technology Acceptance Model (Davis 1989) corresponds to one of the most renowned, analyzed and studied models in literature seeking to understand how and why users accept and use technology. This model is based on Perceived Ease of Use and Perceived Usefulness variables, which predict Intention of Use. TAM2 was created after TAM1

© Springer International Publishing Switzerland 2016
G. Meiselwitz (Ed.): SCSM 2016, LNCS 9742, pp. 279–286, 2016.
DOI: 10.1007/978-3-319-39910-2_26

and explains the intention to use certain technology in terms of social influence and cognitive processes (Venkatesh and Davis 2000). For this purpose, Subjective Norm, Image, Job Relevance, Quality Output, Result demonstrability, Experience and voluntariness constructs are applied. Three years the Unified Theory of Acceptance and Use of Technology was published (Venkatesh et al. 2003), which seek to predict the intended use through the Performance Expectancy, Effort Expectancy and Social Influence variables, which have a definition very similar to the Perceived Usefulness, Perceived Ease of Use and Subjective Norm variables respectively. Facilitating Conditions variables are added, which has a direct effect on the Use Behavior and is defined as the degree to which an individual believes that certain organizational infrastructures and techniques exist to support the use of a system (Venkatesh et al. 2003). The last two new variables correspond to Gender and Age, which, like Experience and Voluntariness, play a role of moderating variables. More recently, UTAUT2 emerges as an UTAUT extension, to study the acceptance and use of technologies in a consumption context (Venkatesh et al. 2012). This model incorporates three new variables, these being Hedonic Motivation, Price Value and Habit.

According to Schneider et al. (2009), in the social networking field, many authors seek to explain the use of Online Social Networks. Users commonly spend more than half an hour interacting with the OSNs while the byte contributions per OSN session are relatively small. Ellison et al. (2007) suggests that Facebook might provide greater benefits for users experiencing low self-esteem and low life satisfaction. As for Twitter, according to Java et al. (2007), people use microblogging to talk about their daily activities and to seek or share information. As for Instagram, motives were positively associated with both usage and self-presentation (Cheung 2014). People use social networks such as Facebook, Twitter and Instagram for the sole purpose of entertainment and maintaining contacts with their friends (Narula and Jindal 2015). As shown, there are various motives for using social networks. According to Brandtzæg and Heim (2009), people use social networks to contact new people, keep in touch with friends and general socialization, which are closely related to the subjective standard. Xu et al. (2012), suggest that user utilitarian gratifications of immediate access and coordination along with hedonic gratifications of affection and leisure could be related to Perceived Usefulness, Perceived Ease of Use and web-site social presence respectively and were positive predictors of Social Network site usage.

3   Methodology

The study considers an initial exploratory review phase of previous history regarding intention to use information and communication technologies, in addition to reviewing the use level and motives of some popular social networks. In a second, conclusive stage, 456 people answer an online questionnaire to learn what motivates them to use social networks. The questionnaire is based on the UTAUT2 model, as explained below, and a direct question is added to clarify the main use that people assign to social networks studied in this article.

The proposed model considers the following variables: Subjective Norm (SN), Perceived Playfulness (PP), Perceived Ease of Use (PEU) and Perceived Usefulness (PU) as predictors of the Intention to Use (IU).

Subjective Norm is defined as the degree in which people have the impression that other people who are important to them believe that they should use a new system (Venkatesh et al. 2003), therefore, the Subjective Norm is closely linked to the intention of using Social Networks (Chen 2014; Li 2011; Pelling and White 2009).

Perceived Playfulness is defined as the pleasure that the individual feels when he or she behaves in a certain way or carries out a particular activity (Moon and Kim 2001), then the Playfulness acts as a predictor of the intention to use Social Networks (Sledgianowski and Kulviwat 2009).

Perceived Ease of Use defined as the degree in which a user believes that using certain technology is free from effort (Davis 1989) and Perceived Usefulness defined as the degree in which a person believes that using certain technology will improve his or her job performance (Davis 1989). As stated, Perceived Ease of Use and Perceived Usefulness are predictors of the Intention to Use a Social Network (Sledgianowski and Kulviwat 2009).

Intention to Use (IU) defined as the set of motivational factors that indicate how much people are willing to try or how much effort they plan to exercise in order to develop a certain behavior (Ajzen 1991).

Figure 1 shows the Structural model with latent variables and proposed relationships.

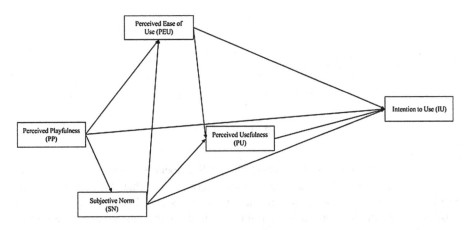

Fig. 1. Proposed model

To achieve the study's objective, the proposed model shown in Fig. 1 was used and five social networks were chosen: Facebook, Twitter, Instagram, WhatsApp, and LinkedIn.

4   Analysis and Results

The most widely used social network is WhatsApp, with 90 % of people who admit using it many times a day, which is closely linked to the characteristics of the application as it is primarily used to exchange instant messages. Facebook also has one of the highest frequencies of use.

Leisure is closely linked to the intention of use for each social network. In fact, Facebook is primarily used for leisure, followed by informative and academic purposes. Similarly, 61.4 % of WhatsApp users use it for leisure, also followed by informative and academic purposes. Instagram is used primarily for leisure unlike LinkedIn that is used primarily for work purposes. Moreover, Twitter is used for informational purposes in 61.6 % of cases and only 30.4 % for leisure as shown in Fig. 2.

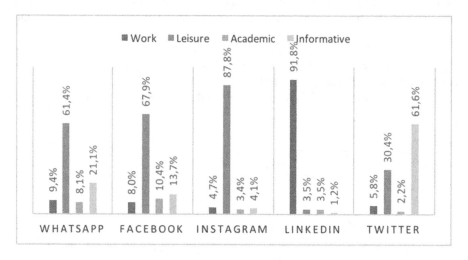

Fig. 2. Purpose of use

Then the intensity of use for each of the studied social networks is analyzed. As shown in Fig. 3, the most widely used social network is WhatsApp, with 98 % of people who admit using it many times a day, which is closely linked to the characteristics of the application as it is primarily used to exchange instant messages. Facebook also has one of the highest frequencies of use. The questionnaire shows that 73.7 % of participants declared using Facebook many times a day and 19.5 % about once a day. As for Instagram, 29.6 % reported not using it while 26 % said they use it many times a day. The least used social network is Linkedin, with 31 % of users who said they do not use it and 37 % who only revise it once a week. Twitter experienced a similar situation, with 29 % of non-users and 22 % who use it once a week.

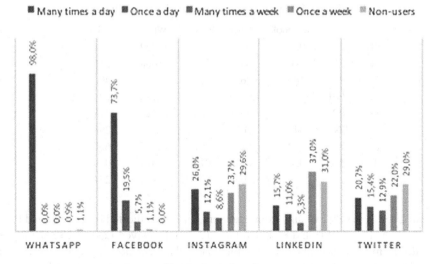

Fig. 3. Intensity of use

Thus taking into account Figs. 2 and 3, it can be assumed that people use more frecuently social networks when the purpose is leisure.

Table 1 shows a reliability analysis performed on the scales used, obtaining satisfactory results across five social networks.

Table 1. Cronbach Alpha for each social network

	Facebook	Twitter	Instagram	Whatsapp	Linkedin
PEU	.882	.919	.907	.891	.916
PP	.780	.854	.811	.770	.796
PU	.804	.840	.847	.765	.884
SN	.844	.874	.822	.864	.909
IU	.833	.899	.889	.832	.899

Subsequently, the structural model was analyzed, obtaining adequate absolute, incremental, and parsimony adjustment for each case. Table 2 shows the standarized estimates resulting from structural equation modeling.

Subjective Norm does not exert a significant influence on Perceived Ease of Use, but it does on Perceived Usefulness. This can be interpreted as individuals perceiving that social networks are more useful to serve his or her purposes when more people close to the individual are using them. Precisely, social networks possess the characteristic of being able to interact with many people. Additionally, Subjective Norm only significantly affects the Intention of use for LinkedIn, Twitter and Whatsapp. Perceived Ease of Use does not exert any significant influence on Intention to Use in any of the 5 social networks. That may be because people also relate the concept of ease-of-use with the Perceived Playfulness variable, and would absorb part of the variance that Perceived

Table 2. Standarized estimates for each social network

	Facebook	Twitter	Instagram	Whatsapp	Linkedin
PEU ← SN	−.028	.055	.033	−.022	.132
PEU ← PP	.620	.641	.665	.668	.616
PU ← SN	.400	.265	.367	.352	.490
PU ← PEU	.101	.032	−.110	.188	.026
PU ← PP	.247	.303	.323	.328	.278
IU ← SN	.042	.265	.013	.116	.298
IU ← PU	.223	.521	.457	.275	.654
IU ← PEU	−.054	−.017	−.014	.074	.029
	.806	.597	.836	.425	.274

Ease of Use effectively explains from intention to use, as indicated by Cheong and Park (2005), Shin et al. (2011) and Park and Ohm (2014). Perceived Ease of Use should be excluded from a user acceptance model for a particular technology or service because it often decreases the reliability and validity of a research model for mobile technologies. It could also be that ease is not important since users have certain experience and habits using these 5 social networks.

Perceived Playfulness proves to be a powerful predictor of Perceived Ease of Use. This corresponds to the issues raised previously about the close relationship that both variables possess, which can be interpreted as the more a person is trained in using a social network, the more willing he or she will be to interact with it, perceiving it to be easy to use. In addition, Perceived Playfulness is the best predictor of Intention to Use Facebook, Twitter, Instagram, and WhatsApp. This was to be expected since these social networks are used for leisure purposes. Considering that Facebook and Instagram had the highest intended use estimators and that the subjective norm is not significant, it can be assumed that these two social networks are mostly used for fun.

In regards to LinkedIn, Perceived Usefulness proves to be the most powerful predictor for Intention to Use, unlike what occurs in the other social networks, where Perceived Playfulness is more influential. In this regard, this social network is mainly used for work purposes, thus, people associate it with being more useful. It is necessary to highlight that people tend to associate the concept of utility with aspects relating to the workplace.

With respect to Twitter, both Perceived Playfulness and Perceived Usefulness are good predictors of Intention to Use. It is noteworthy that this social network is used for informational purposes and secondly for purposes of leisure, concepts related to Perceived Usefulness and Perceived Playfulness variables, respectively.

5 Discussion

Perceived Playfulness turned out to be one of the best determinants when predicting the intention to use Facebook, Instagram, Twitter and WhatsApp, while the best determinant for LinkedIn was Perceived Usefulness. This was also an important variable for Twitter. These results fit perfectly with what results given by the univariate analysis related to purpose of use, which indicate that the top four social networks are used mostly for leisure, looking very are linked to leisure purposes, an aspect linked to Perceived Playfulness, while LinkedIn is used mainly for work, a topic closely linked to Perceived Usefulness. This is also true in a second instance in regards to Twitter.

The study tested an adaptation of the UTAUT2 (Venkatesh et al. 2012) to predict the intended use of five social networks, achieving satisfactory results for all cases. The main contribution of this study is that one cannot make generalizations of social networks since the factors that motivate and influence the intention to use a particular social network depends largely on the use attributed to them. For this reason, Facebook, WhatsApp and Instagram, used primarily for leisure, take particular importance in Perceived Playfulness, unlike LinkedIn, used primarily for work, taking particular importance in Perceived Usefulness.

References

Ajzen, I.: The theory of planned behavior. Organ. Behav. Hum. Decis. Process. **50**(2), 179–211 (1991)

Brandtzæg, P.B., Heim, J.: Why people use social networking sites. In: Ozok, A.A., Panayiotis, Z. (eds.) Online Communities and Social Computing. LNCS, vol. 5621, pp. 143–152. Springer, Heidelberg (2009)

Chen, Y.F.: See you on Facebook: exploring influences on Facebook continuous usage. Behav. Inf. Technol. **33**(11), 1208–1218 (2014)

Cheong, J., Park, M.C.: Mobile internet acceptance in Korea. Internet Res. **15**(2), 125–140 (2005)

Cheung, T.T.: A study on motives, usage, self-presentation and number of followers on instagram (2014)

Davis, F.D.: Perceived usefulness, perceived ease of use, and user acceptance of information technology. MIS Q. **13**, 319–340 (1989)

Ellison, N.B., Steinfield, C., Lampe, C.: The benefits of Facebook "friends:" social capital and college students' use of online social network sites. J. Comput.-Mediated Commun. **12**(4), 1143–1168 (2007)

Java, A., Song, X., Finin, T., Tseng, B.: Why we Twitter: understanding microblogging usage and communities. In: Proceedings of the 9th WebKDD and 1st SNA-KDD 2007 workshop on Web Mining and Social Network Analysis, pp. 56–65. ACM, August 2007

Li, D.C.: Online social network acceptance: a social perspective. Internet Res. **21**(5), 562–580 (2011)

Moon, J.W., Kim, Y.G.: Extending the TAM for a world-wide-web context. Inf. Manag. **38**(4), 217–230 (2001)

Narula, S., Jindal, N.: Use of social network sites by AUMP students: a comparative study on Facebook, Twitter and Instagram usage. J. Adv. Res. Journalism Mass Commun. **2**(2), 20–24 (2015)

Park, E., Ohm, J.: Factors influencing users' employment of mobile map services. Telematics Inform. **31**(2), 253–265 (2014)

Pelling, E.L., White, K.M.: The theory of planned behavior applied to young people's use of social networking web sites. CyberPsychol. Behav. **12**(6), 755–759 (2009)

Schneider, F., Feldmann, A., Krishnamurthy, B., Willinger, W.: Understanding online social network usage from a network perspective. In: Proceedings of the 9th ACM SIGCOMM Conference on Internet Measurement Conference, pp. 35–48. ACM, November 2009

Sledgianowski, D., Kulviwat, S.: Using social network sites: the effects of playfulness, critical mass and trust in a hedonic context. J. Comput. Inf. Syst. **49**(4), 74 (2009)

Smith, C.: DMR (n.d.). http://expandedramblings.com. Accessed 15 Oct 2015

Shin, D.H., Shin, Y.J., Choo, H., Beom, K.: Smartphones as smart pedagogical tools: implications for smartphones as u-learning devices. Comput. Hum. Behav. **27**(6), 2207–2214 (2011)

Venkatesh, V., Davis, F.D.: A theoretical extension of the technology acceptance model: four longitudinal field studies. Manag. Sci. **46**(2), 186–204 (2000)

Venkatesh, V., Morris, M.G., Davis, G.B., Davis, F.D.: User acceptance of information technology: toward a unified view. MIS Q. **27**, 425–478 (2003)

Venkatesh, V., Thong, J.Y., Xu, X.: Consumer acceptance and use of information technology: extending the unified theory of acceptance and use of technology. MIS Q. **36**(1), 157–178 (2012)

Xu, C., Ryan, S., Prybutok, V., Wen, C.: It is not for fun: an examination of social network site usage. Inf. Manag. **49**(5), 210–217 (2012)

Detecting Personality Traces
in Users' Social Activity

Styliani Kleanthous[1(✉)], Constantinos Herodotou[1], George Samaras[1],
and Panayiotis Germanakos[1,2]

[1] Department of Computer Science, University of Cyprus,
CY-1678 Nicosia, Cyprus
{stellak, cherod02, cssamara, pgerman}@cs.ucy.ac.cy
[2] Suite Engineering UX, Products and Innovation,
SAP SE, 69190 Walldorf, Germany

Abstract. The effect that social media have in our lives nowadays is apparent. Many studies focused on how the differences we hold as people due to our personality, reflect our activities online. In this work we aim to exploit reports of previous work to implicitly build a personality model of Facebook users, based on their Facebook activity. An initial evaluation study shows that using Facebook activity data, we can extract information on user personality and at the same time points in further improvements necessary for more accurate personality prediction.

Keywords: Social networks · Big Five personality model · User modeling

1 Motivation

The behavior of users online has been the subject of many studies in social sciences and computing e.g. [1–4]. Results in cognitive psychology, show that the general personality factors predict very well aspects of internet use [4]. In this line, personality traits can be reflected in the activity and navigation of users online [1, 4].

"Big Five" personality domains are described, as five dimensions that define human personality and predict aspects of human behavior. These five dimensions as formulated by Goldberg [5] are: Openness, Conscientiousness, Extraversion, Agreeableness and Neuroticism. In order for a person to be categorized in one of the five dimensions he/she has to answer the "Big Five" personality questionnaire. Most of the studies performed by social scientists on correlating Facebook activity with personality use this questionnaire as a reference point for user personality prediction, and a second questionnaire for 'extracting' the behavior of a user on Facebook e.g. [4, 6].

Similarly, studies coming from the technology perspective consider the "Big Five" questionnaire for extracting the user's personality, but they automatically extract user activity from Facebook offline (e.g. [7–9]). This can be considered as a more unbiased method for Facebook activity extraction since the user is not directly involved in the process. Furthermore, to correlate Facebook activities to the personality of the user, they employ machine learning and data mining techniques e.g. [3, 7, 9]. However, what

© Springer International Publishing Switzerland 2016
G. Meiselwitz (Ed.): SCSM 2016, LNCS 9742, pp. 287–297, 2016.
DOI: 10.1007/978-3-319-39910-2_27

these studies are missing is to feedback the user with the results of his/her personality based on his/her Facebook activity.

Hence, the goal of this work is to take advantage of the results reported on previous theoretical and technical research, particularly in social sciences [1, 4, 6] and computing [2, 7, 8, 10], on which and how, Facebook user activities (e.g. share, like, checkin) relate to the personality of a user. A computational mechanism has been defined for implicitly extracting a user personality model in real time based on the user's activity on Face-book. Within this mechanism a Facebook application has been developed (PersonaWeb app) that allows us to access users' private data and develop a user personality model. The PersonaWeb app is then used to communicate (through visualizations) this information back to the users.

The contribution of this work lays primarily in exploring whether using the data reported on previous research we can: (i) define and implicitly develop a user model in real time, contained of user interaction data and (ii) develop a user personality model, by exploiting the data stored in the user model. Furthermore, through the PersonaWeb app, the user can instantly visually compare the results of his/her personality model extracted, with the results obtained from the "Big Five" personality questionnaire that he/she has answered.

2 Big Five Personality Traits

Before we discuss related technological approaches on extracting personality traits from Facebook it is important to understand how personality traits relate to user, activities and behaviour on Facebook based on the results reported by behavioural and psychology sciences.

Extraversion: People in this dimension have an inherent need to advertise their activities to others and their good mood depends on the feedback they receive from them. People in this category tend to spend more hours in social networking sites [11]. Particularly, in Facebook, they tend to belong to more groups and have more friends [4, 11]. Furthermore, they have the tendency to upload more personal photos than people belonging to other personality dimensions, share more statuses and post more check-ins [7].

Agreeableness: Individuals in this trait are perceived as kind, sympathetic, cooperative, warm and considerate. People who score high on this dimension tend to believe that most people are honest, decent, and trustworthy. The behavior in social networks for people who score high in this dimension, prefer to communicate more with personal messages on Facebook with their friends and be more involved with online games offered in Facebook's API [6]. Furthermore, individuals who fall into this category do not use social networks (i.e. Facebook) for a long time and refrain from making posts on their friends [7, 11].

Conscientiousness: Is a characteristic that defines a person who is being thorough, careful, or vigilant. It is recorded that because people with high conscientiousness are more committed to goals, their activity on Facebook will be decreased in relation with other users of the social network [6]. This implies that they will spend less time in Facebook; they will have fewer friends and they will publish fewer photographs and statuses [10]. In addition, people who fall into this category will rarely like any posts or belong to groups [3].

Neuroticism: This dimension describes people with the tendency to experience strongly negative emotions, such as anger, anxiety, or depression. People characterized by neuroticism, tend to be more frequent users of Facebook since they want to control the information about themselves and their environment [6]. Thus, the most frequent activity they practice is to disseminate information or statements that they approve. In contrast they avoid publishing photos of themselves [11]. Furthermore, neurotics tend to have fewer friends on Facebook, but at the same time, use often the like function in posts of these friends [3, 7].

Openness: Describes people with a general appreciation for art, emotion, adventure, unusual ideas, imagination, curiosity, and variety of experience. People who belong in this dimension are more likely to hold unconventional beliefs. People who are distinguished for their openness to experience, due to their receptivity available for new experiences, will tend to use the social network more to inquire new experiences [7]. They will publish frequently [12] their statuses and they tend to use Facebook's like function in anything that intrigues them [6].

3   Extracting Personality Traits from Facebook

Due to the rapid development of Facebook, compared to other social networks, and due to the enormous amount of information available for most users, many research groups have tried to acquire and exploit the log data in order to draw conclusions in relation to personality. Two main techniques are used and discussed below.

Semi-automated data mining approaches utilize algorithms to extract information from public profiles on Facebook [9, 13]. In any case, the users involved in the study have to complete a personality questionnaire in order for the researchers to get an indication on the users' personality. Data mining algorithms and machine learning [7] are followed in analysing and correlating the activity of users to personality traits. User's replies to the personality questionnaire are used for evaluating the models developed. These studies showed that textual elements [3] and demographic profile information of users can provide indication of user's personality and that indeed personality is closely related to social networks usage. Although data mining algorithms and machine learning approaches are un-obstructive methods for the user, and predict user personality with high accuracy, publicly available information are getting fewer [7] as time passes due to Facebook's new privacy policies and settings. Consequently, the information one can get using this method is not rich and similarly to the previous discussion the user is not directly getting anything back.

A different approach is followed in automated processes. A Facebook application is created that requests user approval to extract their personal activity data hence, richer data for research purposes. In this case, however, to encourage the user to provide access to his data, the application needs to provide some feedback to the user [8].

Although creating Facebook applications for research purposes is becoming a trend among the HCI community [8, 9, 14], here we will focus only on the most relevant approaches to ours. The pioneers of this methodology were the MyPersonality team [9]. The project runs since 2007 (latest reports refer to 7.5 million users to have accessed the MyPersonality Facebook application). The purpose was to extract several Facebook activity and demographic features and correlate patterns of behaviour to personality traits. What the user was getting back through the MyPersonality app was their scores on the psychometric tests they took and nothing related to his Facebook activity.

In [8], classification trees employed in predicting Alternative Five Model personality features. Users required to answer the ZKPQ-60-cc personality questionnaire and in return, the application presented the users with (i) the results of their personality test, (ii) information on similar users who have used the application, (iii) the choice to compare their results with the results of their friends (if they have completed the test) and (iv) the ability to invite their friends to use the application. Although the results show an accurate prediction of 70 % for all traits, the user data extracted were limited to the number of posts in a user's wall, the number of user's friends and the number of months the user used Facebook.

In contrast to previous work, in this paper we are exploring a different approach of exploiting user data extracted from Facebook. Our aim in this work is not primarily to explore the accuracy that can be achieved in predicting personality traits from Facebook activity data (these has been done already in previous work), but to introduce a different approach on how the collected data can be exploited and to also be presented as useful information to the user in real time - all of the approaches mentioned above analyzed the collected data off-line.

4 Computational Framework

A computational framework has been developed following the general framework of adaptive systems proposed by Jameson at [15] and consists of two phases: Data Extraction and Processing, for building the User Model; and User Model Application, for extracting the personality model.

4.1 Facebook Data Extraction for User Modeling

The extraction of Facebook activity data has been done using a Facebook application (PersonaWeb app), which allowed us to get users' permissions for accessing their personal data as input to the framework. The data extracted include publically available information about a user and also private activity data (e.g. friends of a user, posts liked, shares, types of posts liked, checkins, checkins that a user was tagged in, events attended and created etc.).

Additional features have been defined by the authors (e.g. active friends), that can be considered to be a list of friends of a user with whom the user 'regularly' interacts with. In order for a user to be considered as an active friend of a given user, he/she had to publish at least four posts directly on that user's wall, or appear in a Facebook activity together, during a period of a year. The reason for the four posts threshold is for excluding birthday and name-day wishes.

In every user model we keep a vector (nuv) that consists of arithmetic normalized values of the aggregated data collected based on thresholds defined. The thresholds' values defined based on a sample of Facebook users who participated in the study presented in a following section and thus excluded from the overall evaluation sample. After considering reports of Facebook user activity, we defined the activity of 'light' to 'heavy' Facebook usage for each element in Table 1. Elements in nuv can take values from 1 to 5, to simulate the scores of answers in a "Big Five" personality questionnaire. This is used in the extraction, of the user personality model, and the similarities between users in our system.

Table 1. Vector nuv consists of aggregated arithmetic values of user activity on Facebook

Values in nuv
# of likes
# of pages a user is following
# of friends
# of active friends
# of self tags created by a user
# of tags created by other users for a specific user
# of events attended
# of events created
# of checkins created by others and mention a user
# of checkins created by a user
# of status posts made
# of links posted by a user
percentage of user's profile photos with respect to all the photos uploaded
percentage of user's favourite page type with respect to all pages the user likes

4.2 Deriving the User Personality Model

The most important application of the user model in this work is the extraction of the personality of a user. Based on studies mentioned on previous work [1–3, 6–9], we identified Facebook activity that relates positively or negatively and with varied importance to each personality trait (Table 2). In addition, to the positive or negative relevance of an activity to a personality trait, we assigned weights of importance that an activity has, to a personality trait, and can take values from 0 to 1. The process of defining the weights is an initial attempt to experiment with this concept and thus, have been defined based on reports in related work on the importance of Facebook activities for a personality trait [1, 6, 7, 10].

The calculation of the value of each personality trait for a user a is done using Eq. 1 (if activity is positively related) and Eq. 2 (if activity is negatively related). In Eqs. 1 and 2, where ptv can be any of the five personality traits as defined in the "Big Five" model; act_weight is the weight value assigned to an activity (e.g. like, check-in, share); activity$_{ia}$ is the aggregated value of an activity in Table 2 as stored in nuv, for a user.

$$ptv_a = ptv_a + (act\_weight * activity_{ia}) \tag{1}$$

$$ptv_a = ptv_a + (act\_weight * (5 - activity_{ia} + 1)) \tag{2}$$

The extracted personality model for each user is presented to him/her through the PersonaWeb Facebook app, in a graphical way (Fig. 3) along with the results of the Big Five personality test they took.

Table 2. Facebook activity that relates positively or negatively to each personality trait

Personality trait	Positive relevance	Negative relevance
Extraversion	Likes, friends, status, user_checkins, user_events, self_tagprofile_pic	
Agreeableness	Tags, links	Likes, checkins, active_fr
Conscientiousness	page_type	active_fr, status, likes, events, tags, links, pages
Neuroticism	Likes, pages	Friends, profile_pic
Openness	Status, likes, events, pages	page_type

5   PersonaWeb Facebook Application

The purpose of developing the PersonaWeb Facebook App is twofold. Firstly, to be able to get user permission to extract his activity data; secondly, the application allowed us to visualize information kept in the user model and information regarding user results on the personality questionnaire. Initially the user is logging in to the application for the first time and a dialogue box is presented to him asking for his permission to release his data to the application.

If the user clicks accept then a pop-up window appears prompting the user to 'share' his derived personality model on Facebook. At the right-top corner the user can find a button that leads him to the PersonaWeb project web site, where he can find a "Big Five" personality questionnaire. A graphical representation of his Like activity on the social network (Fig. 2) follows. A second graph gives information on pages and their type that the user liked (Fig. 1). Furthermore, the user is becoming aware of (i) the person/page that the most posts he liked come from, (ii) his friend who tagged him most in posts and (iii) the four most recent events he attended.

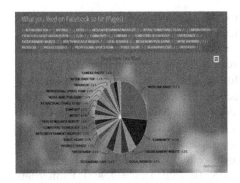

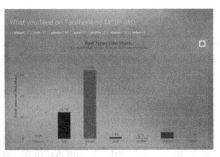

Fig. 1. Graphical statistical analysis of the types of pages a user likes

Fig. 2. Summary of user like activity on different Facebook categories

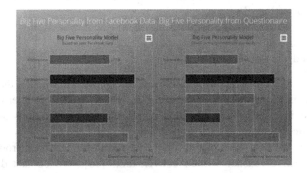

Fig. 3. Personality models of the user as derived from: the questionnaire (right); and Facebook based on activity data (Left)

The second part of the application provides a graphical representation of the user's personality model. It demonstrates the percentage scores of the user on each personality trait. These percentages reflect the user's personality based on his activity and interaction with other users in the social network as discussed above. If the user has completed the personality questionnaire, he can also see a second personality graph based on the results of the questionnaire; in that case he can visually compare the two graphs (see Fig. 3). In different case a message appears followed by a link prompting the user to complete the questionnaire. Below the two personality graphs the user can find an explanation of each Big Five personality trait.

6   Evaluation Study

6.1   Sampling and Procedure

The methodology followed was to perform an initial evaluation study using real Facebook users, who will be willing to fill in the Big Five personality test online and release their data for us to use. Thus, a call for participation was distributed on mailing lists for recruiting volunteers that have active Facebook accounts. This approach allowed us to pull Facebook users of different ages and demographic orientation. The message that was sent, was explaining the reason for the study and the steps that the users had to follow. An additional method for attracting participants was the friend-of -a-friend approach where users shared their personality model results on their Facebook wall through the PersonaWeb app and as a result their friends became aware of the app and joined the study. We allowed eight days for people to access the PersonaWeb app and to complete the "Big Five" personality questionnaire.

Our dataset consisted of 62 active users of Facebook, 38 men and 24 women, with ages between 17 and 59, and average age of 32.08 (Std. Dev = 9.903). Participants were asked to click on a link to the PersonaWeb app, and provide consent for us to extract their activity data. The users were explicitly asked to click on the link provided to complete the "Big Five" personality questionnaire. After the completion of the questionnaire the user was redirected back to the app where he/she could compare both personality models (Fig. 3).

6.2   Data Analysis and Results

The main purpose of this evaluation study was to examine (i) whether the information extracted in the user model reflected the users' activities; and (ii) whether we can utilize results reported in existing literature that correlated personality traits and Facebook activity to predict personality traits in real time.

To approach the first point of this study, we requested feedback from the participants in the form of casual written conversation [16]. We contacted participants through email requesting their comments on whether the information they received through the PersonaWeb Facebook app (e.g. likes, page types, most tagged from, most posts you like come from, events attended, recommendations) were representative of their actions in the social network and represented the current situation of their Facebook usage and their opinion on the recommendation they received. This technique of validating a user model is in line with methods followed in evaluating user modeling and adaptive systems.

25 out of 62 participants replied to our request. The general comments we had were mostly in favor of the information users received but we collected also some constructive criticism as well. Users thought that our system extracted very accurately the "image" of their 'like' activity and they thought that what was presented to them as a decomposition of the 'page types' they are following was indeed and exact useful. Some comments focused in the fact that there was also reflection of their past activity in the extracted information and that this may interfere with inferences done based on the user model. Furthermore, with respect to the last three events attended, the users thought that this was just a reminder of events they attended long time ago and not a feature that added to their experience using this application. On the other hand 5 users reported that this was not a useful feature to have and it should be eliminated. The users appreciated the 'similar users' information communicated to them and mentioned that

they were curious to further explore their similarities to these people, especially since the profile pictures and user names provided were clickable links to that user's profile.

With respect to the second goal of this evaluation, similarly to previous studies mentioned, the results of the "Big Five" personality questionnaire that each user completed were used to compare the two personality models obtained for each user. A Pearson's product-moment correlation employed.

According to the results of the correlation analysis (Table 3), it appears to be a weak positive correlation for the *Extraversion* trait between the two personality models with r = 0.259 at 0.05 significance level. The results in *Agreeableness* trait show a positive but not significant correlation between the two models r = 0.032. Similar to extraversion, *Conscientiousness* trait appears to give a weak positive correlation between the two models with r = 0.281 at the 0.05 significance level. In contrast *Neuroticism* and *Openness* appear to negatively correlate between the two models with r = −0.010 and r = −0.161 respectively.

Table 3. Pearson correlation results between the Big Five personality models extracted based on the questionnaire and the computational model introduced.

Big Five personality trait	Pearson correlation results
Extraversion	0.259
Agreeableness	0.032
Conscientiousness	0.281
Openness	−0.161
Neuroticism	−0.010

The initial results show that the activities considered in our work as important for modeling the personality of the users for the traits of Extraversion, Agreeableness and Conscientiousness reflect in a minimal extend the personality of a Facebook user in our sample. In the case of Openness and Neuroticism the results show that the activities employed are not sufficient and further refinement of the model is needed. These results are not surprising to us since research particularly on social sciences and psychology still report contradictory results on how and which Facebook activities are important for each personality trait in the Big Five model e.g. [1, 10, 14]. Our model is strongly depended on reports of previous research; consequently, our results reflect this contradiction and call for a more refined model definition.

Given the above results we further explored the correlation of activity features we extracted to the personality traits of *Neuroticism* and *Openness*, in an attempt to explain the negative correlations. Initial results show strong positive correlation of Neuroticism with the number of *active friends* a user has and also with the number of *checkins a user is tagged in*. Additionally, consistent with [14] and inconsistent with [10] Neuroticism appears to correlate positively with *like and share* activity on Facebook. A negative relation appears with the number of *events* the user attended. For openness the number of *links* a user shared on Facebook appears negatively related with this trait. This information had not reported on existing literature and hence was not included in our initial personality model. We are currently working on this study to correlate Facebook activity features to other personality traits for improving our models.

7 Conclusion

The motivation behind this work was to implicitly extract a user personality model based on information reported on previous work on activity correlation to personality traits. Compared to previous work, we have used much richer private user data to build a user's personality model and we exploited previous and existing literature from psychology and computing in an innovative way (e.g. real-time computation of the user personality model and instant visualization of the personality prediction results to the user through the Facebook app). However, at this stage we cannot claim statistical comparison of our results with studies in the area of machine learning e.g. [3, 7, 8] primarily due to the limited size of users participated in our evaluation study and due to the work-in-progress state of our work.

In addition to correlating Facebook activities to personality traits we are looking into exploring further the potentials of our approach. For example the assignment of weights of importance to Facebook activities needs to be explored further through several studies in order to see how this can affect the accuracy of predicting the personality model of a user. Although the idea of defining active friends in the user model is in-line with theory and was similar to previous work [8], we believe there is more to 'who can be considered as an active friend' e.g. (textual analysis). Finally, a larger study with more users will provide more accurate results and outlook on the benefits of this approach.

References

1. Amichai-Hamburger, Y., Vinitzky, G.: Social network use and personality. Comp. Hum. Behav. **26**(6), 1289–1295 (2010)
2. Caci, B., Cardaci, M., Tabacchi, M.E., Scrima, F.: Personality variables as predictors of Facebook usage. Psychol. Rep. **114**(2), 528–539 (2014)
3. Golbeck, J., Robles, C., Turner, K.: Predicting personality with social media. In: Proceedings of CHI 2011 Extended Abstracts on Human Factors in Computing Systems (CHI EA 2011), pp. 253–262 (2011). http://dx.doi.org/10.1145/1979742.1979614
4. McElroy, J.C., Hendrickson, A.R., Townsend, A.M., DeMarie, S.M.: Dispositional factors in internet use: personality versus cognitive style. MIS Q. **31**(4), 809–820 (2007)
5. Goldberg, L.R.: An alternative description of personality: the Big-Five factor structure. J. Pers. Soc. Psychol. **59**(6), 1216–1229 (1990)
6. Moore, K., McElroy, J.C.: The influence of personality on Facebook usage, wall postings, and regret. Comput. Hum. Behav. **28**(1), 267–274 (2012)
7. Bachrach, Y., Kosinski, M., Graepel, T., Kohli, P., Stillwell, D.: Personality and patterns of Facebook usage. In: Proceedings of the 4th Annual ACM Web Science Conference (WebSci 2012), pp. 24–32 (2012). http://dx.doi.org/10.1145/2380718.2380722
8. Ortigosa, A., Carro, R.M., Quiroga, J.I.: Predicting user personality by mining social interactions in Facebook. J. Comput. Syst. Sci. **80**(1), 57–71 (2014)

9. Kosinski, M., Stillwell, D., Graepel, T.: Private traits and attributes are predictable from digital records of human behavior. Proc. Natl. Acad. Sci. (PNAS) **110**(15), 5802–5805 (2013)
10. Ross, C., Orr, E.S., Sisic, M., Arseneault, J.M., Simmering, M.G., Robert Orr, R.: Personality and motivations associated with Facebook use. Comput. Hum. Behav. **25**(2), 578–586 (2009)
11. Seidman, G.: Self-presentation and belonging on Facebook: how personality influences social media use and motivations. Pers. Individ. Differ. **54**(3), 402–407 (2013)
12. Markovikj, D., Gievska, S., Kosinski, M., Stillwell, D.: Mining Facebook data for predictive personality modeling. In: Proceedings of the 7th International AAAI Conference on Weblogs and Social Media (ICWSM 2013), Boston, MA, USA (2013)
13. Wald, R., Khoshgoftaar, T., Sumner, C.: Machine prediction of personality from facebook profiles. In: 2012 IEEE 13th International Conference on Information Reuse & Integration (Iri) (2012)
14. Shen, J., Brdiczka, O., Liu, J.: A study of Facebook behavior: what does it tell about your neuroticism and extraversion? Comput. Hum. Behav. **45**, 32–38 (2015)
15. Jameson, A.: Adaptive interfaces and agents. In: Jacko, J.A., Sears, A. (eds.) Human Computer Interaction Handbook, pp. 105–127. CRC Press, Taylor & Francis Group, Boca Raton, NY (2003)
16. Heritage, J., Atkinson, J.M.: Structures of Social Action: Studies in Conversation Analysis. Cambridge University Press, Cambridge (1984)

Domain-Tailored Multiclass Classification of User Reviews Based on Binary Splits

Alexandre Lunardi[1], José Viterbo[1(✉)], Clodis Boscarioli[2], Flavia Bernardini[1], and Cristiano Maciel[3]

[1] Fluminense Federal University (UFF), Niterói, Rio de Janeiro, Brazil
{lunardi,viterbo}@ic.uff.br, fcbernardini@id.uff.br
[2] Western Paraná State University (UNIOESTE), Cascavel, Paraná, Brazil
clodis.boscarioli@unioeste.br
[3] Federal University of Mato Grosso (UFMT), Cuiabá, Mato Grosso, Brazil
cmaciel@ufmt.br

Abstract. Sentiment analysis can be performed using machine learning algorithms to automatically identify the sentiment associated with reviews about products or services available online. In many sentiment analysis practical scenarios, it is necessary to classify reviews in rates between 1 to 5 stars – a multiclass problem. In literature, we found that the best results for reviews classification are those who propose solutions based on binary splits, achieving accuracies above 90 %. As such, we propose a model, based on the Nested Dichotomies algorithm, that performs multiclass classification in successive steps of binary classification operations. For this classifier to be more effective, we propose that the first split should be defined by identifying users' recommendation threshold. We present a case study in which this classification model is applied to a set of subjective data extracted from TripAdvisor, discuss the process of determining the first split and evaluate the accuracy of the proposed model.

Keywords: Sentiment analysis · Recommender systems · Human centered design

1 Introduction

Since the Web 2.0 advent, it is increasingly common to find online valuable opinions or reviews related to products, services, organizations, events and various other items. This is due to the increasing use of social networks, blogs and especially tools that allow users to register their opinions on products or services in e-commerce websites [1]. Capturing and processing such information properly, and discovering the interest of the general public on any item, is of great interest to the business world or to the well-being of a community. The sentiment analysis community is thus developing tools that aim to assist in the recovery and mining of such data [2]. To assist users and online companies, sentiment analysis can be useful in recommender systems to identify if a user's review on a product or service is positive (thumbs up) or negative (thumbs down) [3]. Web users share opinions about the products or services they consume. Therefore, aggregated

G. Meiselwitz (Ed.): SCSM 2016, LNCS 9742, pp. 298–309, 2016.
DOI: 10.1007/978-3-319-39910-2_28

information, such as opinions of web users, can be used in the decision-making process of those that prospect such items. Thus, sentiment analysis can be performed using machine learning algorithms, lexical analysis, keywords or ontologies. While many works propose the classification of the polarity of a review, *i.e.*, positive or negative (binary classification), some researches focus on the inference of ratings (multiclass classification) for the opinions [4]. In this case, the main goal is to classify each opinion in respect to a grade range – typically 1 to 5 stars – and not just as positive or negative.

There are two approaches for multiclass classifier construction. The first one is using learning algorithms constructed for multiclass problems, such as Naïve Bayes, induction of Decision Trees, generalization of Neural Networks, and so on. The second one is based on decomposing the initial multiclass problem into a combination of binary problems. There are two classical techniques for transforming the problem: (i) one-versus-one, where a binary classifier is constructed to distinguish between a pair of classes, and so the number of binary classifiers that compose the multiclass classifier is given by the combination of all classes; and (ii) one-vs-all, where a binary classifier is constructed to distinguish a class against all the other ones. These approaches are commonly used when SVM algorithms are indicated to the problem. A newer approach for decomposing the problem is the one implemented by the Nested Dichotomies algorithms [7], which constructs trees of (all the) possible combinations of class binary splits. This algorithm was not used before in sentiment analysis domain.

In this work, we propose a model based on an adaptation of the Nested Dichotomies algorithm, aiming at reducing the number of trees constructed by the algorithm using domain characteristics, i.e., the first tree division is determined by applying and analyzing questionnaires answered by users of the target domain, in order to identify the users' preference. This paper discusses a methodology to create a model for the classification of user reviews in 5 classes based on binary splits tailored for a specific domain. We present a case study in which the classification model is applied to a set of subjective data extracted from TripAdvisor website (http://www.tripadvisor.com), containing revisions labeled with ratings from 1 to 5. We eventually discuss the process of determining the first division and evaluate the accuracy of the obtained model.

In the next section, we describe other works that focus on sentiment analysis using binary or multiclass classification. In Sect. 3, we discuss the Nested Dichotomies algorithm, in which base our proposal. In Sect. 4, we present our proposal for a domain-tailored multiclass classifier. Finally, in Sect. 5, we draw our conclusions.

2   Related Work

The main research in sentiment analysis aims to measure the positivity of an opinion or review, *i.e.*, to classify it as recommended or not recommended (binary classification). Other works focus on summarization, classification of opinions as either objective or subjective, and inference rating (multiclass classification). Our focus in this work is on ratings classification based on user's opinion. So, this section presents relevant related work on opinion mining using learning algorithm for (i) classifying opinions on positive or negative, *i.e.*, binary classification; or (ii) classifying opinions on three or more classes, *i.e.*, multiclass classification. In some studies, the authors create a scale that varies with the sentiment intensity, for example, five classes: excellent, good, fair, poor and very poor. In other studies, researchers classify opinions based on ratings, where each rate is represented by a number of stars and each star represents a class. This problem is known as inference rating, which is the focus of this work. Further, some works use lexicon models to classify an opinion, or to enrich the (machine) learning process of a classifier. A lexicon model presents norms and conventions of a language, where each word or expression is associated with a probable sentiment.

2.1 Basic Concepts

According to [8], the sentiment analysis or opinions mining is the field of study that examines the attitudes, emotions, feelings and opinions of people related to entities such as products, services, organizations, events, topics and attributes of these entities. Sentiment analysis is a challenging subarea of Natural Language Processing and can approach many problems, from classification in opinion polarity to the summarization process of general feelings about something.

Considering a text t, the initial task in opinions mining consists in deciding whether t is objective or expresses a feeling. In the latter case, t is subjective and express an opinion O, formally represented as a 5-tuple $O = (e, a, s, h, t)$. Where e is the name of the entity or object to which an opinion relates; a is the specific attribute of that entity; s is sentiment of the author in relation to an attribute or entity; u is the author (user) of the opinion; and t is the date (and time, if available) on which the opinion was created. Table 1 shows an opinion O about a hotel e available at the TripAdvisor website. In this example, one can note that the hotel is the entity e, and one of the attributes are the rooms, indicated by a in Table 1. They are classified by the author as "impressive" and "spacious", which denote sentiments (subjective evaluations) of the author about the attribute a (the rooms), indicated by s in Table 1.

Table 1. Example of a user comment about a hotel e

User: UserX (h)
Title: A magnicent building of fading grandeur, redolent of earlier times
Rating: 4
Date: April 28, 2015 (t)
Review: "Ground floor lobbies and suites with art deco design are impressive (s). **Rooms** (a) **are spacious** (s) **with high ceilings and plenty of room in the en suite shower. Yes, lifts are a little slow, the paint is peeling, the plaster cracking, there are stains on the carpet - but hey, everything works, the sheets are well laundered and beds are comfortable".**

The main goal in sentiment analysis is to capture and process opinions generating a list of entities and their ratings, in order to assist a community or a company in better understanding their customer's needs [9]. To [10], the ideal task in sentiment analysis should be processing a set of opinions about a certain entity, generating a list of attributes and aggregating the sentiments related to the attributes.

2.2 Binary Classification

Many of the work on sentiment analysis has focused on binary classification. A summary of the main works in binary classification can be found in [11], where the main features extraction techniques and learning algorithms used in sentiment analysis are highlighted. Among the major works, we can highlight [12], where the authors evaluate the performance of learning algorithms to determine if the sentiment of an opinion is either positive or negative. Using the comments of a movies database, they show that the algorithms are better than humans classification. Even exploring different pre-processing techniques, the assessed learning algorithms did not reach 90 % accuracy.

In [10], the authors created a method for distinguishing positive and negative reviews on two sites: Amazon.com and Clnet. They use different feature selection techniques and evaluate each one, and also test various ways to improve the performance of the lexical analysis method developed by them. By the end, they produced a list for each product, considering the main features extracted from revisions and major revisions for each attribute. Among the challenges they found, they cite inconsistent rating, ambivalence and comparison and small reviews.

Analyzing data from Twitter, in [13] the authors created three databases based on the microblogging messages: positive sentiment, negative sentiment or objective text. These tweets were searched and selected based on emoticons defined as "happy" or "sad". They compared different pre-processing techniques and used Naive Bayes algorithm. As final result, they obtained 60 to 80 % accuracy.

In [14], the authors proposed a new lexicon model for sentiment analysis of restaurants' reviews and showed an improvement on Naive Bayes algorithm. They considered negative words and intensity adverbs in the pre-processing phase. They used SVM algorithm, Naive Bayes and an improved Naive Bayes version, proposed by them. They demonstrate that the proposed Naive Bayes technique, when configured with bigrams + unigrams, shows the best result, reaching an 81.2 % accuracy.

2.3 Rating-Inference Problem or Multiclass Classification

In [15], the authors evaluate the accuracy of humans over the task of determining the rating of a comment. They applied an algorithm based on metric labeling that, in some cases, can outperform some versions of SVM and the human baseline in sentiment classification of data, with three or four classes. As a final result, they obtained a 54.6 % accuracy.

In [16], the authors introduce a new type of data pre-processing, where each review is marked with a score, and the rating is inferred based on the set of scores. The authors claim that the model proposed by them exceeds other works in literature by a significant margin.

In [17], the authors proposed a new search in selection of opinions, in order to estimate the ratings for hotels on sites, where users write comments for a particular service. The rating inference was made based on one or more attributes of the hotel. They used Bayesian Networks, where the calculated rating is estimated for each attribute. Finally, the various attributes form the final rating of a hotel. This method produces the best results for the multiclass classification, with a 73.1 % accuracy.

In [18], the authors built a vector with the intensity of features to represent an opinion, and use this vector as input to the learning algorithms. To create this vector, the proposed system identifies the main characteristics that are relevant to a consumer in the product. From these characteristics, the system quantifies each opinion on hotels, creating an array of opinions. They demonstrate that different characteristics of the product have a different impact on the user's opinion about a hotel. Finally, the system estimates the weight of each product from the intensity vector and estimates the final rating, with a 46.9 % accuracy.

Although focusing on multiclass classification as well, in [6] the authors explored other two types of affective dimensions to classify opinions: the valence and the arousal. They build the feature vectors through tokens extracted considering these two affective dimensions and used a regression model and a SVM algorithm variation to classify a belief in a sense of scale (1–5 scale), obtaining 51.8 % accuracy.

2.4   Sentiment Analysis Applications

In examples ahead, we highlight works focused on different areas ranging from education to social network services. In [19], the authors created a visual analysis of positive and negative reviews of "The Da Vinci Code". They used a visual tool, TermWatch, to construct a multilayer network of terms based on syntactic, semantic and statistical associations. In order to evaluate the terms that have been previously selected, they use a predictive model based on SVM. They used a set of positive and negative reviews as training features. In this case, a review is decomposed into three components which reflect the presence of positive terms, negative and common in both categories.

In [20], the authors created a web recommendation system using text categorization synopsis of movies stored on IMDB, selected from *EachMovie* database. They used three algorithms to build a classifier: kNN, Decisions Trees and Naive Bayes. The final performance of the algorithms is around 60–65 % accuracy, with the decision trees showing best results. However, the difference between the three is negligible.

In [21], the authors used emoticons in order to train learning algorithms with opinions taken from Twitter. In addition to emoticons, keywords from Twittratr site that have positive or negative sentiments were used in training. After testing, they reach about 83 % accuracy with Naive Bayes algorithm. Finally, the authors also provide a website, where the users can know the sentiments about something over existing tweets. The site creates a list of positive, negative and neutral tweets, as well as graphics that show which sentiment is prevalent.

In a work in the education area [22], the authors built a model to evaluate Facebook posts and, by detecting the usual user's humor, check his emotional changes. The application is called *SentBuk*. This information is used in e-learning systems in order to recommend the most appropriate activities in relation to the student's humor in a given period. They built a lexicon classifier and when a large number of sentences is classified, they use these messages as training input to the machine learning algorithm. The best result was obtained using the SVM algorithm with 83 % accuracy.

3 Nested Dichotomies Algorithms

The analysis of related work led us to conclude that the best results are obtained when considering the binary opinion classification, and rating classifiers are more difficult to learn. When rating a product or a service with one to five stars, for instance, sometimes it is difficult to the user to decide between the neighbor numbers. Considering the training instances are in $\mathbb{R}_M$, i.e., there are M features describing the data, the difficult to label the training instances (reviews) into classes (ratings) may lead to diffuse margins between the areas of each pair of classes (ratings) in $\mathbb{R}_M$, which explains the difficulty to learn the classifiers. Thus, exploring techniques to divide the multiclass problem into binary sub-problems may lead to better results.

In [7], the authors proposed dividing a multiclass classification problem into several binary divisions. This method, called Nested Dichotomies (ND), proposes an alternative based on binary classifiers to the One-vs-All (OxA) and the One-vs-One (OxO) traditional approaches. This model consists in constructing trees recursively, where the root node represents a set of classes A, which is divided into two nodes with new mutually exclusive groups of classes B and C. Considering that the multiclass problem has n classes, in the first iteration, the root contains all the n classes, and the two leaves correspond to two disjoint sets of classes, generated by a random division of A. Thus, n-1 divisions are necessary, creating a binary tree with n leaves. A classifier is constructed for each node of the tree that is not a leaf.

For example, a set of five classes needs four divisions and, therefore, four classifiers. This number is smaller than the number of classifiers used by the other two traditional approaches – OxA and OxO. Moreover, the accuracy of ND algorithm, in most cases, exceeds OxA and OxO.

Given a set of classes, it is possible to construct many different trees [23]. So, the original ND algorithm creates a list of k random trees to find an optimal tree model. This number can be informed before the execution ND, and the default is 20 trees in order to find a best result [7].

The final accuracy of the ND classifier is given by the product operator in Eq. 1 [7], where C_{i1} and C_{i2} are two subsets of a division of a set of classes Ci in an internal node i, and $p(c \in C_{i1} \,|\, x, c \in C_i)$ and $p(c \in C_{i2} \,|\, x, c \in C_i)$ are the conditional probability estimated distributions by the two-class model at node i for an instance x.

$$p(c = C|x) \prod_{i=1}^{n-1} \left(I\!\left(c \in C_{i1}\right) p\!\left(c \in C_{i1}|x, c \in C_i\right) + I\!\left(c \in C_{i2}\right) p\!\left(c \in C_{i2}|x, c \in C_i\right) \right) \tag{1}$$

4 Domain-Tailored Multiclass Classification Model

Considering that (i) the results obtained by the binary classification techniques are naturally better than any multiclass classification in sentiment analysis; (ii) to the extent of our knowledge, ND algorithm has not been used for sentiment analysis, specially ratings classification, and (iii) the domain characteristics should be used in the first division, we propose an adaptation of the ND algorithm for rating classification in sentiment analysis to use binary algorithms in sequence to obtain the multiclass classification model.

In this model, the identification of the first two subsets of classes should be determined so that it is more meaningful for the set of users to whom the classifier applies. As such, it is necessary to understand the domain and how the rates will be useful for the users. In the next subsections, we explain our approach to understand a specific sentiment analysis domain and define the classification model by describing our case study on rating hotel reviews.

4.1 Hotel Domain

The hotel domain is frequently used in works that study the rating-inference problem. In this work, we selected a well-known dataset to analyze diverse reviews associated with a rating scale, ranging from 1 to 5. Part of the TripAdvisor reviews reference dataset was used, containing reviews in English. This dataset was used in [24] to find out the latency of the opinion of each individual, and the importance of each aspect in the final rating.

Other works, such as [18], used *Booking.com* reviews to propose a method to infer ratings. As stated before, in this work the ND algorithm was adapted to be applied by the first time on sentiment analysis problem. This will allow to evaluate the performance of this algorithm, which, as shown by [7], outperformed other methods for multiclass domains in other domains.

4.2 Assessing the Influence of Ratings in Hotel Booking

In order to study the domain and assess how the ratings influence the user when he is selecting a hotel, we conducted a survey to verify the user preferences. In all, 131 users answered the survey, and the final result was in line with research found in the *PracticalECommerce* website [25].

First of all, we draw the users general profile. Most of the users who responded to the survey were very young, as 52.3 % of them were between 20 and 29 years old, 31.8 % between 30 and 39 years old and 11.2 % between 40 and 49 years old. Only 2.8 % of the respondents were over 50 years old. and 1.9 % were below 19 years old. In addition, they had high education levels, as 42.0 % of the respondents are graduate, 23.4 % had completed a M.Sc. course and 23.4 % had completed a PhD course. Only 12.1 % had completed only high school. Figure 1 shows two graphs the summarize the profile of the respondents.

To understand the relation of the users with online hotel booking services, we first asked in how many sites on average they search a hotel before making a reservation. All the respondents are regular users of hotels booking online services. Before booking a hotel room, 38.3 % of them search options in one or two different sites, 45.9 % search options in three or four different sites and 15.8 % search in five or more than sites. We then asked them how often they check the ratings of the hotels they might want to book when they are selecting a hotel on an online booking service. While 68.4 % users

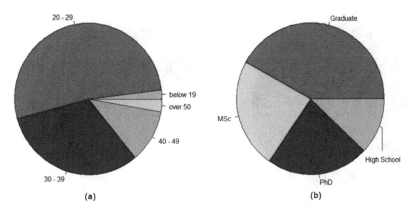

Fig. 1. The profile of the respondents. In (a) we see the age categorization and in (b) we see the education level categorization.

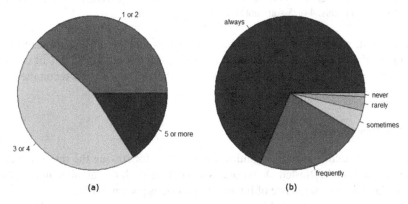

Fig. 2. In (a) we see in how many sites on average the users search a hotel before making a reservation. In (b), we see how often the users check the ratings of the hotels they want to book.

answered they always check, 23.3 % said they check frequently, 4.5 % said they sometimes, 3 % said they check rarely and only 0.8 % said they never check. Figure 2 shows two graphs the summarize these aspects.

To assess how important ratings are for the users in the booking process, initially we asked them if they choose a hotel primarily based on its rating or if they consider other aspects in the first place. We found out that 65.4 % of the users base their decision primarily on the ratings, while only 34.6 % of them would firstly take other aspects in consideration. For those users that base their decision on the ratings, we asked if they would rather select only 5-stars hotels, 4 or 5-stars hotels or 3 to 5-stars hotels (we despised other possibilities in order to make the survey simpler and target our goal). We found out that only 14.9 % of the users would prefer 5-stars hotels, while 46.0 % would prefer a 4 or 5-stars hotels and 39.1 % would choose hotels that are 3-stars or more. Figure 3 shows two graphs the summarize this data.

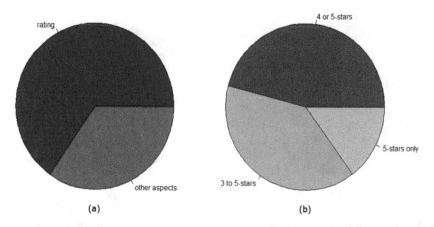

Fig. 3. In (a), we see the percentage of users that choose a hotel primarily based on its rating and those that consider other aspects in the first place. In (b), we the percentage of users that book preferably 5-stars hotels, 4 or 5-stars hotels or 3 to 5-stars hotels.

As a result, we conclude that the two class groups that are most significant for the users in this domain are 1 to 3-stars hotel and 4 or 5-stars hotels, as 46.0 % of the users that base their booking decisions on ratings regard these groups as non-recommendable and recommendable, respectively.

4.3   The Proposed Model

We propose an architecture for a multiclass classifier for solving the rating-inference problem, based on the Nested Dichotomies algorithm. With this architecture we build a single classifier as a sequence of binary classifiers, as shown in Fig. 4.

At first, reviews are divided into two main class groups: "recommended" and "not recommended". From this classification, the class group labeled as "not recommended" is split into two categories: "very bad" and "not so bad". "Not so bad" class group goes through a new process of binary split generating "bad" and "regular" rating groups. Regarding the class group classified as "recommended", this will be split in "good" and "very good". Thus, the final five classes for the views are identified, "very bad", "bad", "regular", "good", "very good", each of which corresponds to star rating on the Likert scale (1–5).

This architecture has been tested with several different base-classifiers, and the best results were obtained with the Naive Bayes algorithm, with a 56.6 % accuracy. Although the final accuracy is less than 60 %, the close accuracy, which is calculated considering correct when an instance is classified as a class neighbor to the correct one [26], exceeds 90 %, as in the use of individual algorithms. Besides, the accuracy of the first classification, which divides the instances in the two groups that are represent the users' preference – not recommended (1, 2 and 3-stars) and recommended (4 and 5-stars) – is 88.9 %. These results overcome many of the earlier works in sentiment analysis, considering the accuracy of the models to binary and multiclass classification. It is worth

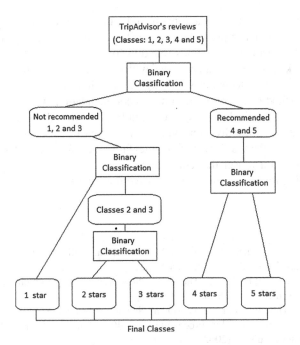

Fig. 4. Binary split model for the inference problem ratings in the hotel booking domain

mentioning also the high accuracy obtained in the classification of the "extreme classes", *i.e.* 1 and 5-stars, which exceeds 75 %. This can be explained by the difficulty in analyzing intermediate classes, due to the similarity between them, while the extreme classes can be more easily discriminated.

5 Conclusion

In this article, we propose a new method for rating-inference problem based on an adaptation of the Nested Dichotomies algorithm for dividing the multiclass rating problem into binary divisions. According to previous researches, this solution may be more appropriate than the typical multiclass to binary divisions approaches One-vs-All and One-vs-One, since Nested Dichotomies algorithm exceeds some multiclass classification models for some datasets [7].

The proposed algorithm is able to divide the classification process so that, in the first split, reviews are already separated as good or bad, tailored to a specific domain. The binary division is more thoroughly analyzed in sentiment analysis works, where opinions are usually grouped in three classes as not recommended and two as recommended. As such, well-known binary division algorithms evaluated in previous studies may be used to build the final classification model without need of adaption to the multiclass problem.

Furthermore, we propose a new stage in the process of defining a final model based on supervised machine learning algorithms that can be used in any multiclass classification domain. In addition to all the common steps in the solution of rating-inference problem, we propose to carry out a domain study, in the form of user's questionnaires or surveys, in order to understand what are the class groups more adequate to the users' preferences and determine the best possible divisions.

In future work, this method can be tested with different datasets to measure performance in relation to other techniques and algorithms already used in the literature. In addition, this method can be used in ratings recommendation system. In this case, an online system could use the knowledge acquired from the overall users' reviews and, at each stage, suggest the best division and indicate the reason for the choice of this division, pointing out which words were fundamental to the suggestion of such a division. This can be useful for a user that could know which words were more important in defining the rating for his review, helping to avoid misclassification.

References

1. Constantinides, E., Romero, C.L., Boria, M.A.G.: Social media: a new frontier for retailers? Eur. Retail Res. **22**, 1–28 (2008). Gabler Verlag
2. Cambria, E., Schuller, B., Xia, Y., Havasi, C.: New avenues in opinion mining and sentiment analysis. IEEE Intell. Syst. **28**(2), 15–21 (2013)
3. Turney, P.D.: Thumbs up or thumbs down? Semantic orientation applied to unsupervised classification of reviews. In: Proceedings of 40th Annual Meeting Association for Computational Linguistics (2002)
4. Pang, B., Lee, L.: Seeing stars: exploiting class relationships for sentiment categorization with respect to rating scales. In: Proceedings of 43rd Annual Meeting Association for Computational Linguistics (2005)
5. Paltoglou, G., Thelwall, M.: A study of information retrieval weighting schemes for sentiment analysis. In: Proceedings of 48th Annual Meeting Association for Computational Linguistics (2010)
6. Paltoglou, G., Thelwall, M.: Seeing stars of valence and arousal in blog posts. IEEE Trans. Affect. Comput. **4**(1), 116–123 (2013)
7. Frank, E., Kramer, S.: Ensembles of nested dichotomies for multi-class problems. In: Proceedings of 21st International Conference on Machine learning (2004)
8. Liu, B.: Sentiment Analysis and Opinion Mining. Morgan Claypool Publishers, San Rafael (2012)
9. Pang, B., Lee, L.: Opinion mining and sentiment analysis. Found. Trends Inf. Retr. **2**(1), 1–135 (2008)
10. Dave, K., Lawrence, S., Pennock, D.M.: Mining the peanut gallery: opinion extraction and semantic classification of product reviews. In: Proceedings of 12th International Conference on WWW (2003)
11. Lunardi, A., Viterbo, J., Bernardini, F.C.: Um Levantamento do Uso de Algoritmos de Aprendizado Supervisionado em Mineração de Opiniões (in portuguese). In: Proceedings of XII Encontro Nacional de Inteligência Artificial e Computacional – ENIAC, pp. 262–269 (2015)
12. Pang, B., Lee, L., Vaithyanathan, S.: Thumbs up sentiment classification using machine learning techniques. In: Proceedings of Conference Empirical Methods in Natural Language Processing (EMNLP), pp. 79–86 (2002)
13. Pak, A., Paroubek, P.: Twitter as a corpus for sentiment analysis and opinion mining. In: LREc 2010 (2010)

14. Kang, H., Seong, J.Y., Han, D.: Senti-lexicon and improved Naïve Bayes algorithms for sentiment analysis of restaurant reviews. Expert Syst. Appl. **39**(5), 6000–6010 (2012)
15. Pang, B., Lee, L.: Seeing stars: exploiting class relationships for sentiment categorization with respect to rating scales. In: Proceedings of 43rd Annual Meeting on Association for Computational Linguistics (2005)
16. Qu, L., Ifrim, G., Weikum, G.: The bag-of-opinions method for review rating prediction from sparse text patterns. In: Proceedings of 23rd International Conference Computational Linguistics (2010)
17. Long, C., Zhang, J., Zhut, X.: A review selection approach for accurate feature rating estimation. In: Proceedings of 23rd International Conference Computational Linguistics (2010)
18. de Albornoz, J.C., Plaza, L., Gervás, P., Díaz, A.: A joint model of feature mining and sentiment analysis for product review rating. In: Clough, P., Foley, C., Gurrin, C., Jones, G.J., Kraaij, W., Lee, H., Mudoch, V. (eds.) ECIR 2011. LNCS, vol. 6611, pp. 55–66. Springer, Heidelberg (2011)
19. Chen, C., Ibekwe-SanJuan, F., SanJuan, E., Weaver, C.: Visual analysis of conflicting opinions. In: 2006 Proceedings of IEEE Symposium on Visual Analytics Science and Technology, pp. 59–66 (2006)
20. Mak, H., Koprinska, I., Poon, J.: INTIMATE: a web-based movie recommender using text categorization. In: Proceedings of IEEE/WIC International Conference on Web Intelligence WI 2003, pp. 2–5 (2003)
21. Go, A., Bhayani, R., Huang, L.: Twitter sentiment classification using distant supervision. Processing **150**(12), 1–6 (2009)
22. Ortigosa, A., Martín, J.M., Carro, R.M.: Sentiment analysis in Facebook and its application to e-learning. Comput. Hum. Behav. **31**, 527–541 (2014)
23. Rodríguez, J.J., García-Osorio, C., Maudes, J.: Forests of nested dichotomies. Pattern Recogn. Lett. **31**(2), 125–132 (2010)
24. Wang, H., Lu, Y., Zhai, C.: Latent aspect rating analysis on review text data. In: 2010 16th Proceedings of ACM SIGKDD International Conference on Knowledge Discovery and Data Mining - KDD 2010, p. 783 (2010)
25. Jiang, Z., Chan, J., Tan, B.C.Y., Chua, W.S.: Effects of interactivity on website involvement and purchase intention. J. Assoc. Inf. Syst. (JAIS) **11**(1), 34–59 (2010)
26. Brooke, J.: A semantic approach to automated text sentiment analysis. Doctoral dissertation, Simon Fraser University (2009)

Social Media in Learning
and Collaboration

Collaboration Support in an International Computer Science Capstone Course

Robert Adams[1] and Carsten Kleiner[2(✉)]

[1] School of Computing and Information Systems, Grand Valley State University,
Allendale, MI 49401, USA
adams@cis.gvsu.edu

[2] Department of Computer Science, University of Applied Sciences & Arts Hannover,
Hannover, Germany
carsten.kleiner@hs-hannover.de

Abstract. Many computer science programs require some kind of culminating "capstone" course where students demonstrate skills learned in their CS curriculum. These capstone courses typically focus on the technical skills that students have learned, but one skill that is becoming more critical in our ever-global world is the ability to work in an international setting. Specifically, working on a team with students from a different country and/or culture. Over the past three years we have successfully offered an international capstone experience requiring students to work on a virtual team with students from a different country. For instructors, the primary challenge in offering such a course is collaboration between the instructors prior to the start of class. For students, the primary challenge is collaboration while the course is underway. This paper examines how we support instructor/instructor, instructor/student, as well as student/student communication and collaboration. This paper highlights how current web-based technologies provide support for collaboration. More specifically at least shared online storage for standard documents such as text or spreadsheets as well as video conferencing facilities are required for all the relations. Additionally, shared code repositories (and corresponding presentation) as well as online and offline messaging is necessary for a satisfactory experience. Software project management platforms provide additional important features. We show how technologies such as GitHub, Google Drive, Google Hangouts and Redmine provided the necessary support in several projects. At the same time other project teams have employed other similar technologies successfully as well. Our hope is that others are encouraged to attempt similar international efforts in order to broaden their students' non-technical skills as all the technologies are already in-place, well-known and stable, thus lowering the barrier for these important international experiences significantly.

Keywords: Computer science capstone course · Collaboration support · International software project · Software engineering in virtual teams · Collaboration tools

© Springer International Publishing Switzerland 2016
G. Meiselwitz (Ed.): SCSM 2016, LNCS 9742, pp. 313–323, 2016.
DOI: 10.1007/978-3-319-39910-2_29

1 Introduction

Many computer science and software engineering programs require some kind of culminating *capstone* course where students demonstrate skills learned in their subject-specific part of the curriculum. Many of these courses focus on a large software development project, and require students to apply their technical (*hard*) skills as well as their non-technical (*soft*) skills to a specific project or implementation. Successful completion of the capstone course demonstrates that students have learned, and can successfully apply, a large subset of the skills learned in prior CS courses. In addition, this course is usually a good dry run for how the future graduates will find their professional workplace.

Although these capstone courses typically focus on the technical skills that students have learned, one skill that is becoming more critical in our ever-global world is the ability to work in an international setting. Like many other CS topics, the meaning of "internationalization" in the curriculum varies. On the technical side, internationalization can mean adapting software to support other languages (e.g., alternate keyboard layouts, and displaying program strings in a different language). As this aspect is very frequently found in practice, there are technological solutions for this issue. The particular solution depends on the specific development language and system architecture, but important foundation to use these properly has usually been laid in technical classes throughout the curriculum. On the non-technical side, internationalization can mean equipping students with the skills necessary to operate within a global company (e.g., managing time zones and working on physically distributed teams). Issues in this area consist of organizational as well as social challenges. It is this latter aspect that we focus on in this paper.

Over the past four years we have successfully offered an international capstone experience as joint effort between Grand Valley State University, Michigan, USA, and the University of Applied Sciences & Arts, Hannover, Germany. Our joint capstone requires students to work on a virtual team with students from a different country. Naturally, offering such a course requires overcoming several challenges for the instructors, as well as for the students. For instructors, the primary challenge in offering such a course is collaboration between the instructors prior to the start of class. For students, the primary challenge is collaboration while the course is underway. This paper examines how we support instructor/instructor, instructor/student, as well as student/student communication and collaboration in an international setting.

This paper is organized as follows: we start with a brief general overview of the course design and how it fits into the two different programs. Thereafter we elaborate on the specific challenges regarding the different collaboration models required throughout the course. Then we suggest technological solutions that help remedy most of the collaboration issues and explain non-technological solutions that are helpful on top. All the suggestions focus on the typical university course setting where budgets are extremely limited. After that we review other work on international capstone courses before we finish with a conclusion and outlook.

2   Course Overview

Before discussing collaboration issues, we provide an overview of the course structure. In the next section we discuss particular challenges of collaboration. Richards [12] identifies several key design choices faced by project-based courses (international or not). Here, we describe and justify our particular pedagogical choices.

One important consideration is team size and team formation. Our choice was for teams of about four students. Our experience confirms that of [11] and [17]: teams with fewer students limit the dynamic, collaborative experience that we wanted students to achieve, and don't accurately reflect the challenges of working on a globally distributed team. Likewise, teams with more than about six students are often overwhelmed by team management issues, especially given the short total time frame of one semester mandated by our curricula. For example, with more than four students, it is often difficult (if not impossible) for students to coordinate their school/work/life schedules to find a common meeting time. We've found that approximately four students presents the right balance between challenge and frustration.

There is broad discussion on whether students should form their own teams or if the instructors should do so. In contrast to [11] and [12], we decided to give students latitude to form their own teams, typically based on the interest in a shared project idea. Students share possible term-length project ideas with each other and from those ideas, self-form teams. The team formation process is moderated by one of the instructors who, after publishing the pool of project ideas, collects student votes for three subjects from this pool. Based on these votes *good* project ideas to be realized will be selected and students assigned. In our experience it is almost always possible to only execute projects with at least four votes while accommodating at least one of the three choices of each student. Even though being able to form their own teams may not accurately reflect the situation in their future professional lives, we note that it provides a boost in motivation due to a shared common interest in the project idea. We have noted that students want to work on their projects because they feel they *own* the project, rather than having it imposed on them. Also having team members that fit well on an emotional level significantly improves motivation. High motivation is extremely important in any software development project [19] and can be difficult to achieve by the instructor if the general project ideas do not suit students.

After teams are formed, teams work cooperatively to create a working software project, as well as several document artifacts. All of these artifacts (and thus the development process) together with due dates are defined in a shared effort by the two instructors before the class starts. Each team reports to only one of the two instructors, so that additional effort on the instructor side due to the international setting is minimized and the students learn to work with a remote product owner. Teams first produce a project prospectus describing their project. Project ideas are generated by the teams themselves, although there is nothing to prevent the instructors from using industry-sponsored projects, or even in-house projects that have been added to the pool of project ideas. Instructors evaluate the prospectus based on content and scope. In terms of content, instructors ensure that the project involves aspects from several different areas of computer science. The project is meant to be a *capstone* experience, and cannot be limited to a single domain of computing (e.g., solely graphics or AI). The prospectus is also evaluated in terms of scope: ensuring that the project is ambitious enough to require the team the entire semester to complete.

After the prospectus is approved, teams conduct a feasibility study to generate a feasibility report and initial burndown chart based on an initial set of items for the product backlog. The feasibility study requires teams to conduct initial research on those areas of the project whose solutions are currently unknown (novel algorithms, data structures, languages, APIs, etc.), and present initial solutions that were discovered. Teams must demonstrate that their target platform, language, libraries are installed on their development machines. Because of the distributed nature of the course, teams must also identify how and where course artifacts will be created. Finally, teams must create a burndown chart based on initial estimates for the items in the product backlog showing the intended timeline for development taking the general course schedule into account.

During the project development phase, teams are required to complete a certain set of items from the backlog to produce a working part of the final product after every sprint. In recent years we have split the semester into 4 sprints, each about 3 weeks in length. After each sprint, teams will generate a sprint report and meet with their instructor to discuss progress to date, and challenges faced. Another important part of every sprint (as well as the preliminary phases) is a peer evaluation that is to be submitted to the instructor individually by each student. The peer evaluations help instructors to identify potential problem spots where intervention by the instructor may be necessary. This is particularly important for issues within the project teams, especially on the social level, that do not show in the intermediate result.

The final result of the term is presented to the entire class. Teams collaboratively create the presentation slides, and must carefully orchestrate the order in which the team members will speak. Besides the course artifacts themselves, teams must also submit periodic peer evaluations. One way of supporting the student's evaluation of their team members is the mandatory use of a version control system [6]. Using the *blame* feature available in systems, instructors can determine how much each student is contributing to a solution. This information helps to support or refute student comments about their peers.

Grading throughout the semester follows a predefined and publicly available grading rubric that has been set by the instructors in a common effort. All grading is done by the instructor that a team reports to with some commonly graded teams in the first two years to align application of the rubrics by the different instructors. The final grades from the percentage results of the grading rubrics, however, are determined by the local instructors in order to align these grades with local specifics of the programs regarding grades.

3   Collaboration Challenges

As noted above, there are several points of collaboration between student/student, instructor/instructor, and instructor/student. In this section we make explicit the challenges and requirements of collaboration at each of these points.

Overall, instructors must agree on the purpose of the course. Without this fundamental agreement, a student's experience in the course would depend highly on who their instructor is. Our goal is to mitigate instructor differences by ensuring a common vision.

Between the instructors, much of the collaboration happens before the class even begins. At minimum, instructors must co-create a syllabus for the course outlining the following items:

- What student learning objectives are central to the course? As with any course in higher education defining the learning objectives for the students is the first central issue to fix. Usually learning objectives for these courses at each individual institution have already been set externally when originally designing the course. The specific collaboration challenge for the instructors is thus to check whether there is a sufficient overlap between those objectives. This can be done virtually (e.g. video conference) but a personal discussion is usually favorable.
- What content do the instructors deliver in class? It is important that all students on the virtual teams start with as equal knowledge regarding software engineering projects as possible. Note though that there is substantial difference in both technical as well as organizational skills even within a single local class. So, at least the same level of variation is to be expected in distributed teams as well. Focus here should be on a common understanding of the development process itself. This collaboration challenge can be solved by exchanging information about prerequisites as well as material to be shared in class. Shared document storage is usually sufficient.
- What software development model/process will students use to create their projects? Similarly to the previous item all students need to work on the same common process model with the same timeline. This can only be achieved if previously agreed and defined by the instructors.
- What deliverables will students be submitting for grading? There should be common understanding and deadlines regarding deliverables throughout the project. As discussed in the previous issue the same development process will be used, thus it should be rather simple to also define common deliverables to be submitted by the students. Usually most of the deliverables are immediate consequences of the chosen process model. Some additional deliverables specific to university courses as opposed to professional software development should be added based on a common decision (i.e. frequent formal peer evaluations).
- How will student deliverables will be graded? Using what criteria? For each of the deliverables mentioned above there needs to be a common set of criteria that will be used to assess the quality. In addition, there should be a common grading rubric (usually percentages have been proven useful). Also, common agreed weights should be used for each of these criteria as well as for overall grading combining grades for all deliverables.
- When will student deliverables be due? After deciding on the process model, deliverables and overall timeline, common due dates for each of the deliverables should be defined. Note that these due dates have to take a potential time difference into account. Due dates for deliverables should be unique for the whole course whereas

presentations may be scheduled individually for distributed teams as close to the presentation times of local teams as possible.

- How will teams be formed and by whom? This is one of the more difficult issues to solve as there are different ways to do this, each with specific advantages and drawbacks. On a meta level it is important that the instructors agree on the process of team formation and decide who will make ultimate decisions in the case of complaints. To a certain degree the formation process depends on other parameters of the course (self-defined projects vs. externally provided, keeping groups of friends on a team vs. purposely separating them). In our setting the process as described above has proven to work well.

After the course begins a whole new set of collaboration challenges arise between the instructor and students, and between the students themselves. Between the instructor and students the main challenges are:

- How to find common meeting times for instructors and students to meet? As teams are distributed, there can be no regular meetings according to the regular university schedule. Thus each team's meeting times with the instructor have to be set individually. As this process tends to be difficult because it extends regular class hours, all parties will need to bring a lot of flexibility. Also, in order to keep organizational overhead minimal an agreed process on how to set these times is necessary.
- How to conduct meetings with students when they are not in the same time zone or country? Whereas the previous challenge already holds true for any distributed team, the international setting with different time zones makes finding common meetings times even more difficult as the number of constraints increases significantly. Thus, a strict process and time-wise flexibility are even more important.
- How to keep track of a team's progress throughout the semester? The deliverables and due dates selected by the instructors should be rather fine-grained in order for the instructor to keep track of the team's progress continuously. In the distributed setting the deliverables are usually the only chances for the instructor to track progress as frequent in-class meetings or informal meetings are not suitable. It is also important to keep an eye on each student's individual participation in the teams. On the other hand the organizational overhead for the instructor must remain manageable.
- How to facilitate communication about a team's performance throughout the semester? Grading of each of the deliverables throughout the project is only helpful if the team gets feedback on their performance shortly after submission. This is particularly important in case of imperfect deliverables to let the team know how to improve the quality for the upcoming artifacts. As this cannot be done in a personal meeting as usual, a way to communicate assessment needs to be defined that is both quick and easy to use.

Finally, the following challenges arise between the students on a team. These are probably the most important challenges as there much more students involved in the class than instructors. In addition there is no natural hierarchy within the student teams so that no ultimately deciding instance is present. Thus easy to use and commonly agreed solutions for these challenges will have to be available in order for the student teams to function properly.

- When and how do the students find common meeting times? Every project work requires some kind of synchronous interaction between team members. In a distributed team apart from local meetings, common meetings can only be virtual and have to observe many time constraints from each participant as well as from the international setting in general. Thus finding suitable meeting times is a real challenge with distributed student teams.
- How are they supported in a continuous team building process? Most components of traditional team building processes are centered on common experiences. These are not really available with distributed teams. It is almost impossible to hold a physical kickoff meeting or perform classical social events supporting team building. New ways of team formation both on the social as well as the organizational level (i.e. roles on the project team) have to be found. Typically those will at least slow the process down significantly which can be problematic given the time constraints of a semester.
- How are they sharing project artifacts (e.g. documents, source code, product backlog)? Throughout the project there is a need to share artifacts within the project team. Those range from simple documents stating ideas or project aspects over documents used as deliverables in the defined process (e.g. sprint reports, product backlogs, burn-down charts) to the source code of the product developed by the team itself. In a distributed team there needs to be a way to provide these sharing capabilities with minimal overhead. As many real-world development teams also operate in a distributed manner this challenge is not as big as it seems. Many professional development teams have faced similar issues and thus well-proven technological solutions are available (see next section).
- How/when are they meeting as a team? Apart from the first challenge which dealt with finding a concrete common meeting time, a related challenge is whether and how often they can be meeting as a team at all. The frequency will definitely be reduced when compared to a local team, so that working style in the project will have to be adjusted to fewer team meetings. This affects many aspects of project work from amount of independent work to level of documentation and ways to make decisions on the team.
- What software development model do they use (e.g. individually, peer programming)? Related to the previous challenge there is also an impact of the distributed team on the software development model. The number of choice is reduced as e.g. pair programming can only be performed by the local parts of a team. This in turn poses a challenge and restrictions on the separation of work within the team which may have to follow geographic aspects more than technical ones.

4   Collaborative Tool Support

According to [20] tools supporting collaboration of student development teams can be grouped into four categories: communication, goal tracking, information distribution (e.g. document sharing and management) and change management. We will focus on the first three of those as change management only impacts the instructor-instructor relationship over several instances of a course and is thus of limited importance for the student teams.

Given the set of challenges described in the previous section, we now discuss tools that were used to address those challenges. As mentioned previously, much of the collaboration between instructors happens before the class begins, and falls into two general types of collaboration: real-time synchronous communication, and asynchronous document creation. Agreement on the general vision and format of the course is best handled synchronously. Face-to-face communication is the best avenue for this, but in this case one instructor was in Germany while the other was in the United States. Therefore, a synchronous communication program like Skype, FaceTime, or Google Hangouts can be used, or if nothing else, a telephone. With synchronous communication instructors can quickly share their ideas for the course, their concerns, and work with the other instructor to create a shared vision for the course. Naturally, this could also be done via email, but the turnaround time makes it less than ideal.

After the general goals of the course are agreed upon, detailed course documents need to be created. We have discovered that an asynchronous document creation system works very well for this. In our particular case, we used Google Drive to collaboratively create course documents and spreadsheets. The course documents included a syllabus and course schedule. The syllabus not only describes the learning outcomes, but the course deliverables, software development methodology to be used, and grading rubrics. Asynchronous collaboration is appropriate because it gives instructors a chance to work on different parts of the documents simultaneously, as well as to thoughtfully respond to edits made by the other instructor. Also, Google Drive's commenting features, as well as its ability to track changes without having to email documents back and forth, ensures that both instructors always have access to the latest version of a document.

During the semester communication between the instructors diminishes except when clarification is required on grading rubrics or how to handle a specific situation with a team. In these cases, our experience is that email is normally sufficient, although a phone call or Skype session to talk through a situation is sometimes warranted.

After the course begins instructors and students start collaborating in earnest. Once again, the challenges fall into two types: the need for real-time synchronous communication, and the need for asynchronous document/artifact sharing. One of the initial challenges is trying to find a common time when teams and their instructors can meet. This is normally accomplished through open source meeting scheduling tools like Doodle [doodle.com]. Because instructors and students are not located in the same country or time zone, meetings must be held online. We have had success using tools like Skype and Google Hangouts, both of which allow for multi-person "conference calls".

Document and artifact sharing (reports, spreadsheets, graphs, etc.) requires some kind of shared storage. We have successfully used Google Drive and Dropbox for this, although some teams choose to host their own websites. Sharing source code is a necessity, and we mandate the use of git. We chose git because it is free, and an industry standard. Some teams choose to share documents by uploading them to their GitHub repositories, as well as using GitHub's wiki feature to create documents, thereby ensuring that all course artifacts are located at the same location.

For our course we also require all students to keep track of the time spent on their project. Many accomplish this by uploading a document or spreadsheet as described above. Other students do this by using an online time tracking tool like Toggl[1]. Toggl allows users to start and stop timers, to specify what was being worked on, and then to generate reports showing time-on-task.

Finally, students on the same team face collaboration challenges, especially when they are not located in the same country. However, even students at the same university often have collaboration challenges due to work schedules outside of school, or family commitments. Like the collaboration between the instructors and teams, collaboration between students can be characterized as either synchronous or asynchronous. Many student teams reported that both Skype and Google Hangouts worked well for them, allowing them to hold live meetings from any location (one student reported that he "attended" a team meeting while his car was stuck in a snowbank on the way to campus). Of course, email also remains a primary tool used to convey information that may not be time-critical. Students also have a need to share artifacts (primarily source code), and this is easily accomplished using tools such as Google Drive and git as described above.

In general, integrated project management systems for software development teams such as Redmine may also provide a good choice as they provide solutions for a fair number of the challenges. They typically focus on the software project specific issues (e.g. wiki, document sharing, version control, issue tracking, time recording), though, still leaving the need for tools solving the communication challenges discussed above.

5   Related Work

The general idea of using distributed student project teams has been documented in the literature for several years, the first notable work being [5] with [1, 3, 10, 17] being more recent. The ideas and challenges mentioned in those papers have been leveraged in our course by re-using some of the ideas and purposely setting it up differently in other aspects. [18] also describes a similar effort compared to ours, but this paper focuses more on the specific collaboration challenges and how those can be solved with recent technological tools that have not been available 10 years ago.

The works just mentioned provide an overall description of course pedagogy. More specific work focuses on overall challenges for distributed teams [16], communication skills [9], student team organization [2], software testing techniques [13], software tools [7, 6], cultural factors influencing success [15], use of Agile and scrum methodologies [14], and student motivation [4]. [20] is a recent paper that categorizes tools used in a software engineering course, but does not elaboration on what those tools were. As discussed above [11, 12] discuss the student team formation process which we did not use here as our setting is different.

Some general work on effective tool support for distributed software development teams away from the University setting also exist, e.g. [8] discussing software quality and [19] explaining how to raise developer motivation in such teams. More papers exist,

---

[1] http://www.toggl.com.

but many are of limited applicability to a university student project as some of the key setup parameters are different (e.g. need for tools complying with no budget, specific student-instructor situation, externally fixed schedule etc.).

6 Conclusions

Many computer science programs require some kind of culminating experience for students, and it is clear that gaining experience working in an international setting is becoming a critical skill. Several schools are incorporating global learning into their capstone courses, and it is likely that other schools are beginning to consider doing the same. The main challenge in developing a course around distributed virtual teams is ensuring sufficient support for collaboration. Over the past three years we have successfully offered an international capstone experience requiring students to work on a virtual team with students from a different country. During that time the number and sophistication of tools that support collaboration has grown dramatically, to the point that lack of tools is no longer a viable argument against virtual teams.

Our experience has been that the need for collaboration among the instructors and students falls into two broad categories: the need for synchronous communication, and the need for asynchronous document sharing. In both cases current open-source tools are sufficient to support distributed software development teams, and these supporting technologies have significantly improved the collaboration of the student teams.

Although a wealth of tools exist in each category, we have successfully run our capstone course using tools that are well-known, well-supported, and completely free. Specifically, both Skype and Google Hangouts are comparable in features and effectively support synchronous discussions. For asynchronous document sharing, Google Drive, Dropbox, and GitHub are more than adequate. Finally, integrated project management systems such as Redmine also provide support for document sharing challenges.

Our hope is that others are encouraged to attempt similar international efforts in order to broaden their students' non-technical skills. All the necessary collaborative technologies are already in-place, well-known, and stable, lowering the barrier for these important international experiences significantly.

References

1. Al-Janabi, S., Sverdlik, W.: Towards long-term international collaboration in computer science education. doi:10.1109/EDUCON.2011.5773118
2. Bruegge, B., Dutoit, A.H., Kobylinski, R., Teubner, G.: Transatlantic project courses in a university environment. doi:10.1109/APSEC.2000.896680
3. Ciccozzi, F., Crnkovic, I.: Performing a Project in a Distributed Software Development Course: Lessons Learned. doi:10.1109/ICGSE.2010.29
4. Clear, T., Kassabova, D.: Motivational patterns in virtual team collaboration. In: Young, A., Tolhurst, D. (eds.) Proceedings of the 7th Australasian Conference on Computing Education, ACE 2005, vol. 42, pp. 51–58. Australian Computer Society Inc., Darlinghurst (2005)

5. Daniels, M., Petre, M., Almstrum, V., Asplund, L., Bjorkman, C., Erickson, C., Klein, B., Last, M.: RUNESTONE, an international student collaboration project. doi:10.1109/FIE. 1998.738780
6. Glassy, L.: Using version control to observe student software development processes. J. Comput. Small Coll. **21**(3), 99–106 (2006)
7. Gotel, O., Kulkarni, V., Scharff, C., Neak, L.: Working Across Borders: Overcoming Culturally-Based Technology Challenges in Student Global Software Development. doi: 10.1109/CSEET.2008.16
8. Gotel, O., Kulkarni, V., Say, M., Scharff, C., Sunetnanta, T.: Quality Indicators on Global Software Development Projects: Does "Getting to Know You" Really Matter? doi:10.1109/ ICGSE.2009.8
9. Johansson, C., Dittrich, Y., Juustila, A.: Software engineering across boundaries: student project in distributed collaboration. doi:10.1109/47.807967
10. Makio, J., Betz, S.: On educating globally distributed software development — A case study. doi:10.1109/ISCIS.2009.5291874
11. Oakley, B., Felder, R.M., Brent, R., Elhajj, I.: Turning Student Groups into Effective Teams. J. Student Centered Learn. **2**(1), 9–35 (2004)
12. Richards, D.: Designing project-based courses: with a focus on group formation and assessment. ACM Trans. Comput. Educ. **9**(1) (2009). Article 2
13. Richardson, I., Moore, S., Paulish, D., Casey, V., Zage, D.: Globalizing Software Development in the Local Classroom
14. Scharff, C., Gotel, O., Kulkarni, V.: Transitioning to Distributed Development in Students' Global Software Development Projects: The Role of Agile Methodologies and End-to-End Tooling. doi:10.1109/ICSEA.2010.66
15. Swigger, K., Alpaslan, F., Brazile, R., Harrington, B., Peng, X.: The challenges of international computer-supported collaboration. doi:10.1109/FIE.2004.1408738
16. Swigger, K., Brazile, R., Serce, F.C., Dafoulas, G., Alpaslan, F.N., Lopez, V.: The Challenges of Teaching Students How to Work in Global Software Teams. doi:10.1109/TEE. 2010.5508836
17. Tabrizi, M.H.N., Collins, C.B., Kalamkar, V.: An international collaboration in software engineering. Proceedings Of The 40th Acm Technical Symposium On Computer Science Education (SIGCSE 2009), pp. 306–310. ACM, New York (2009)
18. van der Duim, L., Andersson, J.: Good practices for educational software engineering projects. In: 29th International Conference on Software Engineering, ICSE 2007, pp. 698– 707. IEEE Computer Society Press (2007)
19. Sach, R., Sharp, H., Petre, M.: Continued involvement in software development: motivational factors. In: Proceedings of the 2010 ACM-IEEE International Symposium on Empirical Software Engineering and Measurement (ESEM 2010). ACM, New York (2010). doi: 10.1145/1852786.1852843. http://doi.acm.org/10.1145/1852786.1852843
20. Knutas, A., Ikonen, J., Ripamonti, L., Maggiorini, D., Porras, J.: A study of collaborative tool use in collaborative learning processes. In: Proceedings of the 14th Koli Calling International Conference on Computing Education Research (Koli Calling 2014), pp. 175–176. ACM, New York (2014). doi:http://dx.doi.org/10.1145/2674683.2674706

Model Based on Learning Needs of Children with Auditory Impairment

Sandra Cano[1($\boxtimes$)], César Collazos[2], Habib M. Fardoun[3], Daniyal M. Alghazzawi[3], and Abdullah Albarakati[3]

[1] LIDIS Group, University of San Buenaventura, Cali, Colombia
Sandra.cano@gmail.com
[2] IDIS Group, University of Cauca, Popayán, Colombia
ccollazo@unicauca.edu.co
[3] King Abdulaziz University, Jeddah, Saudi Arabia
{hfardoun,dghazzawi}@kau.edu.sa

Abstract. This paper presents a model based on the needs of children with an auditory impairment, in which the dual research lines of Human Computer Interaction and Artificial Intelligence are employed in the design of intelligent interactive systems able to meet the requirements of the user. In following a philosophy of user-centered design, different characteristics of children with hearing disabilities are identified, along with AI techniques that could be applied in the model. The main issues involved in designing a user profile and the techniques used in order to create the process of adapting the system to the user are also discussed.

Keywords: Learning styles · Hearing impaired · Human computer interaction · Artificial intelligence

1 Introduction

Information technology is today transforming many different areas, including health and education. Smart, interactive products are able to transmit learning styles in a way that manages to capture children's attention and motivate them in their activities.

Children learn in many different ways. Furthermore, they may be affected by some type of disability, or in different skills that each is able to develop at their own pace. A hearing impaired child acquires cognitive skills at a slower pace than a hearing child. Hearing impaired children therefore require a special education to receive an appropriate educational development.

Adaptive learning is a method that has been incorporated in the area of education. It requires a computer system in order to create a customized learning experience [5, 8]. It has also been used in the area of health, where psychological aspects are taken into account to adapt the level of difficulty of a game to the skills of the user using neural networks [20].

The term first appeared in 1970 in the field of Artificial Intelligence (AI), in order to adapt an educational process to the strengths and weaknesses of each user. It can thus

© Springer International Publishing Switzerland 2016
G. Meiselwitz (Ed.): SCSM 2016, LNCS 9742, pp. 324–334, 2016.
DOI: 10.1007/978-3-319-39910-2_30

be said that an adaptive system has the ability to adjust its operation to the goals, tasks and interests, and adapt other characteristics to the profile of the user [1]. This leads to the consideration of a user model that makes it possible to capture information from users while they interact with the system, to thereby learn about the user and thus classify learning styles according to the needs of the child.

Meanwhile, in the Human-Computer Interaction (HCI) line, specifically the philosophy of User-Centered Design (UCD) is a methodology that follows a process in order to identify the needs of the user. This means that with the help of UCD it is possible to identify the characteristics of the user and with AI analyze the data and intelligently adapt user interfaces according to the skills, behaviors and interests of the user.

The result is that AI techniques are increasingly being used by HCI researchers and the use of machine learning applications in HCI research is visibly increasing. Previous research [23, 24] has mentioned the importance of these two lines in creating smart user interfaces, as user tasks become more and more complicated. AI can help to reduce this complexity for users to provide intelligent adaptive techniques.

In this article, Sect. 2 describes how these two lines, HCI and AI, can contribute in creating a smart model for children with hearing disabilities; in Sect. 3, the learning needs that may be involved in children with hearing impairment are discussed; the conceptual model is then proposed in Sect. 4; and finally, Sect. 5 presents several conclusions and outlines future work.

2   Human-Computer Interaction and Artificial Intelligence

Previous research [1, 2, 4] shows the interest in how the dual lines of Human-Computer Interaction and Artificial Intelligence can contribute to creating a smart, interactive model for children with hearing disabilities. The work proposed by Gonzalez et al. [1] consists in a student model, wherein based on an analysis of the different aspects of the user, the most relevant are selected, such as: personal information, learning styles, personality, context, and psychological aspects. This model is useful for adapting a virtual education system to certain content, and adapting activities to a specific type of user. Furthermore, UCD methodology has been used in order to design interfaces tailored to the user profile.

Adaptive models applied in learning offer an intelligent alternative for adapting content according to user preferences. Adaptive learning models have been used as the basis for building adaptive systems applied to a specific context. In 2008 [8] took the AHAM [7] model as their base, upon which they built a system for learning environments online. The model architecture consists of the following modules: student model, domain model, instruction model, adaptive model, and user interfaces. In 2010, Mascio et al. [5] proposed the design of an intelligent adaptive learning system for people with a low level of text comprehension. The learning system is based on an AHA (Adaptive Hypermedia Architecture) model, consisting of a domain model, user model, environment model and a model of adaptation for the learning process. A set of rules are also included that are correlated with the domain and user models.

User-centered design has meanwhile been the subject of much research, such as [6], which proposes a model of analysis of the user in order to structure the information concerning end users with children between 7-11 years old. In this work, an experimental design was applied, consisting of a set of tasks that each child or the teacher carries out in order to analyze and identify the different characteristics of the users. Moreover, in 2012 [2] with a UCD focus, an analysis was carried out of different types of user model where the most important characteristics, focused on psychological, physical and cognitive aspects, are extracted. These were proposals with the aim of improving levels of usability in the systems and a way of integrating software operation according to the characteristics of the user.

The research works discussed show the importance of integrating these two lines, HCI and AI, in an intelligent adaptation model that helps to provide an interaction and feedback specific to children with hearing disabilities. To design a model of intelligent learning, it is important to focus on the user in order to identify the characteristics that may affect the child's learning. However, the major challenge facing AI is to interpret the activities of the user and predict the objectives correctly [25]. In addition, children with hearing impairment do not behave the same or learn at the same rate as hearing children [21, 22] - so that different levels of difficulty are needed; or some of them have a different method of communication that may affect the context of use and the learning strategies. This leads to the importance of having a model that can adapt to the needs of the child, whether in communication preferences, context of use, or difficulty level, and so on.

3   Learning Needs

Hearing impairment is an obstacle that renders it impossible to process information linguistically through the ear. This is generally known as deafness. Deaf children who do not have hearing aids have only sign language as their communication channel, so they have difficulty developing concepts in a number of areas. However, some deaf children have benefited from hearing aids such as cochlear implants. These children can go on to communicate verbally, and must learn to receive information by means of sounds, so that they need to learn to recognize the sounds via the cochlear implant[1].

Hearing impaired children face different challenges - cognitive, educational and socio-cultural. Hearing children develop language skills through sounds (sound-letter-word meaning), which corresponds from letter to sound. As such, the same learning styles cannot be applied to hearing impaired children as to hearing children. In addition, children with hearing impairments fail to develop their skills at the same pace as hearing children, which makes it difficult to identify problems in the development of their basic cognitive skills and this can affect their progress in the acquisition of learning. In addition, each child learns at a different pace, indicating that different children may have

---

[1] A tiny electronic device that is surgically inserted in the inner ear, given to those with profound or severe levels of deafness.

different learning styles and in turn the different learning styles will correspond to different teaching styles.

A learning style is defined as the strategies that each individual uses when faced with learning new knowledge, in other words the different ways in which an individual may learn, involving cognitive, emotional and physiological traits that can be used as stable indicators as to how users perceive, interact with, and respond to learning environments [13]. It can thus be said that a learning style is made up of one or several teaching models and strategies. A hearing impaired child can be faced with different learning styles, as he has different ways to communicate, such as sign language (visual and gestural communication), lip-reading (visual communication) and oral communication for children with a hearing aid such as a cochlear implant.

A learning model called VARK [19] can be used to classify individuals according to their preference in order to capture and process the information. The VARK model establishes learning strategies according to the sensory preferences of the child, for example: Visual, Auditory, Reading/Writing, and Kinesthetic. A hearing impaired child has greater development in the visual channel [6]; the manner in which these children reach an understanding of the information submitted to them should thus be supported by pictograms. A child with a cochlear implant, however, requires to make use of the auditory channel to learn how to listen. Therefore, a child with hearing disabilities may have different preferences for receiving information. This could be related to the Felder-Silverman learning model [18], which proposes a test to classify the child in the following categories: entry (visual-verbal), perception (sensory-auditory), organization (inductively deductive) processing (active-reflective), and understanding (sequential-global). A problem can occur in the test due to the fact that when the interaction is with children, and particularly those with a hearing impairment, they do not have adequate language skills to respond to the test on their own.

Elsewhere, there are the cognitive skills for each child. These help to classify the level of difficulty and what form the teaching strategies would take. These cognitive skills can be elicited using psychometric tools [27] that assist in determining the interests of the user. Gagne's theory [14] proposes a domain of cognitive, emotional and motor learning, corresponding with intellectual skills, cognitive strategies, verbal information, attitudes, and motor skills. In turn, it proposes a set of tasks to be considered in learning: gaining the attention of the student, informing the child about the objectives, stimulating them, and providing feedback relating to prior learning, offering stimulating material, providing guidance to the child, checking on their performance, providing information, assessing their performance and enhancing retention transfer.

Thus, it can be stated that the more information obtained about the user, learning strategies better suited to their cognitive, motor skills and attitudes can be applied. Furthermore, the learning theories are subject to the learning styles that can be involved in the application that will interact in a smart way with the child.

4   Conceptual Model

The proposed model contains the following blocks: user profile, evaluation techniques, intelligent environments, and classification. As shown in Fig. 1, each block performs certain functions that are borne in mind throughout the adaptive model.

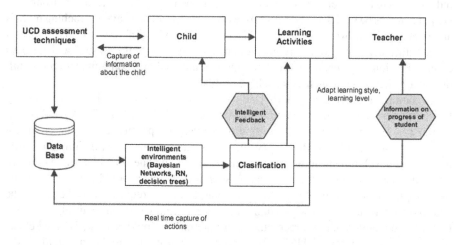

Fig. 1. Model based on the needs of children with a hearing impairment

In **User profile**, the characteristics of the child with a hearing impairment are defined according to their needs. To obtain the information, researchers worked with two organizations: the USAER program (Regular Education Support Service Units) in Aguascalientes, Mexico, a program involving several state schools that accept children with special needs in regular education; and the Institute for Blind and Deaf Children of the Cauca Valley, in Cali, Colombia, who have children with cochlear implants. Information was gathered both for deaf children whose communication channel is sign language or lip-reading and for children with cochlear implants whose channel of communication is oral. The children ranged from 7-11 years.

Following UCD philosophy, a number of different **Evaluation techniques** were carried out on user experience (UX) with the children to identify the user profile. This identification is the continuation of work done in [3], where an analysis model is proposed for deaf children. Through different evaluation techniques adapted to UX, aspects of the children in the teaching of literacy are elicited. A search was also conducted for information from different approaches proposed by authors in the identification of aspects of the user [9–12]. The information obtained was analyzed and the most important aspects for children with hearing impairment were selected, as shown in Table 1.

The identified issues are of use in gathering information about the user, so that the system acquires knowledge about users by means of the various actions carried out, in order to determine which elements to adjust according to their needs. The type of information obtained (Fig. 2) may be of two types: explicit, when the user must register

Table 1. Aspects of user profile

Attributes	Description
Personal information	Involves important information that can be relied upon to define needs and learning level. These comprise Name, Age, Gender, and Academic year.
Skills/abilities	Determine skills that can be taken into account when establishing learning strategies.
Disability (Physical/Cognitive)	Involves the physical auditory disability as well as hearing loss (mild, moderate, moderate-severe, severe or profound), but in turn is related to a cognitive impairment that can occur in children.
Learning styles	Can be defined as the different ways a person gathers, processes, and organizes information. Learning styles can influence user preferences and usually guide the system in adaptation.
Behavior/Academic	A record of dynamic information about the user gained from the various actions performed by the user, e.g. time taken to perform activities, number of activities completed correctly, and so on.
Emotion	The reactions that can be detected from the children on interacting with technology in order to carry out their educational activities.
Motivation	Certain actions carried out by the child, persisting with them until they are completed.

information such as personal data and the type of disability (physical/cognitive); and explicit, when information is captured dynamically as the user interacts with the system, such as cognitive, behavioral/academic, emotion, and motivation.

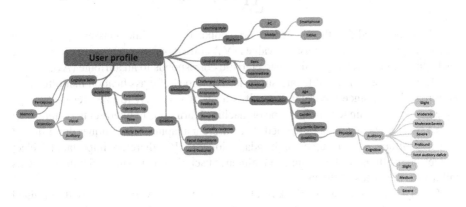

Fig. 2. Taxonomy of user profile.

Emotions are included in the user profile as they are an important part of the driving force of the learning, as they can influence the learning and motivation of the child on trying out the tool. With the aim of fostering motivation, strategies are used that influence such factors, such as challenges, rewards, etc.

To elicit information about cognitive skills in children, psychometric tools are used that can be incorporated as a pre-test within the tool, where the aim is to adjust the level of difficulty of the activities. As a result, the information that is gathered in these different ways is stored in a **database**, where multiple correlations are created between the data and bring about the possibility of creating profiles and trends. As such, the database is a key element because it makes recording and storage of data possible, as well as tracking the performance of the child.

The **intelligent environments** block is related to artificial intelligence approaches. In research to date, the techniques most frequently used are Bayesian networks, decision trees, and neural networks [16, 17]. These techniques are within the branch of machine learning, which aims to develop algorithms that are able to generalize behaviors using information that is unstructured and acquired. Machine learning has automated learning algorithms, including supervised and unsupervised. The task of prediction based on learning styles is related to concept learning, a particular case of supervised learning [15]. This is defined as a correspondence between the inputs (attributes) and desired outputs (classes) of the system. This means that the observations of user behavior that are the inputs of the system help the training of the system in being able to predict future actions of the user.

Bayesian networks determine the probability that an element J belongs to a class C_i, given a set of values $V_{ij}......V_{nj}$ of attributes $\{A_1.......A_n\}$ of element J.

$$P(C_i | A_1 = V_{1j} .... A_n = V_{nj})$$

If the values of the attributes are independent

$$P(C_i) = \prod_{k=1..N} P(A_k = V_{kj} | C_i)$$

It may be noted that the element J corresponds to each child, classes C_i depend on that which it is desired to classify, values (V_{ij}) correspond to each value captured for each child, and each user profile characteristic corresponds to an attribute (A_n).

Decision trees, meanwhile, are supervised methods of classification that offer very high readability, since the training result is a set of very easy to interpret *if-else* type statements. The main idea of this type of machine learning is to interpret the training set with a set of rules that must be learned. The different adaptation techniques differ in cost and may influence the accuracy of the adaptation [26]. It is therefore important to select suitable algorithms, as they in turn can influence user satisfaction in displaying the items tailored to the needs of the users.

Finally, the **classification** block is related to the types of variable that will be trained within the system, i.e. if it is desired to adjust the level of difficulty or according to cognitive skills (attention, perception, memory) of the child so that the system can adjust elements of the user interface. However, it is very important to decide what it is sought to classify, because the number of adaptive models that must be used depends on it.

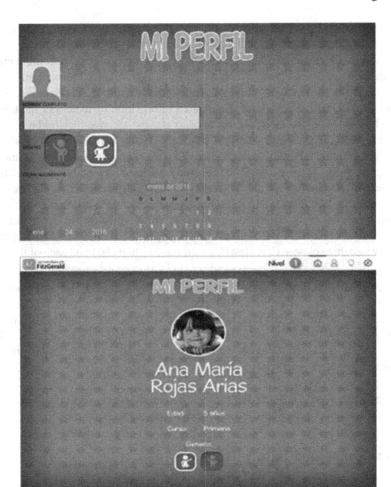

Fig. 3. User interface for data capture

Using this model, decision trees were able to be applied considering the VARK model, which is subject to a condition in the type of disability (physical/cognitive) of the child. In other words, if children have a hearing impairment at a profound level of deafness and do not have a cochlear implant, it means their preference for sensory feedback is visual, so that making use of sounds in a learning tool would not be worthwhile. What is more, if they communicate through sign language, then that ought to be taken into account in the tool. Meanwhile, if it is sought to classify the level of difficulty the child has in relation to the activity, information is gathered from each of the activities carried out using the tool and a record log is kept, where the information is analyzed and the level of difficulty classified (basic, intermediate, advanced) according to that information. The information it is considered important to store is: time that it takes to carry out the activity, the comparison between the frequency of correct and incorrect responses, and the cognitive skills level. The skills level was weighted in a rating between low, medium and high.

To capture information from the user's profile, a user interface was implemented where explicit data is gathered, such as personal information (name, gender, age, course), disability (physical/cognitive) and photo of the child, as shown in Fig. 3.

Once the teacher has registered the explicit information of the child, the tool can begin to be used. The first interface that appears is a pre-test that the child has to take, a psychometric tool that consists of a set of questions designed to assess the basic cognitive skills of the child. The skills assessed are visual attention, perceptual discrimination, and visual memory. The psychometric tool used was based on a study conducted by the department of psychology at the University of San Buenaventura in Cali, where a psychometric model called SONAR has been designed for hearing impaired children.

The information captured from the pre-test is vital for adjusting the level of difficulty of the activities of the tool. Each of the skills tested with the child is taken as a model to classify into three classes $C_i = \{low(L), medium(M), high(H)\}$ and each of the observations made by a child corresponds to $X^{(i)}$ to be used as training data and an $X_j^{(i)}$, which is a characteristic (j) corresponding to an observation of a child (i). Bayesian networks are applied to find the probabilities of each cognitive level, $\{P(L), P(M), P(H)\}$. For the values assigned in low, medium and high, it was considered that if the children manage to score between 0–30 in the assessment, they are classified as low; likewise 30–60 medium; and 70–100 high. The pre-test to be applied in the tool will have a total of 15 questions, distributed as follows: 5 visual attention, 5 perceptual discrimination, and 5 visual memory.

Using this pre-test, it is desired to gather information from the training data and thus apply the most appropriate approach of adaptive learning techniques.

5   Conclusions and Future Work

The relationship between the dual research lines of HCI and AI shows the importance of designing interfaces that can be adapted intelligently to the needs of the user. The adaptation model proposed assists in identifying characteristics of children with hearing disabilities and in turn using the techniques or suitable adaptation algorithms to make a classification according to the outputs desired. HCI is a line of research that can contribute to the requirements of the user model that will be used in AI to employ adaptive algorithms. As future work, it is intended to implement and evaluate the model in a case study on the design of a serious game for teaching literacy to children with hearing impairments that adjusts the level of difficulty of the activity and in turn modifies elements in the presentation.

References

1. González, G., Héctor, M., Duque, M., Nestor, D., Ovalle, C., Demetrio, A.: Modelo del Estudiante para Sistemas Adaptativos de Educación Virtual. Revista Avances en Sistemas e Informática 5(1), 199–206 (2008)

2. Mejía, A., Juárez, R.R., Inzunza, S., Valenzuela, R.: Implementing adaptive interfaces: a user model for the development of usability in interactive systems. In: Proceedings of the CUBE International Information Technology Conference, pp. 1–7 (2012)
3. Cano, S., Muñoz, A.J., Collazos, C.A., Amador, V.: Model for analysis of serious games for literacy in deaf children from user experience approach. In: Proceedings of the XVI International Conference on Human Computer Interaction (2015)
4. Froschl, C.: User modeling and user profiling in adaptive e-learning systems. Master's Thesis. Graz University of Technology (2005)
5. Mascio, T.D., Gennari, R., Vittorini, P.: The Design of an Intelligent Adaptive Learning System for Poor Comprehenders. Cognitive and Metacognitive Educational Systems: Papers from the AAAI Fall Symposium (2010)
6. Narkevicienè, G.A.: Deaf Children's Visual Recall and its Development in School Age, Vytauro Didziojo Universitetas K, p. 52 (2010)
7. de Bra, P., Houben, G.J., Wu, H.: AHAM: a dexter-based reference model for adaptive hypermedia. In: Proceedings of the ACM Conference on Hypertext and Hypermedia (Hypertext 1999), Darmstadt, Germany, vol. 2, pp. 147–156 (1999)
8. Chen, S., Zhang, J.: The adaptive learning based on learning style and cognitive state. In: International Symposium on Knowledge Acquisition and Modeling, pp. 302–306 (2008)
9. Brusilovsky, P.: Methods and techniques of adaptive hypermedia. User Model. User-Adap. Inter. **6**(2–3), 87–129 (1996)
10. Gutiérrez, J., Pérez, T.: Sistemas de Interacción Persona - Computador. En M. Ortega & J. Bravo (Eds.) Sistemas Hipermedia Adaptativos España: Ediciones de la Universidad de Castilla-La Mancha, pp. 159–179 (2001)
11. Frazer, A., Recio-Saucedo, A., Gilbert, L., Wills, G.: Profiling the educational value of computer games. Interact. Des. Architecture(s) J. – IxD&A **19**, 9–27 (2013)
12. Márquez, C.C., Jordán, G.C., Valldeperas, E.M.: Modelo Bayesiano del Alumno basado en el Estilo de Aprendizaje y las Preferencias. Revista IEEE-RITA **4**, 139–146 (2009)
13. Alonso, C., Gallego, D., Honey, P.: Los estilos de aprendizaje. Ediciones Mensajero, Bilbao (1999)
14. Gagné, R.: Las condiciones del aprendizaje. 4ta. edición, México: McGraw-Hill, New York (1985)
15. Mitchell, T.: Machine Learning. McGraw Hill, New York (1997)
16. Rim, R., Amin, M.M., Adel, M.: Bayesian networks for user modeling: predicting the user's preferences. In: 13th International Conference Hybrid Intelligent Systems (HIC), pp. 4–6 (2013)
17. Chen, Q., Norcio, A.F.: A neural network approach for user modeling. In: Conference Proceedings of the System, Man, and Cybernetics. Decision Aiding for Complex Systems, vol 12, pp. 13–16 (1991)
18. Felder, R.: Matters of style. ASEE. Prism **6**(4), 18–23 (1996)
19. Fleming, N.D., Mills, C.: Not Another Inventory, Rather a Catalyst for Reflection. To Improve the Academy **11**, 137–155 (1992)
20. Budiharto, W., Rachmawati, R.N, Ricky, M.Y, Chyntia, B.R.P.: The psychological aspects and implementation of adaptive games for mobile application. In: International Joint Conference on Awareness Science and Technology and Ubi-Media Computing (iCast-UMEDIA), pp. 163–169, pp. 2–4 (2013)
21. Grigonis, A., Narkevicienè, V.: Deaf Children's Visual Recall and Its Development in School Age. Vytauro Didziojo Universitetas K, p. 52 (2010)
22. Marschark, M., Everhart, V.S.: Problem-solving by deaf and hearing students: twenty questions. Deafness Educ int., pp. 65–82 (1999)

23. Tahir, R.: Analyzing the intelligence in user interfaces. In: SAI Intelligent Systems Conference, pp. 674–680 (2015)
24. Henry, L.: User inteface goals. AI Opportunities. AI Mag. **30**(4), 16–22 (2009)
25. Rohrbach, M.: Uwe Schmidt. Intelligent User Interfaces: Modelling the user. University of British Columbia (2008)
26. Gajos, K.Z., Everitt, K., Tan, D.S., Czerwinski, M., Weld, D.S.: Predictability and accuary in adaptive user interfaces. In: Proceedings of the SIGCHI Conference on Human Factors in Computing Systems, pp. 1271–1274 (2008)
27. Anne Anastasi: Test Psicológicos. Ediciones Aguilas, 2da Edición (1968)

A Validated Educational Format in Software Engineering Targeting Students' Collaboration Skills

Carolin Gold-Veerkamp[1]([✉]), Nina Kaelberer[1], Martina Kuhn[2], and Joerg Abke[1]

[1] University of Applied Sciences Aschaffenburg, Würzburger Straße 45,
63743 Aschaffenburg, Germany
{carolin.gold-veerkamp,nina.kaelberer,joerg.abke}@h-ab.de
[2] University of Applied Sciences & Arts Coburg, Friedrich-Streib-Straße 2,
96450 Coburg, Germany
martina.kuhn@hs-coburg.de

Abstract. In the context of the Bologna process the "shift from teaching to learning" is postulated to meet two central goals: To increase the students' employability and to foster needed competencies.

To be in a position to process methods and find solutions for highly complex, abstract, large, and multilayered problems, a Software Engineer has to have a lot of subject knowledge and technical competencies; but above all, he/she has to be able to work in – at least one – team.

For the purpose of preparing the students with professional knowhow and moreover with teamwork skills, the approach shown in this paper supplements an ex-cathedra teaching by a seminar and a project phase. This combination is dedicated to acquire theoretical knowledge in a collaborative and self-directed way. This is done in order to be able to deepen the learned matter, to share content through learning-by-teaching in groups and furthermore to apply the knowledge and skills in a simulated project, which constitutes a realistic situation and teamwork of an engineer as good as possible.

Keywords: Collaboration · Seminar · Project · Education · Wiki · Software Engineering

1 Introduction

Software Engineering (SWE) is hard to teach and learn, because of several different aspects, including a lot of abstract processes, different procedures that have to be used appropriately, the high complexity of problems/tasks and – as a consequence of these facets – the fact that the development of Software has to be done in a team.

Through the implementation of the Bologna Process, the "shift from teaching to learning" [1] is demanded in order to (1) increase the **employability** of students by (2) fostering needed **competencies**. Therefore the students shall gain

© Springer International Publishing Switzerland 2016
G. Meiselwitz (Ed.): SCSM 2016, LNCS 9742, pp. 335–346, 2016.
DOI: 10.1007/978-3-319-39910-2_31

(a) knowledge, (b) abilities and (3) competencies [2, p. 27f.]; listed in ascending order.

The transfer of the active role – and thus also the partial discharge of responsibility – from the teacher to the learner and the shaping of collaboration skills respectively the growth of experiences in a team, can be carried out in combination simultaneously by a guided **collaborative** and **self-controlled** knowledge acquisition and implementation.

The expected/required achievements can be condensed into: A deeper understanding of the subject matter, not only theoretical knowledge, but also the transmission of theory into practice ("realistic" software project – SWP), to work collaboratively and to acquire needed transferable skills (e.g., teamwork, communication, presentation, cooperation skills, conflict ability).

The subsequent section contains information about the context of the project and its intentions (see Sect. 2). In Sect. 3 the didactical approach of the course design in 2014 (see Sect. 3.1) – already published in [3] –and in contrast the planned concept for 2016 are displayed (see Sect. 3.2). Furthermore two major changes will be described in detail (the Story Line and the Grouping Phase; see Sects. 3.3 and 3.4). The two following Sects. 4 and 5 characterise the seminar– the focus of this paper – and the project phase. All of this combined is then summarised in Sect. 6, which includes an outlook containing ideas for improvement.

2   Context, Intentions and Objectives

At the University of Applied Sciences Aschaffenburg the focus is on the degree programme of Mechatronics (B.Eng.); especially on the course "Software Engineering" (5 ECTS) in the fourth semester and the courses "Computer Science I and II" (second and third semester; 5 ECTS each), which form the basic programming skills.

As the students of the Software Engineering course are undergraduates in an engineering subject, Computer Sciences and all related disciplines are not their key thematic area [4, p. 911].

Moreover, Software Engineering covers highly complex and abstract processes and techniques to solve large as well as multilayered problems and is therefore hard to understand, learn and teach.

Thus, the pursued objectives in 2015 and 2016 are:

1. **Activation and motivation:** The students should get activated by the need for self-studying and collaboration. To motivate them, the task is to work jointly on a seminar topic and a project and therefore to support teamwork, which is based on the necessity to orientate themselves within a team. The evaluations show that exactly this aim is the aspect the students like the most throughout the semesters (seminar & project).
2. **Sustainable knowledge:** To avoid "bulimic learning" in the seminar phase, ways to promote a continuous processing shall be implemented and the application of knowledge in a realistic project simulation [5] shall deepen the theoretical knowledge.

3   Didactical Overall Concept of the Course

In 2016 the didactical approach (see Sects. 3.1 and 3.2), which has been invented and tested in the years 2012–2015[1], was further developed on the basis of the design of two years ago (2014, see [3]). Here a short flashback trough the years is given:

- The didactical concept (see Fig. 1) was developed in 2012 (for more information see [6]).
- In 2013 the Wiki was used for the first time. For this, the MediaWiki engine (cf. [7,8]) was utilised.
- Since 2014 Moodle [9] as a learning management system (LMS) and the Moodle-Wiki are exploited. Consequently, all documents and artifacts during the seminar and project phase (see Sects. 4 and 5) are submitted via Moodle. Also central questions for the seminar topics have been generated to improve the quality of the Wiki articles.

To explain the main changes from 2014 [3] to the current (2015/2016) elaboration of the arrangement in detail, the following Subsections deal with the course designs of 2014 and 2016 (Sects. 3.1 and 3.2). Additionally, the Story Line (Sect. 3.3) and the Grouping (Sect. 3.4) are made a subject in this section, which is followed by a detailed look at the seminar and the project phase (Sects. 4 and 5).

3.1   Course Design in 2014

The course Software Engineering has a theoretical (ex-cathedra lectures) and a practical part, which are temporally separated. But their content is highly interrelated, as they both cover central theoretical input, which is of crucial importance for coping with the project phase.

Hence the practical sessions are split into seminar and project phase (see Fig. 1).

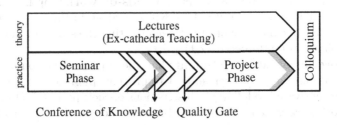

Fig. 1. Principle course design including highlighted evaluations (cf. [3,6])

---

[1] Throughout all years, two evaluations per semester – one after the seminar phase and one at the end of the Semester, i.e. following the project phase – took place.

1. The **lectures** are intended to provide theoretical professional contents in the form of ex-cathedra teaching. As the whole course is supported by the LMS Moodle, the materials for the lectures are available here.
2. The **practical lessons** are sequentially divided into seminar (first third of the semester) and project phase (remaining two thirds of the semester).
   a. The function of the **seminar phase** is to accumulate, compact, share and transfer ("learning by teaching" [10]) expert knowledge in groups self-directedly.
   b. In the **project phase** the students should use knowledge from the seminar and the lecture in a simulated software project. In this part technical as well as transferable skills are required, but also fostered.

3.2 Course Design in 2016

In contrast to 2014 (see Fig. 1), in 2016 (see Fig. 2) – and already in 2015 – some adaptations have been done in order to meet the objectives (Sect. 2):

1. The course is implemented into a **comprehensive "story"**, as the students are supposed to work in "companies", the semester is introduced by the customers for the students to recognize the meaningfulness of the holistic didactical concept to encourage knowledge acquisition (cf. Objective 2-1) and motivation (cf. Objective 2-1).
2. The **grouping** is done in a new format with a long-term prospect and less in small steps as before. Additionally, the students build the groups themselves to motivate them (cf. Objective 2-1).
3. At the beginning of the seminar phase the students **accumulate seminar topics** to strengthen their commitment. This is done in order to promote the self-organised group work (cf. Objective 2-1) and again to foster motivation (cf. Objective 2-1).
4. The **formulations of seminar topics** are revised in order to meet the collection of seminar topics.
5. Because of perennially occuring problems and negative statements – concerning the evaluations of the last years – a **hands-on workshop** introducing the development hardware (Fujitsu Dice-Kit[2]), is given in the first practical session. This is done on account of not demotivating the students while working on the platform (cf. Objective 2-1).
6. The **exercises of and for students** have been part of the course design for some time, but have not been subject to previous publications. The students are more motivated to follow the instructions of their peers (cf. Objective 2-1) while both parties benefit regarding their knowledge (cf. Objective 2-1).

The elements *collecting seminar topics* (see Pt. 3.2-3), *formulating seminar topics* (see Pt. 3.2-4) – as a consequence – and the *exercises of and for students*

---

[2] The Fujitsu Dice-Kit is an evaluation board including a 16-bit micro controller (MB90350) [11], which is used as a development platform in the project phase. It was designed for students.

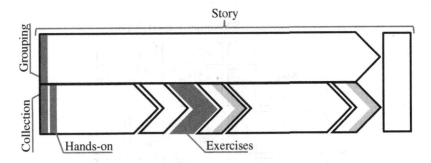

Fig. 2. Changes in the course design from 2014 to 2016

(see Pt. 3.2-6) are main changes in the seminar phase. Section 4 covers the seminar phase, paying special attention to these points (see Sects. 4.2 and 4.4).

The *hands-on workshop* (see Pt. 3.2-5) is introduced in order to support both phases; on the one hand the project phase, where the students have to implement a program for the Dice-Kit, and on the other hand the seminar phase, where the Dice-Kit is one seminar topic to hollow the theme after the hands-on workshop so that the students are prepared for the subsequent project.

The *comprehensive "story"* (see Pt. 3.2-1) as well as the *grouping* (see Pt. 3.2-2) are issues concerning the whole semester and therefore will be explained in detail hereafter (see Sects. 3.3, 3.4).

3.3   Story Line in 2016

Since last year (2015) the course is embedded in a story to raise the students' curiosity right at the beginning of the semester (1st lecture). This is done in order to make the students understand and see the necessity of the knowledge acquisition during the seminar and the lectures; to have the knowledge and tools as background that make the project manageable. This may help to strengthen the motivation of participants and to activate them (see Objective 2-1).

3.4   Grouping in 2016

The grouping is done by the students – with limitations of framework conditions (e.g., lecture plan) – in order to foster motivation.

For a better understanding of the process of grouping, its several steps are summarised in Table 1. The whole approach is also visualised in Fig. 3.

Because of the Story line (see previous Sec.), the decision was made to first separate the practical sessions[3] into two "companies" each (SWP1...6) to show the practical relevance and orientation, although the project phase is preceded by the seminar phase (see step 1 in Table 1).

---

[3] There are 3 parallel running practical sessions with approx. 20 students each and around 60 students each semester.

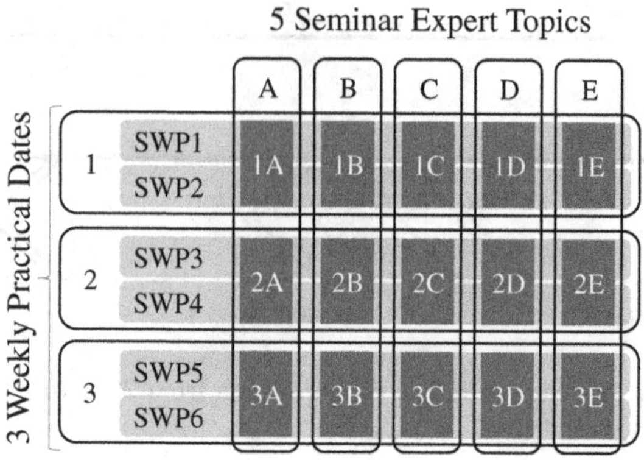

Fig. 3. Grouping in 2016 (cf. [3, p. 286])

Table 1. Grouping process in 2015 and 2016

	Step	Description	Purpose	Outcome
1st Lecture	1	Separation into SWP1...6• (half of group 1/2/3)	Commitment & motivation	Companies created by themselves
		Brain storming in groups: Which know-how do you lack?	First collaboration	Ideas for seminar topics
	2	Collection of topics + clustering (prepared topics A, B, C, D, E)	Commitment & motivation	Seminar topics
		Grouping in 1A, 2A, 3A, 1B, ...◁ to work on topics in seminar phase		
Seminar Phase	3	Work on expert topics	Knowledge acquisition	Wiki articles
	4	Merge of 1A, 2A, 3A to A° (and so on)	Knowledge assurance	Group Wiki articles & posters
		Conference of Knowledge	Knowledge transfer	Shared & transfered knowledge
	5	1st Quality Gate (written test)	Knowledge assessment	Grades for seminar phase
Project Phase	6	"Interchange" to SWP1, SWP2, SWP3, ... (experts of every seminar topic; cf. step 1)	Knowledge application (Wikis as a knowledge platform)	Good team work, artifacts, (project success)
	...	...	...	...

•) 10 students per company; 2 companies each practical session (1, 2, 3)

◁) 4 students (2 from each company "SWP1..6") times 5 (seminar topics A, B, C, D, E) times 3 (practical session 1, 2, 3) = 4 x 15

°) 12 students (4 students x 3 practical sessions 1, 2, 3)

These "companies" have the task to brain storm for needed knowledge, which they will have to acquire by themselves in the seminar phase.

During the seminar phase, the students have to work on one seminar topic (A, B, C, D, E); detailed explanation in Sect. 4. This is done by using Wikis in small groups of two to three students (1E, 2A, 3B, 5C,...; see steps 2 & 3 in Table 1).

To assure the quality of the Wiki contents and to reflect and evaluate the articles, the 15 Wikis (see Fig. 3) are merged into five group articles A, B, C, D and E (see step 4 in Table 1). This also reduces the students' effort to prepare themselves for the intermediate exam (the 1st Quality Gate; see step 5 in Table 1), in which every student has to demonstrate his/her knowledge concerning their own expert topic as well as those of the other groups.

Afterwards, the experts are interchanged (cf. "group or jigsaw puzzle"[4] [13]) and again form the companies (cf. steps 1&6 in Table 1).

4 Seminar Phase

The Wiki is the central tool used throughout the whole seminar phase.

The following Figure (Fig. 4) shows the **functions of the Wiki** (five elements at the top), which are subject of Sect. 4.1. Three more aspects are highlighted here: The **collection of seminar topics** (see Sect. 4.2), the **Conference of Knowledge** (see Sect. 4.3) and the **exercises of and for students** (see. Sect. 4.4).

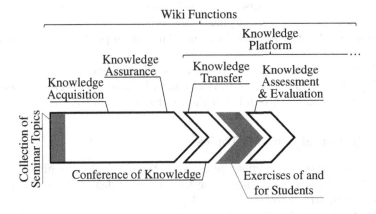

Fig. 4. Seminar phase and Wiki in 2016 with highlighted aspects

---

[4] The jigsaw puzzle/classroom is a similar 10-steps-learning-method to acquire knowledge in a self-directed way and to share it with peers (cf. steps 1–4 in Table 1), because "[j]ust as in a jigsaw puzzle, each piece – each student's part – is essential for the completion and full understanding of the final product" [12]; for more details see [12,13].

4.1 Wiki and Its Functions

The reasoning for using a Wiki instead of a text document is the opportunity to include media-rich contents (cf. [7,8,14]), besides the time- and location-independence, the access via the web and the author role of all team members.

As the publication [3] covers the functions of the Wiki in great detail, the four core functions of the Wiki are listed and explained briefly hereafter – in chronological order (cf. Fig. 4):

1. **Knowledge Acquisition:** The 15 small groups (see Fig. 3) first focus on knowledge acquisition of their topic. The parallelism of group working serves as a quality assurance mechanism.
2. **Knowledge Assurance:** To ensure the quality of the accumulated knowledge, a Conference of Knowledge (CoK) as one part of a Quality Gate was implemented. Three groups with the same seminar topic have to combine and exclude their acquired information in one group article and a poster, in order to regulate the quality and the information depth.
3. **Knowledge Transfer:** The transfer takes place in two parts:
   - The *CoK*, see Fig. 1, to pass on the knowledge and to benefit from learning-by-teaching.
   - The *exercises of and for students*, see. Sect. 4.4, in which the non-experts learn from their peers & the experts learn-by-teaching.

   The knowledge gained from team working is multiplied by the Wiki and spread over the whole semester.
4. **Knowledge Assessment:** The "Quality Gate" (see. Fig. 1 & Table 1-step 5) ensures that every students has gained knowledge of all five seminar topics before they enter the project phase.
5. **Knowledge Platform:** The Wiki is a knowledge platform in two perspectives:
   - To learn for the intermediate exam (see Table 1-step 4).
   - To look up content in the project phase, because experts are present, but their work in the group is not limited to their own topic.

4.2 Collection of Seminar Topics

At the beginning of the seminar phase the students collect seminar topics in order to foster their commitment. The topics are predefined by the laboratory team, but unknown on the students' side.

In the 1st lecture (see Table 1-step 1) the learners get ten minutes to work in the SWP on the question: What do you lack to be able to work collaboratively in your "company"[5]? Afterwards, the elements are collected in plenum and allocated to prepared cluster, which represent the predefined seminar topics.

In advance, the formulations of the seminar topics have been revised in order to – hopefully – meet the expected collection of seminar topics.

---

[5] The term "company" refers to SWP1...6, cf. Table 1.

4.3   Conference of Knowledge

The Conference of Knowledge can be described as an enlarged poster session and is used as a tool of "knowledge forwarding" [3, p. 284]. The students have to create a common poster "in order to illustrate [the key facts of] their seminar topic to the other groups" [3, p. 286]. This method was chosen to make sure that the students spend time on the other seminar subjects [3, p. 285].

4.4   Exercises of and for Students

This element takes place after the development of the Group Wikis and the CoK.

Within the three practical sessions, every seminar topic is deepened[6] by the experts. Hereby, a activation of learners takes place in two parts:

– Activation of experts: Have to find exercises and ways to "teach".
– Activation of peers: Are confronted with other topics and the application of this knowledge in an exercise (e.g., cooking spaghetti as a project management task in 2015).

5   Project Phase

The project phase covers recurrent submissions (see five elements at the top in Fig. 5; cf. seminar topics in Sect. 4) to foster the continuous associated work in the teams.

This phase also contains three customer dialogues per SWP.

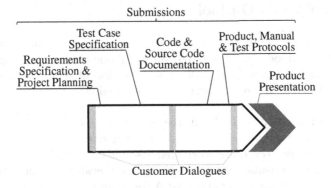

Fig. 5. Project phase in 2016 with highlighted aspects

---

[6] This is done in one practical session (90 min), so every expert team has approx. 15 min for their exercise.

5.1   Roles of the Laboratory Team

As the embedded systems laboratory team of the university at present consists of four persons, it is sensible to have clearly defined roles in the project phase:

- **Lecturer:** In the role of the observer and point of contact for theoretical questions.
- The **Laboratory engineer** answers technical question and lends a hand while progamming.
- The customers' role is embodied by the the **Research assistants**, i.e. they have the time schedule in mind, give feedback to the students.

5.2   Project Tools

The tools in the project phase are nearly covered by every seminar topic (cf. Table 2), except the topic "Requirements".

Table 2. Tools in the project phase on basis of the seminar topics

Seminar topic	Tool	Collaboration aspect
Project management	MS Project [15]	To organize collaboration
Hardware and Programming	Eclipse [16]	
Configuration and version management	SubVersion SVN [17]	To ease collaboration
Documentation (source code documentation & manual)	Doxygen [18]	

6   Summary and Outlook

The course and esp. the Wiki is still implemented in the existing learning management system Moodle [9]. The usage of central questions concerning the seminar topics has been very helpful [3]. The collection of seminar topics worked well, as the students' brain storming overlapped well with the predefined cluster (2015).

Therefore the usage of the Wiki, the collection and formulation of seminar topics have again been proven and should be exploited in 2016.

The teams have been quite motivated last semester (2015). This aspect as well as the linked activation should be the focus of evaluations in 2016.

One rather negative aspect remains: A lot of effort is done to evaluate and grade all the steps and artifacts the students produce during the semester. It is essential to define criteria to be able to grade fair and objective. Different schemes with defined criteria have already been established: e.g., one for the Wikis, one for posters, but also one to give feedback during the project concerning every submission. This was done in order to fasten the review process, to reduce the effort for lab team in general and to increase objectivity.

Could several elements be "outsourced" to the students? On the one hand, this might be too huge a responsibility, partially because they are in the middle of the learning process, i.e. they have no experiences concerning either factual knowledge or giving constructive feedback. On the other hand, students might be able to reflect the work of others and conversely their own.

This aspect has to be discussed.

As the title of this publication promises a "validated educational format", all semesters (2013–2015) have been validated from the students' as well as the lecturers' perspective (cf. Fig. 1[7]), however it is unfortunately beyond the scope of this publication to present these results in detail.

Acknowledgement. The present work as part of the EVELIN project was funded by the German Federal Ministry of Education and Research (Bundesministerium für Bildung und Forschung) under grant number 01PL12022B. The authors are responsible for the content of this publication.

References

1. Wildt, J.: The Shift from Teaching to Learning: Thesen zum Wandel der Lernkultur in modularisierten Studienstrukturen [German]. In: Bündnis, F., 90/Die Grünen im Landtag NRW (ed.) Unterwegs zu einem europäischen Bildungssystem, Ed., Düsseldorf, pp. 14–18 (2003)
2. Weinert, F.E.: Vergleichende Leistungsmessung in Schulen: Eine umstrittene Selbstverständlichkeit [German], ser. Beltz Pädagogik, pp. 17–32. Beltz, Weinheim (2002)
3. Abke, J., Gold, C., Kälberer, N., Kuhn, M.: Collaborative knowledge transfer via Wiki: a project based learning approach in software engineering. In: IEEE 2014 International Conference on Interactive Collaborative Learning (ICL), pp. 283–288 (2014)
4. Rodriguez Perez, S., Gold-Veerkamp, C., Abke, J., Borgeest, K.: A new didactic method for programming in C for freshmen students using LEGO mindstorms EV3. In: IEEE 2015 International Conference on Interactive Collaborative Learning (ICL), pp. 911–914 (2015)
5. Bloom, B.S., Engelhart, M.D., Furst, E.J., Hill, W.H., Krathwohl, D.R.: Taxonomy of Educational Objectives: The Classification of Educational Goals. Handbook I: Cognitive Domain. David McKay Company, New York (1956)
6. Abke, J., Gold, C., Roznawski, N., Schwirtlich, V., Sedelmaier, Y.: A new approach to collaborative learning in software engineering focussed on embedded systems. In: IEEE 2013 International Conference on Interactive Collaborative Learning (ICL), pp. 625–631 (2013)
7. Wikimedia Foundation Std. Mediawiki engine. http://www.mediawiki.org/wiki/MediaWiki. Accessed 02 Feb 2016
8. Ebersbach, A., Glaser, M., Heigl, R., Warta, A.: Wiki: Web Collaboration, 2nd edn. Springer, Heidelberg (2008). ISBN: 978-3-540-35150-4
9. Moodle Pty Ltd. Moodle. https://moodle.org/. Accessed 02 Feb 2016

---

[7] where students' evaluations are highlighted.

10. Grzega, M., Joachim, S.: The didactic model LdL (Lernen durch Lehren) as a way of preparing students for communication in a knowledge society. J. Educ. Teach. **34**(3), 167–175 (2008). http://www.joachim-grzega.de/GrzegaSchoener-LdL.pdf
11. Fujitsu Ltd.: *Fujitsu Dice-Kit*. http://www.robotics.uvc.ro/fujitsu/pdf/ReadMe.pdf. Accessed 02 Feb 2016
12. Network, S.P., Aronson, E.: The jigsaw classroom. http://www.jigsaw.org. Accessed 02 Feb 2016
13. Aronson, E., Blaney, N., Stephin, C., Sikes, J., Snapp, M.: The Jigsaw Classroom. Sage Publishing Company, New York (1978)
14. Erpenbeck, J., Sauter, W.: Kompetenzentwicklung im Netz: New Blended Learning Mit Web 2.0, 1st edn. Luchterhand-Fachverlag, Berlin (2007). (ISBN) 978-3-472-07089
15. Microsoft: MS Project. https://products.office.com/en-ie/Project/project-and-portfolio-management-software. Accessed 02 Feb 2016
16. The Eclipse Foundation: Eclipse. https://eclipse.org/. Accessed 02 Feb 2016
17. Apache Subversion Software Project: Subversion. http://www.subversion.org/. Accessed 02 Feb 2016
18. van Heesch, D.: Doxygen. http://www.doxygen.org. Accessed 02 Feb 2016

Mobile Player Experience Evaluation in RA Geolocalized Serious Games

Carina S. Gonzalez-Gonzalez[1], Habib M. Fardoun[2(✉)], Belén Armas[1], and Abdullah S. AL-Malaise ALGhamdi[2]

[1] Grupo de Interacción, Tecnologías y Educación (ITED),
Computer Engineering and Systems Department,
University of La Laguna, Santa Cruz de Tenerife, Spain
[2] Information Systems Department (IS),
Faculty of Computing and Information Technology (FCIT),
King Abdulaziz University, Jeddah, Saudi Arabia
hfardoun@kau.edu.sa, alu0100696677@ull.edu.es

Abstract. The aim of this paper is to propose the most appropriate tools and techniques to evaluate geolocated video games with augmented reality (RA). To do this, we have studied the assessment tools recommended by leading authors and User Experience (UX) researchers, Playability and Player Experience (PX). Of these instruments and techniques, tools and methods suitable for these types of games were selected. As a study case, it has been taken Progrezz assessment, a platform that allows gamificating real social actions, using this technology as support for mobile augmented reality geographic location. Finally, an organized initial assessment phase guide, which allows a multidimensional measure for UX/PX geolocated mobile games with RA is proposed.

Keywords: Geolocated serious games · AR · UX/PX · Playability

1 Introduction

Currently, there is growing interest in mobile applications and geo augmented reality applications for various purposes, such as marketing, tourism, or serious games [1]. In order to create effective applications, a key aspect is taken into account in the design users design their own experience with the application. Therefore, in this paper we will focus on studying the user experience (UX) [3] and the player experience (PX) [3] to contribute to the design of serious games geolocated augmented reality (RA) [4].

The UX is a developing concept, interdisciplinary, requiring research and study, applied to different systems, devices, contexts and people [2]. Also, the player experience (PX) is influenced by various external and internal factors to the subject [3]. For example, as external factors we find those related to (social, cultural, time, space) context or video game system (gameplay, mechanical, motor, narrative, interface devices, immersion sensors, etc.) [5, 6]. As the player internal factors we can find its own characteristics (e.g., chronological age and gender), psychological and/or physical, their preferences, their playing styles, their mental and cognitive models, among others [6].

© Springer International Publishing Switzerland 2016
G. Meiselwitz (Ed.): SCSM 2016, LNCS 9742, pp. 347–354, 2016.
DOI: 10.1007/978-3-319-39910-2_32

If we want to model and evaluate this experience we find variables and metrics of different types: qualitative and quantitative or concrete and abstract [7]. All this makes the selection tools, methods and suitable for the present case assessment techniques: serious games geolocated of RA.

This paper presents a methodology for evaluating serious games geolocated with RA. This methodology is organized at different times and includes different instruments and mixed evaluation methods. A guide is presented for test configuration. This guide includes the selection of the user group to evaluate, configuration-test/s for geolocation areas, the test script and the different instruments to be used before, during and after the test. The instruments that have been selected and used are types of players' test [8], playability test [6], questionnaires gaming experience [9], focus groups and analysis of logs. This methodology has been validated using a serious game created by the research group, called Progrezz [10–13], which is described in the next section.

2   Progrezz: Serious Geolocated Game with AR

The Progrezz platform is born as a project of free and open-source software (MIT license) that seeks to create a video game designed for smartphones and designed as a web application and it stills in a development state. It aims to intertwine reality with their own history and game mechanics, so there's an energy called "entropy" symbolizes the social imbalance, which has been generated by all those negative actions that manifest in today's society. Starting from this reality, the player is invited to embody a member of a clandestine network of volunteers, seeking to stop civilization's collapse and restore harmony to the world. Using geolocation, the user is provided a stage to explore, where the possibility of finding messages and other items located in the real map is one of the basic mechanics, whose collection is linked to the physical movement of the player to place concrete (Fig. 1).

The utility of the collected objects can advance the story (discovering new mechanical or increasing the level and privileges player), promote events, contain texts advanced players, etc. In addition, you must complete a series of mini games at every step to achieve different objectives. It also seeks that all players can contact other volunteers and identify critical points of the environment through geolocated messages and other resources. Likewise, it is possible to detect and enhance the places where positive actions take place (even contribute economically). That is, the key feature is that users will have the ability to help society while they play and advance in Progrezz. According to the above, it is intended to function as a supportive social network and platform for the dissemination of actions and social movements and voluntary, allowing somehow, visualizes positive actions that happen in our environment both locally and globally. These actions will be reinforced with gamification component surrounding each action carried Progrezz players. Some gameplay elements of Progrezz include territoriality and the feeling of belonging to a global group, adding a sense of solidarity to the game, because the impact is quantified in reality made by the player.

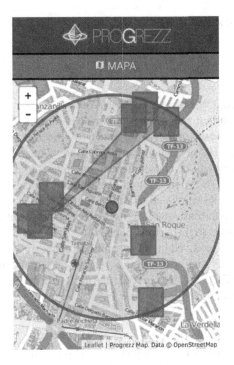

Fig. 1. Progrezz map

In the absence of defined standards or guidelines for evaluating UX geolocated mobile games, this work has been evaluated, selected and adapted different techniques and instruments that allow the evaluation of this platform. Following evaluation designed specifically for this type of mobile games described.

3   Evaluation Proposal

Table 1 shows the phases and activities in which evaluation has organized a mobile game geolocated with RA, as well as the people involved in them are presented.

Table 1. Organization Assessment

Phase	Activities	People
Pre test	- Setting the group, objectives and test area - Prepare test script - Identify and player profile	Evaluators Players
Test	- Evaluate the gaming experience (GEC) [9] via mobile: basic, in-game and post-game	Players
Post Test	- Reviewing group experience (Focus_Group) - Evaluate game's playability - Logs review	Evaluators Players/Experts

We will describe each of the activities carried out to evaluate the geolocated game with RA.

3.1 Pre-test

3.1.1 Set the Group, Objectives and Test Area

The ideal number of participants for the test was determined to be between 10 and 12 people, in order to ensure the proper development of it in a 3-hour session. In addition, the group must be balanced in the number of men and women to avoid bias in gender.

As for the ages, they will be chosen depending on the target audience of the game. For example, in the case of Progrezz, it will be between 18 and 45 years.

The user profile should be related to your level of experience with mobile technologies and geo games. In the case of expert users in geolocated games, they will be asked to act as expert evaluators to inspect the playability of the game.

Also, the goals to be achieved in the test must be correctly located on a map, so that are achieved in a walking tour of the city chosen for the test, the duration of the testing session. In the case of Progrezz, we proceeded to design distribute messages in different streets of the city of La Laguna in Tenerife.

3.1.2 Prepare the Test Script

The test script includes instructions should be given to participants, as well as everything that should be considered for conducting the test: necessary tools, links, resources, etc.

Before starting the test, players must complete the questionnaire on player profile (following Marczewski proposal [8]) so on-line, save the result obtained from it and send it via email to an address given by the evaluators. Here are accessed from the mobile device to the serious game.

In the case of Progrezz, access is performed by using the same browser and login request from a personal account (Facebook, Twitter, Google, Github or Steam). It shall authorize the application to use the GPS location and use your phone camera, in addition to activating the gyroscope (screen rotation). Once the user is in Progrezz account, you can choose from:

– Messages, where you can see unread messages, unread messages, which are available to unlock and fragments of incomplete messages.
– To unlock a message, you must complete a mini game.
– Profile, where the user level and data on the range of vision that is available, according to their level, the distance that must be the fragment to collect to collect it and the accuracy of detecting them will be displayed. In the first few levels players cannot even, post messages on the platform.
– Map where the location of the player and the possible locations of messages shown around. The blue circle indicates the vision range, the red squares areas where you can find messages. The red squares triangles linking together fragments of the same message.
– Scanner, where you can access the viewer augmented reality game. In it they appear blue-green diamonds when we stand before a message fragment to collect.

– The scanner has three modes: camera viewfinder, where you show what is seen directly from the phone's camera viewer augmented reality, where the world increased to the original camera image overlays, and viewer for reality glasses increased, designed for use with glasses Oculus Rift like.

Once inside the game, it will be inserted into the narrative of it. Thus, in Progrezz the player will propose an adventure that is part of a secret society that tries to save the world doing positive social actions. Specifically, for testing has been introduced in the system a total of 17 messages, some of which are divided into fragments as a tutorial. The player's goal is to collect the different messages. To do this, you must move around the map to the red areas and, once there, use the augmented reality viewer to find messages. When the player has the message, you must "capture" for later, you can unlock your reading. Once you have all the fragments of each message, you can access a panel where you collected so far will be displayed. If you want to read one, simply select it, after overcoming a small mini game, its content is displayed onscreen. They have to collect 17 messages to complete the mission.

The test has been designed to be carried out in one day, although the duration will depend largely upon the involvement of the player.

During the game session, the player must pause to complete the questionnaire that will measure the experience during the game. The hyperlink to the questionnaire will be sent to the user during the course of the evaluation.

Once the game session, the user must complete the remaining two modules of the questionnaire gaming experience: the basic module, which will measure the player's experience during the game and post-game module that will measure the feelings of the player once he has stopped playing.

In addition, expert players, who are those who already have experience with similar, such as Ingress, also must complete a questionnaire heuristic that measures factors Playability in different facets, as the intrinsic gameplay, gameplay mechanics, Artistic Playability games the Personal or Social Playability Playability.

Finally, it will be held a Focus Group with test participants to discuss the experience, achieved and frustrated goals, the difficulty of the proposed mission, satisfaction with the goals achieved, possible errors of the platform, the main problems, etc.

3.2 Test: Game Experience Questionnaire (GEQ)

The Gaming Experience Questionnaire (GEQ) [9] has a modular structure comprising: a basic questionnaire, social presence module and a module for post-game.

The three modules are intended to be evaluated immediately after you finish a game session, in the order listed above. The first and second parts are polls feelings and thoughts Player while playing the game; the third part, the post-game module evaluates how players after finished playing feel.

In our case we have developed an in-game version of GEQ, in order to assess the gaming experience in multiple intervals during a game session.

Thus, the following modules are proposed:

- GEQ Basic module: We could say that this is the central part of the GEQ. We will serve to evaluate the gaming experience through seven components: Dipping, flow, competition, positive affect, negative affect, tension and challenge.
- GEQ module In-Game: In-Game GEQ module is the minimum version of the basic questionnaire is used to assess the gaming experience as it takes the game session, which will facilitate the validation of continuous indicators in real time.
- GEQ module Post-Game: The post-game module evaluates how players after having stopped playing felt.

3.3   Post-Test

3.3.1   Focus Group

After users will run the test and, after making the corresponding questionnaires, it is conducted Focus Group session where the highlights of the test are discussed. After the session, a transcript of it is done and proceeds to its qualitative analysis. The phases of this analysis are:

1. Read the transcription and identification of the issues that are most relevant in accordance with the purpose of observation.
2. The process of categorization and coding.
3. Representation of the information collected for each category in a matrix.
4. Obtaining results and drawing conclusions.

3.3.2   Playability

The evaluation of the gameplay should be done by expert users, since a validated questionnaire about the player's experience with different heuristics that allow inspection of different criteria organized into dimensions [2], which measures the quality of use is use a videogame. These quality measures are:

- Satisfaction: Liking or complacency player before the full game or in some specific aspects of it. It can be measured by the percentage of game discovered or unlocked by the number of challenges (primary and secondary) resolved.
- Learning: Easy to understand and master the system, the mechanics of the game and how to interact with it. It can be measured by the number of attempts to challenge and invested according to the intended time.
- Effectiveness: Time and how to use resources to provide fun to the player while it achieves the objectives. It can be measured by the number of shares not carried out according to the time between objectives, goals and challenges.
- Immersion: Ability to believe what is at stake and integrated into the virtual world shown in the game. It can be measured by the time and attempts to challenge and by SAGAT technique [14].
- Motivation: Feature game that moves the person to perform certain actions and persist in them for completion. The percentage of unlocked game and the number of items and secondary objectives achieved can measure it.

- Emotion: Impulse originated involuntary response to stimuli that induce feelings and video game triggers automatic reaction behavior. It can be measured by the Test of emotional grid [15] and by biometric observation and thinking aloud.
- Socialization: Measurement of the elements that promote social factor or group experience; thanks to the reactions engage with other players or with other game characters. The number and type of messages between group members can measure it and the number of shared and used resources.

3.3.3   Logs Analysis

Records of the test participants are analyzed for different regarding the effectiveness and efficiency in achieving the goals of the game metrics, such as:

- Effectiveness on the goal: Number of goals that have been achieved correctly.
- Completed Challenges: Completed challenges number.
- Frequency attempts in achieving goals: Number of attempts to achieve the goal.
- Goal time: Time required by the user to achieve a goal.
- Optimal route: Variability of the route used by the user to achieve the goal against the optimal path.

4   Conclusions

This article has presented a guide for evaluating the user experience (UX) and the player experience (PX) in a geolocated video game that uses augmented reality organized so that to analyze the gameplay as a measure of quality use. This guide was then proposed to evaluate different techniques and methods UX and PX for video games. In addition, it has been applied to a specific case study: Progrezz.

The guide consists of three phases: a phase of pre-test, a test and a posttest. The pre-test phase, comprising various activities, such as setting up the group of participants who will perform, objectives or goals to be achieved and the area of the test. In addition, it should develop the script for the test and identify the player profile, which in our case is selected profiles described by Marczewski. Then, in the test phase, it is important to evaluate the experience in the game. For this we have chosen to select the GEQ questionnaire and an adaptation of it for a test at different intervals during the course of the test. Finally, as the close of the assessment test, conducting a focus group to analyze the main difficulties encountered in performing the test as well as suggestions and proposals for improvement it is proposed. Moreover, expert users should perform a test inspection of the gameplay of the game. Finally, evaluators review the logs obtained from test development in order to obtain metrics effectiveness and efficiency of the game. Following this proposal as a guide for evaluating geolocated mobile games with RA is possible to obtain qualitative and quantitative metrics that allow multidimensional assessment UX/PX as quality video game use. Finally, say that this guide is an initial assessment proposal for a case study where there are standards, but that it should be revised and refined metrics for tighter UX/PX geolocated mobile games with RA.

References

1. Walz, S.P., Deterding, S. (eds.): The Gameful World– Approaches, Issues Applications. The MIT Press, Cambridge (2015)
2. Rusu, C., Rusu, V., Roncagliolo, S., González, C.: Usability and user experience: what should we care about? Int. J. Inf Technol. Syst. Approach (IJITSA) **8**(2), 1–12 (2015). doi:10.4018/IJITSA.2015070101
3. Engl, S., Nacke, L.E.: Contextual influences on mobile player experience– a game user experience model 4. Entertainment Comput. **4**(1), 83–91 (2012). http://dx.doi.org/10.1016/j.entcom.2012.06.001. February 2013, ISSN 1875-9521
4. Bacca, J., Baldiris, S., Fabregat, R., Graf, S., Kinshuk.: Augmented reality trends in education: a systematic review of research and applications. Educ. Technol. Soc. **17**(4), 133–149 (2014)
5. Di Loreto, I.: Social interactive systems design for serious games. In: C. Gonzalez (ed.) Student Usability in Educational Software and Games: Improving Experiences, pp. 174–200. Information Science Reference, Hershey (2013). doi:10.4018/978-1-4666-1987-6.ch008
6. Sánchez, J.L., Iranzo, R.M., Vela, F.L.: Enriching the experience in video games based on playability development techniques. In: C. Gonzalez (ed.) Student Usability in Educational Software and Games: Improving Experiences, pp. 87–117. Information Science Reference, Hershey (2013) doi:10.4018/978-1-4666-1987-6.ch004
7. Nacke, L.E., Drachen, A., Goebel, S.: Methods for evaluating gameplay experience in a serious gaming context. Int. J. Comput. Sci. Sport **9**(2/Special Issue) (2010)
8. Marczewski, A.: A Player Type framework for gamification design. http://www.gamified.uk/user-types/. Retrieved 8 December 2015
9. Brockmyer, J.H., Fox, C.M., Curtiss, K.A., McBroom, E., Burkhart, K.M., Pidruzny, J.: The development of the game engagement questionnaire: a measure of engagement in video game-playing. J. Exp. Soc. Psychol. **45**(4), 624–634 (2009). http://dx.doi.org/10.1016/j.jesp.2009.02.016, ISSN 0022-1031
10. Progrezz website. http://socialmemorycompany.com:9292/pages/client/index.html
11. González-Rodríguez, C.: Módulo de Realidad Aumentada Geolocalizada. Trabajo fin de Grado. Ingeniería Informática. Universidad de La Laguna (2015)
12. Herzog Cruz, D. Progrezz back-end. Trabajo fin de Grado. Ingeniería Informática. Universidad de La Laguna (2015)
13. Armas, B.: Técnicas de evaluación para videojuegos geolocalizados. Trabajo fin de Grado. Ingeniería Informática. Universidad de La Laguna (2015)
14. Endsley, M.R.: Situation awareness global assessment technique (SAGAT). In: Proceedings of the IEEE 1988 National Aerospace and Electronics Conference, NAECON 1988, pp. 789–795. IEEE, May1988
15. Mehrabian, A.: Evidence bearing on the affiliative tendency (MAFF) and sensitivity to rejection (MSR) scales. Curr. Psycho. **13**(2), 97–116 (1994)

Gaggle on the Gavel: Designing an Interactive Website to Create a Community of Lawyers

Sara Anne Hook[✉] and Shilpa Pachhapurkar

Department of Human-Centered Computing,
Indiana University School of Informatics and Computing,
535 W. Michigan Street, Indianapolis, IN 46202, USA
sahook@iupui.edu, shilpach@umail.iu.edu

Abstract. Law is behind other industries and professions in its implementation of technology that could make the practice of law and the delivery of legal services more effective and satisfying. Although there has been considerable development in legal technology over the past few years, research identified the need for an interactive LinkedIn-style online community for lawyers to communicate other lawyers. Such a community would be particularly beneficial for solo practitioners, lawyers in small firms and lawyers in rural communities and would also provide a convenient way to connect with lawyers for referrals and recommendations, for specialized expertise and to develop contacts in different geographic locations. Tentatively titled Gaggle on the Gavel is an attempt to create such a community that would gather a number of attractive features and functionality under one umbrella and be compliant with the rules of professional conduct with respect to client confidentiality, security, advertising and solicitation. A system has been designed, prototyped and revised based on feedback from a focus group of lawyers.

Keywords: Community computing · Information presentation · Interaction design · Legal technology · Interactive community

1 Introduction

In many ways, law is behind other industries and professions in its implementation of technology. Fortunately, a number of legal technology entrepreneurs and academics are designing systems that will make the study and practice of law more efficient and less expensive. New companies are coming into the marketplace to challenge long-standing monopoly-like situations such as have been enjoyed by traditional legal research companies LexisNexis and Westlaw. [1–3] These companies now offer comprehensive practice management systems as well as more targeted software for internal law firm processes such as time-keeping and billing. [4] Websites assist potential clients in locating and connecting with lawyers as well as allow lawyers to promote their services to the public. [5–7] Recent issues of the ABA Journal and other publications have illuminated many attempts to deploy technology to various specialty areas, to make the practice of law more efficient, to create and respond to new areas of practice within the law, and to move the provision of legal services into the 21st century. [8–14] Two

G. Meiselwitz (Ed.): SCSM 2016, LNCS 9742, pp. 355–364, 2016.
DOI: 10.1007/978-3-319-39910-2_33

benefits will be realized from the continued deployment of technology into the field of law: the creation of alternative legal careers, such as in legal operations, legal technology and data protection, in an era where there are too many lawyers [15, 16] and the time this provides for lawyers to fill their intended role as counselors and work on higher-level duties that require the lawyer's skills and expertise rather than more mundane tasks that can be easily accomplished via technology or delegated to support staff. [17] The sheer amount of evidence generated by even a simple court case, along with the need to practice law more efficiently and cost-effectively, means that data analytics and data visualization are needed, including for electronic discovery, litigation management and information governance [18–21].

Our research has identified an unserved niche within the legal technology marketplace. We observed that there was no comprehensive system for lawyers to connect with each other externally in a secure environment that would help them build a professional network of colleagues across the U.S. and even around the world. Our interactive website is intended to provide a LinkedIn-style community specifically for lawyers and will not be available for access by the general public. The tools within our community, called Gaggle on the Gavel, are totally within the lawyer's discretion as to how much of the system he or she wants to use, such as referrals, calendars and tracking of continuing legal education (CLE) seminars and other events, who he or she wants to connect with, and how much information will be shared with external colleagues about cases, career opportunities or research interests. Gaggle on the Gavel will include visualizations that will show trends in the law with respect to the kinds of cases being filed and other issues and statistics that lawyers will be interested in and that will help with strategic planning for law firms. This paper features screenshots from the most recent iteration of Gaggle on the Gavel, provides diagrams of the information architecture and interaction flow, and shares the results of a focus group we conducted in our efforts to design a compelling online community for lawyers.

2 Methods

A thorough review of the literature was conducted to determine the state of technology in law practice. In addition to articles that provided predictions for the future of legal technology, we reviewed articles on document management systems, on the impact of big data on law and legal technology devoted to specific areas, such as intellectual property law and legal research, on entrepreneurs in legal technology and on data visualization, to name but a few. From this research, we determined that although there was increasing attention to developing technology tools for law, there was not an interactive community specifically for lawyers and for lawyers only. Thus, our intent has been to design an interactive community limited to lawyers rather than a website that would be accessible by current and potential clients and the public at large. A review of existing technology indicated that there were many tools for internal law firm management, such as timekeeping, billing and case management as well as productivity tools – either as stand-alone products or as full-featured law firm management systems. Thus, our task became to develop something that was intended for external rather than internal contact management and community-building. We gave our interaction the tentative title of Gaggle on the Gavel, not only because it described our logo of birds sitting on a gavel, one of the two most prominent images of the legal profession, but also because it captured the concept of community. Having at least a tentative title for the system that we were developing helped to move it from the theoretical realm of design into thinking about how it would be promoted and used in the real world of the legal profession.

A number of considerations have informed the development of Gaggle on the Gavel. The prototype and initial design and flow of the website are based on established usability principles and additional expertise in typography. Because of the nature of the profession that Gaggle on the Gavel is being designed for, we have been especially cognizant of setting the right tone with the layout, color scheme, font and logo. By confining the website to lawyers only, it prevents our users from violating the prohibitions related to marketing and advertising as outlined in the ABA Model Rules of Professional Conduct and as adopted, in whole or in part, by the states where the lawyer is licensed to practice. [22–24] Features within Gaggle on the Gavel, including who and what information to share, address the lawyer's duty to safeguard client confidentiality, as embodied under Rule 1.6, Rule 1.9 and 1.18, to name but a few. Thus, in deciding where we would focus our efforts, we were mindful of the need to protect client confidentiality and to not run afoul of the restrictions on advertising and solicitation. Many of these concerns were reduced by not having a website that would be available to the public and by leaving it to the lawyer's discretion about how much to share about a particular case. However, the need for security is paramount, not only to protect what might be private information, but to reassure a lawyer who wants to participate in the community that he or she will not be violating any disciplinary rules or putting confidential client information at risk. Thus, our problem space was defined: a social networking platform that would be attractive, easy to use and allow a lawyer to construct his or her own network for information sharing and support. We saw our community as being especially useful for solo and small firm lawyers as well as lawyers in rural areas, who are often quite isolated as compared with colleagues in large law firms or in major metropolitan areas with active bar associations.

Once we decided that an interactive community was going to be our focus, we needed to develop a "persona" of the typical user and how we would capture these characteristics. The next step in our process was to list all of the features and functionality that we thought would be useful in an interactive community of lawyers. Among the items on our initial list were a place to share cases (but with role-based access and privacy settings in place), a profile page, data visualizations and statistical representations, appointments, calendars and reminders, notifications of conferences and meetings, recommendations, an option to refer cases to lawyers with specific expertise or licensed in a particular location (with privacy settings available), a calculator to track charges or a cost sheet or template if needed for referrals, a knowledge base and a place to select contacts. In the case of recommendations, we decided that developing a rating sheet or questionnaire would be helpful and would allow some consistency in scores. To simplify even further, we considered having Gaggle on the Gavel merely provide an opportunity to endorse a colleague rather than require a rating, with stars used as a designation. At least one commentator has advised lawyers to be careful about endorsements on LinkedIn due to the fact that this may be misleading and appear to be touting expertise that the lawyer may or may not have.

Many states require lawyers to participate in a certain number of CLE hours as a condition of being licensed to practice in that state. Failure to complete the required number of hours can mean disciplinary action, including suspension from practice. Once a year, the body overseeing this may send out a printed report that is outdated. As a result, too many lawyers find themselves registering for expensive CLE seminars in December in order to fulfill their required hours. To address this problem, Gaggle on the Gavel includes a tracking system whereby the lawyer can easily monitor completed and upcoming CLE activities, reducing the risk of a shortage of hours at the end of the reporting period or having to quickly register for expensive seminars that are not in the lawyer's area of interest.

Once the basic design had been developed, we convened a focus group of lawyers and conducted interviews. Our series of 12 questions illuminated the kinds of features that lawyers would be interested in having versus those that were of less interest or that duplicated existing systems. The feedback indicated that an online posting forum would be useful, where lawyers could share interesting information or trends in the law and which would help them develop contacts with other lawyers. Although we had originally planned on including links to reference materials, the lawyers indicated that while this feature might be useful, its utility is sometimes limited and would be very cumbersome to construct. Organization of work through the application would be appreciated, especially if there could be a way to assign priorities to tasks. One important feature that was highlighted in our interviews was a lawyer's need to develop cordial relationships with clients and other lawyers, such as by remembering their birthdays and anniversaries. Thus, a "tickler" system with more than just a name and date would be useful. Because of the way we set out to design Gaggle on the Gavel, with the power for sharing information being the lawyer's choice, confidentiality of information within the system was of less concern to focus group members. Focus group members indicated that what they were most interested in was a feature that would allow them to build a convenient contact list of colleagues working in other areas of the law, including both personal and professional information, so that they could provide referrals and obtain assistance with cases outside of their own areas of practice and jurisdiction. The lawyers were particularly intrigued by data visualizations that would illuminate trends in the law as a way to help them better focus their areas of practice and refine their marketing approaches. An overview of time spent as billable hours, on CLE seminars and in pro bono activities would be useful so that a lawyer could track his or her efficiency. Currently, all these resources are not available under one umbrella. Thus, focus group members indicated that it would be beneficial to have tools such as calendars, reminders, informational content, networking, and practice management tools available within one system. Our original philosophy for Gaggle on the Gavel evolved into a toolbox, with multiple applications being brought together, encompassing both the concept of an interactive community and a convenient dashboard.

More recently, in order to encourage lawyers to provide pro bono legal services to low-income citizens, many states have adopted mandatory pro bono reporting as part of the license renewal process. Yet many lawyers do not have a good way to account for their pro bono activities so that the total hours to report at the end of the year will be accurate. Moreover, one reason that many lawyer have resisted the mandatory reporting rule is because of the difficulty of keeping track of pro bono hours, with a fear that over- or under-reporting will be a cause for disciplinary action. [25] A feature to allow lawyers to capture their pro bono hours contemporaneously has been added to Gaggle on the Gavel.

3   Results

One of the first activities in designing Gaggle on the Gavel was to develop a logo that would be professional and invoke the sense of community, but that would also have a bit of humor to it. Thus, the image of several birds sitting on a gavel, one of the two images most often used to designate the legal profession, was chosen. A variety of color schemes were experimented with before deciding on the combination of black, tan and gold, which would convey a sense of professionalism and be easy to read (Fig. 1).

Fig. 1. Evolution of Gaggle on the Gavel

In order to capture the individual elements and data that would be needed in each specific screen of Gaggle on the Gavel, an information architecture diagram was prepared (Fig. 2).

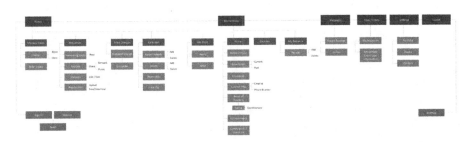

Fig. 2. Information architecture for Gaggle on the Gavel

In order to assure that a user could move smoothly between the various screens within Gaggle on the Gavel, a graphical representation of the journey of a user from initial login to each segment of the system was developed (Fig. 3).

Because Gaggle on the Gavel is, first and foremost, intended to be an interactive community, the system revolves around the opportunity to have a clean, attractive and

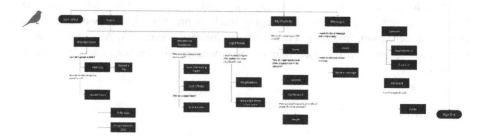

Fig. 3. Interaction flow

compelling profile that is easy to read and update. Among the information that the lawyer can include on his or her profile page are a photograph, basic information about work experience and education, any certifications (provided that these are in compliance with the Rules of Professional Conduct indicating specialization), recommendations, posts and number of contacts. At the top of the screen is a link to the lawyer's portfolio, messages and legal trends, which is a placeholder for visualizations (Fig. 4).

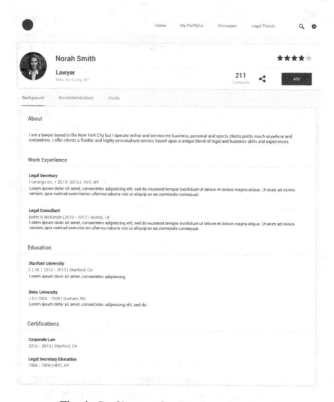

Fig. 4. Profile page for Gaggle on the Gavel

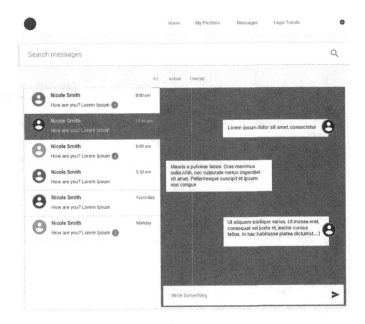

Fig. 5. Inbox for Gaggle on the Gavel

As an interactive community, Gaggle on the Gavel needed an inbox for communication between the lawyer and his or her approved contacts (Fig. 5).

The most useful features of Gaggle on the Gavel are the tracking tools that allow the lawyer to correctly capture CLE hours needed and completed as well as pro bono services provided. Thus, the screen for the CLE personal log is shown. Note that this gives the lawyer an opportunity to add new entries and also keeps track of each category of CLE hours earned, with a convenient graphic at the top of the screen indicating the hours that are pending and an option to print the screen (Fig. 6).

Additional sections of Gaggle on the Gavel - including functionality to manage cases and track charges, a place to save resources such as interesting articles and cases, calendars and job opportunities, and some sample data visualizations - were memorialized using a series of initial wireframes for later revision and refinement.

4   Discussion

The development of the external-looking features of Gaggle on the Gavel has been completed. Another facet of the project that is still under development is one that addresses the concept of a dashboard for capturing a lawyer's productivity, at least in the aggregate. As law firms move away from the billable hour to more of a project-based system as a measure of employee work and the basis for how the client will be charged, it is essential for lawyers to begin to discern how their time is being spent. Among the activities that might be captured on a dashboard are CLE hours, pro bono hours, client hours (including court time, travel time and meetings with clients),

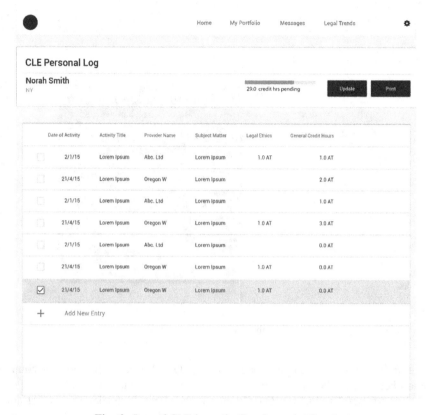

Fig. 6. Log of CLE hours in Gaggle on the Gavel

appointments, meetings that are internal to the law firm (such as partner and management committees), bar association activities and law firm marketing. Even a simple circle or bar chart that shows the relative time spent on each type of activity would be useful. This would be for the lawyer's own use and quite apart from the information gathered and presented by the law firm and used for annual reviews and salary decisions. Like LinkedIn, Gaggle on the Gavel is intended to be something that a lawyer chooses to participate in as an individual professional, rather than a system that is supplied or required by the law firm.

5 Further Work

One of the issues we have grappled with is whether to have a convenient dashboard as part of our interactive community, so that the lawyer can tell, at a glance, the time he or she is devoting to client matters, CLE seminars, pro bono service and law firm marketing activities. On the one hand, we hesitate to duplicate what is already being provided by internal law firm management software. On the other hand, our dashboard was conceived as a simple summary of a lawyer's time, rather than as a detailed designation of each case and event. Another aspect of including a dashboard is how to design a seamless carry-over of time and calendar information from a law firm's internal management software system to Gaggle on the Gavel. This would be problematic for a number of reasons, including the need to provide some sort of software or app for a number of different law firm management systems as well as any security and/or privacy considerations for allowing this type of transmission, being mindful of various rules of professional conduct. We do not want to increase the risk that confidential information about clients or on the law firm's internal operations is inadvertently shared when a lawyer accesses Gaggle on the Gavel. Moreover, the overarching philosophy of Gaggle on the Gavel was that it would be externally focused, and yet this is a tool that is more internal in nature.

Another feature of Gaggle on the Gavel to be developed is data visualizations, which was highlighted as something that focus group members would be interested in having for law firm marketing and long-range planning. This feature also is something that the literature indicates is needed by the legal profession.

References

1. Li, V.: Contracts 2.0: technology rewires the drafting and reviewing of contracts. A.B.A. J. **100**(11), 30–31 (2014)
2. Li, V.: They're no hacks: technology takes center stage as a tool to improve access to justice. A.B.A. J. **100**(10), 66–67 (2014)
3. Talwar, R.: All eyes are on the technology horizon. Peer to Peer **30**(2), 44–48 (2014)
4. Clio: Practice Management Simplified. Res Gestae **58**(6), 26 (2015)
5. Avvo: Find a Lawyer. http://www.avvo.com/find-a-lawyer
6. ZeekBeek. https://www.zeekbeek.com/
7. RocketLawyer. https://www.rocketlawyer.com/
8. Ambrogi, R.J.: Welcoming in: three new products help with client intake. A.B.A. J. **101**(8), 31 (2015)
9. Earl, E.: Beat the computer: law profs develop an analytical tool to help better understand court decisions. A.B.A. J. **100**(12), 12 (2014)
10. Krause, J.: Anti-Corruption tech: a Harvard hackathon brings practicality to political causes. A.B.A. J. **101**(9), 33 (2015)
11. Laird, L.: Parole, prison and compiling data. A.B.A. J. **101**(9), 36 (2015)
12. Tashea, J.: Cleaning records by the thousands. A.B.A. J. **101**(9), 39 (2015)
13. Li, V.: True to transparency. A.B.A. J. **101**(9), 40 (2015)
14. Council, J.: Startups Take Cloud-Based Tech Savvy to Legal Realm. The Indiana Lawyer 26, 4 (May 20-June 2, 2015)
15. Henderson, W.: What the jobs are: new tech, new client needs create a new field of legal operations. A.B.A. J. **101**(10), 36–43 (2015)
16. Hermann, R.L.: 10 Hottest Alternative Legal Careers. Nat. Jurist **25**(3), 12–13 (2016)
17. Odendahl, M.: Returning Lawyers to Their Role as Counselors. The Indiana Lawyer 25, 4, 9 (February 11–24, 2015)
18. Hearsay: Up, Up, Up. A.B.A. J. **101**(6), 13 (2015)
19. King, V.: Data Visualization for Legal: Why You Need It and How to Start. ITLA White Paper. Austin, TX: International Legal Technology Association, pp. 10–16, October 2014

20. Ashtor, J.: The future of patent analysis at Skadden. Peer to Peer **31**(2), 36–38 (2015)
21. Minick, T.: Data analytics for profitable business development. Peer to Peer **31**(2), 56–58 (2015)
22. ABA Model Rules of Professional Conduct (2013). http://www.americanbar.org/groups/ professional_responsibility/publications/model_rules_of_professional_conduct/model_ rules_of_professional_conduct_table_of_contents.html
23. Indiana Rules of Court, Rules of Professional Conduct, Including Amendments made through 30 April 2015. http://www.in.gov/judiciary/rules/prof_conduct/
24. Stafford, D.: Lawyer disciplined over third-party site. The Indiana Lawyer, 7 May 2014. http://www.theindianalawyer.com/article/print?articleId=34087
25. Odendahl, M.: Unpopular Reporting Rule May Spur Volunteerism. The Indiana Lawyer 26, 6 (December 2–15, 2015)

Evaluation of Collaborative Development Environments for Software Engineering Courses in Higher Education

Daniel Kadenbach[✉] and Carsten Kleiner

University of Applied Sciences and Arts Hannover, Hannover, Germany
{daniel.kadenbach,carsten.kleiner}@hs-hannover.de

Abstract. Collaborative Development Environments (CDEs) play a significant role in modern software engineering by integrating multiple crucial tools and functions for the development process at a single point and therefore by providing elemental support for the collaboration of the developers and utilizing synergetic effects through the combination of these tools and social functions. To prepare students optimally they should be trained to use those systems effectively. In this paper we define a criteria list for the evaluation of CDEs to be able to decide which CDE or combination of tools is most suitable for the use in a certain software engineering course in higher education. We build this work on our accumulated experiences and findings of six years of project support for students and scientists in a computer science department.

Keywords: Collaboration · CDEs · Higher education · Software engineering

1 Introduction

Apart from the team of a project itself, projects are primarily being influenced by the environment in which they are carried out. This is especially true for software engineering projects which can enormously benefit (or derogate) from the chosen software tools used to support their development. In every real software project many of these supportive tools are used and together form the collaborative software system of the project. There is a wide variety of categories of these tools and for every category there often are many alternative tools. Also, there are many tools for special purposes, but in most cases there is a common set of tools used in software engineering projects (for example: version control systems like Git or Subversion for source code management, wikis for knowledge management and issue trackers for requirements, task and bug management).

Often these tools are integrated into one system, utilizing the synergetic effects and the overall benefit through generic and social functions, called a Collaborative Development Environment (CDE) or Software Forge. These tools and environments can have a great impact on a project, both in a positive and in a negative way. They often offer ways to improve motivation, learning, reuse of

G. Meiselwitz (Ed.): SCSM 2016, LNCS 9742, pp. 365–372, 2016.
DOI: 10.1007/978-3-319-39910-2_34

knowledge and artifacts and collaboration by improving the visibility, awareness and communication.

It is crucial to teach students of computer science how to work with these tools and environments, which benefits and which challenges they bring along, which different kinds exists, and most importantly: how to choose the right tools (or tool combination) and how to benefit the most from them in the software development process. Students have to learn modern ways of collaboration to be optimally prepared for their later work and to be able to achieve the highest possible quality within their projects and therefore also the greatest personal satisfaction.

Since there are so many different tools it is not an easy task to decide which should be used in software engineering courses in higher education. Apart from learning to use these tools and to collaborate with them, students and the whole organization may also profit from them because (if applied and used correctly) they often offer a higher awareness for and a better access to projects. Therefore it is easier to build common knowledge and to build upon previous projects. Students can learn important skills when they learn how to reuse, improve or extends projects or project parts, because in most cases this is exactly what they will have to do in their later work.

Therefore, we present a categorization of tools and a criteria list to evaluate these tools. This is work in progress. We want to use the criteria list to evaluate different CDEs and tools to be able to find a combination from which the students, staff and organization will have the greatest benefit to offer excellent training, support and collaboration for the carried out projects.

2 Related Work

Much research has already been carried out regarding some of the tools separately and their value in software engineering in general and in higher education. For example the usage of wikis in software engineering projects by students is investigated by Ras in [6] and by Minocha et al in [5]. Al-yahya showed in [1] how to support teamwork skills of students in software engineering courses with wikis.

Vujovic reviews version control systems and investigates how to apply them in software engineering courses in [7] while Cochez et al. analyze how students used git in several computing courses in [2]. Ljubovic et al. investigate how to use repository analysis tools to determine the individual contributions of students in [4].

In contrast to that in this paper we focus on the evaluation of a combination of multiple tools which together form a CDE. Due to the many possible combinations of different tools and to the varying requirements of different environments, it is a non trivial task to evaluate such a system. We are building upon our previous work in [3].

3   Categories of Tools

The most often used categories of tools in software engineering projects from our point of view are summarized in Table 1.

Table 1. Categories of tools and environments

Category	Examples	Description
Version Control Systems	Git, Subversion, Bazaar	Used to manage source files with history and other meta information (who changed what and when) and to provide a single source of information for the project team
Knowledge Management	Dokuwiki, Wordpress, Joomla	Wikis, blogs and content management systems used to document and present projects
Issue Tracker	Bugzilla	For tracking requirements, tasks, bugs and milestones
Project Management	Redmine	Tools to track tasks, resources, responsibilities and project progress
Communication Support	Instant Messenger, Email, mailing lists, forums	Tools to support synchronous or asynchronous communication
Continuous Integration	Jenkins	Tools which provide an automation of the build process
Quality Assurance	SonarQube	Tools for analyzing the quality of source code and documentation, finding security threats, ensuring project quality
Integrated Systems	Redmine, Allura, Trac	Systems which combine multiple of the mentioned functions into one system

These integrated systems are called software forges or collaborative development environments and some are also found in the category of application lifecycle management systems. In particular these systems offer the biggest value for real projects because the combination of functions often utilizes synergetic effects and through their integration they are often more convenient to use than multiple unconnected tools.

When using such supporting tools an important choice has to be made in an organization: should the organization provide these tools and needed infrastructure itself internally or should it use external services from the internet which are often free of charge. The advantages and disadvantages of both choices are discussed in the following.

3.1 Internal (Self Hosted) Tools

The advantages of providing the needed tools and infrastructure yourself in your organization are:

1. It is possible to create an overview of all projects and their tools of the organization and therefore increase the visibility and awareness of those projects to improve the collaboration in the organization. It therefore offers the chance to gather information about all projects at a single place.
2. The organization has full control over all data of its projects. It can decide which data is only shown to members of the organization and which may be visible from the internet. It can protect sensible data and restrict the access in any needed way.
3. Every combination of available tools is possible, since some tools might not be available externally.

The main drawback of this solution is the immense amount of work which has to be constantly invested in providing, maintaining, updating, securing and improving the needed infrastructure. Additionally, more often than not it is not possible to provide suitable tool support for every project, as each project has different needs. Some projects may therefore use external tools nevertheless.

3.2 External Tools

The main advantage of using external tools (for example CDEs like SourceForge or GitHub) is that nearly no work has to be put into the provision of the tools. Often they are also free to use.

One disadvantage can be that often you can only use them for public projects for free, so all project data is available on the internet which is not suitable for many projects, even if it is great for others. Also, you loose full control of your data which can be a crucial point if the data is sensible. Especially in higher education many of the conducted projects have a higher value for their peer group, other students of the same organization, and do not benefit that much from being exposed to the internet.

Another drawback is that it becomes harder for the organization to keep track of all its projects if they are scattered at different locations in the internet. This can make it difficult to strengthen organizational culture and collaboration within the organization. But just this central point of information about all conducted projects can be of such a great value in higher education with its often coherent projects, because it can be a place of interchange, knowledge aggregation, motivation and learning from each other.

Finally, the organization can not ensure the availability of the project data anymore. Some external tools may close their service (as for example Google Code did).

4   Criteria Catalog

In the following we present the criteria we identified to be important for the application of a collaborative environment in a software engineering course in higher education, so that both students and the organization may benefit the most. These criteria will be the key to an evaluation of different systems to find the ones which are best suited for the special requirements in a learning environment. The criteria are divided into four categories:

1. General functions, which mainly contain basic functionality like user authentication or functions which are used across several parts of the system like search functions,
2. tool support, which lists the different supportive tools the system offers,
3. social functions and
4. non-functional requirements.

An overview of the criteria, which are described in more detail in the following section, is given in Table 2.

4.1   General Functions

- User Authentication: Users should be able to register and authenticate to the system easily. There has to be function to recover lost passwords. If the system is used internally, it should ideally provide a way to connect to and use an already existing user database for example via LDAP.
- Project Portal: The system should provide a portal to the projects which it supports. Projects should be visible and browsable in an easy and yet clearly way, so that a user can get an overview of the projects. The system has to offer mature search functions so that a user is able to search for projects and contents in a sensible and effective way.
- Multiple Language Support: The system should support the development of software and documentation for different languages and therefore should offer ways to also offer the project information in different languages.
- Extensibility: A system which is used internally should offer its functions through a well-defined API, so that it can be integrated into existing infrastructure and it should allow the creation of plugins, so that it can be extended to special needs.
- Themes: The theme of the system should be customizable to reflect the organization, so that users feel familiar and a sense of organizational identification and culture can develop.

Table 2. Criteria for CDE evaluation

Category	Criteria
General Functions	User Authentication
	Project Portal
	Multiple Language Support
	Extensibility
	Themes
Tool Support	Version Control System
	Knowledge Management
	Issue Tracker
	File Repository
	Communication Support
	Continuous Integration
	Quality Assurance
Social Functions	Commenting
	Tagging
	Rating
	Gamification
	Code-Review
Non-Functional Requirements	Security and Privacy
	Ease of Use
	Simple Administration

4.2 Tool Support

- Version Control Systems (VCS): Version control systems are a very important tool in software engineering used in most projects. The system therefore should support VCS like Git, Subversion or others. Beyond just offering repositories it should also offer an easy to use view on those repositories, so that users can browse and access them online without the need to check them out. Source code should be displayed with syntax highlighting.
- Knowledge Management: Used to gather and share project experiences and knowledge and to document the software, knowledge management tools like wikis and blogs should be offered.
- Issue Rracker: They can be used to manage and track the progress of requirements, bugs and even tasks, documenting the responsibilities in the project and should be supported. Ideally issues in the issue tracker can reference contents from other tools like commits in the VCS or corresponding pages in wikis.
- File Repository: The system should offer a way to easily upload project files, so that they can be accessed by other users.

– Communication Support: Forums, mailing list and automatic notifications (e.g. for commits in the CVS) should be offered by the system to improve the awareness and communication of its users and to document decisions of project teams.
– Continuous Integration: Ideally the system should also support an automatic build system like Jenkins, so the students are able to learn how to automatize the build process and be prepared for professional software engineering processes.
– Quality Assurance: To improve the project quality it can be of great use if tools can automatically analyze the project and generate reports. In this way the users are instantly rewarded if they improve the quality of the project.

4.3 Social Functions

Social functions are a very important aspect in a CDE to motivate users to create high quality content and to be able to compare the quality of projects. Without these functions and with a growing number of managed projects, users would not be able to find valuable content and the whole system would loose much of its possible benefit.

– Commenting: Users should be able to comment content in the CDE, to give feedback and therefore valuable hints to improve the content and to learn from each other.
– Tagging: Content should be tagable, so that it can be easily found by others. Tags should be proposed by the system based on the already used tags.
– Rating: A rating system of content should be offered, so that the quality of the content can be assessed by the users helping other users to find valuable content. It also creates more motivation for users to improve their content. To improve the quality of the ratings, they should be weighted with the reputation of the users.
– Gamification: Gamification elements can also be used to motivate users to use the system in the desired way and to provide detailed information about their projects.
– Code-Review: A code review from users with high reputation can be used to improve the quality of the source code and to let other users learn from source code in the system, marking exceptionally well written parts or giving hints how to improve other parts.

4.4 Non-functional Requirements

Non-functional requirements are often crucial for the acceptance and effective usage of a CDE. The most important ones which we identified are:

– Security and Privacy: Like for example the use of user names, so that real names are hidden for content which is exposed to the Internet. Additionally, that users can choose which content is exposed to which audience and that confidential information is not accessible by others.

- Ease of Use for End Users: The use of the system must not impose much effort for its users. Therefore it should offer an intuitive user interface and an easy to understand and accessible documentation.
- Simple Administration: Especially for self hosted tools it is important that the administration of these tools is not too cumbersome.

5   Conclusion and Future Work

In this paper we analyzed the categories of tools to support software engineering projects in higher education and presented a criteria catalog to evaluate CDEs. In this way we hope to find the CDEs which will be most suitable to help students learn excellent software engineering techniques and processes, carry out high quality projects with best results and be optimally prepared for their future work.

The next steps will be to actually evaluate different CDEs like SourceForge (Allura), GitHub, Redmine and others on basis of this criteria catalog. Therefore we will evaluate these tools ourselves, but will also let students try out different tools and assess and compare them.

References

1. Al-Yahya, M.: Using wikis to support teamwork skills in software engineering courses. In: 22nd Conference on Software Engineering Education and Training, 2009, CSEET 2009, pp. 142–149, February 2009
2. Cochez, M., Isomöttönen, V., Tirronen, V., Itkonen, J.: How do computer science students use distributed version control systems? In: Ermolayev, V., Mayr, H.C., Nikitchenko, M., Spivakovsky, A., Zholtkevych, G. (eds.) ICTERI 2013. CCIS, vol. 412, pp. 210–228. Springer, Heidelberg (2013)
3. Kadenbach, D., Kleiner, C.: Case-study: How to increase the value of computer science projects in higher education. In: 2012 8th International Conference on Collaborative Computing: Networking, Applications and Worksharing (CollaborateCom), pp. 269–278, October 2012
4. Ljubovic, V., Nosovic, N.: Repository analysis tools in teaching software engineering. In: 2012 IX International Symposium on Telecommunications (BIHTEL), pp. 1–5, October 2012
5. Minocha, S., Petre, M., Roberts, D.: Using wikis to simulate distributed requirements development in a software engineering course. Int. J. Eng. Educ. **24**(4), 689–704 (2008). http://oro.open.ac.uk/15756/
6. Ras, E.: Investigating wikis for software engineering - results of two case studies. In: ICSE Workshop on Wikis for Software Engineering, 2009, WIKIS4SE 2009, pp. 47–55, May 2009
7. Vujovic, V.: Applying a version control system in software engineering classroom. In: International Scientific Conference, 2015, Unitech 2015, Gabrovo, p. 369, November 2015

Exercising Users' Tolerance and Solidarity: A Groupware Application for the Modus Operandi AND

Marlon Jonas de Oliveira Lima[1(✉)], Laura Sánchez García[1],
and Fernanda Eugênio[2]

[1] Informatics Department, Federal University of Paraná, Centro Politécnico,
Jardim das Américas, Curitiba, PR, Brazil
Deoliveiralima.marlon@gmail.com
[2] AND_Lab, R. Poiais de São Bento, Lisbon, Portugal

Abstract. This paper presents the development process of the web application that extends the Question Game giving it support to be played over the internet with a distributed setup. The game scenario is treated as a shared workspace, and the players its users.

1 Introduction

The internet is a crowded place where people can share their opinions at the ease of a click. Given this freedom, manifestations of intolerance are commonly seen over social media and comment sections in all kinds of websites. The virtual nature of communication in social media gives the user a sensation of anonymity, giving the power to say anything without taking the responsibility for those words. Nobody sees who is in the other side of the screen, and that fact helps words of prejudice, intolerance and hate. According to [1] this is the effect of the "online disinhibition" in which an individual behaves differently when using the internet. Among the causes addressed by the author we can highlight:

1. You do not know me (dissociative anonymity): users identity is not always revealed on the internet, and a sense of anonymity provides some type of security to express one's opinions.
2. You can not see me (invisibility): like the anonymity, the fact that in most cases no one is able to physically see a user during an online interaction increases the disnhibition to express one's opinions.
3. See you later (asynchronicity): most Internet communications do not happen in real time, not having to deal a persons reaction decreases the inhibition to say something aggressive or immoral.

Inspired by the primordial question How to live together?, the AND Lab researchers in Lisbon, Portugal, presented the Modus Operandi AND, a set of practices that exercise its users' tolerance and solidarity. This practice can be summed up in one Portuguese word: "reparar"(repair). Which in Portuguese has

© Springer International Publishing Switzerland 2016
G. Meiselwitz (Ed.): SCSM 2016, LNCS 9742, pp. 373–382, 2016.
DOI: 10.1007/978-3-319-39910-2_35

three different meanings that can be translated to "perceive", "stop again" and "repair". First, whenever an event is perceived in your surroundings you must stop your automatic response. Then you must repair your reaction to that specific event. This exercise allows us to analyze situations from different perspectives, allowing a more appropriate and sensible reaction.

The operating mode AND can be exercised by games and workshops. One of the games used by researchers is the Question Game. In this game its participants must interact in a limited scenario with several previously selected objects. Each player can make one modification to the scenario at a time. The game's purpose is to transfer the role of the player for the game itself. Each player must assess how best it can collaborate with the situation presented in the game, then exercising the three steps of "repair".

Up to now, the Question Game can be performed locally with one of the AND Lab researchers. In this context, this paper describes an application that supports the "Question Game", allowing it to be used remotely, distributed and synchronously, maintaining the determinant properties observed in its real world counterpart.

2   Modus Operandi AND

The Modus Operandi AND is a methodology for responsible decision-making, for improvisation contingent sustainable solutions for collaborative composition without a centralized leadership. Created from tools originated from Anthropology and Performing Arts, it has cross-applicability to any area, currently being used not only in the Performing Arts and Human and Social Sciences researches, but also in mediation practices in Clinical Psychology, Education and Pedagogy, Architecture and Urban planning, Political activism. Taking the form of a game with inherent rules from the play itself - that is, situated, provisional, traded act by players and therefore meta-stable - the Operating Mode AND explores the potential of the non-competitive recreational device to exercise the reciprocity skills, the sufficiency of gesture and careful handling, as well as the capabilities of self-observation in the act of sustaining relationships and ethical decision-making in the right timing.

While ethical and aesthetic approach to coexistence and cooperation policies, the Operating AND mode allows anyone to understand and exercise in practice the mechanisms of collaboration, conflict mediation and collective creation - be it in terms of a simple everyday conversation or of a professional design in durational or specific situations.

The present play structure resembles that of a board game, with the difference that in this game there are no predetermined rules, but the rules emerge from the difference in patterns and repetition that appear every time the participants take a position. Thus the game begins by delimiting an area of space, usually with masking tape on the floor to draw an empty square, or using the clean and smooth table top as the "board". This pre-defined space will act as "combined attention zone", allowing to establish an inside (inside the box) and outside (the outside).

The materials with which the game can be played can vary from players own body (with their capacity for action, motion and sound output) to an accidental set of objects, comprising elements in series (office supply, stationery and DIY kits) and unique elements (ornaments, household objects, clothes, toys and used objects).

The game has a minimum of 2 players and no maximum number. Any of the players present can play the game through a "position taking" - that is, the execution of an action within the board with or without the use of objects, duracional or temporarily, with or without trace. The "position taking" is made only through this "mark" on the board, without verbal explanations or direct conversation between the participants, since the conversation will materialize itself through another "position taking" also silent.

From the moment that a "first position" on the board arises, this works as "laboratory accident" for the other participants, and any of them can position himself to establish a relationship with this unforeseen situation - there is no order to the moves, or commitment to everyone to participate. Only the player who has just made a move is restricted and can not do anything in response, thus preventing from controlling the narrative and the unfolding of events. Slowly, with the establishment of the first relationship, then the subsequent relations with this relationship will emerge an immanent pattern. It's complexity depends on the amount of simultaneous relationships that remain between moves. This pattern will be at the same time sustained and transformed throughout the game, working as a common plan of coexistence within which participants negotiate, every round, the balance between their values, opinions and participation in the collective, that is, maintenance of this "material conversation" always alive, fluid and ongoing.

The game is divided in two consecutive phases: "find the game" and "play the game". The phase "find the game" is triggered when a "first position" arises on the board, and is fulfilled when, through the co-positioning, participants can establish together at least one relationship between relations. The minimum number for this to happen is three positions, enabling one first relationship (between the first and the second positions) and then a relationship with this relationship (between the third and the first + second positions). However, the game's starting can be postponed, if player moves do not establish any relationship and/or any relationship between relations. To avoid this risk of breakdown and inherent fragmentation of relationships, the Operating Mode AND proposes that the positions should be as explicit and open as possible, establishing situated and contingent coordinates WHAT, HOW, WHEN and WHERE, avoiding positions based on the response to questions WHY and WHO.

Once found the game, that is, the common plan, the phase "play the game" starts, from at least the fourth position. This phase involves the support of the immanent rules constructed by the collective, preserving its reciprocal character, while avoiding falling into a complementary relationship (that is, stiffening into laws and becoming therefore transcendent rules, with fixed content and predefined roles, features of the "Modus Operandi IS"), or a symmetry relationship (that is, to shift into a competitive behaviour or disperse into an "everything is allowed" disrupting the group, features of the "Modus Operandi OR"). Playing the game with the Modus Operandi AND involves, therefore, while repeating, changing and maintaining the complex set of relationships relations that make up the common plan, balancing repetition and difference doses every round, taking as a criterion the event itself. This task constitutes the main challenge of the "play the game" phase, to "postpone the end", here understood as a synonym for "living together". The evolution of a session of a real execution of the game can be observed in Fig. 1.

The task of "postponing the end" involves continuous responsible care and fine sensitivity to the right timing to continue or change. The Modus Operandi AND proposes that "postponing the end" is made of a double movement: "accept the end" and "anticipate the end". On the other one hand, it is crucial that the

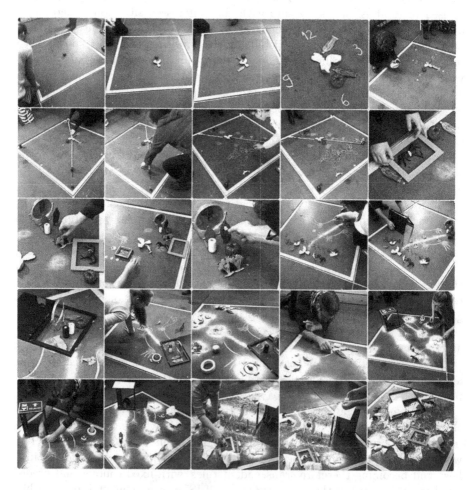

Fig. 1. Question Game session

early phase of "play the game" is marked by "accepting the end", that is, as soon as the "find the game" phase led the group to a common plan, it is essential to understand this will not be endless, using the clarity of the finite nature of things as fuel for a sensitive engagement of the participants in the next phase. At the same time, "postponing the end" will also involve an ongoing effort to "anticipate the end" - not in order to precipitate it, but in order to train attention to the signs of impending accidents or the exhaustion for entering into a loop, in order to take positions that seek to avoid them before they happen.

Thus, through a work bending-and-deploy and direct management of the materiality of events, it is possible to "think with their hands", train the attention to the common, the availability to the unexpected and the pleasure of the community, and to negotiate in practice the golden mean between personal affection and collective events.

Putting on the same plane thinking and doing through the "life model" device afforded by the variable scale board game, the Modus Operandi AND allows direct and experiential investigation of individual and collective mechanisms of coexistence, giving practitioners concrete tools to enhance collaboration processes, peer learning and negotiation of being-together. In particular, it allows each one to realize his own behavioral patterns, contributing to the development of emotional self-regulation skills, self-management of care (selection, focusing and coordination of stimuli), decision making and subsequent implementation. These skills are trained in game mode, to be then "returned" to the human scale of everyday life and social relations, emotional, family and professional practitioners.

3 Methodology

In this section the methodological steps to solve the problem are presented. Due to the great need for fidelity to the original Operating Mode from the Anthropology, regular meetings were held with the researcher that headed the Modus Operandi AND.

3.1 Requirements Specification

During the meetings we discussed how the technological support could assist in the execution of the workshops. As the game requires a complex scenario with various objects available and many possibilities of action, the development of a completely virtual environment proved to be unfeasible as the first approach. Therefore an initial solution was adopted, with the use of a real world scenario, broadcast via video conference to the players, and a mediator in the transmission site to perform the players moves.

To perform an action in the game - "take position" - each participant must answer to a series of questions before acting. The questions to be answered are: "What", "How" and "Where/When." They determine which object will be used and its position in the matrix space time. In a real-world session of the game all these questions must be answered internally and transmitted through the position taking itself. In the digital instance it has to be transmitted by a structured text to the mediator, who will effectively perform them.

The system requirements specification process was developed in three steps. Initially a preliminary use cases document was written, based on the first meeting held with the researcher from AND Lab. Then a mock-up was developed so the researcher could evaluate the systems functionality. After the final review from the researcher a document with the use cases and the scenarios was produced from the use cases fragment structure presented at [2]. A use case diagram can be seen in Fig. 2. There are two actors, the player and the mediator, each one with an own set of possible actions. Each use case has been established in order to offer the most similar experience as possible to the real-world game one.

Fig. 2. Use cases

3.2   Background Research

With the use cases document at hands we could then begin our research of technologies and studies to assist our system's needs. Our main goal was to connect the participants and provide them a environment capable to held a session of the Question Game from begin to end. Computer Supported Cooperative Work

(CSCW) is the study of how people use the technology in relation to hardware and software to work together with shared time and space [3]. So it became the core of our research.

Every technology produced by studies in CSCW area is classified by some authors as Groupware. Although there is a fine line between what is considered CSCW and what is considered Groupware. "The groupware term is used to refer to the technology developed by the research CSCW [4]. [5], presents us a classification system based on "Time" and "Space" of the groupware users, as seen in Fig. 3. Our system requires a synchronous distributed interaction between the users, falling into the third quadrant. Same as video conferencing systems, backing our decision at early steps to use video conference to broadcast the game state to the players.

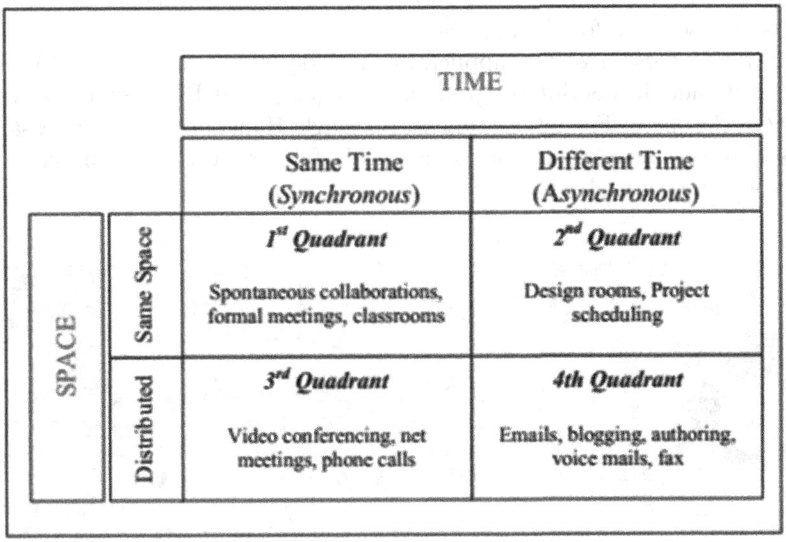

		TIME	
		Same Time (*Synchronous*)	Different Time (*Asynchronous*)
SPACE	Same Space	*1ˢᵗ Quadrant* Spontaneous collaborations, formal meetings, classrooms	*2ⁿᵈ Quadrant* Design rooms, Project scheduling
	Distributed	*3ʳᵈ Quadrant* Video conferencing, net meetings, phone calls	*4th Quadrant* Emails, blogging, authoring, voice mails, fax

Fig. 3. Space x Time diagram Source:[5]

Cooperation is the main characteristic of a groupware application. As presented by [6], the 3 C model of Collaboration says that to collaborate a group has to perform three main activities: communicate, coordinate and cooperate. Additionally, our system require that all communication was done through the positions, no side talks should be allowed. To prevent them, all audios from the participants were muted, and the only way to communicate became through position taking. This decision was not, in fact, operational, but, instead, an innovative feature of the application, since it introduced in the Game of Questions a possibility no available at the real scenario. The coordination can be achieved through the game mechanics itself, so the system must address that to provide an environment capable of coordinating its users actions.

Various technologies are available to extend video conferences functionality. Webinars are powerfull tools that allow participants to send questions to the streamer and review past content at ease. The key feature of a Webinar is the ability to discuss and share information [7]. But they do not provide native means to manipulate or extend this messaging system. With this constraint all coordination responsibilities would fall into the participants hands, making it unfeasible to use "out of the box" Webinars systems.

3.3   Prototype Development

A survey was conducted to evaluate video conferencing solutions available to use within the application. Among the solutions found, the Google Hangouts[1] and the WebRTC[2] emerged. Given the ease of integration between the application to the video conferencing system, Google Hangouts was selected as the video conferencing solution for the application.

The alpha version of the application was developed as a web application using client-side JavaScript programming language and PHP server-side, with a MySQL database. For integration with Google Hangouts it was necessary to encapsulate the entire application in an XML, for it to work as an plugin to the video conferencing tool.

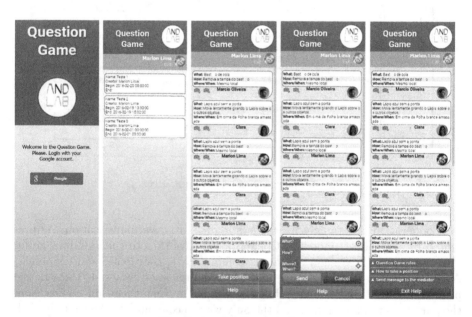

Fig. 4. Application Interface

---

[1] https://hangouts.google.com/.

[2] https://webrtc.org/.

4 Discussion

The solution adopted here was a simple application to exchange text messages in a video conferencing system. The application's difference is in the structure of each message and the tools to help its writing. All messages have been separated into three fields: "What", "How" and "Where/how." In the "What" the user can access a list of the items available for the position taking, facilitating the specification of the item or items needed. And in the "Where/When" the user has the possibility of instead of describing the positions of its statement, it can simply click on the key points of its movement and enumerate to determine the movement path.

Another feature added to the online version of the Question Game was easy access to previous positions. Feature difficult to assimilate the physical version of the game, it would be necessary to keep a photographic record of each position taken by the participants. Each message in the application approved are assigned two images, recording their initial and final state. Thus all participants can track how the scenario has changed along a session of the game.

All features designed to help the user in writing of the positions have been necessary to address the noise introduced by the use of a technology layer between the player and the game. A list of available objects became necessary because the user can not explore space of the game to find out which objects are at your disposal. The functionality of clicking to determine the positions also became necessary by the inability of the player to explore the scenery.

In discussion with the author responsible for the Operating Mode AND it was established that the introduction of technological layer also brought advantages to the practice of the Modus Operandi. Like any statement of position must be performed by text, the practice of outsourcing their wishes in a clear and structured manner assists in carrying Operating AND mode. The dispersed feature of the online game also assists in the implementation of the questions set by removing the noise introduced by any side discussion among participants. Thus each player can focus on the game and not the other players.

5 Conclusion and Future Work

The developed application meet the needs of a distributed synchronous session of the Question Game. The structural model adopted in messages helps players to describe in clear and cohesive way how the positions should be taken. Extra features presented in the application, such as the possibility to consult earlier positions, the assistance while taking the position, making it a more enriching experience for its participants.

As the developed application focus on providing support to the Modus Operandi AND, allowing it to be applied in remote and distributed manner, their use in other areas is restricted. However by adapting the message structure it can be used in any kind of scenario in real time. Providing support for a writing rapidly and dynamically for a specific context.

Two different groups are being formed: users already familiar with the Modus Operandi AND - to provide insights towards the online version's limitations, and novices to the Modus Operandi AND, to contribute with open questions.

These testes are expected to bring fruitfull information in order to develop a new version significantly closer to the physical one, while still taking advantage of the innovative potentiality of technological solutions.

References

1. Suler, J.: The online disinhibition effect. Cyberpsychol. Behav. **7**(3), 321–326 (2004)
2. Dias, F.G., Schmitz, E.A., Campos, M.L.M., Correa, A.L., Alencar, A.J.: Elaboration of use case specifications: An approach based on use case fragments. In: Proceedings of the 2008 ACM Symposium on Applied Computing, ser, SAC 2008, pp. 614–618. ACM, New York (2008). http://doi.acm.org/10.1145/1363686.1363835
3. Grudin, J.: Computer-supported cooperative work: History and focus. Computer **5**, 19–26 (1994)
4. Nielsen, J.: Multimedia and Hypermedia-the Internet and Beyond. Academic Press, Boston (1995)
5. Rama, J., Bishop, J.: A survey and comparison of cscw groupware applications. In: Proceedings of the 2006 Annual Research Conference of the South African Institute of Computer Scientists and Information Technologists on IT Research in Developing Countries. South African Institute for Computer Scientists and Information Technologists, pp. 198–205 (2006)
6. Fuks, H., Gerosa, M.A., Raposo, A.B., de Lucena, C.J.P.: O modelo de colaboração 3c no ambiente aulanet. Informática na educação: teoria & prática **7**(1) (2004)
7. Verma, A., Singh, A.: Leveraging webinar for student learning. In: International Workshop on Technology for Education, T4E 2009, pp. 86–90. IEEE (2009)

International Collaboration for Software Capstone Projects

Alex Radermacher[✉] and Dean Knudson

North Dakota State University, Fargo, ND, USA
{alex.radermacher,dean.knudson}@ndsu.edu

Abstract. Most universities include a senior capstone project as part of their curriculum. These projects are designed to provide students with the opportunity to utilize the skills which they have acquired over the course of their education and to apply them to a large project. Recent trends in software development include increasing globalization and international collaboration both between companies as well as among international teams within an organization. In response to these changes, some instructors of capstone courses have begun to conduct international capstone projects where students in one country are paired with industry companies or other organizations from a different country. This paper presents the results of a survey of educators, software professionals, and former students who have participated in some form of international capstone project. This research is aimed at providing a better understanding of these projects to those who are interested in participating in international capstone projects themselves.

Keywords: Computer science education · Capstone projects · International collaboration

1 Introduction

Including capstone or senior project courses are a common practice for most computer science and software engineering programs and is a recommendation of the Joint Task Force on Computing Curricula [1]. These courses typically involve a small team (usually 3–6 members) of students working on a large project in order to demonstrate their mastery of the different skills and knowledge that they have accrued during their college education. There is no specific format for these capstone courses and many universities have different approaches including service projects for nonprofit organizations [2], projects sponsored by software development industry clients [3, 4], and game programming [5], among several others.

Capstone courses also serve to provide students with an idea of what to expect when they begin their careers in the software development industry, and many employers consider them to be an important experience, similar to having an internship [6]. These experiences allow students to have a better understanding of how software development is commonly practiced in industry.

© Springer International Publishing Switzerland 2016
G. Meiselwitz (Ed.): SCSM 2016, LNCS 9742, pp. 383–392, 2016.
DOI: 10.1007/978-3-319-39910-2_36

However, the software development industry is becoming increasingly globalized [7] and as a result many companies are developing software projects with teams in multiple locations and typically on more than a single continent [8]. This has led educators to call for courses to be taught in a way that incorporates these trends towards greater international collaboration and with globalization in mind [9].

This research focuses on achieving that outcome by providing recommendations or guidelines for educators interested in conducting international projects. To better understand how international capstone projects differ from traditional, local projects, the authors of this work have surveyed educators, software professionals, and former students who have been involved in international capstone projects. The results of this research should assist other universities or industry companies become involved in international capstone projects as well as in the formation of an international capstone exchange that would help facilitate the pairing of universities with international companies.

2   Previous Work

International software projects in an academic setting are hardly a recent phenomenon, and academic studies (in computer science or other related fields) with a focus on international collaboration have been conducted for decades. While there are many publications related to best practices or general guidelines for capstone courses [10, 11], there is relatively little research related to students participating in international software projects.

One study reports on experiences from a course where second-year students at a Canadian university participated in international software development projects and international software engineering research projects [12]. The publication provides many examples of software development or research projects that students participated in with international companies or universities as well as providing guidelines for dealing with international research sponsors.

Another publication describes international collaboration on a research project by senior-level student teams from two universities located in the United States and India [13]. The authors provide a detailed description of the process the different universities went through in order to arrange their international collaboration. A set of general guidelines (e.g., how often to conduct meetings, how instructors should interact with students, etc.) are also provided.

Instructors who led a course where students participated in a software engineering project between student teams in the United States and a non-profit organization in Turkey studied international collaboration from a student perspective [14]. They published a large number of student quotations related to their experiences and difficulties in working on an international software project as well as a list of lessons learned from the international collaboration.

The authors of this research have also published prior research related to international capstone projects including a list of best practices for universities [15], an experience paper based on international collaboration on capstone projects between a US and

Australian university [16], as well as a publication detailing early efforts to establish an international capstone exchange program [17].

This research builds on the previous work by the authors by taking a more systematic approach to understanding how the different participants (i.e., educations, industry professionals, and students) have perceived working on international capstone projects. These additional perspectives on international capstone projects should provide additional support for guidelines when conducting international capstone projects as well an aid for those seeking to begin international collaboration of their own.

3 Study Design and Methodology

In order to expand on the results from previous studies as well as to identify information most relevant for educators or companies considering international capstone projects, we decided to survey the three main stakeholders (i.e., instructors, industry sponsors, and students) involved in capstone projects.

The remainder of this section provides a detailed description of the study, its participants, and the study procedure.

3.1 Research Questions

Before conducting the survey, a set of research questions were developed. These were used to help define the purpose of the research and to guide in the creation of individual survey questions.

1. What additional resources (human, computer, etc.) are required in order for international capstone projects to be successful?
2. What aspects of international capstone projects provide the most difficulty for those involved when compared to local capstone projects?
3. What benefits can the participants of international capstone projects expect beyond those normally found in local or traditional capstone projects.

3.2 Study Subjects

Participants in this study were educators, industry sponsors, or students who had participated in an international capstone project in conjunction with a capstone exchange program started in part by one of the authors at North Dakota State University [17].

We contacted a total of five educators, five industry sponsors, and twenty-four students who had participated in an international capstone project within the last three years. Of these, we received responses from four educators, three industry sponsors, and one student.

3.3 Study Instrument

The instrument used in this study was a short, seven-question survey related to the participants experience with an international capstone project (ICP). The individual survey questions were created using the research questions as a guideline.

Because a majority of the prospective participants were located outside of the U.S., and prior experience of one of the authors in conducting interviews with international participants, a survey was chosen instead of a structured interview in order to make participation easier for international participants and to potentially allow for a higher response rate.

Table 1 below contains a list of survey questions (edited for length) provided to instructors and industry sponsors. Due to the low student response rate, those questions have been excluded as it was felt there was insufficient data for analysis.

Table 1. Survey Questions for Instructors and Industry Sponsors

Survey Questions for Instructors
1) *What experiences (if any) do you feel students received from participating in an ICP that they would not have otherwise received from a typical capstone project?*
2) *What challenges or difficulties have you experienced when conducting an ICP at your university that are less common among typical capstone projects?*
3) *What tools or other resources have you found most useful when conducting an ICP in order to ensure it is more successful?*
4) *What steps or other measures need to be taken in order to ensure a successful outcome when conducting an ICP?*
5) *In what ways (if any) did being paired with another university influence how you were able to set up your capstone exchange?*
6) *To what extent is being paired with another university important for maintaining ICP opportunities?*
7) *Do you have an additional comments of information you feel would be beneficial in improving ICPs?*

Survey Questions for Industry Sponsors
1) *What types of projects do you feel are better (or less) suited for ICPs?*
2) *What challenges or difficulties have you experienced when conducting ICPs at your company that are less common among typical capstone projects?*
3) *What additional resources or requirements do you believe are needed when sponsoring an ICP?*
4) *What added benefits (if any) do you feel there are for companies that sponsor an ICP that are not gained from sponsoring more local capstone projects?*
5) *What additional value or skills (if any) do you feel that students with an ICP experience bring when they join the company?*
6) *To what extent was local university involvement important to your decision to sponsor an ICP?*
7) *Do you have any additional comments or information that you feel would be beneficial in improving ICPs?*

3.4 Study Procedure

All participants were contacted via email by the study authors with a description of the research study, the necessary consent information, and a copy of the survey questions based on the category that participant fell into.

After a low number of responses from former students, an additional request was sent out specifically to students, but it did not yield any additional responses.

4 Results

Results will be broken down by participant group and question. Because there was only a single response from a former student, no detailed analysis is provided for that participant category. Although the student did enjoy the experience, many of the responses to the questions were similar to student responses in previous literature [14].

4.1 Responses from Instructors

Question 1: Student Experiences Gained from an ICP. Instructors felt that international projects provided many opportunities for students that they were less likely to gain from a traditional capstone project. Having an opportunity to learn different cultural and work practices was the most commonly provided answer. Other benefits that were described by multiple participants included having to work across several time zones and needing more rigorous project planning due to reduced interactions. One instructor also indicated that it gave students a good opportunity to improve their everyday English.

Question 2: Challenges Unique to or More Common in an ICP. Time differences were the most widely reported issue that was more particular to international projects than those conducting locally, specifically related to finding meeting times that were convenient for everyone. Another issue was managing expectations as students and industry sponsors from other countries may not be familiar with how capstone projects are conducted at that university. One instructor also noted difficulties due to the alignment of course timelines at different universities.

Question 3: Essential Tools or Resources for an ICP. Skype or some other form of communication tool (video conferencing in particular) was described as absolutely essential. Otherwise commonly used project management software (Redmine, Trello, and GitHub were all mentioned specifically) and other software development tools that are also used with any other capstone project are beneficial.

Question 4: Required Steps or Measures for a Successful Outcome. The most common response by instructors was ensuring that the international industry sponsors had a good understanding of the local practices so that expectations could be better managed. One instructor indicated that it was better to have more frequent contact with international sponsors and that more detailed planning was beneficial when working with an international company for the first time.

Question 5: How Being Paired with Another University Helped. One instructor noted that being paired with another university was critically important and helped connect them with other companies that were interested in conducting an international project. Others noted that it gave them some exposure to other models of conducting capstone projects (e.g., mixed student teams) or different processes and tools.

Question 6: Importance of University Pairing to Maintaining Opportunities. Two instructors indicated that university pairing was important because it allowed them to find replacement sponsors if an international company was unable to participate or had to drop out. Another indicated the benefits of being able to see how other universities conducted their capstone projects and to learn about other processes being used.

Question 7: Additional Comments for Improving ICPs. One instructor commented that it would be interesting to have students teams from several countries collaborate together, although it would likely be difficult to coordinate effectively. Another indicated that an earlier start in terms of project and team selection would be beneficial and one instructor indicated that having aligned semester schedules with other universities would also be helpful.

4.2   Responses from Industry Sponsors

Question 1: Projects Best or Least Suited for ICPs. Several different examples of projects that were not well suited for international student teams were described including those that aren't well-defined initially, projects which require frequent meetings with the customer, or any project that requires a higher degree of cultural understanding in terms of how it will be used by the customer. Projects which were better suited included those where the requirements or constraints were well understood and could be easily communicated or when validation of the software system was easier.

Question 2: Challenges Unique to or More Common in ICPs. All respondents indicated that scheduling meetings due to time zone differences were the largest challenge. One industry sponsor indicated that limited contact made it more difficult to get a feeling for progress and another indicated it made understanding the group dynamic in the student team more difficult.

Question 3: Additional Resources Needed to Sponsor an ICP. Cultural awareness and an understanding of the educational system of the international university that the sponsor is working with were both described as being important for the company. One respondent indicated that it would be beneficial to have clear expectations for both the sponsor and the students.

Question 4: Benefits for Companies Sponsoring an ICP. Two industry sponsors indicated that conducting an international project was important to widening their companies branding or expanding their international presence. One respondent noted that it provided valuable experience in working with people outside of their own country.

Another respondent indicated that it presented an expanded opportunity in terms of hiring new employees.

Question 5: Value of Students with ICP Experience to a Company. There was not much information provided in response to this question, perhaps due to the companies not hiring many or any students with ICP experience. However, one respondent indicated that students who had worked on an international project were likely to have better communication skills as a result of their experience

Question 6: Importance of Local University Involvement. Responses to this question were mixed. One industry sponsor indicated the local university was instrumental in providing this opportunity since they were interested in doing an international project, but were not aware of how to go about doing it. However, another industry sponsor stated that they already have a large number of capstone partnerships and internship programs in place. Another response suggested that it was helpful to have the university involved because they weren't aware of other universities capstone programs or their quality.

Question 7: Additional Comments for Improving ICPs. None of the responses to this question contained any specific suggestions for improvement, but two did note that they felt participating in the international project was useful or and indicated an interest in doing so again in the future.

5 Discussion

This section presents a discussion of the three research questions described in Sect. 3.1 along with additional discussion in Sect. 5.4 including potential reasons for the low student participation rate.

5.1 Research Question 1: Required Resources for ICPs

Video conferencing or other communication tools were identified by participants from both the instructor and industry sponsor categories, although industry sponsors were far more likely to identify a need for understanding the university system that they will be working with as they may not be aware of all of the differences between that university and what they are accustomed to when working with local universities on capstone projects.

Communication tools like Skype and code and project management tools like GitHub are ubiquitous enough or often available at low or no cost that it is not a problem for universities to ensure that these are being used in order to ensure better outcomes for a project. It is also likely that many capstone courses have already incorporated many of these tools or software programs into the traditional projects that are being conducted. However, it would also be beneficial for instructors to compile a set of guidelines for the international companies that they will work with that better describe the culture and the students' level of familiarity with various tools or processes. Having that information up front would help companies and universities better set and manage their expectations when working on international capstone projects.

A set of criteria for selecting projects may also be beneficial to both instructors and sponsors as industry companies did identify a number of different types of projects that were less suited for an ICP, which would be helpful for companies and universities who are participating in an international project for the first time.

5.2   Research Question 2: Challenges Faced with ICPs

Time zone differential was the most commonly identified challenge both by instructors and industry sponsors. Unfortunately this is one challenge that cannot be completely eliminated. Instructors also indicated that differences in the semester schedule between universities also made collaboration with international universities more difficult.

When pairing universities as part of an exchange it may be reasonable to attempt to do so based on time zone differences as well as the similarity of their semester schedule. This becomes easier as the number of participants in an exchange increase, but it may be useful for those universities or companies just beginning to conduct an ICP to keep in mind as it may not always be possible to find a partnership without this issue.

Because frequent or face to face communication is more difficult with ICPs, it is suggested that instructors create student teams more carefully. Members should have experience with the type of project management tools that are necessary to provide information about the project's progress in lieu of direct communication. Although it may not always be possible to find students with experience in the exact tools used by a company, additional experience with any tools in that category may be helpful.

5.3   Research Question 3: Benefits for Participants of ICPs

All respondents (including the single student response) believed that there was some additional benefit participants of international capstone projects. The most commonly identified benefit was exposure to other cultures and practices. Multiple instructors indicated that working with another university as part of a capstone exchanged exposed them to additional tools and processes and industry sponsors felt that international collaboration was a good way to raise awareness for their brand or gain experience working outside of their own country.

One industry sponsor and multiple instructors also felt that students gained valuable experiences from an ICP as well. Improvements in communication ability were the most commonly identified benefit and the single student response indicated that being able to list an international collaborative experience on a CV was beneficial when applying for jobs.

5.4   Other Discussion

One particular aspect of the study that should be discussed is the low participation rate for former students and what could be done to ensure a better response rate in future studies. It is believed that the low response rate may be largely due to a lack of updated contact information. For most of the students contacted as a part of this study, their email address was the previous school supplied email that they may no longer be using or have not forwarded to a new email address.

For future studies it would be beneficial for the authors to spend some additional time to track down current contact information for potential participants rather than relying on potentially out of date information available through the university. One possibility is to ask students currently participating in ICPs to provide future contact information such as a personal email address so that they can be contacted in the future. Otherwise additional effort on the part of authors is required in order to track down current contact information for students who had previously participated in an ICP.

6   Conclusions and Future Work

International capstone projects are perceived as valuable by all of the different participants, however additional steps can be taken to ensure that the additional benefits do not come at such a large expense as to make them less attractive.

This research has provided some additional insights into how international capstone projects can be improved, especially from the perspective of the industry companies who sponsor the different projects as this particular point of view was not as well represented as others in the previous literature related to international collaboration for student projects.

Future work includes developing material to help universities and companies better understand each other's culture, requirements, and expectations in order to make collaboration easier. Additional effort should be made in the future to survey former students who participated in an ICP in order to better understand the problems that they faced as well as how they overcame those challenges. With a better understanding of these issues, conducting case studies of ICPs may also be a valuable future step to better understand how to best arrange and organize these projects.

References

1. ACM/IEEE-CS Joint Task Force on Computing Curricula: Computer Science Curricula 2013. ACM Press and IEEE Computer Society Press. doi:http://dx.doi.org/10.1145/2534860
2. Bloomfield, A., Sherriff, M., Williams, K.: A service learning practicum capstone. In: Proceedings of the 45th ACM Technical Symposium on Computer Science Education (SIGCSE 2014), pp. 265–270. ACM, New York (2014)
3. Gorka, S., Miller, J.R., Howe, B.J.: Developing realistic capstone projects in conjunction with industry. In: Proceedings of the 8th ACM SIGITE Conference on Information Technology Education (SIGITE 2007), pp. 27–32. ACM, New York (2007)
4. Judith, W.C., Bair, B., Börstler, J., Lethbridge, T.C., Surendran, K.: Client sponsored projects in software engineering courses. In: Proceedings of the 34th SIGCSE Technical Sympositum on Computer Science Education (SIGCSE 2003), pp. 401–402. ACM, New York (2003)
5. Parberry, I., Roden, T. Kazemzadeh, M.B.: Experience with an industry-driven capstone course on game programming: extended abstract. In: Proceedings of the 36th SIGCSE Technical Symposium on Computer Science Education (SIGCSE 2005), pp. 91–95. ACM, New York (2005)

6. Radermacher, A., Walia, G., Knudson, D.: Missed expectations: where CS students fall short in the software industry. In: Ellis. B, Kelly, C. (eds.) CrossTalk: The Journal of Defense Software Engineering, vol. 28, no. 1, pp. 4–8. US Air Force STSC in concert with Lumin Publishing, Salt Lake City (2015)

7. Arora, A., Gambardella, A.: The globalization of the software industry: perspectives and opportunities for developed and developing Countries. In: Jaffe, A.B., Lerner, J., Stern, S. (eds.) Innovation Policy and the Economy, vol. 5, pp. 1–32. The MIT Press, Cambridge (2005)

8. Herbsleb, J.D.: Global Software engineering: the future of socio-technical coordination. In: Future of Software Engineering, 2007 (FOSE 2007), pp. 188–198. IEEE Press, New York (2007)

9. Marchant, A.: Teaching ethics in the context of IT and globalization. In: Proceedings of the 5th Conference on Information Technology Education (CITC5 2004), pp. 227–230. ACM, New York (2004)

10. Adams, L., Daniels, M., Goold, A., Hazzan, O., Lynch, K., Newman, I.: Challenges in teaching capstone courses. In: Finkel, D. (ed.) Proceedings of the 8th Annual Conference on Innovation and Technology in Computer Science Education (ITiCSE 2003), pp. 219–220. ACM, New York (2003)

11. Ikonen, M. Kurhila, J.: Discovering high-impact success factors in capstone software projects. In: Proceedings of the 10th ACM Conference on SIG-Information Technology Education (SIGITE 2009), pp. 235–244. ACM, New York (2009)

12. Khmelevsky, Y., Ustimenko, V., Hains, G., Kluka, C., Ozan, E., Syrotovsky, D.: International collaboration in software engineering projects. In: Proceedings of the 16th Wester Canadian Conference on Computing Education (WCCCE 2011), pp. 52–56. ACM, New York (2011)

13. Tabrizi, M.H.N., Collins, C.B., Kalamkar, V.: An international collaboration in software engineering. In: Proceedings of the 40th ACM Technical Symposium on Computer Science Education (SIGCSE 2009), pp. 306–310. ACM, New York (2009)

14. Chidanandan, A., Russell-Dag, L., Laxer, C., Ayfer, R.: In their words: student feedback on an international project collaboration. In: Proceedings of the 41st ACM Technical Symposium on Computer Science Education (SIGCSE 2010), pp. 534–538, ACM, New York, NY, USA (2010)

15. Knudson, D., Slator, B.: Best practices for international capstone projects. In: McBride, R., Searson, M. (eds.) Proceedings of Society for Information Technology & Teacher Education International Conference 2013 (SITE 2013), pp. 1356–1358, AACE, Chesapeake (2013)

16. Knudson, D., Grundy, J.: International capstone exchange – The SUT and NDSU experience. In: Capstone Design Conference (2016, to appear)

17. Knudson, D., Kleiner, C., Sandahl, K.: A preliminary report on establishing an industry based international capstone exchange program. In: Capstone Design Conference 2012

Integrating the Crowd Through Social Media: How Higher Education Can Profit from Viral Mechanisms

Maximilian Rapp[1,2(✉)], Ken White[3], and Markus Rhomberg[2]

[1] HYVE AG, Munich, Germany
maximilian.rapp@hyve.net
[2] Zeppelin University, Friedrichshafen, Germany
markus.rhomberg@zu.de
[3] College of William & Mary, Williamsburg, USA
Ken.white@mason.wm.edu

Abstract. The use of collaboration platforms with social media mechanisms turned out to be an efficient way to integrate costumers and external experts during the innovation processes in companies through Open Innovation. While the governmental sector more and more jumped on that band wagon, higher education hasn't exploited the full potential yet. In this paper we analyze the project "Tomorrow's MBA" of the Mason School of Business at the College of William & Mary, Virginia, and show success factors on how social media can be used on a collaborative and integrative model. Hereby we show that the communication strategy with its diverse online and offline facets is indispensable and highlight the key success factors on how to execute an open innovation project in higher education.

Keywords: Open government · eGovernment · Open innovation · Open education · Communication management · Universities

1 Introduction and Framing

"Tell me and I forget. Teach me and I remember. Involve me and I learn", said once Benjamin Franklin, one of the Founding Fathers of the United States of America. The former president of Pennsylvania had -similiar to Abraham Lincoln- a very strong opinion about the integration of citizens and people in the scope of political, but also educational and social processes. The liberal and open mind of Abraham Lincoln and the well-known Gettysburg Address is often cited in the academic world, especially by modern researchers focused on the impact of citizensourcing, open government or e-government [1] in a digital world [2]. The potential of opening up organizational boundaries in order to co-develop or co-create new products [3], discuss political codes of practice as well as even political party programs [4], was intensively analyzed by the MIT and spread its academically wings over the last couple of years as it is covered in researches especially across innovation, economics, marketing but also public administration. While economically driven research has analyzed open innovation in various facets, social and political science, in a way, had to wait until the Obama legislation in

© Springer International Publishing Switzerland 2016
G. Meiselwitz (Ed.): SCSM 2016, LNCS 9742, pp. 393–404, 2016.
DOI: 10.1007/978-3-319-39910-2_37

2009 to identify a significant number of projects on the integration of citizens in the political process and to analyze their influence on developing collaboratively political and institutional decisions or even political engagement [5]. However, not alone innovative brands and companies integrate creative minds through innovative call for ideas or idea contests as BMW is doing it f.e. to innovate their trunk system or McDonalds to re-invent their Burgers. Instead, historic events show that the public sector used crowdsourcing long before, simply on another level.

Alone in 1869, Napoleon III intended to find a cheaper and more sustainable substitute product for butter to feed his military forces and poor citizens. He engaged the public by initiating an idea contest, which was won by the French chemist Hippolyte Mège-Mouriès by inventing the margarine. As a matter of fact, the government declined any kind of incentive or reward, thus the inventor decided to liquidate his Intellectual Property (IP) to a company called Jurgens, which was later on merged with Unilever. Even a century prior, the British Parliament opened up their demands in order to find a solution to the problem of determining longitude by calling out for ideas under the 1714 Longitude Act [6]. Interestingly enough, the English carpenter and clockmaker John Harrison pocketed 20,000 £ by inventing the marine chronometer, a long-sought after device, which identified the longitude of a ship at sea with a special mechanism for the compensation of temperature fluctuation. It seems with the announcement "A government of the people, by the people and for the people", Lincoln unintendedly transferred this more gamification approach into a normative actuality, into something unexceptional, which passed the status of a theoretical "Leviathan" or "Behemoth" to anchor a bilateral communication flow between top and down or politics and citizens. The major difference more than 150 years later is the medium, as he couldn't know that the integration has potentially been moved or expanded from market place and group of regulars to the Internet with its information and communication technologies (ICTs) or Customer Relationship Management tools (CRM) [1].

However, the new possibilities of government 2.0 or open government have mainly be discussed and identified as an additional channel to integrate and exchange with citizens or people, who are interested, next to more classical platforms like offline workshops, deliberative democracy methods or simply citizen consultation hours. Those still have to be seen as key elements of open integration strategies [7].

Taking a close look on the scholarly literature, it becomes obvious that open innovation and the strategic integration of consumers and citizens are covered closely as such. But, especially the latter leaves various research possibilities open as the public sector has mainly been limited to governments [5] political parties, municipal areas, associations or administration within the Open Government or New Public Management perspective. This excludes the approach and chances of using open innovation regarding another pillar of the public sector, namely educational institutions [8]. While, the discussion about open education in general has led to major findings about the question if higher education should be free of tuition, just a few insights about using open innovation at universities have been delivered [8–10].

Therefore, this paper will focus on the potential benefits and success factors to execute open innovation methods in the scope of higher education, as universities might be private in its origins, but have to be seen as hybrid or assigned to the public agenda.

Hereby, we analyze hands-on data from a project with the public College of William & Mary in Williamsburg, Virginia, USA. The open innovation project focused on co-creating the future of business education through the online idea contest "Tomorrow's MBA". This initiative can be seen as a global pilot in crowdsourcing a strategy outside-the-box, as various target groups have been addressed and integrated during the process. The research data is based on a qualitative approach, as we accompanied the whole process from a scientific point of view and were able to gather qualitative insights, which we highlight in our empirical description. To do so, we first want to achieve a funda-mental theoretical understanding for the topic of open innovation in the public sector. In the end we conclude how this can be successfully applied in higher education by discussing the conclusion and the results of the case "Tomorrow's MBA".

2   Theoretical Background: Using Open Innovation and Crowdsourcing in the Public Sector

The burgeoning literature on open innovation has revitalized firms' interest in purpo-sively opening their business models in order to commercialize not only their own ideas but also external ones. The act of opening up the internal boundaries, f.e. in order to collect consumer insights, collaboratively create new product or service ideas through various online or offline channels, integrate consumers alongside the value chain or outsourcing even product tests to very active users or brand enthusiasts (lead user), leads to an open and more consumer-driven path in innovation (open innovation) [11]. Prom-inent case studies document that companies have discovered the value to be gained from tapping into external sources [12] by referring to empirical evidence that open innovation activities are having a sustainable impact on the companies' success. For instance a survey report by Chesbrough and Brunswicker in 2013 shows that over one third of the surveyed large firms (78 %) have already adopted the approach of innovating openly successfully [13]. In addition, consumers have been found to be valuable partners in gaining need information and creative input [14]. The use cases are different in approach and outcome as examples show; while Bombardier has tried to identify new design concepts for the train of the future, Intel searched together with creative users new use cases for a future technology (Sensing Technology).

Ever since the philosophy of Open Innovation emerged, firms dwelled upon the question which tasks in value creation would be suited for the active integration of consumers (Co-Creation), e.g. through crowdsourcing. Crowdsourcing can be subsumed under the broader concept of co-creation which can be defined as the active, creative and social process, based on collaboration between producers and users that is initiated by the firm to generate value for customers. However, the method itself can be seen as a thriving approach which internalizes a higher level of division of labor engaging external actors in various tasks that had previously been performed by the company itself [15]. In return, participants are incentivized with a reward, which can be intrinsic (f.e. altruism) or extrinsic (f.e. monetary). Hence, researchers dealt with the question of how to successfully design crowdsourcing platforms in the industry context that ignite users' interest in participation, allowing for creative collaboration, and help to build lively social networks [15]. Additionally, Belz et al. point out that especially idea contests have to be seen as promising tool to integrate experts, consumers or citizens from outside the institutional barriers, as gamification and motivational strategies lead to a broad interest and communicational buzz during the campaign [16]. These insights, deduced from the corporate world may offer valuable hints also for the design and management of co-creation platforms in the public sector, especially for the use within higher education, knowing, they may not be directly applicable since public administration differ significantly from companies.

The international rise of this topic is closely connected to new information and communication technologies like social media solutions, wikis and various topic related online groups as well as mobile application, which offer quick access to a large crowd of creative minds at low cost. Social media are at their core based on participation, openness, conversation, community, and connectedness, allowing any internet user to create and exchange his or her own ideas, experience, and expectation [17]. This supports large-scale communication, information sharing, and the coordination among individual citizen, and enables to quickly gather and integrate knowledge from widely dispersed and formerly unconnected groups of people.

The mega-trend of digitalization and open innovation doesn't hold in at economical boundaries. It becomes obvious that citizens in general are used to the rapidity of the internet, collaborative wikis and other dynamic as well as innovative tools, though new ways have to be found to integrate more interactive and social media driven approaches into everyday politics [18]. Furthermore, they expect the adaption of administrations and politics to this level of communication and speed. This expectation covers also the formulation, interpretation and implementation of policies, where significant changes through open government strategies can be achieved. Therefore, the last couple of years have shown that public management, but also political and social science analyzed the potential of online crowdsourcing within the public sector. The broad opportunities given through new ICT and the internet, led to the thriving of the mobilization perspective, which was among others articulated by Norris [19] to have mainly three mechanisms in its core: (1) Internet lowers the costs of gathering and sharing information about politics and is therefore leading to more participation of the disadvantaged; (2) the collaborative structure of the internet leads to a tighter relationship between disengaged citizens and the political world; and (3) the internet bridges the gap of socioeconomic cleavages.

Even though the literature on the use of open innovation in the public sector is growing rapidly, it covers mainly the primary institutions and their need or approach to execute open innovation initiatives like political parties, governments, politicians, administrations or unions. The purpose of this paper, as mentioned above, is to focus on how another institutional backbone of the public service, namely universities, can use the method of crowdsourcing and identify critical success factors. The lack of literature surprises, as you might think the step from opening up companies to consumers or governments to citizens, is logical followed by universities, which are opening up to students or external experts. So, we want to address the following general research question within this paper: (1) How and under which conditions crowdsourcing platforms can be applied to the higher education sector from both a theoretical as well as empirical perspective?

This question is accompanied by seeking answers on (2) factors of success in the process as well as (3) specifications, which have to be considered when implementing open innovation within higher education. Finally, we seek to highlight the objectives that can be reached by realizing a crowdsourcing campaign for universities.

3   Empirical Approach

In order to analyze the research questions we focused on a qualitative approach: the Participatory Action Research Approach [20]. Participatory Action research can be seen as a well-tested and robust method to observe and gain insights on innovation processes. It is defined by trial and error loops that allow for various iterations of planning, acting, observing and reflecting. This process facilitates joint learning among the research team, the participants and other stakeholders that are involved in the research [20]. To gain these insights the research team is accompanying the project team from the William & Mary University from the concept phase to the final evaluation. As part of the participatory approach, qualitative interviews with the project team and responsible persons of the William & Mary University were executed to get in-depth insights about purposes, background, goals, realization, but also implementation of the open innovation project. Additionally, the data given through the registration process on the innovation platform as well as the input from external experts, teaching staff, students etc. through their submissions and input on the platform was analyzed.

This study was conducted over six months and consisted of three phases: (1) the conceptual phase for planning the whole innovation process, (2) the live phase, where the platform was opened up to gather input from the target group and discussion took place and (3) the evaluation phase, where the concept and ideas were condensed and shortlisted for potential implementation. In the following the different phases are described. In order to answer our research questions, we will highlight the success factors as well as the specifications of implementation.

4   Co-creating Tomorrow's MBA

4.1   Conceptual Phase

In 2015, the Mason A. School of Business at the College of William and Mary decided to collaboratively design the future of their MBA. The nucleus of this decision has been the international experience of influential enterprises and organizations, which use co-creation in order to find new trends, innovate their products or improve their services. While different researches have shown that the use of crowdsourcing and methods like innovation contests on social media platforms can be successfully applied in industry and the governmental sector, not many higher education institutions have tested this approach in field and especially for their own use (rather analyzed the data from projects with partners from industry or the public sector). While universities focus on content-driven "products" as the MBA than on physical innovations, the target group differs tremendously from classical open innovation approaches. (Former) MBA students, the teaching staff, business professionals, academics and contestants should come up with new and innovative ideas how the future of the MBA and business administration could like. To combine this goal with a gamification approach to attract the target group, an Online Community was built up with a professional agency, which helped the organization from planning to evaluation. The consortium forged the concept of a social media driven idea contest, where winning ideas will be picked out in the end by an influential jury from the industry to boost the motivation of the target group (e.g. Michael Medline, CEO of Canadian Tire). The award for the winner was mainly intrinsic motivated: The winner's name will be engraved on a Tomorrow's MBA plaque that will be prominently placed in Miller Hall, home to the Mason A. School of Business at William & Mary in Williamsburg, Virginia. In addition, the winner will be featured on the school's website and in a news release as well as getting an interview for the weekly influential podcast of the School. Therefore, the project setting enabled the research team to include the experts as co-researchers and to conduct the action research practically.

Albeit the project's practical manner put some limitations towards the planning and implementation of the action cycles, it allowed the researchers to directly review and perform changes regarding the design of virtual open education platform. Moreover, during the planning phase, different stakeholders from the teaching staff and administration of the college were briefed and decided upon elemental questions like design of the platform, activation and motivation strategy, evaluation process, feedback management or implementation strategies beforehand in a workshop. To guide the community five categories were chosen, where ideas could have been submitted to:

– *Courses, Focus & Skills*: Includes all aspects pertaining to the content in Tomorrow's MBA program or the skills that should be taught and learned in the new Mason A. School MBA program. Relevant content. This could include class offerings, focus or "majors," experiential learning opportunities, partnerships, etc. What should be taught moving forward and what should, no longer, be taught?
– *Formats:* Includes all topics that deal with the fundamental structure of Tomorrow's MBA program. F.e. online, offline or blended model; inclusion of MOOCs or technologies which could be utilized; the academic calendar — semesters, blocks, two-year, one-year, a hybrid, or something new; etc. What should Tomorrow's MBA look like from a format standpoint?
– *Scholarships & Financing*: This includes ideas connected to the steps before students enroll in Tomorrow's MBA program. F.e. new approaches to scholarships; rethinking ways for students and others to finance the program; cost of the program; new and unique ways to raise scholarship funds; etc.
– *Lifelong Learning & Community*: Ideas and innovations that lead to a strong lifelong relationship between each student/graduate and Tomorrow's MBA/the Mason School/William & Mary.
– *Marketing & Branding*: This category includes thoughts, ideas, and innovations pertaining the most effective ways to promote Tomorrow's MBA to prospective students, employers, media and other important audiences. Discussion will include to whom we should communicate and how.

After deciding to launch an eight week ideation campaign on the community (start October 30th with an end on December 23rd 2015), the same group gathered again to submit first ideas on the platform as an initial filling and an additional orientation for the crowd.

4.2 Technical Execution Phase

Based on detailed concept and developed milestones, the online community was finally designed, programmed and eventually tested (Fig. 1).

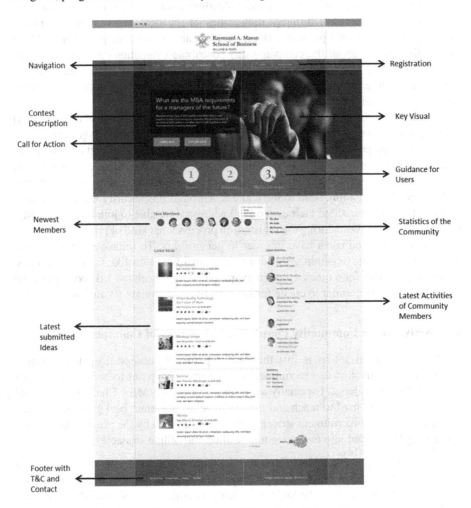

Fig. 1. Landing Page of the collaboration platform (Source: www.tomorrowsmba.mason.wm.edu)

The landing page of the online community was designed to be as user-friendly as possible. Under the logo of the Mason A. School of Business to anchor a quick visual realization of the organization, a navigation menu led to the subpages as (1) the submission form for contributing an idea, (2) an idea pool, (3) a community pool, and (4) to information pages like a detailed contest description or background information about the jurors. Furthermore, a video with the Associate Dean of the School was implemented after the go-live to give a visual and audio explanation of the contest topic. In addition, news feeds were displayed on the vivid landing page to show recent activities from community members as they were able to submit ideas for the future of the MBA, but also to leave comments underneath ideas, evaluations to rank them (the "like" of an idea or a 5-star-Likert scale of different dimensions of an idea) or even write personal messages on each other's pin walls. Hence, visitors and users of the platform could (1) inform themselves about the campaign, (2) contribute evaluations and comments to already uploaded ideas and even (3) participate through own ideas and concepts regarding the given five categories. Users were even able to upload additional content and files like Word, PDF, embedded videos or tag their ideas.

On the top of the page a login/registration box was placed through which registered users were able to sign in and new users could access the registration page, where they could register by providing a user name and e-mail address. This method is particularly necessary, because it guarantees the authenticity of the user. After the registration process, the new user had to activate his account through the verification of the e-mail address by clicking a link send to the address. Through this security mechanism only users that actually provided their own e-mail address were able to join the community. However, we also asked during the registration process what kind of professional background the registered users have in order to get insights. To improve the interactive discussions from the beginning, social media (share) functions like forwarding ideas, Facebook Connect for a quick entry (registration) or a "Facebook Likebox" from the College were used in order to create further attention and initiate a viral buzz.

4.3   Activation & Community Phase: The Importance of Communication

While the technical set-up is just the first step into a successful open innovation campaign, the activation and recruitment of the target group has to be seen as a major communication challenge. Especially within the Tomorrow's MBA Challenge, potential idea generators are hard to reach and usually have an academic background. Hence, a mixture of different recruitment strategies has been realized by the project staff, which can mainly be divided into two categories: online and offline strategies:

- *Cooperation with Blogs and Communities (online)*: Beforehand of the contest, a research phase has highlighted major blogs (like Poets & Quants), communities and forums, which deal with the topic of higher education and business administration. After go-live they were contacted by the project team if they want to share the initiative.
- *Social Media Shares and Social Media Groups (online):* Right after the start of the contest phase the executing agency as well as the College were sharing the contest

through various social media channels like Twitter, YouTube, Facebook, LinkedIn, Xing, Google Plus. Moreover, the official webpages of the College were displaying banners with a link to the community. In addition, closed groups within these social media channels were identified and directly contacted with the wish to share the contest URL.

- *Newsletter (online):* Existing network partners and newsletter recipients were informed throughout the contest phase within different newsletters. Especially the alumni network of the Mason A. School of Business was contacted several times.

- *Contest Webpages (online)*: In general, there are existing webpages, which function as distributor for different contest communities worldwide. Those initiatives like Dare2Compete were addressed by the project team and shared the content.

- *Community Management (online):* As soon as a community starts living due to a certain number of registrations, it has to be managed professionally to motivate the users. Welcoming texts for new users were as important as continuous feedback management from experts of the College to submitted ideas or personal motivation texts on the user's pin walls.

- *Info Stands at Universities (offline):* The project staff tried to acquire students and academics at universities to fill out papers with their ideas, which were uploaded later on the community. Universities like the LMU or the TU in Munich in Germany were targeted for instance.

- *Press Releases (offline)*: Major opinion leaders from the press world like the Virginia Gazette were identified and delivered with a press kit about the campaign. Here all important dates were displayed and the opportunity to get more info via interviews shared with the targeted channels.

- *Meet-Ups & Round Table Discussion (offline)s*: In specific spots like Williamsburg (location of the College) and Munich (location of the agency) or Bayreuth in Germany –mainly at Universities- meet-ups with students, Professors, academics and business professionals were held to sit together on a round-table to discuss major trends, ideas and transfer them directly to the online community.

- *Interviews (offline):* During the contest phase the project staff created a list with academics and Professors within their personal network. In a next step a majority of them were called or met personally (telephone or face-to-face interview) and inter-viewed about their ideas for the future of the MBA. These insights consequently ended up on the community as submitted concepts.

- *Stakeholder Network & Guest Lectures (offline):* Additionally, the project team arranged various guest lectures at Universities, f.e. at the University of Lübeck or the Fresenius School in Germany to share the content of the contest. Moreover, the academical network -especially in the scope of the MBA sphere- was addressed to share the innovative challenge and to activate certain multiplicators.

4.4 Results

During the eight week ideation phase on the innovation community www.tomor-rowsmba.mason.wm.edu 200 ideas from over 5.000 unique visitors from 78 different countries worldwide were submitted. 307 of them registered actively and shared various information about their professional background as well as their contact details. Moreover, 265 comments on shared ideas and 537 evaluations have been made by the community. Interestingly, more than 35 striking press releases, newspaper and blog articles or social media postings were shared and led to a remarkable viral buzz. The influential blog "Poets & Quants" alone named the initiative as one of the top ten innovative projects from universities in 2015. The input will be evaluated by the jury and the teaching staff of the School in 2016 to forge the new MBA for the College (Fig. 2).

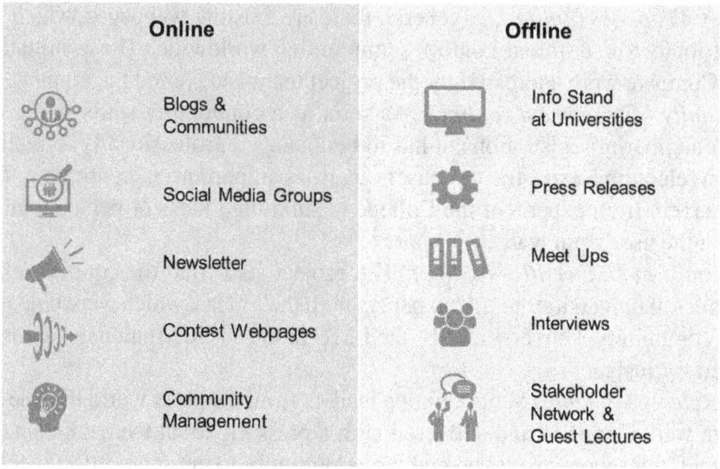

Online	Offline
Blogs & Communities	Info Stand at Universities
Social Media Groups	Press Releases
Newsletter	Meet Ups
Contest Webpages	Interviews
Community Management	Stakeholder Network & Guest Lectures

Fig. 2. Recruitment strategy including social media channels to create viral buzz

5   Conclusion & Further Research

Hence, this research project has shown that the strategic use of social media in a collaborative way leads to a sustainable input from outside the organizational boundaries – with a focus on higher education. Innovative ideas like the use of Hackathons within the MBA program, specific courses for military units, various Apps (e.g. Tinder-App for businesses and students), Learn-how-to-learn modules or future double degree courses described in detail are just a sample of ideas out of 200. In addition, many idea clusters and trends have been spotted through the evaluation process. Here, the faculty was highly involved, as the submitted ideas had to be analyzed and shortlisted to a final top 20 list, which was then discussed with the jury to pick out the winners. As a matter of fact we have seen that even top ideas had to be awarded in the end, the implementation of individual innovative ideas is just half of the success within a competition. All other ideas are still a rich source of inspiration and can be combined, structured or enriched by the faculty and executed as well. In other words: picking out winning ideas through an influential jury doesn't necessarily means that just those ideas could enrich the organization. All others should remain on the radar. Moreover, we highlighted in this paper the various success factors throughout the different phases of the project. While a functioning and user friendly platform is just a small piece of the success jigsaw, the communication strategy mainly decides upon the final results. Interestingly, online channels and social media play a very important role for the viral buzz and marketing effect of the contest, but are way more sustainable when a fruitful combination with offline channels is created. Analyzing the traffic sources of the platform showed that especially facebook groups, blog articles, social media shares and contest pages had a significant effect on the diffusion. While the outcome can be described as very much quantitative and important for the number of registrations and visitors, the offline channels gathered more qualitative input. More than 50 % (102 out of 200 ideas) of the submitted ideas can be referred to personal interviews, info stands at universities or initiated meet-ups.

While this initiative is still a pilot within higher education, the trend of using open innovation and integrating external experts and students in the sector is from our perspective inexorable. Future research could highlight the comparison to projects from the industry or other public innovation communities. Furthermore, the integration and efforts of the faculty during the ideation process and the influence to the overall outcome seems to be an interesting field to analyze.

References

1. Richter, P., Cornford, J.: Customer relationship management and citizenmship: technologies and identities in public services. social. Policy Soc. **7**(2), 211–220 (2008)
2. Brynjolfsson, E., McAfee, A.: The Second Machine Age: Work, Progress, and Prosperity in a Time of Brilliant Technologies. Norton & Company, New York (2014)
3. Füller, J., Mühlbacher, H., Matzler, K., Jawecki, G.: Consumer empowerment through Internet-based co-creation. J. Manage. Inf. Syst. **26**(3), 71–102 (2009)
4. Rapp, M., Hoffmann, C.P., Kröger, N.: Beteiligung an Open Government fördern. HMD Praxis der Wirtschaftsinformatik. **301**(52), 161–171 (2015)
5. Nam, T.: Citizens' attitudes toward Open Government and Government. 2.0. Int. Rev. Admin. Sci. **78**(2), 346–368 (2012)
6. Carter, W.E., Carter, M.S.: The British longitude act reconsidered. Am. Sci. **100**, 102 (2012)
7. Fishkin, J.S.: When the People Speak: Deliberative Democracy and Public Consultation. Oxford University Press, London (2009)
8. Padilla-Meléndez, A., Garrido-Moreno, A.: Open innovation in universities: What motivates researchers to engage in knowledge transfer exchanges: Int. J. Entrepreneurial Behav. Res. **18**(4), 417–439 (2012)
9. Kux, B.: Universities and Open Innovation: a New Research Paradigm. In: Dual, J., Schwyzer, N.: Essays 2030: Visionen für die Zukunft der ETH Zürich. Neue Zürcher Zeitung NZZ libro (2005)
10. Fox, J.: Your Child's Strengths: A Guide for Parents and Teachers. Penguin Group, London (2008)
11. Chesbrough, H., Appleyard, M.: Open innovation and strategy. Calif. Manag. Rev. **50**(1), 57–76 (2007)
12. Nambisan, S., Sawhney, M.: A buyer's guide to the innovation bazaar. Harvard Bus. Rev. **85**(6), 109–118 (2007)
13. Chesbrough, H., Brunswicker, S.: Managing Open innovation in Large firms. Survey Report UC Berkeley & Fraunhofer Insitute for Industrial Engineering, Stuttgart (2013)

14. Sawhney, M., Prandelli, E.: Communities of Creation: managing distributed innovation in turbulent markets. Calif. Manag. Rev. **42**(4), 24–54 (2000)
15. Füller, J.: Refining virtual co-creation from a consumer perspective. Calif. Manag. Rev. **52**(2), 98–122 (2010)
16. Belz, F.M., Silvertant, S., Füller, J., Pobisch, J.: Ideenwettbewerbe. TU Munich, Munich (2009)
17. Kaplan, A.M., Haenlein, M.: Users of the world unite! The challenges and opportunities of Social Media. Bus. Horiz. **53**(1), 59–68 (2009)
18. Collm, A., Schedler, K.: Managing crowd innovation in public administration. Int. Public Manag. Rev. **13**(2), 1–18 (2012)
19. Norris, P.: A Virtous Circle: Political Communication in Postindustrial Societies. Cambridge University Press, London (2000)
20. Checkland, P., Holwell, S.: Action research: its nature and validity. In: Kock, N. (ed.) Information Systems Action Research: An Applied View of Emerging Concepts and Methods, pp. 3–17. Springer, Boston (2007)

Using Liferay as an Interdisciplinary Scientific Collaboration Portal
A Comparative Usability Study of Version 6.1 and 6.2

Günther Schuh[1], André Bräkling[1(✉)], André Calero Valdez[2],
Anne-Kathrin Schaar[2], and Martina Ziefle[2]

[1] Fraunhofer Institute for Production Technology,
Steinbachstraße 17, 52074 Aachen, Germany
{guenther.schuh,andre.braekling}@ipt.fraunhofer.de
[2] Human-Computer Interaction Center, RWTH Aachen University,
Campus-Boulevard 57, Aachen, Germany
{calero-valdez,schaar,ziefle}@comm.rwth-aachen.de

1 Introduction

Interdisciplinary collaboration is seen as a means to solve complex problems that surpass disciplinary boundaries. By combining methods from different disciplines advances can be achieved that were previously inaccessible. In the Cluster of Excellence "Integrative Production Technology for High-Wage Countries" — a research cluster with over 180 staff members from various disciplines — interdisciplinary collaboration is applied intensively. In order to support this collaboration process, we set up a scientific cooperation portal that supports the researchers in various ways.

The web-based portal offers functionality that addresses barriers and benefits of scientific interdisciplinary collaboration [1,2]. As an example, a shared file-space that can be easily accessed from the individual institutes is provided. This file-space supports the researchers as it provides a secure storage location of data that needs to be shared across institutional boundaries. Version control makes sure changes to files will never get lost.

The framework used to create such a portal is the open-source software Liferay[1]. Liferay is a portal solution that comes with several out-of-the-box features that are helpful for scientific collaboration (e.g. the mentioned file-space). Our portal started using the Liferay 6.1 version. In this version some users reported having difficulties in using the portal. Liferay 6.2 comes with several bug fixes and included new features such as:

- *Responsive design:* The design responds flexibly to changing screen sizes. So it can be used on desktop PCs as well as on mobile devices, like smartphones or tablets. Designers and developers can use a preview feature to test their work on different screen resolutions.

---

[1] https://www.liferay.com.

© Springer International Publishing Switzerland 2016
G. Meiselwitz (Ed.): SCSM 2016, LNCS 9742, pp. 405–414, 2016.
DOI: 10.1007/978-3-319-39910-2_38

Fig. 1. The home page of the former Scientific Cooperation Portal using Liferay 6.1. The design was based on the Cluster of Excellence website and dominated by an image slider on top.

- *Several User Interface Refinements:* Beside the general design, also the control elements were recreated. Additionally, the underlying web technologies were updated to provide up-to-date tools for developers.
- *Improved Content Management:* New functionality was added to manage and structure portal contents, e.g., folders to manage content articles, dynamic data structures to define own content types, and a recycle bin to restore erroneously deleted contents.

For further details about Liferay 6.2 improvements, refer to the official Liferay blogs [3,4].

These features promise an improvement in usability, but changing the user interface comes also with switching-costs based on the adjustment to and adaption of new operational concepts. To legitimate these switching costs, which may lead into refusal by the users to work with our cooperation portal, we have to make sure the system usability was actually improved, so that we can expect a long-term increase of satisfaction and acceptance. For this reason, we conducted a comparative usability study of the two used versions, which will allow us to evaluate the supposed usability improvement but also the expected switching costs.

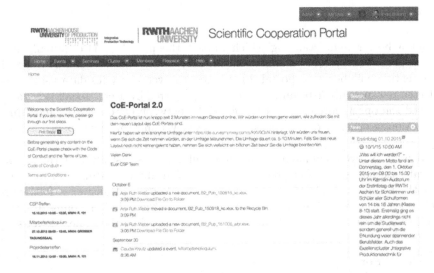

Fig. 2. The home page of the new Scientific Cooperation Portal using Liferay 6.2. The design was based on the Liferay default theme and focused on a very simple and clear structure.

2   Related Work

The scientific cooperation portal was set up to support inter-organizational technology transfer within the Cluster of Excellence. Therefore, we decided to use modern web technologies and social media approaches, which are suitable for this supporting task [5–7].

Our portal meets several functional requirements we identified before [8]: presentation of comprehensive information on technologies or technological know how, presentation of users and their expertise, technology- and application specific information clustering, communication channels et cetera.

Nevertheless user factors must be considered when developing a social software portal that relates to knowledge management and sharing [9]. In particular using such a software in a work environment is fundamentally different than using it in private usage contexts [10]. Users show different sharing behaviors in private and working contexts often moderated by their personality [11]. Often using a social networking site at work comes with new challenges as missing etiquette [12] and differing usage motivation [13]. Neglecting these requirements can lead to rejection of such a tool [14]. Even when individual differences are regarded, one must focus on slick usability [15] to reduce the amount of added complexity into an already stressful researcher life.

All of these findings show, that a successful portal solution depends on a multitude of factors. For this reason, changes to the user interface may cause unpredictable consequences. Accordingly, the preliminarily described user study is mandatory after we updated our existing portal.

3 Method

To get a better understanding which impact the portal update actually has on the perceived system usability, we initially analyzed the general usage of the scientific collaboration portal. In this regard, web analytics data usage was collected to especially determine the features preferred by users. To get this data, we used the open source analytics tool Piwik[2] between October 2013 and April 2015. Among other data, we measured page views and the time spent on each page.

Afterwards, we conducted the actually intended user study in form of two separate studies, which were recorded using the usability testing tool Morae[3]. In both studies, we asked six users to perform tasks and answer a follow-up study. The study was a repeated-measure within-subject design, comparing the usability of versions 6.1 (Fig. 1) and 6.2 (Fig. 2) regarding the same six tasks.

3.1 Task Set

The following tasks were to be performed using both Liferay 6.1 (1st user study) and Liferay 6.2 (2nd user study).

- *Profile Details:* Please validate your personal details. If you find any missing information, please add the information.
- *User Lookup:* Please find person N.N. and send him a personal message.
- *Document Download:* Please locate the protocol of the last colloquium of employees. Please download this document.
- *Calendar:* Please find out when your next project-meeting will take place.
- *Publication Upload:* Your last paper was accepted. Please upload the PDF file from the desktop into its designated location on the server.
- *Community Features:* Your project leader has uploaded a document in your project folder. Please add your feedback on his document by giving it a 4-star rating.

After the tasks were completed, a post-experimental survey was conducted. Here, we measured usability using the system-usability scale. We also measured user satisfaction, expected product use and various independent variables for analyses.

4 Results

We analyzed both all utterances of participants as well as quantitative information from the post-experiment questionnaire.

---

[2] http://piwik.org.
[3] https://www.techsmith.de/morae.html.

4.1 Description of the Sample

All participants were members of the Cluster of Excellence staff and voluntarily took part in the user studies. For the second study regarding Liferay 6.2 we made sure that all participants already knew the previous portal version. We found that at least a third of our participants uses the portal system more than once a month in both studies. Almost all users have been using the portal for longer than 6 months, with a unique exception in the second study. Most researchers reported to use the portal for information purposes (see Fig. 3). Interestingly, the knowledge management purpose decreased for the second study, while the file-space still is one of the most active areas in our portal.

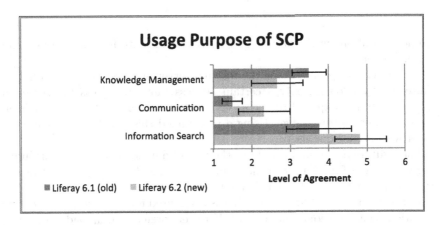

Fig. 3. Reported purpose of usage. Error bars denote standard errors.

4.2 Web Analytics Findings

The web analytics data stated a very clear result: By far, the file-space section was the most-used feature, followed by event information and news. Table 1 gives an overview on relative usage frequency and time by portal section between October 2013 and April 2015. These results also fit the participants' usage purposes as shown in Fig. 3: Predominantly they use the portal for information search.

4.3 Qualitative Findings

Most of the negative feedback we recorded was addressing naming of menu points, which were done similarly in both Liferay versions by us. This means that some participants did not find the naming of menu entries intuitive (e.g. *filespace* instead of *downloads*). Besides that differing levels of menu-depth caused disorientation. Certain menu-levels only contained one sub-menu. This caused the UI-menu to not reveal the mouse-hover-menu. Users mistook this for an error.

Table 1. Relative usage frequence and time by portal section between October 2013 and April 2015.

Section	% of visits	% of time spent
File-space	36.9	60.8
Event information	27.6	12.0
News	21.1	12.5
General cluster information	6.2	3.5
Members	6.0	9.1
Help	1.5	2.1
Seminar sign-up and information	0.7	0.1

Minor irritations were the usage of an American date format in a German research cluster.

A more delicate problem was the internal server architecture. As our server is protected by allowing only a certain address range to access the server, a VPN connection is required to access it. Problematic was that the server itself was outside this address range. Using a proxy fixed this problem, but caused a browser warning for one user.

Almost all users complained about the lack of a good search function. Interestingly, a search function is included in Liferay 6.2, but was disabled in our setting. This issue could thus easily be fixed.

The document management system was configured for the upload of scientific publications (i.e. additional meta-data). Yet users preferred to upload documents as regular documents. Users expected a meta-data auto-detection from pdf files.

A major concern for some users was the continuity of the portal. Users were wondering, what would happen to the data after the funding period of the portal. Researchers demand a software that extends over project funding and can be integrated into several projects, if they are expected to upload and maintain their personal data.

The feature that caused the most trouble is also the seemingly most simple. The calendar behaves differently from outlook and causes slight annoyances for users that normally use outlook to manage their appointments.

The feature most liked by our participants was the member search. The portal supports looking up other researchers and their photos. This was reported to be extremely helpful in a cluster with over 80 active researchers.

Overall, all participants reported that they like the design of the new version and described it as more intuitive than the previous one.

4.4   Comparison of Survey Results

We evaluated the the software using items from the UTAUT, SUS and NPS Scale in both trials. Clear differences can be seen for the items *It is easy for me to use efficiently, I find it easy to use* and *The cluster supports the use.* These

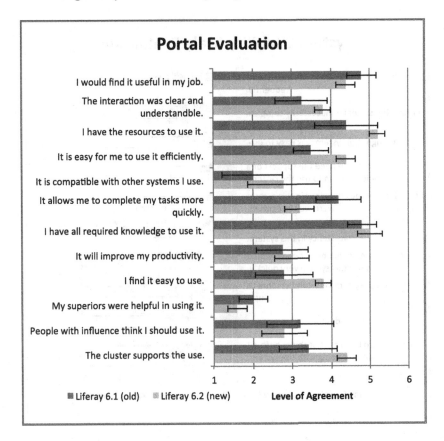

Fig. 4. Usability evaluation according to the UTAUT items. Error bars denote standard errors.

three items show an improvement even for this relatively small sample size. In contrast, the item *It allows me to complete my tasks more quickly* showed a negative effect, which we in part attribute to switching-costs (see Fig. 4).

The System Usability Scale [16] showed an improvement in most measured variables. Variables were measured on a six-point Likert scale and showed an increase of about one standard deviation for most items (see Fig. 5). In particular inconsistencies in the system were removed and people could see other users performing quickly in the system.

The Net Promoter Score [17] increased from 36 to 62 points (see Fig. 6). Beyond this it showed a large reduction in variance, leaving a more homogeneous picture for the second evaluation.

5   Discussion

The usage of "yet another" software for busy researchers must be planned well [14]. When ease of use and usefulness of such a software are not sufficient, social

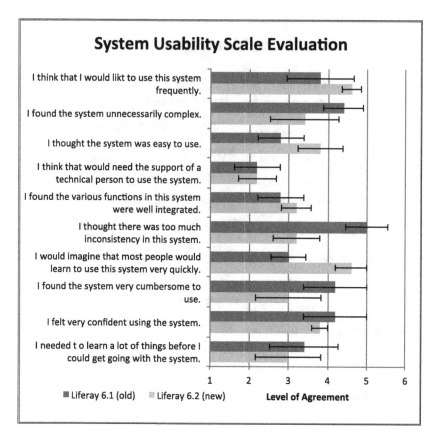

Fig. 5. System usability evaluation according to the SUS items. Error bars denote standard errors.

software is not being used. This problem is amplified by the social nature of social portals. A threshold of users is required to create an agile social community, but if the first users are dissatisfied no social interaction will ever take place.

Our research especially showed, that migrating a software to a complete new user interface may come as a drawback of losing users that already have come accustomed to the user interface of the older version. In our specific case we can argue, that a migration from Liferay 6.1 and 6.2 can be conducted without the loss of users, because the new version improves the usability regardless of switching costs. We also attribute the success in migration to the integration of users in the upgrade process. Menus were renamed according to users expectations and the participants took part in communicating the benefits of the new platform.

Overall, Liferay shows the potential to be used as an open-source research management system when tweaked accordingly. Some of the features, that are a problem for users, are the non-typical calendar and the non-intuitive sub-community management. For the latter, the mental model of how to access a

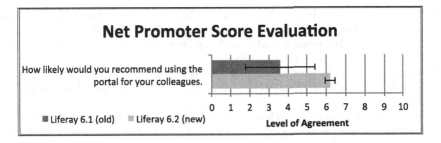

Fig. 6. System usability evaluation according to the Net Promoter Score. Error bars denote standard errors.

sub-community was not immediately clear and thus needs to be improved in the user interface.

5.1 Limitations

Our study was conducted as an exploratory study to both measure and steer the usability and usefulness of our scientific cooperation portal. The relatively small sample size prevent more in depth statistical analyses, but is still helpful in understanding a migration process.

6 Outlook and Future Work

Because of the small quantity of participants, we plan to re-validate our usability findings based on a bigger survey within the Cluster of Excellence. In spring 2016, the new portal version is in use for more than a year, which will allow a new examination without the interference of switching-costs. Overall we plan to continuously monitor the usability of our portal in order to ensure that future migrations can be equally successful.

Acknowledgments. This work was performed as part of the Cluster of Excellence "Integrative Production Technology for High-Wage Countries", which is funded by the excellence initiative by the German federal and state governments to promote science and research at German universities. Furthermore we would like to thank Juliana Brell and Tatjana Hamann, who helped conducting this research.

References

1. Vaegs, T., Calero Valdez, A., Schaar, A.K., Bräkling, A., Aghassi, S., Jansen, U., Thiele, T., Welter, F., Jooß, C., Richert, A., et al.: Enhancing scientific cooperation of an interdisciplinary cluster of excellence via a scientific cooperation portal. In: Full Paper Accepted at the International Conference on E-Learning at the Workplace, 11–13 June 2014

2. Calero Valdez, A., Schaar, A.K., Ziefle, M., Holzinger, A.: Enhancing interdisciplinary cooperation by social platforms. In: Human Interface and the Management of Information. Information and Knowledge Design and Evaluation, pp. 298–309. Springer International Publishing (2014)
3. Falkner, J.: Liferay Portal 6.2 CE Release (2013). https://www.liferay.com/de/web/james.falkner/blog/-/blogs/liferay-portal-6-2-ce-release. Accessed 27 Jan 2016
4. Mesotten, P.: Liferay 6.2 - What's new under the hood? (2014). https://www.liferay.com/de/web/pmesotten/blog/-/blogs/liferay-6-2-what-s-new-under-the-hood-. Accessed 27 Jan 2016
5. Leonardi, P.M.: Social media, knowledge sharing, and innovation: toward a theory of communication visibility. Inf. Syst. Res. 25(4), 796–816 (2014)
6. Leupold, M.: Technologietransfer im Web 2.0 Wie das Wissen heute in die Welt kommen kann. Wissenschaftsmanagement 1 (2010)
7. Czarnitzki, D., Eckert, T., Egeln, J., Elschner, C.: Internetangebote zum Wissens- und Technologietransfer in Deutschland - Bestandsaufnahme, Funktionalität und Alternativen (2000)
8. Schuh, G., Aghassi, S.: Supporting technology transfer with communities and social software solutions. Int. J. Mech. Aerosp. Ind. Mechatron. Eng. 7(11), 1119–1127 (2013)
9. Calero Valdez, A., Schaar, A.K., Bender, J., Aghassi, S., Schuh, G., Ziefle, M.: Social media applications for knowledge exchange in organizations. In: Razmerita, L., et al. (eds.) Innovations in Knowledge Management. ISRL, vol. 95, pp. 147–176. Springer, Heidelberg (2016)
10. Schaar, A.K., Calero Valdez, A., Ziefle, M., Eraßme, D., Löcker, A.-K., Jakobs, E.-M.: Reasons for using social networks professionally. In: Meiselwitz, G. (ed.) SCSM 2014. LNCS, vol. 8531, pp. 385–396. Springer, Heidelberg (2014)
11. Schaar, A.K., Valdez, A.C., Ziefle, M.: User-centered design of business communities. The influence of diversity factors on motives to use communities in professional settings. Procedia Manufact. 3, 645–652 (2015)
12. Calero Valdez, A., Kathrin Schaar, A., Ziefle, M.: Personality influences on etiquette requirements for social media in the work context. In: Holzinger, A., Ziefle, M., Hitz, M., Debevc, M. (eds.) SouthCHI 2013. LNCS, vol. 7946, pp. 427–446. Springer, Heidelberg (2013)
13. Schaar, A.K., Calero Valdez, A., Ziefle, M.: Nutzungsmotivation von sozialen netzwerken im arbeitskontext. In: Exploring Demographics, pp. 657–666. Springer Fachmedien, Wiesbaden (2015)
14. Löcker, A.K., Eraßme, D., Jakobs, E.M., Schaar, A.K., Calero Valdez, A., Ziefle, M.: Yet another platform? motivational factors for using online communities in business contexts. In: Advances in The Ergonomics in Manufacturing: Managing the Enterprise of the Future, vol. 13, p. 152 (2014)
15. Calero Valdez, A., Brauner, P., Schaar, A.K., Holzinger, A., Ziefle, M.: Reducing complexity with simplicity-usability methods for industry 4.0. In: Proceedings 19th Triennial Congress of the IEA, pp. 9–14 (2015)
16. Brooke, J.: SUS: a "quick and dirty" usability scale. In: Usability Evaluation in Industry, pp. 189–194. Taylor and Francis, London (1986)
17. Reichheld, F.F.: The number one you need to grow. Harvard Bus. Rev. 12, 47–54 (2003)

Enterprise Social Media

"Fake It or Make It" – Selfies in Corporate Social Media Campaigns

Tina Gruber-Muecke[1(✉)] and Christiane Rau[2]

[1] Department of Interactive Media and Educational Technologies,
Danube University Krems, Krems, Austria
tina.gruber-muecke@donau-uni.ac.at
[2] Centre of Innovation and Product Management,
University of Applied Sciences Upper Austria, Wels, Austria
christiane.rau@fh-wels.at

Abstract. The usage of selfies has become increasingly popular as a central element in social media campaigns. This study interviewed 9 professionals from marketing agencies to explore the role of selfies in corporate social media campaigns. We identified three distinct types of selfies, i.e. "classic selfies", "polished selfies", and "faked selfies". We found that professionals strive for perceived authenticity of user communication (which is best conveyed by "classic selfies"), while they want to maintain control over the campaigns (e.g. to ensure the aesthetic value and the ad authenticity) leading to the use of "polished selfies" or "faked selfies". As a result of this tension, we identified three distinct approaches agencies and their clients adopt balancing this tension. Our research offers insights how to design and manage selfie campaigns.

Keywords: Social media · Selfie · Corporate branding

1 Introduction

In the modern marketplace, consumers are being empowered within social media platforms and are taking on a more active role as creators, facilitators, and editors of online content, as opposed to being merely passive recipients of information. This transformation of communication and its level of interaction open opportunities for "consumer initiated communication" (CIC). The growing use of smartphones has allowed users to access any type of social networking site with just a few swipes of a finger [1]. In 2015, Instagram has more than 300 million active users [2] and currently 193 million public pictures and videos uploaded to Instagram are hashtagged with the words selfie and selfies [3].

As a reaction to this trend, digital media agencies try to integrate selfies in corporate social media campaigns. A selfie is defined as "a photograph that one has taken of oneself, typically one taken with a smartphone or webcam and shared via social media" [4]. Using selfies in a campaign is a two-folded problem. On the one hand a firm must develop strategies that are congruent with, or suited to, different social media functionalities and the goals of the firm. On the other hand scholars note the increasing importance of authenticity to consumers in developed societies, which goes along with the desire to

© Springer International Publishing Switzerland 2016
G. Meiselwitz (Ed.): SCSM 2016, LNCS 9742, pp. 417–427, 2016.
DOI: 10.1007/978-3-319-39910-2_39

escape excessive commercialization, and with a search for meaning and experiences that feel "real". While previous research focused on the usage of social media as a marketing tool for small business, this paper aims to contribute to the emerging theory about the role and communication of authenticity in marketing and how selfies can be used to interact with potential stakeholders, especially customers, during a social media campaign.

The remainder of this paper unfolds as follows: After presenting the literature on the usage of selfies as a social branding tool, as well as authenticity in corporate branding, we describe the research design. Then we present three types of selfies and distinct ways how marketing agencies include these selfies in their branding campaigns. Finally, we discuss implications for brand management practice.

2 Theoretical Background

2.1 Defining the Selfie Construct

While the usage of selfie is extreme and the usage in social media is increasing [5], its history dates back to an American amateur photographer, Robert Cornelius, and an English inventor, Charles Wheatstone around the year 1840 [6]. Selfies are usually casual, improvised, fast; their primary purpose is to be seen here, now, by other people, most of them unknown, in social networks [7]. A selfie is a self-portrait photograph, typically taken with a hand-held digital camera or camera phone and often shared on social network websites (SNSs) [8]. With new advances of camera phones and digital sharing technologies, mobile photo-sharing has become an important communication activity and an integral part of many people's social lives.

2.2 Usage of Selfies as Social Branding Tool

Social media tools can be used by business organizations of various sizes and types as a marketing tool [9] as they allow business organizations to connect with customers at the right time, directly with lower cost and higher efficiency than other traditional communication tools [10]. This allows social media not only to be used by large business organizations, but also by small and medium enterprises [11]. Regarding social branding, nowadays the most effective marketing channel cannot be bought anymore, but should be earned and owned by companies who successfully utilize social media tools. Companies who connect with their customers and generate organic conversation about their brands. Social media platforms like Instagram are used not only to create content about brands but also to connect customers with others who admire the same brands and share their views. The virtual social networks created by brand admirers are called "brand communities" and the challenge for companies is to develop and extend such communities.

2.3 Authenticity in Marketing

In the recent years attention has focused on authenticity in marketing. Sub-sets of research focus on authenticity of products, services, experiences [e.g. 12–14], brands [e.g. 15, 16], and advertisement [e.g. 17, 18]. Customers increasingly seek for the "real", they demand authenticity and person-to-person interaction [19–21]. According to Gilmore and Pine [20], various factors such as an increase in technology-driven interactions, or a professionalization of commercialized and staged experiences drive this demand.

At the first glance, the concept of authenticity seems to be at odds with professional marketing efforts [18]. Addressing the inherent paradox, the definition of authenticity has been expanded [18] to include two forms of authenticity, i.e. indexical authenticity (the original or the "real" thing) and iconic authenticity (a replica or recreation of the original) [13]. Generally speaking, authenticity is conceptualized as a consumers' perception within a particular context, contrary to an inherent quality of the particular entity itself [18]. This information holds whether the entity is a product, service, a brand or an advertisement.

Brand authenticity is associated with greater purchase intention [15], higher brand equity, and consumers' willingness to pay a price premium [22, 23]. A brand is perceived as authentic if a subjective evaluation of genuineness can be ascribed to a brand [15]. Hold states that "To be authentic brands must be disinterested; they must be perceived as invented and disseminated by parties without an instrumental economic agenda, by people who are intrinsically motivated by their inherent value" [24, p. 83]. The challenge for marketers is to walk the fine line between staying true to an authentic core of the brand while still remaining relevant [25].

Consumers also naturally evaluate the authenticity of an advertisement, which can be perceived to be more or less authentic. Stern defines authentic adverting as conveying "the illusion of the reality of ordinary life in reference to a consumption situation" [17, p. 388]. An ad is evaluated as authentic, if the observers perceive it as reflecting the expected band personality, its particular originality, and its character [18]. Stern points to the importance of stories that convey elements of real life to convince the consumer to accept the illusion as mimetic [17]. Miller shows that ad authenticity positively correlates with ad credibility as well as attitude towards the brand [18]. In a similar vein, Chalmers & Price provide evidence that ad authenticity can influence ad liking [26].

In the recent years, authenticity in the context of digital media communication has received considerable interest. Several authors in particular focus on public affair communication [e.g. 27, 28]. Beyond enabling organizational representatives to communicating with the public, social media provides the possibility to actively integrate "ordinary people" as brand representatives, which are generally perceived as more authentic than faceless organizations, or in the case of public affairs, elite political actors [29, 30]. Gilpin et al. argue that the question of authenticity becomes especially relevant in the context of social media, "as these tools are designed to bring" ordinary people "together in some form" [27, p. 259].

While consumers seem to seek for authenticity, using methods of mass marketing to convey authenticity seems to be at odds with the aim. Beverland and Luxton found that consumers believe that mass marketing undermines claims for authenticity [31]. Consumers might interpret those approaches as attempts of manipulation [24] and over-commercialization, which is inherently contrary to authenticity [23, 32]. Subsequently, Kadirov ask for research exploring how non-traditional advertising – advertisement, which the consumer does not perceive as conventional methods of commercial communication (e.g. guerrilla or covert advertising) influence brand authenticity. In this regard, social media campaigns involving fellow consumers, e.g. by using selfies, might open up new possibilities to communicate authenticity [33].

As social media campaigns and selfies are new, companies seek professional assistance from marketing agencies in designing and implementing campaigns. This leads us to the following research question:

How do marketing agencies use selfies to enhance their brand campaigns?

3 Methodology

We chose an exploratory qualitative research design relying on semi-structured qualitative interviews. A homogeneous sample of marketing agencies representative was chosen to explore the shared sensemaking of the selfie phenomenon in branding campaigns. Interviewees were selected on the basis of their affiliation with a marketing agency and their experience designing and coordinating selfie campaigns for corporate clients. Each interviewee had at least worked on two campaigns for consumer brands. Participants were selected using a snowball sampling technique, starting from professional associates of one of the authors and continuing with participants unknown to the authors. Between July and September 2015, nine face-to-face interviews with respondents from Austrian marketing agencies lasting from 30 min to 2 h (average of 1 h) were conducted (with support from a master student). Interviews included questions exploring selfies such as the usage and integration into social media campaigns, platform for selfies and the selection process of photos for selfie campaigns. In the interviews, respondents talk about 11 branding campaigns.

Interviews were subsequently analyzed following the six phases of thematic data analysis as described in Marshall and Rossman [35]. The coding process was based on a set of pre-defined codes deduced from literature as well as an inductive analysis of the interviews. Reoccurring patterns were organized into themes and are subsequently presented.

4 Findings

The authors structure the presentation of the findings as follows. First, the definitions of selfies as elements of social branding campaigns are presented and second, different categories of selfie campaigns are identified.

4.1 Definition of Selfies

All of the interviewed professionals agreed that different types and variations of selfies exist in social media campaigns. They were asked to give a definition for the term user generated selfie. 7 of 9 mentioned the "classic selfie" as "a photo or picture which the photographer has taken by him/herself". While the traditional definition focuses on the user as generator of the selfie, we found two other types of photos, which interviewees also called selfies. We named them "polished selfies" and "faked selfies". "Polished selfies" refer to "classic selfies" which are edited by a marketing agency before being published, e.g. on advertisement posters. Interestingly, marketing agencies include photos in their campaigns, which rely on a selfie style, but are indeed professionally photographed images. They referred to these photos also as "selfies" even if the production of the images is contrary to the prevalent definition of selfies. We named them "faked selfies" (Table 1).

Table 1. Type of selfies in corporate social media campaigns

Type of selfie	Description	Origin
"classic selfie"	Photo of an user which the user has taken him or herself	User generated
"polished selfie"	Photo of an user which the users has taken him or herself, but which has been professionally edited by a marketing agency	User and marketing agency generated
"faked selfie"	Photos deliberately generated by marketing agencies conveying the image of a selfie while being professionally photographed.	Professional photographer or advertising agency generated

While in the prevalent definition, only the user as creator and image content is mentioned, marketing professionals point to the importance of defining the setting in which a selfie is taken allowing also for motion and change. Extending the prevalent definition, an expert pointed to the active role of the user:

> *"When the user takes a visualization of him/herself and interacts on the visualization."(Expert E, p. 4)*

Our findings show, that experts distinguish selfies in which the users have to photograph themself with objects, performing particular tasks or being in critical situations (e.g. doing extreme sports).

These results demonstrate that from the perspective of advertising agencies a variety of selfies is considered for corporate social media campaigns. Hence, it is critical to decide which type should be used and how this visualization can be integrated in an authentic way into a campaign. Although the interviewees use different notions of the term selfie, they all agreed that a selfie used in a campaign is not always entirely user generated but could be altered by a media agency for the particular purpose of a campaign or even being a professionally photographed image in the style of a selfie.

4.2 Types of Selfie Campaigns

After the definition of selfies as an element of social media campaigns, the second part focuses on the identification of categories of selfie campaigns. The results from the interviews show three categories of selfie campaigns developed by marketing agencies.

4.2.1   User Empowering Selfie Campaigns

In these campaigns, users are asked to post their selfies on social media platforms of their choice. Mostly, they are requested to include pre-defined hashtags in their posts to enable the marketing agency to retrieve the selfies. The main activities of the marketing agency in this category of campaigns are done in the preparation phase. Interviewees stated that they have to carefully define which content should be shown in the selfie. Additionally, the visual appearances of the announcement of the campaigns as well as the prices to be won by the users have to be determined. Interviews revealed several factors motivating marketing agencies and their clients to choose user empowering selfie campaigns. First, clients receive a high-amount of user-generated content. Expert B summarizes the importance of user-generated content as follows:

> *"The user shifts from king to emperor when creating content!" (Expert B, p. 3)*

Second, integrating users by asking them to upload and share selfies takes user involvement to a new level. The following quote illustrates that interaction of customers always played an important role in advertising but the integration of users as producers and distributors of selfies increases the opportunity for interaction. Expert F explains:

> Selfie campaigns allow *"a higher level of interaction with the customer compared to"* customer participation marketing campaigns *"in the past and also compared to asking customers to fill out forms on a website." (Expert F, p. 2)*

Third, this approach potentially allows the client company to reach a high number of recipients in a cost-effective and timesaving way. Expert C states:

> *"As a company we cannot produce such an amount of pictures in such a small amount of time as well as the opportunity to distribute the content in a fast way." (Expert C, p. 2)*

Users not only produce the content, but also share it in a very fast way. For instance, Expert B mentioned the use of incentives such as vouchers or points as instruments for enhanced sharing:

> *"In reaction to points or vouchers the user shares the photo and this results in higher traffic and sharing for the campaign." (Expert B, p. 3)*

In a similar vein, expert A states:

> *"The customers advertises the product for you, we create the sharing infrastructure." (Expert A, p. 4)*

Fourth, enabling users to share and discuss their content potentially facilitates the formation of communities of followers. This in turn might increase brand loyalty. Expert C and F state:

> *"A well prepared selfie campaign allows to build communities of followers and also creates advertising reach." (Expert C, p. 1; Expert F, p. 1)*

Finally, compared to professionally crafted marketing messages, interviewees believe that customers perceive the testimonials of other customers as more authentic, as expert I points out:

"What other customers say about a product is more appreciated than what the company itself says (...) If I see persons similar to myself using the product or the service, of course, I trust them more than a company that promotes its stuff in the best way possible." (Expert I, p. 2)

4.2.2   Agency Controlled Selfie Campaigns

Agency controlled selfie campaigns are characterized by an involvement of the marketing agency as a mediator within the selfie campaign. The campaigns take place at a pre-defined platform. All of the professionals mentioned that they will search for an appropriate existing social media platform in case that it is not provided by the client. Users are asked to upload their selfie on this platform (e.g. a company website or facebook). Expert C explains:

"(...) the user can upload the photo on a platform he is familiar with which means there is no need for explaining or giving additional in-formation to the user." (Expert C, p. 2)

The agency filters the user-generated selfies for publications on the platform. Hence, contrary to the user empowering selfie campaigns, the agency controls the content being published.

The selected selfie as a visual element either remains original ("classic selfie") or is adapted by the marketing agency to increase its appeal ("polished selfie").

Professionals reported that brand ambassadors, e.g. celebrities, are integrated in the marketing of such a social media campaign. Authentic brand ambassadors should act as influencers stimulating the participation and involvement of the users. Expert D explains the role of brand ambassadors:

"If you want to create a contest or interaction with the brand with a selfie-campaign, then I need brand trust, therefore in advance I need an awareness campaign in order to create trust and to enhance the brand publicity. One way is to select "brand ambassadors" for selfie campaigns as they allow to generate advertising with high authenticity." (Expert D, p. 4)

Expert B. considers Influencers important because:

"Ideally in this way, user can be convinced to directly or indirectly sell the product for you." (Expert B, p. 1)

Marketing agencies are motivated to choose agency controlled selfie campaigns, because "the user create a personal connection to the company and brand" (Expert I, p. 1) and "they enable the agency to identify the exact target group through the personal connection" (Expert F, p. 1), but contrary to the user empowering selfie-campaigns, the agency can still select the selfies to be published considering their brand image, as well as their target group from a pool of user-generated selfies. Furthermore, selfies can be visually adjusted to comply with the demands of the client company.

4.2.3   Agency Designed Campaign Integrating Selfies

In the third category of selfie campaigns, agencies design a marketing campaign and integrate "polished selfies" of brand ambassadors or "faked selfies" of photographic models as visual images. Following this approach the agency is in full control of the content of the selfie. If "faked selfies" are integrated, suitable photographs in selfie style are consciously designed. Usually more preparation is necessary to produce selfie-campaigns with objects, as Expert H. illustrates:

"[...] typical challenges for the campaign are the location, the house rule, organizational tasks if the product should be shown with the selfie." (Expert H, p. 4)

The creation and selection of the appropriate selfie is critical. Expert G states:

"In general it depends upon the target group. I would select and offer something, which no one did before in this way. Something funny, surprising or shocking." (Expert G, p. 3)

Generally, the selection of the "faked selfie" or the "polished selfie" to be included in the marketing campaign is done in cooperation with client. The client decides which selfie should be included to create an authentic advertisement for the particular company.

Considerations of corporate identity regulations or brand owners' demands can lead to the selection of this campaign category. Indeed, if a strong adaption to formal regulations is required, user generated selfies would have to be corrected and adapted. "Faked selfies" of photographic models or deliberately chosen "polished selfies" of brand ambassadors are communicated to benefit from the selfie trend. Expert C outlines:

"Selfies are a famous trend phenomenon and they are well known to the average citizen." (Expert C, p. 1)

Table 2 summarizes the authors identified three categories of selfies used in social media campaigns, starting from campaigns with low involvement of the agency and ending with campaigns which are entirely designed by the agency without any user involvement.

Table 2. Categories of corporate social media selfie campaigns with agency involvement

Selfie campaign	Type of selfie included	Description
User empowering selfie campaign	"Classic selfie"	• Agency designs the call for selfies • Users post the selfies on a social media platform of their choice
Agency controlled selfie campaign	"Classic selfie" "Polished selfie"	• Agency pre-defines social media platforms for users' selfie upload • Agency decides which selfie is published • Agency can include brand ambassadors to advertise for the selfie campaign
Agency designed campaign integrating selfies	"Polished selfie" "Faked selfie"	• Agency designs a marketing campaign • Agency includes selected polished selfies of brand ambassadors or faked selfies of photographic models as marketing instrument

5 Discussion and Conclusion

This study contributes to the debate that adequate use and effectiveness of social media is critically affected by the level of professional management because social media activities can not only result in positive effects but they can also cause negative consequences for the company [36]. We focused our research on business-related factors for selecting and implementing selfies in corporate social media campaigns.

We found that marketing agencies can be supportive for translating strategies into persuasive visuals in corporate social media campaigns and identified three different categories how selfies are used as a campaign element in order to enhance interaction with customers. We also note that using user-generated selfies have an impact on campaign involvement and sharing of campaigns.

After categorizing different selfie campaigns we point to the situational conflict faced by professionals from advertising agencies when conceptualizing campaigns for companies as their clients. While the company asks for professional management of a selfie campaign, the marketing agency must have a plan to address the trade-off between a desired high level of user interaction in a campaign and the need for control and intervention in such a campaign (in terms of selecting the adequate platform, visual and communication elements). In order to reduce information asymmetry between the agency and the client, we suggest a coordinated campaign preparation and the clear definition of the role and responsibility of the marketing agency especially when the question of ad authenticity through real life customers is concerned.

However, because of our small sample size, we cannot rule out experience as a potential influence on the selection of selfies for corporate social media campaigns. Future studies that sample greater numbers of advertising professionals, perhaps with the use of a survey method, may be able to refine the role of filtering and the usage of polished or faked selfies in a social media campaign.

Finally, while our findings analyzed the role of media agencies, it would be interesting for future research to do research on the consumer's perception of the emotional authenticity of the different selfie categories.

References

1. Vranica, S.: A 'Crisis' in Online Ads: One-Third of Traffic Is Bogus. Wall Street Journal (2014)
2. Golding, N.: How many 'likes'? Does your business have a place on Instagram? http://blogs.brighton.ac.uk/ng132/2015/04/20/how-many-likes-does-your-business-have-a-place-on-instagram/
3. Svelander, A., Wiberg, M.: The practice of selfies. Interactions **22**, 34–38 (2015)
4. OxfordWords blog: Oxford Dictionaries Word of the Year 2013: Selfie (2013). http://blog.oxforddictionaries.com/press-releases/oxford-dictionaries-word-of-the-year-2013/. [Accessed 01/30/2016] (2013)
5. Deller, R.A., Tilton, S.: Selfies as charitable meme: charity and national identity in the #nomakeupselfie and #thumbsupforstephen campaigns. Int. J. Commun. **9**, 1788–1805 (2015)

6. Sorokowski, P., Sorokowska, A., Oleszkiewicz, A., Frackowiak, T., Huk, A., Pisanski, K.: Selfie posting behaviors are associated with narcissism among men. Pers. Individ. Differ. **85**, 123–127 (2015)

7. Saltz, J.: Art at arm's length: a history of the selfie. N.Y. Mag. **47**, 71–75 (2014)

8. Samani, H.: Take a Selfie with Brand; Effective Approach or Not? https://www.researchgate.net/publication/274509342_Take_a_Selfie_with_Brand_Effective_Approach_or_Not

9. Birkner, C.: Sharing the LOVE. Mark. News **45**, 11–12 (2011)

10. Luxton, S., Reid, M., Mavondo, F.: Integrated marketing communication capability and brand performance. J. Advertising **44**, 37–46 (2015)

11. Kaplan, A.M., Haenlein, M.: Users of the world, unite! challenges Opportunities Soc. Media Bus. Horiz. **53**, 59–68 (2010)

12. Carroll, G.R., Wheaton, D.R.: The organizational construction of authenticity: an examination of contemporary food and dining in the US. Res. Organ. Behav. **29**, 255–282 (2009)

13. Grayson, K., Martinec, R.: Consumer perceptions of iconicity and indexicality and their influence on assessment of authentic market offerings. J. Consum. Res. **31**, 296–312 (2004)

14. Fuchs, C., Schreier, M., van Osselaer, S.M.J.: The handmade effect: what's love got to do with it? J. Mark. **79**, 98–110 (2015)

15. Napoli, J., Dickinson, S.J., Beverland, M.B., Farrelly, F.: Measuring consumer-based brand authenticity. J. Bus. Res. **67**, 1090–1098 (2014)

16. Bruhn, M., Schoenmüller, V., Schäfer, D., Heinrich, D.: Brand authenticity: towards a deeper understanding of its conceptualization and measurement. Adv. Consum. Res. **40**, 567–576 (2012)

17. Stern, B.: Authenticity and the textual persona: postmodern paradoxes in advertising narrative. Int. J. Res. Mark. **11**, 387–400 (1994)

18. Miller, F.: Ad authenticity: an alternative explanation of advertising's effect on established brand attitudes. J. Curr. Issues Res. Advertising **36**, 177–194 (2015)

19. Fine, G.A.: Crafting authenticity: the validation of identity in self-taught art. Theor. Soc. **32**, 153–180 (2003)

20. Gilmore, J.H., Pine II, J.B.: Authenticity: What Consumers Really Want. Harvard Business Review Press, Boston (2007)

21. Holt, D.B.: Poststructuralist lifestyle analysis: conceptualizing the social patterning of consumption on post-modernity. J. Consum. Res. **23**, 326–350 (1997)

22. Beverland, M.B.: Crafting brand authenticity: the case of luxury wines. J. Manag. Stud. **42**, 1003–1029 (2005)

23. Beverland, M.B.: Building Brand Authenticity: Seven Habits of Iconic Brands. Palgrave Macmillan, Basingstoke (2009)

24. Holt, D.B.: Why do brands cause trouble? A dialectic theory of consumer culture and branding. J. Consum. Res. **29**, 70–90 (2002)

25. Keller, K.L.: Conceptualizing, measuring, and managing customer-based brand equity. J. Mark. **57**, 1–22 (1993)

26. Chalmers, T.D., Price, L.L.: Perceptions of authenticity in advertisements: negotiating the inauthentic. Adv. Consum. Res. **36**, 72–75 (2009)

27. Gilpin, D., Palazzolo, E., Brody, N.: Socially mediated authenticity. J. Commun. Manag. **14**, 258–278 (2010)

28. Grow, G., Ward, J.: The role of authenticity in electoral social media campaigns. First Monday **18**, 1–15 (2013)

29. Coleman, S., Moss, G.: Governing at a distance – politicians in the blogosphere. Inf. Polity **13**, 7–20 (2008)

30. Montgomery, M.: The uses of authenticity: speaking from experience in a UK election broadcast. Commun. Rev. **4**, 447–462 (2001)
31. Beverland, M.B., Luxton, S.: Managing integrated marketing communication (IMC) through strategic decoupling: how luxury wine firms retain brand leadership while appearing to be wedded to the past. J. Advertising **34**, 103–116 (2005)
32. Kadirov, D., Varey, R.J., Wooliscroft, B.: Authenticity: a macromarketing perspective. J. Macromarketing **24**, 73–79 (2014)
33. Kadirov, D.: Private labels ain't bona fide! Perceived authenticity and willingness to pay a price premium for national brands over private labels. J. Mark. Manag. **311**, 773–1798 (2015)
34. Marshall, C., Rossman, G.B.: Designing Qualitative Research. SAGE Publications, Thousand Oaks (1999)
35. Scheiner, C.W., Eder, A., Goranova, M., Baccarella, C., Voigt, K.I.: The use and evaluation of social media by new enterprises in Germany – an empirical analysis. In: Proceedings of the International Marketing Trends Conference, Venice (2014). http://www.marketing-trends-congress.com/archives/2014/pages/PDF/084.pdf. Accessed 31 Jan 2016

Social Media in User Entrepreneurship

Hari Suman Naik[(✉)] and Kathrin M. Möslein

Friedrich-Alexander-University Erlangen-Nuremberg, Nuremberg, Germany
{harisuman.naik,kathrin.moeslein}@fau.de

Abstract. User entrepreneurs develop innovative products or services for their needs and then found firms to commercialize their innovations. Their ability to coordinate the innovation related efforts is vital for both these steps. Drawing upon six cases on user entrepreneurial firms, the study explores how user entrepreneurial firms use social media, highlighting firm resources that are associated with social media and give them a competitive advantage. It was seen in these six technology based firms that social media was used for outside-in, Spanning as well as inside-out resources, especially external relationship management, market responsiveness, new product/service development and technology development.

Keywords: User innovation · User entrepreneurship · Social media · Resources and capabilities

1 Introduction

Users often develop innovative products or services that do not exist in the market to meet their needs. When these innovations also address the needs of a larger population, then users can start commercially offering them in the market. Users engage in collective creative activity prior to firm formation, often in communities, that result in improvement of their ideas and initial market validation [1]. Social media applications such as blogs, social networking sites, content communities etc. [2] have been the backbone of communities and are vital for coordinating innovation and entrepreneurial activities, especially among smaller firms. This study explores how user entrepreneurs use social media, with an emphasis on resources that give them a competitive advantage. With the help of six cases of user entrepreneurial firms, it identifies resources of these firms that are associated with social media.

The following section provides the necessary literature background on user entrepreneurship and social media, which is followed by sections on the detailed research design, findings, discussion, and conclusion.

2 Literature Background

The following section reviews literature that forms the necessary background for this study. It starts out with an introduction to user innovation and subsequent of user entrepreneurship. It then describes the role of social media in firms and the research gap of social media in user entrepreneurship.

© Springer International Publishing Switzerland 2016
G. Meiselwitz (Ed.): SCSM 2016, LNCS 9742, pp. 428–436, 2016.
DOI: 10.1007/978-3-319-39910-2_40

2.1   From User Innovation to User Entrepreneurship

Users of products or services often know their needs better than manufacturers. Manufacturers can discover this need information, but in many situations, these needs are too "sticky" i.e., they do not get easily transferred from the user to the manufacturer [3]. In these cases, users have developed their own innovative solutions[1] that satisfy their specific and unmet needs. Numerous studies have shown that both user firms and end users are sources of innovation in processes as well as new products [4]. User firms as sources of innovation have been seen in various industrial sectors. Some examples are in semiconductors [5], security software [6] and financial services [7]. End users of consumer goods have also developed significant innovative ideas as can be seen in various products used in extreme sports such as biking [8], kayaking [9] etc. and also in open source software [10]. Users are sometimes assisted by manufacturers e.g. who offer them toolkits to innovate [11] or by hosting user communities where their ideas branch out and evolve and as they share their ideas or creations among their network [12]. It has led to steadily improving capabilities for users to design and to coordinate their innovation related efforts which drives user innovation [13].

Sometimes, these users who develop prototypes that meet their unmet needs, realize that they could commercialize their innovative product or service and stumble into entrepreneurship [14]. User entrepreneurs are quite prevalent (for instance, 46.6 percent of firms founded in 2004 and survived to year five in the United States were founded by users), and they are different from regular manufacturers. They are predominantly innovative, and have a prevalence of venture capitalist funding, have a high human capital, successfully generate revenues, and have a higher share of women and minority groups [15]. They also have lower estimates on financial returns and profit thresholds than regular manufacturers [1]. Shah and Tripsas differentiate between professional user entrepreneurs and end user entrepreneurs. Professional user entrepreneurs founded a firm around an innovation that resulted in use in a previous job or business. This gives them a high work experience and they are likely to have previous entrepreneurial experiences and tend to have a higher rate of return, when compared to end user entrepreneurs. End user entrepreneurs build firms around innovations that developed from their personal use [1].

The user entrepreneurship process is different from regular entrepreneurship in two ways. The first difference is that the process of setting up a firm is emergent. Even before the concept of the entrepreneurial venture started, the user experienced a problem or need that was unmet by existing solutions in the market. The user then develops a prototype product for personal use, which generated interest among other users. The second difference is that user communities play a significant role in development and diffusion of the innovation much before firm formation. These communities consist of loosely affiliated users who participate voluntarily form a vital role in motivating users, building upon existing ideas, and even testing prototypes. The level of interest of community members validates of it only solves the idiosyncratic needs of the user or has commercial potential by solving the needs of a larger

---

[1] 'Solutions' is used to refer to products, services or a combination of both in this paper for better readability.

population [14]. In this process, users may innovate and develop a solution for unmet needs in one industry and then shift to another industry where there is an opportunity to commercialize [16]. Social media plays a vital role in online user communities and are valuable to nascent firms. The relationship between social media and firms is discussed further in the next section.

2.2   Role of Social Media in Firms

The importance of user communities in the process of user entrepreneurship hints at a strong role of social media and associated technologies. The term social media (often used interchangeably with social networks and Web 2.0) is used to refer to internet-based applications that build on the ideological and technological foundations of Web 2.0 and that allow the creation and exchange of user generated content. Categories of social media include blogs, social networking sites, virtual social worlds, collaborative projects, content communities and virtual game worlds [2]. Social media applications aim to engage users and have features to generate initiate and circulate new and emerging sources of online information [17]. Firms can thus use social media to engage users with the eventual goal of generating profit. Firms use social media for marketing and customer relationship management, networking within and outside the organization, recruitment and other miscellaneous activities [18].

While established firms may be conservative and use social media only to mitigate risks of not having an online presence, smaller firms may be more inclined to use social media to create additional value. This is because SMEs have often struggled to adopt technology due to their lack of skills and resources when compared to bigger firms. Social media has massively reduced the barriers of SMEs in terms of skills and resources and allowed them to effectively compete with much larger organizations that enjoy efficiencies of scope and scale [19]. It is used widely by SMEs for marketing and customer relationships management [20] in both B2B [21] as well as B2C contexts [22].

2.3   Social Media for User Entrepreneurs

While many of the benefits of social media that apply to SMEs may be seen in user entrepreneurs, SMEs are quite heterogeneous and differ vastly. SME owner-managers differ in their age, education level, attitude towards the internet, preference for face to face interactions, strategies for growth etc. [23]. Hence, the technically comfortable user entrepreneurs [15] can be quite different in their use of social media to other older SME owner-managers, say for example in the French hotel industry [24]. Furthermore, user entrepreneurs may be more inclined to look for rapid market growth when compared to more conservative family owned SMEs [15]. This leads us to treat user entrepreneurs differently thereby resulting in the research question of how user entrepreneurs use social media and how does it give them a competitive advantage.

3   Research Design

As this area is relatively unexplored, an exploratory case study approach was adopted [25]. The study uses a multiple non-embedded case study based on data from six user entrepreneurial firms in the information technology industry. The data is used to theorize about the use of social media for competitiveness following an inductive approach [26–28]. Using six cases fits within the recommendation of using four to ten cases of Eisenhardt that allow sufficient data without too much complexity and do cross case analysis [26].

3.1   Data Sample

The empirical field for this study was restricted to firms in the field of information technology. For identifying a suitable sample of user entrepreneurial firms, two approaches were taken. The first was to identify firms who had previously developed innovative prototypes for use needs and are on the look out to commercialize their solutions. To do this, we selected nascent firms competing in entrepreneurial events around the field of information technology that have already user-evaluated prototypes. Out of these events, an entrepreneurship academy themed around Internet of Things that followed the approach of creating prototypes for their user needs and later commercializing them was selected. The top three teams from this academy continued to develop their prototypes and aim to bring their prototypes into production.

The second approach was to search broadly for established start-ups that were founded by users, within the theme of information technology. After exploring through various entrepreneurship communities, platforms, and Facebook groups, our search for cases was restricted to the crowdfunding platforms Kickstarter and Indiegogo. Crowdfunding campaigns on these platforms related to information technology were then filtered to those that mention a user need as the origin of the innovation. The first

Table 1. Sample of firms for cases

Name	Solution	Employees	Started
SensePro	Gesture sensing device to control Gopro action cameras	5	2015
JAMS wearables	Modular wearable bracelet so users can choose the right sensors to track their personal data that match their needs.	4	2015
Drone in	Drone based advertising service	3	2015
FreeWavz	Wire-free smart earphones which can monitor heart rate and fitness	<10	2007
OpenElectrons	Robotics systems based on Raspberry Pi and Arduino	5	2002
Sher.ly	Private cloud solution for sensitive data sharing with secure access control	6	2013

50 campaign owners were then contacted using a short survey to find out if they had indeed developed the idea based on their needs and hence were indeed user entrepreneurs [15]. Based on 13 responses to this survey, seven firms were detected as user entrepreneurial out of which three were available for interviews. The firms sampled for the case study are described in Table 1.

3.2   Data Gathering and Analysis

Data gathering for the cases began by collecting all published documentation of the firms online including profiles published on social media, entrepreneurship platforms, and crowdfunding campaigns. Individuals from these six firms were interviewed using a set of semi-structured questions that could be adapted to the interviewee. The interviews were recorded and transcribed. Any questions not covered in the interviews were further covered through email exchanges with the interviewees.

The data gathered through these multiple sources was analysed through a coding scheme based on the theoretical perspective of resource-based view [29] in the context of information systems [30]. Information systems (IS) assets and capabilities (Outside In, Spanning and Inside Out as in Table 2 that are social media based in the cases were identified and coded for the different steps in the user entrepreneurship process model outlined by [14]. The coded statements were used to organize and evaluate the data.

Table 2. Typology of IS resources from [30]

Outside-In	Spanning	Inside-Out
• External relationship management • Market responsiveness	• IS business partnerships • IS planning and change management	• IS Infrastructure • IS technical skills • IS development • Cost effective IS operations

4   Findings

Considering the data sample of high-tech user entrepreneurial firms, the use of social media is pervasive in all six cases, but is done in different ways. The first three cases of firms (SensePro, JAMS Wearables, and Drone-In) had working prototypes but were not yet at the stage of commercializing their products are presented first. They used social media for external relationship management. All three had facebook and twitter profiles to build strong community networks, where they regularly posted updates of the status of their prototypes and funding events in which they participated. The goal of these activities was to create a buzz around their new product or service idea, which could give them greater visibility during funding events and a momentum to enter into future crowd funding campaigns. This is clearly seen in the case of Drone-In.

"Social media has allowed us to effectively have free advertising and exposed us to different people from different backgrounds who are interested in the services we hope

to offer. It has been a great way to throw ourselves into the public domain and we have used it stir the conversation on drones in general. It has allowed us to reach out to potential partners and investors in new innovative tech... also given us a great deal of collateral and proof of concept when we've approached investors, the were able to see the support the idea had and how much time and effort had been invested in the project."

All three firms had their own web pages used for displaying their innovative solutions, features and user testimonials, and as a point of contact for the future. However, at this stage of the entrepreneurial process, they relied on their public social network pages to log their experiences rather than posting on dedicated blog pages. Market responsiveness was very important for the firms as they strived to differentiate themselves from competing and substitute solutions. This was done by regularly scanning various social media platforms and ensuring that they were always flexible to adapt their solutions to meet changing needs.

OpenElectrons relies on user communities for market sensing and customer linking. By following the maker movement and being regularly part of conferences like the Maker Faire, they are connected to new needs and then present it in online forums.

"Lego Mindstorms is a very small, tight community. There are forums, there are groups, and we are connected into those groups. There are people who know us from there and recommend our products through other users. They present it on the forums. That is how people know us. So it is pretty much from word-of-mouth."

Sher.ly used targeted advertising features on blogs and social networking sites to reach the right target group for their secure and private data storage.

"We advertise on blogs and we publish a lot of stories about our solution. What is the best benefit and what is the best use case, how you can benefit from it and how we can simplify things you do. So there are various things you can do. We try to focus, that means that when we talk to a specific group, we are trying to talk to specific people, for example not teenagers"

Social media did not play a major role in managing internal partnerships of SensePro, JAMS wearables or Drone-In. Instead, they played a role in keeping the firm members motivated and dedicated towards success. As these three firms relied on open source electronics for their solutions, they continuously relied on forums and blogs of related suppliers and communities (e.g. Arduino microcontrollers) to improve their technical IT skills, build knowledge assets and to experiment with new technology.

FreeWavz and Sher.ly both had close relationships with blogging sites, which they use to promote themselves. FreeWavz also used a public relations firm to manage promotions on social media based outlets.

"We also have a public relations firm. We use that as a help. There have been articles written about us. Then we have some additional promotions and discussions going on for some magazines that want to include reviews of our product so they also want to include us in reviews of top technology products and headphone products."

Hence, the user entrepreneurial firms used social media for their resources and capabilities that could give them a competitive advantage, which ranged from having market sensing to developing knowledge assets. These are summarized in Table 3.

Table 3. Identified resources and capabilities associated to social media in the six user entrepreneurial firms

Identified resource/capability	Associated types of social media	Examples from cases
Manage external relationships	Content communities Social networking sites	Find customers through Mindstorms community Find partners through facebook/twitter
Market responsiveness	Social networking sites	Monitor profile pages of competition
Business Identified resources and capabilities associated to social media	Blogs	Posting product reviews on blogs
Planning and Change Management	Content communities, Collaborative projects	New product ideas in communities
IS infrastructure	Social networking sites	Employee motivation through facebook posts
Technology development	Blogs, Content Communities, Collaborative projects	Using open source Arduino and associated content

5   Discussion and Conclusion

The paper studied six cases of user entrepreneurial firms to identify their use of social media and the role of social media in their competitiveness. Freely available social media services provide scalable models for market responsiveness and market relationships, building brand loyalties and collaborative activities with other organizations and their customers. The interlinking between different various social media platforms exacerbates this effect, allowing user entrepreneurs to tap customers who use multiple platforms and build loyalty around their brands. Integration of e-commerce functionalities in social media provides further value to small-scale user entrepreneurs. Social media based IS resources [30] are not located within the firm but are readily available and the way they are used result in their effectiveness.

This research provides further contributions to the nascent fields of social media in user entrepreneurship. User entrepreneurship is poised to take off with users getting further access to production capabilities and better funding opportunities. Its findings are relevant to potential and existing user entrepreneurs looking to learn from previous experiences of other potential and existing user entrepreneurs. While this market segment is relatively niche [1] in comparison to the general social media market, social media firms can incorporate advance features that improve their offerings to small entrepreneurs, especially those with a background in user entrepreneurship.

References

1. Shah, S., Tripsas, M.: When do user innovators start firms? A theory of user entrepreneurship. SSRN eLibrary **20**, 1–42 (2012)
2. Kaplan, A.M., Haenlein, M.: Users of the world, unite! the challenges and opportunities of social media. Bus. Horiz. **53**, 59–68 (2010)
3. von Hippel, E.: "Sticky information" and the locus of problem solving: implications for innovation. Manag. Sci. **40**, 429–439 (1994)
4. Bogers, M., Afuah, A., Bastian, B.: Users as innovators: a review, critique, and future research directions. J. Manag. **36**, 857–875 (2010)
5. von Hippel, E.: The dominant role of the user in semiconductor and electronic subassembly process innovation. IEEE Trans. Eng. Manag. **2**, 60–71 (1977)
6. Franke, N., von Hippel, E.: Satisfying heterogeneous user needs via innovation toolkits: the case of Apache security software. Res. Policy **32**, 1199–1215 (2003)
7. Oliveira, P., von Hippel, E.: Users as service innovators: the case of banking services. Res. Policy **40**, 806–818 (2011)
8. Lüthje, C., Herstatt, C., von Hippel, E.: User-innovators and "local" information: the case of mountain biking. Res. Policy **34**, 951–965 (2005)
9. Baldwin, C.Y., Hienerth, C., von Hippel, E.: How user innovations become commercial products: a theoretical investigation and case study. Res. Policy **35**(9), 1291–1313 (2006)
10. Von Krogh, G., von Hippel, E.: Special issue on open source software development. **32**, 1149–1157 (2003)
11. von Hippel, E.: PERSPECTIVE: user toolkits for innovation. J. Prod. Innov. Manag. **18**, 247–257 (2001)
12. Franke, N., Shah, S.: How communities support innovative activities: an exploration of assistance and sharing among end-users. Res. Policy **32**, 157–178 (2003)
13. von Hippel, E.: Democratizing innovation: the evolving phenomenon of user innovation. J. Fur Betriebswirtschaft. **55**, 63–78 (2005)
14. Shah, S., Tripsas, M.: The accidental entrepreneur: the emergent and collective process of user entrepreneurship. Strateg. Entrep. J. **1**, 123–140 (2007)
15. Shah, S., Smith, S.W., Reedy, E.J.E.: Who are User Entrepreneurs? Findings on Innovation, Founder Characteristics, and Firm Characteristics (The Kauffman Firm Survey). SSRN Electron. J. (2012)
16. Haefliger, S., Jäger, P., Von Krogh, G.: Under the radar: industry entry by user entrepreneurs. Res. Policy **39**, 1198–1213 (2010)
17. Correa, T., Hinsley, A.W., de Zúñiga, H.G.: Who interacts on the Web?: the intersection of users' personality and social media use. Comput. Human Behav. **26**, 247–253 (2010)
18. Kim, W., Jeong, O.-R., Lee, S.-W.: On social Web sites. Inf. Syst. **35**, 215–236 (2010)
19. Harris, L., Rae, A.: The revenge of the gifted amateur … be afraid, be very afraid …. J. Small Bus. Enterp. Dev. **16**, 694–709 (2009)
20. Derham, R., Cragg, P., Morrish, S.: Creating Value: An SME and Social Media. In: PACIS 2011 Proceedings, p. 53 (2011)
21. Michaelidou, N., Siamagka, N.T., Christodoulides, G.: Usage, barriers and measurement of social media marketing: AB exploratory investigation of small and medium B2B brands. Ind. Mark. Manag. **40**, 1153–1159 (2011)
22. Christodoulides, G.: Branding in the post-internet era. Mark. Theor. **9**, 141–144 (2009)
23. Chua, A., Deans, K., Parker, C.M.: Exploring the types of SMES which could use blogs as a marketing tool: a proposed future research agenda. J. Inf. Syst. Small Bus. **16**, 117–136 (2009)

24. Nakara, W.A., Benmoussa, F.Z., Jaouen, A.: Entrepreneurship and social media marketing: evidence from French small business. Int. J. Entrep. Small Bus. **16**, 386 (2012)
25. Yin, R.K.: Case Study Research: Design and Methods (2009)
26. Eisenhardt, K.M.: Building theories from case study research. Acad. Manag. Rev. **14**, 532–550 (1989)
27. Glaser, B.G.: The constant comparative method of qualitative analysis. Soc. Probl. **12**, 436–445 (1965)
28. Glaser, B.G., Strauss, A.: The Discovery of Grounded Theory, p. 1967. Weidenf & Nicolson, London (1967)
29. Day, G.S.: The capabilities of market-driven organizations. J. Mark. **58**, 37 (1994)
30. Wade, M., Hulland, J.: Review: the resource-based view and information systems research: review, extension, and suggestions for future research. MIS Q. **28**, 107–142 (2004)

Cruel Intentions? – The Role of Moral Awareness, Moral Disengagement, and Regulatory Focus in the Unethical Use of Social Media by Entrepreneurs

Christian W. Scheiner[1(✉)], Katja Krämer[1], and Christian V. Baccarella[2]

[1] Institute of Entrepreneurship & Business Development, Universität zu Lübeck,
Lübeck, Germany
{christian.scheiner,katja.kraemer}@uni-luebeck.de
[2] Chair of Industrial Management, Friedrich-Alexander-Universität Erlangen-Nürnberg,
Nürnberg, Germany
christian.baccarella@fau.de

Abstract. Unethical behavior of entrepreneurs in the use of social media can have detrimental effects, both for the own entrepreneurial firm and also on competitors. In order to understand why entrepreneurs show unethical behavior a conceptual framework is developed in this paper, linking motives for financial gains, moral awareness, moral disengagement, and the tendency to make unethical decisions in the use of social media. This paper offers therewith insights into the cognitive processes of entrepreneurial decision-makers with respect to moral reasoning and ethical decision-making.

Keywords: Moral disengagement · Moral awareness · Regulatory focus theory · Social media · Unethical behavior · Conceptual framework · Entrepreneur

1 Introduction

In a business context, decision-makers are continuously and increasingly challenged to find solutions to moral dilemmas where demands of different stakeholders have to be considered although they hold opposing moral beliefs and standards [1, 2]. This is especially the case in marketing, where a bridging function between the company and its environment is fulfilled. Hence, a balance between organizational demands on the one side and demands from customers and the broader public on the other side has to be found. Decision-makers in companies have often been criticized to disproportionally prioritize the demands of the company leading to the application of deceptive advertisements, the manipulation of consumers, or the usage of inferior materials in products affecting its durability negatively. While those examples can be clearly detected as morally wrong, there exists a wide spectrum of decisions where ambiguity is given. Is it for instance morally acceptable to use non-informative appeals during broadcast periods in which the largest proportion of the audience are children, who may not be aware of the persuasion tactics of marketers or are too young to resist them [3]?

© Springer International Publishing Switzerland 2016
G. Meiselwitz (Ed.): SCSM 2016, LNCS 9742, pp. 437–448, 2016.
DOI: 10.1007/978-3-319-39910-2_41

Within the last decade, social media enlarged the toolkit of decision-makers in marketing. In that context, social media represents a paradigm shift in the way companies interact with their customers. Despite its relative newness, social media channels and related monitoring activities have become essentials for the communication and brand strategy of organizations [4–6]. Researchers and practitioners alike agree that social media applications, such as Facebook or Twitter, have changed the nature of marketing and brand management dramatically [5].

Social media is especially attractive for entrepreneurial firms [7], as it is less expensive than traditional marketing tools [8], offering the opportunity to reach a large audience by maintaining a close relationship at the same time [9]. A panel study among 1,972 entrepreneurial firms in North America showed that more than 90 % used Facebook, more than 70 % Twitter, nearly 60 % LinkedIn, more than 50 % video sharing, about a quarter photo sharing services, more than 30 % review sites and almost 25 % location-based services [10]. Given the importance of social media for entrepreneurial firms, a focus is given to entrepreneurs in this study.

Due to the impact of social media on marketing and marketers, it is necessary to gain insights into the cognitive processes of entrepreneurs with respect to moral reasoning and ethical entrepreneurial decision-making. In order to better understand these aspects, a theoretical framework is developed in this paper that integrates moral awareness and moral disengagement to provide a profound basis to explore the use of social media by entrepreneurs.

2   Theoretical Background

2.1   Social Media and Unethical Behavior

Based on the collaborative and interactive components of the Internet, social media can be defined as "a group of Internet-based applications [...] that allow the creation and exchange of user-generated content" [11, p. 61]. The rapid technological developments in communication technologies in the last decades represent a drastic change of familiar social patterns and lead to altered beliefs and motivators for action [12]. Social media has democratized information and now allows almost unlimited interactivity. This is why the borders between message creators and message receivers became blurred with the result that consumers are able make their voices heard more easily.

Social media has experienced tremendous growth in recent years. It is estimated that almost one third of the world's population is already using social media applications [13], which underlines the huge potential that social media holds for businesses from all fields and industries. Companies can now quite literally reach a worldwide audience at the push of a button. The fact that social media applications offer the possibility to interact with a specific target audience in a very cost-effective way allows especially entrepreneurs with limited financial resources to grow their business and maintain their competitiveness [8].

The sheer unlimited connectivity and the at least theoretical anonymity in the World Wide Web in conjunction with unanswered legal questions, offer many possibilities for ethically questionable or wrong behavior [14]. However, not only consumers can display morally or ethically questionable behavior on social media, but also corporate employees or even entrepreneurs. In order to avoid possible legal consequences, Elefant [15, p. 1], for instance, proposes therefore several best practices and guidelines for US utilities engaging in social media. She argues that the "naturally free-flowing world of social media" offers several possibilities to negatively impact codes of conduct, regulations or compliance issues.

Research has discussed the disclosure of personal information on social networking sites (SNS) as one possible way to engage in an unethical way on social media [16, 17]. Customers' or employees' exposed private information on SNS could be used in an immoral manner [18]. Moreover, due to an increasing number of linked online services (e.g. Facebook and the photo sharing platform Instagram), social media users could lose control over their private content (e.g. private pictures), because companies might gain access to it more easily [19]. Another form of misconduct on social media stems from improper use of anonymity. The New York Times reports the case of John Mackey, one of the founders of Whole Foods Market, who used an online pseudonym to anonymously praise his own company and to discredit a competitor [20]. So-called "flogs" (fake blogs) represent further corporate unethical behavior on social media. In the case of flogs, companies instruct an advertising agency to create a fictitious blog of a supposedly independent character, who writes about a product or a company in a very positive way. Various cases of fake blogs have been discovered and have put corporate officials under pressure [21].

The literature overview revealed that there are plenty of ways that firms can behave unethically on social media. The fact that particularly entrepreneurs can benefit from opportunities arising from social media creates a major dilemma for them: On the hand, social media offers wide-ranging opportunities to boost their business. On the other hand, many of these opportunities can include ethically questionable business practices. This raises the question of how unethical behavior of entrepreneurs on social media can be explained. The next section therefore builds on that and offers a solid theoretical basis to explain entrepreneurial moral misconduct in a social media setting.

2.2 Moral Disengagement

Based on the criticism that psychological theories of moral agency rather tend to focus on the moral thought to the neglect of the moral conduct, researchers started to focus on the exploration of why individuals show unethical behavior, e.g. [22–26].

The behavior of people who are confronted with moral issues are usually guided and regulated by their moral agency [23]. In this vein, moral agency refers to being "embedded in a broader socio-cognitive self-theory encompassing self-organizing, proactive, self-reflective, and self-regulatory mechanisms rooted in personal standards and linked to self-sanctions" [23, p. 193]. Individuals can, however, detach themselves from certain moral problems they face in certain situations "by selectively disengaging their moral self-sanctions from detrimental social policies and practices" [24, p. 10]. Having said that, people in such situations are able to act in an unethical, detrimental, and harmful manner and pursue related activities with freedom from the restriction of self-censure [24–26].

Bandura [22] argued that eight psychosocial mechanisms enable individuals to morally disengage from own moral standards that lead to a destructive and unethical behavior: namely moral justification, euphemistic labeling, advantageous comparison, displacement of responsibility, diffusion of responsibility, disregarding or distortion of consequences, dehumanization, and attribution of blame.

The concept of moral disengagement already found its entrance in management, and particularly, in entrepreneurship research. Recent research of Baron et al. [26] focus on the causes for unethical decision making amongst entrepreneurs that might have destructive effects on their companies, involved stakeholders, and themselves. Results show that the entrepreneurs' motivation for financial gains is positively related to moral disengagement. Moreover, the findings show that moral disengagement is positively related to the tendency to make unethical decisions amongst their sample of founding entrepreneurs [26].

2.3 Regulatory Focus Theory

Self-regulation, and in particular, the regulatory focus theory are increasingly in the center of interest in entrepreneurship research to gain an in-depth understanding of behavioral patterns amongst entrepreneurs and founders. Self-regulation, in general, refers to "the psychological processes by which individuals exercise control over their cognitive, emotional, and behavioral processes" [27, p. 622]. This means that individuals control their own actions and behavior by focusing on both strategies for goal setting and achievement.

The regulatory focus theory is based on the hedonic principle, which states that individuals try to avoid pain and seek contentment [27–30], and the self-discrepancy theory, which distinguishes the ideal self, the ought self, and the actual self [31]. The regulatory focus theory suggests that individuals try to fulfill their duties and try to achieve their goals at the same time [29, 30] in order to bring the actual self in alignment with the ideal and the ought selves. Two generic modes govern, therein, own behavior. An emphasis is either placed on the minimization of the discrepancy between actual and the ought self or on reducing the difference between the actual and the ideal self [30–32]. Whereas individuals with a promotion focus are motivated by growth and advancement needs, individuals with a prevention focus are rather motivated by security- and safety-related needs [27–30]. These two foci and the related diverging motives form the basis on which each individual builds its objectives and standards. As a consequence, promotion-focused individuals concentrate on their ideals (e.g. hopes, wishes) they aim to achieve. These individuals emphasize the existence of positive outcomes when they strive for their ideals. On the other side, prevention-focused individuals concentrate on and view their goals by means of duties or responsibilities that should be attained. Thus, these individuals emphasize the absence of negative outcomes [27–30]. Promotion and prevention pride are, however, typically not correlated with each other and are not mutually exclusive [33]. Entrepreneurs' behavior can, hence, be guided by a promotion and a prevention pride [34, 35].

3 Propositions and Framework Development

Previous research has uncovered a multitude of motives why individuals pursue self-employment as a career choice, e.g. [36–40]. Scheinberg and MacMillan [41] conducted a study in eleven countries and found that individuals were motivated by "need for approval", "need for independence", "need for personal development", "welfare considerations", and "perceived instrumentality of wealth". Birley and Westhead [38] confirmed these findings in their study with 405 managers of entrepreneurial firms, but added "tax reduction and indirect benefits" and "follow role models" as further reasons. Robichaud et al. [40] differentiate between "independence and autonomy", "family security", "intrinsic rewards", and "extrinsic rewards". Gatewood et al. [42] explored cognitive factors of potential entrepreneurs. Based on their findings, they argue that an identification of a market need, independence and autonomy, the perception of a high reward (e.g. financial), the desire to use knowledge and experience, the enjoyment of being self-employed, and the desire to prove that it can be realized are main motives for starting a business. Another line of research distinguishes in the search for entrepreneurial motivation between necessity-driven and opportunity-driven motivation. While it is argued that necessity-driven entrepreneurs are motivated by push factors (especially unemployment), pursue opportunity-driven entrepreneurs this career path for pull factors such as social status and profit [43].

Within the identified motives, the motive for financial gains is a recurrent and fundamental element in explaining why individuals have chosen an entrepreneurial career. Baron et al. [26] argue, therefore, that financial gains are a primary motive for entrepreneurship and that this motive is suitable to explain the conduct of entrepreneurial behavior. In line with this notion, we focus in our paper solely on motivation for financial gains.

Concerning the relationship of motive for financial gains and moral disengagement, Litzky et al. [44] argue that financial gains can cause different types of unethical behavior in a general business context. Employees purchase or damage, for instance, organizational property without authorization, they show hostile and aggressive behavior towards co-workers and other individuals, they violate existing standards in ensuring product consistency, or they put other individuals intentionally at a disadvantage. Baron et al. [26] examined the relationship of motive for financial gains and moral disengagement in an entrepreneurial setting and found they are positively related. As general and entrepreneurial findings indicate a general interdependence between financial gains and moral disengagement, we propose that this effect also exists in the use of social media as marketing tool by entrepreneurs.

Proposition 1: Entrepreneurs' motive for financial gains is positively related to moral disengagement in the use of social media.

Rogers et al. [45] argue that the Internet has created a new space where unique possibilities for deviant and malign behavior can be found reaching from criminal to misbehaving. The focus of this article is set on misbehaving behavior and defines unethical behavior as something that is "quasi legal and [does] not "constitute serious criminal acts but nevertheless [constitutes] nonconformance to a given set of norms that are accepted by a significant number of people in society" [46, p. 447]. Anonymity [47] reducing the chances of being detected and held accountable [47], and the remote nature of online behavior leading to a sense of disinhibition [46, 48] are seen as the base for deviant conduct. A phenomenon where deviant online behavior can frequently be observed is online firestorms. Pfeffer et al. [49, p. 118] define online firestorms "as the sudden discharge of large quantities of messages containing negative [Word-of-Mouth] and complaint behavior against a person, company, or group in social media networks". Firestorms are especially suitable to illustrate unethical behavior because of the nature of messages in such occurrences. These are predominantly expressed opinions, often not based on facts, and highly emotional [49].

Deviant behavior is, in general, not limited to a specific group with socio-demographic or psychographic characteristics. DeMarco [50] argues, for instance, that the Internet is increasing the chances that even 'good kids' show deviant or even criminal behavior. In order to misbehave from an ethical standpoint, people have to disengage at least to some extent from their normally occurring self-regulatory process that impedes them to act in a way that is contradicting and maybe violating their own moral standards [25]. Based on these general findings and the findings of Baron et al. [26] that moral disengagement is given in the tendency to show unethical behavior among entrepreneurs, it can be assumed that moral disengagement is in play also when entrepreneurs conduct deviant behavior in the use of social media.

Proposition 2: Entrepreneurs' moral disengagement is positively related to the tendency to make unethical decisions in the use of social media.

Together, Propositions 1 and 2 suggest an influence of moral disengagement on the relationship between motive for financial gains and the tendency to unethical behavior in the use of social media.

Proposition 3: Moral disengagement mediates the relationship between entrepreneurs' motive for financial gains and the tendency to make unethical decisions in the use of social media.

Following the regulatory focus theory, two regulating modes (promotion focus, prevention focus) serve as the motivational base for behavior [30, 31].

Entrepreneurs with a promotion focus are motivated by factors relating to ideal self-states and are more inclined to potential gains [35]. Because of that motivation, these factors can be more easily accessed and reach consciousness faster [32]. Individuals with a promotion focus pay, therewith, greater attention to moral issues impacting the achievement of ideal-self states and future benefits [35]. The more promotion focus regulates the behavior of an entrepreneur, the greater is the influence on moral awareness.

Proposition 4: Promotion focus influences the moral awareness of an entrepreneur in the use of social media.

When entrepreneurs are driven by a prevention focus, they will be more attentive to factors, which are related to ought self-states and potential losses [35]. In such cases, entrepreneurs are more vigilant towards moral issues that bear the risk of violating ought self-states and future losses. This motivation affects furthermore the accessibility of information and the speed with which stimuli reach consciousness [32]. The more prevention focus is distinguished in an entrepreneur, the more moral awareness is influenced.

Proposition 5: Prevention focus influences the moral awareness of an entrepreneur in the use of social media.

Butterfield et al. [51, p. 982] define moral awareness as "a person's recognition that his or her potential decision or action could affect the interests, welfare, or expectations of the self or others in a fashion that may conflict with one or more ethical standards". Moral awareness is, therewith, not fixed and outside of the sphere of influence of situational and motivational factors.

The motive for financial gains illustrates such a factor. A study by Pittarello et al. [52] provides evidence that the motive for financial gains influences awareness via the perception accuracy. In their study, perception tasks were given to participants. In cases where self-interest in the form of financial gains could be served, the perception accuracy decreased; especially when participants could use ambiguity as an excuse to justify dishonest behavior.

Proposition 6: Entrepreneurs' motive for financial gains is negatively related to the moral awareness of entrepreneurs in the use of social media.

The core element of Bandura et al. [25] concept of moral disengagement highlights the distorting effect of moral justification, euphemistic labeling, advantageous comparison, displacement of responsibility, diffusion of responsibility, disregarding or distortion of consequences, dehumanization, and attribution of blame on perceiving the consequences of conduct morally adequately. Barsky [53] argues, therefore, that moral awareness is compromised by moral disengagement by reducing or neglecting the consequences of unethical conduct.

Proposition 7: Moral disengagement is negatively related to the moral awareness of entrepreneurs in the use of social media.

As moral awareness enables individuals to become aware of and recognize moral issues [54], moral awareness serves as a moral compass. The higher moral awareness, the higher the likelihood to detect moral issues and to act in line with own existing moral standards. At the same time, low moral awareness decreases the sensitivity to unethical conduct and consequences. Hence, entrepreneurs with a low level of moral awareness are less concerned with moral implications and choose the options that are serving their goals to a greater extent. Where ethical implications are completely overlooked, Palazzo et al. [55] use the term "ethical blindness".

The interdependency of the level of moral awareness determines the moral behavior of entrepreneurs especially where moral dilemmas or moral ambiguity is given. Recent research by Pittarello et al. [52] was able to show that ambiguity was used to justify morally wrong conduct in order to keep a feeling of moral behavior when people have to choose between honesty and self-interest. In their experiments, participants showed a misperception of presented information in favor of tempting information, which enabled them to improve their outcome in the experiment.

The existence of prior knowledge about the consequences of unethical behavior affects the intention to behave ethically positive [56]. Studies by Scheiner et al. [7] and Agnihotri et al. [57] indicate that the general knowledge about the use of social media is rather limited. Agnihotri et al. [57] showed, for instance, that social media is still not fully accepted and established in the area of sales. They found, for instance, that only 9 % of salespeople reported a social media-concerned focus in their company. Reasons were control, cost and time concerns, a lack of knowledge on senior management level, and missing valid and reliable measures for success. When the general knowledge about social media is rather limited, it can be assumed that knowledge about ethical concerns is also rather narrow, which in turn influences moral awareness.

Proposition 8: Entrepreneurs' moral awareness is negatively related to the tendency to make unethical decisions in the use of social media.

Together, Propositions 6 and 8 suggest an influence of motive for financial gains on the relationship between moral awareness and the tendency to make unethical decisions in the use of social media.

Proposition 9: Moral awareness mediates the relationship between entrepreneurs' motive for financial gains and the tendency to make unethical decisions in the use of social media.

Together, Propositions 7 and 8 suggest an influence of moral disengagement on the relationship between moral awareness and the tendency to make unethical decisions in the use of social media.

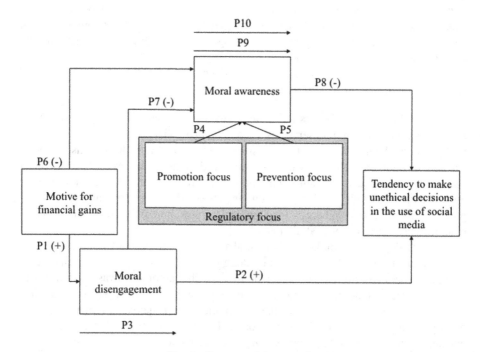

Fig. 1. Conceptual framework

Proposition 10: Moral awareness mediates the relationship between moral disengagement and the tendency to make unethical decisions in the use of social media.

Figure 1 summarizes the propositions linking motive for financial gains, moral disengagement, moral awareness, regulatory focus theory, and the tendency to make unethical decisions in the use of social media by entrepreneurs.

4   Conclusion

The main goal of our study was to provide a comprehensive framework that explains unethical behavior of entrepreneurs in the use of social media. Therefore, we developed a set of propositions, linking for the first time motives for financial gains, moral disengagement, moral awareness, promotion and prevention focus, and entrepreneurs' tendency to make unethical decisions in a social media setting.

Motivated by the increasing importance of social media and the expanding possibilities to utilize social media for entrepreneurial purposes, the theoretical framework provides causal relationships between these basic constructs. Thus, our framework builds on existing research while extending its explanatory power to the field of entrepreneurship and social media research.

The framework offers a solid foundation for further studies empirically testing our proposed relationships and thus contributes to the development of a theory of unethical behavior in social media.

References

1. Rahim, M.A., Garrett, J.E., Buntzman, G.F.: Ethics of managing interpersonal conflict in organizations. J. Bus. Ethics **11**(5–6), 423–432 (1992)
2. Erench, W., Allbright, D.: Resolving a moral conflict through discourse. J. Bus. Ethics **17**(2), 177–194 (1998)
3. Resnik, A., Stern, B.L.: An analysis of information content in television advertising. J. Mark. **41**, 50–53 (1977)
4. Samanta, I.: The effect of social media in firms' marketing strategy. J. Mark. Oper. Manag. Res. **2**(3), 163–173 (2012)
5. Tiago, M.T., Veríssimo, J.M.: Digital marketing and social media: Why bother? Bus. Horiz. **57**(6), 703–708 (2014)
6. Mangold, W.G., Faulds, D.J.: Social media: the new hybrid element of the promotion mix. Bus. Horiz. **52**(4), 357–365 (2009)
7. Scheiner, C.W., Eder, A., Goranova, M., Voigt, K.-I.: The use and evaluation of social media by new enterprises in Germany – an empirical analysis. In: Proceedings of the 13th International Marketing Trends Conference, Venice (2014)
8. Kahle, L.R., Valette-Florence, P.: Marketplace lifestyles in an age of social media: theory and method. M.E. Sharpe, Armonk (2012)
9. Lacho, K., Marinello, C.: How small business owners can use social networking to promote their business. Entrepreneurial Executive **15**, 127–134 (2010)

10. Dornaus, E.: Constant contact fall 2011 attitudes and outlooks survey (2011). img.constantcontact.com/docs/pdf/fall-2011-attitudes-and-outlooks-survey-key-findings.pdf. Assessed 1 February 2016

11. Kaplan, A.M., Haenlein, M.: Users of the world, unite! the challenges and opportunities of social media. Bus. Horiz. **53**(1), 59–68 (2010)

12. Bandura, A.: Social cognitive theory of mass communication. Media Psychol. **3**(3), 265–299 (2001)

13. We are social: Digital, social & mobile in 2015 (2015). http://wearesocial.net/blog/2015/01/digital-social-mobile-worldwide-2015/. Assessed 1 February 2016

14. Sweetser, K.D.: A losing strategy: the impact of nondisclosure in social media on relationships. J. Public Relations Res. **22**(3), 288–312 (2010)

15. Elefant, C.: The "power" of social media: Legal issues & best practices for utilities engaging in social media. Energy Law J. **32**, 1–57 (2011)

16. Boyd, D.M., Ellison, N.B.: Social network sites: definition, history, and scholarship. J. Comput. Mediated Commun. **13**(1), 210–230 (2007)

17. Lehavot, K., Ben-Zeev, D., Neville, R.E.: Ethical considerations and social media: a case of suicidal postings on facebook. J. Dual Diagn. **8**(4), 341–346 (2012)

18. Pai, P., Arnott, D.C.: User adoption of social networking sites: eliciting uses and gratifications through a means–end approach. Comput. Hum. Behav. **29**(3), 1039–1053 (2013)

19. Hansson, L., Wrangmo, A., Soilen, K.S.: Optimal ways for companies to use Facebook as a marketing channel. J. Inf. Commun. Ethics Soc. **11**(2), 112–126 (2013)

20. Martin, A.: Whole Foods Executive Used Alias. The New York Times (2007). http://www.nytimes.com/2007/07/12/business/12foods.html. Assessed 1 February 2016

21. Macnamara, J.: Public relations and the social: how practitioners are using, or abusing, social media. Asia Pac. Public Relat. J. **11**(1), 21–39 (2010)

22. Bandura, A.: Social Foundations of Thought and Action. Prentice-Hall, Englewood Cliffs (1986)

23. Bandura, A.: Moral disengagement in the perpetration of inhumanities. Pers. Soc. Psychol. Rev. **3**(3), 193–209 (1999)

24. Bandura, A.: Impeding ecological sustainability through selective moral disengagement. Int. J. Innov. Sustain. Dev. **2**(1), 8–35 (2007)

25. Bandura, A., Barbaranelli, C., Caprara, G.V., Pastorelli, C.: Mechanisms of moral disengagement in the exercise of moral agency. J. Pers. Soc. Psychol. **71**(2), 364–374 (1996)

26. Baron, R., Zhao, H., Miao, Q.: Personal motives, moral disengagement, and unethical decisions by entrepreneurs: cognitive mechanisms on the "slippery slope". J. Bus. Ethics **128**(1), 1–12 (2014)

27. Tumasjan, A., Braun, R.: In the eye of the beholder: how regulatory focus and self-efficacy interact in influencing opportunity recognition. J. Bus. Ventur. **27**(6), 622–636 (2012)

28. Crowe, E., Higgins, E.T.: Regulatory focus and strategic inclinations: promotion and prevention in decision-making. Organ. Behav. Hum. Decis. Processes **69**(2), 117–132 (1997)

29. Higgins, E.T.: Making a good decision: value from fit. Am. Psychol. **55**(11), 1217–1230 (2000)

30. Buliga, O., Scheiner, C.W., Voigt, K.-I.: Business model innovation and organizational resilience: towards an integrated conceptual framework. J. Bus. Econ. (forthcoming). http://link.springer.com/article/10.1007%2Fs11573-015-0796-y. Assessed 1 February 2016

31. Higgins, E.T.: Self discrepancy: a theory relating self and affect. Psychol. Rev. **94**(3), 319–340 (1987)

32. Higgins, E.T.: Promotion and prevention: regulatory focus as a motivational principle. Adv. Exp. Soc. Psychol. **30**, 1–46 (1998)

33. Higgins, E.T., Friedman, R.S., Harlow, R.E., Idson, L.C., Ayduk, O.N., Taylor, A.: Achievement orientations from subjective histories of success: promotion pride versus prevention pride. Eur. J. Soc. Psychol. **31**(1), 3–23 (2001)

34. Shah, J.Y., Higgins, E.T., Friedman, R.S.: Performance incentives and means: how regulatory focus influences goal attainment. J. Pers. Soc. Psychol. **74**(2), 285–293 (1998)

35. Bryant, P.: Self-regulation and moral awareness among entrepreneurs. J. Bus. Ventur. **24**(5), 505–518 (2009)

36. Shane, S., Kolvereid, L., Westhead, P.: An exploratory examination of the reasons leading to new firm formation across country and gender. J. Bus. Ventur. **6**(6), 431–446 (1991)

37. Carter, N.M., Gartner, W.B., Shaver, K.G., Gatewood, E.J.: The career reasons of nascent entrepreneurs. J. Bus. Ventur. **18**(1), 13–39 (2003)

38. Birley, S., Westhead, P.: A taxonomy of business start-up reasons and their impact on firm growth and size. J. Bus. Ventur. **9**(1), 7–31 (1994)

39. Cassar, G.: Money, money, money? a longitudinal investigation of entrepreneur career reasons, growth preferences and achieved growth. Entrepreneurship Reg. Dev. **19**(1), 89–107 (2007)

40. Robichaud, Y., McGraw, E., Roger, A.: Toward the development of a measuring instrument for entrepreneurial motivation. J. Dev. Entrepreneurship **6**(2), 189–201 (2001)

41. Scheinberg, S., MacMillan, I.C.: An 11 country study of motivations to start a business. In: Kirchhoff, B.A., Long, W.A., McMullan, W.E., Vesper, K.H., Wetzel Jr., W.E. (eds.) Frontiers of Entrepreneurship Research, pp. 669–687. Babson College, Wellesley (1988)

42. Gatewood, E., Shaver, K., Gartner, W.: A longitudinal study of cognitive factors influencing start-up behaviors and success at venture creation. J. Bus. Ventur. **10**(5), 371–391 (1995)

43. Verheul, I., Thurik, R., Hessels, J., van der Zwan, P.: Factors influencing the entrepreneurial engagement of opportunity and necessity entrepreneurs. EIM Research reports March, 1–24 (2010)

44. Litzky, B.E., Eddleston, K.A., Kidder, D.L.: The good, the bad, and the misguided: How managers inadvertently encourage deviant behaviors. Acad. Manag. Perspect. **20**(1), 91–103 (2006)

45. Rogers, M., Smoak, N., Liu, J.: Self-reported deviant computer behavior. Deviant Behav. **27**(3), 245–268 (2006)

46. Selwyn, N.: A safe haven for misbehaving? an investigation of online misbehavior among university students. Soc. Sci. Comput. Rev. **26**(4), 446–465 (2008)

47. Freestone, O., Mitchell, V.: Generation Y attitudes towards e-ethics and internet-related misbehaviours. J. Bus. Ethics **54**(2), 121–128 (2004)

48. Denegri-Knott, J.: Consumers behaving badly: deviation or innovation? Power struggles on the web. J. Consum. Behav. **5**(1), 82–94 (2006)

49. Pfeffer, J., Zorbach, T., Carley, K.M.: Understanding online firestorms: negative word-of-mouth dynamics in social media networks. J. Mark. Commun. **20**(1–2), 117–128 (2014)

50. DeMarco, J.: It's not just fun and war games – juveniles and computer crime (2001). http://ipmall.info/hosted_resources/CyberCrime/usamay2001_7.pdf . Assessed 6 February 2016

51. Butterfield, K.D., Treviño, L.K., Weaver, G.R.: Moral awareness in business organizations: influences of issue-related and social context factors. Hum. Relat. **53**(7), 981–1018 (2000)

52. Pittarello, A., Leib, M., Gordon-Hecker, T., Shalvi, S.: Justifications shape ethical blind spots. Psychol. Sci. **26**, 794–804 (2015)

53. Barsky, A.: Investigating the effects of moral disengagement and participation on unethical work behavior. J. Bus. Ethics **104**(1), 59–75 (2011)

54. Rest, J.R.: Moral Development: Advances in Research and Theory. Praeger, New York (1986)

55. Palazzo, G., Krings, F., Hoffrage, U.: Ethical blindness. J. Bus. Ethics **109**(3), 323–338 (2012)

56. Watley, L.D., May, D.R.: Enhancing moral intensity: the roles of personal and consequential information in ethical decision-making. J. Bus. Ethics **50**(2), 105–126 (2004)
57. Agnihotri, R., Kothandaraman, P., Kashyap, R., Singh, R.: Bringing "social" into sales: the impact of salespeople's social media use on service behaviors and value creation. J. Pers. Selling and Sales Manag. **32**(3), 333–348 (2012)

Unleash Your Brand! Using Social Media as a Marketing Tool in Academia

Timm F. Trefzger[1](✉) and Domenique Dünfelder[2]

[1] School of Business and Economics, Friedrich-Alexander-Universität Erlangen-Nürnberg, Nürnberg, Germany
timm.trefzger@fau.de
[2] stilbezirk, Nürnberg, Germany
d.duenfelder@stilbezirk.de

Abstract. This article presents a guiding framework on how to use social media as a marketing tool for academic researchers. We present fundamentals of a modern communication strategy, which is tailored to the needs of scholars and highlights the importance of personal brands, especially in academia. We offer concrete recommendations regarding target audiences and discuss various social media channels, including researcher-specific platforms such as SSRN, Mendeley, or ResearchGate. We then present an organizational approach to managing social media activities on a daily basis. In particular, we outline a workflow that can be used to efficiently manage social media activities. Because various social media sites differ fundamentally not only in their architecture but also in regard to their optimal use, we finally point out operational recommendations to increase effectivity throughout a researcher's portfolio of social media channels.

Keywords: Social media · Social networking sites · Academia · Personal branding · Self-marketing · Content marketing · Social network analysis

1 Personal Branding and Social Media in Academia

Academic researchers who use Twitter to inform their followers about a recently published article, universities that post stories on Facebook about alumni and corresponding career paths, research institutes that present their profiles on LinkedIn – a growing number of examples illustrates that different stakeholders in academia increasingly start to use social media to communicate with their audiences. On the one hand, this development is not surprising, since social media has already become an established element of the marketing mix for most companies and offers a wide range of opportunities [1, 2]. On the other hand, most academic researchers probably do not fully seize the manifold opportunities of this new world of online communication. But why should a researcher engage on social media sites?

Firstly, the emergence of social media has fundamentally simplified communication. Especially for individuals, it is today easier and more cost-effective than ever before to get in contact with others around the world. Consequently, researchers' associated

© Springer International Publishing Switzerland 2016
G. Meiselwitz (Ed.): SCSM 2016, LNCS 9742, pp. 449–460, 2016.
DOI: 10.1007/978-3-319-39910-2_42

organizations (e.g. the university they work for) have relinquished control over communication, reputation and branding to the individuals who are associated with those organizations. Secondly, competition between researchers is increasing and a long-term academic career is hard to achieve. A survey across 8,216 researchers at 68 UK higher education institutions has revealed that there is a mismatch between career expectations and realistic career possibilities among academics [3]. It is therefore of utmost importance that researchers face competition and differentiate themselves from others.

Today, in many cases, high-quality research alone might not be enough to stand out from other scholars. In response, we argue that perceptual aspects will play an increasingly important role as a differentiator. This issue is especially addressed by the concepts of personal branding and self-marketing, which have been frequently discussed in comparable contexts [e.g. 4]. Self-marketing includes all "activities undertaken by individuals to make themselves known in the marketplace" [5, p. 590], and personal branding builds on the premise "that everyone has a personal brand" [5, p. 590]. Both concepts address the same idea, namely to transfer marketing and branding principles from a corporate environment to individuals (hereafter only referred to as "personal branding"). The aims of personal branding are both to be known in the marketplace (for example as a potential employee) and to differentiate from others.

By transferring personal branding to the context of academic researchers, the question may arise of 'what the personal brand of an academic researcher is'. We argue, in fact, that researchers' personal brands are fundamentally determined by their activities [6]. Depending on the research environment and personal preferences, there is a broad variety of activities that researchers can engage with. It is a common assumption that peer-reviewed journals and academic conferences constitute the main research process and output. However, many researchers are also involved in teaching activities or sometimes serve as consultants for companies or even governments. Ultimately, the individual portfolio of activities determines their personal brand as a researcher.

Against this background, a key task of aspiring scholars will be to build their personal brand as researchers. For this purpose, social media is perfectly suited to support this process [7]. In response, we present a guiding framework for academic researchers that will help to fully embrace the opportunities that social media sites can offer. Academics will learn (or deepen their knowledge) on how to utilize social media sites to communicate their personal brand. Although we will focus primarily on an individual's perspective, the suggestions of this article might also be beneficial for academic organizations, such as universities or research institutes, which can use this article to reflect on their current social media strategies. Our framework is based on a review of articles from academic journals, the business press, as well as on discussions with representatives of social media agencies and social media managers of large corporations.

2   A Communication Strategy in Academia

2.1   Notice that You Act in a Network

As already discussed, the emergence of social media has shifted the power of communication in favor of individuals. Thereby, social media has forced us to view both organizations and individuals as a network of players standing on the same field (see Fig. 1). Before social media, organizations mainly had to take care of their own brand. Today, however, individuals associated with an organization have their own digital identities, represented through an increasing engagement on social media sites. This leads to a greater interdependency among organizations and individuals in terms of their communication activities. For example, a university today has its official website and is moreover present on several social media platforms. Yet, the individuals working for the university, such as professors or other researchers, increasingly build their own digital identities on social media platforms.

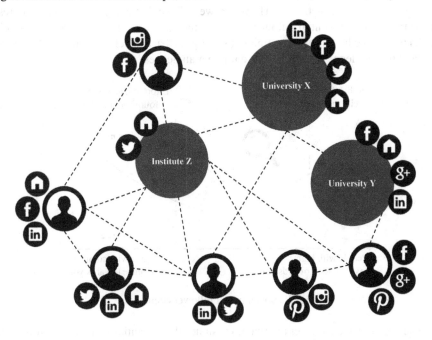

Fig. 1. Digital network of players in the academic sphere (example)

Social network analysis [8, 9] suggests that the members of a network significantly influence each other. If one player, for example, has a very good reputation (e.g. a university), this reputation is automatically passed on to the associated individuals. It is, however, possible that negative perceptions of individual network members harm others in the network. As a foundation of those effects, the concept of word of mouth (WOM) communication plays a central role [10], because it emphasizes the power of communication activities within a network, which can hardly be controlled by individuals within this entity. Of course, the effects suggested by social network analysis and WOM have been valid before the emergence of social media [11]. Nevertheless, the effects of WOM become even more powerful in the online environment, as social media helps to distribute information faster than in offline networks [9, 12]. By that, social media has strengthened individual members of those new networks compared to traditional offline social networks, and has thus enhanced the dynamics and complexity within those networks. Because of this mutual dependency, we argue that it is important that all players in a network are aware of their great responsibility to build and communicate their (personal) brands in a way that the network can benefit. In the following, we present concrete ideas about how to organize researchers' social media activities.

2.2   Identify Your Target Audiences

The foundation of all communication activities is an understanding of the target audiences [13]. In fact, there is a broad variety of different stakeholders who could be interested in a researcher's activities. However, we believe that many researchers underestimate the extent of potential followers on social media. We have thus developed a simple model (social media follower continuum; see Fig. 2) that can help to illustrate the potential (and the challenge) to reach different target audiences.

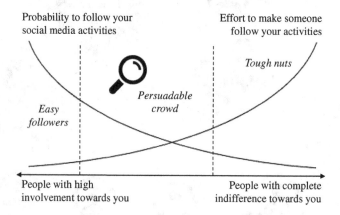

Fig. 2.   Social media follower continuum

The social media follower continuum assumes that potential social media followers (people who follow your activities on social media) can be aligned between opposite ends of a continuum. On the one hand, there are people with high involvement or interest towards you. Those people can be described as *easy followers* because it might not be hard to win them as followers. Probably, most stakeholders who know you in person are *easy followers*, such as colleagues, close business partners or even family members and friends. It is also possible that students become *easy followers* when, for example, certain course information is regularly communicated via a social media platform. On the other hand, there might probably exist people with complete indifference towards you because they are characterized with no direct or indirect involvement or interest towards you. We call those people *tough nuts*, because it is difficult – and probably not necessary – to convince them to follow your activities.

Between *easy followers* and *tough nuts*, there is the *persuadable crowd*. This group is composed of different (potentially) interested parties, who do not follow you automatically, but who might be interested in your activities (now or in the future). For example, there are people who are interested in a certain topic and who want to follow thought leaders in that specific field. As a result, they continuously decide which experts to follow on e.g. Twitter depending on their perception of those experts. The subsequent question is how to provide relevant content to members of the *persuadable crowd*, aiming to persuade them to follow your social media activities.

Against this background, we suggest identifying existing – but also aspired – target audiences. For most academic researchers, the international research community in a certain field might be an important target audience. Students with an interest in offered teaching activities might be another target audience. In addition, surrounding firms or institutes could be a further target audience, which might be interested in your activities. Overall, the identification and understanding of different target audiences are fundamental during the following phase of content creation. Only if you understand who your target audiences are, you can adequately communicate with them [13].

2.3   Embrace the Idea of Content Marketing and Select Valuable Content for Your Audience

Based on the identification of your target audiences, it is important to understand their needs and the topics they are interested in, because this understanding is fundamental to answer the question of what to communicate. The idea of sharing content that is relevant and valuable to your target audiences is referred to as content marketing [14]. The concept has increasingly gained importance, especially in the field of digital marketing [15]. A reason for this is that social media users are confronted with a growing amount of content every day. Therefore, the relevance and value of content from a user's perspective are increasingly important when it comes to the question of whether to engage with a social media post or not. This importance is further emphasized by the uses and gratifications (U&G) theory.

U&G theory suggests that individuals strive to receive gratifications through their media usage [16]. As a result, social media users adjust their online behavior according to their gratifications. On social media sites, studies have shown that users search for entertainment, information and social interactions [e.g. 17, 18]. Content strategies of academics should therefore consider these findings and provide content that fulfills the needs of their target audiences, because communication effectiveness is closely related to it.

Against this background, it can be useful to establish certain content categories, which are specifically designed for the already defined target audiences. For example, a researcher in the field of entrepreneurship could publish information about (own) research articles, pictures from academic conferences, interesting and valuable information about entrepreneurship in general, tutorial videos about what is important when founding a company or behind-the-scenes pictures of his/her work day. As you can imagine, there are a lot of possibilities to generate interesting and valuable content for your target audiences.

Barack Obama can serve as a lively example for the establishment of a content category. On a regular basis, Barack Obama has published pictures which have portrayed him as a nice and accessible person, for instance, when he went for lunch with his staff at a public burger restaurant. Another example would be a picture of him in the Oval

Office of the White House, playing around with a football during a meeting. These examples show that Barack Obama has obviously established "behind-the-scenes" content as a central content category of his communication strategy. One could also argue that this part of his content strategy has been successful, because many people, in fact, see him as a nice and accessible person.

When content categories are established, the goal is to find and publish valuable content on a regular basis. However, it might be not entirely clear which online channels are suitable for the communication purposes of academic researchers. In the next section, we therefore outline different types of social media sites.

2.4   Communication Channels: Which Platform to Use?

The landscape of social media sites is continuously changing in terms of new sites evolving and others losing relevance [19]. From a researcher's perspective, of course, not all social media platforms are reasonable to engage on. For example, it might not be necessary to become active on the video messaging application Snapchat, because – up to now – it is not at all a suitable channel for researcher-related content and is mostly used by teenagers. However, there exist platforms where it is not as easy to decide whether to use them or not. The mobile photo-sharing and social networking service Instagram, for example, is hardly suitable to communicate new research articles, but could be a great channel to (visually) tell stories about your life as a researcher (e.g. at academic conferences), with the aim of adding some shine to this life and thereby sharpen your personal brand. In general, we suggest to stay open for new emerging platforms and to continuously reflect on the landscape of platforms in regard to their potential for your own portfolio of used social media platforms. In the following, we elaborate on different types of social media sites.

First of all, social networking sites, such as Facebook and Twitter, are generally used both in a private and business context [20]. With currently more than 1.5 billion users, Facebook is the most popular social media platform [21]. Although the site is primarily used for private purposes, most brands are present with their own fan pages. Also for researchers, Facebook offers great potential, because of the high number of active users. Next to Facebook, Twitter might also be a suitable channel for your communication activities, because the micro blog has continuously evolved to a network, which is especially used by organizations to publish all sorts of information [22]. Simultaneously, users follow interesting organizations, thought leaders, magazines etc. to assess relevant information.

Social networking sites, which are primarily used in the business context, are called business networking sites [2]. Currently, the (by far) most used business networking site is LinkedIn. Individuals can create personal profiles and connect with their peers. Originally, most people on LinkedIn used the platform mainly to showcase their resume. In recent years, LinkedIn has moved away from the static platform it has been in the beginning but has evolved to an increasingly active network. Today, next to individuals' profiles, most companies, universities and institutes are present on LinkedIn and use the platform increasingly as a communication channel. For academic researchers, LinkedIn is a great platform to stay in touch with other researchers and to stand out by publishing content, which is valuable for their network.

Another important piece in the portfolio of useful social media sites is networking platforms and content communities that specifically focus on academic researchers (e.g. SSRN, Google Scholar, Mendeley, ResearchGate). Those platforms are greatly suitable to showcase your research and to also connect with other researchers. Although there are already several of those platforms, it has been recently noticeable that various sites continuously emerge into a combination of networking platform and content community. The Social Science Research Network (SSRN, www.ssrn.com), for example, is devoted to the dissemination of scientific research but has recently announced that they will further expand the possibilities of creating personal profiles. Another example is Mendeley (www.mendeley.com), which has been primarily used as a program to manage research articles. Yet, the possibility to also showcase research papers and to get in contact with other researchers has changed the way Mendeley is used today. A third example is ResearchGate (www.researchgate.net). It is also a social networking site, aiming to connect researchers worldwide and offering the possibility to present research papers. Finally, Google Scholar (www.scholar.google.com) has already evolved into an important platform for most researchers, due to the presentation of popular citation indices (e.g. h-index), which are increasingly important in academia. In contrast to established platforms, relatively new websites such as ACADEMIA (www.academia.edu) are emerging, having a similar value proposition to ResearchGate.

Regardless of your decision on which sites to be present, it is important that your profile is always updated on all sites you are active on. For this, you can use, for example, an Excel sheet with each row containing a published paper. The columns are then used for all the platforms on which you want to publish your research papers (either just the reference or the actual file). Thereby, it is relatively simple to keep the overview, although you have profiles on several sites.

A further and important cornerstone within a social media strategy is a non-social-media-website, on which you can publish information about your activities in detail. This could be your affiliated organization's official website or another website that you control yourself. As we will describe below, the optimal publication of content on social media sites requires one to present content in a very short way, because a short message length is more effective or even obligatory (e.g. Tweets on Twitter cannot have more than 140 characters). Therefore, it is necessary on social media sites to publish posts that include a link to your non-social-media-website, where the content is presented in more detail for those who want to further engage with this content.

3   Organizing Your Social Media Management

3.1   Polish Your Profiles Across All Platforms

Before you engage in the daily work of social media management, it is important to review your profiles on all platforms you are present on. It is not only important that all profiles look and feel professional, but it is also necessary that all profiles are aligned to your overall (personal) brand strategy. Decide which pictures and copy texts (e.g. your biography) you want to use, and distribute these elements across your platforms. If it is necessary, adjust the elements according to the needs of individual sites. By that approach, a consistent look and feel across platforms is ensured, although there might be reasonable adjustments because of varying platform architectures or mechanisms.

3.2   Establish a Workflow

Since most academic researchers do not employ social media managers who are responsible for their social media activities, it is of great importance to establish a workflow that minimizes the overall social media effort, but yet ensures professional social media communication. We consider the social media workflow as a process that includes more people than the individual researcher because researchers often work in a team. As a consequence, our process can be used by individuals and by teams, as the overall mechanisms remain the same.

We suggest a continuously running, three-step process that organizes the workflow according to content creation, preparation and communication (see Fig. 3). The basic idea is to avoid that people think too much towards single channels ("What can I do on Facebook today?"), because it can be considered as not efficient to think about channels separately. Instead, the content should be in the center of all considerations. After you have decided what content is worth sharing, you have to select suitable channels and prepare the content for publication. In the following, we elaborate on these three phases of social media management.

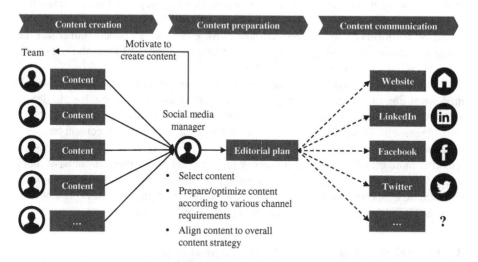

Fig. 3.   Social media management workflow

In the content creation phase, possible content has to be collected. It is important that everyone who participates in this task is open for topics that are possibly interesting for the already defined target audiences. Stanford University, for example, has implemented a series for their social media channels, in which they introduce members of the staff. One episode was a story on an employee who has been preparing sandwiches on the Stanford campus for 40 years. The story was presented in an emotional way and received a high amount of positive user interaction. This example illustrates that the openness for relevant and interesting stories is an important element during the content creation phase. It is furthermore crucial that content creation does not only involve the detection of relevant content, but also the generation of shareable media such as (good) pictures or videos (a photo taken with your smartphone is better than no photo!). The content has then to be sent to a central position, which is controlled by the person responsible for content preparation. For example, the content could be centrally saved on a shared network drive or by using a web service such as Dropbox or Google Drive.

In the second phase, the person who is responsible for content preparation (referred to as *social media manager*) has to select and prepare the content for publication. Because of the platform differences, it is of particular importance to optimize the content according to the individual requirements of the selected channels. The social media manager is moreover responsible that the content is aligned to the overall content strategy. When researchers work alone, they have to fulfill both the role of content creators, as well as the role of the social media manager. When researchers are working in a team, it might be beneficial that the social media manager is a person with a great affinity for social media and communication.

In the content communication phase, the social media manager publishes the content on various platforms. Since it might not always be reasonable to publish every kind of content on all platforms, the social media manager has to decide on which platforms a certain story should be published. For example, a photo showing you at a conference dinner in Venice might be worth sharing on Facebook, but not applicable for LinkedIn, because LinkedIn – up to now – is typically used for more "serious" content. Since it can be quite confusing to maintain the overview about different posts on various social media platforms, we recommend using an editorial plan (see Fig. 4). In the simplest form, an Excel spreadsheet can be used to plan the posts and to note on which platforms a post should be published. Thereby, it is easy to maintain control over the communication activities across platforms at all times.

#	Post	Date	Attachment	Comment	Facebook	Twitter	LinkedIn	University Website	Research Gate	Google Scholar	...
1	Paper accepted (Journal of XXX)	30-Jul-16	Picture	Include link in the text	YES	YES	YES	YES	YES	YES	
2	Paper presentation (AOM)	3-Aug-16	Video	Include link in the text	YES	YES	YES	YES			
3	Conference dinner (AOM)	5-Aug-16	Picture	-	YES						
4	Business Horizon article on XXX	9-Aug-16	Picture	Include link in the text		YES	YES				
...	...										

Fig. 4. Editorial plan (simplified example)

3.3   Understand Your Channels and Strive for Operational Excellence

If you decide to engage on a certain social media site, it is of utmost importance to completely understand the rules and mechanisms of the channel, and to strive for operational excellence. But why is this so important? Firstly, on social networking sites, your posts have to compete with posts of users' friends or simply with funny cat videos. In addition, most users are confronted with a very large amount of information and decide very fast whether to further engage with a certain post or to continue scrolling down the almost endless list of posts in their timeline. It is therefore important that your post catches users' attention (see also U&G theory, which is explained above). Secondly, the high amount of content has led social networking sites to filter posts to a certain degree. In this context, the amount of post interaction is very important, because it determines the number of people who will potentially see a post in their news feed. On Facebook, for example, the initial number of likes, comments and shares that a post receives indicates the "relevance" of the post, assessed by the mysterious and frequently cited "Facebook algorithm". This relevance subsequently determines how many users will see the post in their timeline. Consequently, the degree of post interaction in terms of likes, comments, and shares will significantly affect the number of people who will potentially engage with its content. It is therefore essential to design posts the "right" way to maximize post popularity – but what is the "right" way?

Several empirical studies have already focused on the antecedents of post popularity on social networking sites [e.g. 23, 24]. Those studies have shown that posts with attached pictures and videos are significantly more successful in terms of user interaction compared to posts including other attachments such as links to external websites. It was moreover found that a short amount of text is beneficial because social networking sites are typically used to access information very fast.

Although prior studies have often focused specifically on Facebook or Twitter, we assume that revealed findings can also be transferred to other platforms. In general, to optimize social media effectiveness, posts should include an appealing or interesting picture or video. A short text can serve as an appetizer for those who want to know more about the featured message. The text might also include a link, which directs interested users to a more detailed presentation of the content on, for example, your university's official website. With this approach, the content is presented at different detail levels, and interested users can decide how deep they want to engage with your content. To further reduce the amount of text in a post, we recommend the use of short links (e.g. bit.ly). We furthermore want to emphasize that, on social networking sites, it is important to publish content on a regular basis [1]. It is hard to say what the best frequency is, as it also depends on the platform. Three to five posts per week might be a reasonable frequency for researchers to publish on their social networking sites. However, since social media sites are highly dynamic, it can also be beneficial to publish more, if the content is valuable to the target audiences.

Finally, it has to be stated that the above-mentioned ideas on how to reach operational excellence on social media sites have to be understood as a first step only. Researchers who want to successfully engage in this sphere may have to read through a few of those numerous guidebooks, which can be found on the Internet, and might also have to consider the following statement of an unknown author: "Social media is a lot of fun when it is done right. But when it is done right, it is even more work."

4 Conclusion

Studies comparing academics' career expectations and realistic career possibilities indicate that academic researchers already face a high level of competition, and differentiation becomes increasingly critical. Although scholars' most important quality indicator is their research output, perceptional aspects become more and more important to differentiate from others. Therefore, self-marketing and personal branding can be used to actively shape public perception in a favorable way. For this purpose, social media sites offer great potential. Our article has therefore presented a guiding framework for researchers on how to utilize social media to effectively build their personal brand. Of course, this article is not a final answer to all open questions in the field of social media; nevertheless, it might have opened your mind in regard to the great opportunities social media can offer, especially in academia.

Acknowledgements. We used icons made by Bogdan Rosu, SimpleIcon, and Zurb from www.flaticon.com.

References

1. Kaplan, A.M., Haenlein, M.: Users of the world, unite! The challenges and opportunities of social media. Bus. Horiz. **53**(1), 59–68 (2010)
2. Mangold, W.G., Faulds, D.J.: Social media: the new hybrid element of the promotion mix. Bus. Horiz. **52**(4), 357–365 (2009)
3. Gibney, E.: Researchers' "unrealistic" hopes of academic careers. Times Higher Education (2013). https://www.timeshighereducation.com/news/researchers-unrealistic-hopes-of-academic-careers/2007247.article. [Cited 9 Feb 2016]
4. Peters, T.: The brand called you. Fast Company **10**, 83–88 (1997)
5. Shepherd, I.D.H.: From cattle and coke to charlie: meeting the challenge of self marketing and personal branding. J. Mark. Manag. **44**, 589–606 (2005)
6. Labrecque, L.I., Markos, E., Milne, G.R.: Online personal branding: processes, challenges, and implications. J. Interact. Mark. **25**(1), 37–50 (2011)
7. Harris, L., Rae, A.: Building a personal brand through social networking. J. Bus. Strategy **32**(5), 14–21 (2011)
8. Borgatti, S.P., Foster, P.C.: The network paradigm in organizational research: a review and typology. J. Manag. **29**(6), 991–1013 (2003)
9. Kane, G., Labianca, G., Borgatti, S.P.: What's different about social media networks? A framework and research agenda. MIS Q. **38**(1), 275–304 (2014)
10. Brown, J.J., Reingen, P.H.: Social ties and word-of-mouth referral behavior. J. Consum. Res. **14**(3), 350–362 (1987)
11. Granovetter, M.S.: The strength of weak ties: a network theory revisited. Sociol. Theory **1**, 201–233 (1983)
12. Trusov, M., Bucklin, R.E., Pauwels, K.: Effects of word-of-mouth versus traditional marketing: findings from an internet social networking site. J. Mark. **73**(5), 90–102 (2009)
13. Kotler, P., Armstrong, G.: Principles of Marketing. Pearson, Harlow (2014)
14. Harad, K.C.: Content marketing strategies to educate and entertain. J. Financ. Plann. **26**(3), 18–20 (2013)

15. Steimle, J.: What Is content marketing?. Forbes (2014). http://www.forbes.com/sites/joshsteimle/2014/09/19/what-is-content-marketing/#572453151d70. [Cited 1 Feb 2016]

16. Stafford, T.P., Stafford, M.R., Schkade, L.L.: Determining uses and gratifications for the internet. Decis. Sci. **35**(2), 259–288 (2004)

17. Brandtzaeg, P.B., Heim, J.: A typology of social networking sites users. Int. J. Web Based Communities **7**, 28–51 (2011)

18. Park, N., Kee, K.F., Valenzuela, S.: Being immersed in social networking environment: Facebook groups, uses and gratifications, and social outcomes. CyberPsychol. Behav. **12**(6), 729–733 (2009)

19. Kietzmann, J.H., Hermkens, K., McCarthy, I.P., Silvestre, B.S.: Social media? Get serious! Understanding the functional building blocks of social media. Bus. Horiz. **54**(3), 241–251 (2011)

20. Hughes, D.J., Rowe, M., Batey, M., Lee, A.: A tale of two sites: Twitter vs. Facebook and the personality predictors of social media usage. Comput. Hum. Behav. **28**(2), 561–569 (2012)

21. Statista. Leading social networks worldwide as of January 2016, ranked by number of active users (in millions) (2016). http://www.statista.com/statistics/272014/global-social-networks-ranked-by-number-of-users/. [Cited 9 Feb 2016]

22. Burton, S., Soboleva, A.: Interactive or reactive? Marketing with Twitter. J. Consum. Mark. **28**(7), 491–499 (2011)

23. Trefzger, T.F., Baccarella, C.V., Voigt, K.-I.: Antecedents of brand post popularity in Facebook: the influence of images, videos, and text. In: Proceedings of the 15th International Marketing Trends Conference, pp. 1–8, Venice (2016)

24. De Vries, L., Gensler, S., Leeflang, P.S.H.: Popularity of brand posts on brand fan pages: an investigation of the effects of social media marketing. J. Interact. Mark. **26**(2), 83–91 (2012)

Hold the Line! The Challenge of Being a Premium Brand in the Social Media Era

Timm F. Trefzger[1(✉)], Christian V. Baccarella[1],
Christian W. Scheiner[2], and Kai-Ingo Voigt[1]

[1] School of Business and Economics,
Friedrich-Alexander-Universität Erlangen-Nürnberg, Nürnberg, Germany
{timm.trefzger,christian.baccarella,
kai-ingo.voigt}@fau.de
[2] Institut für Entrepreneurship und Business Development,
Universität zu Lübeck, Lübeck, Germany
christian.scheiner@uni-luebeck.de

Abstract. Social media represents a substantially new way of communicating with customers. Whereas marketers used to spread their messages without receiving any direct feedback or reactions, customers now have the possibility to instantly reply to companies' communication efforts. Adapting to altered communication patterns poses a huge challenge especially for premium brands. On social media, premium brands are not anymore able to entirely rely on their huge marketing budgets but rather need to embrace and utilize newly emerged communication approaches. This study examines a sample of 1156 car brand posts of US Facebook pages and reveals that premium brands possess specific characteristics in their communication strategy. Our findings offer valuable insights into marketing communication activities of premium brands on social media sites.

Keywords: Premium brands · Social media · Social networking sites · Brand posts · Automotive · Appeals · Communication strategy · Content analysis

1 Introduction

In the last decade, social media has evolved into an integral part of daily life. Simultaneously, it is becoming more and more common to communicate digitally with each other. This transformation of communication behavior has also fundamentally changed the way of how companies approach their customers [1]. Whereas marketers used to spread their messages without receiving any direct feedback or reactions, customers now have the possibility to instantly reply to companies' communication efforts [2]. Marketers need to consider these changed circumstances when positioning their brand in order to maintain their competitiveness. Simmons [3] therefore suggests to embrace the transformational nature of the Internet and urges companies to adapt their branding strategies to it. The paradox, in this case, is that social media allows addressing individualistic needs while being able to create a sense of community at the same time. This increased complexity of relationships, however, changed traditional and proven

© Springer International Publishing Switzerland 2016
G. Meiselwitz (Ed.): SCSM 2016, LNCS 9742, pp. 461–471, 2016.
DOI: 10.1007/978-3-319-39910-2_43

marketing communication methods and calls for more sophisticated branding approaches [4].

Especially for premium brands, adapting to altered communication patterns poses an enormous challenge. Premium brands can typically be differentiated from non-premium brands according to their product superiority and perceived prestige, which can increase purchase likelihood and allows companies to command a price premium [5, 6]. In order for customers to accept higher prices, premium brands need to justify and defend their "premiumness", for example, through extensive marketing communication activities [7]. On social media, premium brands are not able anymore to entirely rely on their huge marketing budgets, but rather need to embrace and utilize new communication approaches. Therefore, premium brands need to find new ways to communicate their premiumness to potential customers in the virtual sphere, where the borders between the traditional marketing mindset and new ways of company-consumer-relationships are blurred and permeable.

Although there has been a rise of studies in the field of social media, more research is required in order to examine causal relationships of social media communication activities [8]. Moreover, to the best of our knowledge, this study is the first attempt to explore premium brands' communication activities in the context of social media. Due to the growing importance of social media for marketing purposes and the need for premium brands to align their branding strategies with changed communication patterns, the purpose of this explorative study is therefore to examine the communication strategies of premium brands in a social media setting.

Thus, this study analyzes social media marketing practices of automobile premium brands regarding their social media communication activities and compares their effectivity with a control group of non-premium brands. The car industry is a suitable object for studying the marketing efforts of premium brands, because, for many customers, prestige and exclusivity are strong reasons for choosing a car brand [9].

This paper is structured as follows. We start with a brief overview of social media and the characteristics of premium brands. We end this overview with three explorative research questions, which set the direction for the following empirical analysis. This analysis examines communication activities of premium brands and a non-premium control group on a popular social media website. After the presentation of the results, we discuss our findings and give some practical implications.

2   Theoretical Overview: Social Media and Premium Brands

For a long time, companies were able to carry out marketing activities in one direction. Individuals had no choice but to consume information without having the possibility to question it or to exchange opinions with others. Hence, companies used to have the information sovereignty, giving them the necessary instruments to guide opinions according to their will and their benefit. Given the case, for example, of deceptive advertising, it has been difficult for customers to share their discontent with like-minded peers [10]. All this changed fundamentally when social media shifted communication patterns to the digital world. Now, consumers can easily interact with each other whenever and wherever they want.

Social media include a wide range of different applications and services, such as micro-blogging sites (e.g. Twitter), video sharing platforms (e.g. YouTube) or social networking sites (SNS) (e.g. Facebook) [1]. The connecting element among all social media applications is the fact that mainly users generate the content available on these sites [11]. The increasing importance of social media applications and the huge amount of social media users has also attracted considerable interest among marketers. Especially SNS have recently gained importance for corporate branding purposes. On SNS, companies can create a digital presence and are therefore able to gather customers or interested social media users at relatively low costs [12]. Facebook, currently the most popular SNS [13], offers companies the possibility to create so-called fan pages, which allow interested users to follow the activities of a brand. Companies can interact with their followers by sharing posts, including e.g. pictures, videos or links [14]. This direct interaction makes it possible to strengthen the bond between a brand and its (potential) customers [15].

The transforming impact of social media particularly poses challenges for premium brands. Premium brands can broadly be defined as brands that are typically associated with a certain degree of exclusivity. Moreover, products of premium brands generally possess superior product attributes, such as an excellent quality or a high technological level [5]. The concept and perception of "premiumness" are closely related to the concept of luxury and whose meaning has significantly evolved over the last decades. In that context, Brun and Castelli [16] give an extensive overview of the development of the nature of luxury. They argue that although premium products can include some connecting characteristics such as superior technical performance, global reputation or premium quality, the perception of luxury remains highly subjective and depends on the differences of consumers' profiles. Moreover, the authors describe the ongoing dilution and democratization of luxury with the emergence of different forms of the so-called "new luxury", which is targeted at the upper middle class. Through, for example, line extensions, companies can reach new customer segments with relatively low financial effort and risk [9]. Similarly, Truong et al. [17] report about recent efforts of premium brands to target the mass market (also referred to as "masstige", a term combining the words "mass" and "prestige"). The challenge for premium brands is, however, to keep their prestigious image, while becoming affordable for some part of the mass market. Truong et al. [17] illustrate this risky trade-off using the example of the premium car manufacturer BMW and argue that the prestige of a premium brand such as BMW could be seriously damaged "when every single teacher drives one of the brand's cars" [17, p. 381].

Managing the balancing act between maintaining a prestigious image and maximizing sales is even more difficult in the context of social media. Traditionally, companies could build strong brands by heavily investing in marketing activities to create brand equity [18]. Social media changed that. In their article "Will social media kill branding?", Kohli et al. [19] argue that branding will become more and more transparent, which means that established brands have to fight harder to maintain their competitive advantage. The authors further state that the "reigns of leading brands will be shortened" [19, p. 40], which indicates that former strong brands are in danger of losing their competitive edge. The fact that huge marketing budgets are not as important anymore to effectively utilize social media applications for branding purposes increases the pressure for premium brands to find ways to stand out and to remain perceived as premium. Hence, premium brands need to carefully plan their social media communication strategies and need to conscientiously check the nature of the information they want to communicate to their customers.

It was already mentioned that premium brands are connected with certain characteristics that are perceived as premium. It was also already mentioned that social media allow almost unlimited interaction and can be used to form a strong relationship with customers. The key question in a digital environment is therefore how premium brands can utilize social media to share and maintain their premium brand image. More specifically, the challenge for premium brands is how to frame their communication activities in order to match message content with benefits their premium customers seek to fulfill [20]. Subsequently, social media messages need to contain certain premium appeals that help brands to be perceived as premium. For example, in their analysis of prestige-seeking consumers, Vigneron and Johnson [21] find that buyers are looking for specific values when consuming prestige products, namely: perceived conspicuous value, perceived unique value, perceived social value, perceived hedonic value, and perceived quality value. Similarly, Vernette and Hamdi-Kidar [20] identify several attributes of consumers' luxury perception. The identified attributes can be categorized into an impressive (e.g. excellent quality or elegance) and an expressive (e.g. rarity, uniqueness or exclusivity) dimension. Their study emphasizes the notion that although the perception of premiumness is generally subjective, consumers do associate certain features and signals with a premium brand.

The above-mentioned discussion clearly underlines that premium brands need to have a distinct social media communication approach to differentiate themselves from non-premium brands in order to be perceived as premium. It is assumed that premium brands need to be more active and more consistent in communicating their messages on social media to compensate the loss of information sovereignty. Premium brands therefore need to address and integrate specific signals and appeals that are perceived by their potential buyers as premium into their marketing communication activities. We thus assume that clear differences between communication activities of premium brands and non-premium brands need to exist. In order to analyze these differences, our study focuses on corporate communication activities on the popular SNS Facebook. Therefore, our study is guided by the following research questions:

Research Question 1:	On social networking sites, do premium brands achieve higher overall brand page popularity and higher overall post interaction than non-premium brands?
Research Question 2:	On social networking sites, do premium brands possess a specific pattern in the communication of premium appeals (e.g. superior quality, performance, design, luxury)?
Research Question 3:	On social networking sites, do premium appeals especially affect post interactivity of premium brands?

3   Methodology

3.1   Sample and Coding Procedure

To examine the behavior of brands in securing their premium brand status, the SNS Facebook was chosen because of its high popularity. As a research object, we chose the automotive industry. Due to their undisputed premium brand approach, Audi, BMW, and Mercedes-Benz were selected as premium brands [22, 23]. Additionally, a control group of non-premium brands was built to reveal the characteristic behavior of premium brands and to identify specific strategies in securing their premiumness. Consequently, 558 brand posts of premium brands were collected and compared with 598 brand posts of non-premium brands. Ford, Honda, and Nissan comprised the non-premium brand control group.

During data collection in December 2014, the brands' US Facebook pages were accessed and posts that have been published before November 2014 were manually saved as screenshots. We considered a time span of around five weeks between the newest posts and data collection to be sufficient (see e.g. [24]) because post interaction happens very fast on social networking sites. For every brand, we collected 200 posts. Finally, we had to exclude some posts with photo albums, because they received a second round of user interaction after the brands added additional photos to already existing albums.

We extensively trained four undergraduate students to perform the coding of the posts. They were then assigned to one of two independent coding teams (two coders per team) and both teams processed the whole sample. Thereby, we could review coding objectivity by assessing reliability measures. For all included variables, we individually calculated intercoder reliabilities by using the proportional reduction in loss (PRL) approach, which was developed by Rust and Cooil [25]. No variable showed a PRL value lower than the recommended minimum level of 0.7. Therefore, we can assume that the coding offers a sufficient level of measurement objectivity.

3.2   Measures

As a measure of overall brand page popularity, we collected the number of followers (number of page likes). As post interaction variables, we individually assessed the number of likes, comments, and shares for every brand post. Since the brand pages in our sample differed in terms of the number of total followers, we adjusted post interaction measures by the number of page likes for every post (e.g. for likes: number of post likes divided by the number of page likes [of the respective brand] multiplied by 1 million). Thereby, we generated adjusted interaction measures, which offer meaningful insights about how much interaction a certain post has received among one million followers. For OLS regressions, we took the natural logarithm of the number of likes, comments, and shares. Due to the nature of the logarithm function, we transformed the zeros into 0.00001. Finally, we searched for typical premium brand appeals. In particular, we examined whether a post – explicitly and primarily – communicated quality aspects, performance aspects, information about the technological level, design or aesthetics aspects, and/or aspects that are related to luxury, status, or prestige.

For OLS regressions, we included several control variables into our considerations, because prior research has indicated the influence of other variables on post interaction (e.g. [26, 27]). First of all, we captured various post attachments. Namely, it was determined whether a post included one picture, more than one picture, a video, or none of these options. Message length was evaluated by counting the number of text lines (no text, 1–2 lines, 3–5 lines, more than 5 lines). We furthermore controlled whether a post was a shared post (from another Facebook page) as well as whether a post was posted on the weekend.

4 Findings

4.1 Descriptive Statistics

The first research question asked whether premium brands are successful in achieving higher popularity of their brand pages and in terms of overall post interaction (see Table 1). On average, there is a tendency that premium brands excel in this aspect. However, Audi (premium brand) reveals to have fewer followers compared to Nissan (non-premium brand).

In regard to post interaction, our findings show that premium brand posts have received a lot more likes per one million followers than posts from the control group ($F = 86.545$, df = 1, $p = .001$). Interestingly, we found an opposite relationship for comments, where premium brand posts have received clearly fewer comments per one million followers than the control group ($F = 32.101$, df = 1, $p = .001$). No significant difference ($p > .1$) was detected for the number of post shares.

Table 1. Brand page popularity and overall post interaction means

	N	Number of page likes	Adjusted post interaction means[a]		
			Likes**	Comments**	Shares
Premium brands	*558*	*15.10 m*	*1040.0*	*11.4*	*51.6*
Audi	197	9.41 m	1073.2	10.0	48.4
BMW	192	19.03 m	1289.3	15.0	61.2
Mercedes-Benz	169	16.85 m	718.0	8.9	44.6
Control group	*598*	*5.85 m*	*491.6*	*21.9*	*42.6*
Ford	200	2.91 m	648.7	35.9	75.0
Honda	198	3.61 m	498.9	17.5	33.1
Nissan	200	11.02 m	327.3	12.2	19.6
Total	*1156*		*756.3*	*16.8*	*47.0*

Note: *p < .05; **p < .01; ***p < .001 (ANOVAs comparing interaction means of premium and non-premium brands); [a] Calculation e.g. for likes: Average post likes/Page likes * 1 million

The second research question asked whether premium brands possess a specific pattern in communicating premium appeals (see Table 2). In fact, premium brands communicated *performance aspects* in their posts more often than the control group ($\chi 2 = 8.565$, df = 1, p = .003). Moreover, *design/aesthetics* was particularly communicated more often by premium brands (8.4 %; $\chi 2 = 37.991$, df = 1, p = .000). In addition, the premium appeal *luxury/status/prestige* was not used at all by the control group. This appeal was yet identified in 5.6 % of the premium brand posts ($\chi 2 = 34.138$, df = 1, p = .000). *Quality aspects* were rarely communicated. Nonetheless, non-premium brand posts explicitly contained this appeal more often (3.0 %) than premium brands (1.3 %; $\chi 2 = 4.205$, df = 1, p = .040). Although premium brands communicated the *technological level* more often, no significant difference could be found regarding this appeal (p > .1).

Table 2. Use of premium appeals

Premium appeals	Premium		Control Group		Total	
	Count	%	Count	%	Count	%
Performance aspects**	159	28.5	126	21.1	285	24.7
Design/aesthetics***	118	21.1	50	8.4	168	14.5
Technological level	92	16.5	86	14.4	178	15.4
Luxury/status/prestige***	31	5.6	0	0.0	31	2.7
Quality aspects*	7	1.3	18	3.0	25	2.2

Note: N = 1156; *p < .05; **p < .01; ***p < .001 (non-parametric chi-square analysis comparing premium and non-premium control group).

4.2 Effects on Post Interaction

The third research question asked whether premium appeals have an influence on post interactivity and whether this influence is especially given for premium brands. Therefore, we conducted six OLS regression models. We individually considered likes, comments, and shares model for both premium and non-premium brands (see Table 3). Overall, all regression models are significant (ps = .000) and explain the variance of the dependent variables sufficiently well (11.8 % $\leq$ R2s $\leq$ 38.2 %; 10.0 % $\leq$ adj. R2s $\leq$ 36.7 %).

The findings reveal that the use of certain appeals can have an impact on interaction measures. In fact, the communication of *performance aspects* generally affected all interaction measures positively. The communication of information about *the technological level* of the products had a significant positive effect only on the number of comments and shares in the premium brand models (M3, M5). Moreover, *design/aesthetics* aspects revealed to have also a positive effect, especially for the premium brands. No significant effects on post interaction could be detected for *quality aspects* as well as for the *luxury/status/prestige* appeal.

468   T.F. Trefzger et al.

Table 3. Estimation results of regression analyses

Variables	Likes[a] model		Comments[a] model		Shares[a] model	
	Premium M1	CG M2	Premium M3	CG M4	Premium M5	CG M6
Premium appeals						
Performance aspects	.322**	.706***	.235*	.448**	.532***	.673***
Design/aesthetics	.361	.335*	.436***	.528*	.727***	.491
Technological level	.207	−.074	.337**	−.176	.555**	.274
Luxury/status/prestige	−.060	.	−.122	.	.113	.
Quality aspects	.487	.055	.620	.210	.745	−.029
Control variables and constant						
Post attachments						
1 picture	1.129***	1.225***	.594*	1.155***	1.066*	1.182***
>1 picture	1.775***	1.225***	1.064***	1.227***	1.565***	1.334***
Video	.463	.751***	.606*	1.012***	1.399***	2.055***
Message length						
1–2 text lines	1.059***	.310	.745**	.333	1.641***	−.242
3–5 text lines	1.191***	−.068	.818**	−.195	1.670***	−.358
>5 text lines	.945**	.056	.470	.095	1.370***	.019
Shared post	−.964***	.138	−.968***	.128	−1.496***	−.852**
Weekend post	−.268*	−.098	−.321**	−.352	−.367*	−.354
Constant	6.791***	5.781***	3.100***	2.691***	2.874***	3.307***
Model statistics						
N	558	598	558	598	558	598
F-value	25.842	11.862	15.649	6.541	16.170	8.118
p-value	.000	.000	.000	.000	.000	.000
R^2	.382	.196	.272	.118	.279	.143
Adj. R^2	.367	.179	.255	.100	.261	.125

Note: [a] Natural logarithm; *p < .05; **p < .01; ***p <.001; CG = non-premium control group.

5   Implications and Conclusion

Given the findings of our study, it can be concluded that premium brands follow a distinct social media communication approach. Generally, they are more successful regarding overall brand page popularity and interactivity measures. In comparison to the control group, premium brands were, in average, able to clearly gather more brand page likes. Thereby, premium brands can use this fact and win back social media-related losses of information sovereignty by controlling content and by being able to guide exchanged information between users on their brand pages.

Concerning the overall interactivity measures, a mixed, more negative picture is drawn. In fact, premium brands were able to gain significantly more likes than the control group, but failed, however, in terms of comments and shares. In particular, premium brand posts received significantly less comments than the posts of the control group. No difference was found for the number of shares. For premium brands, these shortcomings in shares and especially comments contain an immediate threat for securing their premium brand status. Premium brands must therefore develop adequate measures to increase the level of interactivity in regard to these aspects.

Regarding the use of premium appeals, clear hierarchies for premium brands and the control group become visible. Premium brands communicated *performance aspects* most frequently, followed, in that order, by *design/aesthetics*, *technological level*, *luxury/status/prestige*, and *quality aspects*. For the control group, a different hierarchy of premium appeals was detected. The most frequently communicated appeal *performance aspects* was followed by the appeals *technological level*, *design/aesthetics*, and *quality aspects*. These findings show that premium brands specifically emphasize *performance aspects* as well as *design/aesthetics* aspects, whereas in the control group, *performance aspects* and information about the *technological level* were more important.

In contrast to that hierarchical perspective, a direct comparison of the overall use of premium appeals revealed that premium brands communicate *performance aspects*, *design/aesthetics*, and *luxury/status/prestige* more often than the control group. In addition, *quality aspects* were communicated less frequently. It is moreover striking that there is no difference in the use of the appeal *technological level*.

Considering the effectiveness of post appeals, clear recommendations can be given to premium brands in securing their premium brand status. The regression analyses showed that the use of certain premium appeals significantly affects interactivity of brand posts. Highlighting *performance aspects* improved the level of interactivity in every aspect. Likes, comments, and shares were significantly increased. Despite its general benefits on communication effectiveness, *performance aspects* might, however, not be suitable to secure the premium brand status, as this positive effect was concurrently given for both groups. Conversely, the appeals *technological level* and *design/aesthetics* offer this valuable opportunity. *Technological level* led to an increase in comments and shares, specifically for premium brands. Moreover, the appeal *design/aesthetics* unfolded a significantly positive effect solely on the number of shares for premium brands.

Given the general weakness in receiving interaction in terms of post comments, premium brands should start to highlight their technological level more intensively. Therefore, a different usage proportion concerning premium appeals could be a starting point, highlighting more technological and design-related aspects. Our findings additionally indicate that a stronger emphasis on these appeals would offer the possibility to excel non-premium brands in regard to post shares.

Another interesting finding concerned the usage of the *luxury/status/prestige* appeal, even if it had no impact on interactivity. Only premium brands used this appeal in the analyzed social media posts. Vernette and Hamdi-Kidar [20] as well as Vigneron and Johnson [21] pointed to the importance of this aspect in fulfilling customer expectations that are associated with a premium brand. Therefore, we suggest that premium brands should include this appeal more often into their social media messages. It was already mentioned that the perception of premium is at risk to be diluted through line extensions and brand stretches [17]. Thus, premium brands need to communicate prestige aspects more intensively, for example in our case by posting pictures of super sports cars, in order to maintain their premium image, despite the fact that their product portfolio might tell a different story.

With the rise of social media, premium brands are challenged to secure their premium brand status under completely new conditions. This paper therefore reveals patterns of communication behavior of premium brands on SNS and, additionally, gives direct recommendations in order to create, protect, and strengthen a premium brand status.

References

1. Mangold, W.G., Faulds, D.J.: Social media: the new hybrid element of the promotion mix. Bus. Horizons. **52**(4), 357–365 (2009)
2. Patterson, A.: Social-networkers of the world, unite and take over: a meta-introspective perspective on the Facebook brand. J. Bus. Res. **65**(4), 527–534 (2012)
3. Simmons, G.J.: "I-Branding": developing the internet as a branding tool. Mark. Intell. Plann. **25**(6), 544–563 (2007)
4. Simmons, G.J.: Marketing to postmodern consumers: introducing the internet chameleon. Eur. J. Mark. **42**(3/4), 299–310 (2008)
5. Quelch, J.A.: Marketing the premium brand. Bus. Horizons. **30**(3), 38–45 (1987)
6. Steenkamp, J.-B.E.M., Batra, R., Alden, D.L.: How perceived brand globalness creates brand value. J. Int. Bus. Stud. **34**(1), 53–65 (2003)
7. Baccarella, C.V., Scheiner, C.W., Trefzger, T.F., Voigt, K.-I.: Communicating high-tech products – a comparison between print advertisements of automotive premium and standard brands. Int. J. Technol. Mark. **11**(1), 24–38 (2016)
8. Brettel, M., Reich, J.-C., Gavilanes, J.M., Flatten, T.C.: What drives advertising success on Facebook? An advertising-effectiveness model measuring the effects on sales of "likes" and other social-network stimuli. J. Advert. Res. **55**(2), 162–175 (2015)
9. Kirmani, A., Sood, S., Bridges, S.: The ownership effect in consumer responses to brand line stretches. J. Mark. **63**(1), 88–101 (1999)
10. Olson, J.C., Dover, P.A.: Effects deceptive of advertising. J. Mark. **15**(1), 29–38 (1978)

11. Kietzmann, J.H., Hermkens, K., McCarthy, I.P., Silvestre, B.S.: Social media? Get serious! Understanding the functional building blocks of social media. Bus. Horizons. **54**(3), 241–251 (2011)

12. Laroche, M., Habibi, M.R., Richard, M.-O.: To be or not to be in social media: how brand loyalty is affected by social media? Int. J. Inf. Manage. **33**(1), 76–82 (2013)

13. Statista: Leading social media websites in the United States in October 2015, based on share of visits (2016). http://www.statista.com/statistics/265773/market-share-of-the-most-popular-social-media-websites-in-the-us/. [Cited 11 Feb 2016]

14. McCorkindale, T.: Can you see the writing on my wall? A content analysis of the Fortune 50s Facebook social networking sites. Public Relat. J. **4**(3), 1–14 (2010)

15. Barwise, P., Meehan, S.: The one thing you must get right when building a brand. Harvard Bus. Rev. **88**(12), 80–84 (2010)

16. Brun, A., Castelli, C.: The nature of luxury: a consumer perspective. Int. J. Retail. Distrib. Manage. **41**(11/12), 823–847 (2013)

17. Truong, Y., McColl, R., Kitchen, P.J.: New luxury brand positioning and the emergence of masstige brands. J. Brand. Manage. **16**(5–6), 375–382 (2009)

18. Keller, K.L., Lehman, D.R.: Brands and branding. Mark. Sci. **25**(6), 740–759 (2006)

19. Kohli, C., Suri, R., Kapoor, A.: Will social media kill branding? Bus. Horizons. **58**(1), 35–44 (2015)

20. Vernette, E., Hamdi-Kidar, L.: Consumer meaning making: the meaning of luxury brands in a democratised luxury world. Int. J. Mark. Res. **55**(4), 2–20 (2013)

21. Vigneron, F., Johnson, L.W.: A review and a conceptual framework of prestige-seeking consumer behavior. Acad. Mark. Sci. Rev. **1999**, 1 (1999)

22. Oliver, N., Schab, L., Holweg, M.: Lean principles and premium brands: conflict or complement? Int. J. Prod. Res. **45**(16), 3723–3739 (2007)

23. Zoellner, F., Schaefers, T.: Do price promotions help or hurt premium-product brands? J. Advert. Res. **55**(3), 270–283 (2015)

24. Sabate, F., Berbegal-Mirabent, J., Cañabate, A., Lebherz, P.R.: Factors influencing popularity of branded content in Facebook fan pages. Eur. Manage. J. **32**(6), 1001–1011 (2014)

25. Rust, R.T., Cooil, B.: Reliability measures for qualitative data: theory and implications. J. Mark. Res. **31**(1), 1–14 (1994)

26. De Vries, L., Gensler, S., Leeflang, P.S.H.: Popularity of brand posts on brand fan pages: an investigation of the effects of social media marketing. J. Interact. Mark. **26**(2), 83–91 (2012)

27. Trefzger, T.F., Baccarella, C.V., Voigt, K-I.: Antecedents of brand post popularity in Facebook: the influence of images, videos, and text. In: Proceedings of the 15th International Marketing Trends Conference, pp. 1–8, Venice (2016)

Author Index

Printed in the United States
By Bookmasters